Twelve Lectures on Multilingualism

MM Textbooks

Advisory Board:
Professor Colin Baker, *University of Wales, Bangor, UK*

Professor Viv Edwards, *University of Reading, Reading, UK*

Professor Ofelia García, *Columbia University, New York, USA*

Dr Aneta Pavlenko, *Temple University, Philadelphia, USA*

Professor David Singleton, *Trinity College, Dublin, Ireland*

Professor Terrence G. Wiley, *Arizona State University, Tempe, USA*

MM Textbooks bring the subjects covered in our successful range of academic monographs to a student audience. The books in this series explore education and all aspects of language learning and use, as well as other topics of interest to students of these subjects. Written by experts in the field, the books are supervised by a team of world-leading scholars and evaluated by instructors before publication. Each text is student-focused, with suggestions for further reading and study questions leading to a deeper understanding of the subject.

All books in this series are externally peer-reviewed.

Full details of all the books in this series and of all our other publications can be found on http://www.multilingual-matters.com, or by writing to Multilingual Matters, St Nicholas House, 31–34 High Street, Bristol BS1 2AW, UK.

MM Textbooks: 15

Twelve Lectures on Multilingualism

Edited by
David Singleton and Larissa Aronin

MULTILINGUAL MATTERS
Bristol • Blue Ridge Summit

This book is dedicated to our sons:
David's sons Christopher and Daniel
and Larissa's son Michael-Gil'ad

DOI https://doi.org/10.21832/SINGLE2067
Library of Congress Cataloging in Publication Data
A catalog record for this book is available from the Library of Congress.
Names: Singleton, D. M. (David Michael), editor. | Aronin, Larissa, editor.
Title: Twelve Lectures on Multilingualism/Edited by David Singleton and Larissa Aronin.
Description: Bristol; Blue Ridge Summit: Multilingual Matters, [2019] |
  Series: MM Textbooks: 15 | Includes bibliographical references and index.
Identifiers: LCCN 2018028667 | ISBN 9781788922067 (hbk : alk. paper) |
  ISBN 9781788922050 (pbk : alk. paper) | ISBN 9781788922098 (kindle)
Subjects: LCSH: Multilingualism.
Classification: LCC P115 .T94 2019 | DDC 306.44/6–dc23 LC record available at
  https://lccn.loc.gov/2018028667

British Library Cataloguing in Publication Data
A catalogue entry for this book is available from the British Library.

ISBN-13: 978-1-78892-206-7 (hbk)
ISBN-13: 978-1-78892-205-0 (pbk)

Multilingual Matters
UK: St Nicholas House, 31–34 High Street, Bristol BS1 2AW, UK.
USA: NBN, Blue Ridge Summit, PA, USA.

Website: www.multilingual-matters.com
Twitter: Multi_Ling_Mat
Facebook: https://www.facebook.com/multilingualmatters
Blog: www.channelviewpublications.wordpress.com

Copyright © 2019 David Singleton, Larissa Aronin and the authors of individual chapters.

All rights reserved. No part of this work may be reproduced in any form or by any means without permission in writing from the publisher.

The policy of Multilingual Matters/Channel View Publications is to use papers that are natural, renewable and recyclable products, made from wood grown in sustainable forests. In the manufacturing process of our books, and to further support our policy, preference is given to printers that have FSC and PEFC Chain of Custody certification. The FSC and/or PEFC logos will appear on those books where full certification has been granted to the printer concerned.

Typeset by Nova Techset Private Limited, Bengaluru and Chennai, India.
Printed and bound in the UK by Short Run Press Ltd.
Printed and bound in the US by Thomson-Shore, Inc.

Contents

About the Authors — vii
Introduction — xiii

Part 1: Multilingualism in Society and Education

Lecture 1: What is Multilingualism? — 3
Larissa Aronin

Lecture 2: Applied Linguistics and Multilingualism — 35
Danuta Gabryś-Barker

Lecture 3: The Psycholinguistics of Multiple Language Learning and Teaching — 65
Britta Hufeisen and Ulrike Jessner

Lecture 4: Educational Policy and Multilingualism — 101
Jasone Cenoz and Durk Gorter

Part 2: Aspects of Individual Multilingualism

Lecture 5: Multilingual Individuals — 135
John Edwards

Lecture 6: Cross-linguistic Influence and Multiple Language Acquisition and Use — 163
Gessica De Angelis

Lecture 7: Motivation and Multilingualism — 179
Ema Ushioda

Lecture 8: Age and Multilingualism — 213
Carmen Muñoz and David Singleton

Part 3: The Psycholinguistics and Neurolinguistics of Multilingualism

Lecture 9: The Psycholinguistics of Multilingualism — 233
Julia Festman

Lecture 10: The Neurolinguistics of Multilingualism — 271
McLoddy Kadyamusuma, Eve Higby and Loraine Obler

Part 4: Forms of Multilingualism in the Past and Present

Lecture 11: Historical Multilingualism 299
Kurt Braunmüller

Lecture 12: Receptive Multilingualism 329
Jan D. ten Thije

Subject Index 365

About the Authors

Editors

David Singleton took his BA at Trinity College Dublin and his PhD at the University of Cambridge. He is an Emeritus Fellow of Trinity College Dublin, where he was, until his retirement from that institution, Professor of Applied Linguistics. He now holds the title of Professor Emeritus at the University of Pannonia, Veszprém (Hungary) and Professor at the State University of Applied Sciences, Konin (Poland). He has served as President of the Irish Association for Applied Linguistics, as Secretary General of the International Association of Applied Linguistics (AILA) and as President of the European Second Language Association (EUROSLA). David's publications number more than 200, his books and articles ranging across a wide spectrum of topics but focusing mainly on cross-linguistic influence, the second language lexicon, the age factor in language acquisition and multilingualism. He is the co-author of *Key Topics in Second Language Acquisition* (Multilingual Matters, 2014) and *Beyond Age Effects in Instructional L2 Learning* (Multilingual Matters, 2017). He is the founding editor and continuing co-editor of the Multilingual Matters SLA book series. In 2015 David received the EUROSLA Distinguished Scholar Award and in 2017 he was awarded Honorary Membership of AILA.

Larissa Aronin is an Associate Professor at the Oranim Academic College of Education (Israel). She is a former Secretary and a founding member of the International Association of Multilingualism. Larissa was a Visiting Scholar at the Department of Linguistics and Philosophy in the School of Humanities, Arts and Social Sciences at the Massachusetts Institute of Technology (USA) (2014) and a KIVA Guest Professor at the Technical Universität Darmstadt (Germany) (2016). She has published about 100 articles and books on various topics in the domain of multilingualism and has opened up new research avenues in areas of the material culture of multilingualism and of dominant language constellations. Larissa has published in a range of international journals on a wide array of topics connected with multilingualism such as *The International Journal of the Sociology of Language*, *The International Journal of Multilingualism* and *Language Teaching*. She is the co-author of *Multilingualism* (with David Singleton; John Benjamins, 2012), has contributed to *The Encyclopedia of Applied Linguistics* (Wiley-Blackwell, 2013) and is the co-editor of *The Exploration of Multilingualism: Development of Research on L3, Multilingualism and Multiple Language Acquisition* (with Britta Hufeisen; John Benjamins, 2009) and *Current Multilingualism: The New Linguistic Dispensation* (with David Singleton, Joshua Fishman and Muiris Ó Laoire; De Gruyter, 2013). Larissa is an Advisory Board Member of *Language Teaching* (CUP) and an editorial board member of a number of peer-reviewed journals.

Contributors

Kurt Braunmüller (Hamburg University) received his degrees from Tübingen (Dr Phil) and Freiburg University (Dr habil) and was thereafter Heisenberg Fellow at Kiel University. He is member of several Scandinavian scientific academies. Kurt's main interests lie in Scandinavian and Germanic linguistics, especially in contact linguistics and multilingualism and in historical Germanic linguistics, but also in linguistic and typological changes in general. He has conducted research projects on Low and High German-Scandinavian language contact during the Middle Ages and in early Modern Times (era of the Hanseatic League), on Latin impact on Ancient/Runic Germanic and on the historical development of Scandinavian syntax. He has also investigated the possibilities and problems of inter-Scandinavian communication and of Faroese-Danish bilingualism. He further published on the typology of Germanic and Proto-Germanic (as a contact language). Among Kurt's 20 book publications are a comprehensive survey of the five (six) modern Scandinavian languages, *Die skandinavischen Sprachen im Überblick* (3rd edn, Francke, 2007; 2nd edn translated into Norwegian, Novus, 1998) and a historical investigation into the typology of the Germanic languages, *Syntaxtypologische Studien zum Germanischen* (Narr, 1982). He was co-editor of *The Nordic Languages: An International Handbook of the History of the North Germanic Languages* (De Gruyter, 2002/2005). His further publications comprise more than 130 (academic) articles and around 50 reviews.

Jasone Cenoz Iragui is Professor of Research Methods in Education at the University of the Basque Country, UPV/EHU. Her research focuses on multilingual education, bilingualism and multilingualism. Her publications include *Teaching Through Basque* (Multilingual Matters, 2008), *The Multiple Realities of Multilingualism* (co-edited with Elka Todeva; De Gruyter Mouton, 2009), *Towards Multilingual Education* (Multilingual Matters, 2009) and *Multilingual Education: Between Language Learning and Translanguaging* (co-edited with Durk Gorter; Cambridge University Press, 2015). She has been guest speaker at a large number of European universities and also in North America, Asia, Australia and New Zealand. Jasone is on the board of a number of scientific journals and she is past President of the International Association of Multilingualism. She received the Spanish Association of Applied Linguistics Research Award in 2011.

Gessica de Angelis is Assistant Professor of Applied Linguistics at the Centre for Language and Communication Studies and Fellow of Trinity College Dublin. Her main research interests are in second/third language acquisition, cross-linguistic influence, multilingual language development and multilingualism and education. Gessica is the author of *Third or Additional Language Acquisition* (Multilingual Matters, 2007). She is also the co-editor of *New Trends in Crosslinguistic Influence and Multilingualism Research* (Multilingual Matters, 2011), *Learning and Teaching in Multilingual Contexts: Conceptual, Sociolinguistic and Educational Perspectives* (Multilingual Matters, 2014) and *Crosslinguistic Influence and Crosslinguistic Interaction in Multilingual Language Learning* (Bloomsbury, 2015). She is former Vice President of the International Association of Multilingualism (2009–2011; 2011–2013).

About the Authors

John Edwards was born in England, educated there and in Canada, and received his PhD from McGill University. After working as a Research Fellow at the Educational Research Centre in Dublin he moved to Nova Scotia, where he became Professor of Psychology at St Francis Xavier University. He is a member of several psychological and linguistic societies, as well as scholarly organizations for the study of ethnicity and nationalism. He is a Fellow of the British Psychological Society, the Canadian Psychological Association and the Royal Society of Canada. John is now a Senior Research Professor at St Francis Xavier University (Antigonish), Adjunct Professor, Graduate Studies, at Dalhousie University (Halifax) and Visiting Professor at Minzu University (Beijing). John's main research interest relates to the establishment, maintenance and continuity of group identity, with particular reference to language. He has lectured and presented papers on this topic in many countries and his work has been widely translated. He is the editor of the *Journal of Multilingual and Multicultural Development* (Routledge). He is also the editor of the Multilingual Matters book series for the Bristol publisher of the same name, a series that now comprises more than 150 titles. John's books include *Multilingualism* (Penguin, 1995), *Language and Identity* (Cambridge, 2009), *Language Diversity in the Classroom* (Multilingual Matters, 2010), *Minority Languages and Group Identity* (John Benjamins, 2010), *Multilingualism: Understanding Linguistic Diversity* (Continuum/Bloomsbury, 2012) and *Sociolinguistics: A Very Short Introduction* (Oxford University Press, 2013).

Julia Festman is Professor of Multilingualism at the Pedagogical University Tyrol (Austria). From 2013 to 2016 she was head of the interdisciplinary diversity and inclusion research group at the University of Potsdam (Germany), where she worked on the acquisition of reading and writing in 3rd grade mono- and multilingual children. Before that she was a post-doc at the Potsdam Research Institute for Multilingualism at the University of Potsdam. Julia received a DFG grant to join Thomas Münte's team at the Institute of Psychology/Neuropsychology at the University of Magdeburg (2005–2010) as a post-doc working on executive functions, bilingualism and EEG. In 2004 she obtained her PhD on the topic of psycholinguistics and trilingualism at Bar Ilan University (Israel) and was a visiting scientist in the cognitive psychology department at the University of Exeter (UK) and in 2002 in the Institute for Psycholinguistics at the University of Leipzig (Germany).

Danuta Gabryś-Barker is Professor of English at the University of Silesia, Katowice (Poland), where she lectures and supervises MA and PhD theses in applied linguistics, psycholinguistics and especially in second language acquisition and multilingualism. She has published approximately 150 articles and the books *Aspects of Multilingual Storage, Processing and Retrieval* (Wydawnictwo Uniwersytetu Śląskiego, 2005) and *Reflectivity in Pre-service Teacher Education* (Wydawnictwo Uniwersytetu Śląskiego, 2012). Danuta has also edited 15 volumes, among others for Multilingual Matters, Springer and the University of Silesia Press. She has been the co-editor-in-chief of the *International Journal of Multilingualism* (Taylor & Francis/Routledge) since 2010 and the co-founder and co-editor-in-chief of the journal *Theory and Practice of Second Language Acquisition* (University of Silesia Press) since 2015.

Durk Gorter is Ikerbasque Research Professor at the University of the Basque Country UPV/EHU, Donostia-San Sebastián. He is leader of DREAM, the Donostia Research Group on Education and Multilingualism, and also the editor of *Language, Culture and Curriculum*. Previously he was Head of the Department of Social Sciences at the Fryske Akademy in Ljouwert/Leeuwarden (the Netherlands) and also full Professor in the Sociolinguistics of Frisian at the University of Amsterdam. Durk carries out research on multilingual education, linguistic landscapes and comparative studies of European minority languages. Some of his recent publications include *Multilingual Education: Between Language Learning and Translanguaging* (co-edited with J. Cenoz; Cambridge University Press, 2015), *Minority Languages in the Linguistic Landscape* (co-edited with H. Marten and L. Van Mensel; Palgrave Macmillan, 2012) and *Minority Languages and Multilingual Education* (co-edited with V. Zenotz and J. Cenoz; Springer, 2014).

Eve Higby received her PhD in speech-language-hearing sciences from the City University of New York Graduate Center. She is currently completing a postdoctoral research fellowship in psychology at the University of California, Riverside. Her work focuses on language and cognitive processes in bilingualism and aging and on how language experience affects brain structure and function. Eve has published on multilingualism and the brain, language in aging and cross-linguistic influence in bilingualism. She is working on the second edition of the book *Language and the Brain* (Cambridge University Press) together with Loraine Obler, Ioulia Kovelman and Kris Gjerlow.

Britta Hufeisen received her PhD at Kassel University (Germany) in 1990 and her Habilitation at Darmstadt University (Germany) in 1999. After being an Assistant Professor of German Applied Linguistics at the University of Alberta (Canada) for almost four years in the early 1990s, she worked at Darmstadt University and has been a full Professor of Linguistics and Multilingualism since 2006. She has been Adjunct and Guest Professor at universities in, among others, Alberta (Canada), Falun and Göteborg (Sweden), Kuala Lumpur (Malaysia), Amman (Jordan) and Ho Chi Ming (Vietnam). In research Britta focuses on multiple language learning and plurilingual whole school policy. In both areas she has published extensively both nationally and internationally. She has been a plenary speaker all over the world and supervises numerous PhD students.

Ulrike Jessner is Professor at the University of Innsbruck (Austria) and the University of Pannonia, Veszprem (Hungary), where she has a role as one of the founding members of the International Doctoral School of Multilingualism. She has published widely in the field of multilingualism with a special focus on the acquisition of English in multilingual contexts. She is the co-author of *A Dynamic Model of Multilingualism* (with Philip Herdina; Multilingual Matters, 2002) which pioneered DSCT in language acquisition research. She has been engaged in the development of the research area of third language acquisition/ multilingualism as a founding member and President of the International Association of Multilingualism. Ulrike chairs the Regional Educational Competence Centre 'German & Multilingualism' and is founding editor of the *International Journal of Multilingualism* and the book series Trends in Applied Linguistics (with Claire Kramsch, UC Berkeley). Supported by her research group DyME (Dynamics of Multilingualism with English) Ulrike is currently involved in two large-scale kindergarten projects in Tyrol (funded by the Tyrolean government) and in the trilingual Ladin kindergartens in South Tyrol (commissioned by the Bolzano Province). With her work on metalinguistic awareness in multilingual learning, she opened up a new research avenue in multilingual learning and teaching ('Metacognition in multilingual learning: A DMM perspective', in Bjørke, Dypedahl and Haukås (eds) *Metacognition in Language Learning and Teaching*, Routledge, 2018).

McLoddy Kadyamusuma is an Assistant Professor at the State University of New York at Fredonia in the communication sciences and disorders department. His primary interests are in language assessment and treatment in neurologically impaired multilingual individuals. His other interests include the effect of linguistic experience and musical training on language processing in native and non-native speakers of tonal languages.

Carmen Muñoz is Full Professor of Applied English Linguistics at the University of Barcelona (Spain). Her research interests include the effects of age and context on second language acquisition, young learners in instructed settings, individual differences, bilingual/multilingual education and multimodality in language learning. She is the founder and coordinator of the GRAL research group at the University of Barcelona, where she has coordinated a dozen research projects, among them the BAF Project (*Age and the Rate of Foreign Language Learning*, Multilingual Matters, 2006), and the Spanish team in the EU-funded ELLiE (Early Language Learning in Europe) project. Carmen's recent publications include the article 'The role of age and proficiency in subtitle reading: An eye-tracking study' in *System* (2017), and 'Tracing trajectories of young learners: Ten years of school English learning' in *ARAL* (2017). In recent years she has been granted the ICREA Academia award by the Catalan Government and the Distinguished Scholar award by EuroSLA.

Loraine Obler is a Distinguished Professor in the speech-language-hearing sciences programs at the City University of New York Graduate Center. She is the co-author of *The Bilingual Brain: Neuropsychological and Neurolinguistic Aspects of Bilingualism* (with Martin Albert; Academic Press, 1978). She has also published *Language and the Brain* (with Kris Gjerlow; Cambridge University Press, 1999). Loraine's research interests include language changes associated with healthy aging and dementia, bilingual aphasia and the cross-language study of agrammatism.

Jan D. ten Thije is an Associate Professor at the Utrecht Institute for Linguistics and lecturer at the Department of Languages, Literature and Communication. He was previously an associated professor ('Hochschuldozent') at the Department for Intercultural Communication at Chemnitz University of Technology (1996–2002), visiting professor at the Department for Applied Linguistics at Vienna University (2001), and lecturer and researcher at the Department for General Linguistics (University of Amsterdam) (1994–1996). Jan studied general linguistics and Dutch language and culture in Amsterdam (University of Amsterdam) and received his PhD at Utrecht University (1994) with research focusing on intercultural discourse in advisory institutes. His main fields of research concern institutional discourse in multicultural and international settings, lingua receptiva/receptive multilingualism, intercultural training, language education and functional pragmatics. He coordinates the Masters programme in intercultural communication at the Department of Languages, Literature and Communication at

Utrecht University. He is editor-in-chief of the *European Journal for Applied Linguistics* (EuJAL) published by Mouton de Gruyter and series editor of *Utrecht Studies in Language and Communication* (USLC) published by Brill Publications, Leiden.

Ema Ushioda is Professor and Head of Department at the Centre for Applied Linguistics, University of Warwick. She has worked in language education since 1982 and has conducted in-service workshops on motivation and autonomy for language teachers from many countries. Her main research interests are language learning motivation, learner autonomy, sociocultural theory and teacher development, and she has published widely in these areas. Ema's recent books include *International Perspectives on Motivation: Language Learning and Professional Challenges* (Springer, 2013), *Teaching and Researching Motivation* (co-authored by Z. Dörnyei, Pearson, 2011) and *Motivation, Language Identity and the L2 Self* (co-edited by Z. Dörnyei, Multilingual Matters, 2009). Ema is the co-editor (with Z. Dörnyei) of a special issue of *The Modern Language Journal* (2017) on 'Beyond global English: Motivation to learn languages in a multicultural world', and is currently working on a research monograph on ethical perspectives on language learning motivation research, and also a third edition (with Z. Dörnyei) of *Teaching and Researching Motivation*.

Introduction

Larissa Aronin and David Singleton

This volume is intended to provide a comprehensive overview of multilingualism and sheds light on the ways in which the use and acquisition of languages are changing in contemporary society. The volume is organized into 12 lectures, each dedicated to a particular topic of importance and each accompanied by questions for student reflection and suggestions for further reading. The lectures in question are written by leading researchers in the various areas of multilingualism and provide state-of-the-art accounts of the field. The topics covered are among the most interesting and fundamental areas commonly taught in multilingualism studies and the most in demand for multilingualism courses. Our hope is that dealing with these diverse viewpoints and approaches will encourage in the reader the development of informed and creative thinking on multilingualism.

At this time multilingualism is at its peak as a focus of attention among both academics and lay people. The current powerful appeal of multilingualism is evidenced by the explosion of scholarship around it and by the term itself becoming something of a 'buzzword'. Indeed, the number of professionals and practitioners whose daily activities require a better understanding of multilingualism is growing. The phenomenon is being intensively researched and taught in its various dimensions – from neurolinguistics and cross-linguistic interaction to multiple language teaching, language policy and intercultural understanding.

Development in the field of multilingualism studies, especially intense in the last two decades, has yielded a wealth of thought-provoking research and multidisciplinary findings. This introduction will briefly discuss: (1) some aspects of the broad evolution of language research; (2) the characteristics of the 'multilingual stage' of awareness of language and languages; (3) the issue of the relationship between bilingualism and multilingualism (in the sense of tri + lingualism); and (4) this volume's aims and content.

Stages of Awareness of Language and Languages

Language became a topic of particular scholarly concern during the 19th century. From this time on, we can point to three stages of societal awareness with regard to language and languages: *monolingual*, *bilingual* and *multilingual* (Aronin & Singleton, 2012: 19–32). The partition into three stages is admittedly rough and ready; the stages are not strictly tied to any exact dates and times, nor are they neatly discrete. The different stages of awareness of language and languages do not relate to the number of languages in use in given societies; rather, they signal predominant perceptions and practices, reflecting the social ideas and predispositions with regard to both scientific and everyday interest in language.

The role assigned to language at a particular time and in a given society roughly coincides with social organization and contemporary ideology. In earlier times it was important that people were able to use language at all, any language; the fact that people used ***a*** language was significant in itself. With the formation and strengthening of nation-states, the principle 'one nation-one language' became a watchword and ***the*** operative language came to the forefront – French for France, German for Germany, etc. Today's discourse is on languages.

The 'monolingual stage'

From the end of the 19th century onwards the philosophy of language tended to ask 'general questions about language as such' (Lacey, 2001: 172). Language as a human possession was at the centre of philosophers' attention. Scholars investigated in this connection an abstract, pure, arbitrary system devoid of real-life context: 'philosophers became interested in language for what they could get out of it for philosophy' (Cooper, 1973: 4). As for linguists who dealt with specific languages, they mostly had purely theoretical and linguistic-schematic goals (see, for example, Bloch & Trager, 1942; Chomsky, 1957; Katz, 1972; de Saussure, 1916; Whorf, 1956). The existence of individuals with more than one language competence at their disposal was treated as abnormal and peripheral. Hence the application of the term *monolingual stage*, despite the existence of millions of bilingual and multilingual people in the world from our earliest beginnings. Monolingual ideology regarded the monolingual user, who was supposed to have perfect knowledge of his/her native language, as the norm. As a consequence, the monolingual native speaker became a default point of departure in education and social assessment. The second language (L2) user was by definition deficient, according to common wisdom.

This notwithstanding, the monolingual stage delivered a great deal of data about language and languages which remain of enormous value. The monolingual paradigm, with its valuable philosophical and linguistic insights (and its increasingly rejected biases) still subsists today.

The 'bilingual stage'

The *bilingual stage* is characterized by a widening of purview to include people using two languages. Bilingual individuals came into the spotlight as societies felt a need to investigate social, psychological, ethical, educational, and other issues connected with immigration of one kind and another. From the mid-20th century, bilingualism became a salient issue in areas such as politics, economics and the cognitive sciences. Already early in the 20th century a number of seminal contributions in this perspective had appeared, and from the 1960s onwards came a real upsurge in interest in bilingualism. The realities of immigration and of children growing up bilingually (see, for example, Singleton *et al.*, 2013a) sparked studies in the psycholinguistics and psychology of biculturalism and bilingualism. There was also an expansion of research horizons connected to the growing interest in individual identity (see Aronin & Singleton, 2012: 20–32).

An important outcome of the bilingual stage was the realization that the 'bilingual is not the sum of two monolinguals' (Grosjean, 1989, 1992), that the L2 learner is not a failing, underachieving imitator of a native speaker, but a language user in his/her own right (Cook, 1992, 1993). This key insight signified an important first threshold in the development of thinking about the acquisition and use of more than one language (Aronin & Hufeisen, 2009b). It has to be said that in practice, individuals, users and organizational policies still often hang on to the monolingual perspective. Although bilinguals and L2 users are acknowledged and investigated, the monolingual paradigm still de facto retains its position insofar as the native-speaker ideal remains an unspoken presence in the discussion of language acquisition goals and attainments (see, for example, Canagarajah, 2016: 440).

The 'multilingual stage'

With the passing of time, the bilingual stage gave way to the current *multilingual stage* of society's awareness of language and languages. The stage is so named because of the recognition of the determinative role of multilingualism in the new linguistic dispensation. This multilingual stage of awareness finds expression in the experience and acknowledgment of global changes related to languages and their use, and in the coming to grips with the fact that that virtually every facet of human life depends, directly or indirectly, on multilingual social arrangements and multilingual individuals (Aronin & Singleton, 2012; Aronin *et al.*, 2013). In the field of multilingualism studies, the new stage of awareness of language and languages is signalled by a second threshold, that is, the marking, in many quarters, of a clear distinction between bilingualism and multilingualism (Aronin & Hufeisen, 2009b). At this stage there has ubiquitously arisen the realization of an acute need to get to grips with multilingualism – to deepen our understanding of its nature, to maximize its benefits (Bastardas-Boada, 2012; Matras & Robertson, 2015) and to face up to its challenges (Blackledge & Creese, 2010; Jessner & Kramsch, 2015).

What Characterizes the 'Multilingual Stage' of Awareness of Language and Languages?

In general, linguistics, in all its subfields, is coming to focus more and more explicitly on a multiplicity of languages. This change of focus has been partly inspired by neuroscience research (see Andrews, 2014; Kadyamusuma *et al.*, this volume). The focus on comparisons among multilinguals in this research is methodologically a crucial step forward, as Festman points out (2012: 209); in previous decades neurolinguistics research tended to compare monolingual groups to strictly bilingual groups. Researchers now compare multilingual speakers to other multilingual speakers. One can point, for example, to Festman's distinction between 'switching' and 'non- switching' multilinguals (Festman, 2012, this volume) or to Wattendorf *et al.*'s (2014) investigation into sentence processing in early and late multilinguals.

In the social domain of multilingualism research, the basic concepts of multilingualism that feature are undergoing transformations. The meanings of *language, dialect, language proficiency* and *mother tongue* in their relation to contemporary society reflect the dynamic nature of multilingualism (Vasanta, 2011). The meanings of *society* and *community* have also changed in accordance with sociolinguistic transformations. The image of a homogeneous 'speech community' that was previously taken for granted (as well as those of 'mother tongue' and 'foreign language') is also undergoing a substantial makeover. Now, when referring to the reality of dealing with multiple languages, we speak about 'hybridizing identities' (Bailey *et al.*, 2016) and employ the terms applied to these sociolinguistic patterns and practices, such as *languaging, translanguaging* (García, 2013; Otheguy *et al.*, 2015), *super-diversity* (Vertovec, 2007) and *dominant language constellations* (Aronin, 2006, 2016).

Methods of research and ways of problem solving in language practices that were considered 'safe' and accepted as working for two languages may not always work for three or more languages. It is argued that new questions are posed and new methods of investigation and new solutions need to be looked for in order to deal with situations involving multiple languages (see Aronin & Hufeisen, 2009a; Aronin & Jessner, 2014). In regard to the proposed differences between bi- and tri + -lingualism, a number of models have been suggested which seek to demonstrate the relevant differences. For example, the factor model proposed by Hufeisen (2005, 2010) talks of the difference between learning an L2 and a third language (L3); whereas the learner of an L2 is a complete novice to non-native language learning, in the case of acquiring an L3 a learner already has the experience of learning his first additional language. Another well-known model, the dynamic model of multilingualism (DMM) proposed by Herdina and Jessner (2002), contextualizes individual language learning within the framework of dynamic systems theory.

Also, with respect to the judgments regarding the nature of multilingualism, ideas have swung from seeing it as dangerous and unwelcome to an absolutely positive perception of multilingualism, now coming to rest at a view of multilingualism as a complex phenomenon, the evaluation of which depends on many factors in any particular instance. Overall, rather than operating, as in traditional research, on the basis of binary oppositions (mono versus bi; native versus non-native; host versus immigrant; English versus LOTE), a range of nuances, individual cases, diverse circumstances and various outcomes are now taken into account in multilingual research. *Complex rather than simple* is now accepted as the nature of multilingual reality (see Muñoz & Singleton, this volume; Ushioda, this volume). Such complexity is also seen in the emergence of the dominant language constellation approach, which considers the everyday use of a set of languages as a complex, normative pattern of language use (see Aronin, 2016; Aronin, this volume).

Multilingualism is currently treated holistically, as a continuum rather than as a series of separate, self-contained phenomena (see, for example, Cenoz, 2009; Cenoz & Gorter, this volume; Hornberger, 2004). Similarly, one notes the employment of spatial metaphors referring to the covering or crossing of space, as in scales and their intercrossing intersection or conversion (Bailey *et al.*, 2016) and a 'geographical' perspective expressed in the terms *-scape, -trans* and the like as in *linguascape*, or in terms of socio-geopolitical divisions as in *urban spaces, translocal, Asian cosmopolitans*. The inner features of the multilingual are clearly also of interest. Here belongs the idea of competence embracing *intercultural competence, symbolic competence* and of course *multicompetence* (Cook, 1992, 1993; cf. Singleton, 2016). Byram *et al.* (2002: 30) note that intercultural competence includes reference not only to knowledge and understanding, but also to the 'ability to make the strange familiar, and the familiar strange (savoir être), to step outside their taken for granted perspectives, and to act on the basis of new perspectives (savoir s'engager)'. According to Kramsch (2008: 400), 'symbolic competence is the ability not only to approximate or appropriate for oneself someone else's language, but to shape the very context in which the language is learned and used'.

Intense involvement with societal dimensions is another feature of present multilingual research. More issues, topics and theories emphasizing environment and milieu have emerged 'unpacking the significance of context' (Bailey *et al.*, 2016: 313). Current multilingual research deals impressively with various societal aspects of language acquisition and use, such as receptive multilingualism (see ten Thije this volume). Referring to neurolinguistics research, Festman (this volume) writes: '[t]here seems to be a shift in the selection of participant groups: no longer are differences between mono- and bilingual processing in focus, but rather between subgroups of bi- and multilinguals or between bi- and multilinguals'. Of course, linguistic research has always provided some insights relative to the users of the languages in question. On the whole, research into the monolingual stage did not, however, provide answers to and, importantly, did not *mean* to provide answers to social issues. With the advance of bilingualism awareness such issues came to the fore; for example, there was increasing discussion of the ways in which immigrants acquired their host country's language and the wisdom of their abandoning or maintaining their original language.

The study of multilingualism, even in its most specialized aspects such as neuroscience, concerns society, since language as a form of social activity physically changes brain topography and functions. Societal dimensions are similarly to be found, for example, in treatments of cross-linguistic influence (De Angelis, this volume) and applied linguistics (Gabryś-Barker, this volume). The authors of each lecture in this volume, even when discussing non-societal topics (e.g. Edwards on individual multilingualism; McLoddy, Higby and Obler on the physiological processes taking place in the brain; Braunmüller on historical multilingualism), feel the need to start their arguments by describing, even if in very general terms, what they think multilingualism is and necessarily touch upon social background.

Bilingualism and Multilingualism: The Same or Different?

The core feature that makes bilingualism different from multilingualism (in the sense of tri + -lingualism) is their respective levels of complexity (Aronin & Jessner, 2015). In complexity studies, complexity status is assigned to systems with more than two variables. Starting with systems involving three variables, outcome is considered inherently uncertain, influenced by spontaneous inner and extrinsic influences. If we employ traditional logical considerations – indeed, common sense – we arrive at similar conclusions regarding differences in mental operations involved in the use and acquisition of one, two or three and more languages. If we are dealing with just one entity, our cognizing is focused on that one particular phenomenon. When there are two entities in play, any generalizations or predictions we make are constrained by that duality. But with *three* entities, the range of variation in outcomes, interconnections and possible predictions opens up considerably.

The criteria for defining lower or higher levels of complexity used in various fields of human activity can be reduced to the following three factors: (1) number of items involved, such as the number of steps, algorithms, symbols, parts, etc.; (2) the intensity of the phenomenon, the amount of effort required in its processing; and (3) the rate and density of items under review. In the language domain, adding just an L3 or even just one skill of an L3 increases the number of active elements and possibilities, and augments the information, interactions and emergent qualities and variables to a much greater degree than when one language increases to two. With an L3 the aspects that become more dense are myriad – lexical proliferation and complexity (see, for example, Singleton, 2012), number of grammar options to express an idea, etc. Arguments based on logic and on complexity thinking have been substantiated by empirical findings in neurolinguistics, applied linguistics and pragmatics, as well as by fresh puzzling facts with regard to multilinguals which cannot be accounted for using explanations employed in the case of bilinguals.

Among these data are findings pointing to new emergent qualities, to a 'system shift' (De Angelis, 2005) after the passing of a certain threshold. The threshold in question is the mastery and use of an additional language after two are already in place. The study by De Angelis is on lexical transfer between non-native languages and 'illustrates a type of behaviour that speakers of two languages do not display', which leads her to infer that '[t]he interaction between non-native languages cannot be assumed to be governed by the same principles that govern the interaction between the native and one non-native language' (De Angelis, 2005: 14). Kemp (2007) investigated language learning strategies and found very specific tendencies in regard to how multilinguals use grammar learning strategies, which point to the possibility that 'compared to L2 learning, augmentation in number and frequency of strategies used occurs to a greater extent during the acquisition of the third language, increasing more gradually in additional languages' (Kemp, 2007: 257). In the area of pragmatics of early multilingual development, Safont-Jordà

(2012: 112) found 'quite a different pattern' in the use of politeness strategies in the L3 in a longitudinal case study on interaction between Catalan, Spanish and English. The differential impact of being trilingual rather than bilingual in education, and on interactions between friends and family, has also been intensively researched (see Henry, 2011; Lanza & Svendsen, 2007).

Another kind of data which has appeared recently is both puzzling and thought provoking because the findings are not in line with the logic of research on bilinguals. Such are, for example, the findings on switching costs and response times. Switching costs in bilinguals are mostly asymmetric. That is, response time is reported as longer when the switch is from the L2 to the first language (L1) than vice versa (Kroll *et al.*, 2008). It appears that switching costs in trilinguals are not so pronounced as might have been expected in the light of research on bilinguals and that multilinguals may thus have stronger executive control (Ansaldo *et al.*, 2008; Festman, 2012). In addition, no asymmetry in switching costs were found in multilinguals, whether in the switching cost between their L1 and a low-proficiency L3, nor between their L2 and the less proficient L3 (Costa *et al.*, 2006). In the same way, we have the 'out of line' finding of Cedden and Şimşek (2012), who found that the representation of an L3 in the mind provides an advantage for executive control processes compared to bilinguals. Another relevant finding is from a study on syntax acquisition, where Strik (2012) found that 'trilingual children do not show more difficulties with *wh*-questions in Dutch than bilingual children' (Strik, 2012: 58). The question arises: How is it that, with all the complexity of three languages as compared to two, it is not reported that trilinguals have more difficulties and need significantly more time and effort? We can see that the logic of expectation traditionally applied in regard to mono- and bilingual processes does not seem to function here. It is no surprise then, that researchers in neuroanatomy, neurophysiology and neurofunctionality more and more often differentiate between bi- and tri + -lingualism (Andrews, 2014: 1) – in tune with the differentiation of bilingual and multilingual paradigms increasingly made by sociolinguists and applied linguists.

Goral (2012: 721) observes that 'it is plausible that multilinguals are unique in their ability to learn an additional language and their ability to activate or inhibit their other languages while communicating in one'. Similarly, Higby *et al.* (2013: 68) state that '[w]hile some studies of multilingualism have shown similar results to what has been seen in studies of bilinguals, certain unique properties of multilinguals are beginning to be noticed, particularly regarding early language representation, gray matter density, and speed of lexical retrieval' (cf. Festman, this volume). To summarize, we have reason to believe that 'with more experience in learning an additional language (as opposed to the first experience in learning one) different mechanisms develop that wouldn't exist without having learnt and used the second additional language, that is, L3' (Aronin & Jessner, 2015: 280). The answer, then, to the question as to whether bilingualism and multilingualism are the same would appear to be: 'bilingualism and multilingualism are close and overlapping in many ways, but as a bilingual turns into a multilingual, quantitative and qualitative differences become deeper, to the extent that the nature of the emerging [...] phenomena changes' (Aronin & Jessner, 2015: 277).

Overview of the Book

This book is divided into four parts, each focusing on a major broad theme in multilingualism. The lectures in **Part 1** introduce the reader to the foundations of multilingualism as a human practice. Traditionally, the importance of languages is manifested in the learning and teaching of certain languages and in particular educational practices and policies. Accordingly, the first four lectures deal with societal multilingualism, language learning and teaching and language policies.

Lecture 1 by **Larissa Aronin** gives a general theoretical view of multilingualism as a societal phenomenon and as a field of practice and research. The lecture emphasizes the significance of current multilingualism for society, points to differences between 'current' and 'historical' multilingualism, and defines the notion of the 'new linguistic dispensation', commenting on its main features, properties and tendencies. The two – seemingly opposite – trends of the 'new linguistic dispensation' are discussed not only in regard to their apparent contrary directions, but also in regard to their intensive interaction. The concept of dominant language constellation is added to the mix, underlining and further shedding light on the complexity of current sociolinguistic patterns in respect of multilingualism.

Lecture 2 by **Danuta Gabryś-Barker** concentrates on selected areas of research where multilingualism informs applied linguistics. These include lines of research dealing with fairly recently defined notions such as multilinguality, multicompetence and multilingual language awareness, as well as more traditional concepts such as code-switching. The lecture extensively dwells on the topics of the lexicon and cross-linguistic influence (which are also dealt with in Lectures 3 and 10) from the applied linguistics point of view. In addition, the chapter contains a brief overview of research on emotions and affectivity as they connect to language teaching and learning.

Lecture 3 by **Britta Hufeisen** and **Ulrike Jessner** focuses on multiple language learning and teaching (MLLT), which refers to getting to grips with more than two languages in tutored instruction and in a natural context. The lecture presents basic concepts, terminology and scenarios of MLLT and provides a rich and systematic overview of the research on theory and practice in the learning of and instruction in L3 and further foreign languages (L4, L5, Ln) in diverse areas of psycholinguistics, sociolinguistics and applied linguistics. The lecture devotes space to the three central theoretical models of multiple language learning and ends with a description of the multilingual whole-school language curriculum.

Lecture 4 by **Jasone Cenoz** and **Durk Gorter** sets out the existing educational policies for multilingualism. The authors explain that multilingual classes do not necessarily imply multilingual education, and they focus on the types and continua of multilingual education. The need and the ways to move from bilingual to multilingual education receive special treatment in the lecture. In particular, the lecture refers to current issues in respect of educational policies for speakers of minority and majority languages, and discusses teaching though the minority language (as in the Basque Country, Catalonia, New Zealand and France). The chapter also touches on the challenges faced by minority languages in education and multilingual pedagogical practices.

Part 2, Aspects of Individual Multilingualism, gathers together lectures referring to important aspects of individual multilingualism and multilingual identity.

Lecture 5 by **John Edwards** starts with a summary of his classic account of societal multilingualism, its role in human history and society and its varieties. Turning then to multilingual individuals, Edwards discusses multilingual competence, drawing on the research literature, on literary vignettes and on historical facts. The discussion of individual multilingualism inevitably commingles with references to societal and historical conditions, which provide food for thought and for insights. Translation phenomena are accorded a place in this lecture too. The author talks about multilingual self-assessment, language choice, code-mixing and code-switching and even the choice of personal names by and for multilingual individuals in various individual contexts. An important part of the lecture is devoted to the exceptional multilingualism of various people, from highly educated, famous personalities to 'savants' and autistic individuals. The author discusses the perennially debated issues of whether multilinguals are 'smarter' than others and whether 'the most talented among them [are] also stranger than others'.

Lecture 6 by **Gessica De Angelis** delivers an overview of early research on cross-linguistic influence, providing clarification of concepts which have often been misunderstood. The author gives an account of ideas about cross-linguistic influence starting with Weinreich, Lado, Corder and Selinker, and then moves to the research of the 1970s with its focus on patterns of non-native development and the quest to identify sources of language transfer in addition to the L1. The subsequent discussion dealing with the direction of cross-linguistic influence and combined influences, as well as with overt and covert transfer, is particularly enlightening. Current perspectives on positive and negative transfer are then treated and the long-debated issue of the role of internal versus external factors in triggering or constraining cross-linguistic influence. The reader will also find an overview of studies on language distance and psychotypology, that is, the learner's individual perception of similarity/difference between languages – a factor much discussed in the relevant literature. Such factors as L2 status, or foreignness, and recency of use are also duly discussed in the lecture.

In **Lecture 7** by **Ema Ushioda** the reader will find methodically and meticulously discussed issues of motivation which are relevant to and important for the analysis of both individual and societal multilingualism. The lecture tackles social, cultural, political, sociological and psychological dimensions of motivation and offers critical perspectives on motivation and multilingualism. Distinguishing between bi- and multi-, the lecture supplies a history of the research on motivation in second language acquisition (SLA) and also deals with motivation in respect of learning multiple languages. The author draws out 'some insights relevant to understanding how learning multiple languages may have different motivational characteristics from learning a single second language'. Supplying practically important knowledge for teachers and education providers, the author provides examples from various parts of the world and different educational settings. In the last section of the lecture Ushioda briefly refers to research designs, methodologies and instruments suitable for investigating language learning motivation in the context of multilingualism.

Lecture 8 by **Camen Muñoz** and **David Singleton** enters into one of the longest running and most heated debates in the language acquisition domain, that which concerns the role of age of onset in the ultimate attainment of target language proficiency. The lecture discusses multilingual acquisition beginning at different ages, differentiates between the outcome of naturalistic and formal instructional learning conditions, and is critical of the use of the monolingual, native yardstick for successful, ultimate attainment. It considers the evidence for and against the maturational constraints notion and, while not ruling any possibility out, generally casts a cold eye on the sustainability of an absolutist version of the critical period hypothesis. On a more practical level, the reader will also find in this lecture some perhaps surprising answers to questions related to the part played by age in rendering school learners multilingual.

The components of **Part 3, The Psycholinguistics and Neurolinguistics of Multilingualism**, relate to the internal mechanisms of multilingual abilities and performance.

Lecture 9 by **Julia Festman** focuses on individual multilingualism from the perspective of the three crucial questions of psycholinguistics: (1) How do we organize language knowledge? (2) How do we process language? (3) How do we acquire language? Trilingual processing and production, trilingual competence and the trilingual speaker's language modes are also explored in comparison with those of monolinguals and bilinguals. The lecture discusses the distinction between trilingualism and bilingualism and devotes special attention to what is meant by 'the psycholinguistics of multilingualism'. The lecture also deals with the mechanisms underlying language choice and language switch.

Lecture 10, produced by the team of researchers **McLoddy R. Kadyamusuma, Eva Higby** and **Loraine Obler**, outlines how the brains of those who speak two or more languages are organized. It sets out to give currently available answers to core questions in the neurolinguistics of multilingualism which interest both lay people and professionals alike: whether multilinguals have different neural mechanisms for processing language, and whether there is one brain mechanism for all languages or if processing is specific to each language. The authors summarize what we know about the cognitive consequences of multilingualism in the healthy brain and also devote much of the lecture to the effects of multilingualism during ageing, focusing on dementia, aphasia and other neurodegenerative conditions.

The final part of the book, **Part 4, Forms of Multilingualism in the Past and Present**, illustrates the diversity of forms that multilingualism can take in time, space and culture, containing two chapters that analyse multilingual practices in the past and present.

Lecture 11 by **Kurt Braunmüller** focuses in the main on the most obvious feature of multilingualism, namely language contact – in society and 'in the brain'. He points out that while this can lead to language change, both divergent and convergent between the languages in question in different circumstances, it can also be favourable in some contexts to an absence of change, i.e. stability. He also makes the point that where contact-induced change occurs it may be either augmentative, increasing or enlarging systems, or reductive, tending in the other direction. Among the rich array of other topics he discusses in his treatment of the diachronic consequences of language contact are language standardization and language change resulting from the incomplete acquisition of a contact language. The lecture ends with a useful survey of different kinds of multilingualism in language history.

The final **Lecture 12** is devoted to the concept of receptive multilingualism and its related concepts. Overviewing the research on interaction between different and closely related languages and the feature of mutual intelligibility, **Jan D. ten Thije** lists the contexts in which receptive multilingualism occurs, considers its occurrence in cross-border communication, in particular regions and in specific transnational and international institutions, companies and the media, and analyzes interaction strategies.

References

Andrews, E. (2014) *Neuroscience and Multilingualism*. Cambridge: Cambridge University Press.

Ansaldo, A.I., Marcotte, K., Scherer, L. and Raboyeau, G.G. (2008) Language therapy and bilingual aphasia: Clinical implications of psycholinguistic and neuroimaging research. *Journal of Neurolinguistics* 21 (6), 539–557.

Aronin, L. (2006) Dominant language constellations: An approach to multilingualism studies. In M. Ó Laoire (ed.) *Multilingualism in Educational Settings* (pp. 140–159). Hohengehren: Schneider Publications.

Aronin, L. (2016) Multicompetence and dominant language constellation. In V. Cook and Li Wei (eds) *The Cambridge Handbook of Linguistic Multicompetence* (pp. 50–76). Cambridge: Cambridge University Press.

Aronin, L. and Hufeisen, B. (2009a) Methods of research in multilingualism studies: Reaching a comprehensive perspective. In L. Aronin and B. Hufeisen (eds) *The Exploration of Multilingualism: Development of Research on L3, Multilingualism and Multiple Language Acquisition* (pp. 103–120). Amsterdam: John Benjamins.

Aronin, L. and Hufeisen, B. (2009b) Crossing the second threshold. In L. Aronin and B. Hufeisen (eds) *The Exploration of Multilingualism: Development of Research on L3, Multilingualism and Multiple Language Acquisition* (pp. 155–160). Amsterdam: John Benjamins.

Aronin, L. and Jessner, U. (2014) Methodology in bi- and multilingual studies: From simplification to complexity. *AILA Review* 27, 56–79.

Aronin, L. and Jessner, U. (2015) Understanding current multilingualism: What can the butterfly tell us? In C. Kramsch and U. Jessner (eds) *The Multilingual Challenge* (pp. 56–79). Berlin: De Gruyter.

Aronin, L. and Singleton, D. (2012) *Multilingualism*. Amsterdam: John Benjamins.

Aronin, L., Fishman, J., Singleton, D. and Ó Laoire, M. (2013) Introduction. Current multilingualism: A new linguistic dispensation. In D. Singleton, J. Fishman, L. Aronin and M. Ó Laoire (eds) *Current Multilingualism: A New Linguistic Dispensation* (pp. 1–23). Berlin: Mouton de Gruyter.

Bailey, A.J., Canagarajah, S., Lan, S. and Devereux, G.P. (2016) Scalar politics, language ideologies, and the sociolinguistics of globalization among transnational Korean professionals in Hong Kong. *Journal of Sociolinguistics* 20 (3), 312–334.

Bastardas-Boada, A. (2012) *Language and Identity Policies in the 'Glocal' Age: New Processes, Effects, and Principles of Organization*. Barcelona: Generalitat de Catalunya, Institut d'Estudis Autonòmics.

Blackledge, A. and Creese, A. (2010) *Multilingualism: A Critical Perspective*. London: Bloomsbury Academic.

Bloch, B. and Trager, G.L. (1942) *Outline of Linguistic Analysis*. Baltimore, MD: Linguistic Society of America/Waverly Press.

Byram, M., Gribkova, B. and Starkey, H. (2002) *Developing the Intercultural Dimension in Language Teaching: A Practical Introduction for Teachers*. Strasbourg: Council of Europe.

Canagarajah, S. (2016) Crossing borders, addressing diversity. *Language Teaching* 49, 438–454.

Cedden, G. and Şimşek, Ç.S. (2012) The impact of a third language on executive control processes. *International Journal of Bilingualism* 16 (3), 1–12.

Cenoz, J. (2009) *Towards Multilingual Education: Basque Educational Research from an International Perspective*. Bristol: Multilingual Matters.

Chomsky, N. (1957) *Syntactic Structures*. The Hague: Mouton.

Cook, V. (1992) Evidence for multi-competence. *Language Learning* 42 (4), 557–591.

Cook, V. (1993) *Linguistics and Second Language Acquisition*. London: Macmillan.

Cooper, D.E. (1973) *Philosophy and the Nature of Language*. London: Longman.

Costa, A., Santesteban, M. and Ivanova, I. (2006) How do highly proficient bilinguals control their lexicalization process? Inhibitory and language-specific selection mechanisms are both functional. *Journal of Experimental Psychology: Learning, Memory, and Cognition* 32 (5), 1057–1074.

De Angelis, G. (2005) Multilingualism and non-native lexical transfer: An identification problem. *International Journal of Multilingualism* 2 (1), 1–25.

de Saussure, F. (1916) *Cours de Linguistique Générale*. Paris: Payot. (English translation (1959) *Course in General Linguistics*. New York: McGraw.)

Festman, J. (2012) 'Multilingual brains': Individual differences in multilinguals – a neuropsycholinguistic perspective. In K. Braunmüller and C. Gabriel (eds) (2012) *Multilingual Individuals and Multilingual Societies* (pp. 207–220). Amsterdam/Philadelphia, PA: John Benjamins.

García, O. (2013) Informal bilingual acquisition: Dynamic spaces for language education. In D. Singleton, J. Fishman, L. Aronin and M. Ó Laoire (eds) *Current Multilingualism: A New Linguistic Dispensation* (pp. 99–118). Berlin: Mouton de Gruyter.

Goral, M. (2012) Multiple languages in the adult brain. In M. Faust (ed.) *The Handbook of the Neuropsychology of Language* (pp. 720–737). Oxford: Blackwell.

Grosjean, F. (1989) Neurolinguists, beware! The bilingual is not two monolinguals in one person. *Brain and Language* 36, 3–15.

Grosjean, F. (1992) Another view of bilingualism. In R. Harris (ed.) *Cognitive Processing in Bilinguals* (pp. 51–62). Amsterdam: North-Holland.

Henry, A. (2011) Examining the impact of L2 English on L3 selves: A case study. *International Journal of Multilingualism* 8 (3), 235–255.

Herdina, P. and Jessner, U. (2002) *A Dynamic Model of Multilingualism: Perspectives of Change in Psycholinguistics*. Clevedon: Multilingual Matters.

Higby, E., Kim, J. and Obler, L.K. (2013) Multilingualism in the brain. *Annual Review of Applied Linguistics* 33, 68–101.

Hornberger, N. (2004) The continua of biliteracy and the bilingual educator: Educational linguistics in practice. *International Journal of Bilingual Education and Bilingualism* 7 (2/3), 155–171.

Hufeisen, B. (2005) Multilingualism: Linguistic models and related issues. In B. Hufeisen and R.J. Fouser (eds) *Introductory Readings in L3* (pp. 31–45). Tübingen: Stauffenburg Verlag.

Hufeisen, B. (2010) Theoretische Fundierung multiplen Sprachenlernens – Factorenmodell 2.0. *Jahrbuch Deutsch als Fremdsprache* 36 (2010), 191–198.

Jessner, U. and Kramsch, C. (eds) (2015) *The Multilingual Challenge*. Berlin: De Gruyter.

Katz, J.J. (1972) *Linguistic Philosophy: The Underlying Reality of Language and its Philosophical Import*. London: Allen & Unwin.

Kemp, C. (2007) Strategic processing in grammar learning: Do multilinguals use more strategies? *International Journal of Multilingualism* 4 (4), 241–261.

Kramsch, C. (2008) Ecological perspectives on foreign language education. *Language Teaching* 41 (3), 389–408.

Kroll, J.F., Bobb, S.C., Misra, M. and Taomei, G. (2008) Language selection in bilingual speech: Evidence for inhibitory processes. *Acta Psychologica* 128, 416–430.

Lacey, A.R. (2001) *A Dictionary of Philosophy*. London and New York: Routledge.

Lanza, E. and Svendsen, B.A. (2007) Tell me who your friends are and I might be able to tell you what language(s) you speak: Social network analysis, multilingualism, and identity. *International Journal of Bilingualism* 11, 275–300.

Matras, Y. and Robertson, A. (2015) Multilingualism in a post-industrial city: Policy and practice in Manchester. *Current Issues in Language Planning* 16 (3), 296–314.

Otheguy, R., García, O. and Reid, W. (2015) Clarifying translanguaging and deconstructing named languages: A perspective from linguistics. *Applied Linguistics Review* 6 (3), 281–307.

Safont-Jordà, M.P. (2012) A longitudinal analysis of Catalan, Spanish and English request modifiers in early third language learning. In D. Gabryś-Barker (ed.) *Cross-linguistic Influences in Multilingual Language Acquisition* (pp. 99–114). Berlin: Springer.

Singleton, D. (2012) Multilingual lexical operations: Keeping it all together ... and apart. In J. Cabrelli Amaro, S. Flynn and J. Rothman (eds) *Third Language Acquisition in Adulthood* (pp. 95–114). Amsterdam: John Benjamins.

Singleton, D. (2016) A critical reaction from second language acquisition research. In V. Cook and Li Wei (eds) *The Cambridge Handbook of Linguistic Multicompetence* (pp. 502–520). Cambridge: Cambridge University Press.

Singleton, D., Regan, V. and Debaene, E. (eds) (2013a) *Linguistic and Cultural Acquisition in a Migrant Community*. Bristol: Multilingual Matters.

Singleton, D., Fishman, J.A., Aronin, L. and Ó Laoire, M. (eds) (2013b) *Current Multilingualism: A New Linguistic Dispensation*. Berlin: Mouton de Gruyter.

Strik, N. (2012) Wh-questions in Dutch: Bilingual and trilingual acquisition compared. In K. Braunmüller and C. Gabriel (eds) (2012) *Multilingual Individuals and Multilingual Societies* (pp. 47–61). Amsterdam/Philadelphia, PA: John Benjamins.

Vasanta, D. (2011) (Re)searching multilingualism in India: A critical review of concepts. *Journal of Indian Speech Language and Hearing Association* 25 (2), 71–81.

Vertovec, S. (2007) Super-diversity and its implications. *Ethnic and Racial Studies* 6, 1024–1054.

Wattendorf, E., Festman, J., Westermann, B., *et al.* (2014) Early bilingualism influences early and subsequently later acquired languages in cortical regions representing control functions. *International Journal of Bilingualism* 18 (1), 48–66.

Whorf, B.L. (1956) Language, mind, and reality. In J.B. Carroll (ed.) *Language, Thought and Reality: Selected Writings of Benjamin Lee Whorf* (pp. 246–270). Cambridge, MA and New York: MIT Press and Wiley.

Part 1

Multilingualism in Society and Education

Lecture 1

What is Multilingualism?[1]

Larissa Aronin

Introduction

Multilingualism is a complex, vibrant and ever-intriguing phenomenon. Today the significance of multilingualism has spilled over its local and private roles into having a much broader, global importance and it is one of the most essential social practices in the world.

The term *multilingualism* is used here to refer to the use of three and more languages and is distinguished, where appropriate, from bilingualism, the use of two languages. In this perspective bilingualism is taken to be a special case of multilingualism rather than vice versa. This position will be further explained later in this lecture where, rather than taking the similarities between bilingualism and multilingualism for granted, we consider the meaningful differences between the two.

The question 'What is multilingualism?' is not as simple as it looks at first sight. Decades have been spent on heated discussions about what kind of person a multilingual is. Definitions and descriptions of various communities which are labelled as multilingual vary in their accounts. The basic understanding of what multilingualism is often diverges for researchers depending on their differing backgrounds and ideologies. Definitions include: 'Multilingualism is the *presence* of a number of languages in one country or community or city'; 'Multilingualism is *the use* of three or more languages'; and 'Multilingualism is *the ability* to speak several languages'. In this last sense, multilingualism is widely regarded as 'a natural state of humankind' (Flynn, 2016).

In addition, neuroscientists discuss multilingualism in the context of the way the brain is organized among those who speak multiple languages.

The above accounts suffice for general acquaintance with different dimensions of multilingualism. Still, there is so far no simple, short and 'one size fits all' answer to the question 'What is multilingualism?'. This lecture will show why we should not expect one. Instead, it will acquaint the reader with the forms, appearances and key features of multilingualism. It will discuss the basic terminology and concepts of multilingualism, introduce the fundamentals that have been established in the field so far, mention some theories and concepts suggested and employed for the study of multilingualism and provide an update on its most recent developments. In the lecture, multilingualism will be considered in a general sense mostly as a societal phenomenon.

Forms of Multilingualism

Individual and societal multilingualism

It is convenient and logical to distinguish between **individual** and **societal multilingualism**. This said, we must acknowledge that the domains of individual multilingualism and societal multilingualism are not clear cut. They are closely interwoven. Human language is a collective phenomenon (Andrews, 2014: 49; Donald, 2004) and it is impossible to study individual multilingualism without considering its societal dimensions. And the opposite is also true: societal multilingualism cannot be understood without knowing how multilingualism affects individuals.

Individual multilingualism relates to the personal sphere and covers the acquisition and use of several languages by an individual. It deals with an individual's ability to master, and appropriately use, two or more languages, and includes language-related physical abilities and neurological processes taking place in the brain, in healthy, challenged and gifted individuals. Those researching individual multilingualism are interested in the emotions and attitudes of learners and speakers of multiple languages in relation to their own and others' languages. Such researchers also study and compare the life trajectories of users of different constellations of languages, and investigate how such individuals benefit from, or are challenged by, the set of languages in their life. The term plurilingualism is sometimes used instead of *individual multilingualism*, especially in Francophone scholarship and documents of the European Union. The individual aspects of multilingualism are discussed in their own specific lecture (Lecture 5 by John Edwards) and are also dealt with in other lectures in this volume.

The term *societal multilingualism* refers to the contexts, circumstances, order, manner and routines of use of languages in different kinds of communities, organizations and groups. People are not only aware of, but often regulate their language practices through the way they deal with the language varieties they know, and by introducing additional language varieties into their communal life. Societies have a prescribed or expected linguistic behaviour, associated with the particular position or status of languages in a family, school, nation and country. Language-related events going beyond an established frame are also a matter of interest for sociolinguists, applied linguists and sociologists of language. How multiple language varieties intersect in society, what the status and social opportunities of people are who use particular languages in certain multilingual contexts, what the language policies and practices are and how they change with time – all these issues are within the scope of societal multilingualism (Edwards, 2007). Also, multilingualism may impact on how the language(s) one uses influence how easily one can obtain medical help, publish an article, write a complaint and get a job in a multilingual country. Likewise, such details as whether one has a container in one's kitchen on which the word 'bread' is written in an indigenous or a lesser used language, rather than in an official language of a country, are matters of societal multilingualism.

By *societal multilingualism* we mean the organized and unorganized language practices with three and more languages and the handling of more than two languages by some or all members of a society, as well as the implications of these practices and this handling for the society and its members. 'Handling' involves language policies, attitudes, language behaviour and the assumptions underlying such behaviour in a particular community, all in the context of three and more languages being dealt with.

The existence of societal multilingualism in a country or region does not mean that the country or region in question is peopled by equally multilingual citizens. There are communities and territories where multiple languages coexist side by side. That is, in some countries speakers use their own languages but not so much the other languages of the community; they do not normally know and do not have to know or use all the languages spoken in this territory. When many languages simply coexist in a territory, without the necessity of all of them being used by all the citizens, it can be called *proximate multilingualism*. Switzerland, with its principle of territoriality, is a good example of proximate multilingualism. Although this country is considered one of the oldest multilingual countries in Europe, its citizens do not need to use all four official languages of the Swiss Confederation: German, French, Italian and Romansch. A single language (e.g. Italian in Ticino, German in Zurich, Glarus, Lucerne, Nidwalden, Obwalden) is recognized as official in most cantons for use in all domains of social communication. Only a few cantons are officially bilingual: Bienne and Freiburg, as well as the federal capital Berne with French and German as official languages. There is also the trilingual canton of Graubünden, where German, Romansh and Italian are official languages. People can manage very well using just one official language of a canton.

In many localities we encounter a wide range of degrees to which languages simply exist separately side by side, or are interfused in the language practices of the citizens. This range runs from indifference to languages other than one's own to active interaction and tight language contact. In the proximal type of societal multilingualism, people speaking minority languages may live in linguistic and cultural bubbles, or may live their lives using only immigrant languages without mastery of an official majority language. Where there is predominance of the proximate type of multilingualism in a society, some speakers who master a set of the important languages will serve as mediators between the language communities.

The second form of societal multilingualism which has proliferated recently, often spreading to territories formerly characterized by the proximate form, is the *integrative* form of societal multilingualism. The integrative form denotes the situation where people not only encounter other languages of the context but actively use them. Integrative multilingualism is increasingly frequent owing to the globalization processes of migration and technological advance. The integrative and proximate forms of multilingualism are at opposite extremes of a continuum; there is a range of intermediate forms – less integrative and more integrative – in between.

Historical and current multilingualism

In order to deal with multilingualism practically, and for the sake of theoretical understanding, it is useful to come to some conclusions about whether multilingualism existed in the past, or if is a totally new phenomenon. To answer this question let us first turn to the adjacent fields of anthropology, ethnology and history.

They inform us that multilingualism is a specifically human feature and has been characteristic of humans for thousands of years. Language is involved in human evolution in an intricate way and language is a quality distinguishing our species from others. Notably, *many* languages have been spoken from the dawn of human interaction. Barnard (2016: 134) maintains that with *Homo sapiens* and possibly Neanderthals, who had bigger brains than *Homo sapiens*, '[m]ultilingualism was the norm, and multilingual peoples were made up of individuals from different linguistic backgrounds, whose groups intermarried and passed on both their genes and their linguistic diversity'. Looking at more recent history, we see that the social nature of language and ideas about it roughly parallel stages of societal evolution and organization, varying under changing historical circumstances (see Table 1.1).

This table broadly suggests that for the earliest communities, the fact of the existence of human language was important in itself. At this stage, whether in the form of a proto-language or embracing many particular communication systems, it served humans as a tool of communication and cognition and distinguished humans from other species.

Later in history, with the establishment of nation-states in Europe, language became a consolidating tool for the development of a civil society. A particular language or language variety from among those used within a nation's borders was often selected to play a unifying role and to enhance political and economic development in a country. During both waves of the development of individual nation-states, the first in the 15th–18th centuries (the Netherlands, Scotland, England, United States, France) and the second in the

Table 1.1 *Stages of societal organization and language patterns*

Stage of societal organization	Language crucial as
Tribal	*A* language
Nation-states	*The* language
Globalization: centralization and localization	Langua**ges**

Source: After Aronin (2005: 9).

19th century (Sweden, Spain, Norway, Portugal, Greece, Belgium, Hungary, Denmark, Romania, Italy, Canada, Japan, Germany, Iceland and Bulgaria), the European territories divided into nation-states which were typically each identified by one language. It was *the language*, e.g. French in France, High German in Germany, Spanish in Spain, that was called upon to represent communal identity, shared experiences and interests.

Today, in postmodern times, multiple languages organized in unitary groups are important (dominant language constellations are discussed later in this lecture). The particular form and essence of multilingualism is time dependent and follows changes in social existence.

In earlier times, particular languages and even single specific skills were instrumental in subserving a variety of facets of human existence as the backdrop to multilingualism. Multilingualism as a phenomenon was useful but not crucial for the maintenance and advancement of communities and groups. Normally, in various localities and communities, one factor came to the fore as especially useful. At other times and in other places another linguistic skill would become useful for advancement of the particular group. For instance, elsewhere we have referred to Ancient Egypt, where the skill of writing was more significant than the presence of multiple languages in the vast country (Aronin & Singleton, 2012: 44–45).

Previous multilingual contexts mainly dictated particular points of emphasis in the use of several languages or their specific single skills necessitated by particular aims or needs. We can infer that multilingualism of the past was largely circumstantial and unevenly spread between groups and individuals for a variety of purposes. Specific limited (not necessarily unimportant) aims needed to be attained, but such attainment did not define the development of humanity nor was it crucial for such development. Multilingualism in the past had different tasks and aims. It was local and patchy, whereas it is (contrastingly) systematically and overarchingly global now.

Our current day-to-day existence and social behaviour, accompanied by language, differ markedly from those of previous generations. While the three basic components of multilingualism, 'user, environment and language' (Aronin & Singleton, 2012), endure through centuries, they also keep mutating, thus inducing changes in the resultant type of multilingualism. In other words, the same but ever-changing elements each time generate different varieties of social practice, different kinds of multilingualism. Flores and Lewis (2016: 98, emphasis added) rightly treat 'language practices and language categories as *sociopolitical emergences* that are produced by the specific histories and contemporary contexts of interlocutors'.

We can conclude this section as follows. The presence and the use of many languages in human societies as well as the human ability to use many languages have existed since long ago. However, the manifestations, configuration and role of multilingualism have been different in different periods relating to circumstances and the stage of human development. Emphasizing these meaningful changes, I refer to the forms of multilingualism which occurred in the past as **historical multilingualism**, and that unfolding today as **current multilingualism**. The specificity of the multilingualism of our own times will be elaborated on in the next section.

The Key Features of Current Multilingualism

Current multilingualism differs from the previous social linguistic arrangements in many ways. Ignoring the transformations would be like saying that technology has not changed throughout history on the basis that we still use the wheel, which was allegedly invented in the late Neolithic period. In the following we will discuss the characteristic features of postmodernity inextricably linked to current language practices and the key features of current multilingualism.

Globalization as a context and the driving force

The scope of multilingualism has broadened immensely to the extent that it now covers the whole world. Even the countries that were until recently considered strictly monolingual, such as Japan and Iceland, are now experiencing an influx of languages and multilingual speakers. Current multilingualism is suffusive, being part and parcel of most current human activities. In late postmodern times multilingualism has gradually developed into a phenomenon crucial in its role in and impact on human civilization. It is central to the progress and maintenance of modern civilization (Aronin & Singleton, 2012).

What has led to such fundamental worldwide changes in the way people use their languages? Globalization is frequently invoked in this connection, and current multilingualism is linked to its basic processes such as mobility, diversity and technological innovation. These notions came under intensive discussion in the late 20th century and are often mentioned as characteristic only of more recent times.

In fact, many social processes and phenomena which we think of as appearing only recently are not really new, but rather have undergone transformation with time. Globalization itself is said to have started long ago, with the voyage of Christopher Columbus to the New World in 1492. Therefore, it is important to understand how mobility, diversity, complexity and the technological advances of today feature in the reality of multilingualism.

Mobility is one of the features deemed to be the cause of diversity of the current multilingualism. Yet scholars point out that people have always been on the move. Most recent anthropological research suggests that human language *preceded* the migrations of our species across the globe. Barnard (2016) believes that language had begun before modern humans populated the earth: '[w]hen humans first arrived in Australia, they arrived with language, having used it on their migration and after their fortuitous settlement on the continent' (Barnard, 2016: 134). In the Middle Ages in Europe the roads were full of pilgrims, priests and wandering soldiers, and carriages bringing families and their luggage from villages to towns and back. Chaunu (1966) describes the ways in which improving transport in Europe facilitated the flow of people and trade, resulting in remarkable economic effects for some places. Early modern history (see, for example, Betteridge, 2007; Schilling, 2008) also presents us with evidence of significant movements of individuals, populations and goods around Europe.

We often encounter claims of an unprecedented increase of migration in recent times. It is true that the number of immigrants has increased in the last century and a half. But considering that the overall number of people on Earth has also swelled, the proportion of migrants has actually decreased. The exhaustive study of demographers Czajka and de Haas (2014) convincingly demonstrates that what actually changed in regard to migration is not its scope but the migratory trajectories, distance and destinations, especially in Europe. The patterns and meaning of migration have altered as well. Alternating between different cities, countries and continents has become 'normal' as opposed to one-way migration in earlier times. Contemporary migration is more visible, and receives more attention from researchers because it is more intense and more crucially intertwined with the fabric of society.

Technological advance in our times may seem pertinent only to our period, but scholars tell us that the previous eras' breakthroughs in technology appeared perhaps even more drastic to their contemporaries. Radical technological improvements have been occurring for a long time and some scientists claim that the emergence of such technologies stunned contemporaries not less and perhaps more than the internet and modern-day sophisticated appliances impress us. It has to be acknowledged, on the other hand, that the transformations wrought by communication technology have brought crucial changes to linguistic practices.

Yet another concept of globalization discussed in connection with multilingualism is **diversity** and **superdiversity**. In 2007 Steven Vertovec introduced the concept of 'superdiversity' in the field of social science. His intention was to address *'a changed set of conditions and social configurations* which call for a multi-dimensional approach to understanding contemporary processes of change and their outcomes' (Vertovec, 2014, italics in original). The author of this concept specified that transformative 'diversification of diversity' 'has not just occurred in terms of movements of people reflecting more ethnicities, languages and countries of origin, but also with respect to a multiplication of significant variables that affect where, how and with whom people live' (Vertovec, 2014: n.p.). No doubt the sociolinguistic diversity and superdiversity of language variants, language users and linguistic practices and situations that has ensued is part of this global process (Pavlenko, 2019).

One more important novelty that has entered the globalization discourse is a *complexity* or *emergence perspective*. According to this, the world is not only complex in the meaning of 'complicated', as simply compiled of many elements, but complex, assuming that the whole is greater than the sum of its parts. *Emergent phenomena*, which are the products of multiple *interactions* of elements, acquire properties that are different from the properties of the components of a phenomenon. Illustrations easily come from organic and physical nature: bacterial infections, hurricanes, communities of ants, as well as dunes, formed by interaction with the flow of air or water, are all emergent phenomena. When individuals create societies, the actions of individuals come together in ways that have always been among the most difficult to explain. No wonder complexity is an increasingly valued perspective in applied linguistics (see, for example, De Bot, 2004; Larsen-Freeman & Cameron, 2008) and multilingualism (Aronin & Jessner, 2015; Jessner, 2013). Teachers, social workers, doctors, psychologists and administration workers are becoming aware that multilingualism is complex, and has to be dealt with accordingly.

When discussing complexity as a feature of today's multilingualism it is important to remember that not all systems are complex in the same way. The degree of complexity is defined by quantifiable criteria. While bilingualism and multilingualism are both complex phenomena, multilingualism has a higher degree of complexity than bilingualism (see more on this in Aronin & Jessner, 2015). In tri-plus multilingualism the number of steps, algorithms, symbols, parts and aspects are more numerous and denser than in bilingualism. This might, for example, have to do with the number of words for the same situation available to a language user, or the number of grammar options available to express an idea. There are seven language modes (Grosjean, 2001) available for a trilingual as compared to a bilingual's three. The use and acquisition of three languages clearly contains more information than with two: one more language system with one more lexicon, grammar and pronunciation system, an accompanying third culture, and also a much wider metalinguistic awareness about how the third set of systems relates to the other two, separately and together. Obviously, there are differences of complexity between cross-linguistic interactions involving three languages as compared with those involving just two. Differentiation in tri-plus multilingualism is more diverse and numerous; it increases exponentially, also due to cross-linguistic interactions. For instance, the specific accent in the third language (L3) may be the result of influences from the second language (L2) and first language (L1), and may also vary from individual to individual. Thus, taking all of the above into account, multilingualism comes through as a phenomenon less predictable and of a more complex order than bilingualism. This situation refers to various emergent phenomena, including differences between individual multilinguals, the atmosphere in particular multilingual schools, the mini-community status of multilingual families, varieties of global English, the appearance of new languages and new linguistic varieties and also the localization and representation of processing elements in each particular trilingual-multilingual brain.

To conclude, we can say the following. Being part and parcel of globalization, multilingualism is inherently involved in its main processes. Globalization processes, such as migration and technological advance and characteristics such as superdiversity and complexity, reflect multilingualism practices.

The distinctive features of current multilingualism

Multilingualism as distinct from bilingualism

There is no doubt that bilingualism and multilingualism have much in common. Both are defined as the ability in an individual to use at least one language in addition to the mother tongue or, in a community or a country, the use or existence of more than one language. But similarity does not mean identity. Beyond observable surface characteristics and despite the power of the tradition of conflating bilingualism and multilingualism, the distinction between the two is becoming increasingly apparent (Aronin & Hufeisen, 2009; Cenoz & Genesee, 1998; Cenoz *et al.*, 2001). From the previous section we have seen that multilingualism is essentially more complex than bilingualism. Multilingualism is distinct from bilingualism in other essential ways. Scholars in different disciplines have found *systemic differences* between bilingualism and multilingualism. These findings defy the longstanding assumption of laypeople, and even of some researchers, that processing, acquiring and using three and more languages are essentially the same as processing, acquiring and using only two languages, that it is 'just adding one more language'. The increasing amount of data we receive from neurolinguists, psycholinguists and sociolinguistics scholars as well as ordinary daily observations and experiences do not allow us easily to equate bilingualism and multilingualism. Thus, recent research in neurolinguistics refers to multilingualism as opposed to bilingualism quite explicitly (Andrews, 2014). Higby *et al.* (2013: 68) note that 'certain unique properties of multilinguals are beginning to be noticed, particularly regarding early language representation, gray matter density, and speed of lexical retrieval'. Flynn *et al.* (2004: 4–5) argue that 'a comparison of L1 and L2 acquisition alone [...] is not sufficient in terms of our understanding of the human capacity for language. We need to investigate the acquisition of a third language (L3) in order to unconfound certain factors left confounded in L1/L2 acquisition.' These and other studies leave little doubt that, with further experience in additional language learning as opposed to the first experience in additional language learning, different mechanisms develop that would not exist if the person had not learnt and used the second additional language (L3).

Various studies have detected a 'threshold', a 'system shift' or other qualitative events marking the transition from bilingualism to multilingualism. Applied linguists and sociolinguists seem to have come to a consensus that with acquisition of the L3, important changes occur. Berkes and Flynn found that the performance of the L3 study group on relative clauses was undeniably better than that of the L2 group and postulated that 'results would indicate that enhancement took place in the learners' syntactical knowledge due to multilingual experience' (Berkes & Flynn, 2012: 10). This is enormously important in terms of the implications of multiple language acquisition for language teaching. In the area of pragmatics and early multilingual development, determining interaction between Catalan, Spanish and English in a longitudinal case study, Safont-Jordà (2013: 112) found 'quite a different pattern' in the use of politeness strategies in the L3. The results of this longitudinal study confirmed the dynamic and qualitative change that takes place in L3 acquisition. Kemp (2007) found very specific tendencies in how multilinguals use language learning strategies, that the more languages learners knew, (a) the greater the number of grammar learning strategies they used and (b) the more frequently they used them. These are important quantitative data, but they also point to a possible threshold effect for the use of grammar learning strategies, which 'may mean that, compared to L2 learning, augmentation in number and frequency of strategies used, occurs to a greater extent during the acquisition of the third language, increasing more gradually in additional languages' (Kemp, 2007: 257). In her study of non-native lexical transfer De Angelis (2005: 14) analyzed data that 'illustrates a type of behaviour that speakers of two languages do not display, highlighting the uniqueness of multilinguals' behavior, and the need to view multilinguals as unique learners and speakers, rather than as bilinguals with additional languages'. De Angelis proposed a 'system shift', understood as a shift in lexical knowledge from a source to a guest system, and stated that 'the interaction between non-native languages cannot be assumed to be governed by the same principles that govern the interaction between the native and one non-native language' (De Angelis, 2005: 14).

These and other *significant differences* between bilingualism and multilingualism have crucial implications for research and practical dealings with multilingualism – both in the area of language acquisition and for societal outcomes. One of the practical outcomes of the distinction is a new understanding of and consequent approach to the organization of *trilingual education* as distinct from the education of trilinguals and from bilingual education (see, for example, Cenoz & Jessner, 2009). Owing to the realization of the specific nature of multilingualism, other novel issues of importance appear in the field, some of them specific solely to multilingual, but not bilingual, phenomena, such as the issues of prior knowledge of bilinguals in the process of learning subsequent languages. Among the newly emerging issues of importance are trilingual early development (Braun & Cline, 2014), minority languages, education via minority language (see Lecture 4 on multilingual education by Jasone Cenoz & Durk Gorter, this volume), new language varieties (see, for example, Kirkpatrick, 2007), world Englishes and English in its various functions (e.g. as a global language, as a lingua franca, as a second language), increased focus on linguistic rights (e.g. Coetzee-Van Rooy, 2010), managing multilingual populations (e.g. Matras & Robertson, 2015), and cross-linguistic interactions between the non-native languages (see Lecture 6 by Gessica de Angelis, this volume).

The accumulated data from a diversity of disciplines that point to the divergence of bilingualism and multilingualism from physiological, cognitive, emotional, pedagogical and social points of view are significant because they carry crucial implications as to how we deal with the phenomena of societal and individual bi- and multilingualism. Aronin and Jessner (2015: 281) concluded that '[b]ilingualism and multilingualism are close, and overlapping in many ways, but, as a bilingual turns into a multilingual, the phenomenon diverges (bifurcates), quantitative and qualitative differences become deeper, to the extent that the nature of the emerging phenomena changes'.

There are also some puzzling facts discovered with regard to multilinguals *which cannot be explained in ways used for bilinguals*. The issue of trilingual switching costs is one of them. One would expect that trilinguals should need longer response times as compared to bilinguals when switching from one language to the other simply because of the amount of data to be suppressed (languages not used at the moment). Bilingual research has supplied evidence that the switching cost in bilinguals is mostly asymmetric: the response time is reported as longer when switching from the L2 to the dominant L1 than from the L1 to the weaker L2, and not vice versa. This is interpreted as deriving from the need to inhibit the dominant L1 more intensively when producing words in the less dominant L2 (Kroll *et al.*, 2008, in Goral, 2012). With trilingual participants in tests, the situation with switching cost is different; it is less clear and harder to explain. It seems that switching costs in trilinguals are not as pronounced as might be expected. It is obvious that the investigation of multilingualism requires theories, concepts and research methods of its own (Aronin & Hufeisen, 2009; Aronin & Jessner, 2014).

Models specific to multilingualism

The conceptual base of multilingualism as a field of study has inherited many theories which have been developed in regard to bilingualism over the years and includes theoretical explanations of language contact, alternation and code-switching, interference, diglossia, bilingual speech processing (e.g. Levelt's 1989 speaking model), social meaning and language structure, etc. Some of the models created to explain bilingualism are relevant to multilingualism too. Nevertheless, while bilingual theories and models contribute to multilingualism studies, they alone do not suffice for a comprehensive explanation of multilingualism, mainly owing to the increased level of complexity in multilingualism.

Several models have been put forward to specifically explain multilingual and not bilingual phenomena. Most of the existing multilingualism models refer to the process of multiple language acquisition. These are the factor model by Britta Hufeisen (1998, 2010), the role-function model by Sarah Williams and Björn Hammarberg (Hammarberg, 2001, 2009), the multilingual processing model proposed by Franz-Joseph Meißner (2003) and the dynamic model of multilingualism (DMM) developed by Philip Herdina and Ulrike Jessner (2002) (see more on these models in Lecture 3 of this volume). One model, the biotic model of multilingualism proposed by Larissa Aronin and Muiris Ó Laoire (2004), is largely sociolinguistic in its perspective. It takes a broad holistic view of the multilingual individual and multilingualism, and is developed along the lines of the complexity approach. This model is more general and attempts to account for the whole identity of the multilingual, including the cognitive, societal and personal (e.g. emotional) aspects (Gabryś-Barker, 2005; Lecture 2, this volume).

The above-presented models of multilingualism are specifically constructed with the aim of describing and explaining the nature of multilingualism and multilingual users/learners. These models distinguish between bilingualism and multilingualism, that is, between bilinguals and tri+-linguals. All of them propose universals for multilingualism, and multiple language acquisition processes and phenomena. Each model has its own field of reference and focuses on various aspects from a variety of theoretical points of view. Together, they complement and reinforce each other (Marx & Hufeisen, 2003). All these models of multilingualism hold that interrelations between the language systems of multilinguals are central, and all the relevant systems are in use in parallel (either actively or passively). All models acknowledge the active role of previously acquired languages in learning a new one.

Methodology of multilingualism

Once one accepts the distinction between bi- and multilingualism on theoretical and practical levels, the reliability, adequacy and appropriateness of bilingual methods used for research in multilingualism comes under scrutiny. Time-honoured methods of psycholinguistic and sociolinguistic research, including research approaches and instruments that range from questionnaires and observations to tests and experiments, continue to be rightly and intensively employed by researchers (Hornberger & Corson, 1997; Li Wei & Moyer, 2008).

With that, it has become increasingly clear that not all the methods of bilingualism are easily adaptable for multilingual situations. Scholars have realized that for a long time the difference between bilinguals and multilinguals and bilingualism and multilingualism has been ignored, or its appropriate study has been frequently avoided, owing to perceived difficulties. Recent literature includes cases where in bilingual experimental studies at least some of the participants were actually tri- and more-linguals, which rendered the findings less reliable.

The greater complexity of the field of research, study design and identification of groups and individuals, etc. all present methodological challenges for researchers of multilingualism. Not all the methods used in bilingualism studies take account of the specific complex nature of multilingualism; therefore, not all of them are appropriate for its study. For this reason new methods for taking a global look at complex phenomena and processes have been developed. These are, in the first place, complexity methods and conceptualizations of various kinds.

As for complexity methods, Larsen-Freeman and Cameron (2008: 241) advocate their use, on the grounds that '[r]eductionism does not produce satisfying explanations that are respectful to the interconnectedness of the many nested levels and timescales that exist'. They elucidate that when investigating complex phenomena from a complexity/DCT perspective, '...the nature of explanation changes, cause and effect no longer operate in the usual way'. Researchers of multilingualism via dynamic systems/complexity also suggest the adoption of modified research methodologies, ranging from ethnography, formative experiments and action research to longitudinal, case study, time-series approaches, micro-developmental studies, computer modelling and brain imaging, and the combination of a number of methodologies, in order to be able to provide valid answers to new research questions (Larsen-Freeman & Cameron, 2008: 241–250; see also Verspoor *et al.*, 2011).

A number of methods especially appropriate for multilingualism can be gathered together under the umbrella term of *conceptualizations*. The methodology of conceptualization has evolved gradually and has grown exponentially in recent years (Aronin, 2017). Conceptualizing, or applying theoretical thinking, entails interpretation of data from a number of viewpoints. This can include clarifying terms, developing new concepts and constructs and applying novel perspectives to already studied phenomena. The whole field of multilingualism, and specific areas within it, are being conceptualized.

Among the conceptualizations belongs the deployment of a set of concepts and constructs in bilingualism and multilingualism which can serve as methods or lenses of examination per se. Here we can identify the *affordances perspective* (Gibson, 1977, 1979), *multi-competence* (Cook, 1992, 2013a) and *dominant language constellations* (Aronin, 2006, 2016). Using *metaphors* as a way of exploring bilingual and multilingual reality has proved to be especially useful (e.g. Hornberger, 2002).

In addition, *particular lines of research, in themselves, act as a methodology* for the wider area of multilingualism. This means that the concepts, the theories and the particular methods and techniques of the disciplines involved are applied to multilingualism studies. These streams of research advance the current study of multilingualism by addressing it from different vantage points.

This especially happens with interdisciplinary strands of research when methods that are now in use are appropriated from both neighbouring and distant disciplines. For instance, investigation of 'the material culture of multilingualism' focuses on material objects as they influence, modify or determine multiple language use and acquisition. The material culture of multilingualism perspective draws on ethnology, anthropology, sociology and linguistics and consequently employs the methods and techniques of all the disciplines involved and also has the material objects as subjects of research. The study of materialities in the multilingual context not only injects a wealth of additional data previously deemed irrelevant, but also allows an unorthodox approach and research questions to deal with established issues in multilingualism.

In the same way, *historical multilingualism studies* serve as a methodology for research and use historical and linguistic methods and techniques (Bloemendal, 2015; Braunmüller & Ferraresi, 2003; Rindler-Schjerve & Vetter, 2007). Finally, the budding field of the *philosophy of multilingualism* (as distinct from philosophy of language) is an overarching, global methodology of conceptualization in multilingualism (Aronin & Singleton, 2013).

Recently, an issue of the joint appropriateness of methods for bilingualism and multilingualism has emerged. There is a kind of overlap where some methods are appropriate for both bilingualism and multilingualism research. Saying that, some methods of bilingualism are not appropriate for multilingualism and some methods only work and are appropriate for use when dealing with three and more languages.

Diversity of societal multilingualism

Societal multilingualism is not uniform throughout the globe; rather, it is extremely diversified in today's world. We can see particular manifestations of societal multilingualism as various forms of 'sociopolitical emergences' (Flores & Lewis, 2016: 98) that are produced by specific histories and contexts.

A fascinating variety of multilingual language practices can be found in different geographical locations. European/Western multilingualism or, as it sometimes called, 'multilingualism of the Old World', has been the dominant focus of research in multilingualism. Another longstanding line of research describes and examines Indian multilingualism (Annamalai, 2006; Kachru *et al.*, 2008).

Multilingualism in India has its own face. A huge number of languages, almost 6600, belonging to at least four language families – Indo-European, Dravidian, Austro-Asiatic and Tibeto-Burman – is not the only exceptional feature of Indian multilingualism. The daily use of many of these languages is a norm rather than something out of the ordinary. Thousands of mother tongues, mostly minority languages, are typically maintained throughout the years because of the fundamental values peculiar to language use in India. Whether speakers of languages which are widely distributed across India or speakers of languages with few users, all tend to preserve and perpetuate their language varieties. India is noted for having the largest number of home languages, as well as for maintaining the home language across generations even when the population migrates to another linguistic area (Pandit, 1979).

India's many thousands of languages are not used evenly throughout the country and across populations. It is typical that a state contains a mixture of speakers of many languages rather than speakers of one or two. The transparency and fluidity of boundaries between languages (Khubchandani, 1997) helps speakers move between various patterns of language use in different domains of their daily life, 'to glide from one language to another' (Annamalai, 2008: 228). Major regional languages (vernaculars) are accepted nationally, while other languages are accepted as dialects of particular regions. The noticeable differences in the domains of use, the functions and the prestige of languages make some researchers speak about the hierarchical nature of multilingualism in India, characterized by a double divide – one between the elitist languages of power (e.g. English, Hindi) and the major regional languages (vernaculars), and the other between the regional languages and the tribal ones (Mohanty, 2010: 131).

The sociolinguists of Africa have long insisted that along with clear similarities to the rest of the world, African multilingualism is very special in many ways, and has been developing into its present state for centuries (Anchimbe, 2007; Banda, 2009; Coetzee-Van Rooy, 2010; Makoni & Meinhof, 2003). Most African states are multilingual to varying degrees, and the list of outstandingly multilingual countries includes: Nigeria, with 514 languages; Cameroon, with 279 languages; Sudan, with 134 languages; Chad, with 132 languages; Tanzania, with 129 languages; and the Central African Republic, with 69 languages (Lewis, 2009). The special type of multilingualism existing in African contexts 'is characterised by the coexistence of oral and written, foreign and indigenous, official and non-official, pidginized and non-pidginized languages used for distinct and less-intervening purposes' (Anchimbe, 2007: 9). As pointed out by Makoni and Meinhof (2003: 6), a speaker of a particular language may be regarded as a mother tongue speaker even if that person does not speak the language fluently, but has mastered the cultural and often religious practices of the community. How these language varieties are accommodated within the societies and which issues emerge as more critical for each particular country are significant questions if we want to understand the specific versions and patterns of multilingualism, and multilingualism as a whole.

The diversity of multilingual arrangements and practices is also seen in the recent interest devoted to particular multilingual practices in locally confined societies. Here attention is centred on heteroglossic 'social groupings of a small and manageable size', 'mainly in areas not or relatively recently exposed to Western settlements and Western ideas of nation-states and standard language ideologies' (Lupke, 2016: 41). **Small-scale multilingualism** is a particular type of multilingualism 'to designate balanced multilingualism practiced in meaningful geographical spaces sustaining dense interaction and exchange at their interior'. The author believes that the study of such societies, which are likely to constitute 'the primal human condition' (Evans, 2013) advances our understanding of the social conditions that have shaped language use and language structure for most of human history.

On the same grounds of the perceived predominance of attention to 'Western' multilingualism and the disregard of other multilingual settings, a group of sociolinguists and applied linguists have come up with the concept of **southern multilingualisms** (https://southernmultilingualisms.org/). They focus on 'the experiences, knowledge and expertise that southern and marginalized communities have of multilingualism and diversity' and see the advantage of focusing on these settings in finding out how knowledge and expertise may be exchanged in reciprocal and respectful ways among marginal and mainstream communities located in Southern and Northern settings of the world.

Terms have appeared reflecting the novelty of the emergent features of language practices. Such terms include, for example, **metrolingualism** and **truncated multilingualism**. Metrolingualism is defined as 'the contemporary practice of creative uses, or mixing of different linguistic codes in predominantly urban contexts, transcending established social, cultural, political and historical boundaries, identities and ideologies' (Jaworski, 2014: 134). Truncated multilingualism is the descriptive term referring to an individual mastery of multiple languages, defined as 'linguistic competencies which are organized topically, on the basis of domains or specific activities' (Blommaert *et al.*, 2005). This approach attempts to account for the unexpected manifestations of multilingualism in the real world, when not complete languages but their parts are used, according to need.

Multilingual practices refer not only to what is 'given' at present. They are also being re-evaluated and modified with regard to particular educational perspectives. The concept and term 'translanguaging' appeared about 10 years ago to refer to multiple languages as a valuable resource. It is developing within the theoretical dimension differently from the code-switching approach. The latter, a more traditional view, emerges from viewing named languages such as English, French and Dutch as separate monolingual codes which could be used without reference to one another, and thus operates with the concepts of borrowing, calques and language interference (MacSwan, 2017). The translanguaging school of thought (García, 2013; García & Kleyn, 2016; Otheguy *et al.*, 2015) calls for a vision of multiple languages transgressing language borders. According to this increasingly widespread view, bilinguals have one linguistic repertoire from which they strategically select features in order to communicate effectively. Researchers promoting translingual practices in education (Canagarajah, 2011) argue for the educational value of allowing bilingual students in school to use their entire language repertoire, rather than sticking to the separate use of different named languages.

To sum up the section on key features of current multilingualism, we can say the following. Although the study of multilingualism largely stems from the study of bilingualism, multilingualism is now widely seen as a separate field of study with its own subject matter, models, theories and methods of research. Multilingual practices are extremely diverse, as are the perceptions of these practices on the part of scholars and users.

In this section we saw that global changes coupled with the complex and emergent nature of multilingualism have resulted in a meaningful transformation of language practices. The changes refer to the way in which languages are perceived, treated and used. In the next section we will discuss some particular changes in language practices.

Part 1: Multilingualism in Society and Education

Distinctive Language Practices in Current Multilingualism

This section is devoted to the distinctive language practices of current multilingualism, in particular, the ways we perceive, treat and use languages.

Language nominations: The way we perceive and treat languages

With thousands of languages spread across the world, with most countries becoming multilingual and with the recognition of many previously ignored languages, pidgins and dialects, there emerged the need to somehow situate them by mentally marking their roles in respect of individuals and within societies. **Language nominations** serve this purpose. Language nominations are specific language appellations that are assigned to various named languages and dialects according to their perceived role for particular individuals or communities. Language nominations are used in addition to the names of languages, such as Spanish, Norwegian or Russian. They include, for example, *'official language'*, *'majority language'*, *'indigenous language'*, *'immigrant languages'*. For example, Danish is an *official* and *national language* in Denmark. Danish is a *minority* language attaching to Danish communities in Norway, Sweden, Spain, the United States, Canada, Brazil and Argentina and also a *home language* for around 15–20% of the urban population of Greenland. How do language nominations emerge?

Some language nominations appear in state documents. This, for instance, happened in India, where according to the English Language Amendment Bill, English is an *associate language*. In Canada, The Canadian Official Languages Act made English and French the *official languages* of the country.

A top-down imposition of language nominations is not the only and not their most frequent origination. In the last decades especially, language nominations have been discussed and proposed by sociolinguists and applied linguists in addressing specific practical situations. Consider the *heritage language* nomination which was selected from a number of options by language professionals in North America (Kagan, 2005; Wiley, 2001). The motive was the upsurge of interest on the part of the grandchildren of immigrants in the languages of their forebears. Sociolinguists and applied linguists felt compelled to construct and define the term in reference to such languages. Coining this term allowed educators to develop a basic definition of a heritage language learner who is different in important ways from the traditional foreign language student. The term serves a very practical purpose and refers to a language learner who is raised in a home where a non-English language is spoken, who speaks or at least understands the language in question and who is to some degree bilingual in that language and in English (Wiley, 2001).

A number of language nominations were consciously worked out because of the urgent need for the management and protection of minority languages. In order to ensure more favourable provisions concerning the status of regional or minority languages, the legal regime of persons belonging to 'minorities' and the recognition of the regional or minority languages as an expression of cultural wealth, the nominations of *regional* and *minority languages* were issued by the Council of Europe (European Charter for Regional or Minority Languages 1992; see http://www.ifa.de/fileadmin/pdf/abk/inter/ec_ets_148.pdf, accessed 21 March 2018).

The nominations provided by scholars do not necessarily coincide with those created for the same languages by ordinary language users. Language nominations evolved naturally, by way of popular coinage, expressing a shared popular understanding of the role of a given language and a common attitude to it. In this case nominations carry emotional connotations and advert to the value and role currently assigned to a given language by a particular community. For example, *mother tongue, home language* and *native language* traditionally carry connotations of origin, permanency and inseparable emotional ties, while *foreign language* points to distance from one's way of life and culture and usefulness for particular purposes such as tourism or reading (Aronin & Singleton, 2010; Aronin *et al.*, 2011).

Not only do language nominations indicate the role of particular language for a person, they also point to the function of the language in a community. Such terms may convey subjective evaluation about the position that a society has allocated to a specific language in a specific place and period of time. Therefore, they have become vital for teachers, social workers and other interested parties. Language teaching is different according to how one defines a language. Today it is important to distinguish between *English as a second language, English as a lingua franca* and *English as a foreign language* in the context of writing syllabi, courseware and textbooks, determining the hours for teaching in a school, or selecting appropriate vocabulary and grammar (Cook, 2013b). The distinction between the *second* and the *third language* is crucial when it comes to experiment design in applied linguistics, establishing ways of teaching and learning languages and dealing with the identity of a multilingual.

The fact that languages in addition to their proper names (e.g. Turkish, French) necessarily also have language nominations may be thought of as 'going without saying', but in fact it has significant theoretical and practical implications. Language nominations reflect a range of perceptions regarding languages on the part of those who speak them and on the part of those who may appraise or deal with languages and their speakers. The nomination applied to English, French, Portuguese and German in the African context – the 'colonial' or 'received' languages, carrying certain connotations immediately clear to those aware of these nominations – involves attitude and historical political load, which is indicative of how these terms should and should not be used.

The careful naming of languages that can be official de facto but are not official *de jure* (as in the case of English in Israel and in some African countries, or English as an associate language in India) indicates the sensitivity of matters connected with languages and their status in society. In this sense, language nominations mirror the dominant discourse in a particular society. Annamalai (2006) points out that in India the English Language Amendment Bill declared English to be an associate language 'until such time as all non-Hindi States had agreed to its being dropped'. This has not yet occurred, and it is still widely used. For instance, it is the only reliable means of day-to-day communication between the central government and the non-Hindi states. The view of the English language among many Indians has gone from associating it with colonialism to associating it with economic progress, and English continues to be an official language of India.

In recent decades, language nominations have increased in number and significance. They had not been in such active use in earlier times. An illustrative example from the past would be from the work of the learned and sophisticated Renaissance scholar, Erasmus of Rotterdam. Wesseling (2015: 36) testifies that Erasmus almost never used the name of his native tongue, *Hollands*: 'Erasmus rarely refers to his native language by name, with the exception of *De recta pronuntiatione*, in which he occasionally compares features of pronunciation in a few regional dialects within the Low Countries.'

At present such nominations are used, proposed and changed across the world by language users, researchers and official bodies, and in connection with many and varied issues in politics, education and healthcare. The considerable proliferation of language nominations is a remarkable development and has occurred in the context of current multilingualism. The phenomenon of the global proliferation of language nominations in numbers and in significance, rather than the existence of nominations per se, is a novel one, specific to the conditions of current multilingualism.

Dominant language constellation: The way we use languages

If language nominations reveal how we *perceive* and *treat* languages, dominant language constellations show how we *use* multiple languages in today's world. Languages and language skills are subjected to re-evaluation and restructuring in terms of the mode of their use by groups and by individuals. Global and local trends dictate that the human language faculty is often expressed via a number of languages rather than a single language. Traditionally, in sociolinguistics, language teaching and language acquisition, the mastery and deployment of many languages is described using the concept of **language repertoire**.

Language repertoires

The concept of language repertoire evolved from a monolingual perspective. Under the name 'verbal repertoire' it was famously deployed by Gumperz (1964: 137–138), who used it to refer to the sum of various skills in one language. Later the notion of language repertoire was expanded to include more than one language, as 'an individual's particular set of skills (or levels of proficiency) that permit him or her to function within various registers of (a) language(s)' and the 'totality of linguistic varieties shared by the group as a whole' (Pütz, 2004: 227; Schiffmann, 1996: 42). Today we speak of language repertoires as comprising various language skills from three and more languages. We can imagine a language repertoire as the sum of all the linguistic skills in one, two, three or more languages, an asset, resource or a store possessed by an individual or a group. Contemporary language repertoires may contain a long list of skills in many languages accumulated with the help of mobility, new media and technologies, all of which make languages more available.

The linguistic 'unit of circulation' of today, however, may be neither a single named language (English, French or Dutch), nor the entire language repertoire. Although the notion of language repertoire has been and still is relevant for sociolinguistics, this notion alone is insufficient for the understanding and advantageous use of languages in the contemporary world. In view of late postmodern changes and challenges, we have to reconsider the way we look at our linguistic assets. The global extension of repertoires due to the increased availability of languages for learning and use often makes their treatment too complicated and unfocused. There appeared the need for an additional concept, for both theoretical and practical purposes, elucidating how contemporary humans use their languages.

Given a person's constraints in terms of time, efforts and energy, it is not possible for an individual to use all his/her language resources on a daily basis. This common observation was supported by George Kingsley Zipf (1901–1950), an American linguist and philologist who studied statistical occurrences in different languages. His principle of least effort postulates that animals, people and even well-designed machines will naturally choose the path of least resistance or 'effort'. Indeed, in our day-to-day lives, no matter how many languages and skills we have in our repertoire, we usually use only part of this language repertoire. Such a constellation of the individual's most important languages at a particular period of his/her life is called a **dominant language constellation**.

Dominant language constellation

To represent the pattern of grouping of languages in use at a given time, the concept of dominant language constellation (DLC) was proposed by Aronin (2006, 2016). It denotes the group of person's most expedient languages, functioning as an entire unit and enabling an individual to meet all his/her needs in a multilingual environment. The DLC includes only a person's most useful and used languages, rather than all the languages known to them as would be the case for language repertoire. Unlike a language repertoire, a DLC comprises the languages which, together, perform the most vital functions of language.

Language repertoire and DLC are mutually complementary. A DLC is an active part of one's language repertoire. At the same time, there are a number of significant differences between the two concepts. For a more nuanced theoretical distinction, the difference between language repertoire and DLC is summarized in the Table 1.2.

Table 1.2 *Language repertoire versus dominant language constellation*

Language repertoire	*Dominant language constellation*
Relates to the **totality** of an individual's or a community's linguistic skills	Concerned with the **vehicle languages** which stand out as being of prime importance
Originated from and **remains highly relevant to monolingualism**	**Specifically appropriate to multilingualism**
Each language is seen and **dealt with separately**	The languages of a constellation are **treated as a unit**
A repertoire is about resources	**DLC is about active usage**

Put simply, the main difference between a language repertoire and a DLC is that a language repertoire is 'what we have' – a sum of skills, an asset and a resource that an individual or a group possesses; a DLC, on the other hand, is 'what we do' – the way we use languages.

While the repertoire of multilinguals may include five, six, seven, eight or more languages, the typical so-called 'Western' DLC comprises three languages. It is often the case that a DLC comprises an international language (e.g. English, German, French, Russian), a regionally important language and a local one. In the Russian Federation there may be DLCs with just two languages. The number of DLC languages is, of course, different in India and African countries, where the kind of multilingualism and the number of habitually used languages is greater (see, for example, Anchimbe, 2007; Banda, 2009). DLCs in Indian, Pakistani or African contexts require special consideration. Multilingualism in India, for example, features innumerable multitudes of languages, constellations of languages in use and patterns of their deployment (see, for example, Kachru *et al.*, 2008). A convenient way to present the language unit is to use DLC maps (see Figure 1.1).

The DLC map in Figure 1.1 gives an account of the use of languages by Rose, a Christian teacher of English in an Arab sector school in Israel. Rose reported either full or partial mastery of eight languages; this is her language repertoire. Being a Catholic, Rose hears mass in Latin in church on Sundays and Church holidays. Therefore, she can speak and comprehend Latin to a limited degree. Her repertoire also includes Italian, Spanish and Brazilian Portuguese,

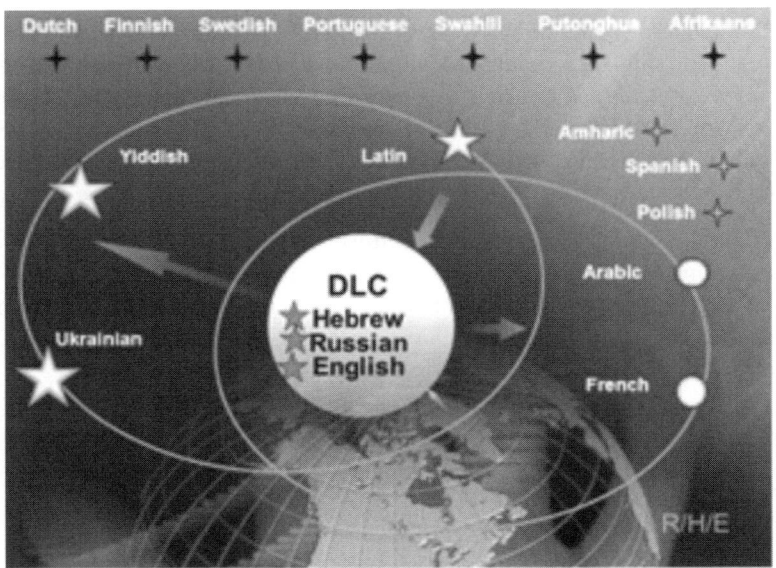

Figure 1.1 'Rose'. Arabic community Israel. Language repertoire and dominant language constellation

Notes: Five-point stars: languages of language repertoire. Circle planets: repertoire languages with weaker knowledge or seldom used. Four-point stars: languages a person is exposed to in their close environment and often understands – whether separate words and phrases or more; it can be either a heritage language in a family or a language often heard due to social proximity, whether by wish or by circumstance.

which she learnt on her own. The skills in these languages serve Rose mostly for enjoyment: watching TV programmes and listening to songs and for occasional travel. But her main languages are depicted in the centre of the DLC map. Rose's DLC comprises Spoken Arabic, Hebrew and English. In all of these three languages Rose's proficiency is excellent. As formal Arabic, *Alfusha*, is considered by the speakers as a separate language variety from *Amia*, Spoken Arabic, used only in specific situations, the latter is the variety Rose included in her DLC. Formal Arabic is not in her DLC, but is a part of Rose's repertoire which she mostly uses at school for writing formal letters and carrying out official school matters.

An assortment of DLCs, common for particular populations, can coexist in the same physical space. For example, among the communal DLCs in Australia we can find English/Polish/German, Latvian/English and Bosnian/German/English. In Argentina there is a population whose DLC consists of Welsh, English and Spanish; in Hungary someone's vehicle languages may be Romanian, Hungarian and German.

It is typical under the new linguistic dispensation to have a number of DLCs in a country, for example, in Germany: Polish/German, Polish/German/English, Turkish/German and Russian/German/English. In Switzerland, in the canton of Ticino there are people for whom English/German/French or Italian/French/German are crucial. In a Romansh valley there is a small population of quadrilinguals with Romansh/German/Italian/French. And these are only some of many DLCs deployed in Switzerland. Given that traditional linguistic maps are still in the 'one-state-one-language' era and no longer reflect the multilingual reality of contemporary communities and countries, perhaps the linguistic makeup of the world might be better presented via typical DLCs, rather than according to single languages.

DLC is a comparatively stable pattern of organization which continuously creates or recreates itself by transforming or replacing its components or undergoing continuous changes. The operation of three or more languages in concert, and in particular their *interaction*, gives DLCs their dynamism as they co-evolve in a variety of diverse contexts and times. An example of such transformations in the configuration and dominance of languages within the same DLC is the case of a multilingual who habitually puts to use his vehicle languages: Mandarin, German and English. His repertoire is considerably wider and includes Korean,

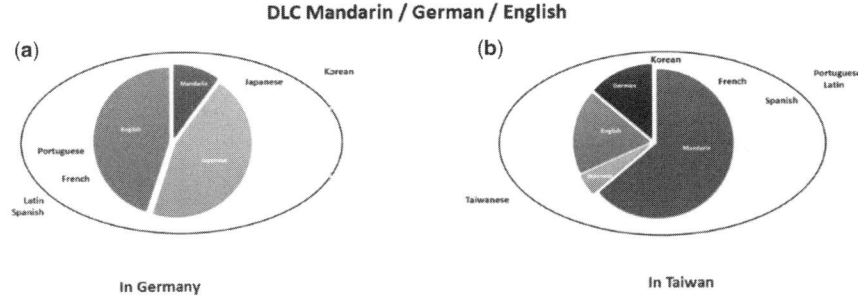

Figure 1.2 Maps for dominant language constellation of Mandarin/German/English: (a) DLC in Germany; (b) DLC in Taiwan (Courtesy Anonymous, 2016)

Part 1: Multilingualism in Society and Education

Japanese, French, Latin and other languages. The maps (see Figures 1.2a and 1.2b) show the fluctuation of DLC elements during a year when the student shuttled between Germany, where he studies, and Taiwan where one of his parents originates from. During this year the make-up of the DLC, i.e. *which* languages constituted his DLC, remained the same but, depending on the context he lived in, the degree of how dominant his different languages were or how intensively he had to use each of them changed (see Figure 1.2b).

A DLC constantly adapts itself to the environment and personal needs. Another case study by a PhD student of a German university and Sri Lankan national (Kannangara, 2017) describes the dynamics of a personal DLC across a longer timespan (Figure 1.3). Kannangara traced the evolution of her personal DLC, Singhalese/English/German, on the basis of the amount of usage of the languages across important periods of her life.

The above studies demonstrate that DLCs are often subject to shifts during an individual's lifespan. Personal life events and/or sociohistorical changes may cause some languages to leave a DLC, drift into the category of 'languages that happen to be known' and become dormant; other languages may come to the forefront and enter a DLC. Personal DLCs are indicative of the dependency on different languages in a given social context, and of some degree of personal choice regarding the use of languages. DLC mapping and analysis is a potent tool for identity investigation and intercultural studies.

The languages of the DLC are not separate languages in a strict sense; rather, together they form one workable language unit. The several languages of a DLC together carry out all language functions that human language is responsible for. They serve as a means of communication, cognition and expression of identity. Moreover, a DLC is not just the sum of the languages constituting it. It is an entity that possesses characteristics beyond

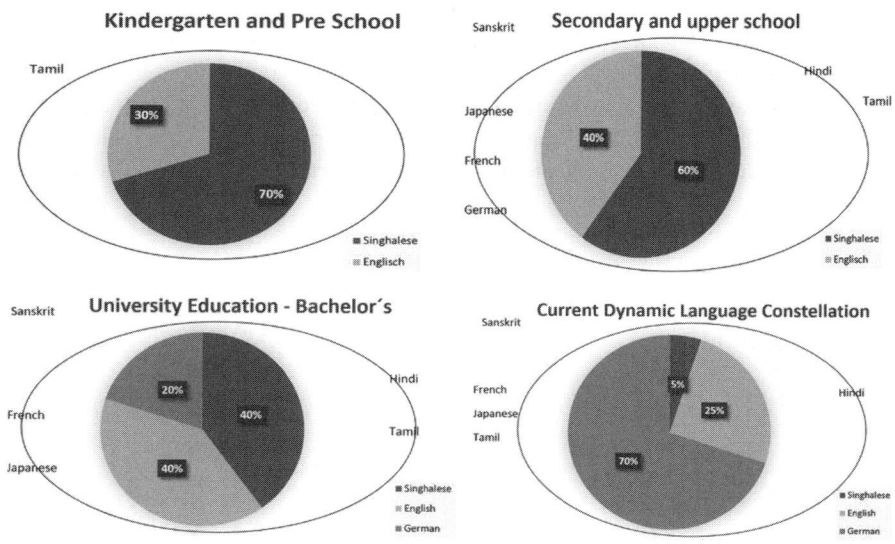

Figure 1.3 Selected dominant language constellation maps with Singhalese/English/German (after Kannangara 2017)

the sum of its parts. The linguistic qualities and social functioning of a language are not the same when it is used in a constellation, as compared to when it is used separately in a monolingual mode. A DLC is always context bound and reflects social rhythm and timing. A DLC is manageable, immediately indicative of the linguistic behaviour of individuals and communities. The DLC approach opens up a host of novel questions. Among these are the following: How do particular languages work together in a particular context? Do languages of a DLC dominate one another, or work strictly according to a certain configuration? What happens in the brain of their user? How do languages cooperate in one brain and how do they together contribute to a person's identity?

For instance, consider the range of colour terms in different languages (Berlin & Kay, 1969). If an individual's DLC contains languages, one of which has four basic colours, another six and the third 11 colour terms, which perception of colours is actually at work with this multilingual? Does she/he discern a maximum of colours according to the 11-colour term language? Or does the distinction operate depending on which language is in use at the time? A similar question can be posed regarding the differences among DLC languages in relation to word order in numbers (*einundzwanzig* in German versus *twenty-one* in English or *двадцать один* in Russian), differing forms of address, and other intra-DLC variations.

There appears to be an assortment of particular DLC patterns for specific contexts and languages. Studying DLC patterns, we enter the thrilling world of complexity to which languages, their use and acquisition undoubtedly belong. It can easily be seen how productive a search for patterns and patterning in multilingual populations and in education can be (Aronin & Jessner, 2015). The DLC approach represents the current pattern of language use, and shifts the focus from the investigation of separate languages to the exploration of their constellations, away from the monolingual perspective. Employing the concept of DLC enables realistic management of the phenomenon of multilingualism, sensitivity to multiple changes and diversity of the ways in which people use their languages.

New Linguistic Dispensation

The overall order of things with regard to languages in contemporary society can be described by the concept of the **new linguistic dispensation** (Aronin & Singleton, 2008, 2012). The word 'dispensation' means system, order, arrangement, government or organization of a nation, community, etc., especially as existing at a particular time. We define the new linguistic dispensation as an emergent linguistic-social condition, characterized by unique properties and developments, expressed in global and local patterns. It affects big and small communities, nations and countries. Regularities and patterns characteristic of the new linguistic dispensation apply to firms, parties, interest groups, armies, churches and individuals.

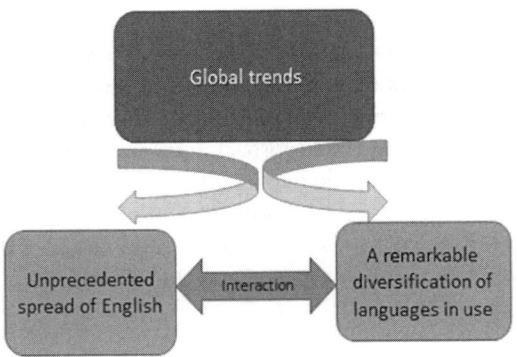

Figure 1.4 New linguistic dispensation: the two trends

Fishman (1998) described the shifts in the contemporary sociolinguistic situation as characterized by two major trends (see Figure 1.4).

1. An unparalleled spread of the use of English as an international language.
2. A remarkable diversification of the languages in use.

The new linguistic dispensation includes monolingual, bilingual and multilingual arrangements (see Figure 1.5). These are spread unequally across the globe. Since virtually every facet of human life depends on multilingual social arrangements and multilingual individuals, directly and indirectly (Aronin & Singleton, 2012; Aronin *et al.*, 2013), the principal component of the new linguistic dispensation both in its scope and in its role is *multilingualism*. Concomitantly, there are many bilingual spaces, and monolingual niches, which are mostly local.

Multilingualism is the defining, *inherent* part of the new linguistic dispensation.
Multilingual language practices at community, institutional and collective levels are the vehicle of the new linguistic dispensation, and play a central role in it. Transnational and multinational business companies and educational, cultural and political organizations like

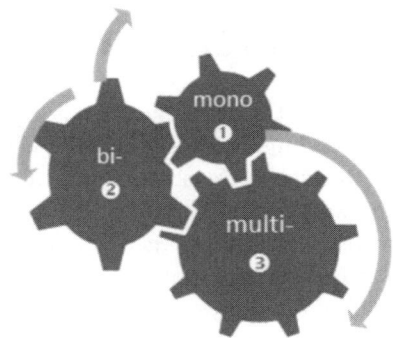

Figure 1.5 New linguistic dispensation embraces multi-, bi- and monolingual arrangements

the EU, etc. are based on multilingual linguistic arrangements (although this does not mean that these arrangements work smoothly and equally for all the languages). Members of small language communities have to know regional and official languages and languages of wider communication; at the same time they often promote, revive and sustain their indigenous languages. Thus multilingualism is vital both at the global and local levels.

The interaction between the three kinds of arrangements – mono-, bi- and multi-, with the prominent role of multilingualism – produces the reality of a new linguistic dispensation in each particular local context, and globally (Aronin, 2015). Even with multilingualism playing a leading role globally, it is possible that in some cases monolingual or bilingual approaches are justified for teaching or for dealing with individuals and communities, even in the multilingual context.

Conclusions

Multilingualism is an inherent human trait. It denotes both the ability of humans to use three and more languages, and social situations where such capacity is utilized. The use of multiple languages accompanying human activities is behaviour unique to humans. Anthropologists mention multilingualism from the dawn of humanity. Current multilingualism is a global phenomenon, intermixed within the main globalization processes, and plays a central role in maintaining and advancing contemporary global civilization.

In this lecture we have distinguished between the forms of societal multilingualism: proximate versus integrative and historical versus current. We have given an account of the essential differences between bilingualism and multilingualism and the theoretical models and methodology of multilingualism.

The distinctive features of current multilingualism include but are not limited to the unprecedented scope and breadth of distribution, complexity, extreme diversity and fluidity, ubiquitously manifesting various 'sociopolitical emergences' (Flores & Lewis, 2016: 98) and its active crucial role for human society.

Multilingual language practices differ not only from those of the past, but are extremely diversified in today's world. They are characterized by a diversity of users, languages and, in particular, a diversity of multilingual arrangements across the world and communities.

The hallmark feature of current multilingualism is the drastic change in how languages are used. Today neither single languages nor the entire language repertoire serve as units of language circulation. Notably, sets of languages labelled as dominant language constellations are the prevailing patterns of language practices now.

We also discussed the proliferation of language nominations which define and describe the role of each particular language in particular contexts. Finally we defined the new linguistic dispensation which is manifested in patterns and dispositions of contemporary human activity. The new linguistic dispensation includes monolingual, bilingual and multilingual arrangements. Of these, multilingualism is the leading component of the new dispensation.

Questions for Students' Reflection

1. What is the difference between current and historical multilingualism? Why is it important to distinguish between the two?

2. Describe the concept of the new linguistic dispensation. How are monolingual, bilingual and multilingual arrangements accommodated within it?

3. Explain the concepts of dominant language constellation and language repertoire. How are they similar and how are they different? How are they interrelated?

4. Why is multilingualism of the utmost importance in the contemporary world?

5. What are the two thresholds in the development of knowledge about multilingualism in human society?

6. Categorization task:

    a. Fill in the table and categorize terms and concepts. Some are done for you. select from: (i) behaviour; (ii) reality, that is, situation, human practices; (iii) theoretical construct, abstraction; (iv) quality, characteristic.

    b. Add your own comments and examples and discuss them in class.

Term and/or concept	Definition explanation	Categorization	Your comments, ideas and considerations
Multilingualism			
Bilingualism			
Plurilingualism			
Social multilingualism			
Individual multilingualism		Ability	
Proximate and integrative forms of social multilingualism			
Translanguaging			
Dominant language constellation (DLC)			
New linguistic dispensation			
Current multilingualism			
Historical multilingualism		Type of	
Diversity, superdiversity		Quality, characteristic	
Multilingual language practices			
Translanguaging			
Language repertoire			
Language community			

> c. Choose three terms or concepts and explain the connection between them. (i) Explain how three other terms/concepts are different. (ii) Draw a scheme/figure showing the interrelation of some of these terms/concepts; this can be that one concept or term subsumes others, or that they represent different views, or represent different levels of generalization ...

Note

(1) This lecture draws and expands upon previous work.

Suggestions for Further Reading

Hufeisen, B. and Fouser, R.J. (eds) (2005) *Introductory Readings in L3.* Tübingen: Stauffenburg Verlag.

References

Anchimbe, E.A. (ed.) (2007) *Linguistic Identity in Postcolonial Multilingual Spaces.* Newcastle-upon-Tyne: Cambridge Scholars.

Andrews, E. (2014) *Neuroscience and Multilingualism.* Cambridge: Cambridge University Press.

Annamalai, E. (2006) India: Language situation. In K. Brown (ed.) *Encyclopedia of Language & Linguistics* (pp. 610–613). Boston, MA: Elsevier.

Annamalai, E. (2008) Contexts of multilingualism. In B.B. Kachru, Y. Kachru and S.N. Sridhar (eds) *Language in South Asia* (pp. 223–234). Cambridge: Cambridge University Press.

Aronin, L. (2005) Theoretical perspectives of trilingual education. *International Journal of the Sociology of Language* 171, 7–22.

Aronin, L. (2006) Dominant language constellations: An approach to multilingualism studies. In M. Ó Laoire (ed.) *Multilingualism in Educational Settings* (pp. 140–159). Hohengehren: Schneider.

Aronin, L. (2015) Current multilingualism and new developments in multilingual research. In P. Safont-Jordà and L. Portoles (eds) *Multilingual Development in the Classroom: Current Findings from Research* (pp. 1–27). Newcastle-upon-Tyne: Cambridge Scholars.

Aronin, L. (2016) Multicompetence and dominant language constellation. In V. Cook and Li Wei (eds) *The Cambridge Handbook of Linguistic Multicompetence* (pp. 142–163). Cambridge: Cambridge University Press.

Aronin, L. (2017) Conceptualizations of multilingualism: An affordances perspective. *Critical Multilingualism Studies* 5 (1), 7–42. See http://cms.arizona.edu/index.php/multilingual/article/view/109/163.

Aronin, L. and Hufeisen, B. (eds) (2009) *The Exploration of Multilingualism: Development of Research on L3, Multilingualism and Multiple Language Acquisition*. Amsterdam: John Benjamins.

Aronin, L. and Jessner, U. (2014) Methodology in bi- and multilingual studies: From simplification to complexity. *AILA Review* 27 (*Research Methods and Approaches in Applied Linguistics: Looking Back and Moving Forward*) 27, 56–79.

Aronin, L. and Jessner, U. (2015) Understanding current multilingualism: What can the butterfly tell us? In C. Kramsch and U. Jessner (eds) *The Multilingual Challenge* (pp. 271–291). Berlin: De Gruyter.

Aronin, L. and Ó Laoire, M. (2004) Exploring multilingualism in cultural contexts: Towards a notion of multilinguality. In C. Hoffmann and J. Ytsma (eds) *Trilingualism in Family, School and Community* (pp. 11–29). Clevedon: Multilingual Matters.

Aronin, L. and Singleton, D. (2008) Multilingualism as a new linguistic dispensation. *International Journal of Multilingualism* 5 (1), 1–16.

Aronin, L. and Singleton, D. (2010) Affordances and the diversity of multilingualism. *International Journal of the Sociology of Language* 205, 105–129.

Aronin, L. and Singleton, D. (2012) *Multilingualism*. Amsterdam: John Benjamins.

Aronin, L. and Singleton, D. (2013) Multilingualism and philosophy. In C.A. Chapelle (ed.) *The Encyclopedia of Applied Linguistics* (pp. 3951–3954). New York: Wiley-Blackwell.

Aronin, L., Ó Laoire, M. and Singleton, D. (2011) The multiple faces of multilingualism: Language nominations. *Applied Linguistics Review* 2, 169–190.

Aronin, L., Fishman, J., Singleton, D. and Ò Laoire, M. (2013) Introduction. In D. Singleton, J.A. Fishman, L. Aronin and M. Ò Laoire (eds) *Current Multilingualism: A New Linguistic Dispensation* (pp. 3–23). Berlin: Mouton de Gruyter.

Banda, F. (2009) Critical perspectives on language planning and policy in Africa: Accounting for the notion of multilingualism. *Stellenbosch Papers in Linguistics PLUS* 38, 1–11.

Barnard, A. (2016) *Language in Prehistory*. Cambridge: Cambridge University Press.

Berkes, E. and Flynn, S. (2012) Enhanced L3...Ln acquisition and its implications for language teaching. In D. Gabryś-Barker (ed.) *Cross-linguistic Influences in Multilingual Language Acquisition* (pp. 1–22). Berlin: Springer.

Berlin, B. and Kay, P. (1969) *Basic Color Terms: Their Universality and Evolution*. Berkeley, CA: University of California Press.

Betteridge, T. (ed.) (2007) *Borders and Travellers in Early Modern Europe*. Farnham: Ashgate.

Bloemendal, J. (ed.) (2015) *Bilingual Europe: Latin and Vernacular Cultures. Examples of Bilingualism and Multilingualism c. 1300–1800*. Studies in Intellectual History Vol. 239. Leiden/Boston, MA: Brill.

Blommaert, J., Collins, J. and Slembrouck, S. (2005) Spaces of multilingualism. *Language and Communication* 25 (3), 197–216.

Braun, A. and Cline, R. (2014) *Language Strategies for Trilingual Families: Parents' Perspectives*. Bristol: Multilingual Matters.

Braunmüller, K. and Ferraresi, G. (eds) (2003) *Aspects of Multilingualism in European Language History*. Amsterdam: John Benjamins.

Canagarajah, A.S. (2011) Translanguaging in the classroom: Emerging issues for research and pedagogy. *Applied Linguistics Review* 2, 1–28.

Cenoz, J. and Genesee, F. (eds) (1998) *Beyond Bilingualism: Multilingualism and Multilingual Education*. Clevedon: Multilingual Matters.

Cenoz, J. and Jessner, U. (2009) The study of multilingualism in educational contexts. In L. Aronin and B. Hufeisen (eds) *The Exploration of Multilingualism* (pp. 119–135). Amsterdam: John Benjamins.

Cenoz, J., Hufeisen, B. and Jessner, U. (eds) (2001) *Looking Beyond Second Language Acquisition: Studies in Tri- and Multilingualism*. Tubingen: Stauffenburg.

Chaunu, P. (1966) *La Civilisation de l'Europe classique*. Paris: Arthaud.

Coetzee-Van Rooy, S. (2010) The importance of being multilingual. Inaugural lecture 6/2010. North-West University Vaal Triangle Occasional Papers, Vanderbijlpark.

Cook, V.J. (1992) Evidence for multi-competence. *Language Learning* 42 (4), 557–591.

Cook, V.J. (2013a) Multi-competence. In C. Chapelle (ed.) *The Encyclopedia of Applied Linguistics* (pp. 3768–3774). New York: Wiley-Blackwell.

Cook, V.J. (2013b) ELF: Central or atypical form of SLA? In D. Singleton, J. Fishman, L. Aronin and M. Ó Laoire (eds) *Current Multilingualism: A New Linguistic Dispensation* (pp. 27–44). Berlin: Mouton de Gruyter.

Czajka, M. and de Haas, H. (2014) The globalization of migration: Has the world become more migratory? *International Migration Review* 48 (2), 283–323.

De Angelis, G. (2005) Multilingualism and non-native lexical transfer: An identification problem. *International Journal of Multilingualism* 2 (1), 1–25.

De Bot, K. (2004) The multilingual lexicon: Modelling selection and control. *International Journal of Multilingualism* 1 (1), 17–32.

Donald, M. (2004) The definition of human nature. In D. Rees and S. Rose (eds) *The New Brain Sciences: Perils and Prospects* (pp. 34–58). Cambridge: Cambridge University Press.

Edwards, J. (2007) Societal multilingualism: Reality, recognition and response. In P. Auer and Li Wei (eds) *Handbook of Multilingualism and Multilingual Communication* (pp. 447–467). Berlin and New York: Mouton de Gruyter.

Evans, N. (2013) Multilingualism as the primal human condition: What we have to learn from small-scale speech communities. Keynote address at the 9th International Symposium on Bilingualism, Singapore.

Fishman, J. (1998) The new linguistic order. *Foreign Policy* 113 (Winter), 26–40.

Flores, N. and Lewis, M. (2016) From truncated to sociopolitical emergence: A critique of super-diversity in sociolinguistics. *International Journal of the Sociology of Language* 241, 97–124.

Flynn, S. (2016) What do we mean by 'Development' in multilingual language acquisition: Where do we start, where do we end and how do we get there? Plenary presentation at the 10th

International Conference on Third Language Acquisition and Multilingualism, 1–3 September, University of Vienna.

Flynn, S., Foley, C. and Vinnitskaya, I. (2004) The cumulative-enhancement model for language acquisition: Comparing adults' and children's patterns of development in first, second and third language acquisition of relative clauses. *International Journal of Multilingualism* 1 (1), 3–16.

Gabryś-Barker, D. (2005) *Aspects of Multilingual Storage, Processing and Retrieval*. Katowice: Wydawnictwo Universitetu Śląskiego.

García, O. (2013) Informal bilingual acquisition: Dynamic spaces for language education. In D. Singleton, J.A. Fishman, L. Aronin and M. Ó Laoire (eds) *Current Multilingualism: A New Linguistic Dispensation* (pp. 99–118). Berlin: Mouton de Gruyter.

García, O. and Kleyn, T. (2016) *Translanguaging with Multilingual Students: Learning from Classroom Moments*. New York and Abingdon: Routledge.

Gibson, J.J. (1977) The theory of affordances. In R. Shaw and J. Bransford (eds) *Perceiving, Acting and Knowing* (pp. 67–82). New York: Wiley.

Gibson, J.J. (1979) *The Ecological Approach to Visual Perception*. Boston, MA: Houghton Mifflin.

Goral, M. (2012) Multiple languages in the adult brain. In M. Faust (ed.) *The Handbook of the Neuropsychology of Language* (pp. 720–737). Blackwell.

Grosjean, F. (2001) The bilingual's language modes. In J. Nicol (ed.) *One Mind, Two Languages: Bilingual Language Processing* (pp. 1–22). Oxford: Blackwell.

Gumperz, J. (1964) Linguistic and social interaction in two communities. *American Anthropologist* 66 (6), 137–153.

Hammarberg, B. (2001) Roles of L1 and L2 in L3 production and acquisition. In J. Cenoz, B. Hufeisen and U. Jessner (eds) *Cross-linguistic Influence in Third Language Acquisition: Psycholinguistic Perspectives* (pp. 21–41). Clevedon: Multilingual Matters.

Hammarberg, B. (ed.) (2009) *Processes in Third Language Acquisition*. Edinburgh: Edinburgh University Press.

Herdina, P. and Jessner, U. (2002) *A Dynamic Model of Multilingualism: Perspectives of Change in Psycholinguistics*. Clevedon: Multilingual Matters.

Higby, E., Kim, J. and Obler, L.K. (2013) Multilingualism in the brain. *Annual Review of Applied Linguistics* 33, 68–101.

Hoffmann, C. and Ytsma, J. (eds) (2004) *Trilingualism in Family, School and Community*. Clevedon: Multilingual Matters.

Hornberger, N. (2002) Multilingual language policies and the continua of biliteracy: An ecological approach. *Language Policy* 1 (1), 27–51.

Hornberger, N.H. and Corson, D. (eds) (1997) Research methods in language and education. *Encyclopaedia of Language and Education, Vol.8*. Dordrecht: Kluwer.

Hufeisen, B. (1998) L3-Stand der Forschung-Was bleibt zu tun? In B. Hufeisen and B. Lindemann (eds) *Tertiärsprachen. Theorien, Modelle, Methode* (pp. 169–183). Tübingen: Stauffenburg.

Hufeisen, B. (2010) Theoretische Fundierung multiplen Sprachenlernens – Factorenmodell 2.0. *Jahrbuch Deutsch als Fremdsprache* 36, 191–198.

Jaworski, A. (2014) Metrolingual art: Multilingualism and heteroglossia. *International Journal of Bilingualism* 18 (2), 134–158.

Jessner, U. (2013) Dynamics of multilingualism. In C. Chapelle (ed.) *The Encyclopaedia of Applied Linguistics* (pp. 1798–1805). Wiley: Blackwell.

Kachru, B.B., Kachru, Y. and Sridhar, S.N. (eds) (2008) *Language in South Asia*. Cambridge: Cambridge University Press.

Kagan, O. (2005) In support of a proficiency-based definition of heritage language learners: The case of Russian. *International Journal of Bilingual Education and Bilingualism* 8 (203), 213–221.

Kannangara, S. (2017) The evolution of personal dominant language constellation. Paper presented at 11th International Symposium on Bilingualism, 11–15 June, Limerick.

Kemp, C. (2007) Strategic processing in grammar learning: Do multilinguals use more strategies? *International Journal of Multilingualism* 4 (4), 241–261.

Khubchandani, L.M. (1997) *Revisualizing Boundaries: A Plurilingual Ethos*. New Delhi: Sage.

Kirkpatrick, A. (2007) *World Englishes: Implications for International Communication and English Language Teaching*. Amsterdam: John Benjamins.

Kroll, J.F., Bobb, S.C., Misra, M. and Taomei, G. (2008) Language selection in bilingual speech: Evidence for inhibitory processes. *Acta Psichologica* 128, 416–430.

Larsen-Freeman, D. and Cameron, L. (2008) *Complex Systems and Applied Linguistics*. Oxford: Oxford University Press.

Levelt, W.J.M. (1989) *Speaking: From Intention to Articulation*. Cambridge, MA: MIT Press.

Lewis, M.P. (ed.) (2009) *Ethnologue: Languages of the World* (16th edn). Dallas, TX: SIL International. See http://www.ethnologue.com/.

Li Wei and Moyer, M. (eds) (2008) *The Blackwell Guide to Research Methods in Bilingualism and Multilingualism*. Oxford: Blackwell.

Lüpke, F. (2016) Uncovering small-scale multilingualism. *Critical Multilingualism Studies* 4 (2), 35–74.

MacSwan, J. (2017) A multilingual perspective on translanguaging. *American Educational Research Journal* 54 (1), 167–201.

Makoni, S. and Meinhof, U. (2003) Introducing applied linguistics in Africa. In S. Makoni and U.H. Meinhof (eds) *Africa and Applied Linguistics. AILA Review* 16, 1–12. Amsterdam: John Benjamins.

Marx, N. and Hufeisen, B. (2003) Multilingualism: Theory, research methods and didactics. In G. Bräuer and K. Sanders (eds) *New Visions in Foreign and Second Language Education* (pp. 178–203). San Diego, CA: LARC Press.

Matras, Y. and Robertson, A. (2015) Multilingualism in a post-industrial city: Policy and practice in Manchester. *Current Issues in Language Planning* 16 (3), 296–314.

Meißner, F.-J. (2003) EuroComDidact: Learning and teaching plurilingual comprehension. In L. Zybatow (ed.) *Sprachkompetenz – Mehrsprachigkeit – Translation. Akten des 35. Linguistischen Kolloquiums, Innsbruck, 2–22 September 2000* (pp. 33–46). Tübingen: Narr.

Mohanty, A.K. (2010) Languages, inequality and marginalization: Implications of the double divide and Indian multilingualism. *International Journal of the Sociology of Language* 205, 131–154.

Otheguy, R., García, O. and Reid, W. (2015) Clarifying translanguaging and deconstructing named languages: A perspective from linguistics. *Applied Linguistics Review* 6 (3), 281–307.

Pandit, P.B. (1979) Perspectives on sociolinguistics in India. In W.C. McCormick and S.A. Wurm (eds) *Language and Society: Anthropological Issues*. The Hague: Mouton.

Pavlenko, A. (2019) Superdiversity and why it isn't: Reflections on terminological innovation and academic branding. In B. Schmenk, S. Breidbach and L. Küster (eds) *Sloganization in Language Education Discourse*. Bristol: Multilingual Matters.

Pütz, M. (2004) Linguistic repertoire/Sprachrepertoire. In U. Ammon, N. Dittmar, K. Mattheier and P. Trudgill (eds) *An International Handbook of the Science of Language and Society/Ein Internationales Handbuch zur Wissenschaft von Sprache und Gesellschaft* (2nd edn) (pp. 226–231). Berlin: Walter de Gruyter.

Rindler-Schjerve, R. and Vetter, E. (2007) Linguistic diversity in Habsburg Austria as a model for modern European language policy. In J. ten Thije and L. Zeevaert (eds) *Receptive Multilingualism: Linguistic Analyses, Language Policies and Didactic Concepts* (pp. 49–70). Amsterdam: John Benjamins.

Safont-Jordà, P. (2013) Early stages of trilingual pragmatic development: A longitudinal study of requests in Catalan, Spanish and English. *Journal of Pragmatics* 59, 68–80.

Schiffmann, H. (1996) *Linguistic Culture and Language Policy*. New York: Routledge.

Schilling, H. (2008) *Early Modern European Civilization and its Political and Cultural Dynamism*. Lebanon, NH: UPNE (University Press of New England).

Verspoor, M., De Bot, K. and Lowie, W. (2011) *A Dynamic Approach to Second Language Development: Methods and Techniques*. Amsterdam: John Benjamins.

Vertovec, S. (2014) Reading 'Super-Diversity'. In B. Anderson and M. Keith (eds) *Migration: A COMPAS Anthology*. Oxford: COMPAS. See http://compasanthology.co.uk/wp-content/uploads/2014/02/Vertovec_COMPASMigrationAnthology.pdf.

Wesseling, A.H. (2015) Latin and the vernaculars: The case of Erasmus. In J. Bloemendal (ed.) *Bilingual Europe: Latin and Vernacular Cultures. Examples of Bilingualism and Multilingualism c. 1300–1800* (pp. 30–49). Leiden/Boston, MA: Brill.

Wiley, T. (2001) On defining heritage learners and their speakers. In J.K. Peyton, D.A. Ranard and S. McGinnis (eds) *Heritage Languages in America: Preserving a National Resource* (pp. 109–142). McHenry, IL: Delta Systems.

Zipf, G. (1949/1965) *Human Behavior and the Principle of Least Effort: An Introduction to Human Ecology*. New York and London: Hafner.

Lecture 2

Applied Linguistics and Multilingualism

Danuta Gabryś-Barker

Applied Linguistics and Its Selected Areas with Multilingual Focus

It is not easy to define applied linguistics univocally since it does not represent one scholarly domain but often assumes linguistics to be at its core. A consensus has never been reached, however. The term was first used as a scientific domain in the late 1940s, demonstrating the connections between the practice of teaching foreign languages and linguistic theory, at a time when structural linguistics and psychological theories of behaviourism resulted in the audio-lingual method of teaching foreign languages. It brought about the opening of applied linguistic programmes at various academic institutions (e.g. at the University of Edinburgh, 1956), the creation of its own organization (AILA – *Association Internationale de Linguistique Appliquée*, 1964), monograph publications (e.g. Corder, *The Edinburgh Course in Applied* Linguistics, 1973) and the beginning of several scholarly journals (*Language Learning*, 1948; *TESOL Quarterly*, 1967; and later *Applied Linguistics*, 1980 and *Annual Review of Applied Linguistics*, 1980). The central concern with theoretical linguistics evolved over time and applied linguists conceived applied linguistics to be a multidisciplinary science (Kaplan, 2002). Its initial interest in applying purely linguistic theories to language teaching and learning was broadened to other areas of study related to language instruction, acquisition and use.

Thus, over time, applied linguistics became a truly interdisciplinary domain of study, embracing psycholinguistic and sociolinguistic issues, language education and policy, and most importantly second language acquisition (SLA) and foreign language teaching and learning. Now applied linguists, rather than moving within pure domains, focus on problem-solving issues related to language in their research, for example in teaching and learning problems, language policy translation issues and language pathology, as well as on many others.

This diversity of problems requires that those involved in applied linguistic research and its practical application have knowledge first of linguistic theories and language teaching and learning, but also of psychology and neurology, sociology, policy and educational planning, curriculum building, assessment and teacher training, among many other fields (Kaplan, 2002: ix). Additionally, developments in the field of linguistics itself (e.g. the emergence of cognitive and corpus linguistics) created the need for their applications in teaching and learning, alongside the need for new methods of data collection and analysis. On the other hand, because of more focus on individual learner differences and the development of learner autonomy, more knowledge is required from the applied linguist in relation to psychological issues in affectivity – motivation, attitudes and the learning theories of cognitive psychology. Thus, applied linguistics became a much more demanding discipline requiring new resources from other scholarly fields of study. This multidisciplinary approach is very strongly reflected in the choice of relevant research methods and the greater focus on qualitative types of research from social sciences methodology (ethnography, case studies) rather than the quantitative approaches of the past. In this lecture I will focus on the applied linguistics limited to the constructs and issues involved in multilingual foreign language learning.

The selection of areas of study presented in this lecture is designed to draw on the major concepts in multilingual research. Some early studies in multilingualism can be regarded as contributing to the development of applied linguistics in respect of individual language development, as well as the role of contextual factors in this development. More recent studies tend to be concerned with linguistic issues such as the concept of multicompetence, the multilingual mental lexicon, language processing in cross-linguistic consultations (language transfer focus) and code-switching at different language levels (semantic, syntactic). As mentioned earlier, the multidisciplinary character of applied linguistics and quantitatively and qualitatively different types of research in the case of multilingualism require a broader scope of research methods, deploying qualitative research with more attention. Thus a brief commentary on what is fairly new to the language studies methods used in multilingual research follows the content focus of the lecture.

Bilingualism versus Multilingualism

The researchers in the field of multilingualism use the term multilingualism in various ways. Some of them assume that it embraces bilingualism (also in the case of some of the contributors to this volume), whereas others see bilingualism and multilingualism as separate phenomena. I subscribe to the latter view, considering them to be separate areas of study. Thus, in my understanding, the contribution of research into multilingualism to the field of applied linguistics has to be seen as deriving from the differences between bilingualism and multilingualism. These differences clearly consist in:

- different and more varied contextual patterns of acquisition/learning;
- quantitative differences as more languages are processed in the mind of a learner;
- qualitative differences due to language typology, both linguistic (language distance) and psychological;
- an extended possibility of interactions between different languages being acquired, both in terms of interference and facilitation;
- prior knowledge facilitating the new cognitive information based on both L1 and L2 competence;
- more extensive (previous) learning experience itself;
- an enhanced state of metalinguistic and strategic awareness. (after De Angelis, 2007)

The contextual diversity of acquisition/learning processes of a greater number of languages than in the case of bilingualism creates different patterns of development. In the case of three languages, four patterns are possible (Table 2.1), but this becomes even more elaborate in the case of four or more languages involved (Table 2.2).

Both the complexity and highly individual character of multilingual development make its study a real challenge (Aronin & Jessner, 2015), with very diversified outcomes in relation

Table 2.1 *Possible patterns of a trilingual development*

Languages	Sequence of acquisition/learning	Context
L1 → L2 → L3	All the languages are acquired consecutively	Fully formal learning at school, when foreign languages are introduced at different times
L1/L2 → L3	A bilingual child acquiring another language consecutively	Partially naturalistic with a child in a mixed-marriage family acquiring/learning another language either naturalistically (immigrants) or through instruction
L1 → L2/L3	Foreign languages are learned after L1 was acquired	Fully formal, a typical example of two foreign languages learned simultaneously at school through formal instruction
L1/L2/L3	All the three languages are acquired simultaneously	A fully naturalistic acquisition, e.g. in an African context, when there is a basic tribal, a higher status tribal language used in more formal contexts, and a lingua franca which might be the legacy of colonial times, usually English, French or Portuguese

Table 2.2 *Second language acquisition (SLA) versus multilingual acquisition (MLA)*

Second language acquisition	Multilingual acquisition
L1 → L2 (compound bilingualism)	L1 → L2 → L3
L1 + L2 (coordinate bilingualism)	L1 → L2/L3
	L1/L2 → L3
	L1/L2/L3
	L1 → L2 → L3 → L4
	L1 → L2/L3 → L4
	L1 → L2 → L3/L4
	L1 → L2/L3/L4
	L1/L2 → L3 → L4
	L1/L2 → L3/L4
	L1/L2/L3 → L4
	L1/L2/L3/L4

Source: After Cenoz (2001: 40).

to *multicompetence, language transfer* and *the multilingual mental lexicon of a multilingual* in comparison with a bilingual language learner/user. Also, the variety of acquisition patterns of three (or more) languages creates *an affectively complex situation* (among others, different motivations, attitudes and preferences in the use of L1, L2, Ln) for a prospective multilingual in relation to the learning and use of each language, and needs to be discussed here.

The Dynamics of Multicompetence

Discussion of the construct of multilinguality and multicompetence and their complexity was started by Cook (1991). He sees it as 'The compound state of mind with two (three) grammars (p.112). A bilingual/multilingual mind is different from that of a monolingual with respect to the fact that knowledge of L1 is different from knowledge of L2/Ln, and the metalinguistic awareness of language of a multilingual is increased due to his/her knowledge of multiple language systems. This obviously has an impact on the cognitive processing involved in L1 and L2/L3 on the level of comprehension and production. There is an ongoing debate as to whether multicompetence is holistic; that is to say, do L1, L2 and Ln systems merge? Is there only one complex grammar system or several separate ones? Or alternatively, is some part of it shared by languages and some part of it functioning separately for each language?

Various scholars have concerned themselves with the concept of multicompetence (Table 2.3). It seems that most of the experimental evidence supports the multicompetence model seen as holistic. This is exemplified by the fact that the mental lexicon of a multilingual demonstrates a close relationship between L1 and L2/Ln. Phonological, lexical

Table 2.3 *Focus on the concept of multicompetence and its evolution*

Name	Year	Definition
Cook	1991	*A different state of mind*
Clyne	1997	*Multilateral competence* (linguistic and procedural)
Cenoz and Genesee	1998	An individual ability to use several languages effectively
Hoffmann	1999	Linguistic and functional ability in all languages of a multilingual user
Kesckes and Papp	2000	A common underlying conceptual base and a multilingual processing device
Aronin and Ó Laoire	2001	An ecosystem
Herdina and Jessner	2002	A complex psycholinguistic system and a holistic perception
Aronin	2006	*The dominant language constellation*
Cook	2016	*Three premises of multicompetence*
Murahata, Murahata and Cook	2016	Research questions and methodology of multicompetence

and syntactic processing in L2/Ln are not separate and demonstrate relations and consultations between languages. This is again evidenced, for example, in users'/learners' code-switching between different languages. Additionally, recent research shows that the hypothesis claiming that foreign languages are stored in a different brain hemisphere (the right one) from the mother tongue (the left) is to be rejected. Their localization in brain areas is not separate for different languages but rather demonstrates complex links and overlaps (Gabryś-Barker, 2005).

An interesting discussion on the nature of multicompetence and multilinguality is offered by Aronin and Ó Laoire (2001), who look at it from an ecological perspective:

> We use the term eco as an analogue of the ecological phenomenon intrinsic to the nature cycle, emphasizing the essential dynamics of growth, change, fluctuation, input, absorption and decay; while stressing the entity of multilingualism. (Aronin & Ó Laoire, 2001: 2)

This approach emphasizes the state of constant change a multilingual person experiences due to the interaction of the various linguistic systems of L1, L2, L3 and Ln. The interaction obviously has to introduce various modifications at different levels of linguistic knowledge and competence and, as a consequence, in modifications in language performance. This approach points to possible processes of language deterioration in its different elements, labelled as language attrition, but it also emphasizes the evident development and progress of other language elements (Figure 2.1).

Aronin (2016) discusses the relation between multilinguality and multicompetence and asks a question:

> How is multilinguality related to multi-competence? Multi-competence is a largely linguistic perspective, which emphasizes the specific qualities and abilities of the whole group of individuals – those who speak more than one language. It celebrates the *ability and the quality* that all bi- and multilinguals share. Multilinguality is a unique

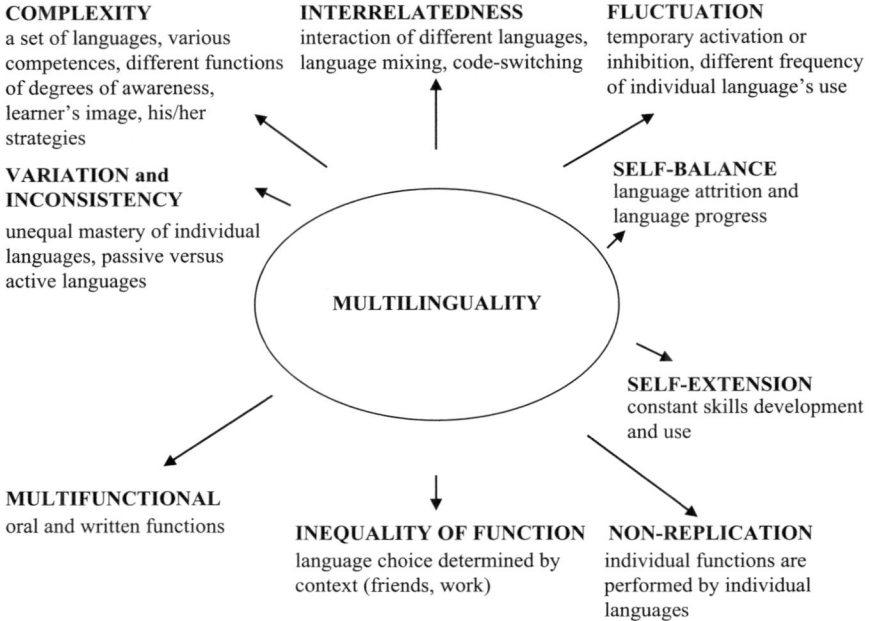

Figure 2.1 Multilinguality seen as an ecosystem
Source: Adapted from Aronin and Ó Laoire (2001: 2–4).

personal characteristic for tri- and multilinguals, the foundation of which is multi-competence. It is multi-competence that shapes the identity of a multilingual in accordance with each particular environment. (Aronin, 2016: 145, emphasis in original)

As can be seen, multicompetence and multilinguality are very individual phenomena that cannot be measured and described in fixed patterns. Their complexity derives from the individual multilingual language learner/user and his or her learning and psycholinguistic profile, as well as contextual factors (for a fuller discussion of these, see Aronin, 2016; Aronin & Jessner, 2015; Aronin & Ó Laoire, 2001).

Most recently, the construct of multicompetence has been offered by Cook who believes that:

Multi-competence thus covers the knowledge and use of two or more languages by the same individual or the same community. At some level, all the languages form part of one overall system, with complex and shifting relationships between them, affecting the first language as well as the others. (Cook, 2016: 2)

According to him, the three premises of multicompetence are:

Premise 1. Multi-competence concerns the total system for all languages (L1, L2, LN) in a single mind or community and their inter-relationships (...)

Premise 2. Multi-competence does not depend on the monolingual native speaker (...)

Premise 3. Multi-competence affects the whole mind, i.e. all language and cognitive systems, rather than language alone. (Cook, 2016: 9–16)

Earlier, Herdina and Jessner (2002), in their discussion of multicompetence (and multilinguality), emphasize its complexity by stating that the major quality of multilingualism (and multicompetence) is its dynamic character. Their *dynamic model of multilingualism* (DMM; Herdina & Jessner, 2002) considers multilingual development from a psycholinguistic perspective and describes it as a holistic process, as featuring in dynamic systems research in sciences such as biology, physics, mathematics or neuroscience. In short, dynamic systems research assumes that:

- The whole is more than the sum of its parts.
- The whole determines the nature of its parts.
- The parts cannot be understood if considered in isolation from the whole; the parts are dynamically interrelated or dependent. (Herdina & Jessner, 2002: 150)

The main emphasis is put here on the holistic, mutually related and interacting quality of any system. Herdina and Jessner go further by pointing to the following features of multilingualism: non-linearity, maintenance, reversibility, stability, interdependence, complexity and change of quality observed in multilingual development (Table 2.4).

Table 2.4 *Dynamic model of multilingualism*

Quality	Focus
Non-linearity	Language development is not steady and linear but slows down or accelerates depending on the individual circumstances in which it takes place.
Maintenance	The ability to use and function in a certain language (languages) presupposes that some degree of maintenance of a given language (languages) has to be observed. The larger the number of languages involved is, the greater the effort to maintain them will be. Language attrition may occur.
Reversibility	Language attrition is a reversible process provided that the resources become available again, i.e. the effort needed to maintain the language will be restored.
Stability	Individual language stability plays a role in language development: If the learner can freely vary the amount of effort, this process of adaptation to environmental pressure will obviously increase system stability as a desired effect. (Herdina & Jessner, 2002: 92)
Interdependence	Multilingual development according to the DMM is not a development of individual language systems, but one dynamic system of interdependent language development of individual systems constantly converging and diverging to create multilingual competence.
Complexity	Complexity consists in interaction of multiple factors in a holistic and non-linear manner.
Change of quality	This interdependence leads to a change in the quality of a multilingual language system in terms of: • learning skills (prior learning experience); • language management skills (metalinguistic and strategic awareness); • language maintenance skills.

Source: Based on Herdina and Jessner (2002).

The non-linearity of multilingual processing is demonstrated in the relation between *language acquisition effort* (LAE) and *language maintenance effort* (LME). LAE and LME result in *general language effort* (GLE). They describe the progress made due to the individual effort of a language user/learner on the level of learning and preservation of the languages learnt. The concept of language transfer is central to this model but redefined as *cross-linguistic interaction* (CLIN), seen now as a dynamic characteristic. Other phenomena connected with language processing such as code-switching and borrowing from (multiple) language sources, as in the case of a multilingual language user (L1, L2, L3, Ln), represent aspects of CLIN.

It was research on multilingualism that brought to the fore the dynamic character of language development processes and also redefined language transfer as a form of cross-linguistic consultation (discussed below, in the section on The Multilingual Mental Lexicon).

In studying multicompetence and its dynamic and complex characteristics, Aronin (2006) introduced the concept of *dominant language constellation* (DLC), which is:

> the constellation of one's dominant languages is a group of one's most important (vehicle) languages, functioning as an entire unit, and enabling an individual to meet all needs in a multilingual environment (Aronin, 2006; Aronin & Ó Laoire, 2004; Aronin & Singleton, 2012). The Dominant Language Constellation includes only the most expedient languages for a person, rather than all the languages known to them, as would be the case in language repertoire. Unlike a language repertoire, a DLC comprises the languages which, together, perform the most vital functions of language. (Aronin, 2016: 146)

Such an understanding of the concept of DLC illustrates the uniqueness of every multilingual person, but at the same time it relates to the multilinguality of a community in which an individual functions and becomes 'an interface between the individual and the communal' (Aronin, 2016: 160). Thus, as Aronin points out, studying DLC should relate on at least two levels:

> (1) sociolinguistic, in zooming into how, in which proportions and for which results and implications constellations of languages are used in society in communities; (2) in the realm of language acquisition, how multi-competence emerges to be what it is, in the framework of a set of particular languages. (Aronin, 2016: 160–161)

Aronin claims that the DLC model of studying and individual and societal multilingualism can provide systematic data on how individuals cope with their multilinguality in daily interactions and in the challenges of functioning in multilingual communities.

Discussion of the complex character of multicompetence is continued and more recently presented by Aronin and Jessner (2015), in which they look at the complexity approach as most relevant to studying multilingualism:

> It is necessary to (a) shift the mental attitude concerning multilingual phenomena, (b) apply complexity approaches to the researching, or (re) interpreting data of current

and previous research and (c) treat multilingualism the way complexity phenomena should be treated, focus on new possibilities for research by reflecting on its essential nature, which is distinct from mono- and very often also, from bilingualism. (Aronin & Jessner, 2015: 288)

The need to adopt the complexity approach to studying multicompetence is necessary, according to Aronin and Jessner (2015), as multilingualism has to be seen as a more complex phenomenon than bilingualism, exhibiting the characteristic features of open complex systems, which are 'characterized by irregularity, fuzziness, sensitivity to initial conditions, liability to predictions of general trends or directions, rather than established exact rule-bound regularities' (Aronin & Jessner, 2015: 288).

Language Transfer and Code-switching in Multilinguals

The phenomenon of language transfer was initially defined by Odlin (1993: 27) as '(...) the influence resulting from similarities and differences between the target language and any other language that has been previously (and perhaps imperfectly) acquired'. In this understanding, language transfer will occur when:

- the TL (target language) element has not been acquired because of insufficient input or no input at all;
- the TL element has been internalized by the learner but he/she cannot access/activate it at the moment of performance (especially in immediate tasks such as speaking);
- the rules acquired are not sufficient/complete and do not account for all necessary applications;
- the rules can only be approximated to, e.g. the English system of indefinite and definite articles. (Gabryś, 1999: 170)

Compared with language transfer studies in SLA, research in the multilingual context becomes much more complex, as Heidrick (2006) explains:

> In contrast to the traditional approach to SLA transfer theory which takes into account only the native language (L1) and the target language, TLA [third language acquisition – *addition by author*] researchers seem to support the inclusion of the previously learned non-native languages when they claim that a comprehensive theory of transfer must include prior knowledge of non-native languages. (Heidrick, 2006: 1)

Such an understanding led researchers, right from the start of research on language transfer, to look closely at language errors resulting from language transfer due to language typology and psychotypology (perceived language distance) (Ringbom, 1987;

Sharwood-Smith & Kellerman, 1986), but also at errors due to the role of language specificity (language markedness) and non-structural factors, learner age or his/her learning history (context, methods of teaching and learning) (Alonso-Alonso, 2002).

In multilingualism studies, the term language transfer – previously often identified with interference rather than viewed as a positive influence – is now also seen as an added value. Thus the new term cross-linguistic interaction (CLIN; or cross-linguistic consultations) is used. Among others, Jessner (2003) offers a new perspective on the phenomenon of CLIN, suggesting that it consists of language consultations of learners in which they activate different languages by means of different strategies such as avoidance, simplification and over-monitoring. As mentioned earlier, she also sees CLIN not just as language transfer but also as embracing such phenomena as code-switching (CS) and borrowing. In this, Jessner follows the line of thinking of Sharwood-Smith and Kellerman (1986), who much earlier coined the term *cross-linguistic influence* (CLI), and defines language transfer from a broader perspective, meaning not only transfer but also language phenomena such as avoidance, borrowing or CS.

Studies on cross-linguistic influences in multilingual settings look mostly at negative transfer as a result of L1 or L2 influence on L3 comprehension and production. Many of these deal with lexical issues but there are also studies relating to phonological transfer or pragmatic aspects. What is interesting in these studies is that they take a new perspective on language transfer and see it as a dynamic process in which each language in the possession of a multilingual person performs a role in this process. Table 2.5 presents a selection of the fairly numerous studies on CLIN in the multilingual context, demonstrating a wide variety of research interest in this area of multilingualism.

An interesting area of CLIN can be found in the studies focusing on lexical transfer. In his early study on lexical transfer, Ringbom (2001) focused on cross-linguistic influences in trilingual comprehension, pointing to the perceived language distance, formal cross-linguistic similarity, the language of input and language proficiency as determinants in processing strategies and the types of errors occurring. He observed that lexical transfer errors can relate to both form and meaning and can be classified into five distinctive categories: language switches, coinages (hybrids and blends), deceptive cognates, calques and semantic extensions. Ringbom also explained that lexical errors, for instance switches and coinages, derive from 'insufficient awareness of intended linguistic form, instead of which (a modified form of) an L2 word is used' (Ringbom, 2001: 65). They result in the creation of a non-existent item in the TL, a so-called foreignized word, which is an example of foreignizing used as a processing/production/communication strategy. He gives the following example: *The* hillow *was hidden in the cupboard* (Finnish *hillo* = jam) (discussed in detail in Gabryś-Barker, 2005).

Research shows that the proportion of different types of errors observed in bilingual/multilingual language users changes with their growing language proficiency. Form-focused transfer is mostly dominant in the early stages of language learning, since it is

Table 2.5 *Selected studies on cross-linguistic interaction in multilinguals*

	Focus	*Comment*	*Sample studies*
1.	Role of metalinguistic awareness in CLIN and prior language knowledge	Metalinguistic awareness having more impact than language proximity. Need to encourage learners' comments on similarities and differences between languages, thus developing their metalinguistic awareness.	Jessner (2003) Gibson and Hufeisen (2003) Gabryś-Barker (2005)
2.	CLIN as a phenomenon of competing language systems in multilingualism	The activation of a multilingual's other languages (L1, L2) when there are insufficient L3-specific entries in the mental lexicon to produce a meaningful utterance.	Dewaele (2001) Longxing Wei (2003a)
3.	Role of language proficiency in multilingual processing	A less advanced L3 learner relied heavily on her L2 articulatory system, which changed with growing L3 competence. The same was observed in the case of grammatical processing. L2 is activated more often than L1, roles are assigned to each language (e.g. L2 as a supplier).	Cook (1992) Hammarberg (2001) Herwig (2001) Peyer *et al.* (2010)
4.	Role of (psycho)typology	Competence in L2 (and not necessarily L1) close typologically to L3 facilitates its acquisition. Perceived similarity between languages encourages transfer between them. The role of typology in the organization of the multilingual lexicon.	Leung (2005) Gibson *et al.* (2001) Ringbom (2011) Cenoz (2003)
5.	CLIN at the lexical level	Cross-linguistic interaction in the MML, the focus on culture-specific concepts. Parasitic model of lexical retrieval in multilinguals.	Gabryś (2001) Gabryś-Barker (2005) Ecke (2015)
6.	Interaction between cognate words	Facilitative aspects of cognate words in language processing (lexical priming tasks, translation).	Lemhofer *et al.* (2004) Otwinowska-Kasztelanic (2011)
7.	Code-switching in the multilingual context	The role of individual variation demonstrating the positive attitude towards CS stems from tolerance of ambiguity, cognitive empathy and low neuroticism.	Dewaele and Li Wei (2014)

(Continued)

Table 2.5 *(Continued)*

	Focus	*Comment*	*Sample studies*
8.	CLIN at the level of morphosyntax	Selected issues of grammatical structure such as aspect, modal particles or subjunctive.	Angelovska and Hahn (2012) Kresič and Gulan (2012) Włosowicz (2012)
9.	Pragmatic aspects of CLI	Interaction of languages in different contexts of its use.	Tymczyńska (2012) Ringbom (2012)

believed that vocabulary size (width) and organization (depth) are first determined by formal language characteristics and not semantic ones (Ringbom, 2001: 65). It seems that the differences in error frequency are linked to a gradual progression from organization by form to organization by meaning with growing L3 proficiency. Both dimensions of lexical competence, vocabulary size and vocabulary organization develop as the learner's proficiency improves. Improved lexical proficiency comprises not only a larger vocabulary but also a more structured organization of the lexicon with a larger number of associative links, predominantly semantic, for each word. Similar results were observed in a study of trilingual language users' performance in a set of translation tasks (Gabryś-Barker, 2005). The main focus was on the influence of the language of input on language processing. In both cases the language of input that brought about the lexical transfer was noted. It was observed, for example, that instances of CS into L1 in L1 input processing and into L2 in L2 input processing were quite common.

The issue of the CS of multilinguals was taken up by Dewaele (2008, 2010) to discover that it is related to strong emotions but also to the type of interlocutor and conversation topic. To continue research on this phenomenon, Dewaele and Li Wei (2014) designed a follow-up online questionnaire looking at inter-individual variation in the CS of 2070 subjects across the world to determine the factors that contribute to positive or negative attitudes to CS. Analysis of the data showed that positive attitudes to CS stem from high levels of tolerance of ambiguity, cognitive empathy and low levels of neuroticism. It also demonstrated that both low-level speakers and advanced speakers present more positivity towards CS. Additionally, sociobiographical variables such as learning history or present life in a linguistically/ethnically diverse context promote positive attitudes. In other studies on CS in a multilingual context, a new term, translanguaging, appears to describe this phenomenon (García & Li Wei, 2013). It is seen now as a desirable phenomenon, respecting all the languages and individual choice of their use by a multilingual (Cenoz & Gorter, 2015).

Studies on lexical transfer and also syntactic transfer in the context of multilingual language acquisition and learning have contributed to research on the mental lexicon of a multilingual person, as they demonstrate the cross-language consultations (or interactions) that occur in the brain when lexical search, access and finally retrieval of a lexical item (a lexical entry) result in its articulation as a syntactically correct and semantically meaningful utterance.

The Multilingual Mental Lexicon

Defining the mental lexicon and its complexity

One of the levels of linguistic competence crucial for language use, in both monolingual and multilingual contexts, is language users' possession of words, namely their lexical competence. Singleton (2000: 161) points to the importance of one's lexical competence, stressing that it is 'an important dimension of language that needs to be addressed in any description of the phenomenon of language or indeed in the description of any particular language'. Lexical competence comprises different types of lexical knowledge, not only of individual words, but also of the mutual relations between them, as well as reference to meaning outside language reality. Being a lexically competent language user means acquiring the denotative meaning of words, the hierarchical relations between words (those of superordination and subordination within a given semantic field), the relations of homonymy, synonymy and antonymy, items marking discourse continuity, the connotations that given words carry and awareness of the metaphoric nature of these wordsand expressions.

Different aspects of the development of lexical knowledge, such as storage of lexical items and their retrieval from memory, processing words in L1, L2, Ln and their mutual connections, and generally the way in which this internal inventory of words is being organized and structured in a multilingual mind, constitute knowledge about one's mentallexicon.

Early in the years of studying the mental lexicon, Emmorey and Fromkin (1988) describe it as:

> that component of grammar in which information about individual words and/or morphemes is entered, i.e. what a speaker/hearer of a language knows about the form of the entry (its phonology), its structured complexity (its morphology), its meaning, its semantic representation), and its combinatorial properties (its syntactic, categorical properties) (...) also orthographical or spelling representation. (Emmorey & Fromkin, 1988: 144)

The entries in a mental lexicon are stored in the form of lemmas carrying semantic and syntactic information and lexemes, that is to say, the morphosyntactic and phonological characteristics of lexical entries (Levelt, 1989). As mentioned earlier, they form connections at different levels, thus developing a network of lexical entries. In other words, a mental lexicon can be defined as an internal inventory of lexical items and phrases and the way they are stored. It should also be seen as a conceptual system composed of concepts and their linguistic phonological and orthographic realizations; at the same time, lexical processing access and retrieval as evidence of the working structure of the mental lexicon should be strongly emphasized.

Just as Singleton (2000) underlines the central importance of lexical descriptions of language, Cenoz *et al.* (2003) provide very convincing support for the need to research multilingualism as a common linguistic phenomenon by stressing the crucial importance of the study of a multilingual mental lexicon (MML). It seems to be one of the central aspects of successful language behaviour in terms of both linguistic and communicative competence. The centrality of vocabulary or more precisely one's mental lexicon (words and their interconnections in our brain and memory) can be judged from the abundance of research done in the area of vocabulary learning in the mother tongue and L2. Fairly new and fast-developing research in multilingualism is very much based on the findings, and on adapting methodologies, from L2 vocabulary research – as occurred in the parallel case of L2 vocabulary research in its early stages, when reference was made to L1 processes. It was L1 models that were adapted for the purposes of investigating the L2 mental lexicon phenomena. Although still in its initial stages, L3 mental lexicon studies cover a fair amount of ground, questioning and presenting as yet tentative conclusions concerning the major areas of interest, such as:

- the relationships between the L1, L2 and L3 mental lexicons in the learner's mind (interconnectivity: dependence or independence?);
- the ways of processing different languages;
- the structure of different languages in the mind;
- accessing (selectively or non-selectively) words in the mind;
- the role of language typology in lexical retrieval;
- the strategies used in recall processes (for an overview, see Gabryś-Barker, 2005).

The areas of MML study do not differ greatly from the research focus in L2 mental lexicon work and mainly look at the notion of language transfer, understood now as cross-linguistic consultations between languages, and the dynamic interaction of multiple languages. It may be assumed that the discussion of the integration and separation of mental lexical systems is an even more complex issue than in the case of the L2 mental lexicon. The multiplied variables involved in structuring and processing the languages – be they the increased number of languages available (and possible directions and degrees of connectivity) or the complexity and variety of social language use determinants and different personal characteristics (contexts of acquisition/learning and use, preferences, dominance, etc.) – all make this research area more tentative than in the case of bilingualism. Additionally, the disputed status of languages in the possession of the multilingual, which can be understood as L2, L3 or Ln, adds to the difficulty. It is debatable if it is the order of acquisition of each, or the competence in, or an individual's perception of a given language, or all of these, which go together to constitute the status of the languages involved.

To sum up, the complexity of MML and research in this area stems mainly from:

- the increased number of languages available (and possible directions and degrees of connectivity);
- the complexity and variety of social language use determinants;
- different personal characteristics (contexts of acquisition/learning and use, preferences, dominance, etc.).

It seems then that a lot of different patterns of multilinguality or more specifically MMLs need to be investigated by means of a more complex research methodology. This has led to a wider range of research methods being used in studying MML. These embrace:

- think-aloud techniques, in which verbalized data can show the ways in which the multilingual processes individual languages, their degree of activation (selection) and its purposes (discussed later in this lecture);

- retrospection, in which multilinguals reflect upon their perspective on their learning experiences, which can contribute to investigating multilinguals' language awareness;

- neurological imaging techniques, which allow a researcher to locate the areas of responsibility for different languages in the brain, which can develop understanding of how an MML is organized (separation and integration).

Theories of the mental lexicon in L1 and L2/Ln

Early theories of lexical processing have led to a whole variety of models describing the phenomenon of the L1 mental lexicon, later adapted in descriptions of the L2 mental lexicon and to some extent in hypothetical L3 mental lexicon models. These models see lexical processing as an online phenomenon, which accommodates both acoustic and linguistic (contextual) information, and assumes that lexical items are stored on phonological, semantic and syntactic levels. The major difference lies in the sequence and mode of interaction between the three levels and different types of information available for processing (for discussion, see Singleton, 2000).

The study of MML is a fairly new and fast developing area of multilingualism research and for some aspects of it monolingual approaches are being adopted, as for example in the case of the *interactive activation model*, expanded into *multilingual interactive activation* (Dijkstra, 2003). What we know so far is still fragmentary and hypothetical. In his introductory discussion on MML, Müller-Lance (2003) summarizes what has been still to some extent erratically evidenced in studies on MML:

- in the development of L3 lexical competence it is a language acquired that plays a more significant role than L1;

- the memorization of L3 words is easier if they are similar to words in other languages;

- the first syllable is more important for lexical transference than the last one;

- association responses in the language the learner is more proficient in are semantic, whereas a lower proficiency yields phonetic responses;

- associations are different for those who acquired their L2/L3 compared with those who learnt them at school;

- interlingual cognates facilitate transference strategies.

Most comprehensive in its scope is a monograph on MML, *The Multilingual Lexicon*, edited by Cenoz *et al.* (2003). It is a compilation of studies on different aspects of MML structure, storage, language processing and retrieval (Table 2.6).

Table 2.6 *Multilingual mental lexicon (MML) studies*

	Aspects of MML	Comment	Author
1.	Multilingual interactive activation (MIA)	A parallel word recognition in all languages; depending on frequency and proficiency levels, no special processing mechanisms other than in L2 required, an extension of a bilingual model (*interactive activation model*; McClelland & Rumelhart, 1981). The non-linguistic (expectation, instruction) and linguistic (syntactic, lexical) factors effect language activation or deactivation.	Dijkstra (2003)
2.	The transfer-appropriate processing framework	Word-completion tasks demonstrate that the structure of an L3 ML depends on conceptual features of a word; learner competence. Multilingual language processing occurs at the prelinguistic and conceptual level and at the semantic-conceptual-lexical level. Passive and active competence in languages (L2/L3) influence the speed of word completion.	Schönpflug (2003)
3.	Activation of lemmas in an MML	A single MML; lemmas assigned to each language, interlanguage transfer at the conceptual and morphological level, responsible for errors, role of competence.	Longxing Wei (2003a)
4.	Parasitic character of an MML	Transfer between all the languages of an MML and at all representational levels decides about its structure; it is dependent on individual learner differences (learning history, language(s) and word characteristics and contextual factors (task, mode and modality)). The results show that cross-linguistic interaction at the form level comes from a speaker's L3, at the conceptual level from L2, and at the frame level from L1, so L2 seems to be most significant.	Hall and Ecke (2003)
5.	Language typology and language activation	Typological closeness between languages results in interaction between them; however, individual, contextual and linguistic factors can result in different cross-linguistic consultations.	Cenoz (2003)
6.	Connective model of MML (a strategy model of multilingual learning)	The significant role of learning experiences (acquisition versus learning), inferencing strategies, access filter (e.g. *germanophone* versus *romanophone*) and use of Krashens's monitor; thus there are three types of MML organization: the multilinguoid, the bilinguoid and the monolinguoid individuals, depending on the strength of cross-linguistic connections. Languages may not be separated in the MML: motivation and interaction with the target language more important than proficiency, time and acquisition order.	Müller-Lance (2003)
7.	Formulaic expressions in MML	A tentative conclusion that formulaic sequences for different languages function separately in a ML; two ways of activation: recall of a chunk (if learnt as such) or accessed through grammatical analysis.	Spöttl and McCarthy (2003)

In the most recent publication on the MML, Szubko-Sitarek (2015) focuses on multilingual lexical recognition in the mental lexicon of L3 users, pointing out the role performed by visual modality as well as cognate facilitation in structuring the lexicon. A similar area of investigation was taken up earlier by Dijkstra (2007), in which he pointed out the role of context in multilingual processing and also the role of visual and auditory modalities in these processes.

Integration versus separation

One of the major multilingual lexicon issues investigated concerns relations between languages in an MML, that is, the integrationist and separatist points of view. In his critical evaluation of earlier MML studies, Singleton (2003) points out that evidence concerning the two major approaches, separation versus integration of languages in an MML, heavily inclines towards the integrative view. At the same time, however, contrary evidence cannot be wholly rejected. This issue has yet to be resolved by more recent studies. Various published studies carried out in the area of the mental lexicon support these differing positions and so no definite answer can be arrived at. It seems legitimate to argue that perhaps different types and degrees of interconnectivity make some parts of the mental lexicon more integrated and others more separate.

In a thorough overview of studies and arguments for or against the two approaches to the L2/Ln mental lexicon, Singleton (2003) provides support for both positions (Table 2.7).

Singleton (1999) and others (Alonso-Alonso, 2002; Ringbom, 2001) discuss the factors that may have an impact on the structure of a multilingual lexicon but also on the activation of a lexical item, which results in a certain degree of separation or integration. The nature of a learning environment (naturalistic versus formal instruction) and amount of exposure to each language will influence the degree of separation or integration within one MML, as the amount of contact with L1 vocabulary may influence the connections between the two lexicons. The elimination of the L1 in certain domains of life will cause language attrition on the lexical level and the L2 mental lexicon may function more independently – being more often the language of choice. There would therefore be no need for direct connections (Gabryś-Barker, 2005).

Also, language proficiency and language dominance in multilingual competence, expressed as functional competence, will determine the structure of one's MML. The separate social domains of home versus work versus school of a bilingual's functioning will tend to cause structure changes in the mental lexicons in L1, L2 and L3. The naturalistic setting will promote the development of separate or partially overlapping lexicons for both languages, which will be very much determined by the language dominance factor. Learning transfer resulting from methods, techniques and learning strategies will also shape an MML. Perhaps one of the major shaping factors will be the perceived and real typological distance between languages, their similarities and differences (Gabryś-Barker, 2005).

The context of formal instruction which occurs in a classroom setting gives a bi- or multilingual much more restricted access and exposure to language. It is specifically

Table 2.7 *Evidence for integration or separation of languages in a multilingual mental lexicon*

Evidence in support of integrationist view
• Cross-linguistic influence observed in bilingual/multilingual production: examples of transfer errors in Ln lexical choices made (sources: L1 or L2 lexis); use of calques (literally translated words).
• Learning strategies employed by multilinguals: examples of strategies based on the other language(s) such as: associations, use of cognate words or false friends.
• Bilingual behaviour: examples of intrasentential (within one sentence) CS, i.e. unintentional insertion of words/phrases from the other language, foreignizing (adapting L1 forms to fit L2/L3 formal rules, of phonetics or morphology, for example).
• Communication strategies observed: examples of subconscious CS, slips of a tongue.
• Reaction times: examples of quicker reaction times in the retrieval of cognate words (a quicker access to the lexicon because of the proximity of cognates).
• Translation tasks: examples of incorrect lexical choices made, for instance the use of words semantically similar but with different contextual restrictions (semantic extension).
Evidence in support of separatist view
• The modularity hypothesis: examples of different specialized modules in the mind cooperating in only a limited way; the post-pubertal learning of L2 is seen as occurring in isolation from L1.
• Language typology: examples of marked formal differences between languages making multilinguals draw analogies from more familiar rules within one language system.
• Language loss/aphasia: languages are recovered selectively; language disorders may affect one of the languages and not the others; also different areas of language functioning may be influenced by brain lesions.
• The ability to distinguish and select appropriate language in a multilingual context: examples of communicative sensitivity and selectivity, for instance in the case of bilingual children following the pattern of one-parent-one-language (a choice of language determined by the language of a parent in mixed-nationality parents).

Source: Based on Singleton (2003).

limited in vocabulary selection, which is not determined by the natural conditions of language use in communication, as it is in authentic L2/Ln settings, but by the lesson topic and syllabus followed. Additionally, foreign language instruction is still most often delivered in the mother tongue, which additionally limits learners' exposure to L2/Ln lexis. As a result, L2/Ln language learners become more L1 dependent and consequently the structures of their lexicons may become more integrated in a bilingual dictionary-like fashion. Additionally, the teaching methods used in a foreign language classroom may have a significant impact on the way the mental lexicon of a learner will be structured, how a lexical entry will be accessed and ultimately retrieved in a foreign language. It can be observed that:

> The traditional overt vocabulary teaching methods or practice of rote learning of bilingual lists of words are only occasionally supplemented with guessing techniques and discovery learning. Traditional methodology heavily relying on L1 as a linguistic resource and reference system brings about the integration of L1 and L2/Ln lexis, often manifested in lexical transfer from the mother tongue, examples of unintentional code-switches or falling into the trap of *false friends*. (Gabryś-Barker, 2005: 52)

To sum up, the factors that will have an impact on the structure of an MML are:

- learning environment: natural or classroom setting, degree of exposure to a certain language;
- language dominance in multilingual competence: functional competence;
- language proficiency in each language;
- learning transfer (the influence of methods, techniques and learning strategies);
- the type of linguistic task to be performed, the perceived and real typological distance between languages (Alonso-Alonso, 2002; Gabryś-Barker, 2005; Ringbom, 2001; Singleton, 1999, 2000).

Despite a growing number of studies in this area of multilingualism, there is an ongoing discussion as to how to approach the issues raised by the MML.

Methods in Researching Multilingualism

This lecture also seeks to demonstrate how research on multilingualism has impacted research methodology in applied linguistics, mostly by expanding it beyond quantitative methods, implementing mixed methodology and an interdisciplinary perspective. Researching multilingualism, which is a highly complex and idiosyncratic phenomenon with a multiplicity of interacting variables and dynamic contexts, entails a more widespread use of qualitative research, focusing on multilinguals' own language evidence, among other forms, expressed in narrative texts as representing autobiographical memories.

Simultaneous introspection

A good example of this in MML research is the more extensive use of research methods hitherto used only sporadically, such as thinking aloud and retrospection (Gabryś-Barker, 2010). Introspective methods have been used in language acquisition (LA) research for over 30 years. Their use reflects a shift in emphasis from the language product to the process that underlies generation of this product. Introspective reports became empirical tools of measurement of human behaviour in psychology a long time ago, whereas they have gained recognition as a research method in LA only fairly recently. The development of cognitivism in L2/FL teaching and learning allowed for the introduction of introspection as a valid and reliable method of research. The use of introspective methods came into being with the challenge to the hegemony of behaviouristic theory, which explained the mechanisms and structure of cognitive processes of the human mind by stimulus-response formula. Its inadequacy led to a feeling of dissatisfaction among applied linguists and made them look for methods that would enable them to probe the subjects' internal states.

The term *introspection* means to reflect, to look inside oneself. When formalized and applied as a research method, it means to verbalize one's own thoughts and thinking processes. In language studies, in practical terms it means that subjects are asked to verbalize all their thoughts and emotions when performing a language task. So it is the process of externalizing what goes on in one's brain either at a given moment (simultaneous introspection), on completion of a certain action (consecutive introspection) or after a time lapse (retrospection). Each verbalization is understood as deriving from the cognitive process that underlies it. As a result, verbalization must comply with all the constraints that have been identified for cognitive processes. In turn, cognitive processes consist of a set of sub-processes, which follow one another and are being transformed under the influence of a series of information processes. Information is stored in short-term memory (STM – with a limiting capacity of about 15–20 seconds) and in long-term memory (LTM – with permanent storage but slow access time). Information just received is stored in STM and is easily retrieved and articulated at the time of performing a task (Gabryś-Barker, 2011: 122).

Verbalized data can show the ways the multilingual processes individual languages, their degree of activation (selection) and their purposes (Table 2.8).

Table 2.8 *Verbalized introspection data in different areas of multilingualism research*

General focus (objective)	*Specific focus (examples)*
1. Cognitive 2. Affective 3. Social	1. Strategies of recall 2. Comments on success and/or failure of performance 3. Asking for assistance in performance of the task
Declarative versus procedural knowledge	Comments on grammatical/lexical rules versus comments on strategies
Modality of language use: 1. Spoken versus written 2. Receptive versus productive 3. Combination of the above	1. Verbalized comments versus those in the written text 2. Comprehension comments versus produced language solutions
Continuity of the verbalization process versus a discrete research aspect	1. Focus on pauses (as marked in TAPs) in the verbalization processes 2. Focus only on the researched phenomena, e.g. errors, strategies, etc.

In think-aloud protocols (TAPs) the data can be analyzed as demonstrating different levels of processing, cross-linguistic influences and affectivity. This verbalization is to a certain extent an explicit manifestation of both controlled and automatic processing. It is also a kind of monologue or dialogue with oneself in the mother tongue or any other language known to the multilingual. Table 2.9 presents the use of simultaneous introspection on its

Table 2.9 *Simultaneous introspection in multilingual acquisition studies*

	Type of language tasks used	**Research focus**	**Year**
Study 1:	Translation of the text from L2 (English) into L3 (Italian)	• learner profile (approach to the task, metalinguistic awareness, language transfer)	1995
Study 2:	Translation from L2 (English) into L3 (Italian) (English/Italian)	• language transfer at the level of lexis and syntax • transfer of training • language competence in language transfer	1998
Study 3:	Translation from L1 (Polish/Portuguese) into L2 (English) Translation from L2 (English) into L3 (German)	• lexical search processes • acquisition versus learning • transfer of training	1999
Study 4:	Translation (as above)	• the influence of the language of input (L1 versus L2) on the TL output • implicit versus explicit processing • lexical transfer	2005
Study 5:	Translation (as above)	• inner/private speech • activation of individual languages • levels of metalinguistic awareness	2005
Study 6:	Translation of a semi-authentic text	• interlingual language transfer in syntactic processing • transfer of training (explicit metalinguistic knowledge) • the affective dimension of language processing	2008

Source: Gabryś-Barker (1995–2008).

own or combined with retrospection in researching the MML and focusing on the metalinguistic awareness of a multilingual, cross-linguistic influences in MML, lexical search patterns and transfer of learning, as well as transfer of training.

Narrative in its different forms

The past two decades have brought about the development and spread of narrative research in different disciplines: from anthropology, psychology, education, language studies and linguistics to communication studies. What is more, enquiry into narrative is often interdisciplinary (Gabryś-Barker, 2013b). Studies using narratives offer more individualized understandings; thus they are most appropriate for the investigation of multilinguality phenomena. Narratives are employed as a research tool in the so-called 'autobiographical method' (Denzin, 1978), which embraces various forms of narratives: diaries, biographies, letters and memoirs. Narratives allow a researcher to carry out an in-depth analysis of subjective feelings, appraisals and experiences. These should be taken into consideration, as they are the driving motives for any activity. Importantly, one should also consider the context in which the subject lives and functions, as it determines to a great extent his/her interpretations and ways of expressing them. A variety of data – both diachronic (the subject's past) and present day – has value for the researcher. Narratives are important as they allow a researcher to focus 'on the meanings that people ascribe to their experiences (...) narrative inquiry concerns more than can be observed in daily practice. It also investigates the different ways in which people interpret the social world and their place within it' (Trahar, 2011: 48). Thus, multilinguals' perspectives on their learning experiences can also contribute to the picture of their multilinguality.

Although well-known tools such as questionnaires are still universally used in studying multilingualism (e.g. Dewaele, 2008; Dewaele & Pavlenko, 2001–2003), narrative texts in the form of autobiographical narratives or diaries are also employed more and more frequently (e.g. Gabryś-Barker, 2005, 2013b; Pavlenko, 2005). They allow a researcher to grasp the complexity of a topic investigated through its open form, allowing for data-driven qualitative paradigms of studies. Analysis of narratives also considers the context in which the subject lives and functions, as it determines to a great extent his/her interpretations and ways of expressing them. It is believed that every form of this type of data has value for a researcher.

There also exist multilingualism studies that look at the language development of a multilingual person by incorporating narratives as a data collection tool. Among other things, they can focus on the issues such as:

- language biographies (Busch, 2012);
- the profiles of multilinguals (Gabryś-Barker, 2013b);
- language processing in multilingual thinking (Gabryś-Barker, 2013a);
- age and proficiency levels as factors in a multilingual profile (Gabryś-Barker & Otwinowska-Kasztelanic, 2012).

Conclusions

As statistical data show, multilinguality is not a rare phenomenon and most people are to some extent multilingual. Individual multilinguality is seen as the ability to understand and use more than two languages, and multilinguals may differ in their preferences for different languages in different contexts and for different functions. Multilingualism does not affirm that this functionality has to be balanced, but rather stresses the multiplicity of possible profiles of a multilingual language user. The complexity of individual multilinguality derives not only from the multiplicity of languages (three or more) involved, but also from individual learner differences such as learning histories or ways of functioning in different languages. This complexity requires an individual approach to the issues of language(s) development and achievement; for this reason, the case study is a legitimate and extensively used research paradigm for studying multilinguals and multilingualism. The focus on an individual and not just on statistically verified models of numerous language users is characteristic of multilingualism research.

The contribution of multilingualism research to applied linguistics has to be valued for its introduction of a multidisciplinary perspective in researching language learning. This perspective not only requires focus on language itself but also pays attention to psychological, social and educational aspects of language learning (as other lectures in this volume illustrate). This multidisciplinary approach is also manifest in multilingualism research insofar as it makes use of science research paradigms and a scientific understanding of constructs such as multilinguality itself, multicompetence and its dynamic character (Aronin & Ó Laoire, 2001; Herdina & Jessner, 2002). In so doing, this approach redefines them from a more multidisciplinary vantage point.

One of the most significant contributions that multilingualism research has made is in the development of qualitative methods of research and models of qualitative content analysis (QCA; e.g. Mayring, 2000). Here, the use of learner experiences as expressed in their autobiographical memories (narratives) is most prominent. Also when studying cross-linguistic influences, one of the methods employed of pioneering importance is introspection – in the form of thinking aloud (simultaneous introspection) and retrospection (combining introspection and narratives).

A strong element in multilingualism research focuses on the advantages of being multilingual and in this way promotes multilinguality. Studies have contributed to the revival of minority languages such as Basque in Spain (Cenoz, 2009; Gorter *et al.*, 2014) or Frisian in Holland (Ytsma & Van der Schaff, 2001), where multilingualism research is very influential and has consequences for educational reform in language instruction on the one hand, and in raising the ethnic and identity awareness of speakers of those languages on the other. Thus multilingualism research, in its study of minority languages, is not just linguistic analysis but also has important sociopolitical consequences for language communities.

One of the areas where studying multilingual development builds on the traditions of bilingualism studies is language transfer, now redefined as cross-linguistic influence (CLI) and cross-linguistic interaction (CLIN). These studies, as can be seen in the earlier overview presented in this lecture, also expand bilingualism research paradigms and take a different perspective on language transfer. In multilingualism research it is seen as providing evidence of how language development occurs, emphasizing both its facilitative and impeding influences. In multilingual CLI/CLIN studies, there is also attention given to the role of similarities in language transfer in demonstrating how dominant and peripheral languages in one's repertoire can facilitate their mutual functioning (Ringbom, 2007). Additionally, the related issue of code-switching on the intersentential level (discourse) is not believed to be an undesirable manifestation of learner confusion in language activation but is an example of *translanguaging*, a positive characteristic of plurilingualism (i.e. individual multilinguality) (García & Li Wei, 2013).

Research in multilingualism plays a role not only in developing our knowledge of what we understand about language processing, learning and use, but also has pragmatic implications for actual multiple language learning and instruction. The burgeoning research in multilingualism, with its increasing studies and further findings, should percolate into educational practice at the level of foreign language(s) instruction, especially now that two foreign languages are obligatory in most of the programmes of study in European schools. Findings concerning cross-linguistic influences and metalinguistic awareness (and their role in multilingual language development) can be used in designing language programmes for multilinguals which would allow them to use their prior knowledge more consciously. There is also a place for improvement in teacher training programmes, which should aim to prepare teachers of foreign languages who are able to accommodate and make use of their multilingual learners' knowledge of two (or more) languages.

Questions for Students' Reflection

1. *'In paying attention to the language practices of young people in urban settings, we see new **multilingualisms** emerging, as the young people create meanings with their diverse linguistic repertoires. We see the young people (and their parents and teachers) using their eclectic array of linguistic resources to create, parody, play, contest, endorse, evaluate, challenge, tease, disrupt, bargain and otherwise negotiate their social worlds.'* (Blackledge & Creese, *Multilingualism: A Critical Perspective*, New York: Continuum, 2010)

   Can you think of examples to illustrate the above quotation? Why do the authors use the term multilingualism in the plural, *multilingualisms*?

2. When can we call a person trilingual, quadrilingual and *Ln* lingual? Discuss the following criteria: *degree of proficiency, degree of functional capability, intelligibility*. Can you think of any other criteria?

3. Would you agree with the statement that perhaps there are no longer monolingual people? If so/if not, what arguments would you put forward to illustrate/to reject this belief?

4. Comment on the advantages of the multilingual over the bilingual language learner/user and compare the contextual patterns of bilingual and multilingual development.

5. Discuss the ecological approach to multilinguality based on the model of Aronin and Ó Laoire (2001).

6. Think of possible ways of defining the multilingual mental lexicon by completing the following sentence:

   The multilingual mental lexicon is like ...

7. Think of a mini-research project that would illustrate how we recall words from our multilingual mental lexicon.

8. Why does research in multilingualism make extensive use of qualitative methods and tools of study?

Suggestions for Further Reading

Aronin, L. and Singleton, D. (2008) Multilingualism as a new linguistic dispensation. *International Journal of Multilingualism* 5 (1), 1–16.

Aronin, L. and Singleton, D. (2012) *Multilingualism*. Amsterdam and Philadelphia, PA: John Benjamins.

Bowles, M.A. (2010) *The Think-Aloud Controversy in Second Language Research*. New York and London: Routledge.

Cenoz, J. and Gorter, D. (eds) (2015) *Multilingual Education: Between Language Learning and Translanguaging*. Cambridge: Cambridge University Press.

Cenoz, J., Hufeisen, B. and Jessner, U. (eds) (2003) *The Multilingual Lexicon*. Dordrecht: Kluwer Academic.

Cook, V. and Li Wei (eds) (2016) *The Cambridge Handbook of Linguistic Multicompetence*. Cambridge: Cambridge University Press.

Gabryś-Barker, D. (2005) *Aspects of Multilingual Storage, Processing and Retrieval*. Katowice: University of Silesia Press.

Gabryś-Barker, D. (ed.) (2012) *Cross-linguistic Influences in Multilingual Language Acquisition*. Heidelberg and Berlin: Springer.

Herdina, P. and Jessner, U. (2002) *A Dynamic Model of Multilingualism: Perspectives of Change in Psycholinguistics*. Clevedon: Multilingual Matters.

Mayring, P. (2000) Qualitative content analysis. *Forum: Qualitative Social Research* 1 (2). Available at www.qualitative-research.net (accessed 7 July 2018).

Pavlenko, A. (2007) *Emotions and Multilingualism*. Cambridge: Cambridge University Press.

References

Alonso-Alonso, R. (2002) *The Role of Transfer in Second Language Acquisition*. Vigo: Universidade de Vigo.

Angelovska, T. and Hahn, A. (2012) Written L3 (English): Transfer phenomena of L2 (German) lexical and syntactical properties. In D. Gabryś-Barker (ed.) *Cross-linguistic Influences in Multilingual Language Acquisition* (pp. 23–40). Berlin and Heidelberg: Springer.

Aronin, L. (2006) Dominant language constellations: An approach to multilingualism studies. In M. Ó Laoire (ed.) *Multilingualism in Educational Settings* (pp. 140–159). Hohengehren: Schneider Publications.

Aronin, L. (2016) Multi-competence and dominant language constellation. In V. Cook and Li Wei (eds) *The Cambridge Handbook of Linguistic Multicompetence* (pp. 142–163). Cambridge: Cambridge University Press.

Aronin, L. and Jessner, U. (2015) Understanding current multilingualism: What can the butterfly tell us? In C. Kramsch and U. Jessner (eds) *The Multilingual Challenge* (pp. 271–292). Berlin: De Gruyter.

Aronin, L. and Ó Laoire, M. (2001) Exploring multilingualism in cultural contexts: Towards the notion of multilinguality. In J. Ytsma and M. Hooghiemstra (eds) *Proceedings of the Second International Conference on Trilingualism*. Leeuwarden: Fryske Akademie (CD).

Aronin, L. and Ó Laoire, M. (2004) Exploring multilingualism in cultural contexts: Towards a notion of multilinguality. In C. Hoffmann and Y. Ytsma (eds) *Trilingualism in Family, School and Community* (pp. 11–29). Clevedon: Multilingual Matters.

Aronin, L. and Singleton, D. (2008) Multilingualism as a new linguistic dispensation. *International Journal of Multilingualism* 5 (1), 1–16.

Aronin, L. and Singleton, D. (2012) *Multilingualism*. Amsterdam and Philadelphia, PA: John Benjamins.

Busch, B. (2012) Language biographies: Approaches to multilingualism in education and linguistic research. In B. Busch, A. Jardine and A. Tjoutuku (eds) *Language Biographies for Multilingual Learning*. Occasional Paper No. 24. Cape Town: PRAESA.

Cenoz, J. (2001) The effect of linguistic distance, language status and age on cross-linguistic influence in third language acquisition. In J. Cenoz, B. Hufeisen and U. Jessner (eds) *Cross-linguistic Influence in Third Language Acquisition* (pp. 8–20). Clevedon: Multilingual Matters.

Cenoz, J. (2003) The role of typology in the organization of the multilingual lexicon. In J. Cenoz, B. Hufeisen and U. Jessner (eds) *The Multilingual Lexicon* (pp. 103–116). Dordrecht: Kluwer Academic.

Cenoz, J. (2009) *Towards Multilingual Education: Basque Educational Research from an International Perspective*. Bristol: Multilingual Matters.

Cenoz, J. and Genesee, F. (eds) (1998) *Beyond Bilingualism: Multilingualism and Multilingual Education*. Clevedon: Multilingual Matters.

Cenoz, J. and Gorter, D. (eds) (2015) *Multilingual Education: Between Language Learning and Translanguaging*. Cambridge: Cambridge University Press.

Cenoz, J., Hufeisen, B. and Jessner, U. (2003) Why investigate the multilingual lexicon? In J. Cenoz, B. Hufeisen and U. Jessner (eds) (2003) *The Multilingual Lexicon* (pp. 1–10). Dordrecht: Kluwer Academic.

Clyne, M. (1997) Some of the things trilinguals do. *International Journal of Bilingualism* 1, 95–116.

Cook, V. (1991) The poverty-of-the stimulus argument and multicompetence. *Second Language Research* 7, 103–117.

Cook, V. (1992) Evidence for multicompetence. *Language Learning* 42 (4), 557–591.

Cook, V. (2016) Premises of multi-competence. In V. Cook and Li Wei (eds) *The Cambridge Handbook of Linguistic Multicompetence* (pp. 1–25). Cambridge: Cambridge University Press.

Corder, P. (1973) *The Edinburgh Course in Applied Linguistics*. Oxford: Oxford University Press.

De Angelis, G. (2007) *Third or Additional Language Acquisition*. Clevedon: Multilingual Matters.

Denzin, N.K. (1978) *Sociological Methods*. New York: McGraw-Hill.

Dewaele, J.M. (2001) Activation or inhibition? The interaction of L1, L2 and L3 on the language mode continuum. In J. Cenoz, B. Hufeisen and U. Jessner (eds) *Cross-linguistic Influence in Third Language Acquisition: Psycholinguistic Perspectives* (pp. 69–89). Clevedon: Multilingual Matters.

Dewaele, J.-M. (2008) The emotional load weight of *I love you* in multilinguals' languages. *Journal of Pragmatics* 40, 1753–1780.

Dewaele, J.M. (2010) *Emotions in Multiple languages*. Basingstoke: Palgrave.

Dewaele, J.M. and Li Wei (2014) Attitudes towards code-switching among adult mono- and multilingual language users. *Journal of Multilingual and Multicultural Development* 1, 235–251.

Dewaele, J.M. and Pavlenko, A. (2001–2003) *Bilingualism and Emotions*. Web questionnaire, University of London.

Dijkstra, T. (2003) Lexical processing in bilinguals and multilinguals. In J. Cenoz, B. Hufeisen and U. Jessner (eds) *The Multilingual Lexicon* (pp. 11–26). Dordrecht: Kluwer Academic.

Dijkstra, T. (2007) The mental lexicon. In M.G. Gaskell (ed.) *The Oxford Handbook of Psycholinguistics*. Oxford: Oxford University Press (published online 2012).

Ecke, P. (2015) Parasitic vocabulary acquisition, cross-linguistic influence and lexical retrieval in multilinguals. *Bilingualism: Language and Cognition* 18 (2), 145–162. See www.academia.edu (accessed 29 December 2015).

Emmorey K. and Fromkin, V. (1988) The mental lexicon. In F. Newmeyer (ed.) *Linguistics: The Cambridge Survey, Vol. 3. Language: Psychological and Biological Aspects* (pp. 129–149). Cambridge: Cambridge University Press.

Gabryś, D. (1995) Introspection in second language learning research. *Kwartalnik Neofilologiczny* 3 (95), 271–291.

Gabryś, D. (1998) The phenomenon of transfer in L3 learning from a psycholinguistic perspective: A case study. In *ISAPL '97 Proceedings* (pp. 409–414). Porto: Universidade do Porto.

Gabryś, D. (1999) Cross-linguistic influences in L3-learning. In M. Wysocka (ed.) *On Language Theory and Practice, Vol. 2* (pp. 169–182). Katowice: University of Silesia Press.

Gabryś-Barker D. (2001) A cross-cultural aspect of the interaction of languages in the mental lexicon of a multilingual learner. In J. Cenoz, B. Hufeisen and U. Jessner (eds) *Looking Beyond Second Language Acquisition: Studies in Tri- and Multilingualism* (pp. 97–110). Tübingen: Tübingen Verlag.

Gabryś-Barker, D. (2005) *Aspects of Multilingual Storage, Processing and Retrieval*. Katowice: University of Silesia Press.

Gabryś-Barker, D. (2008) Syntactic processing in multilingual performance (a case study). In D. Gabryś-Barker (ed.) *Morphosyntactic Issues in Second Language Studies* (pp. 86–106). Clevedon: Multilingual Matters.

Gabryś-Barker, D. (2010) Turn on your TAP: Memory in language processing. *Linguarum Arena, Revista do Programa Doutoral em Didactica de Lingua da Univerisdade do Porto* 1 (1), 25–42.

Gabryś-Barker, D. (2011) Introspective methods in researching multilingualism. Paper presented at *Quantitative Content Analysis Seminar, November, Lepizig Universität*.

Gabryś-Barker, D. (2013a) Face to face with one's thoughts: On thinking multilingually. In M. Pawlak and L. Aronin (eds) *Essential Topics in Applied Linguistics and Multilingualism: Studies in Honor of David Singleton* (pp. 185–204). Heidelberg: Springer.

Gabryś-Barker, D. (2013b) The profile of a multilingual. In *Proceedings of the Tenth Annual Conference of the Polish Association for the Study of English: PASE Papers in Linguistics, Translation and TEFL Methodology* (pp. 185–198). Krakow: Jagiellonian University Press.

Gabryś-Barker, D. and Otwinowska-Kasztelanic, A. (2012) Multilingual learning stories: Threshold, stability and change. *International Journal of Multilingualism* 9 (4), 367–384.

García, O. and Li Wei (2013) *Translanguaging: Language, Bilingualism and Education*. London: Palgrave Macmillan.

Gibson, M. and Hufeisen, B. (2003) Investigating the role of prior language knowledge. In J. Cenoz, B. Hufeisen and U. Jessner (eds) *The Multilingual Lexicon* (pp. 87–102). Dordrecht: Kluwer Academic.

Gibson, M., Hufeisen, B. and Libbon, G. (2001) Learners of German as L3 and their production of German prepositional verbs. In J. Cenoz, B. Hufeisen and U. Jessner (eds) *Cross-linguistic Influence in Third Language Acquisition* (pp. 138–148). Clevedon: Multilingual Matters.

Gorter, D., Zenotz, V. and Cenoz, J. (eds) (2014) *Minority Languages and Multilingual Education*. Berlin: Springer.

Hall, C. and Ecke, P. (2003) Parasitism as a default mechanism in L3 vocabulary acquisition. In J. Cenoz, B. Hufeisen and U. Jessner (eds) *The Multilingual Lexicon* (pp. 71–86). Dordrecht: Kluwer Academic.

Hammarberg, B. (2001) Roles of L1 and L2 in L3 production and acquisition. In J. Cenoz, B. Hufeisen and U. Jessner (eds) *Cross-linguistic Influence in Third Language Acquisition* (pp. 21–41). Clevedon: Multilingual Matters.

Heidrick, I. (2006) Beyond the L2: How is transfer affected by multilingualism? Teachers College Columbia Working Papers in TESOL and Applied Linguistics, Vol. 6, No. 1. *The Forum*, 1–3.

Herdina, P. and Jessner, U. (2002) *A Dynamic Model of Multilingualism: Perspectives of Change in Psycholinguistics*. Clevedon: Multilingual Matters.

Herwig, A. (2001) Plurilingual lexical organization: Evidence from lexical processing in L1-L2-L3-L4 translation. In J. Cenoz, B. Hufeisen and U. Jessner (eds) *Cross-linguistic Influence in Third Language Acquisition: Psycholinguistic Perspectives* (pp. 115–137). Clevedon: Multilingual Matters.

Hoffmann, C. (1999) Trilingual competence: Linguistic and cognitive issues. *Applied Linguistic Studies in Central Europe* 3, 16–26.

Jessner, U. (2003) The nature of cross-linguistic interaction in the multilingual system. In J. Cenoz, B. Hufeisen and U. Jessner (eds) *The Multilingual Lexicon* (pp. 45–56). Dordrecht: Kluwer Academic.

Kaplan, R.B. (ed.) (2002) *The Oxford Handbook of Applied Linguistics*. Oxford: Oxford University Press.

Kesckes, J. and Papp, T. (2000) Metaphorical competence in trilingual language production. In J. Cenoz and U. Jessner (eds) *English in Europe: The Acquisition of a Third Language* (pp. 99–120). Clevedon: Multilingual Matters.

Kresić, M. and Gulan, T. (2012) Interlingual identifications and assessment of similarities between L1, L2, and L3: Croatian learners' use of modal particles and equivalent modal elements. In D. Gabryś-Barker (ed.) *Cross-linguistic Influences in Multilingual Language Acquisition* (pp. 63–80). Berlin and Heidelberg: Springer.

Lemhofer, K., Dijkstra, T. and Michel, M.C. (2004) Three languages, one ECHO: Cognate effects in trilingual word recognition. *Language and Cognitive Processes* 19 (5), 585–611.

Leung, Y.I. (2005) L2 vs L3 initial state: A comparative study of the acquisition of French DPs by Vietnamese monolinguals and Cantonese-English bilinguals. *Bilingualism: Language and Cognition* 8 (1), 39–61.

Levelt, W. (1989) *Speaking: From Intention to Articulation*. Cambridge, MA: MIT Press.

Longxing Wei (2003a) Activation of lemmas in the multilingual mental lexicon and transfer in third language learning. In J. Cenoz, B. Hufeisen and U. Jessner (eds) *The Multilingual Lexicon* (pp. 57–70). Dordrecht: Kluwer Academic.

Longxing Wei (2003b) Lemma congruence between languages as an organizing principle in intrasentential codeswitching. *Lingua* 2, 183–186.

McClelland, J.L. and Rumelhart, D.E. (1981) An interactive activation model of context effects in letter perception. An account of basic findings. *Psychological Review* 88 (5), 375–406.

Müller-Lance, J. (2003) A strategy model of multilingual learning. In J. Cenoz, B. Hufeisen and U. Jessner (eds) *The Multilingual Lexicon* (pp. 117–132). Dordrecht: Kluwer Academic.

Murahata, G., Murahata, Y. and Cook, V. (2016) Research questions and methodology of multi-competence. In V. Cook and Li Wei (eds) (2015) *The Cambridge Handbook of Linguistic Multicompetence* (pp. 26–49). Cambridge: Cambridge University Press.

Odlin, T. (1993) *Language Transfer*. Cambridge: Cambridge University Press.

Odlin, T. (2012) Reconciling group tendencies and individual variation in the acquisition of L2 and L3. In D. Gabryś-Barker (ed.) *Cross-linguistic Influences in Multilingual Language Acquisition* (pp. 81–97). Berlin and Heidelberg: Springer.

Otwinowska-Kasztelanic, A. (2011) Awareness and affordances: Multilinguals versus bilinguals and their perceptions of cognates. In G. De Angelis and J.M. Dewaele (eds) *New Trends in Crosslinguistic Influence and Multilingualism Research* (pp. 1–18). Bristol: Multilingual Matters.

Pavlenko, A. (2005) *Emotions and Multilingualism*. New York and Cambridge: Cambridge University Press.

Peyer, E., Kaiser, I. and Berthele, R. (2010) The multilingual reader: Advantages in understanding/decoding German sentence structure when reading German as an L3. *International Journal of Multilingualism* 7 (3), 225–239.

Ringbom, H. (1987) *The Role of the First Language in Foreign Language Learning*. Clevedon: Multilingual Matters.

Ringbom, H. (2001) Lexical transfer in L3 production. In J. Cenoz, B. Hufeisen and U. Jessner (eds) *Cross-linguistic Influence in Third Language Acquisition* (pp. 59–68). Clevedon: Multilingual Matters.

Ringbom, H. (2007) *Cross-linguistic Similarity in Foreign Language Learning*. Clevedon: Multilingual Matters.

Ringbom, H. (2011) Error analysis. In J.-O. Östman and J. Verschueren (eds) *Pragmatics in Practice* (pp. 149–152). Amsterdam. John Benjamins.

Ringbom, H. (2012) Multilingualism in a football team: The case of IFK Mariehamn. In D. Gabryś-Barker (ed.) *Cross-linguistic Influences in Multilingual Language Acquisition* (pp. 185–197). Berlin and Heidelberg: Springer.

Schnöpflug, U. (2003) The transfer-appropriate-processing approach and the trilingual's organization of the lexicon. In J. Cenoz, B. Hufeisen and U. Jessner (eds) *The Multilingual Lexicon* (pp. 27–44). Dordrecht: Kluwer Academic.

Sharwood-Smith, M. and Kellerman, E. (eds) (1986) *Crosslinguistic Influence in Second Language Acquisition*. Oxford: Pergamon.

Singleton, D. (1999) *Exploring the Second Language Mental Lexicon*. Cambridge: Cambridge University Press.

Singleton, D. (2000) *Language and the Lexicon: An Introduction*: London: Edward Arnold.

Singleton, D. (2003) Perspectives on the multilingual lexicon: A critical synthesis. In J. Cenoz, B. Hufeisen and U. Jessner (eds) *The Multilingual Lexicon* (pp. 167–176). Dordrecht: Kluwer Academic.

Spöttl, C. and McCarthy, M. (2003) Formulaic utterances in the multilingual context. In J. Cenoz, B. Hufeisen and U. Jessner (eds) *The Multilingual Lexicon* (pp. 133–152). Dordrecht: Kluwer Academic.

Szubko-Sitarek, W. (2015) *Multilingual Lexical Recognition in the Mental Lexicon of Third Language Users*. Berlin and Heidelberg: Springer.

Trahar, S. (2011) *Developing Cultural Capability in International Higher Education: A Narrative Inquiry*. London: Routledge.

Tymczyńska, M. (2012) Trilingual lexical processing in online translation recognition. The influence of conference interpreting experience. In D. Gabryś-Barker (ed.) *Cross-linguistic Influences in Multilingual Language Acquisition* (pp. 151–168). Berlin and Heidelberg: Springer.

Włosowicz, T. (2012) Cross-linguistic interaction at the grammatical level in L3 reception and production. In D. Gabryś-Barker (ed.) *Cross-linguistic Influences in Multilingual Language Acquisition* (pp. 131–150). Berlin and Heidelberg: Springer.

Ytsma, J. and Van der Schaff, A. (2001) *Frisian: The Frisian Language in Education in the Netherlands*. Regional Dossiers Series. Ljouwert: Mercator-Education.

Lecture 3

The Psycholinguistics of Multiple Language Learning and Teaching

Britta Hufeisen and Ulrike Jessner

Introduction

In many contexts in the world more than one language is used on a daily basis. Multilingualism can be encountered as an institutional, societal, discursive and individual phenomenon. In multilingual contexts it is common that language skills are developed in various languages for their use in certain domains but that the language proficiency in some of the languages can be limited.

The Council of Europe has specified the European goal of becoming multilingual in its request that each member state provide its citizens with the opportunity to learn at least two foreign languages besides their first language(s) (Council of Europe, 2008). Furthermore, one of the languages learned should preferably be a language of wider communication and the second should be a neighbouring or minority language. This would mean, for instance, that somebody living in Germany should be competent in German, and learn English, French or Spanish as the language of wider communication, Polish or Danish as one of the neighbouring languages, or Turkish or Russian as a minority language. This person might also already be proficient in German and Turkish because he or she has a Turkish background. A second example would be that of an Austrian citizen who is proficient in German (and possibly a second language of minority communication), learning Spanish or English as a language of wider communication, plus Croatian or Italian as a minority and/or neighbouring language.

In line with these political and educational developments, a significant amount of linguistic research in the field of multiple language learning has recently evolved both within Europe and worldwide. Today multilingualism is interpreted as a phenomenon which views language choice and proficiency as necessarily dependent on use in specific domains of life, thereby moving away from the notion of multiple monolingualism (Baker, 2001). Scholars working in the area of third language acquisition and multilingualism are interested in the exploration of the most important factors guiding the language learning process in a multilingual context. The process of becoming and the state of being multilingual are not only a matter of multilingual competencies and literacies or even dialectal competencies, but also require a level of intercultural sensitivity, and an awareness of all three.

The aim of this lecture is to provide an introduction to this research with teaching examples stemming from a mainly European perspective with the aim of providing ideas for application to other contexts. Its emphasis will be not so much on the learning of a first foreign language, but instead highlights the learning of a second foreign language (L3) and further foreign languages (L4, L5, Ln). Multilingualism research is taking place in diverse areas, including psycholinguistics (e.g. the effects of multiple language learning on the individual), sociolinguistics (e.g. the effects of multiple language learning on the community and/or society) and applied linguistics (e.g. the effects of multiple language learning on the structured process of instruction and the effects of specific instructional processes on the learning of second and further foreign languages).

Therefore, this lecture will first introduce the terminological framework used in the literature on multiple language learning and teaching. This will be followed by an overview of research to date on theory and practice in learning and instruction. Finally, challenges for future studies will be discussed as stimulation for furthering research in multilingualism.

Basic Concepts: Definitions and Scenarios

Defining multiple language learning

In this lecture the main terms which are in use in research on multiple language learning will be discussed. Overall, such concepts differ from traditional research terminology concerned with bilingualism or the learning of two languages (i.e. classical second language acquisition (SLA) research).

Multiple language learning not only refers to the learning of more than two languages in tutored instruction (third, fourth or nth language learning, for which the term third language acquisition (TLA) is used), but the term also refers to the learning of a second or third or fourth (foreign) language (L3, L4, Ln) in a natural context.

Being multilingual means being proficient in more than two languages, as is the case with language users who grow up or live with three or more languages. This could include proficiency in languages such as Finnish, Swedish and Sami in Northern Finland; languages such as Turkish, Kurdish and German in Germany; an Italian dialect, standard Italian and Slovenian in the North East of Italy; or Arabic, English and Tyrolean dialect in Austria.

Becoming multilingual can evolve from being surrounded by more than two languages on a daily basis. Such a situation might be expected, for example, of an individual growing up in Switzerland who becomes proficient in Romansh, Italian and German. However, it could just as easily apply to a person who grows up with just one first language and then learns two or more languages in the course of his/her school career.

It is important to note that such a viewpoint represents a contrast to earlier and common beliefs that the prefix 'multi' indicates 'more than one', with the consequence that multilingualism is often erroneously used as a synonym for bilingualism only and that multiple language learning is somehow identical to learning a first foreign language (L2).

However, researchers of multilingualism take the strong stand that bilingualism, trilingualism or quadralingualism should be regarded as specific subtypes of multilingualism. That is, the learning of a first foreign language (L2 learning), a second (L3 learning), a third (L4 learning), a fourth (L5 learning), etc. all should be regarded as specific processes of multiple language learning as much as bilingualism does not equal trilingualism. Likewise, trilingualism (or second foreign or additional language learning) is not to be treated simply as extended bilingualism and extended SLA but as a specific subtype of multilingualism and multiple language learning in its own right. The very recent multilingual turn in SLA studies, as discussed by May (2015), also seems to open new perspectives on the necessity of the distinction between SLA/bilingualism and TLA/trilingualism or multilingualism.

The justification for a distinction between bilingualism and multilingualism is increasing empirical evidence which demonstrates that learning a third (or fourth, fifth, etc.) language is a completely different process from learning a second language (for an overview, see Aronin & Hufeisen, 2009; De Angelis, 2007). It is crucial to take into account the fact that the L3 learner relies on a different set of previous knowledge from that which the L2 learner is equipped with. This previous knowledge marks a different starting point for the onset of the learning of a subsequent further language. The result is often a faster and more carefully planned language learning process on the part of the learner, as will be discussed below in more detail.

So far, little attention in L3 research has been focused on specific variants within one language or language family (e.g. Frisian/Dutch/German). This would also include dialectal variants and standard variants in combination with foreign languages or different social registers. In the course of time it is expected that these linguistic situations will be studied to a greater extent. Within the framework of current research into multiple language learning, a differentiation is made between societal and individual multilingualism.

However, this lecture will not go into detail about societal multilingualism and will instead concentrate on individual multilingualism as a result of multiple language learning, as we believe in a constant interaction between the social and individual level of language learning, as explicated below.

A number of researchers representing a multilingual standpoint argue that all (!) types of language learning and acquisition – even L1 acquisition – should be classified as multilingual learning. In this view, the study of multiple language learning and of the multilingualism that results from this learning provides a prototypical theoretical umbrella for the study of language acquisition as a whole. These researchers believe that only the study of multilingualism can provide insights into the language acquisition processes as a whole (Cenoz *et al.*, 2003a; Flynn *et al.*, 2004; Herdina & Jessner, 2002).

Multiple language learning scenarios

The process of acquiring or learning three or more languages is characterized by diversity and complexity. This complexity mainly concerns the routes and the influential factors in TLA. In SLA, one can distinguish between two kinds of routes: that is, growing up with two languages in the family or the community, or learning an L2 in a tutored instruction setting once the primary L1 acquisition has been finished. In TLA, the number of routes of acquisition multiplies, as described by Cenoz (2000). With respect to three languages, she describes at least four prototypical types of the succession of languages:

- Simultaneous acquisition of L1/L2/L3: a child may grow up with three (or more) languages simultaneously; this could also be called triple first language acquisition.
- Consecutive acquisition of L1 > L2 > L3: a monolingual speaker starts learning his/her L2 in Grade 5 and his/her L3 in Grade 7, both in a tutored fashion.
- Simultaneous acquisition of L2/L3 after acquiring the L1: a monolingual speaker starts learning his/her L2 and L3 simultaneously in Grade 6 at secondary school.
- Simultaneous acquisition of L1/L2 before learning the L3: a child who is growing up bilingually starts learning another language at school at an early age.

There is a wide variety of possible combinations of TLA and multilingual development that match these four prototypical scenarios which could include the following:

- An adolescent student starts learning yet another foreign language in Grade 12 after she has already learned/started learning a first foreign language in school starting in Grade 5.
- A child who grows up with two migrant languages may start learning the regional variety in kindergarten and commence learning the standard variety of the host country and typical foreign languages at school.
- A university student who has already learned two foreign languages at school starts learning a new language at the age of 27.

- A child who grows up with a dialect might acquire the standard variant in kindergarten and start learning foreign languages at school.
- A middle-aged employee, after having used her L3 French in professional circumstances, begins to learn a new foreign language, Mandarin.
- A learner has learned a first and a second foreign language after having acquired the L1, but he or she does not continue learning or using the L2 until 20 years after finishing school.

The number of routes of learning increases with the number of languages, so that in their overview of forms of the acquisition of seven languages Todeva and Cenoz (2009: 7) present 32 possibilities.

These various scenarios show the multitude of possible language combinations and the complexity of multilingualism as a linguistic phenomenon. They also show that much more complex possible research methods have to be developed in order to study these complex phenomena effectively and systematically, as indicated in Aronin and Hufeisen (2009) and Aronin and Jessner (2014).

Researching Multiple Language Learning

Early research

Although L3 has only recently received more systematic attention from a small but increasing part of the linguistic community, researchers such as the German Maximilian Braun who wrote about multilingualism as early as 1937 defined multilingualism as the 'active and passive comprehensive proficiency in two or more languages' (Braun, 1937: 115, our translation). He differentiated between learning and acquisition and believed that it was determination and aptitude that guided the language learning process and its success. Later on, Vildomec (1996) published a monograph on multilingualism, in which he dealt with the learning styles of his multilingual subjects in a kind of anecdotal way. Some years later, Naiman *et al.* (1996) had already worked on the language learning strategies of the *good language learner*, that is, the experienced language learner.

In the late 1960s and early 1970s, typical research questions were concerned with interferences between the three or more languages of a learner (Stedje, 1976; Zapp, 1979). Data usually consisted of production data of learners at school and university and generally concentrated on the negative effects of the interactions of the various languages in the learners' minds. Such research often resulted in warnings for the foreign language classroom teacher to make sure that the multiple languages the students had in their heads were carefully separated and that no connection among them should be allowed, made or even emphasized. It was only during the late 1980s and early 1990s that the positive aspects of the existence of several languages in the minds of the learners were investigated and exploited in search of new pedagogical concepts. For example, Thomas (1987) and Ringbom (1987) found that learners who were already competent in two languages learned an Lx as their L3 more effectively than monolingual learners learning the same Lx as their L2. They also drew attention to individual learner phenomena, such as determination, motivation, aptitude, attitude and learning style.

Current research

Over the last 20 years, interest in L3 learning has grown considerably, along with general interest in multilingualism (for detailed overviews on TLA research, see Aronin & Hufeisen, 2009; Cenoz et al., 2001a, 2001b, 2003b; De Angelis, 2007). Recent research has looked into the differences and similarities between the processes of learning a L2 versus those of learning an L3.

The biannual L3 conferences on Third Language Acquisition and Multilingualism, the first of which took place in 1999 at the University of Innsbruck, Austria, have continuously attracted an increasing number of participants, which led to the founding of the International Association of Multilingualism in 2003. The *International Journal of Multilingualism* was launched in 2004. Over the past few years a variety of methodological approaches have been developed to investigate multilingual phenomena (described in more detail below).

With respect to TLA, the following main areas of research can be characterized:

a. sociolinguistic studies which investigate multilingual communities and use in multilingual contexts such as in children growing up with three languages;

b. psycholinguistic studies which deal with the multilingual individual learner, thereby mainly focusing on cross-linguistic influence and multilingual awareness, as discussed in more detail below;

and

c. applied studies which take into account the specifics of the learning context, the conditions and products of such learning, and the possible consequences for the foreign language learning classroom.

Sociolinguistic aspects of multiple language learning

L3 research from a sociolinguistic perspective focuses on such linguistic situations as can be found in regions where minority languages exist. For example, Turkish migrants in Germany might use Turkish and German in daily life and be learning English as their L3 in tutored instruction. In some European regions, minority languages are used as autochthonous languages. For example, in the Basque Country, a part of the population is bilingual in Spanish and Basque and the younger generations tend to study English as a third language. Likewise, in Catalonia, most people are bilingual in Spanish and Catalan, and again English is learned as a third language. In the northern part of the Netherlands, the citizens of

Friesland use Frisian and Dutch on a daily basis and children learn English as their third language from an early age at school. In Austria, where the majority of the population speak German as a dominant language, there are bilingual enclaves like the one in Carinthia where Slovenian and German are used together, and another in Burgenland where Hungarian or Croatian and German are used on a daily basis. Here again, the bilingual children come into tutored contact with English as their third language. Additionally an increasing number of refugees, who are already bi- or even multilingual, have started learning the languages of their new environments plus English as a fourth or fifth language.

On the other hand, in Cyprus, although there are two official languages, this does not necessarily mean that all the citizens are bilingual. The same applies in Switzerland with its four official languages, French, German, Italian and Romansh. Not all citizens speak all four languages: some might be competent in two of the official languages and learn L3 and L4 in school; others might have a migrant language background, speak a Swiss German dialect in daily life, use standard German as L3 in official situations and learn L4 and L5 at school.

These examples show how manifold the linguistic situations may become once the minority languages, dialectal variants and other migrant and heritage languages which are part of an individual learner's repertoire are included in the study of multiple language learning. With this in mind, one can see that in a number of European countries English is learned as an L3 (or L4, L5 or L6, respectively), although from a standard language point of view it appears to be the first foreign language in tutored instruction (Cenoz & Jessner, 2000; Jessner, 2006; Jessner & Cenoz, 2007). Hoffmann (2000) introduced the term 'multilingualism with English' to refer to this phenomenon both as a societal and an individual phenomenon (see also Stavans & Hoffmann, 2015).

Apart from English as L3, there are also other typical L3s, such as German, which are the focus of L3 research. As mentioned above, German might be learnt by children with a Turkish or Kurdish language background in Germany. Or French as an L3 might be learnt by immigrants from Asia who come to Belgium. Yet another example is provided by bilingual immigrant children living in an Arabic and/or Berber family from Morocco who then acquire Dutch as an L3 in the Netherlands.

Among the topics of L3 research, the prestige of language variants is studied with respect to language choice: prestige influences the speaker's willingness to maintain a migrant, heritage or minority language in a possibly new environment, as well as his or her attitudes towards learning additional languages. Whether a language is maintained in a new environment depends very much on the prestige of this language in this context. For instance, in a Polish family in an Austrian or German context, the younger generation might decide not to maintain the Polish language but to acquire other, seemingly more prestigious languages at school and university such as Spanish or Italian. Lately, ethnolinguistic vitality as a more appropriate term has been introduced to discuss the complexity of language development in relation to language prestige and distinctive identity. Lasagabaster and Huguet (2007) published a large-scale questionnaire study on the attitudes of pre-service teachers towards L3 learning and/or multilingualism in a number of officially bilingual contexts in Europe such as Ireland, Malta, Wales, Friesland, the Basque Country, Catalonia and Galicia.

Aronin and Ó Laoire (2004) studied multilingual situations and contexts in countries such as Israel and Ireland with respect to the effects on an individual learner's repertoire. They describe these situations as instances of *individual multilinguality*, which is obviously linked to the fact that '[d]ifferent aspects of life often require different languages', which is called the complementarity principle by Grosjean (2010: 29ff.; see also Aronin on the dominant language constellation below).

Psycholinguistic perspectives on multiple language learning

Psycholinguistic research in the domain of L3 is concerned with the multilingual individual and individual processes of multiple language learning and use. Examples include studies focusing on the tri- or respectively more than three – multilingual learner, and developmental patterns of multilingual development such as language maintenance, attrition and loss, as well as the characteristics of multilingual production and their underlying cognitive mechanisms. Over the last years the main fields of psycholinguistic research on L3 learning have included cross-linguistic influence and multilingual awareness. These two areas will be discussed briefly in the following sections.

Cross-linguistic influence

Interaction in the sense of cross-linguistic influence between languages in TLA is a more complex phenomenon than cross-linguistic influence in SLA, which in traditional studies was viewed as being influenced by the mother tongue only. Not very long ago Cook (2003) pointed towards a bilateral relationship in cross-linguistic influence in bilingual studies.

In a multilingual system, however, cross-linguistic influence not only takes place between the L1 and the L2, but also between the L2 and the L3, and the L1 and the L3. Cross-linguistic influence can result in processes and products such as transfer of linguistic units, transfer of L2 language learning strategies into L3 learning, or language loss of the L2 due to the recent learning of the L3 (recency effect, e.g. Hammarberg, 2001). Aiming to capture such unforeseen effects in syntax, Flynn *et al.* (2004) proposed a cumulative enhancement model for language acquisition. They argue that the L1 does not play a privileged role in the language acquisition process as other languages concur in influencing target language development (see also Leung, 2005). In a migration context, both the L2 or the L3 or the L2 and the L3 can jeopardize the maintenance of the L1 and, as a consequence, result in language attrition (see also Jessner, 2003).

A number of studies have provided evidence that the L2 fulfils a particular role during the learning of a further foreign language, which in the literature has been referred to as L2 status. It appears that L3 learners and users do not simply fall back on their L1 in their L3 production and reception, but rather on their L2. The L2 seems to take over the role of a source, default and supplier language during production of the L3, especially when the L3 learner has not yet reached a high level of competency in the L3 (Hufeisen, 1991).
In research specifically on the learning of an L3 of Indo-European origin, results showed that L3 learners whose L1 is typologically unrelated to the L2 and/or L3 tended to transfer linguistic and language learning knowledge from their L2 and not from their L1

(e.g. Bartelt, 1989; Cenoz, 2001; Hufeisen, 1991). This finding has been corroborated by studies which have investigated learners whose complete language repertoire consists of Indo-European languages (De Angelis, 2005a, 2005b). In a Canadian study, Tremblay (2006) found that L2 exposure can influence the learners' ability to use their L2 knowledge in order to overcome their lexical deficits in their L3. A higher level of L3 proficiency, on the other hand, appears to correlate with a lower level of frequency with which the L2 intrudes during L3 production.

In recent work on cross-linguistic influence in multilingual systems it became clear that the factor of multilingual awareness needs more attention. It is argued that research needs to encompass more work dedicated to cross-linguistic interaction which per se (or as defined in the Dynamic Model of Multilingualism, see below) focuses on both linguistic and cognitive aspects of multilingual development (see De Angelis *et al.*, 2015). Several factors related to multilingual awareness in its forms metalinguistic awareness and language (learning) awareness have been identified as salient in cross-linguistic processes in TLA which are:

- *Psychotypology*. It appears that perceived linguistic distance between languages has more impact on cross-linguistic influence than the factual linguistic distance. In other words, learners who believe their L2 and L3 are related find many parallels between the two. They will then find it easier to learn the L3 than those learners who cannot detect any similarities between their L2 and their L3, even though linguistically there may be many (Hammarberg, 2001).

- *Recency of use*. The longer an L2 has not been used by the speaker, the lower its cross-linguistic influence on the L3 (Hammarberg, 2001). Please note also that an increasing number of language attrition studies have contributed to a better understanding of the processes of gradual language decay (see, for example, the special issue of *International Journal of Bilingualism* on language attrition, edited by De Leuw *et al.*, 2013).

- *Level of proficiency in the target language*. The higher the language proficiency level in the L3 the weaker the cross-linguistic influence of L2 on L3 is (Hammarberg, 2001).

- *The foreign language effect* or the tendency of L3 language learners to activate the first foreign language. Especially in the early stages of L3 learning, learners do not only tend to activate their L2- as opposed to L1-related knowledge for production and reception tasks in the L3, but also in connection with L3-specific learning strategies (Hufeisen, 1991; Meisel, 1983).

- *The learners' perception of correctness* of an L3-target word (De Angelis & Selinker, 2001; see also Hall & Ecke, 2003).

Hammarberg (2001), Cenoz (2003b) and Jessner (2006) discovered that L3 learners tend to activate all their languages during L3 performance, which has been confirmed in an increasing number of studies since then (see, for example, *International Journal of Multilingualism*). Jessner (2006) found, for instance, that the majority of bilingual (German and Italian) adult students from South Tyrol activated German and Italian in order to counteract lexical deficiencies during production in their L3 English for various reasons. German, the dominant language in most cases, acted as a kind of springboard for the detection of lexical deficits, whereas Italian was used as a confirming agent after the cognate in the target language was activated. These studies also support Green's (1986) model of language activation. Furthermore, the activation of languages is related to what Grosjean (2001) refers to as language mode. The concept of language mode deals with the variable conditions in multiple speech situations. The language choice in a certain situation is governed by the language mode; that is, it depends on the language mode how many languages are activated in a speech situation. Depending on variables such as the speaker's language mixing habits, the usual mode of interaction, the presence of monolinguals, etc., the speaker can be in mono-, bi- or trilingual mode.

Multilingual awareness

Today it is widely assumed that life with two or more languages can lead to linguistic and cognitive advantages (Bialystok & Cummins, 1991). In a number of studies carried out in the Basque Country and in Catalonia (Cenoz, 1991; Cenoz & Valencia, 1994; Muñoz, 2000; Sagasta, 2003; Sanz, 1997) it was found that bilingual children outperformed monolinguals in the acquisition of English as a foreign language. These cognitive advantages are linked in the learner to a heightened level of metalinguistic awareness, creative or divergent thinking, communicative sensitivity and experience in language learning (see also Cenoz, 2003a).

Jessner (2006) defines linguistic awareness in multilinguals as an emergent property of multilingual proficiency and as consisting of at least two dimensions in the form of cross-linguistic awareness and metalinguistic awareness. Cross-linguistic awareness refers to the learner's implicit and explicit awareness of the links between the language systems. Cross-lexical consultation, or 'how bi- and multilinguals search for words in their other languages when they meet linguistic problems in the target language' (Jessner, 2008a: 278) has been a subject of interest for a number of researchers. We find examples of cross-linguistic consultation in multilingual production as documented in think-aloud protocols (Jessner *et al.*, 2016). Participants tended to draw from German (L1) and/or French (L3) when they did not find the right word or expression in English (L2):

- German/German dialect CLINs:
  ... small rain, just a few: <L1.ger> Tropfen [drops] <L1.ger> ... (Excerpt eldü_01)
  ... the man has –ahm– long hair, <L1.terdia> halt (xx) also, Bart ischt des [you know (xx) so, beard is this] <L1.gerdia> ... (Excerpt kado_01)
- French CLINs:
  ... and her they (.) <L3.fr> bon [well] <L3.fr> I don't see their faces ... (Excerpt mila_02)
  ... short black hair (.) an a <?> <L3.fr> barbe [beard] <L3.fr> ... (Excerpt pama_02)

Other examples stem from instances of cross-linguistic lexical influence from English (L2) on Italian (L3) which occurred in spontaneous written production:

- *(...) und ich schreibe* molto delizioso *weil* delizioso *denke ich dass das schon das richtige Wort ist* delizioso *weil in Englisch ist es auch* delicious *ähm* [= ?un dessert] era molto delicioso *(...)*

> [and I'll write *molto delizioso* because I think *delizioso* is the right word *delizioso* because in English it is also *delicious* ähm [= ?*un dessert*] *era molto delicioso*]

Jessner also points out that metalinguistic and metacognitive awareness play an important role in the development of the language learning strategies of multilingual learners and users (Moore, 2006). Due to their experience in learning languages, multilingual learners use different and often also more strategies compared to monolingual students learning their first foreign language (cf. Jessner, 2017; McLaughlin, 1990).

That expert learners outperform novice learners has also been evidenced in a number of studies with a focus on strategy building (e.g. Ender, 2007; Mißler, 2000; Müller-Lancé, 2003). Kemp (2007) detected a threshold effect for the use of grammar learning strategies, such that diversification in and augmentation of strategy use occurs to a greater extent during the acquisition of an L3.

More recently in two Greek studies a positive relationship between degrees of plurilingualism and strategy use was found. The results of the large-scale study by Psaltou-Joycey and Kantaridou (2009) indicated that the trilingual students used more strategies more frequently than bilinguals, especially those strategies that promote metalinguistic awareness, and that more advanced trilinguals made more frequent use of strategies. Furthermore Mitits (2015), in her large-scale study, concentrated on the question as to whether multilingual early adolescent language learners transfer language learning strategies from their L2 Greek to FL English and found that the multilinguals exceeded the monolinguals in the use of strategies for learning EFL.

In two large-scale studies on linguistic awareness in language attrition carried out in both Tyrolean and South Tyrolean contexts (LAILA and LAILA-BICS), during one of the tasks young adult students were asked to produce introspective think-aloud protocols during the decoding of a Romanian text, a language hitherto unknown to the students. At the time of the study the German speaking students in both contexts were acquainted with at least three languages (English/Latin and/or Italian or French) during their school career. The think-aloud protocols show that the students use compensatory strategies and a high degree of creativity in the application of problem-solving activities. The examples from the LAILA and LAILA-BICS studies give extensive proof of the emergent properties of the multilingual users within the strategic processing when dealing with an unknown foreign language in a multilingual complex system.

The examples evidence the study participants' metalinguistic awareness (MLA) and cross-linguistic awareness (XLA)/knowledge and interaction (CLIN) based on language typology and grammatical awareness as well as language transfer endorsed by the use of supporter languages such as German, English, French, Italian and Spanish, as well as Latin.

In addition, the findings in multilingual strategy development show strong tendencies in strategy application, quantity and use, and it becomes obvious that there is indeed a difference between more and less experienced language learners in their strategic processing when encountering a novel and unknown linguistic system. The strategies applied evidently differ from mono- and bi-, but to a certain extent also to less experienced multilingual language learners not only in terms of quantity and quality, therefore demonstrating the realm of the multilingual (M-) factor in different sociolinguistic settings (Jessner & Török, 2017; see also Török, 2017 on the M-factor).

Application of L3 research in school and university settings

Interest in the application of research on multilingual learning has considerably increased over the past few years. As the above discussion shows, results from a number of such research projects carried out over a period of 15 years have been included in the discussion. Research questions have dealt with various aspects of multilingual instructed learning and teaching methods in their specific school contexts.

L3 research in school and university settings is often conducted as action research projects. Most of these research projects come up with specific suggestions concerning their application in real learning situations. As an example, the complex project *EuroCom European Intercomprehension* will be introduced as follows.

The assumption behind the EuroCom project is that etymological similarities and parallels between languages of the same language family can be applied to the learning process of another language of a specific language family when one language of that family has already been learned. For example, if a learner has already learned French as their L2 or L3, it is assumed that the learning of additional languages of the Romance language family such as Portuguese, Catalan or Romanian should not be difficult if certain techniques are applied during the process of getting acquainted with the seemingly new language. The method of learning and instruction is based on the Seven Sieves, which are linguistic techniques with which the languages in question are compared. These techniques facilitate the continual construction of hypotheses about the new target languages (see also the discussion of Meißner's model below). By applying these techniques, the learner is expected to acquire receptive knowledge of the target languages in a very short time in order to be able to read texts. All three European language families have been used for such intercomprehension projects: the Romance languages (EuroComRom: Klein & Stegmann, 2000), the Germanic languages (EuroComGerm: Hufeisen & Marx, 2014) and the Slavic languages (Slavic Intercomprehension: Tafel, 2009). Klein (2004) tested this concept with 14–15-year-old pupils at secondary school who were intrigued by the idea of learning several languages at the same time. They reported enjoying trying to apply the specific seven techniques in order to help decipher texts in a seemingly unknown language (see also recently Kordt, 2015a, 2015b).

Theoretical Models of Multiple Language Learning

Parallel to these chiefly empirical research activities, attempts have been made to develop theoretical models of multiple language learning. Three models which have received particular attention in both the scientific community and among practitioners will therefore be discussed in greater detail: Herdina & Jessner's Dynamic Model of Multilingualism, Hufeisen's Factor Model, and Meißner's plurilingual processing model.

Dynamic Model of Multilingualism (Herdina & Jessner, 2002)

The language development of multilingual speakers is a complex and dynamic process. In sciences such as meteorology, mathematics, ecology, physics and psychology, dynamic systems theory and or complexity theory (DSCT) has been applied to complex problem solving for some time now, but only recently has applied linguistics started using it as a conceptual metaphor (see De Bot *et al.*, 2007; Larsen-Freeman & Cameron, 2008).

The Dynamic Model of Multilingualism (DMM) applies DSCT to multilingual development and use (Herdina & Jessner, 2002; Jessner, 2008a) since both the complexity and variability of multilingual development lend themselves to the use of this thinking metaphor. In the DMM a holistic perspective of multilingualism, which presents a necessary presupposition of a DSCT perspective, is taken. Such a view assumes that the changing parts of a system are dynamically interrelated and that they not only influence one another's development but also the development of the system as a whole. Hence the multilingual speaker is described as a unique but competent speaker-hearer (Grosjean, 1985) and therefore is not comparable to a monolingual speaker (Jessner, 2014). Therefore a holistic approach which is applied in the DMM, originally developed by Grosjean (1985), was taken up by Cook in his concept of multicompetence (e.g. Cook, 1991; Li Wei & Cook, 2016; see also below). However, in both of their approaches the relationship between the dynamics of language development and holism has not been discussed.

According to DSCT the multilingual system is characterized by features such as non-linearity, reversibility and complexity. Due to the perceived communicative needs of a multilingual individual, language choice and hence the development of the multilingual system changes over time, which can also result in language attrition and/or loss. Figure 3.1 (based on Herdina & Jessner, 2002: 124, Fig. 29b) models the development of a multilingual system; that is, it shows how the speaker develops language proficiency in more than two languages over a certain period of time. While the primary language system of the speaker remains dominant during this time, the secondary or incipient system undergoes development. The development of the third system is dependent on the acquisition of the first two systems, which in certain cases takes place at the same time, as in simultaneous bilingualism. In fact, a closer look at the figure shows that transitional bilingualism forms an integrative part of the development of the third system. In this case, learner bilingualism, as it was called by Herdina and Jessner (2002: 125) to show that bilingualism forms part of multilingualism, concerns the second and the third system and forms part of overall multilingual development.

Sometimes reactivation takes place after a certain period of time or languages are simply no longer used and can be replaced by others. Variability in the process depends on sociological, psychological and individual factors; thus the context of learning, be it natural

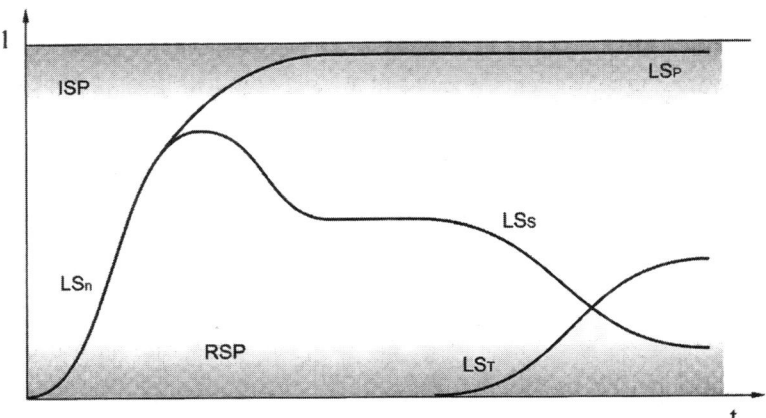

Figure 3.1 Learner multilingualism: overall development
Notes: LS_n = prior language system(s); LS_p = primary language system; LS_s = secondary language system; LS_T = tertiary language system; ISP = ideal native-speaker proficiency; RSP = rudimentary speaker proficiency; t = time; l = language level.
Source: Herdina and Jessner (2002: 124).

or instructed, always plays a crucial role. In this way, DMM represents an autonomous model of multilingualism, serving both as a bridge between SLA and bilingualism and as a model which explicitly focuses on more than two languages.

In consequence, multilingual proficiency (MP) can be defined as the dynamic interaction between the various language systems (LS_1, LS_2, LS_3, LS_n, etc.), cross-linguistic interaction (CLIN) and the M(ultilingualism)-factor or effect, as can be seen in the following crude formula: $LS_1/LS_2/LS_3/LS_n$ + CLIN + M-factor = MP.

The model language systems are seen as interdependent and not, contrary to the perception of traditional transfer research, as autonomous. This means that the behaviour of each individual language system in a multilingual system largely depends on the behaviour of previous and subsequent systems and it would therefore not make sense to look at the systems in isolation. The concept of cross-linguistic interaction also integrates cognitive transfer, as discussed by Cummins (e.g. 1991) in his interdependence hypothesis and by Kecskes's (e.g. 2000 with Papp) common underlying conceptual basis. These are non-predictable cognitive effects of the development of the multilingual system which determine the development of the systems themselves.

The M-factor, which is described as an emergent property of the multilingual system, is responsible for the catalytic effects of L3 learning. The skills and abilities which have been identified as responsible for the detected differences between second and third language learning, particularly in the case of a second foreign language, lead to an increase in metalinguistic and metacognitive awareness, as well as a heightened communicative sensitivity (see also the Factor Model below). The core component of the M-factor is multilingual awareness, which is composed of meta- and cross-linguistic awareness and is considered *the* key factor in multilingual learning and use (e.g. Jessner, 2006, 2008a, 2014). Metalinguistic awareness (MLA) 'refers to the ability to focus attention on language as an object in itself or to think abstractly about language and, consequently, to play with or manipulate language' (Jessner, 2006: 42). In DMM terms, the acronym MLA refers to both multilingual awareness – the umbrella term for MLA and XLA – and metalinguistic awareness.

From a DSCT perspective, multilingual systems are not comparable to monolingual systems, as the former include components which monolingual systems lack, as even those components shared by both systems have a different level of significance within the multilingual system. The main difference between bilingualism and multilingualism is the degree of complexity. Not all the systems are complex in the same way. It is the interaction, not the mere number of agents, factors or parts that matters in complexity. 'Complex' (not to be confused with 'complicated' which means 'compiled of many elements' and therefore not necessarily complex) involves multiple active interactions between the parts which lead to countless, often unpredictable, outcomes.

The criteria for defining a lower or higher level of complexity can be condensed into the number of items involved, such as the number of steps, algorithms, symbols, parts, etc. The quantifiable measures that testify to a higher or lower degree of complexity are the intensity of a phenomenon, the amount of effort required, the rate and the density of items under review. All these factors lead us to believe that multilingualism is more complex than bilingualism (see more on this in Aronin & Jessner, 2015).

Factor Model (Hufeisen, 2010)

This model describes the factors that constitute the conditions for the initial stages that learners go through in their language learning processes while acquiring an L1, and learning an L2, an L3 and an L4/Lx. Each of these factors consists of a group of aspects which share similar features, and accompanying the acquisition of each language (from L1 to L2, from L2 to L3), a new bundle of factors is added to the factor complexity. The decisive and concomitant factors for acquiring an L1 are:

- *Neurophysiological factors*, which constitute the basis and the precondition for general language learning/acquisition, production and reception capability. If one of these factors is lacking or is flawed, language acquisition will be difficult, deficient or will fail (Gopnik *et al.*, 1999).
- *Learner external factors*, which include features such as sociocultural and socio-economic surroundings, culture-specific learning traditions, and the type and the amount of input the learner is exposed to. Lack of sufficient or qualitatively adequate input will result in difficult or deficient language acquisition/learning.

The following factors and their features are distinguished and added as applying to the L2 learning process in this model, shown in Figure 3.2:

- *Emotional factors* exert an enormous influence on the language learning process. They include features such as anxiety, motivation or acceptance of the new target language by

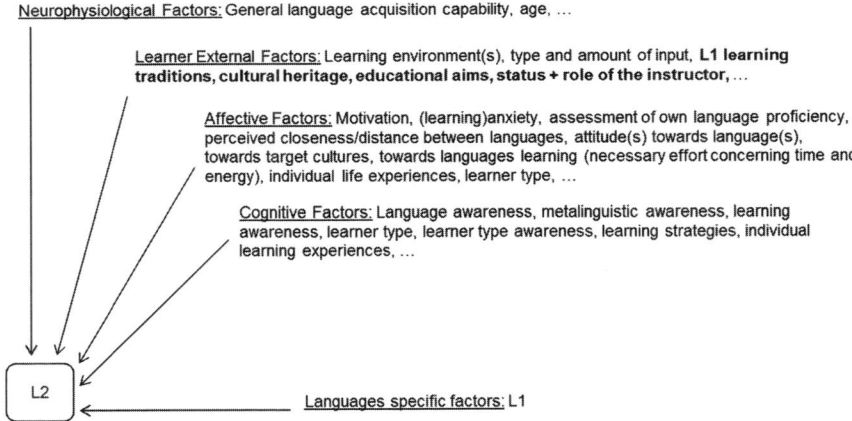

Figure 3.2 Hufeisen's Factor Model: learning a second language

the learner. For instance, a feeling of anxiety can result in a retarded or obstructed language learning process (cf. Dewaele, 2002).

- *Cognitive factors* include language awareness, linguistic and metalinguistic awareness, learning awareness, knowledge of one's own learner type and the ability to employ learning strategies and techniques.
- *Linguistic factors* consist of the learner's L1(s).

The focus of Hufeisen's model lies on the salient differences between learning an L2 and learning an L3. In fact, it is these differences that constitute the justification for the rejection of (extended) L2 models for L3 learning. This model makes the assumption that, in the initial stages of learning an L2, the learner is completely inexperienced and therefore unfamiliar with the process of learning an additional language. An L3 learner, by contrast, is expected to already be acquainted with the *foreign language learning process* and has (consciously or subconsciously) already collected individual techniques and strategies to deal with this type of learning situation, albeit with differing degrees of ultimate success. It is quite likely that the learner has already intuitively discovered his/her learner type and can act accordingly to further his/her own L3 language learning success. This state of affairs serves as justification for a further L3-specific set of factors which do not apply to the L2 learning process:

- *Foreign/second language learning-specific factors*, such as individual L2 learning experiences, (explicit or subconscious) foreign language learning strategies and interlanguages of other previously learned languages.

The linguistic factor-bundle will then expand accordingly, from merely the L1(s) to L1(s) and L2, which will then probably take over the role of a *bridge language* on the way to the L3 (Hufeisen, 1991). In fact, recent studies show that the L2 takes over the role of a bridge language even if the L1 and the respective target language L3 are more closely related to

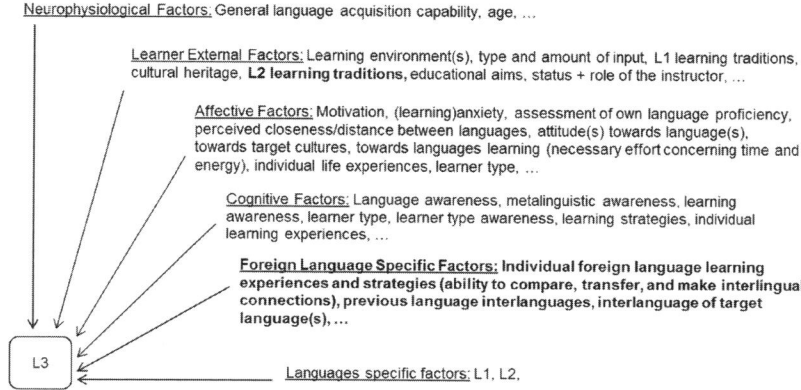

Figure 3.3 Hufeisen's Factor Model: learning a third language

each other than the L2 and the L3 (Hufeisen, 2000). In other words, L3 learners have specific language knowledge and competencies at their disposal which are simply non-existent for L2 learners.

Stage 3 of the model (Hufeisen, 2010), which consists of four stages as introduced above (acquisition of L1, learning of an L2, learning of an L3), can be illustrated as shown in Figure 3.3.

Stage 4 of Factor Model shows the learning of an L4, L5, Ln, and thus can be considered an expansion of Stage 3. Factors expand, such as the language-specific factor now consisting of L1, L2, and L3 and Ln are added, but so far there is no evidence that new factor bundles have to be added.

The Factor Model not only attempts to illustrate the prototypical language learning process of multiple languages but can also be used in the analysis of concrete and specific learning situations. Factors interact with each other such that if one factor or factor complex changes, there is a corresponding impact on the whole learning situation. Each learner develops his or her own specific factor complexity in which certain factors turn out to be predominant, thereby exerting a strong influence on the given learning situation. Other factors might weaken in significance and become less relevant during an individual's learning process.

Empirical studies show that new factors might arise. Vidgren (2017) found in her study with Finnish 16-year-old pupils that they thought the factor 'time and work expenditure' very relevant for their effort to learn foreign languages; they even reported choosing their languages according to the estimated time and work expenditure necessary in order to reach good grades. So far, this factor has not been mentioned in this model. Vidgren suggests introducing a new factor bundle which she would label generally as *learner practical factors* (*lernpraktische Faktoren* in the German original version). She argues that time and work expenditure can neither be assigned to the learner external factors nor to the learner internal factors. Further empirical research will find more factors that exert a relevant influence on the foreign language learning process, and the model will then have to be adjusted accordingly.

Multilingual Processing Model (Meißner, 2004)

At the core of Meißner's multilingual Processing Model, which he situates at the interface of constructivist learning theory and multilingualism pedagogy (EuroComDidact, cf. Meißner, 2002), is a spontaneous learner grammar. This model is the theoretical basis for most EuroCom projects which we have mentioned several times in this lecture.

Meißner's model describes and explains the processes at work during the beginning stages of reading in an unknown language (ideally belonging to a language family that is familiar to the learner). The precondition for the application of these processes is that a learner is proficient in at least one foreign language (such as Russian) when learning another closely related one (such as Polish or Ukrainian). The learner's task is to employ specific strategies to quickly and systematically understand a text in the as yet unknown language. These underlying processes, which facilitate the understanding of the new language, are based on the assumption that learners will systematically employ their knowledge of previously learned languages in the attempt to make sense of the new text and to construct hypotheses about structure(s) in the new language. In doing so, it is expected that the learner will continually formulate and reformulate hypotheses about the new language, thereby constructing a *spontaneous hypothesis learner grammar*. This hypothesis-led construction process works especially well when the languages involved are related to each other and when the learner grammar is initially based to a greater extent on previously learned language systems, rather than on the target language system. This element is the main difference from Selinker's notion of interlanguage (Meißner, 2004: 47). In Meißner's view, it is only in the course of the language learning process that the spontaneous grammar is continuously revised and developed in the direction of the target language's structures and lexicon. The previously learned foreign language closest in genetic type to the new target language takes over the role of a *bridge language*. This bridge language functions as a matrix against which the new structures and lexicon are contrasted and compared. The existence of such (a) bridge language(s) is the precondition for the establishment of a spontaneous grammar. In addition, the following conditions hold: there must be an etymological relationship between the languages; the learner needs to be proficient in the bridge language(s); and finally, the learner needs to receive instruction in how to use the knowledge of previously learned languages as bridge languages. Only when these three conditions are met can the spontaneous grammar be established and continue to develop. In this process, the grammar undergoes four distinct stages (note that the model applies to receptive and not to productive skills).

In the first stage, after the first encounter with the new target language, a first spontaneous grammar of the language is hypothesized or constructed by the learner. Initial and rudimentary understanding is facilitated by the bridge language (for example, for a native speaker of Arabic, L2 English would help with the initial decoding of L3 German). The spontaneous hypothesis grammar is revised continuously, thereby being extended or enlarged dynamically as the target language input is systematically compared to previous hypotheses about the target language.

In the second stage, an interlingual correspondence grammar is created via the spontaneous grammar, which in turn constructs interlingual correspondence rules. These rules switch between previous linguistic knowledge of the bridge language(s) and the increasing knowledge of the new target language system. Over time, these rules come to resemble the target language's more and more closely. Noteworthy features of this interlingual correspondence grammar include instances of transfer between the source language(s) and the target language.

In the third stage, a multilingual intersystem is constructed which stores and saves all successful (as well as unsuccessful) interlingual transfer processes. This intersystem consists of transfer bases which provide the learner with a general framework for decoding and understanding the new language. The Multilingual Processing Model contains six such transfer bases: communicative strategy transfer; transfer of interlingual processing procedures; transfer of cognitive principles; transfer as pro- or retroactive overlap; learning strategy transfer; and lastly, transfer of learning experiences.

In the fourth and final stage, learning experiences in the target language are stored as a collection of metacognitive strategies. Over the course of time, the learner gradually constructs a multilingual knowledge system containing both positive and negative correspondence rules. These rules can be applied when the learner is confronted with written or spoken texts. The rules can then be altered, revised and extended when another language system is introduced, as shown in Figure 3.4.

From the above it should become clear that the three models greatly differ in their attempt to illustrate multilingual learning and its application to multilingual teaching. They differ as well from a scientific point of view as they provide theoretical modelling of different

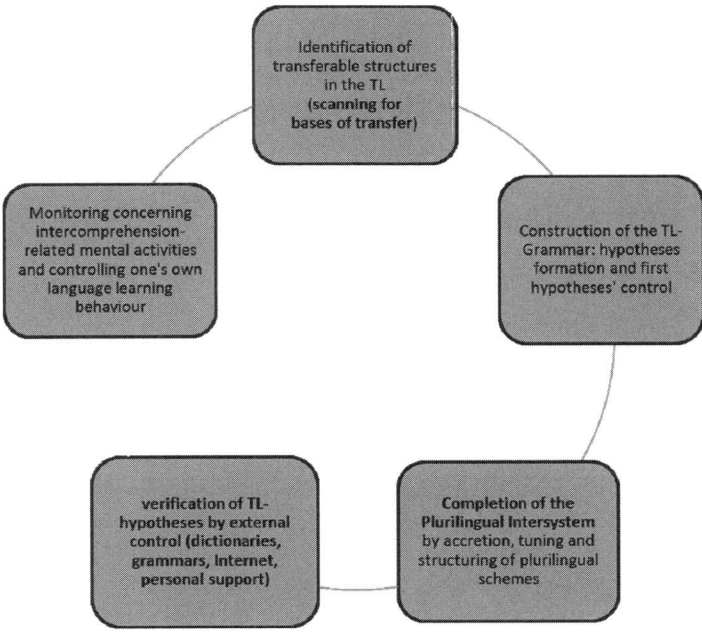

Figure 3.4 Meißner's Multilingual Processing Model (2004)

aspects of multilingual learning and each stems from different theoretical backgrounds. Hufeisen describes in detailed form the factors in first, second and third language learning by putting an emphasis on foreign language learning in the classroom and differences between these types of instructed learning. Herdina and Jessner pay tribute to Hufeisen's work in their holistic perspective of multilingualism but also put particular emphasis on the dynamics and complexity of multilingual development, thereby providing a bridge between processes and products of all types of multilingualism (ranging from first to multiple language development). In contrast, Meißner's model must be regarded as an attempt to explain processing in multilingual learners as a result of one particular teaching method applied in multilingual teaching. So whereas Hufeisen and Meißner focus on instructed learning in their models, Herdina and Jessner include all forms, that is, natural and instructed learning forms, into their model.

Multilingualism in the Classroom: Instructing and Learning First, Second, Third and Further Languages

The models and empirical studies described above entail particular consequences for the classroom, both for learners and for teachers, and also for school development. The fact that a learner's language and metalinguistic competencies grow with each additional (foreign) language experience invites a shift from L2 to multilingual pedagogical practices (as introduced by Jessner, 2008b; Jessner *et al.*, 2016) which will be discussed in later sections. Most research – often in the form of classroom and action research projects – has until now concentrated solely on the learner perspective.

Learner perspective: Multilingual awareness-raising activities in the classroom

The key aspects in this section are summarized as follows:

- the process of contrasting languages and raising metalinguistic and cross-linguistic awareness;
- building on prior language knowledge: tertiary language learning and EuroCom in the multilingual classroom in Europe;
- languages in use, perceiving languages as connected instead of as isolated, accepting multiple perspectives and applying and expanding language learning strategies.

Various empirical studies have provided evidence that such specific strategies can be both learned and taught in learning contexts (see Marx, 2005; Neuner-Anfindsen, 2005). Learners can, for instance, learn how to read and understand texts by systematically referring back and forth within their whole language repertoire in order to make educated guesses about new language vocabulary and content (see Meißner's spontaneous hypothesis grammar above). They can learn how to develop sensitivity to the similarities and parallels between their previous and their new languages. They can also learn how to create for themselves a multilingual mode of thinking, so that they are not simply focusing on the target language, thereby restricting themselves to the target language mode during their learning process. By exploiting this kind of multilingual mindset, they have the opportunity to find out more about their individual learner style or type, which will in turn help with the later organization of their learning process with the goal of maximally benefiting from their learning efforts. These efforts could include the creation of systematic vocabulary, grammar, tables, etc. once they have developed an understanding of their own approach to learning (see Jessner, 2017).

Further multilingual language learning tools might include keeping a personal vocabulary notebook or starting a foreign language portfolio containing words and phrases from all the languages in their individual language repertoire. Previously learned languages can be used and discussed within the classroom context by instructors and learners alike as bridge languages. Acknowledging the existence of previous languages and recognizing their status as useful pedagogical tools is an automatic means of promoting the new language learning process. Both learners and instructors need to be made explicitly aware, however, that the benefits of such a multilingual approach in the classroom will outweigh any deficits in the form of interferences as perceived by many who still work from a monolingual perspective.

In her seminal study, Allgäuer-Hackl (2017) provides strong evidence for the success of multilingual training in an Austrian school context. In a long-term study carried out in an Austrian school, the development of multilingual awareness was investigated (see also Allgäuer-Hackl & Jessner, 2013). The testing population (aged 17–18 years) took part in a multilingual training seminar provided as a non-obligatory, additional course by two teachers at the secondary school. The languages the students had learnt during their school career were English, French, Italian and Spanish. They all came from a German-speaking environment, where an Allemanic German dialect is used together with standard German as a medium of instruction. In this *Multilingual Seminar*, the students obtain insights into how languages work, study positive transfer and interferences, acquire language learning strategies and practise oral skills in the languages they are learning, at the same time as carrying out multilingual tasks, thereby developing receptive skills in further languages, through the EuroCom approach, for example. Allgäuer-Hackl's research questions centred on the linguistic and cognitive effects that such multilingual training has on the participants' multilingual awareness. It was found that seminar participants significantly outperformed non-participants in tasks that require enhanced metalinguistic and cross-linguistic awareness. Furthermore, the participants profited from the training with regard to their individual language proficiency. Positive transfer was observed in all directions (L2 on further languages, but also L4 on L3 or L2, L2 on L1, and vice versa) and participants used more languages from their repertoire as supporter languages and used them more frequently than non-participants. Additionally, the training increased the participants' awareness of language learning strategies and enhanced their motivation to improve the languages learnt and/or learn other languages. Interestingly enough, the participants also outperformed the peer group in tasks that had not been practised before, thus pointing to the emergence of new qualities in the multilingual training group.

Allgäuer-Hackl's work is to be seen as both inspiring and complementary to a number of other studies carried out by the DyME (Dynamics of Multilingualism with English) research group at Innsbruck University in both the Tyrolean and the South Tyrolean school context (see Jessner et al., 2016). Hofer (2015); Hofer and Jessner (2016), for instance, investigated the development of meta- and cross-linguistic awareness in pupils aged eight to nine years attending a bilingual programme in South Tyrol. The aim of the study was to discover whether there is an influence or what kind of influence multilingual education has on the multilingual awareness of the learners and consequently on the level of proficiency in three languages in contact, namely Italian, German and English. Data were collected in two Italian primary schools in Bolzano, where two classes of the bilingual education programme ($n = 40$) were compared to two other classes in a traditional setting ($n = 44$). The research questions concerned (a) their multilingual awareness and (b) the level of proficiency in each of the languages. Proficiency tests (reading/listening comprehension, sentence completion, etc.) were administered in all three languages. In addition, participants' metalinguistic abilities were tested using an abridged version of the MAT-2 (Pinto et al., 1999). The statistical analysis revealed that pupils from the CLIL class significantly outperformed both control groups in each test. This result supports earlier studies focusing on English as an L3 from other European contexts such as Spain and Finland, as already indicated. At the same time, the study demonstrates that the L1 of the schoolchildren actually profits from contact with other languages. This is a clear indication that early and extensive exposure to an L2 and/or L3 can promote and enhance learners' MLA and their proficiency in their first, second and third languages. In their investigation of 8th grade trilingual learners in South Tyrol, De Angelis and Jessner (2012: 62) found positive effects of the L2 on the L1, confirming that students with a higher proficiency level in the German L2 also wrote longer texts in Italian L1. De Angelis and Jessner showed that pupils' written productions in L2 German and L3 English were positively correlated and even seemed to have a positive effect on their overall academic achievement.

This was also confirmed by Traxl (2015), who found that in a German-Italian immersion primary school in Innsbruck the nine-year-old bilinguals outperformed their peers in a conventional setting in both English and their level of metalinguistic awareness, thereby confirming Hofer's work. What all three multilingual programmes have in common are special training sessions in which the pupils are made familiar with metalinguistic and metacognitive knowledge derived from multilingual expert learners.

Based on intensive experience in the multilingual classroom, Jessner et al. (2016) have cited implications for the classroom, such that L2 pedagogy is extended to a pedagogy of multilingualism. They delineate principles for a pedagogy of multilingualism based on DSCT thinking and research findings, with a special focus on metalinguistic and cross-linguistic awareness in experienced or trained multilinguals. Multilingual activities can be designed for multilingual classes but also adapted to foreign language classes in such a way that they support the development and use of the target language. They can also be integrated into subject language teaching in general and will, as we claim, contribute to more efficient (language) learning and teaching, given the fact that every language in the students' repertoire, including heritage languages, will benefit. In fact it is not enough for language teachers to work together to ensure an understanding of differences and similarities between the languages learnt and taught in a school. Instead, specific training in multilingual awareness raising activities in special training sessions is required in order for everyone in the classroom to profit from a multilingual teaching approach (Jessner et al., 2016).

Finally, an etymological approach to English language teaching (Jessner, 2006: Chapter 5) is suggested in order to serve as a new didactic tool to encourage the learning of other languages, even in countries where English predominates as the L2. In such an approach the enormous number of Romance elements in the English language would naturally be emphasized, not only in order to raise multilingual awareness in the language learning classroom but also to foster multilingual learning in students over the long term. Thus English could function as a bridge language in multilingual learning contexts, an idea which can be seen as related to European Intercomprehension, described above.

Additionally, English which has a special status on the European continent can be taught as a new language for all children in schools with a high percentage of migrant children, as English is learnt by all pupils as a type of more neutral language than the national language – apart from being the third or even fourth language in the children's repertoire in most cases. This also applies to CLIL programmes using English, even with an early start in kindergarten or primary school (Egger & Lechner, 2012).

It should also be noted that quite recently in English speaking contexts the ESL (English as a second language) learner has been exchanged by the EAL (English as an additional language) learner, thereby working from a multilingual rather than an L2 perspective. As correctly pointed out by Harmer (2015: 50), other languages than English should be allowed into the English classroom to help the students with transfer of knowledge and the development of techniques and strategies. But from his perspective also, clear guidelines for the use of other languages should be agreed on in order to maximize the benefits of the students' multilingualism.

Teacher perspective: Teachers as language users

Prerequisites for such a multilingual teaching approach as mentioned above are various conditions from the teacher and teaching perspectives. Student teachers and teachers need to create and extend their own multilingual awareness in order to develop the concept of multilingual competence in the classroom (Jessner et al., 2016), ideally not just in the foreign language classroom, but also in the L1 classroom, the heritage language classroom and the subject classroom. L2 instructors would have a specific responsibility as mediators to lay the foundation of foreign language learning for their learners. This entails the willingness and ability to cooperate on a regular basis on all sides so that a multilingual teaching approach can be developed, not merely in single sessions but systematically over all subjects, classes and age groups.

This goal is based on the assumption that every teacher, no matter of which subject(s), is a language user who needs to know her tool *language* for the instruction process as well in reference to the content. This awareness raising would naturally take place on the job, but should ideally already have begun during her or his university education. It would then be implemented during teacher training and in-service training, not just in language classrooms but in classrooms where all subjects are taught. Not to mention that a successful teacher needs to be an experienced language learner herself (see also Ellis, 2016).

Whole-school language curriculum: PlurCur®

In terms of language education, school development and education policy, there is also a need for the creation and implementation of multilingual whole-school curricula as introduced by Hufeisen (2011a, 2011b, 2015) and illustrated in Figure 3.5.

This prototypical curriculum has been piloted in projects such as PlurCur® (Allgäuer-Hackl *et al.*, 2015) or EOL (https://www.ecml.at/ECML-Programme/Programme2016-2019/Learningenvironmentswhereforeignlanguagesflourish/tabid/1865/Default.aspx). They eliminate the separation of languages in school and university by way of combining language learning systematically with content learning. With this approach, the learning curve within the framework of L3 instruction and learning will be steeper and faster as learners will now be more competent in the foreign language learning process and more language sensitive in dealing with non-linguistic subjects. The content subjects will profit from a higher language awareness level in learners and teachers and classroom time can then be used for concentrating on the content.

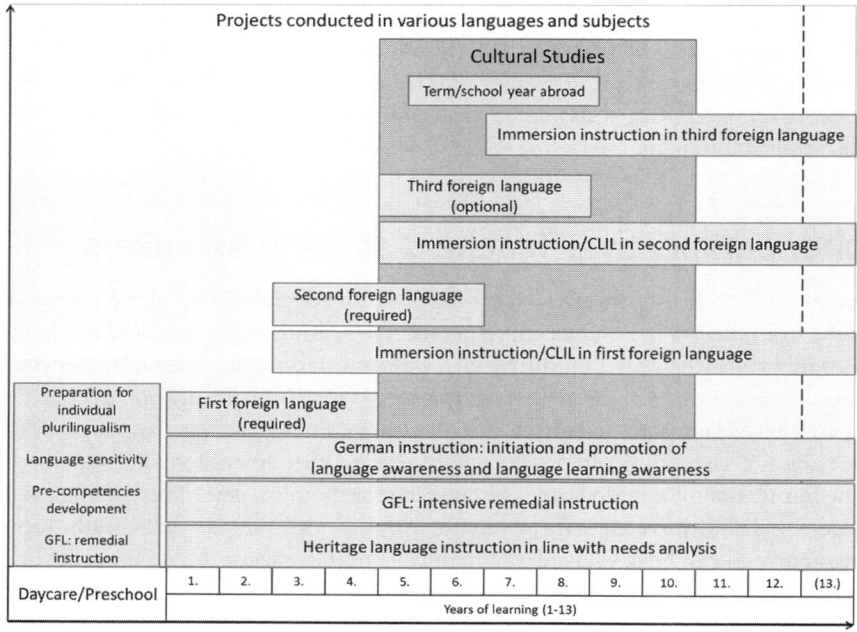

Figure 3.5 Prototype of a multilingual whole-school curriculum (Hufeisen)

The implication of such a new curricular policy would mean a greater initial focus on receptive as opposed to productive skills, on language learning strategies in contrast to concrete language input, and finally on the learners' own activities in their search for hypotheses about the new target languages L3, L4, Ln rather than on the introduction or explanation of grammar. Research results show that learners enjoy including all their languages (including heritage), into their everyday life at school and into specific subjects (see Henning, 2015 on a multilingual theatre workshop). They also show how the pupils' attitude towards their own multilingualism improves, how the potential linked to this multilingualism changes and how the learners' multilingual awareness rises.

Introducing a concept of multiple language acquisition and learning to the school curriculum or even a multilingual whole-school curriculum can, of course, not be the sole responsibility of L3 or Ln teachers alone. This responsibility must not only be shared by all language instructors (including instructors of any given L1) and content subject instructors, but by the respective school boards and education ministries, and – last but not least – by the parents. L2 instructors would have a specific responsibility as mediators to lay the foundation of foreign language learning for their learners. It is therefore important that they do not teach the language in question in the typically isolated fashion that is still often the case today: in Austria or Germany, teachers of English as a typical L2 usually refer neither to the L1s in a given learner group, nor do they prepare the way for the later L3 learning process.

Textbooks have recently been introduced which refer explicitly to previously learned languages and which emphasize similarities with other languages. This approach strengthens cross-linguistic comparison strategies (see, for example, the German textbook for Latin *Salvete* or for Spanish *Encuentros*). A prototypical L3 textbook normally begins at a very high level from a very early learning stage, just because there is no need for the usual simple beginner exercises (see, for example, the textbook for German as a foreign language *DeutschCom*). In fact, researchers recommend starting with complex texts from the outset. These challenges will encourage the learners to employ their already acquired knowledge about language and languages and – more importantly – about the language learning process itself.

Controversial Issues and Questions for Future Research

Research into the learning and use of multiple languages

More research is needed in areas of the world where societal and individual multilingualism is viewed, acted upon and engaged in differently compared to the (Anglo)-/European centred approaches discussed above. Such studies should, for example, focus on the impact of cultural factors of the foreign language learning process and thus provide new paths to innovative research methods.

Indeed, factors such as L1 cultural learning styles seem to have such a significant impact on successful foreign language learning that they overshadow other factors designed to encourage success. Ouédroago (2005), for example, documents that methodological and strategic language learning approaches which include factors such as language awareness, learning strategies or learning awareness do not work well in countries like Burkina Faso (Africa). The oral learning style of these multilinguals in this culture does not value or emphasize such cognitive aspects as highly as in the typical language classrooms of the Western hemisphere.

Kärchner-Ober (2009) reports that her learners in Malaysia experienced greater difficulties than she had anticipated when they were encouraged to apply previous language learning knowledge. This is due to the proficiency levels of the languages used in Malaysia not being sufficiently developed which, as a result, means that they cannot be used as a tool in a subsequent foreign language learning process. As well, the application of previously learned knowledge as an act of self-initiated learning is not part of her Asian students' learning tradition. What Kärchner-Ober finds is that her learners have developed competencies or proficiency levels in their various languages that are limited to specific domains. The linguistic goal for these speakers is to be able to function appropriately in different everyday situations in Malaysia; however, they are not fully competent, proficient or fluent in any one of these various languages. It should be noted that this phenomenon nevertheless manifests itself in a very positive fashion as the language competencies in question exactly match the individual and societal communicative needs of the learners/speakers.

It is clear that there are still many more and very specific aspects of individual multilingualism that merit further research. Future research on multilingual awareness, for instance, could include more studies of individual learning biographies as a means to isolate and measure the influence of factors or factor complexes from different perspectives. One such example is the narrative collection of multilingual linguists by Todeva and Cenoz (2009). In this volume, which offers insights into the multilingual development of the contributors, the link between the biographies included in the volume and a DSCT approach to multilingual development is provided. In this way, they offer new perspectives for working from both an emic, the learner's, and an etic, the scholar's perspective.

While a wide assortment of traditional methods of psycholinguistic and sociolinguistic research continue to be intensively employed by researchers of bi- and multilingualism, it has become clear that the understanding of multilingualism as a phenomenon in its own right calls for multilingualism-specific research methods. As multilingualism and multilingual development cannot be investigated with monolingual-oriented assessment tools, as already suggested above, there is a need for future research to develop specific L3/multilingualism research methods.

There are an increasing number of studies attesting to the dissimilarity of bilingualism and multilingualism from a variety of disciplines including socio- and psycholinguistics.

The puzzling additional qualities evidenced in multilingual learners have been linked to phenomena such as the 'threshold effect' and 'system shift', and amount to what was labelled by Herdina and Jessner (2002) as the *M(ultilingualism)-factor* or by Hufeisen (2010) as *foreign language specific factors*.

An additional language beyond two languages crucially raises the level of complexity of learning and how they are used. Compared to research in bilingualism, the range of findings, outcomes and interconnections in multilingualism increases exponentially as, importantly, the variation does. This fact has significant implications for the methodology of research.

Bilingualism and multilingualism are close and overlapping in many ways, but as a bilingual develops into a multilingual the quantitative and qualitative differences become more intense, to the extent that the nature of the emerging phenomena changes, as explicated in both the Factor Model and the DMM (see also Aronin & Hufeisen, 2009). There are new trends in research methodology of which DSCT and conceptualizations such as multicompetence, affordances (Kordt, 2015a, 2015b) and dominant language constellation should be mentioned (Aronin, 2016). Additionally, metaphors as a way of exploring bilingual and multilingual reality have proved to be useful (for more details, see Aronin & Jessner, 2014). Specific lines of research as employed in historical multilingualism studies serve as a methodology of research which applies historical and linguistic methods and techniques. The material culture of multilingualism perspective draws on ethnology, anthropology, sociology and linguistics, consequently employing the methods and techniques of all the disciplines involved (see Aronin & Singleton, 2008).

Research in multiple language(s) teaching

Specific teaching methods, i.e. those which deliberately take into consideration a learner's multilingual past, present and possible future, will have to be developed and studied. The need then arises for targeted research methods designed to measure the success rate of these new teaching methods. What needs to be tested in carefully controlled experiments is whether new teaching instruction materials which take the learners' previous languages and language learning experiences into account actually demonstrate advantages over traditional teaching materials.

Further investigation is needed in order to verify the assumption that language learners who have English as their first foreign language tend to learn later foreign languages to a significantly lower degree than those learners whose first foreign language is not English (Krumm, 1999). Does the learning of English obstruct the learners' interest in learning additional foreign languages and if so, why exactly? On the other hand, we need to know more about the fact which affordances the learning of an L3 or Lx activates with reference to L2 (mainly English; Kordt, 2015a).

Further research is needed in order to find out how efficient any kind of multilingual whole-school curriculum is, which types and forms would work in various regions of the world and which subjects and languages can be included in such a curriculum (Hufeisen, 2011a).

Finally, further research in multilingual education and pedagogy should be directed at establishing new norms and forms of teacher training (Hufeisen, 2015). This research has to deal with the definition of what types of teachers this new type of language instruction requires. Studies should find out if it is useful to offer joint courses such as language acquisition theory to future language teachers, irrespective of the language they teach. Intervention studies have to check how far language teaching students profit from joint introductions to multilingual teaching methodology and to what degree future L1 and heritage language teachers have to be involved in this awareness-building process. The implementation of the results of these studies into every day teaching will have to be evaluated. Research results will also have a far-reaching impact on local, regional and national education policies.

Research on the university education of future multilingual teachers and language-sensitive (subject) teachers and on the multilingual perspective of school development and education policy is still lacking. No doubt specific research will have to be designed by incorporating specific research methods which combine linguistic features with education and policy features. Further clarity in these areas would, as a next stage, aid in positively influencing the in-service training of all teachers working in schools, universities and other educational institutions and not only those directly involved in language teaching.

Questions for Students' Reflection

1. What are the differences between second language learning and third language learning?
2. What are the differences between bi- and multilingualism?
3. Which factors play a crucial role in the Dynamic Model of Multilingualism?
4. Explain the meaning and relevance of the 'foreign language learning specific factors' in the Factor Model.
5. What is EuroCom?
6. How can multilingual teaching methods be applied to your context?
7. Why is language awareness raising a very important aspect for (future) teachers of all subjects?
8. What are the advantages and disadvantages of joint courses and seminars on, for example, language acquisition theory for all students of all language subjects? Compare and decide. Explain your decision.
9. Which seminars on multilingualism would you like to see in your programme? Which would you have liked to take while you were at university?
10. What would your ideas and ideals look like for your own multilingual whole-school curriculum?

Suggestions for Further Reading

Clyne, M. (2003) *Dynamics of Language Contact*. Cambridge: Cambridge University Press.

Moore, D. (2006) *Plurilinguismes et Ecole*. Paris: Didier.

References

Allgäuer-Hackl, E. (2017) Multilingual/metalinguistic awareness in school contexts within a dynamic systems and complexity theory perspective. The effects of training on multiple language use and multilingual awareness. PhD thesis, University of Innsbruck.

Allgäuer-Hackl, E. and Jessner, U. (2013) Mehrsprachigkeitsunterricht aus mehrsprachiger Sicht: Zur Förderung des metalinguistischen Bewusstseins. In E. Vetter (ed.) *Professionalisierung für sprachliche Vielfalt. Perspektiven für eine neue Lehrerbildung* (pp. 111–147). Baltmannsweiler: Schneider Hohengehren.

Allgäuer-Hackl, E., Brogan K., Henning, U., Hufeisen, B. and Schlabach, J. (eds) (2015) *MehrSprachen? – PlurCur!: Berichte aus Forschung und Praxis zu Gesamtsprachencurricula*. Baltmannsweiler: Schneider Hohengehren.

Aronin, L. (2016) Multicompetence and Dominant Language Constellation. In V. Cook and L. Wei (eds) *The Cambridge Handbook of Linguistic Multicompetence* (pp. 142–163). Cambridge: Cambridge University Press.

Aronin, L. and Hufeisen, B. (eds) (2009) *The Exploration of Multilingualism: Development of Research on L3, Multilingualism and Multiple Languages*. Amsterdam: John Benjamins.

Aronin, L. and Jessner, U. (2014) Methodology in bi- and multilingual studies: From simplification to complexity. *AILA Review* 27 (1), 56–79.

Aronin, L. and Jessner, U. (2015) Understanding current multilingualism: What can the butterfly tell us? In U. Jessner and C. Kramsch (eds) *The Multilingual Challenge. Cross-disciplinary Perspectives* (pp. 271–292). Berlin and New York: Mouton de Gruyter.

Aronin, L. and Ó Laoire, M. (2004) Exploring multilingualism in cultural contexts: Towards a notion of multilinguality. In C. Hoffmann and J. Ytsma (eds) *Trilingualism in Family, School and Community* (pp. 11–29). Clevedon: Multilingual Matters.

Aronin, L. and Singleton, D. (2008) Multilingualism as a new linguistic dispensation. *International Journal of Multilingualism* 1 (1), 1–16.

Baker, C. (2001) *Foundations of Bilingual Education and Bilingualism* (3rd edn). Clevedon: Multilingual Matters.

Bartelt, G. (1989) The interaction of multilingual constraints. In H.W. Dechert and M. Raupach (eds) *Interlingual Processes* (pp. 151–177). Tübingen: Narr.

Bialystok, E. and Cummins, J. (1991) Language, cognition, and education of bilingual children. In E. Bialystok (ed.) *Language Processing in Bilingual Children* (pp. 222–232). Cambridge: Cambridge University Press.

Braun, M. (1937) Beobachtungen zur Frage der Mehrsprachigkeit. *Göttingische Gelehrte Anzeigen* 199 (4), 8–130.

Cenoz, J. (1991) *Enseñanza-Aprendizaje del Inglés como L2 o L3*. Leoia: Universidad del País Vasco.

Cenoz, J. (2000) Research on multilingual acquisition. In J. Cenoz and U. Jessner (eds) *English in Europe: The Acquisition of a Third Language* (pp. 39–53). Clevedon: Multilingual Matters.

Cenoz, J. (2001) The effect of linguistic distance, L2 status and age on crosslinguistic influence in third language acquisition. In J. Cenoz, B. Hufeisen and U. Jessner (eds) *Cross-linguistic Influence in Third Language Acquisition: Psycholinguistic Perspectives* (pp. 8–20). Clevedon: Multilingual Matters.

Cenoz, J. (2003a) The additive effect of bilingualism on third language acquisition: A review. *International Journal of Bilingualism* 7 (1), 71–88.

Cenoz, J. (2003b) Cross-linguistic influence in third language acquisition: Implications for the organization of the multilingual mental lexicon. *Bulletin VALS-ASLA* 78 (1), 1–11.

Cenoz, J. and Jessner, U. (eds) (2000) *English in Europe: The Acquisition of a Third Language*. Clevedon: Multilingual Matters.

Cenoz, J. and Valencia, J.F. (1994) Additive trilingualism: Evidence from the Basque Country. *Applied Psycholinguistics* 15 (1), 197–209.

Cenoz, J., Hufeisen, B. and Jessner, U. (eds) (2001a) *Looking beyond Second Language Acquisition: Studies in Tri- and Multilingualism*. Tübingen: Stauffenburg.

Cenoz, J., Hufeisen, B. and Jessner, U. (eds) (2001b) *Cross-linguistic Influence in Third Language Acquisition: Psycholinguistic Perspectives*. Clevedon: Multilingual Matters.

Cenoz, J., Hufeisen, B. and Jessner, U. (2003a) Why investigate the multilingual lexicon? In J. Cenoz, B. Hufeisen and U. Jessner (eds) *The Multilingual Lexicon* (pp. 1–9). Dordrecht: Kluwer.

Cenoz, J., Hufeisen, B. and Jessner, U. (eds) (2003b) *The Multilingual Lexicon*. Dordrecht: Kluwer.

Cook, V.J. (1991) The poverty-of-the-stimulus argument and multicompetence. *Second Language Research* 7 (2), 103–117.

Cook, V.J. (2003) The changing L1 in the L2 user's mind. In V.J. Cook (ed.) *Effects of the Second Language on the First* (pp. 1–18). Clevedon: Multilingual Matters.

Council of Europe (2008) *White Paper on Intercultural Dialogue 'Living Together As Equals in Dignity'*. Strasbourg: Council of Europe. See http://www.coe.int/t/dg4/intercultural/Source/White%20 Paper_final_revised_EN.pdf (accessed 7 August 2017).

Cummins, J. (1991) Language learning and bilingualism. *Sophia Linguistica* 29 (1), 1–194.

De Angelis, G. (2005a) Interlanguage transfer of function words. *Language Learning* 55 (3), 379–414.

De Angelis, G. (2005b) Multilingualism and non-native lexical transfer: An identification problem. *International Journal of Multilingualism* 2 (1), 1–25.

De Angelis, G. (2007) *Third or Additional Language Acquisition*. Clevedon: Multilingual Matters.

De Angelis, G. and Jessner, U. (2012) Writing across languages in a bilingual context: A dynamic systems theory perspective. In R. Manchón (ed.) *L2 Writing Development: Multiple Perspectives* (pp. 47–68). Berlin and New York: Mouton de Gruyter.

De Angelis, G. and Selinker, L. (2001) Interlanguage transfer and competing linguistic systems. In J. Cenoz, B. Hufeisen and U. Jessner (eds) *Cross-linguistic Influence in Third Language Acquisition: Psycholinguistic Perspectives* (pp. 42–58). Clevedon: Multilingual Matters.

De Angelis, G., Jessner, U. and Kresic, M. (eds) (2015) *Crosslinguistic Influence and Crosslinguistic Interaction in Multilingual Language Learning*. London: Bloomsbury Academic.

De Bot, K., Lowie, W. and Verspoor, M. (2007) A dynamic systems theory to L2 acquisition. *Bilingualism: Language and Cognition* 10 (1), 7–21.

De Leuw, E., Opitz, C. and Lubińska, D. (2013) Dynamics of first language attrition across the lifespan. *International Journal of Bilingualism* 17 (6), 667–674.

Dewaele, J.-M. (2002) Psychological and sociodemographic correlates of communicative anxiety in L2 and L3 production. *International Journal of Bilingualism* 6 (1), 23–28.

Egger, G. and Lechner, C. (eds) (2012) *Primary CLIL Around Europe. Learning in Two Languages in Primary Education*. Marburg: Tectum Verlag.

Ellis, E. (2016) *The Plurilingual TESOL Teacher: The Hidden Languaged Lives of TESOL Teachers and Why They Matter*. Berlin: Mouton de Gruyter.

Ender, A. (2007) *Wortschatzerwerb und Strategieneinsatz bei mehrsprachigen Lernenden. Aktivierung von Wissen und erfolgreiche Verknüpfung beim Lesen auf Verständnis einer Fremdsprache*. Baltmannsweiler: Schneider Hohengehren.

Flynn, S., Foley, C. and Vinnitskaya, I. (2004) The cumulative-enhancement model for language acquisition: Comparing adults' and children's patterns of development in first, second and third language acquisition of relative clauses. *International Journal of Multilingualism* 1 (1), 3–16.

Gopnik, A., Kuhl, P. and Meltzoff, A. (1999) *The Scientist in the Crib. Minds, Brains, and How Children Learn*. New York: William Morrow.

Green, D. (1986) Control, activation and resource: A framework and a model for the control of speech in bilinguals. *Brain and Language* 27 (1), 210–223.

Grosjean, F. (1985) The bilingual as a competent but specific speaker-hearer. *Journal of Multilingual and Multicultural Development* 6 (1), 467–477.

Grosjean, F. (2001) The bilingual's language modes. In J. Nicol (ed.) *One Mind, Two Languages: Bilingual Language Processing* (pp. 1–22). Oxford: Blackwell.

Grosjean, F. (2010) *Bilingual: Life and Reality*. Cambridge, MA: Harvard University Press.

Hall, C. and Ecke, P. (2003) Parasitism as a default mechanism in L3 vocabulary acquisition. In J. Cenoz, B. Hufeisen and U. Jessner (eds) *The Multilingual Lexicon* (pp. 71–86). Dordrecht: Kluwer.

Hammarberg, B. (2001) Roles of L1 and L2 in L3 production and acquisition. In J. Cenoz, B. Hufeisen and U. Jessner (eds) *Cross-linguistic Influence in Third Language Acquisition: Psycholinguistic Perspectives* (pp. 21–41). Clevedon: Multilingual Matters.

Harmer, J. (2015) *The Practice of English Language Teaching*. Harlow: Pearson Education.

Henning, U. (2015) Begleitstudie zu vielsprachigem Theaterspiel. Spracheinstellungen qualitativ erforschen. In E. Allgäuer-Hackl, K. Brogan, U. Henning, B. Hufeisen and J. Schlabach (eds)

MehrSprachen? PlurCur!: Berichte aus Forschung und Praxis zu Gesamtsprachencurricula (pp. 107–123). Baltmannsweiler: Schneider Hohengehren.

Herdina, P. and Jessner, U. (2002) *A Dynamic Model of Multilingualism: Perspectives of Change in Psycholinguistics.* Clevedon: Multilingual Matters.

Hofer, B. (2015) *On the Dynamics of Early Multilingualism: A Psycholinguistic Study.* Berlin, New York: Mouton de Gruyter.

Hofer, B. and Jessner, U. (2016) Multilingualism at the primary level in South Tyrol: How does multilingual education affect young learners' metalinguistic awareness and proficiency in L1, L2 and L3? *Language Learning Journal* 44 (3), 1–12.

Hoffmann, C. (2000) The spread of English and the growth of multilingualism with English in Europe. In J. Cenoz and U. Jessner (eds) *English in Europe: The Acquisition of a Third Language* (pp. 1–21). Clevedon: Multilingual Matters.

Hufeisen, B. (1991) *Englisch als erste und Deutsch als zweite Fremdsprache – Empirische Untersuchung zur zwischensprachlichen Interaktion.* Frankfurt: Peter Lang.

Hufeisen, B. (2000) How do foreign language learners evaluate various aspects of their multilingualism? In S. Dentler, B. Hufeisen and B. Lindemann (eds) *Tertiär- und Drittsprachen. Projekte und empirische Untersuchungen* (pp. 23–39). Tübingen: Stauffenburg.

Hufeisen, B. (2010) Theoretische Fundierung multiplen Sprachenlernens – Faktorenmodell 2.0. *Jahrbuch Deutsch als Fremdsprache* 36 (1), 200–207.

Hufeisen, B. (2011a) Gesamtsprachencurriculum: Überlegungen zu einem prototypischen Modell. In R.S. Baur and B. Hufeisen (eds) *'Vieles ist sehr ähnlich': Individuelle und gesellschaftliche Mehrsprachigkeit als bildungspolitische Aufgabe* (pp. 265–282). Baltmannsweiler: Schneider Hohengehren.

Hufeisen, B. (2011b) Drei ausgewählte Merkmale eines Gesamtsprachencurriculums: Interkulturelle Studien, Deutsch als Zweitsprache und Textkompetenz. *Die Neueren Sprachen* 2, 45–55.

Hufeisen, B. (2015) Zur möglichen Rolle der sog. klassischen Sprachen für Gesamtsprachencurriculumskonzepte. In S. Hoffmann and A. Stork (eds) *Lernerorientierte Fremdsprachenforschung und -didaktik* (pp. 45–57). Tübingen: Narr.

Hufeisen, B. and Marx, N. (2014) EuroComGerm – Die Sieben Siebe. *Germanische Sprachen lesen lernen* (2nd edn). Aachen: Shaker.

Jessner, U. (2003) On the nature of crosslinguistic interaction in multilinguals. In J. Cenoz, B. Hufeisen and U. Jessner (eds) *The Multilingual Lexicon* (pp. 45–55). Dordrecht: Kluwer.

Jessner, U. (2006) *Linguistic Awareness in Multilinguals: English as a Third Language.* Edinburgh: Edinburgh University Press.

Jessner, U. (2008a) A DST model of multilingualism and the role of metalinguistic awareness. *The Modern Language Journal* 92 (2), 270–283.

Jessner, U. (2008b) Teaching third languages: Findings, trends and challenges. *Language Teaching* 14 (1), 15–56.

Jessner, U. (2014) On multilingual awareness or why the multilingual learner is a specific language learner. In M. Pawlak and L. Aronin (eds) *Essential Topics in Applied Linguistics and Multilingualism. Studies in Honor of David Singleton* (pp. 175–184). Vienna: Springer.

Jessner, U. (2017) Language awareness in multilinguals: Theoretical trends. In J. Cenoz, D. Gorter and S. May (eds) *Language Awareness and Multilingualism* (pp. 19–29). Cham: Springer International.

Jessner, U. and Cenoz, J. (2007) Teaching English as a third language. In J. Cummins and C. Davison (eds) *The Kluwer Handbook on English Language Teaching* (pp. 155–167). New York: Springer.

Jessner, U. and Török, V. (2017) Strategies in multilingual learning: Opening new research avenues. In S.E. Pfenninger and J. Navracsics (eds) *Future Research Directions for Applied Linguistics* (pp. 192–214). Bristol: Multilingual Matters.

Jessner, U., Megens, M. and Graus, S. (2016) Crosslinguistic influence in third language acquisition. In R. Alonso Alonso (ed.) *Crosslinguistic Influence in Second Language Acquisition* (pp. 193–214). Clevedon: Multilingual Matters.

Kärchner-Ober, R. (2009) *'The German Language is Completely Different from the English Language.' Gründe für die Schwierigkeiten des Lernens von Deutsch als Tertiärsprache nach Englisch bei malaysischen Studenten mit verschiedenen nicht-Indo-Europäischen Erstsprachen. Eine datenbasierte, sozio-ethnografische Studie*. Tübingen: Stauffenburg.

Kecskes, I. and Papp, T. (2000) *Foreign Language and Mother Tongue*. Mahwah, NJ: Lawrence Erlbaum.

Kemp, C. (2007) Strategic processing in grammar learning: Do multilinguals use more strategies? *International Journal of Multilingualism* 4 (4), 241–261.

Klein, H.G. and Stegmann, T. (2000) *EuroComRom – Die sieben Siebe: Romanische Sprachen sofort lesen können*. 2 Editiones EuroCom 1. Aachen: Shaker.

Klein, S.H. (2004) *Mehrsprachigkeitsunterricht an der Schule. Protokoll einer 25-stündigen EuroComRom-Unterrichtsreihe mit Präsentations-CD für Lehrer*. Editiones EuroCom 22 (1). Aachen: Shaker.

Kordt, B. (2015a) Die Affordanzwahrnehmung von SchülerInnen bei der schulischen Umsetzung des EuroCom-Konzepts – Einblicke in eine explorativ-interpretative Studie. In E. Allgäuer-Hackl, K. Brogan, U. Henning, B. Hufeisen and J. Schlabach (eds) *MehrSprachen? PlurCur!: Berichte aus Forschung und Praxis zu Gesamtsprachencurricula* (pp. 85–106). Baltmannsweiler: Schneider Hohengehren.

Kordt, B. (2015b) Sprachdetektivische Textarbeit. *Praxis Fremdsprachenunterricht* 4, 4–9.

Krumm, H.-J. (ed.) (1999) *Sprachen – Brücken über Grenzen. Deutsch als Fremdsprache in Mittel- und Osteuropa*. Vienna: Eviva.

Larsen-Freeman, D. and Cameron, L. (2008) *Complex Systems and Applied Linguistics*. Oxford: Oxford University Press.

Lasagabaster, D. and Huguet, A. (eds) (2007) *Multilingualism in European Countries*. Clevedon: Multilingual Matters.

Leung, Y.-K.I. (2005) K2 vs. L3 initial state: A comparative study on the acquisition of French DPs by Vietnamese monolinguals and Cantonese-English bilinguals. *Bilingualism: Language and Cognition* 8 (1), 39–61.

Li Wei and Cook, V. (eds) (2016) *The Cambridge Handbook of Linguistic Multi-Competence*. Cambridge: Cambridge University Press.

Marx, N. (2005) *Hörverstehensleistungen im Deutschen als Tertiärsprache. Zum Nutzen eines Sensibilisierungsunterrichts in 'DaFnE'*. Baltmannsweiler: Schneider Hohengehren.

May, S. (2015) *The Multilingual Turn: Implications for SLA, TESOL and Bilingual Education*. New York and London: Routledge.

McLaughlin, B. (1990) The relationship between first and second languages: Language proficiency and language aptitude. In B. Harley, P. Allen, J. Cummins and M. Swain (eds) *The Development of L2 Proficiency* (pp. 158–174). Cambridge: Cambridge University Press.

Meisel, J.M. (1983) Transfer as a second-language strategy. *Language and Communication* 3 (1), 11–46.

Meißner, F.-J. (2002) EuroComDidact. In D. Rutke (ed.) *Europäische Mehrsprachigkeit. Analysen – Konzepte – Dokumente* (pp. 45–64). Aachen: Shaker.

Meißner, F.-J. (2004) Modelling plurilingual processing and language growth between intercomprehensive languages. In L.N. Zybatow (ed.) *Translation in der globalen Welt und neue Wege in der Sprach- und Übersetzerausbildung*. Innsbrucker Ringvorlesung zur Translationswissenschaft II (pp. 1–57). Frankfurt am Main: Peter Lang.

Mißler, B. (2000) Previous experience of foreign language learning and its contribution to the development of learning strategies. In S. Dentler, B. Hufeisen and B. Lindemann (eds) *Tertiär- und Drittsprachen. Projekte und empirische Untersuchungen* (pp. 7–22). Tübingen: Stauffenburg.

Mitits, L. (2015) *Language Learning Strategies and Multilingualism: Monolingual EFL and Multilingual EFL/L2 Greek Learners in Greek Secondary Education*. Kavala: Saita Publications.

Moore, D. (2006) *Plurilinguismes et Ecole*. Paris: Didier.

Müller-Lancé, J. (2003) *Der Wortschatz romanischer Sprachen im Tertiärspracherwerb*. Tübingen: Stauffenburg.

Muñoz, C. (2000) Bilingualism and trilingualism in school students in Catalonia. In J. Cenoz and U. Jessner (eds) *English in Europe: The Acquisition of a Third Language* (pp. 157–178). Clevedon: Multilingual Matters.

Naiman, N., Fröhlich, M., Stern, H.H. and Todesco, A. (1996) *The Good Language Learner*. Clevedon: Multilingual Matters.

Neuner-Anfindsen, S. (2005) *Fremdsprachenlernen und Lernerautonomie. Sprachlernbewusstsein, Lernprozessorganisation und Lernstrategien zum Wortschatzlernen in Deutsch als Fremdsprache*. Baltmannsweiler: Schneider Hohengehren.

Ouédroago, D. (2005) Mehrsprachigkeit und Deutschunterricht in Burkina Faso. Welche Strategien zur Verbesserung der Lehr- und Lernmethoden? Paper read at the International Conference for Teachers of German, August, Graz, Austria.

Pinto, M.A., Tinone, R. and Trusso, F. (1999) *Metalinguistic Awareness. Theory, Development and Measurement Instruments*. Pisa: I.E.P.I.

Psaltou-Joycey, A. and Kantaridou, Z. (2009) Foreign language learning strategy profiles of university students in Greece. *Journal of Applied Linguistics* 25 (1), 107–127.

Ringbom, H. (1987) *The Role of L1 in Foreign Language Learning*. Clevedon: Multilingual Matters.

Sagasta, P. (2003) Acquiring writing skills in a third language: The positive effects of bilingualism. *International Journal of Bilingualism* 7 (1), 27–42.

Sanz, C. (1997) L3 acquisition and the cognitive advantages of bilingualism: Catalans learning English. In L. Díaz and C. Pérez (eds) *Views on the Acquisition and Use of a Second Language* (pp. 449–456). Barcelona: Universitat Pompeu Fabra.

Stavans, A. and Hoffmann, C. (2015) *Multilingualism*. Cambridge: Cambridge University Press.

Stedje, A. (1976) Interferenz von Muttersprache und Zweitsprache auf eine dritte Sprache beim freien Sprechen – ein Vergleich. *Zielsprache Deutsch* 1 (1), 15–21.

Tafel, K. (2009) *Slavische Interkomprehension. Eine Einführung*. Tübingen: Narr.

Thomas, J. (1987) The role played by metalinguistic awareness in second and third language learning. *Journal of Multilingual and Multicultural Development* 9 (1), 235–247.

Todeva, E. and Cenoz, J. (eds) (2009) *The Multiple Realities of Multilingualism*. Berlin: Mouton de Gruyter.

Török, V. (2017) Building on the M-factor: Strategies in decoding an unknown language. PhD thesis, University of Innsbruck.

Traxl, C. (2015) Metalinguistic awareness in primary school children: English as a third language. Diploma thesis, University of Innsbruck.

Tremblay, M.-C. (2006) Crosslinguistic influence in third language acquisition: The role of L2 proficiency and L2 exposure. *CLO/OPL Ottawa* 34 (1), 109–119.

Vidgren, N. (2017) Deutsch nach Englisch und Schwedisch – Subjektive Theorien finnischer DaF-Lernender über das Lernen von mehr als einer Fremdsprache und die zwischensprachliche Interaktion. Baltmannsweiler: Schneider.

Vildomec, V. (1963) *Multilingualism*. Leyden: Sythoff.

Zapp, F.J. (1979) Verzahnung von Zweit- und Drittspracherwerb. In G. Walter und K. Schröder (eds) *Englisch* (pp. 9–14). Munich and Wien: Oldenburg.

Journals

International Journal of Multilingualism. Routledge/Taylor & Francis.

Textbooks

DeutschCom

Breitsameter, A., Vicente, S. and Cristache, C. (2009) *deutsch.com 2, Arbeitsbuch*. Ismaning: Hueber.

Breitsameter, A, Aßmann, J., Vicente, S. and Cristache, C. (2011) *deutsch.com 3, Arbeitsbuch*. Ismaning: Hueber.

Neuner, G. (ed.) (2008) *deutsch.com 1, Kursbuch*. Ismaning: Hueber.

Neuner, G. (ed.) (2009) *deutsch.com 2, Kursbuch*. Ismaning: Hueber.

Neuner, G. (ed.) (2011) *deutsch.com 3, Kursbuch*. Ismaning: Hueber.

Vicente, S., Cristache, C., Neuner, G., Kirchner, B. and Szakály, E. (2008) *deutsch.com 1, Arbeitsbuch*. Ismaning: Hueber.

Encuentros

Amann, K. *et al.* (2003) *Encuentros 1. Nueva Edición. Lehrwerk für den Spanischunterricht.* Berlin: Cornelsen.

Salvete

Althoff, U. *et al.* (2006) *Salvete. Neue Ausgabe. Texte und Übungen 1.* Berlin: Cornelsen.

Web pages

www.eol.ecml.at (accessed 31 July 2017).

www.plurcur.ecml.at (accessed 31 July 2017).

Lecture 4

Educational Policy and Multilingualism

Jasone Cenoz and Durk Gorter

Multilingualism in School Contexts: An Introduction

Multilingualism is common in school contexts for historical, social, political and economic reasons. Multilingualism in education takes many forms. In some cases schoolchildren have different home languages, as can happen in big cities with a diverse population but increasingly in smaller cities and towns as well. It can also occur where there is not great linguistic diversity but the school language and the home language are different. These multilingual classes are common now because of colonization, globalization and the mobility of the population. Multilingual classes do not necessary imply multilingual education, because the school may not have multilingualism as an aim and students have to learn the language of the state or the host country in educational systems that aim at monolingualism.

Multilingualism can also be one of the educational goals in a school, region or state. In this case the educational system makes provisions for teaching languages either as subjects or integrating language and content. This does not necessarily mean that the students' first language (L1) is one of the languages to be learned. In fact, almost 40% of the world population does not have access to education in their L1 (Walter & Benson, 2012). As Heugh (2013: 231) explains when analyzing language policy in education in South Africa, 'one of the key factors in student underachievement had to do with the failure to teach literacy well enough and long enough in the language best understood by students'.

Nowadays and due to the spread of English as a language of international communication, many schools all over the world include English in the curriculum, either as a school subject or as a language of instruction. Other strong languages such as French, Spanish or German can also be learned at school and even languages that have a weaker social status. The weak status of a language may be associated with the limited number of speakers of the so-called minority languages (for example, Navajo in the US or Frisian in the Netherlands; Gorter, 2001), or their limited functions in society (for example, Quechua in Peru or Berber in Morocco) even when the demography is strong.

All decisions on multilingual education are part of language policy. As Hélot and Ó Laoire (2011) point out:

> All schools and educational institutions, whether they realize it or not, operate from and within a certain policy. While certain languages are selected to be taught, only certain standard varieties are accepted; while other languages are introduced at earlier or later points in learners' education, some remain in the margins or are expected to be taught outside of the school system. (Hélot & Ó Laoire, 2011: xiv)

According to Spolsky (2009: 4), language policy has three interrelated components:

- Language practices are 'the observable behaviors and choices', that is, the way language is actually used.
- Language beliefs or ideology: the most important beliefs are 'the values or statuses assigned to named languages, varieties, and features'.
- Language management is defined as the 'explicit and observable efforts by someone or some group that has or claims to have authority over the participants in the domain to modify their practices and beliefs'.

Language policy can affect different areas and one of the most crucial is education. Another important point related to language policy is that declared policies do not always reflect the real policies because there are hidden agendas (Shohamy, 2006). For example, it is not necessary to have a strong policy against a weak language because a policy of not supporting the weak language will contribute to making it weaker and this may be the hidden goal of such a policy.

Educational policies on multilingualism are related to different background factors. The policy to reinforce the teaching of English in many countries in the world is associated with the international importance English has as a lingua franca. The link between educational policies and political factors can also be seen in the changing status of minority languages in Spain in the last decades of the 20th century. After many years of exclusion, Basque, Catalan and Galician became co-official languages in their regions in the late 1970s and early 1980s and were strongly reinforced because of their use in education.

Multilingual Education for Speakers of Minority Languages

Minority languages are defined in the *Charter for Regional or Minority Languages* of the Council of Europe (1998) as 'languages that are traditionally used within a given territory of a state by nationals of that state who form a group numerically smaller than the rest of the state's population and [are] different from the official language(s) of that state'. Minority languages such as Welsh in the UK or Frisian in the Netherlands share the same territory with English or Dutch which are the dominant state languages or majority languages. Minority languages are defined by their status as compared to the majority language. A minority language such as Catalan with approximately 10 million speakers has a minority status as compared to Spanish in Spain but has more speakers than other European state languages such as Danish, Greek or Swedish.

There are other labels to refer to minority languages. Terms such as 'heritage' or 'indigenous' languages are more common in North America. The term 'heritage language' includes the languages of immigrants, refugees and indigenous groups (see, for discussion on nomenclature, Extra & Gorter, 2007).

Some minority languages are 'unique' because they are spoken in one or more than one state but are nowhere the official dominant or majority language of a state (Cenoz & Gorter, 2008). An example of a 'unique' minority language is Breton, which is spoken according to some estimates by approximately 200,000 speakers in the French region of Brittany. Another example is Quechua, which is spoken by approximately 10 million speakers in several countries (Ecuador, Peru, Bolivia, Argentina, Chile and Colombia) but is not the dominant language in any of them. Other minority languages are not unique because they are at the same time the dominant language of a neighbouring state. For example, German is a minority language in South Tyrol in Italy but is the majority language of Germany and Austria.

Minority languages are very important in the study of multilingualism because speakers of minority languages are in most cases multilingual. They usually learn the majority language from an early age and in many cases they also learn English as an international language.

The situation of minority languages

Many minority languages are small and are regarded as 'endangered' or 'vulnerable' in the *UNESCO Atlas of the World's Languages in Danger* (Moseley, 2010). For example, in Brazil there are 97 languages that are considered vulnerable and 81 are endangered. In New Zealand there is one vulnerable language, Māori. In the UK, Welsh and Scots are vulnerable and eight other languages are endangered.

Fishman (1991, 2001) proposed the Graded Intergenerational Disruption Scale, a continuum of eight stages for assessing language loss or disruption. Stage 8 indicates near total extinction of the language while Stage 1 indicates the least disruption. This

Table 4.1 *Stages of the Graded Intergenerational Disruption Scale*

Stage 8	Reconstructing the language and adult acquisition of the language.
Stage 7	Cultural interaction in the language primarily involves the older generation of the community.
Stage 6	The intergenerational and demographically concentrated family-home-neighbourhood-community: the basis of mother-tongue transmission.
Stage 5	Schools for literacy acquisition, for the old and for the young, and not in lieu of compulsory education. Many minority languages start promotional activities with adult classes and out of school lessons for children.
Stage 4b	Public schools for minority children, offering some instruction via the minority language, but substantially under control of the dominant language group.
Stage 4a	Schools in lieu of compulsory education and substantially under curricular and staffing control of the minority.
Stage 3	The local/regional work sphere, among both minority and majority speakers.
Stage 2	Local/regional mass media and governmental services.
Stage 1	Education, work sphere, mass media and government operations at higher and nationwide levels.

Source: Adapted from Fishman (1991: 395; 2001: 466).

framework is intended both as a diagnostic tool and as a guide to plan actions to reverse language shift from the minority to the majority language. The stages are described in Table 4.1.

According to Fishman (1991: 399) the most important element of language maintenance is Stage 6, intergenerational mother tongue transmission. He considers that languages in Stages 8–5 are on the 'weak side' while languages in Stages 4–1 are on the 'strong side'. Fishman highlights the importance of language learning at home and in the community. Schools are considered very important for language learning but they cannot be the sole agent of revitalization.

Minority languages in education

The position of minority languages in education can range from the very strong position of having the minority language as the main language of instruction to the very weak position of making no provision for the minority language in the curriculum. The most common positions are intermediate, that is, to study the minority language as a subject or as the language of instruction only for some subjects. The teaching of minority languages is more widespread in preschool and primary education than in secondary and higher education. Table 4.2 summarizes the situation of three minority languages in education to illustrate this point.

Corsican is a Romance language spoken on the Mediterranean island of Corsica in France. According to the sociolinguistic survey of the Corsican language (Collectivité de Corse, 2013), there are between 86,800 and 130,200 speakers of Corsican. Approximately a quarter of pre-primary and primary school children have Corsican as the language of

Table 4.2 *Teaching through the minority language*

Corsican, France	Approximately 24.53% of pre-primary and primary school pupils are enrolled in bilingual courses with up to 50% of lessons. Only 6.71% of pupils in secondary school have Corsican as one of the languages of instruction (Fusina & Arrighi, 2012).
Māori, New Zealand	Approximately 15.8% of Māori students attend Māori-medium education but less than 7% attend the intensive programme with Māori as the main language of instruction for 81–100% of the school time (Hill & May, 2014).
Catalan in Catalonia, Spain	Approximately 96% of pupils in primary school and 81% of pupils in secondary school have Catalan as the language of instruction for all subjects except for Spanish and English language classes (Areny *et al.*, 2013).

instruction but only 6.7% of all students in secondary education have Corsican as the language of instruction. As is the case in many other regions where minority languages are spoken, the percentage of secondary school students with Corsican as one of the languages of instruction is lower than in primary education. In New Zealand, Māori is spoken by about 150,000 speakers, or 21.3% of the Māori population (see also Benton, 2015). As we can see in Table 4.2, only 7% have Māori as the main language of instruction. The situation is quite different in the case of Catalonia, where Catalan is the language of instruction for the majority of the population in primary and secondary schools. Catalan is a co-official language, along with Spanish, in Catalonia and two other Spanish regions, Valencia and the Balearic Islands. Māori is the official language of New Zealand alongside English, but Corsican in France does not have an official status.

The status of a language can have an impact on its use in education but there are other factors affecting education, such as the linguistic distance between the minority and the majority language, the geographical spread of the minority or the size of the language. When the majority and minority languages are typologically related, such as Catalan and Spanish, it is easier to spread the use of the minority language in education because there are fewer comprehension problems. When the minority and majority languages are unrelated, such as Māori and English, it is necessary to devote more time to teaching the minority language at school. The size of the minority language is an important factor because there can be more opportunities to use the language outside school and also more possibilities to have qualified teachers. When the minority language is used in several countries and it is a state language there can be more teaching resources available as well.

Education through the minority language generally aims at maintaining and developing the minority speakers' L1. However, the revival of minority languages in some regions such as Wales or the Basque Country and the official status of the minority language have attracted speakers of the majority language to multilingual programmes with the minority language as the main language of instruction. These programmes are at the same time enrichment programmes for students with the minority language as an L1 and immersion programmes for speakers of the majority language.

Challenges faced by minority languages in education

The use of minority languages in education has some special characteristics. Programmes using minority languages are in most cases bilingual or multilingual programmes, because even if the minority language is the main language of instruction the state language is also included in the curriculum and in many cases other languages as well. The use of minority languages in education faces some challenges which can be seen in Table 4.3.

Table 4.3 *Challenges faced by minority languages in education*

1.	Legal status and funding
2.	Standard language
3.	Teachers' proficiency in the minority language
4.	Teaching materials
5.	Language use
6.	From bilingualism to multilingualism

Legal status

This is one of the main challenges to the use of many minority languages in education. There is much diversity in the legal status of minority languages and some countries have stronger policies than others to protect and develop them. The status of minority languages cannot be separated from socio-economic and sociopolitical consequences (May, 2000). For example, minority languages in Spain such as Galician, Catalan or Basque acquired a co-official status along with Spanish in the late 1970s, while there was an active policy against them in the previous decades.

The Council of Europe established the *Charter for Regional or Minority Languages* (Council of Europe, 1998) to protect the use of minority languages in education and other domains. The Charter is a legal document which so far has been ratified by 25 states (see Table 4.4).

Table 4.4 *States that have signed and ratified the Charter and the languages covered*

States (25): Armenia, Austria, Bosnia and Herzegovina, Croatia, Cyprus, Czech Republic, Denmark, Finland, Germany, Hungary, Liechtenstein, Luxembourg, Montenegro, Netherlands, Norway, Poland, Romania, Serbia, Slovakia, Slovenia, Spain, Sweden, Switzerland, Ukraine and the United Kingdom
Languages (79): Albanian, Aragonese, Aranese, Armenian, Assyrian, Asturian, Basque, Beás, Belarusian, Bosnian, Bulgarian, Bunjevac, Catalan, Cornish, Crimean Tatar, Croatian, Cypriot Maronite, Czech, Danish, Finnish, French, Frisian, Gagazu, Galician, German, Greek, Hungarian, Inari Sami, Irish, Istro-Romanian, Italian, Karaim, Karelian, Kashub, Krimchak, Kurdish, Kven Finnish, Ladino, Lemko, Leonese, Limburgish, Lithuanian, Low German, Lower Saxon, Lower Sorbian, Lule Sami, Macedonian, Manx Gaelic, Meänkieli, Moldovan, Montenegrin, North Frisian, North Sami, Polish, Romani, Romanian, Romanch, Russian, Ruthenian, Sater Frisian, Scots, Scottish-Gaelic, Serbian, Skolt Sami, Slovakian, Slovenian, South Sami, Swedish, Tatar, Turkish, Ukrainian, Ulster Scots, Upper Sorbian, Valencian, Vlach, Welsh, Yenish, Yezidi, Yiddish

The Charter covers a total of 79 languages used by minorities in Europe. Some of these languages are covered in one state but not in another. For example, Basque and Catalan are covered in Spain but not in France where they are also spoken. Some of the languages are majority languages in a kin state and others are unique minorities. Some countries have only ratified part of the Charter and there are eight countries that have signed the Charter but have not followed up with ratification. The Charter establishes measures to promote the use of regional and minority languages in education, judicial authorities, administrative authorities and public services, media, cultural activities and facilities, economic and social, such as transfrontier exchanges.

According to the Charter, minority languages can be school subjects or languages of instruction and they should be present at different levels of education from preschool education through university and higher level education, including adult courses and teacher training, as well as the teaching of history and culture in relation to minority languages. In Table 4.5 two examples of the legal text and the different levels of ratification regarding the use of minority languages in preschool education and university and higher education can be seen.

There has been some improvement in the situation of minority languages in education in Europe in countries that have ratified the Charter. For each level of education, the state can choose among the measures according to the situation of each language. Apart from the Charter, in some European countries there are binding legal regulations regarding the use of languages in education. Minority languages are used more at preschool and primary school levels than at secondary school and higher education levels. The legal recognition of

Table 4.5 *European Charter for Regional or Minority Languages*

With regard to education, the Parties undertake, within the territory in which such languages are used, according to the situation of each of these languages, and without prejudice to the teaching of the official language(s) of the State:
Article 8a on Preschool Education
i. to make available preschool education in the relevant regional or minority languages; or
ii. to make available a substantial part of preschool education in the relevant regional or minority languages; or
iii. to apply one of the measures provided for under i and ii above at least to those pupils whose families so request and whose number is considered sufficient; or
iv. if the public authorities have no direct competence in the field of preschool education, to favour and/or encourage the application of the measures referred to under i to iii above.
Article 8e on University and Higher Education
i. to make available university and other higher education in regional or minority languages; or
ii. to provide facilities for the study of these languages as university and higher education subjects; or
iii. if, by reason of the role of the State in relation to higher education institutions, subparagraphs i and ii cannot be applied, to encourage and/or allow the provision of university or other forms of higher education in regional or minority languages or of facilities for the study of these languages as university or higher education subjects.

a minority language in education is usually a necessary step for funding its use as the language of instruction.

Standard language

One frequent challenge for minority languages is the development of a standard variety of the language for its use in education. It is common for minority languages to have different varieties and not one single standard variety for use in education. Many minority languages have been used more orally than in writing and the most common language at school has been the majority language. Outside school, the majority language has also been the main language in areas such as the media, business, administration and public services. Majority languages also went through processes of standardization, as in the case of English, French or Spanish in the 17th and 18th centuries. Some minority languages such as Galician, Basque or Catalan have a standard unified variety of the language that is used in education.

Teachers' proficiency in the minority language

This is a challenge often faced by minority languages that are unique in one or more countries (Cenoz, 2008). The weak tradition of using minority languages in education in the past is reflected in the lack of trained teachers who are proficient speakers of the minority language. For example, training for teachers of languages such as Kashubian (Poland), Māori (New Zealand), Quechua (Peru) or Frisian (the Netherlands) has to be provided in the regions where these languages are spoken. When the minority language is the state language of a neighbouring country there are more possibilities for finding teachers. For example, teachers trained in Germany can teach in minority language education in Italy or Belgium.

Teaching materials

The situation of teaching materials is a real challenge in education in the case of unique minorities because educational materials have to be developed for a limited market. There are more possibilities for teaching materials in the case of minority languages that are also majority languages in other countries, but they have to be adapted to national and regional curricula.

Language use

An additional challenge for minority languages is that because speakers are also proficient in the majority language they may use the majority language as the default language in communication. This is common in the case of any minority language but even more so when minority languages are also learned by speakers of the majority language. For example, a recent survey on the use of Welsh indicates that 'Just over one in five Welsh speakers felt most comfortable using Welsh, just over a quarter felt equally comfortable using both languages and over half of Welsh speakers felt most comfortable using English' (Welsh Government, 2015: 48). The data from the most recent sociolinguistic survey of

Basque (Basque Government, 2012) indicate that 39.6% of Basque speakers in the Basque Autonomous Community use more Basque than Spanish and 22.3% as much Basque as Spanish. The rest of the speakers who are bilingual in Basque and Spanish use more Spanish than Basque. These data confirm the minority position of Welsh and Basque. It is to be expected that even if minority languages have an important role in education they are not always used among students. The challenge of language use is very important for minority languages because they face the risk of being used just as school languages and not for everyday communication.

From bilingualism to multilingualism

Another challenge for minority languages in education in non-English speaking countries is the need to move from bilingual to multilingual education. Traditionally, language policy in education considered the majority and minority languages when establishing their roles in the school curriculum. Foreign languages were also taught but were not considered as important as other school subjects. Nowadays the teaching and learning of English has become very important worldwide and educational policies including minority languages need to include at least three languages, except in cases where English is the majority language as in Welsh or Māori schools. Therefore, the challenge is to develop proficiency in not only two but three languages. Some examples of this situation include: Frisian, Dutch and English in Friesland, the Netherlands (Gorter, 2005); Mongolian, Chinese and English in the Inner Mongolian Autonomous Region of China; or Aymara, Spanish and English in Bolivia.

In sum, learning through minority languages has special characteristics related to the role of the minority and majority languages in the family, at school and in society in general. It is common for speakers of minority languages to face a mismatch between home and school language or between school and community language.

The use of minority languages in education shows that programmes that aim at maintaining and developing the minority language along with other languages are associated with positive academic outcomes (Cenoz & Gorter, 2005; see also Gorter *et al.*, 2014a).

The experiences of multilingual education including minority language are often not well known outside the areas of use of the minority languages. However, these programmes integrate content and language teaching in two or more languages and their pedagogical practices can be an important reference for other multilingual programmes.

Multilingual Education for Speakers of Majority Languages

In the previous section we have seen that speakers of majority languages are sometimes enrolled in educational programmes with a minority language as the language of instruction. In this case they learn the minority language which is used as the medium of instruction along with students who speak the minority language as an L1. Although this is common in some areas where minority languages are spoken, it is more common for speakers of majority languages to learn languages of wider communication such as English. In this section, we focus on multilingual education for speakers of majority languages by looking at programmes that use a second or foreign language as the language of instruction to teach content, or what is usually known as content-based instruction.

Content-based instruction (CBI) has been defined as 'the concurrent study of language and subject matter, with the form and sequence of language presentation dictated by content material' (Brinton *et al.*, 1989: vii). There are many types of CBI but the basic characteristic is that academic content is taught in the second or foreign language. According to Met's (1998) continuum of content and language integration, some programmes are mainly focused on content and can be called 'content driven', whereas others focus more on language and can be called 'language driven'. When a physics class deals with different types of energy and the focus is on analyzing the specific characteristics of energy, the focus is on content even if the class is taught through the medium of English in a context where English is a second or foreign language. CBI on different types of energy could also take place in the English language class by reading a text or conducting a project on this topic but paying more attention to language. In this case it would be 'language driven'. Both lessons combine the learning of curricular content and language learning but they adopt a different focus. CBI can take place at all educational levels: preschool, primary, secondary or higher education levels.

Immersion programmes

Immersion programmes have been considered 'the quintessential model of content-based L2 instruction' (Genesee & Lindholm-Leary, 2013: 3). The first immersion programme started in Quebec, Canada in 1965. This programme, like most immersion programmes in Canada, aimed at English speaking children and used French as the language of instruction for some school subjects. The label 'immersion' usually refers to programmes that use the additional language for at least 50% of academic instruction in primary school (Tedick *et al.*, 2011). Swain and Johnson (1997: 6–8) considered that an immersion programme had the core features shown in Table 4.6.

These features do not define all immersion programmes. For example, immersion programmes in Catalan or Basque for speakers of Spanish as L1 are often mixed with

Table 4.6 *Core features of immersion programmes*

1.	The L2 is the medium of instruction
2.	The curriculum is the same as for L1
3.	Overt support exists for the L1
4.	The programme aims for additive bilingualism
5.	Exposure to the L2 mainly in the classroom
6.	Students enter with similar levels of L2
7.	The teachers are bilingual
8.	The classroom culture is that of the L1

Table 4.7 *Examples of immersion programmes*

	Languages	Types	Characteristics
Canada	English L1 French L2	Early-Middle-Late Partial-Total	Increasing number of students with other home languages. Approximately 10% of the students without English as L1 are in French immersion programmes.
Finland	Finnish L1 Swedish L2 English L3 German L4	Early Total followed by Partial	Less than 1% of the total school population of Finland, but can get to 50% in some municipalities
Basque Country	Spanish L1 Basque L2 English L3 French L4	Early Total Early Partial	Originally aimed at speakers of Basque as L1 who are in the same classes as speakers of Spanish as L1. Most students in the Basque Autonomous Community have instruction through the medium of Basque, reaching 90%.

students with Catalan or Basque as a second language (L2) and those students do not enter the immersion programme with similar levels of L2. Swain and Lapkin (2005) considered that the core features also need to be adapted in the case of Canadian immersion because nowadays many students in immersion programmes do not speak English at home but other languages instead. In these cases schools do not offer overt support for the L1 and the classroom culture is not that of the L1. Immersion programmes can be found in different countries. Some examples can be found in Table 4.7.

Canadian immersion programmes can be different according to the intensity of the use of the L2 and the level at which the programme is implemented (Genesee & Lindholm-Leary, 2013). There are total and partial immersion programmes and early, middle and late immersion programmes. Early total immersion programmes have 100% of the school time in the L2 (French) in kindergarten but the percentage of French-medium instruction goes down to approximately 50% in later years. Partial immersion refers to programmes with approximately 50% of the school time in the L2. Middle immersion begins in Grades 3 or 4 when students are 8/9 or 9/10 years old, with French immersion for about 80% of the time. Late immersion starts in Grades 6 or 7 when students are 11/12 or 12/13 years old, with 60–75% of French instruction.

Björklund *et al.* (2014) explain how Swedish immersion for Finnish-speaking children in Finland usually starts at the age of four or five. In the first years, only Swedish is used, but from age seven onwards the L1 and L3 (English in most cases) are also part of the curriculum. An optional fourth language is added later. Finnish and Swedish are used as the medium for the teaching of content while the L3 or L4 are taught as school subjects. Swedish immersion in Finland does not reach 1% of the population but in some municipalities it can reach 50% of the students.

Gorter *et al.* (2014b) explain the Basque immersion models for Spanish speaking children in the Basque Autonomous Community. These models offer early partial or early total immersion in Basque. In this context, partial immersion means 50% of Basque instruction and total immersion means approximately 80% of Basque instruction. Immersion starts in preschool and goes on until the end of secondary school. Spanish and English are taught as school subjects in the case of total immersion but English has become an additional language of instruction in recent years. Most students in the Basque Autonomous Community (80%) are enrolled in Basque-medium instruction but this is not immersion for students with Basque as the L1. Students in the partial immersion programme usually have Spanish as their L1. The programme with Basque instruction for 80% of the school curriculum was originally designed as an enrichment programme using the minority language for Basque L1 speakers, but it has attracted a large number of Spanish L1 speakers. Therefore, this programme is now also an immersion programme for students who do not speak Basque at home.

Evaluations of immersion programmes indicate positive linguistic and academic outcomes (Björklund *et al.*, 2014; Cenoz, 2009; Genesee & Lindholm-Leary, 2013; Gorter *et al.*, 2014b; Tedick & Wesely, 2015). Immersion students' development of the L1 is similar to students in non-immersion programmes even if they have fewer hours of instruction in the L1. At the same time, immersion students' achievement in the L2 is much higher than in the case of students who are not in immersion programmes. Their level in the L2 is similar to that of L1 speakers for comprehension skills but it usually does not reach the level of native speakers for production skills. Immersion students also achieve the same level of competence in academic subjects as non-immersion students.

Content and language integrated learning

CBI has undergone an important development in Europe in recent years in second and foreign languages with content and language integrated learning (CLIL) programmes. Both CBI and CLIL are used as umbrella terms and they take different forms. What are the differences between CBI and CLIL? Cenoz (2015) analyzed the essential and accidental properties of CBI and CLIL and found that there are no differences between CBI and CLIL regarding their essential properties (see also Cenoz *et al.*, 2013). The list of properties can be seen in Table 4.8.

The essential properties used to compare CBI and CLIL are the criteria used by Baker (2011) to identify different types of bilingual education. According to these properties, CBI and CLIL are the same. In both cases the medium of instruction is the L1 and an additional language and both CBI and CLIL aim at multilingualism without replacing the L1 with the L2. Both CBI and CLIL aim at pluralism and enrichment as societal and educational aims and the typical child in these programmes is a speaker of the majority language. The prototypical CBI/CLIL programmes are usually taught by content teachers of different content subjects with a second or foreign language as the language of instruction. They share the same essential properties and are not pedagogically different from one another.

There can be some differences regarding the accidental properties of CBI and CLIL because they are linked to specific educational contexts and because their origin is different. CBI programmes were developed in the context of bilingual education in Canada where English

Table 4.8 *Essential and accidental properties of content-based instruction (CBI) and content and language integrated learning (CLIL)*

		CBI	**CLIL**
Essential properties	Medium of instruction	L1 and additional	L1 and additional
	Language aims	Multilingualism	Multilingualism
	Societal and educational aims	Pluralism and enrichment	Pluralism and enrichment
	Typical type of child	Majority language	Majority language
Accidental properties	Target language	French, Basque, Welsh, English	English
	Native versus non-native teachers	Native and non-native teachers	Non-native teachers
	Starting age	Kindergarten, primary or secondary education	Primary or secondary education
	Origin	Canada 1960s	Europe 1990s

is the majority language. CLIL programmes have their origin in the teaching of English (and in some cases other foreign languages) in Europe. CLIL programmes are not as intensive as immersion programmes and they are usually limited to the teaching of one or two subjects through the medium of English or another foreign language. Immersion programmes can be considered as a type of CBI or CLIL programme with at least 50% of the teaching conducted through the second or foreign language. There is a great diversity of programmes included under the umbrella terms CBI and CLIL. There can also be differences regarding having native or non-native teachers or the starting age, but these are accidental properties and do not make CBI and CLIL different.

Immersion programmes have a strong tradition of research on their effectiveness as compared to other types of CBI or CLIL programmes (Cenoz *et al.*, 2013). Research on CLIL has compared CLIL and non-CLIL groups of learners and has reported higher achievement in English for CLIL learners but has not looked at the outcomes regarding L1 and academic achievement in content to the same extent (Coyle, 2007; Lorenzo *et al.*, 2010). It also remains to be proved whether the positive results in the L2 are due to the integration of language and content or to the amount of exposure to the target language.

CBI and CLIL are typically aimed at speakers of majority languages but as we have already seen some immersion programmes are at the same time enrichment programmes to promote the L1 of speakers of less dominant languages. For example, programmes that have Welsh or Basque as the main language of instruction have students with the majority and the minority language as home languages. The aim of these programmes is to promote the minority language not only among L1 speakers but also among speakers of the majority language.

Another type of immersion programme is the two-way immersion programme. One of the main aims of these programmes, developed in the United States, is to facilitate the academic progress and acquisition of English language skills in the case of schoolchildren who do not have English as their home language. Most two-way immersion programmes are in English and Spanish but there are also programmes in other languages such as

Chinese, Korean or French (Genesee & Lindholm-Leary, 2013). Two-way immersion programmes have speakers with English as the L1 and speakers with another home language as an L1 in the same class. Some programmes start with more intensive exposure to the non-English language in the first years and then the proportion moves to 50/50. Evaluations of these programmes report positive linguistic and academic outcomes (Genesee & Lindholm-Leary, 2013; Tedick & Weseley, 2015). These programmes have some points in common with European immersion programmes in minority languages but also important differences. European programmes with a minority language as the language of instruction have as their aim the protection of the minority language and the reinforcement of the use of the minority language in society at large, which is not generally the aim of two-way immersion programmes in the United States.

CBI and CLIL programmes are an important contribution to the development of multilingual education. There are different types of programmes because they have developed in contexts that have specific characteristics, but they are all based on the integration of language and content. Cenoz *et al.* (2013) highlight the importance of sharing pedagogical practices across contexts and conduct research that can be generalized to different contexts. Another important point to take into consideration is the dynamics of society and CBI/CLIL programmes. Nowadays it is no longer valid to consider that students in these programmes are homogeneous in their language and culture. Globalization including the increasing mobility of the population can be seen all over the world. CBI/CLIL programmes should take into account the diversity of the school population and value their multilingual and multicultural contribution.

Types of Multilingual Education

The previous two sections include information about some widespread multilingual programmes for speakers of minority and majority languages. They also give an idea of the diversity of situations in which multilingualism in education takes place. This section will start by summarizing some distinctions in bilingual education and different types of bilingual education. Then a model to compare different types of multilingual education aiming a multilingualism and multiculturalism will be explained. Multilingual education can be understood as education that aims at achieving competence in more than two languages but it is used extensively as a synonym of bilingual education.

Types of bilingual education

Many years ago Lambert (1974) made a distinction between additive and subtractive bilingualism. Additive bilingualism takes place in situations where the L2 does not replace the L1, such as Canadian immersion or immersion in minority languages for speakers of majority languages. In the case of subtractive bilingualism, the L1 is seen as an obstacle for academic development and it takes place when the L1 is replaced by the L2 and there are no provisions for the L1 at school. This is the situation of many speakers of less dominant or minority languages all over the world.

A well-known distinction can be made between elite and folk bilingualism (De Mejía, 2013). Elite bilingualism is a prestigious type of bilingualism that is voluntary and optional and it is usually in languages of wider communication. In contrast, folk bilingualism is not voluntary because becoming bilingual is a necessity for speakers of minority languages.

According to the linguistic background of the students and the aims of the school, some broad categories have been distinguished: transitional, maintenance and enrichment programmes (Baker, 2011; May, 2008). In the case of *transitional programmes*, the child's L1 is replaced by the majority language. These programmes also imply cultural assimilation and their aim is monolingualism in the majority language. In the case of *maintenance* and *enrichment programmes*, the L1 is not replaced by the L2. Maintenance programmes aim to form a solid basis in the L1 so the L2 is developed more easily. They aim for bilingualism and biliteracy but in quite a limited way because the L1 is not developed or extended. Enrichment programmes aim for bilingualism and biliteracy and aspire to cultural pluralism. An additional type of programme is heritage language programmes, which are similar to enrichment programmes but aim at reinforcing an endangered language.

Baker (2011) distinguishes strong and weak forms of bilingual education according to the language background of the child, the language of the classroom, and the linguistic, societal and educational aims. A summary of the different types can be seen in Table 4.9. It also includes 'monolingual forms of bilingualism', that is, programmes that do not aim at bilingualism but take place in contexts where there is a majority and a minority language. The typology is very broad because it also includes the teaching of a second or foreign language as a subject as a weak form of bilingual education. Most educational systems in the work could be included in one or more of these categories because English or other languages are taught as foreign languages in most programmes and nowadays there are minorities in many parts of the world. It can be said that the typology is very comprehensive.

In spite of this, it is difficult to fit all the types of multilingual education into the different categories of Baker's (2011) typology. As we have already seen, many programmes include not only two languages but three or more. Another difficulty is that there is a wide range of situations in many of the types of bilingual education identified in this typology. For example, the category 'maintenance/heritage language' refers to indigenous, regional minorities and immigrant languages, and these situations can often have different demographics, status and legal protection. On the other hand, there seems to be some overlap between the segregationist and separatist categories, which Baker (2011) considers as not being very common.

The continua of multilingual education

The great diversity of programmes and the need to consider multilingual education rather than bilingual education creates the need for other perspectives when analyzing different types of bilingual and multilingual education. Cenoz (2009) proposed the *continua of multilingual education* as a tool to describe, compare and evaluate different types of multilingual education within a country or internationally. This model represents the

Part 1: Multilingualism in Society and Education

Table 4.9 *Typology of bilingual education*

Monolingual forms of education for bilinguals	Mainstream/submersion Structured immersion	Speakers of minority languages are taught through the majority language.
	Mainstream/submersion with withdrawal classes	Speakers of minority languages are taught through the majority language but they have compensatory lessons in the majority language.
	Segregationist	Monolingual education through a minority language.
Weak forms of bilingual education	Transitional	Minority L1 used temporarily for teaching until students are proficient in the majority language.
	Mainstream with foreign language teaching	Majority L1 only exposed to other languages as school subjects.
	Separatist	Teaching through minority language only to protect minority language.
Strong forms of bilingual education	Immersion	Students with L1 as a majority have at least 50% of the time though the medium of a second language.
	Maintenance/heritage language	At least half of the curriculum time in minority language aiming at bilingualism and biliteracy.
	Two way/dual language	Majority and minority language students and both languages used as languages of instruction.
	Mainstream bilingual	Two majority languages as languages of instruction.

Source: Adapted from Baker (2011).

features of multilingual education as continua rather than in close categories. The model includes specific educational variables inside a triangle and also linguistic variables and sociolinguistic variables both at the macro and micro levels (Figure 4.1).

The continua of multilingual education model distinguishes different types of multilingual education by looking at linguistic, sociolinguistic and educational factors. In this model, multilingual education is used to refer to programmes that aim at developing proficiency in two or more languages without including the monolingual forms of education for bilinguals identified by Baker (2011). A class or school may be sometimes called bilingual or multilingual because students speak different home languages, but if the programme does not aim for maintenance or enrichment of two or more language it is not considered a type of multilingual education.

The continua of multilingual education model highlights the interaction of linguistic, sociolinguistic and educational variables. The triangle represents educational variables and they are affected by linguistic distance and the sociolinguistic context. The effect of

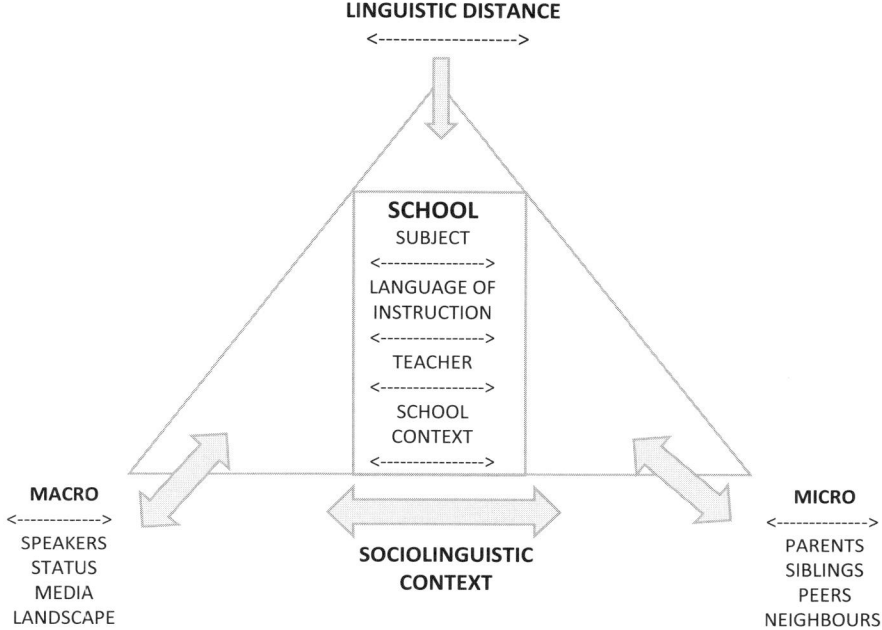

Figure 4.1 Continua of multilingual education
Source: Cenoz (2009).

linguistic distance is unidirectional but the social context has a bidirectional effect because it can influence educational variables but at the same time it can be influenced by them. Schools are part of society and their educational aims and the type of children enrolled in multilingual programmes will be closely related to the social context. At the same time, education contributes to shaping that social context and an increasing level of multilingualism and multiculturalism at school can have an effect on society at large.

Apart from considering the complexity of education by including different types of linguistic, sociolinguistic and educational variables, the use of continua highlights the dynamics of education and society.

Linguistic distance is one of the factors to take into consideration when comparing different types of multilingual education. Languages that are closely related to one another share aspects of their syntactic structure, phonological system or lexis. Less distant languages may be easier to learn than unrelated languages. For example, Dutch, Frisian and English, which are the three languages in the curriculum in the province of Friesland in the Netherlands, are all Germanic languages and share more structural and phonetic aspects than other languages. Japanese and English are more distant and they do not share the same script. In the continua of multilingual education model, the distance between languages is placed on a continuum without using absolute categories. Linguistic distance is relative and languages are not only 'related' or 'unrelated' but there can also be different degrees in their relationship. Linguistic distance can influence the design of the different programmes and the need to devote more or fewer hours to the different languages either as subjects or as languages of instruction. It can also have some influence in the degree of multilingualism of the teachers.

At the sociolinguistic level, the continua of multilingual education model makes a distinction between the macro and micro levels. The macro level looks at variables such as the number of speakers of the different languages, their status nationally and internationally, and their use in the media or in the linguistic landscape. When two multilingual programmes are compared at this level, one will be more multilingual than the other if the school is located in a context that is more linguistically diverse. The micro level includes the languages used at home with the parents, siblings or the extended family and the languages students use with their peers or in the community. The sociolinguistic context is considered 'more multilingual' if there is more linguistic diversity in the students' social networks.

The educational variables include four continua: subject, language of instruction, teacher and school contexts. When comparing multilingual programmes, each of these variables can be more or less multilingual.

Most multilingual programmes, even if they are CBI/CLIL programmes, have specific subjects to teach language (language arts classes). There can be important differences in the curriculum regarding this factor. The programme can have two or more languages and introduce them at different ages. Another aspect that can make a programme more multilingual is the integration of the different languages. Therefore a programme with more languages, with more exposure to different languages and with integrated curricula will be closer to the multilingual end of the 'subject continuum' than a programme with only one second or foreign language which is introduced in later grades for a few hours per week and without coordinating its curriculum with the main language of instruction.

Apart from teaching languages as subjects, most multilingual programmes use second or foreign languages as languages of instruction. In this case, the programme will be more multilingual when more languages are used to teach content and when there is coordination between teachers and syllabuses of different languages.

The continuum 'teachers' will imply more multilingual positions when there are more multilingual teachers who are proficient in different languages and they have specific training for multilingual education including CBI- or CLIL-specific training. Therefore, it covers not only pre-service or in-service linguistic training but also training in teaching methodology.

The continuum 'school context' refers to the linguistic landscape of the school and the use of languages inside the school for communication between teachers, supporting staff, students and parents, including informal conversations, meetings and written information. If more than two languages are used for these functions the programme of education will be closer to the more multilingual end of the continuum.

The use of continua to distinguish different multilingual programmes has some advantages but also some difficulties. The main advantage is that it consists of more open than closed categories and allows for a wide diversity of situations. As it is a more dynamic approach without fixed categories it allows for changes within the same programme that can become more or less multilingual in the different continua. However, this model also has the difficulty of placing a specific programme along each of the continua in an accurate way.

In this section, two different ways to approach the great diversity of bilingual and multilingual educational programmes have been described. The first approach is based on distinctions based on fixed categories so as to establish a typology for classifying the different programmes. The second approach uses continua which are open and can be more dynamic.

The Multilingual Classroom

Multilingual education has traditionally focused on the acquisition of competence in different languages, and languages have been considered as separate entities. This position is associated with monolingual ideologies and hardens boundaries between languages. This language separation ideology is well rooted and has been referred to as 'parallel monolingualism' (Heller, 1999: 271), 'two solitudes' (Cummins, 2005: 588), 'separate bilingualism' (Blackledge & Creese, 2010) or 'One Language Only (OLON) or One Language at a Time (OLAT) ideology' (Li Wei, 2011: 374). This monolingual approach has been criticized because it is not in accordance with the way languages are learned and used in social contexts (see, for example, Cenoz & Gorter, 2013, 2015). New approaches to multilingual education focus on individual agency, taking into account the way multilingual speakers' resources interact in the social context.

These new trends are conceptualized in different ways and using different terms. For example, Canagarajah (2013) uses the term 'translingual practices' and considers that communication transcends individual languages as can be seen in Table 4.10. Canagarajah (2013) also considers that communication transcends words because language is only one of the semiotic resources used in communication along with symbols, icons and images.

Table 4.10 *Communication transcends individual languages*

'Languages' are always in contact with and mutually influence each other.
Users treat all available codes as a repertoire in their everyday communication.
Users don't have separate competences for separately labelled languages.
Languages are not necessarily at war with each other; they complement each other in communication.
Text and talk don't feature one language at a time; they are meshed and mediated by diverse codes.
Meaning doesn't arise from a common grammatical system or norm.
Language patterns are always open to negotiation and reconstruction.
Communication involves treating languages as 'mobile resources'.

Source: Canagarajah (2013: 6–7).

In this section we will look at multilingual policies and practices that emphasize the use of the whole linguistic repertoire in the educational context.

Focus on multilingualism

'Focus on multilingualism' is an approach to language teaching and research in the context of multilingual education. It is a holistic approach which looks at the ways in which multilingual students can use their multilingual knowledge and communicative resources more effectively (Cenoz & Gorter, 2011). Focus on multilingualism has three dimensions: the multilingual speaker, the whole linguistic repertoire and the social context, as can be seen in Table 4.11.

Table 4.11 *The dimensions of focus on multilingualism*

Focus on multilingualism	The multilingual speaker: fluid, dynamic competence
	The whole linguistic repertoire
	The social context

The multilingual speaker

The communicative skills of multilingual speakers are different from those of monolingual speakers. Monolingual and multilingual speakers use their linguistic resources in different ways depending on the speaking context and interlocutor, but there are differences in the resources they can use because multilingual speakers have resources from two or more languages at their disposal. A multilingual speaker may interact in some similar contexts in two or more languages, but there may be contexts in which the multilingual speaker is accustomed to interacting in one language only. For example, a bilingual Spanish-English speaker may discuss a movie in two languages but only feels comfortable when talking or singing to a small child in one of the languages. The type of competence a multilingual speaker has in one language is difficult to isolate without considering the other language because they are intertwined. Multilingual speakers navigate between languages according to the context and they cannot be considered less competent than monolingual speakers because they are not accustomed to using all the languages they know for all the contexts. In fact, multilingual speakers can communicate more effectively in more situations and with a larger number of interlocutors.

In spite of this, the competence of multilingual speakers is still very often measured from a monolingual perspective in comparison to the ideal native speaker of one single language. This tradition was criticized many years ago by Grosjean (1985, 2008) who proposed the holistic approach to bilingualism and by Cook (1992) who proposed the concept of multicompetence. These approaches are more adequate than monolingual approaches because multilingual speakers are not failed monolinguals but competent users of several languages who have a unique linguistic profile.

Focus on multilingualism considers that the communicative competence of multilingual speakers is fluid, not fixed but dynamic. It is fluid because there are no fixed boundaries between languages and it is dynamic because the competence in each of the languages can develop according to the context.

The whole linguistic repertoire

In contrast to the trend to separate the different languages spoken by multilinguals in order to avoid interference, focus on multilingualism considers the whole linguistic repertoire. Languages support one another at the cognitive level. Research on L3 acquisition shows that bilinguals have advantages when learning additional languages because of their enhanced metalinguistic awareness and their expanded linguistic repertoire (Cenoz, 2013; Cenoz & Jessner, 2009). The languages previously learned can have a scaffolding function when learning additional languages. This can be seen clearly in Todeva's (2009) narrative (see Table 4.12).

Table 4.12 *Todeva's perception of scaffolding at the lexical level*

Tapping into one's prior linguistic knowledge becomes quite easy once one learns, with experience, to see beyond phonological and graphological variations. Through the years I realized, for instance, that even though my L1 is a Slavic language, it shares many words with French, Italian, English, and German. Some of this shared lexicon is the result of direct borrowing from these four languages, while another part came from Latin. This awareness of lexical units belonging to multiple languages greatly facilitated my vocabulary learning in Spanish.

Source: Todeva (2009: 61).

Furthermore, another reason to consider the whole linguistic repertoire is that multilingual speakers communicate using resources that can be identified as belonging to one or more languages. Cross-linguistic interaction studies indicate that it is multidirectional (Cenoz & Gorter, 2011; De Angelis & Dewaele, 2011; Jarvis & Pavlenko, 2008). The comment in Table 4.13 shows the perception of cross-linguistic influence that Kamanga (2009), a multilingual speaker of several African languages and English, has about his own experience.

The strict separation of languages in language classes and CBI/CLIL can prevent students from using their own resources. In contrast with the widespread tradition of separation, focus on multilingualism considers that the languages in multilingual speakers' repertoire need to be activated in order to support each other and enhance metalinguistic awareness.

Table 4.13 *Kamanga's perception of cross-linguistic influence*

My speech demonstrates all kinds of crosslinguistic influence: influence from one mother tongue to another; from a mother tongue to a second language; from a mother tongue to a third language; from a second language to a mother tongue; and from a second language to a third language. However, I am not yet sure if I also exhibit influence of any of my third languages on either my second language or any of my first languages.

Source: Kamanga (2009: 124).

The social context

Multilingualism has a social dimension because multilingual speakers acquire and use languages while engaging in language practices in a social context. The analysis of multilingual discourse practices shows that multilingual speakers are creative using elements from different languages. This can be seen in the social practices of communication in situations in which the monolingual norms of the school are not enforced. Musk (2010) conducted a study among Welsh-English bilingual secondary school students and reported their mixed language practices:

> By adopting a participant perspective, it has emerged that the default medium used by these young people in informal discussions is a mixed code; Welsh is primarily the base language, but with English insertions (words and phrases). It is the default medium insofar as it is unmarked and carries no extra meaning. In other words, it is a seamless bilingual medium, whereby the boundaries between languages or codes are at most only loosely maintained, that is, Welsh tends to provide the syntactic framing. (Musk, 2010: 195)

Focus on multilingualism considers the competence of multilingual speakers who can shape their communicative context while engaging in language practices (see also Kramsch, 2009; Kramsch & Huffmaster, 2015). Multilingual speakers can communicate using resources from different languages in some contexts and also in a single language in others.

Translanguaging

One of the concepts that has gained currency in the last few years is translanguaging. As Lewis *et al.* (2012a) point out, the term '*trawsieithu*', which was later translated from Welsh into English as translanguaging, was first used by Welsh educationalist Cen Williams in the 1980s. It referred to the use of two languages, Welsh and English, for teaching and learning within the same lesson in a planned and systematic way. Students get oral or written information in one language and use the information in the other language so that input is in one language and output is in the other language. For example, students can prepare a poster in English and explain it in Welsh or read a history text in Welsh and discuss it in English (Beres, 2015). The basic idea is to use one language to reinforce the other so that the information is fully understood.

Lewis *et al.* (2012b) give an example of a translanguaging activity in a geography lesson in primary school with 7–9-year-old pupils. The activity has the following steps:

- *Reading text*. The class reads information in English on 'Fair Trade' on the internet.
- *Question-answer for comprehension*. The teacher asks questions about the meaning of specific terms in the text and the students can respond in both Welsh and English.
- *Teacher's explanation*. The teacher explains some specific terms in Welsh.
- *Teacher's summary*. The teacher summarizes the text in Welsh.

- *Task.* The teacher asks students to complete a poster in Welsh so as to explain 'Fair Trade' as a good idea.

This example shows that English and Welsh alternate for different parts of the activity and that translanguaging is planned for pedagogical purposes. Lewis *et al.* (2012b) identify two types of translanguaging in bilingual education in Wales: teacher-directed translanguaging and pupil-directed translanguaging. Teacher-directed translanguaging is used mainly as a planned and structured activity that is used as scaffolding by the teacher. Pupil-directed translanguaging has less support from the teacher and takes place with students who can work independently and already have a good command of both languages.

Baker (2011) explains that translanguaging can have four potential advantages, as shown in Table 4.14. Some of these potential advantages have also been highlighted in other contexts. Studies in L2 classes or bilingual education have identified different functions for the use of the L1 (Lin, 2015). Some of these functions are related to classroom management and others to comprehension and feedback. McMillan and Turnbull (2009) suggest that code-switching can be a valuable strategy for vocabulary learning when words have no cognates in the L1 and are difficult to explain. Even though more research is needed to confirm the possible advantages of using the L1 in the classroom, Macaro (2009) highlights the potential problems in not using the L1 as a resource:

> What emerges is an increasing possibility that banning the first language from the communicative second language classroom may in fact be reducing the cognitive and metacognitive opportunities available to learners. (Macaro, 2009: 49)

In spite of these advantages, Jones and Lewis (2014) consider that translanguaging can also pose a risk in the case of minority languages because it may trigger the use of the majority language (see also Cenoz & Gorter, 2017):

> Although the deliberate and systematic use of two languages in the classroom can be of advantage to children's learning, careful consideration must be given to the sociolinguistic contexts of schools, especially in situations where a minority language coexists with a majority language as media of instruction. It has been observed that there is a tendency in Welsh-medium schools in predominantly English-speaking areas to control the use of translanguaging, as there is a growing concern that allowing the use of English texts for translanguaging purposes might be a stepping-stone for introducing more of the majority language (English). This is of particular concern to educators in areas where the minority language (Welsh) is already marginalized in the community outside the school. (Jones & Lewis, 2014: 168–169)

Table 4.14 *Potential advantages of translanguaging*

It may promote deeper and fuller understanding of the subject matter.
It may help students develop oral communication and literacy in their weaker language.
The dual use of languages can facilitate home–school cooperation.
It may support the integration of speakers with different degrees of fluency.

Source: Baker (2011: 289–290).

The concept of translanguaging has been extended beyond the specific pedagogical practices of alternating the languages used for input and output (García, 2009; García & Li Wei, 2014). In this way translanguaging refers to spontaneous practices in communication. It is 'the process by which bilingual students and teachers engage in complex discursive practices in order to "make sense" of, and communicate in, multilingual classrooms' (García & Sylvan, 2011: 389). An important difference between the original concept of translanguaging developed in Wales and the extended use of spontaneous translanguaging is the following: '... translanguaging for me is an approach to bilingualism that is centered not on languages, but on the observable communicative practices of bilinguals' (García, 2011: 147). According to this view, translanguaging is different from code-switching because the concept of code-switching assumes that separate languages exist.

> The notion of code switching, understood by most informed scholars in a dynamic and creative fashion as the expressive transgression by bilingual speakers of their two separate languages. (Otheguy *et al.*, 2015: 282)

According to this view, languages are not linguistic objects because they are socially constructed (see also Makoni & Pennycook, 2007) and translanguaging is:

> the deployment of a speaker's full linguistic repertoire without regard for watchful adherence to the socially and politically defined boundaries of named (and usually national and state) languages. (Otheguy *et al.*, 2015: 283)

This view of translanguaging has important consequences not only in education because educators should recognize and value multiple repertoires and contribute to the legitimization of discursive practices that include elements from the whole linguistic repertoire.

Translanguaging has also been studied as related to identity. Creese and Blackledge (2015: 21) consider that language does not necessarily equal identity. They analyze the relationship between translanguaging and identity in complementary schools in the UK. These schools teach heritage language and culture in languages such as Bengali, Chinese or Gujarati and are run by the language communities outside the official school hours. Creese and Blackledge (2015: 33) discuss how the study of translanguaging can be useful for studying the complex identities of the students because identities are performed 'through the deployment of certain linguistic resources in certain ways'.

Multilingual pedagogical practices

The influence of multilingual views that consider the resources multilingual speakers have in their whole linguistic repertoire imply different teaching strategies and activities in the language classroom. Not all scholars use the term translanguaging for these practices and, as Shohamy (2011: 419) points out, 'There are clearly multiple ways of moving within a multilingual continuum'. However, if translanguaging is understood in its original meaning as developed in the context of Welsh-English bilingual education, other multilingual pedagogies can also be understood as an extension of the alternation of input-output pedagogy.

Table 4.15 *Characteristics of strategies*

Strategic integration into literacy instruction.
Purposeful planning and explicit teaching.
Explicit guidance to promote higher order thinking.
Focus on group and collaborative projects.
Bidirectional (Spanish to English and English to Spanish).

Source: See Escamilla *et al.* (2013: 69).

Cummins (2007) criticizes monolingual assumptions and proposes pedagogical strategies such as translation, focusing on cognates or the creation of dual-language multimedia books and projects (see also Cummins, 2017). Similar strategies have been proposed by Escamilla *et al.* (2013) in the context of English-Spanish bilingual education in the United States. The characteristics of these strategies to develop cross-language connections can be seen in Table 4.15.

Lyster *et al.* (2013) reported a pedagogical intervention to develop metalinguistic awareness in morphology by focusing on English and French in Canada. The results of the intervention indicate that this approach can have a positive effect on morphological awareness.

Arteagoitia and Howard (2015) reported positive results for Spanish speaking students when activating their knowledge of cognates. In this study, 230 middle school students in the United States improved their vocabulary and reading comprehension in English after a pedagogical intervention based on Spanish-English cognates.

The Landako project on translanguaging in a trilingual school in the Basque Country is carrying out a pedagogical intervention based on focus on multilingualism (Cenoz & Gorter, 2011), which emphasizes the development of language awareness and metalinguistic awareness. It focuses on cognates, morphological awareness and writing skills across three languages – Basque, Spanish and English – and also uses the alternation of input and output as in translanguaging in Wales. The project is still in its first stages but the feedback from students and teachers is very positive.

An important aspect to be developed when multilingual pedagogies are implemented is a multilingual focus in evaluation. Shohamy (2011) considers that language testing is lagging behind the development of multilingual teaching:

> Although dynamic, diverse, and constructive discussions of multilingual teaching and learning are currently taking place within language education field, the phenomenon is completely overlooked in the assessment field that continues to view language as a monolingual, homogenous and often still native like construct. There seems to be lack of coordination between the two disciplines of teaching and testing. (Shohamy, 2011: 419)

Shohamy (2011: 247) proposes some ideas for language testing such as multilingual tasks that allow test takers to mix languages ('What is viewed in monolingual tests and criteria as interference is viewed here as a more effective way to transmit language'), or tests in which the questions are given in two languages in order to allow for full comprehension.

Another important contribution in multilingual assessment is the development of a bilingual rubric to evaluate writing skills. Escamilla *et al.* (2013) propose assessing Spanish and English writing using the same rubric. The rubric has two parts, one quantitative and one qualitative. The quantitative part offers the possibility of giving scores for both languages for content, structural elements and spelling. The qualitative part offers the possibility of evaluating bilingual strategies that can be associated with learning two languages at the discourse, sentence, word and phonics level. The rubric also contains language-specific approximations that are not necessarily linked to the simultaneous development of the two languages.

Conclusions

In sum, multilingual education is spreading in different parts of the world because of globalization, the spread of English, the revitalization of minority languages and the mobility of the population. School classes in many parts of the world accommodate students who speak different home languages and have multilingualism among their educational goals. However, there is often a mismatch between the home languages and the languages in the curriculum. Multilingual education can be aimed at minority and majority language students. Both types have some specific characteristics but also common elements that can be shared.

Nowadays there is a trend to integrate content and language in CBI/CLIL programmes as an efficient way to learn a second or additional language at the same time as academic content. There is also a need for integration of all the languages multilingual speakers or emergent multilinguals have in their whole linguistic repertoire. This integration can provide learners with more resources based on their own use of languages and can bring together multilingual discursive practices and school pedagogies.

Questions for Students' Reflection

1. Find somebody who speaks a minority language. Did they learn it at home or at school? Did they learn how to read and write in the minority language? Do they use the minority language now?

2. Compare two schools you know by using the continua of multilingual education model in order to see how multilingual they are. Are there differences at the linguistic, sociolinguistic or educational levels?

3. Which are the main advantages and disadvantages of using the whole linguistic repertoire for teaching and learning languages as proposed by focus on multilingualism? Can it be done in all contexts?

> 4. Translanguaging can be understood in different ways. How has the original pedagogical concept of translanguaging extended in recent years? Can you give some examples of translanguaging from your own experience?

Suggestions for Further Reading

Cenoz, J. and Gorter, D. (eds) (2015) *Multilingual Education: Between Language Learning and Translanguaging*. Cambridge: Cambridge University Press.

Cenoz, J. and Gorter, D. (2011) Focus on multilingualism: A study of trilingual writing. *The Modern Language Journal* 95, 356–369; doi:10.1111/j.1540-4781.2011.01206.x.

García, O. and Li Wei (2014) *Translanguaging: Language, Bilingualism and Education*. Basingstoke: Palgrave Macmillan.

Gorter, D., Zenotz, V. and Cenoz, J. (eds) (2014) *Minority Languages and Multilingual Education*. Berlin: Springer.

Lin, A.M.Y. (2015) Conceptualising the potential role of L1 in CLIL. *Language, Culture and Curriculum* 28 (1), 74–89; doi:10.1080/07908318.2014.1000926.

References

Areny, M., Mayans, P. and Forniès, D. (2013) *The Catalan Language in Education in Spain*. Ljouwert and Leeuwarden: Mercator European Research Centre on Multilingualism and Language Learning. See https://www.mercator-research.eu/fileadmin/mercator/documents/regional_dossiers/catalan_in_spain_2nd.pdf.

Arteagoitia, I. and Howard, E.R. (2015) The role of the native language in the literacy development of Latino students in the U.S. In J. Cenoz and D. Gorter (eds) *Multilingual Education: Between Language Learning and Translanguaging* (pp. 89–115). Cambridge: Cambridge University Press.

Baker, C. (2011) *Foundations of Bilingual Education and Bilingualism* (5th edn). Bristol: Multilingual Matters.

Basque Government (2012) *Fifth Sociolinguistic Survey: Basque Autonomous Community, Navarre and Iparralde*. Donostia-San Sebastián: Basque Government, Ministry of Culture. See http://www.euskara.euskadi.net/r59-738/en/contenidos/informacion/sociolinguistic_research2011/en_2011/2011.html.

Benton, R.A. (2015) Perfecting the partnership: Revitalizing the Maori language in New Zealand education and society 1987–2014. *Language, Culture and Curriculum* 28 (2), 99–112.

Beres, A. (2015) An overview of translanguaging: 20 years of 'giving voice to those who do not speak'. *Translation and Translanguaging in Multilingual Contexts* 1 (1), 103–118; doi:10.1075/ttmc.1.1.05ber.

Björklund, S., Mård-Miettinen, K. and Savijärvi, M. (2014) Swedish immersion in the early years in Finland. *International Journal of Bilingual Education and Bilingualism* 17 (2), 197–214; doi:10.1080/13670050.2013.866628.

Blackledge, A. and Creese, A. (2010) *Multilingualism: A Critical Perspective*. London: Continuum.

Brinton, D., Snow, M.A. and Wesche, M. (1989) *Content-based Second Language Instruction*. New York: Newbury House.

Canagarajah, S. (2013) *Translingual Practice: Global Englishes and Cosmopolitan Relations*. Abingdon: Routledge.

Cenoz, J. (2008) Achievements and challenges in bilingual and multilingual education in the Basque Country. *AILA Review* 21, 13–30.

Cenoz, J. (2009) *Towards Multilingual Education: Basque Educational Research from an International Perspective*. Bristol: Multilingual Matters.

Cenoz, J. (2013) The influence of bilingualism on third language acquisition: Focus on multilingualism. *Language Teaching* 46, 71–86; doi:10.1017/S0261444811000218.

Cenoz, J. (2015) Content-based instruction and content and language integrated learning: The same or different? *Language, Culture and Curriculum* 28, 1–24.

Cenoz, J., Genesee, F. and Gorter, D. (2013) Critical analysis of CLIL: Taking stock and looking forward. *Applied Linguistics* 35 (3), 243–262; doi:10.1093/applin/amt011.

Cenoz, J. and Gorter, D. (2005) Trilingualism and minority languages in Europe. *International Journal of the Sociology of Language* 171, 1–5.

Cenoz, J. and Gorter, D. (eds) (2008) Multilingualism and minority languages: Achievements and challenges in education. *AILA Review* 21 (special issue).

Cenoz, J. and Gorter, D. (2011) Focus on multilingualism: A study of trilingual writing. *The Modern Language Journal* 95, 356–369; doi:10.1111/j.1540-4781.2011.01206.x.

Cenoz, J. and Gorter, D. (2013) Towards a plurilingual approach in English language teaching: Softening the boundaries between languages. *TESOL Quarterly* 47 (3), 591–599; doi:10.1002/tesq.121.

Cenoz, J. and Gorter, D. (2015) Introduction: Theory and practice of multilingual education. In J. Cenoz and D. Gorter (eds) *Multilingual Education: Between Language Learning and translanguaging*. Cambridge: Cambridge University Press.

Cenoz, J. and Gorter, D. (2017) Minority languages and sustainable translanguaging: Threat or opportunity? *Journal of Multilingual and Multicultural Development* 38 (10), 901–912; doi.org/10.1080/01434632.2017.1284855.

Cenoz, J. and Jessner, U. (2009) The study of multilingualism in educational contexts. In L. Aronin and B. Hufeisen (eds) *The Exploration of Multilingualism* (pp. 119–135). Amsterdam: John Benjamins.

Collectivité de Corse (2013) *Direzzione di a Lingua Corsa*. Ajaccio: Inchiesta sociolinguistica lingua corsa. See http://www.corse.fr/linguacorsa/Inchiesta-sociolinguistica-nant-a-a-lingua-corsa_a123.html.

Cook, V. (1992) Evidence for multi-competence. *Language Learning* 42, 557–591.

Council of Europe (1998) *European Charter for Regional or Minority Languages*. ETS 148. Strasbourg: Council of Europe. See http://www.coe.int/t/dg4/education/minlang/.

Coyle, D. (2007) Towards a connected research agenda for CLIL pedagogies. *International Journal of Bilingual Education and Bilingualism* 10, 543–562.

Creese, A. and Blackledge, A. (2015) Translanguaging and identity in educational settings. *Annual Review of Applied Linguistics* 25, 20–35.

Cummins, J. (2005) A proposal for action: Strategies for recognizing heritage language competence as a learning resource within the mainstream classroom. *The Modern Language Journal* 89, 585–592.

Cummins, J. (2007) Rethinking monolingual instructional strategies in multilingual classrooms. *Canadian Journal of Applied Linguistics* 10, 221–240.

Cummins, J. (2017) Teaching for transfer in multilingual school contexts. In O. García, A. Lin and S. May (eds) *Bilingual and Multilingual Education* (pp. 103–115). Encyclopedia of Language and Education Series. Berlin: Springer; doi:10.1007/978-3-319-02258-1_8.

De Angelis, G. and Dewaele, J.M. (eds) (2011) *New Trends in Crosslinguistic Influence and Multilingualism Research*. Bristol: Multilingual Matters.

De Mejia, A.M. (2013) Elite/folk bilingual education. In *The Encyclopedia of Applied Linguistics*. London: Blackwell; doi:10.1002/9781405198431.wbeal0361.

Escamilla, K., Hopewell, S., Butvilofsky, S., Sparrow, W., Soltero-González, L., Ruiz-Figueroa, O. and Escamilla, M. (2013) *Biliteracy from the Start: Literacy Squared in Action*. Philadelphia, PA: Caslon.

Extra, G. and Gorter, D. (2007) Regional and immigrant languages in Europe. In M. Hellinger and A. Pauwels (eds) *Language and Communication: Diversity and Change*. Handbooks of Applied Linguistics, Vol. 9 (pp. 15–52). Berlin: Mouton de Gruyter.

Fishman, J. (1991) *Reversing Language Shift*. Clevedon: Multilingual Matters.

Fishman, J. (ed.) (2001) *Can Threatened Languages be Saved? Reversing Language Shift, Revisited: A 21st Century Perspective*. Clevedon: Multilingual Matters.

Fusina, J. and Arrighi, J.M. (2012) *The Corsican Language in France*. Ljouwert and Leeuwarden: Mercator European Research Centre on Multilingualism and Language Learning.

García, O. (2009) *Bilingual Education in the 21st Century*. Oxford: Wiley-Blackwell.

García, O. and Li Wei (2014) *Translanguaging: Language, Bilingualism and Education*. Basingstoke: Palgrave Macmillan.

García, O. and Sylvan, C.E. (2011) Pedagogies and practices in multilingual classrooms: Singularities in pluralities. *The Modern Language Journal* 95 (3), 385–400.

Genesee, F. and Lindholm-Leary, K. (2013) Two case studies of content-based language education. *Journal of Immersion and Content-based Education* 1, 3–33; doi:10.1075/jicb.1.1.02gen.

Gorter, D. (2001) A Frisian update of reversing language shift. In J.A. Fishman (ed.) *Can Threatened Languages be Saved? Reversing Language Shift: A 21st Century Perspective* (pp. 215–233). Clevedon: Multilingual Matters.

Gorter, D. (2005) Three languages of instruction in Fryslân. *International Journal of the Sociology of Language* 171, 57–73.

Gorter, D., Zenotz, V. and Cenoz, J. (eds) (2014a) *Minority Languages and Multilingual Education*. Berlin: Springer.

Gorter, D., Zenotz, V., Etxague, X. and Cenoz, J. (2014b) Multilingualism and European minority languages: The case of Basque. In D. Gorter, V. Zenotz and J. Cenoz (eds) *Minority Languages and Multilingual Education: Bridging the Local and the Global* (pp. 278–301). Berlin: Springer.

Grosjean, F. (1985) The bilingual as a competent but specific speaker-hearer. *Journal of Multilingual and Multicultural Development* 6, 467–477.

Grosjean, F. (2008) *Studying Bilinguals*. Oxford: Oxford University Press.

Heller, M. (1999) *Linguistic Minorities and Modernity: A Sociolinguistic Ethnography*. London: Longman.

Hélot, C. and Ó Laoire, M. (2011) Introduction: From language education policy to a pedagogy of the possible. In C. Hélot and M. Ó Laoire (eds) *Language Policy for the Multilingual Classroom* (pp. xi–xxiii). Bristol: Multilingual Matters.

Heugh, K. (2013) Multilingual education policy in South Africa constrained by theoretical and historical disconnections. *Annual Review of Applied Linguistics* 33, 215–237.

Hill, R. and May, S. (2014) Balancing the languages in Māori-medium education in Aotearoa/New Zealand. In D. Gorter, V. Zenotz and J. Cenoz (eds) *Minority Languages and Multilingual Education* (pp. 159–176). Berlin: Springer.

Jarvis, S. and Pavlenko, A. (2008) *Crosslinguistic Influence in Language and Cognition*. New York: Routledge.

Jones, B. and Lewis, G. (2014) Language arrangements within bilingual education. In E.M. Thomas and I. Mennen (eds) *Advances in the Study of Bilingualism*. Bristol: Multilingual Matters.

Kamanga, C.M.M. (2009) The joys and pitfalls of multiple language acquisition. The workings of the mind of a simultaneous multilingual. In E. Todeva and J. Cenoz. (eds) *The Multiple Realities of Multilingualism* (pp. 115–134). Berlin: Mouton de Gruyter.

Kramsch, C. (2009) *The Multilingual Subject*. Oxford: Oxford University Press.

Kramsch, C. and Huffmaster, M. (2015) 'Multilingual practices in foreign language study'. In J. Cenoz and D. Gorter (eds) *Multilingual Education Between Language Learning and Translanguaging* (pp. 114–136). Cambridge: Cambridge University Press.

Lambert, W.E. (1974) Culture and language as factors in learning and education. In F.E. Abour and R.D. Meade (eds) *Cultural Factors in Learning and Education* (pp. 91–122). Bellingham, WA: 5th Western Washington Symposium on Learning.

Lewis, G., Jones, B. and Baker, C. (2012a) Translanguaging: Origins and development from school to street and beyond. *Educational Research and Evaluation: An International Journal on Theory and Practice* 18 (7), 641–654; doi:10.1080/13803611.2012.718488.

Lewis, G., Jones, B. and Baker, C. (2012b) Translanguaging: Developing its conceptualisation and contextualization. *Educational Research and Evaluation: An International Journal on Theory and Practice* 18 (7), 655–670; doi:10.1080/13803611.2012.718490.

Lin, A.M.Y. (2015) Conceptualising the potential role of L1 in CLIL. *Language, Culture and Curriculum* 28 (1), 74–89; doi:10.1080/07908318.2014.1000926.

Li Wei (2011) Multilinguality, multimodality, and multicompetence: Code- and modeswitching by minority ethnic children in complementary schools. *The Modern Language Journal* 95, 370–384.

Lorenzo, F., Casal, S. and Moore, P. (2010) The effects of content and language integrated learning in European education: Key findings from the Andalusian bilingual sections evaluation project. *Applied Linguistics* 31, 418–442.

Lyster, R., Quiroga, J. and Ballinger, S. (2013) The effects of biliteracy instruction on morphological awareness. *Journal of Immersion and Content-Based Language Education* 1, 169–197; doi:10.1075/jicb.1.2.02lys.

Macaro, E. (2009) Teacher use of code-switching in the second language classroom: Exploring 'optimal' use. In M. Turnbull and J. Dailey-O'Cain (eds) *First Language Use in Second and Foreign Language Learning* (pp. 35–49). Bristol: Multilingual Matters.

Makoni, S. and Pennycook, A. (2007) Disinventing and reconstituting languages. In S. Makoni and A. Pennycook (eds) *Disinventing and Reconstituting Languages* (pp. 1–41). Clevedon: Multilingual Matters.

May, S. (2000) Uncommon languages: The challenges and possibilities of minority language rights. *Journal of Multilingual and Multicultural Development* 21 (5), 366–385.

May, S. (2008) Bilingual/immersion education: What the research tells us. In J. Cummins and N.H. Hornberger (ed.) *Bilingual Education* (2nd edn) (pp. 19–34). Encyclopedia of Language and Education series. Berlin: Springer.

McMillan, B. and Turnbull, M. (2009) Teachers' use of the first language in French immersion: Revisiting a core principle. In M. Turnbull and J. Dailey-O'Cain (eds) *First Language Use in Second and Foreign Language Learning* (pp. 15–34). Bristol: Multilingual Matters.

Met, M. (1998) Curriculum decision-making in content-based language teaching. In J. Cenoz and F. Genesee (eds) *Beyond Bilingualism: Multilingualism and Multilingual Education* (pp. 35–63). Clevedon: Multilingual Matters.

Moseley, C. (ed.) (2010) *UNESCO Atlas of the World's Languages in Danger* (3rd edn). Paris: UNESCO. See www.unesco.org/culture/languages-atlas/en/atlasmap.html.

Musk, N. (2010) Code-switching and code-mixing in Welsh bilinguals' talk: Confirming or refuting the maintenance of language boundaries? *Language, Culture and Curriculum* 23 (3), 179–197; doi:10.1080/07908318.2010.515993.

Otheguy, R., García, O. and Reid, W. (2015) Clarifying translanguaging and deconstructing named languages: A perspective from linguistics. *Applied Linguistics Review* 6 (3), 281–307.

Shohamy, E. (2006) *Language Policy: Hidden Agendas and New Approaches*. Abingdon: Routledge.

Shohamy, E. (2011) Assessing multilingual competencies: Adopting construct valid assessment policies. *The Modern Language Journal* 95 (3), 418–429.

Spolsky, B. (2009) *Language Management*. Cambridge: Cambridge University Press.

Swain, M. and Johnson, R.K. (1997) Immersion education: A category within bilingual education. In R.K. Johnson and M. Swain (eds) *Immersion Education: International Perspectives* (pp. 1–16). Cambridge: Cambridge University Press.

Swain, M. and Lapkin, S. (2005) The evolving sociopolitical context of immersion education in Canada: Some implications for program development. *International Journal of Applied Linguistics* 169, 169–186; doi:10.1111/j.1473-4192.2005.00086.x.

Tedick, D.J. and Wesely, P.M. (2015) A review of research on content based foreign/second language education in US K-12 contexts. *Language, Culture and Curriculum* 28 (1), 25–40; doi:10.1080/0790 8318.2014.1000923.

Tedick, D.J., Christian, D. and Fortune, T.W. (2011) The future of immersion education: An invitation to 'dwell in possibility'. In D.J. Tedick, D. Christian and T.W. Fortune (eds) *Immersion Education: Practices, Policies, Possibilities*. Bristol: Multilingual Matters.

Todeva, E. (2009) Multilingualism as a kaleidoscopic experience: The mini universes within. In E. Todeva and J. Cenoz (eds) *The Multiple Realities of Multilingualism* (pp. 53–74). Berlin: Mouton de Gruyter.

Walter, S. and Benson, C. (2012) Language policy and medium of instruction in formal education. In B. Spolsky (ed.) *The Cambridge Handbook of Language Policy* (pp. 278–300). Cambridge: Cambridge University Press.

Welsh Government (2015) *Statistics on Welsh Language Use in Wales 2013–2015*. Cardiff: Welsh Government and Welsh Language Commissioner. See https://www.statisticsauthority.gov.uk/wp-content/uploads/2016/02/Assessment-Report-321-Statistics-on-Welsh-Language-Use-in-Wales.pdf.

Williams, C. (2002) *Extending Bilingualism in the Education System. Education and Lifelong Learning Committee Report*. Cardiff: National Assembly for Wales. See http://www.assemblywales.org/3C91C7AF00023D820000595000000000.pdf.

Part 2

Aspects of Individual Multilingualism

Lecture 5

Multilingual Individuals[1]

John Edwards

Introduction

Multilingualism is a psychological, social and cultural phenomenon that has always been important. The political dynamics of regions whose populations are linguistically heterogeneous are necessarily and obviously different from those where most inhabitants speak the same language – and this applies to polities both great and small, to countries and to empires. Less democratic states may of course pay less attention to the internal mosaics of ethnicities, cultures and languages, but even totalitarian regimes must give at least some attention to them, if only for manipulative and essentially Machiavellian reasons.

Where languages are in question, tolerance on the part of government has historically played an important part in maintaining popular acquiescence. Such tolerance need owe nothing, however, to favourable official perspectives on ethnolinguistic diversity; on the contrary, it usually reflects a lack of concern. In the empires of the Romans, the Ottomans, the Habsburgs and the British, few in power cared what languages the toiling classes spoke. Why would they? So long as peace was preserved and taxes were paid, why should the court elites worry about the languages used by their subjects? And, from their lowly position, what would the peasants know or care about the languages of their masters? Gellner (1983: 127) points out that, in the replacement of one ruler by another, any language alteration – whether, for example, 'the new Pasha [spoke] Arabic, Turkish, Persian, French or English' – was generally of very little import indeed.

The matter of religion was generally more important than language – hence the idea of *cuius regio, eius religio* (the religion of the ruler is the religion of his subjects) – much more important, given the greater divisive potential of religious differences. Sometimes, of course, religion and language have marched together. In 19th century Russia, 'polonization' in Lithuania was associated with Catholicism, a threat to the official Orthodox Church. At about the same time, anti-French sentiment in Flanders had a strongly religious tone and, for some ultramontane Catholics, language activism was but an aspect of larger religious motivations.

Benign linguistic neglect is a perfectly understandable official stance in many settings. If, however, the patriotism of citizens comes into question, then attempts to encourage it via official practice or legislation may very well have a linguistic component. A focus on language here is generally underpinned by concerns about ethnic heterogeneity, and is particularly noticeable when new political arrangements have come into force. In revolutionary France, for example, fewer than half the inhabitants of the country were actually French speaking, and many regional varieties were seen by the new political masters as buoys marking dangerous reefs. Abbé Grégoire, the head of the French Education Commission, surveyed the situation in 1790: he found that French was essentially the language of the elite, coexisting with *'trente patois différents'* – varieties that ought to be eliminated in the interests of national unity. Little wonder, then, that in July 1794 all languages other than French were proscribed.

Macro-level considerations of multilingualism can and should prompt more fine-grained enquiry. After all, whether we consider historical and contemporary language policies enacted or supported by authority, or the great – and, indeed, often significantly greater – importance of unofficial pressures and postures, we almost immediately reflect upon the quotidian practices, desires and abilities of those whose presence has occasioned linguistic rule and routine.

What is Multilingualism?

Multilingualism is obviously a widespread global phenomenon, and statistically much more common than monolingualism. Its emergence is easily understood, and one or two causal factors predominate. There is, first of all, the simple movement of people. Immigrants to a new country bring their languages into contact with each other and with those of existing populations. Territorial expansion is another type of migration, with similar results. Sometimes, as with imperialist and colonial expansion, it is not necessary for large numbers of people to physically move; they may 'move' their language into contact with others through military and economic pressures which require but a handful of soldiers, merchants and bureaucrats. Thus, a few thousand people ruling the Indian subcontinent brought about a massively expanded base for English among a population that now is well over 1 billion; it is estimated that about 1 in 10 Indians have some level of English fluency, for most of whom it is a second or subsequent language. Confederations of different language communities also give rise to both personal and societal multilingualism: the German, French, Italian and Romansch speakers in Switzerland are a good example here; so, to a lesser extent, are the French and Flemish in Belgium. Other political arrangements conducive to multilingualism are countries arising from more arbitrary or involuntary amalgamations. These often result from colonial boundary marking and country creation; modern examples are found in Africa, Asia and the Middle East. Border areas often stimulate multilingualism, too. Beyond these macro-level underpinnings of multilingualism, more fine-grained cultural and educational motivations have always served to expand language repertoires – whether or not (as we shall see) a desire or possibility exists for ordinary conversational use.

Stavans and Hoffmann (2015: 137) pose the question: 'multilingual individuals – who are they?' The obvious 'frame of analysis', as they point out, is simply the social multiplicity of languages and cultures, some forms of which I have just described. At the individual level, they differentiate 'natural' multilinguals – those whose fluencies arise more or less informally – from those whose expanded repertoire is a function of education. This then leads them to a little typology of multilingual speakers, using the criteria of 'age and sociocultural context of acquisition and use' (Stavans & Hoffmann, 2015: 141). There are, of course, a great many variations possible, especially when one folds in the host of other factors that figure in multilingualism: degrees of competence, areas of use, status of the several languages, linguistic attitudes and beliefs, and so on.

Generally speaking, earlier views of multilingualism saw it as necessarily underpinned by some rough equivalence or balance among the varieties in question; later ones have allowed much greater variations in competence. Developments here have been driven by increasingly nuanced awareness of the different dimensions of competence that can be reasonably borne in mind. Consider, first, that there are four basic language skills: listening, speaking, reading and writing. Consider further the possible subdivisions: speaking skill, for example, includes what may be quite divergent levels of expression in vocabulary, grammar and accent. There is thus a substantial number of elements which figure in the assessment of multilingualism, and it rarely follows that strength in one is necessarily mirrored by strength in another. Rough assessments of relative proficiency are almost always possible – and, as we shall see, extremes of ability are easily visible (or audible) – but subtle differences may prove troublesome if (as part of scholarly enquiry, for instance) we want to compare individuals or groups, or if we wish to study the relationship between multilingualism and other personality traits. (Intelligence is one of the most studied features here, something to which we shall shortly turn.)

At a very simplistic level, we might say that everyone is multilingual. That is, there is no-one in the world (no adult, anyway) who does not know at least a few words in languages other than the maternal variety. If, as an English speaker, you can say *c'est la vie* or *gracias* or *guten Tag* or *tovarisch* – or even if you only understand them – you clearly have some 'command' of a foreign tongue. Such a minimum capability, of course, will not suggest multilingual ability to many readers. If, on the other hand, you are like George Steiner, who claims equal fluency in English, French and German, and who further claims that, after rigorous self-examination – of which language emerges spontaneously in times of emergency or elevated emotion, which variety is dreamt in, which is associated with the earliest memories – no one of the three seems dominant, then multilingualism does seem a rather more apt designation (see Steiner, 1992). The point here, of course, has to do with the *degree* of competence – or, more accurately, the degrees of varying facets of linguistic competence – necessary to underpin a meaningful designation of 'multilingual'. Even at this juncture, readers will probably understand that no firm answers, no general metrics, are likely to be found. One of the recurring approaches in the literature, however, has centred on the assessment of relative 'balance' – but even here, it is easy to see the difficulty in giving the multilingual accolade to someone who is 'perfect' in French, German and English, while withholding it from another whose fluencies are well developed but less symmetrical. (These three languages are cited, incidentally, because they are Steiner's, and because he has made the interesting observation that his sort of 'primary multilingualism' may reflect an 'integral state of affairs' quite unlike the multilingualism that has emerged over time from monolingual beginnings.)

There has been virtually no research on the consequences for identity (see below) of multilingual tapestries so closely woven as Steiner's seem to be, but one imagines that there are subtleties here that go far beyond simple additive relationships. As noted, it is notoriously difficult to define and assess multilingualism, and perhaps rigorous examination would reveal important imbalances even in polyglots like Steiner. Nonetheless, more attention to deep-seated multiple fluencies is surely indicated. Of course, the Steiners of the world (and the Conrads, Nabokovs, Kunderas, Stoppards, and all the rest) have the literary and intellectual power to reflect in meaningful ways upon their fluencies. Steiner (1992) has written famously about the 'extraterritoriality' of multilingual writers; Ilan Stavans argues that monolingualism is a form of oppression (see Kellman, 2000); others, from Goethe to Eliot, have argued over the ability – particularly the poet's ability – to be fully expressive beyond the *muttersprache*. It would be good to have reports from more mundane multilingual quarters, too.

There seems little doubt that, beyond some fairly low threshold, the development of multilingual abilities may have consequences for one's sense of psychological and social identity. Furthermore, it is entirely plausible that any changes will increase as language fluencies deepen and widen. A rough-and-ready distinction has been drawn between those whose linguistic expansions are instrumental in nature and those who see them as part of more integrative moves towards another cultural community. While perceived necessity probably underpins both postures, and while they rarely exist in some static or compartmentalized parallelism, it is easy to see that involvement in a broad language-and-culture nexus is more necessary and/or more attractive to some than to others. This in turn implies more of those identity consequences just noted. At one level, these might reveal themselves in a Whorfianism of the 'weaker' sort – an expanded linguistic patterning of thoughts, attitudes and habits.

At a deeper psychological level, much of interest rests on the degree to which multilinguals possess either several (theoretically) separately identifiable systems of language – from each of which they can draw, as circumstances warrant – or some sort of language 'pool' to which the different varieties contribute, according to their relative degrees of development and fluency. As Hamers and Blanc (2000) point out, we are far from having compelling empirical data here. It is hardly surprising, then, that when we consider the possible effects of multilingual competences on personality traits, the findings are sparse, the limitations great and the conclusions insubstantial. It is interesting that, in their massive study of bilingualism, Baker and Jones (1998) give only six pages (out of more than 750) to a section on personality.

There are of course long-held popular (and, sometimes, academic) perceptions that multilinguals must have some sort of 'split' personality: two or more individuals in one, as it were; a recent investigation is that of Dewaele and Nakano (2013); see also Ramírez-Esparza *et al.* (2006) and, for an excellent overview of multilingualism generally, and the personal characteristics of multilinguals specifically, Aronin and Singleton (2012). Grosjean (1982, 2010) and others have noted that bilinguals, at least, sometimes report that their language choices draw out, and draw upon, different personalities. But, as Baker and Jones (1998) and Hamers and Blanc (2000) note, the evidence here is anecdotal at best. Indeed, we could go a little further and point to the large logical and rational difficulties which some several-in-one arrangement would create. On the other hand, there is some evidence that language choice may implicate different *aspects* of personality: informants are liable to give slightly different pictures of themselves, depending on the language used in interviews and on questionnaires. They may make different responses to objective or projective probes, responses may be more emotional through one variety (typically, but not inevitably, their maternal language), they may more strongly affirm their sense of ethnic identity in one language than in another, and so on (see, for example, studies by Ervin, Guttfreund, Bond and others, usefully summarized in Hamers & Blanc, 2000). The fact that different social settings and variations in language-affect linkages lead to different patterns of self-presentation clearly does not imply separate personalities, although it does suggest an enhanced repertoire of possibility.

It is interesting and important to consider the significance of multilingual fluencies that may link an individual to more than one linguistic, cultural or ethnic community. Could a sense of 'multiple belonging' undergird those feelings of 'multiple personality' noted above – feelings that are at once inaccurate *sensu stricto*, but often compelling? Is the allegedly enlarged language-personality-allegiance nexus the assumed origin of the expanded acuity and awareness that some have claimed for bilingual and multilingual individuals? The short answers to these sorts of questions are all positive, or potentially positive, in a world where complicated patterns of social relations are made more intricate still by a very wide range of linguistic capabilities. Of course, a great deal of multilingualism has very little emotional significance: the purely instrumental fluencies needed to conduct simple business transactions do not, after all, represent much of an excursion from one's original base camp. This is probably a rather larger category than is often thought: even substantial linguistic breadth need not in itself imply emotional or psychological depth – it may simply reflect the exigencies of a complicated public life.

What seems to be the most important underpinning of multilingualism – of language *use*, of course, but also of at least the more formal contexts of language acquisition – has to do with real or perceived *need*. This is the thread that runs all the way from the multilingual agora to the academic study. In almost all cases, then, multilingualism is a practical affair; few people become or remain multilingual on a whim. (There have always been those, of course, who delight in language learning for its own sake, and we shall meet some of them shortly.) A generally observed corollary is that individual abilities in two, three or more languages will not be equal. Indeed, we can predict that they will extend more or less as far as circumstances demand – anything else would be uneconomical. In the literature on formal language learning, much is often made of the importance of favourable motivation but, beyond the classroom, necessity is the great motivator, a force that can ride roughshod over personal attitudes and inclinations. Most historical changes in personal and group language use owe much more to immediate exigencies than they do to attitude. The adoption of English by the broad Irish population, for example, was not accompanied by favourable attitudes, although there was a rather grudging acknowledgment of instrumental pressures. Motivations in such 'real-life' settings are quite unlike those that operate at school – although they often produce deeper and more permanent expansions of language capabilities.

Multilingual Competence

Here is a self-description of James Murray, the first editor of the *Oxford English Dictionary*, found in his grand-daughter's delightful biography (Murray, 1977). It is part of his letter of application for a position with the Keeper of Printed Books at the British Library – a post he did not get, incidentally:

> I possess a general acquaintance with the languages and
> literature of the Aryan and Syro-Arabic classes ... with several
> [languages] I have a more intimate acquaintance as with
> the Romance tongues, Italian, French, Catalan, Spanish, Latin
> and in a less degree Portuguese, Vaudois, Provençal and
> various dialects. In the Teutonic branch I am tolerably
> familiar with Dutch ... Flemish, German, Danish.
> In Anglo-Saxon and Moeso-Gothic my studies have been
> much closer ... I know a little of the Celtic, and am at
> present engaged with the Sclavonic [sic], having
> obtained a useful knowledge of Russian. In the Persian,
> Achaemenian Cuneiform and Sanscrit [sic] branches,
> I know for the purposes of Comparative Philology.
> I have sufficient knowledge of Hebrew and Syriac to read
> at sight the O.T. ... to a less degree I know Aramaic Arabic,
> Coptic and Phenician [sic]. (Murray, 1977: 70)

And here is a linguistic description of Paulin Djité, a friend and colleague of mine:

> [He] grew up in Côte d'Ivoire speaking French and Wè at home, and
> Yoruba, Baoulé and Dyula with playmates and others. His education
> was through French, English and Spanish. As an adolescent,
> he added Attié, Gouro, Koulango, Dida and Bété to his
> linguistic repertoire, along with a more passive knowledge
> of Ewe and other varieties. (Edwards, 2012: 32)

These vignettes reveal various points along the multilingual spectrum: in fact, monolinguals (and most bilinguals) would see them as revealing quite formidable capabilities. Members of powerful or dominant communities will often complain about the tremendous difficulties involved in language learning. In the modern world, English and American monolinguals often seem to feel as if there exists some inherited lack of foreign language aptitude. This is sometimes accompanied by expressions of envy for those multilingual Africans, Asians and Europeans, and sometimes (more subtly) by a linguistic smugness reflecting a deeply held conviction that, after all, those clever 'others' who don't already know English will have to accommodate in a world made increasingly safe for Anglophones. All such attitudes, of course, reveal more about social dominance, convention – and, indeed, perceived necessity (or the lack of it) – than they do about aptitude.

The first vignette illustrates the wide range of language competence that is possible for an educated, intelligent and committed person with fairly specific requirements. It is certainly true that Murray had, from a young age, 'a sort of mania for learning languages; every new language was a new delight, no matter what it was, Hebrew or Tongan, Russian or Caffre' [Kaffir – now a derogatory term – by which Murray probably meant Xhosa] (Murray, 1977: 32). The variety here does indeed suggest an undisciplined passion, but his chief interests were always with 'grammar and structure ... [I] rarely did enough at the vocabulary' (Murray, 1977: 32). As a lexicographer, Murray had little or no need for oral fluency in many languages. His chief requirements were as follows: first, a reading knowledge of several languages; secondly, a broad acquaintance with the lexicons and grammars of many more varieties; thirdly, some comprehension of variant orthographies. Nonetheless, Murray's multilingualism was of a higher than usual nature – and notes on 'polyglossia' will be found below.

Regardless of how it may seem to monolinguals, the second vignette in fact highlights a rather 'ordinary' life – although Paulin Djité is a well-known contemporary scholar of language policy, planning and development. In this description we see an example of the wide competences of people who would probably not think of themselves as linguistically unusual or particularly talented. The portrayal here reveals a range of abilities which – while they may be somewhat greater in *degree* – are not different in basic principle from those possessed by the majority of people around the world.

Bilingual or multilingual competence has sometimes reflected and supported upper-class boundaries. In earlier times, not to have known Latin or Greek or French in addition to one's mother tongue would have been unthinkable for educated people – although perhaps 'unthinkable' in the same way that not having servants would have been. Such 'élite' capacities, however, are far removed from the mundane necessities fuelling the much more common – and often much more extensive – 'folk' varieties: humbler citizens have also been multilingual from earliest times. The fact that most global citizens possess at least some level of multilingual competence surely indicates that adding second and subsequent languages to one's repertoire is not a particularly remarkable feat – after all, many (probably the majority) of those citizens are poorly educated at best, and are not found in what most would consider the upper cultural and economic echelons of society. We know it was necessary under the Ptolemies to acquire Greek, even for quite minor posts, and Athenian slaves – representatives of the lowest class of all – were often bi- or multilingual as they were pressed into domestic service (Lewis, 1976).

In short, to be multilingual is not the aberration supposed by some whose fluencies are less well developed – particularly by those who speak only a 'big' language. It is in fact the global norm; as already implied, monolingualism is much less common than the sorts of expanded repertoires illustrated in the opening vignettes. The linguistic myopia that is so often a feature of monolingual perspectives is sometimes accompanied by a narrow cultural awareness and – if we move for a moment from the personal to the social level – can be seen to be reinforced by state policies which typically elevate only one language to official status. Thus, while there exist something like 5000 languages in about 200 countries, only a quarter of all states recognize more than one language. As well, even in those countries in which two or more varieties have legal status, one language is usually predominant, or has regional limitations, or carries with it disproportionate amounts of social, economic and political power. Switzerland, for example, with its recognition of German, French, Italian and Romansch, shows clear linguistic dominance for one variety at the canton level, and the four languages are not anything like equal in cross-community utility. Singapore also has four official languages – English, Mandarin, Tamil and Malay – but the latter two are much less important than the former pair. Ireland constitutionally recognizes both Irish and English, but the first has, increasingly, only symbolic significance in the general life of the country. And so on.

Equally, coming to terms with the extent and depth of multilingualism can be influenced by official policy, and this is particularly so in linguistically heterogeneous states. To stay with Singapore: all citizens there are placed in one of the four linguistic groupings noted earlier – which can result in 'mother tongues' being assigned. Even though Indians in Singapore may speak Malayalam or Gujerati (for example), the policy selects Tamil as 'their' language; similarly, although relatively few Chinese are Mandarin mother-tongue speakers (Hokkien, Teochew and Cantonese are the major variants), that variety is 'assigned' to them. In 1980 a case was reported of a civil servant who was ethnically Chinese but who had Malay as a mother tongue and English as a second language. Permission was refused for him to sit an examination in Malay because it was deemed 'only natural' that one should be competent in one's mother tongue – designated here, on Singaporean principles, as Mandarin (see Edwards, 1995). (Policy changes in 1990 mean that Indian Singaporeans are no longer 'assigned' Tamil; non-Mandarin speakers of Chinese 'dialects' seem not to have been given similar flexibility.)

A lecture on individual multilingualism is not the place to provide many details about the phenomena that widespread societal multilingualism necessitates. These include the use of lingua francas or 'link languages': the so-called 'languages of wider communication' (that is, varieties that have achieved regional or global dominance); restricted or limited linguistic forms whose diminished scope is at once easy to master and sufficient for communicative purposes (most notable here are pidgin and creole varieties); and constructed or 'artificial' languages (Esperanto being the best known in this category). It *is* necessary, however, to say something about translation, the other great 'bridging' mechanism, since – as we shall see – it can have immediate and personal relevance in surprising ways.

Apart from the most elementary word-for-word exercises – rarely useful, as the Roman statesman Cicero pointed out when advising against translating *verbum pro verbo* – every act of translation involves interpretation and judgment. This means that translation happens within as well as across languages. Indeed, even the simplest of conversations between speakers of the same language can require the oral equivalent of 'reading between the lines', and it is only through a constant process of translation (and periodic re-translation) that we maintain links with our own literature and our own culture. Most translators respect the general admonition of John Dryden who, when translating Virgil in the late 17th century, reported that he 'thought fit to steer betwixt the two extremes of paraphrase and literal translation; to keep as near my author as I could without losing all his graces'. The idea, as Dryden went on to say, was to try and make the poet 'speak such English as he would himself have spoken, if he had been born in England, and in this present age' (Edwards, 1995: 49). Three centuries later, the point was generalized by the classicists Émile Rieu and Leonard Tancock as 'the law of equivalent effect'. (The views of Tancock and Rieu are most easily consulted in remarks found in the Penguin translations of Zola's novels, notably *l'Assommoir* and *Germinal* (1970 and 1954 editions, respectively).)

For present purposes we may note that, however accurate the translation, it can occasion psychological concerns and social tensions. As Steiner (1992: 244) put it, 'there is in every act of translation – and specially where it succeeds – a touch of treason. Hoarded dreams, patents of life are being taken across the frontier.' And what are 'patents of life', if not the psychological collections of past and present that are unique – or are felt to be unique, at any rate – to ourselves, both as individuals and as group members? This suggests that, at some levels or in some circumstances and contexts, translation may not be entirely welcomed. Talleyrand, for instance, once observed that speech was given to human beings so that they could disguise their thoughts (see Edwards, 1995: 47). While this may seem a twisted application of a sophisticated communicative tool, we should remember here that the private and 'in-group' use of particular languages and language varieties in the construction and transmission of myths, legends and religious beliefs has long been important – important, and potentially threatened by the work of translators. There are clear demonstrations that translation can be blasphemous: some groups believe that the name of God is never to be uttered, others reserve this honour for a priestly caste, and still others argue that *no* language at all is adequate for religious purposes. The Quakers, for instance, prefer silent worship, for only then may God's own 'still, small voice' be heard (I *Kings* XIX: 12).

An informal Whorfianism tells us that every language interprets and presents the world in a somewhat different way, that the unique wellsprings of group consciousness, traditions, beliefs and values are intimately related to a given variety. So, translation may mean the revealing of deep matters to others, and cannot be taken lightly. The translator, the one whose multilingual facility permits the straddling of boundaries, is a necessary quisling. But necessity is not invariably associated with comfort, and not even their employers care very much for spies. Is it any wonder, then, that proverbial expressions in several languages reflect deep concerns about the crossing of language borders? To cite only two: the Italian *traduttori, traditori* and the Hungarian *fordítás, ferdítés* both equate translation with treachery or distortion.

Part 2: Aspects of Individual Multilingualism

Multilingual Self-assessment and Ascription

We can perhaps bring cross-language matters more firmly into individual contexts if we consider internal fluencies and choices, on the one hand, and linguistic ascription, on the other. The first of these phenomena has to do with switching behaviour of one sort or another; it has a large literature and can be treated very briefly here. Bilingual and multilingual individuals clearly have choices available that are denied to monolinguals: they can switch or mix their language use within or across utterances and interlocutors. In his classic volume, Weinreich (1953: 1) wrote that all such 'deviation from the norms of either language' may be referred to as *interference*. It seems evident, however, that not every switch from one language to another results from the unwelcome intrusion which this term suggests. Indeed, speakers often switch for emphasis, because they feel that the *mot juste* is found more readily in one of their languages than in another, or because of their perceptions of the speech situation, changes in content, the linguistic skills of their conversational partners, degrees of intimacy, and so on. Some writers have thus opted for the more neutral term *transference,* which implies, among other things, a greater element of volition: 'sometimes I'll start a sentence in English *y terminó en español*' (as Poplack's 1980 title runs).

The idea of *transference* notwithstanding, it is psychologically revealing to discover that attitudes towards switching behaviour are often negative, and that unfavourable perceptions here are not held by monolinguals alone. *Tex-Mex, Franglais, Japlish* and many other similar terms are often encountered, and they usually have pejorative connotations. Multilingual speakers have themselves considered their switching behaviour to be 'embarrassing', 'impure', 'lazy', or even 'dangerous', even though the reasons they give (as noted above) for moving among their languages make a great deal of sense (Edwards, 2013a). Indeed, it seems obvious that maximizing one's communicative efficiency must be a favourable state of affairs. In short, multilingual individuals possess not only the style-shifting available to all speakers, but also the language-shifting that is unavailable to their monolingual counterparts. It is hard to imagine that this is anything but a valuable addition.

Generally speaking, the mixing and switching made possible by multilingualism *has* been seen positively throughout history, often as a marker of status. In the Middle Ages, those European scholars, diplomats and aristocrats who possessed lingua franca Latin as well as their vernacular(s) enjoyed lives of privilege far removed from those of the masses. Indeed, members of social élites have often pointed, themselves, to the advantages of multiple fluencies. The 13th-century English Franciscan, Roger Bacon – known as 'Doctor Mirabilis' – wrote in his *Opus Tertium* that 'notitia linguarum est prima porta sapientiae' (knowledge of languages is the doorway to wisdom). Charles V, the 16th-century Holy Roman Emperor, observed that 'quot linguas calles, tot homines vales', meaning that one is worth as many people as languages known. When French came into international prominence, it was a new 'link language' but also the preferred medium of the elite. In

Sobieski's Polish court, in Catherine's St Petersburg, in Frederick's Berlin, and in many other royal quarters from the 17th century onwards, it was the language of aristocratic prestige.

While there have always been dissenting views, examination generally reveals that the criticisms are not of multilingualism per se but rather of linguistic capacities unaccompanied by intellectual depth. In his short essay, *Of Education*, first published in 1644, John Milton suggested:

> though a linguist should pride himself to have all the tongues that Babel cleft the world into, yet if he have not studied the solid things in them as well as the words and lexicons, he were nothing so much to be esteemed a learned man as any yeoman or tradesman competently wise in his mother-dialect only. (Milton, 1958 [1644]: 319–320)

At about the same time, the poet Samuel Butler wrote that 'he that has many Languages to express his Thoughts, but no thoughts worth expressing, is like one that can write all hands, but never the better Sense' (De Quehen, 1979: 11).

Personal names, both chosen and ascribed, can be important in this context and, indeed, it is something of a pity that onomastic study is not a little more prominent in sociolinguistics and the sociology of language. The names Faith, Felicity, Patience and Joy are modern reminders of Puritan practices, in which godly virtues were made into names. 'Increase Mather' was an important figure in 17th-century Massachusetts and 'Praisegod Barebone' gave his name to a parliamentary assembly of 1653. More elaborate naming also occurred along the lines of 'Fight-the-Good-Fight Jones' and 'Fear-the-Lord Smith'. Contemporary first names like Courage, Goodwill, Blessed, Lordwin, Goodluck and Withus remain popular in parts of Africa, legacies of colonialism and proselytism. Such naming choices may seem to say little of direct relevance to multilingual capacities, but one imagines that they all bear to some extent upon such important psychological factors as self-esteem and social inclusion or exclusion – to say nothing of prejudicial attitudes and perceptions. There are some pointed instances here. Rolihlahla Mandela recounts how, on his first day at school, the teacher (Miss Mdingane) told him that his new name would be Nelson. It is not surprising, then, to find that indigenous names are often taken up again in postcolonial settings. In South Africa, the Premier of the Eastern Cape went from Arnold to Makhenkesi, the Defence Minister from Patrick to Mosioua.

Group names are of interest here, too, particularly where unwanted external impositions come to dominate – and in some instances become internally adopted. Thus, some of the Dakota ('the friends') became known as Sioux ('snakes'), an abbreviation of a term bestowed upon them by enemies. Many Inuit consider the earlier term 'Eskimo' to be a derogatory reference to them as eaters of raw meat. While the Welsh call themselves *Cymry* (meaning something like 'fellow countrymen'), the English name for them derives from the Anglo-Saxon *w(e)alh*, via the Germanic *Wälsche* ('stranger', 'foreigner' or even 'barbarian'). The Khoisan speakers of southern Africa call themselves *Khoekhoe* ('men of men'), but the Dutch called them Hottentots ('stammerers'). Barbarians and stammerers: the terms are in fact closely associated. The first, signifying all that is brutal, uncouth and tasteless, is derived from a Greek term for the latter.

If readers imagine that we have strayed a little too far from the individual to the group here, they may like to bear in mind the fact that sharing a name (a group nomination, a surname, an epithet) with others does not rule out a simultaneous importance at the most intimate personal level. Similarly, the topic to which I turn next – attitudes to language varieties – is at first blush more social than psychological. Again, however, it is easy to understand how multilingual inclinations, directions and capacities can be affected by widely held assessments. Furthermore, when some of these reflect powerful political and religious views, the implications at the individual level become even more pointed.

So, from ascriptions to attitudes is not such a huge leap. While contemporary scholarship has demonstrated that no language or dialect is intrinsically 'better' or 'worse' than any other, this was not always the received wisdom (nor, of course, does it always extend very far beyond the academic cloisters today). The longstanding historical sense was that one's own language was superior to others in various ways. Thus, Richard Carew, a 16th-century poet and antiquary, argued for the 'excellency' of English, going on to note that Italian was 'pleasant, but without sinews', that French was 'delicate, but ever nice as a woman', that Spanish was 'majestical but fulsome', and that Dutch was 'manlike, but withal very harsh'. Two centuries later, Antoine de Rivarol observed that French was synonymous with clarity, and that English, Greek, Latin and Italian were mediums of ambiguity. In the late 18th century, George Lemon wrote about the 'purity and dignity, and all the high graceful majesty' of English – while reflecting on French 'flimsiness', Italian 'neatness', Spanish 'gravity' and the 'native hoarseness and roughness' of Germanic varieties. Many similar examples can easily be found, in many literatures. Perhaps it is only necessary to add that these views – representing the scholarship of the day, remember – extended well into modern times. Edward Higginson, in his English grammar of 1864, stated that 'there is not, nor ever was, a language comparable to the English'. Within the language, too, there is no shortage of modern expressions of preference. In 1932, the scholar-editor Robert Chapman saw Standard English as 'one of the most subtle and beautiful of all expressions of the human spirit'; in 1934, Henry Wyld – an eminent lexicographer and philologist – suggested that 'no unbiased listener would hesitate in preferring RS [Received Standard English: the modern-day Received Pronunciation (RP)] as the most pleasing and sonorous form'; for these several citations, and for Vallancey's observation in the next paragraph, see Edwards (1995: 6–7, 89, 95).

An examination of 'smaller' languages – particularly during times of attempted maintenance and revival – reveals that such strongly stated linguistic sentiments are not the sole preserve of large and imperial varieties. Towards the end of the 19th century, Irish was extolled for its 'perfection' and 'independence', which were so pronounced that it must clearly have been one of the first languages spoken on earth; indeed, an 18th-century scholar-soldier, Charles Vallancey, held that the origins of Irish lay with Carthage, that the language was a 'Punic-Celtic' compound, and that Ireland itself was the 'Thule of the Ancients'. Irish was seen as ideally suited for musical expression, and it was claimed that Irish vocal organs were naturally adapted for Gaelic speaking – Irish was already in the heads of non-Irish speaking Irishmen, so to speak, and teaching it therefore involved a drawing-out rather than a putting-in.

Exceptional Multilingualism and its Ramifications[2]

Erard (2012) provides a useful overview of polyglots and 'hyperpolyglots'. The latter term was applied by Hudson (2003) to describe individuals knowing more than six languages. Erard raises the ante to 11, but the precise number need not detain us here: the point is simply that, among multilinguals, some few have quite extraordinary abilities. He suggests four basic cornerstones of polyglossia: (a) a capacity for sustained study; (b) a 'superior ability to switch among languages'; (c) an excellent memory; (d) some advantageous neurological underpinnings (Erard, 2012: 268–269). While some of the fascination that 'super-linguists' have for us is that they 'seem to have leapfrogged the banality of method', they tend in fact to rely upon quite ordinary – not to say tedious, or dull – practices. They have the capacity, however, to 'make the banality more productive. Their minds *enjoy* the banality' (Erard, 2012: 269).

Erard builds his book around Cardinal Giuseppe Mezzofanti (1744–1849), as did Russell (1858) – whose work, which provides a hundred-page discussion of polyglots both ancient and modern – should be better known. Mezzofanti, who became a librarian in the Vatican, spoke – as nearly as one can determine (see below, particularly Watts, 1859) – about 50 languages with some fluency. He took every opportunity to talk with native speakers; beyond this, it is clear that he devoted a great deal of time to learning languages, sometimes in ways that most would find extremely boring. For example, when visiting the library in Bologna where Mezzofanti worked before going to Rome, Erard found stacks of flashcards in many languages, most of them written in the Cardinal's own hand. While clearly a very atypical linguist, Mezzofanti's actual capabilities are not particularly clear, and some of the more detailed information that we have about him reveals considerable variation in estimates of his linguistic scope and depth and, indeed, on the important matter of just what it means to 'know' a language.

Erard reports criticisms, along the lines that Mezzofanti never came out with anything creative: 'he has not five ideas', one fellow priest said (Erard, 2012: 5). Mezzofanti reminded one German visitor of a parrot: 'he does not seem to abound in ideas' and he often repeats himself. Another visitor – and Mezzofanti had many, some of them quite famous – said that he 'rather studies the words than the subject of what he reads' and referred to his 'empty unreflecting word-knowledge': he is, she wrote, best understood as 'one of the curiosities of the Vatican' (Watts, 1852: 119–121). Watts himself, while styling Mezzofanti 'the greatest linguist the world has ever seen', yet points out that 'he was a linguist only and not a philologist', and that 'in an age which was remarkable for the vastness of its discoveries in the field of philology, the great linguist did absolutely nothing' (Watts, 1852: 124–125).

A polyglot to whom I have recently given some close attention is Solomon Caesar Malan (1812–1894), a Victorian clergyman, scholar – and polyglot (Edwards, in press). A clerical contemporary provides a brief summary of Malan's linguistic accomplishments (Tuckwell, 1900: 95–96). By the time he went up to Oxford in 1833, he had fluent French, German,

Spanish and Italian; in fact, Malan asked if he might write some of his papers in French, German, Spanish, Italian, Latin or Greek – rather than in English. (His request was denied.) He was also 'well advanced' in Hebrew, Sanskrit, Arabic and other oriental varieties. As a professor in Calcutta, he added Chinese, Japanese and 'the various Indian, Malay, Persian tongues'. His library included books in 'more than seventy languages, the majority of which he spoke with freedom ... he published twenty-six translations of English theological works, in Chinese and Japanese, Arabic and Syriac, Armenian, Russian, Ethiopic, Coptic.' (Malan donated his library to the Indian Institute at Oxford; it included material in 105 languages.) Tuckwell also notes that, in his frequent 'Eastern rambles', Malan was able to 'chat in market and bazaar with everyone whom he met'. Malan himself, in an 1872 letter to his wife, wrote: 'This is life! Talking thirteen languages a day – Jews, Turks, Infidels – I like the Turks best' (Malan, 1897: 273).

During his lifetime, Malan prepared a collection of psalms and prayers 'in more than eighty languages and scripts' (Malan, 1897: 162), and made translations of the Lord's Prayer in 71 languages: these range from the biblical varieties, to Asian, European and even two Pacific languages (Fijian and Māori). His *magnum opus*, however, was a three-volume set of *Notes on the Book of Proverbs* (1889–1893). These notes were bound, expanded and re-bound over more than 50 years. There are more than 16,000 of them, and the author's guiding impulse was his conviction 'that there is not a verse in the Book of Proverbs which does not find abundant parallels in Eastern literature' (Malan, 1897: 398). The vast majority of the notes are from oriental and non-Christian sources, reflecting more than 40 different languages.

Malan was clearly an exceptional example of multilingual talent, but what do we know about Malan the man? It seems that some of his psychological characteristics are relatable to his linguistic skills in important ways – and this will become clearer when we move into the next section. Here we may note that, while a formidable scholar whose talents ranged beyond remarkable linguistic abilities (Malan was an accomplished carpenter, musician, artist, naturalist and biblical exegete), the extent of his activities has suggested breadth without depth. Chadwick (1970) is most pointed here, when he refers to a mind lacking in 'critical sense'. Deficiencies in this vital capacity do indeed undercut originality of endeavour, and energetic application and a powerful work ethic are insufficient remedies. The most interesting personality characteristics attributed to Malan are ones that reinforce this central point. An intelligent and hard worker, Malan was disdainful and sometimes arrogant about intellectual and other pursuits that were not his own. He was unswervingly opinionated, possessed of a self-righteous sense of certainty. Despite his talents and his robust opinions, Malan seemed insecure once outside his self-generated and self-sustained borders – and insecurity can very easily coexist with disdain and intractability. He was quite thin-skinned, lashing out at criticism (which he was quick to detect) with reactions that were often of an ad hominem nature. Given this, it is perhaps unsurprising that Malan was unwilling to place himself in scholarly positions where he might be observed and found wanting, even though he was offered prestigious Oxford appointments.

His powerful work ethic, so evident in his intense and lengthy scholarly productions, reveals the collector's obsessive concern with completeness. Malan was a man who valued 'system', order, routine and categorization, and in his academic works we see a marriage of these values with his language fluencies – all in the ultimate service of an almost archival concern with what are essentially elaborate *lists*. One will find in these works the fruits of a type of intelligent activity that does not rely chiefly upon originality or innovation, upon that all-important critical sense mentioned by Chadwick. (This does not necessarily detract from the potential usefulness of Malan's work, of course: scholar-archivists assemble, collate and sometimes interpret material that will be grist for the mills of others.)

Polyglossia, 'savants' and the autistic spectrum

The amazing linguistic capacities of some polyglots are sometimes found in those 'savants' who also demonstrate exceptional – but, as we shall see, limited – musical, mathematical and other skills. Treffert (1989) highlights three pivotal features of the 'savant syndrome': neurological anomalies, inherited and/or acquired aptitudes, and powerful and reinforced motivation – and we could almost invariably add excellence in memory and systematization to the list. There is some agreement that the achievements of many, perhaps most, savants are in fact based on 'an essentially normal mental-processing capacity allied to unusually intense and long-lasting attention, concentration and involvement in particular interests' (Howe, 1991: 162; see also Foer, 2011). This takes nothing away from their extraordinarily rare achievements, of course, but – coupled with the fact that they generally coexist with normal (or, in some instances, subnormal) abilities in other spheres of life – it does suggest that we are not dealing with miracle-workers. Still, 'the demonstration that an individual can be simultaneously gifted and retarded continues to be a source of bafflement' (Howe, 1991: 65). Smith (2005: 39) notes that 'savants [are] people with an island of startling ability in a sea of disability: people like "Rainman" made famous by Dustin Hoffman's portrayal of an autistic savant in the film of that name'. How are we best to understand such people, this coexistence of extraordinary, if narrow, talent with broad incapacities?

In April 2014, BBC2 aired a programme called *Living with Autism*, presented by Uta Frith (see also Frith, 2014). It revealed that, while about 80% of autistic individuals are unable to live independently, many have quite special talents. While perhaps one in ten has extraordinary abilities – the calendrical or 'lightning' calculators, for instance – as many as one in three seems to have *some* notable skills (in music, memory, etc.). Beyond memory, other common autistic traits include task repetition and practice (often obsessive), generally in the service of creating systems and patterns, as well as social inadequacies in which communication is impaired. Monologic communication, especially when scripted, means that making formal presentations – including, most interestingly, discussing one's own autism – on familiar subjects, in familiar settings, is possible for some. Nonetheless, autistic individuals – even those referred to as 'high-functioning' – often have frustrating and anxious social lives, in which they cannot understand the actions and words of others, and where they fail to understand jokes, banter and metaphor. Imitation can reduce stress here – a process not unlike the social 'modelling' that is so useful for all people.

The single descriptor 'autism' has now generally given way to the term 'autism spectrum disorder'. This is important (and relevant here) because it highlights a more nuanced approach and in fact suggests that the traits of autistic individuals are very often ones that, in less dominant form, are found in a great many people (some would, in fact, say 'most people'). Simon Baron-Cohen, interviewed on that BBC programme, thus argues that very few of us would be at zero on any plausible scale of autism. As one of the most prominent contemporary investigators of autism, Frith describes herself as obsessive in her work, sometimes socially awkward, and so on. In general, 'autistic-like' traits – including compulsiveness, perfectionism, systematicity, eccentricity and energetic devotion to specific tasks – are widely detectable, particularly among scholars and others of above-average intelligence whose work often rests upon these qualities. Tendencies to systematize might particularly help to explain why 'scientists score higher than nonscientists on a test that measures autistic traits' (Erard, 2012: 230).

Citing the work of Baron-Cohen, Erard (2012) notes that some polyglots seem 'near-autistic', that certain neurological features and anomalies have been suggested as underlying factors in their extraordinary abilities – and that some have an 'extreme male brain' (possibly higher levels of testosterone, that is to say). Baron-Cohen has also suggested that 'systematizing' is a frequent element in autism. Maleness and making lists: one of Erard's informants said that 'I don't know many women who collect stamps or coins', suggesting to the author – and perhaps to us – that we might see 'polyglottery as a kind of collecting behavior, perhaps an obsessive one' (Erard, 2012: 228); in any event, 'famous language learners, language accumulators and language geeks tend to be men' (Erard, 2012: 101). Collecting often involves a search for completeness, or perfection, and obsessions or compulsions are not uncommonly found among savants, whether clinically autistic or not – and, among these, we may wish to include some of the most amazing multilinguals.

Daniel Tammet (born in 1979) is a 'high-functioning' autistic savant, a member of a very small group (perhaps 100 worldwide) of so-called 'prodigious savants'. He has been the subject of television documentaries, and is a published author. His articulate capacity for self-description makes him a particularly valuable subject for scientific study. Tammet knows 10 languages and, in a famous demonstration, he learned Icelandic in a week, becoming sufficiently fluent to be interviewed on television in Reykjavik. Nonetheless, he cannot (for example) drive a car: he would be overwhelmed by all the detail.

Polyglossia and personality: A concluding remark

With what we know about polyglots in general, about the personality characteristics that all of us probably possess – but which attain extraordinary dimensions in very few people – and from my potted 'case study' of Solomon Caesar Malan, we can venture some broad conclusions about pronounced multilingual competence. Polyglots clearly benefit from very good memories, from the capacity for sustained and focused application, and from a dogged – if not obsessive or compulsive – persistence. Despite enlarged interests and abilities, they are often more collectors and systematizers than either creators or innovators. Here we might also recall Chadwick's accusation of poor 'critical sense' – a point that, if true, would go some way towards explaining why remarkable abilities do not always lead to remarkable scholarship.

Thomas Carlyle wrote about genius resting on the ability to take great trouble, which has given rise to the more common aphorism that it is an 'infinite capacity for taking pains'. The achievements of many savants, wherever they may fall along the autistic spectrum, very often reveal assiduous and unremitting application to tasks, linguistic and otherwise. At the same time, we should not bestow the title of 'genius' too readily. (One thinks here of the title of Howe's (1991) book, in which savants are seen as having 'fragments of genius' – and, indeed, of many more informal assessments of abilities that seem magical and mysterious.) Indeed, if we go back to Carlyle's rather unpoetic formulation, we read that the 'transcendent capacity of taking trouble' is a necessary but insufficient condition for works of genius: the words 'first of all' immediately follow what has just been cited (Carlyle, 1859: 407).

Multilingualism and Intelligence

Most of the research on this topic has dealt specifically with bilinguals; as we shall see, however, it is broadly applicable to more than linguistic duality. Valian (2015a) points out that researchers would not generally expect important differences, in terms of any cognitive advantages accruing from language repertoire expansion, between bilinguals and multilinguals. Indeed, she writes that 'bilingualism should be understood to include knowledge of any number of languages beyond one' (Valian, 2015a: 3) – not the most elegant phrasing, perhaps, but one sees her point. (This section, it should be noted, does not deal with some of the interesting work on language learning and brain alteration and/or 'growth'; see Edwards (1995) and, for good recent summaries, Mårtensson *et al.* (2012) and the recent special issue of the *International Journal of Bilingualism* devoted to 'multilingual brains' (Reiterer & Festman, 2014)).

The idea that one's personality expands with extra languages has been a very common one, as we have seen. We have also seen that some have demurred. Both attitudes touch, of course, on the possible cognitive advantages that multilingualism might or might not confer. This has continued to be a much debated matter, and has – for almost a century – attracted the attention of language specialists. Otto Jespersen wrote that 'it is, of course, an advantage for a child to be familiar with two languages: but without doubt the advantage may be, and generally is, purchased too dear ... the brain effort required to master the two languages instead of one certainly diminishes the child's power of learning other things' (Jesperson, 1922: 148). A few years later, in 1930, John Firth, a doyen of mid-20th-century British linguistic scholarship, observed that, while 'the average bilingual speaker ... has two strings to his bow', one is 'rather slacker than the other' (Firth, 1970: 211). Generally speaking, early work supported these opinions, implying some finite cognitive capacity which, if it were enlarged in one way must necessarily be restricted in another. Some of the research was conducted at a time of great concern over the alleged 'feeble-mindedness' of the immigrants flooding into North America and elsewhere (largely in the Anglophone world). It was widely felt in these largely monolingual settings that multilingualism was a handicap, and that intelligence was positively correlated with greater English fluency.

Florence Goodenough, one of the few women prominent in psychology at the time, considered that 'the use of a foreign language in the home is one of the chief factors in producing mental retardation' (Goodenough, 1926: 393). In such a climate – one in which the mental capabilities of both immigrants and some indigenous inhabitants were thought to require eugenic intervention – it is hardly surprising that linguistic characteristics would attract attention. Nonetheless, ill-conducted research and undisguised racism did give way to more carefully controlled studies, work which began to suggest no strong relationship between intelligence and multilingualism; controlling for sex, age, social class and other important variables became common procedure, and the lack of such control was increasingly seen to have produced the negative associations found (or assumed) previously.

A turning point came in the early 1960s, when findings showing a *positive* relationship between intelligence and bilingualism began to appear. Peal and Lambert (1962) reported that ten-year-old bilingual children in Montreal outperformed their monolingual counterparts on both verbal and non-verbal intelligence tests, suggesting greater mental agility. They were quite aware, however, that correlation need not imply causation: did greater mental flexibility cause or follow expanded language skills? Other limitations included the degree of bilingualism among the children and the general socio-economic representativeness of the sample. Nonetheless, studies now tended to highlight the apparently advantageous cognitive effects of bilingualism.

Commenting on this developing trend some time ago, I noted the initial correlation-causation difficulty. Not only is the directionality linking measurements of intelligence with linguistic competences uncertain, but we must also bear in mind that in many instances where correlations have been demonstrated, their presence is accounted for by other variables entirely – known or unknown. As well, there are problems of defining and assessing both multilingual skills and intelligence, and in ensuring comparability between groups of bilinguals and monolinguals (see also Valian, 2015b). These all suggested that 'strong conclusions about bilingualism and cognition are not warranted' (Edwards, 1995: 70). Furthermore:

> Being bilingual (or multilingual, for that matter) is unlikely
> to mean any significant increase in cognitive and intellectual
> skills ... It would be perverse, however, to deny that bilingualism
> can represent another *dimension* of one's capacities, and in that
> sense be a repertoire expansion. I see nothing controversial about
> this, just as I would see nothing controversial in the statement that a
> number of years' devotion to the study of great literature can
> lead to a heightened or, at least, altered sensitivity to the
> human condition. (Edwards, 1995: 71)

Some very recent findings in this important area have, however, suggested that certain cognitive strengths *are* associated with bilingual competence, and the work of Bialystok and her colleagues has been central. Bialystok (2009) argued, for example, that bilingualism is associated with improved cognitive functioning and, in a later paper (Bialystok, 2010), that bilingual children solve certain tasks more quickly than do monolinguals, particularly those involving the processing of complex stimuli. Moreno *et al*. (2010) extended the work from children to adults and, indeed, Bialystok's most recent work is concerned with investigating bilingualism across the lifespan. In a further development, it has been suggested that expanded language competence may ameliorate the symptoms of Alzheimer's disease (see Bialystok *et al.*, 2007, 2014a; Craik *et al.*, 2010; Woumans *et al.*, 2015). The larger 'cognitive reserves' of bilingual speakers are seen to provide the advantage here. As can be imagined, these findings have attracted considerable media attention (see Bates, 2010, for a representative piece). As a careful scholar, Bialystok – like Peal and Lambert before her – has pointed to limitations and uncertainties, as well as to areas in which the performance of bilinguals is *not* better than that of their monolingual counterparts.

Notwithstanding this commendable caution, however, many researchers in the area – on the basis of a large and growing literature – have come to accept that adding languages improves cognitive abilities. In a recent article, Genesee (2015: 6) provides an admirable summary; not only does it reflect much contemporary thinking, but it also touches (very briefly, of course) on the reasoning behind that thinking; it is worth citing at length here:

> research has shown that bilingual individuals enjoy certain neurocognitive advantages in comparison with monolinguals. A bilingual advantage has been demonstrated in the performance of tasks that call for selective attention (e.g., Bialystok, 2001), including tasks that require focusing, inhibiting, and switching attention during problem solving, for example. It has been argued that learning and using two languages calls for selective attention to minimize interference between languages and ensure their appropriate use; this, in turn, enhances the development of executive control processes in general, not only in linguistic domains. These advantages have been found in both childhood and adulthood (Bialystok, Craik, Klein and Viswanathan, 2004) and are most evident in bilinguals with relatively advanced levels of proficiency in two languages and who use their two languages actively on a regular basis (Bialystok, Peets and Moreno, 2014b). (Genesee, 2015: 6)

The language–intelligence linkage has been closely re-examined in a recent issue of *Bilingualism: Language and Cognition* which is almost entirely devoted to bilingualism, cognition and aging (Abutalebi & Clahsen, 2015). There is an introductory piece (Valian, 2015a), ten very short 'peer comments', and a general response (Valian, 2015b). The important phenomenon of 'executive control' (as mentioned by Genesee, above) is central here. Such 'control' or 'executive function' is allegedly implicated in a wide variety of cognitive processes. Valian, however, points out that language–intelligence relationships are inconsistent because 'individuals vary in the number and kinds of experiences they have' (Valian, 2015a: 3), many of which constitute challenges that may sharpen cognitive acuity. Such remarks may be taken as broad support for the cautions expressed earlier; see also Kirk *et al.* (2014). More pointedly, Valian's analyses suggest that expanded language repertoires are 'inconsistently correlated with superior executive function and delayed onset of dementia' and that '*all* speakers (mono- or bilingual) have non-linguistic ways of improving executive function' (Valian, 2015a: 3). Valian returns to this point in her closing pages, and – with special regard to language and the effects of aging – makes the eminently sensible argument that there are no doubt 'many underlying mechanisms' that may contribute (Valian, 2015a: 19). And, in her second paper, Valian (2015b) writes that it may well be the *effort* involved in managing more than one language that provides any advantages multilingualism may have over monolongualism. Indeed, while cautiously supporting the 'bilingual advantage', she writes that 'there is a benefit of bilingualism, but bilingualism competes with other sources of benefits' (Valian, 2015b: 47).

Klein (2015: 29) writes that, with Peal and Lambert's study helping to dispel the inaccurate notion that bilingualism might be detrimental, 'through her "myth-dispelling" efforts and prodigious empirical output, Bialystok has pushed the pendulum of opinion in the opposite direction'. While, in an earlier and quite comprehensive overview, Hilchey and Klein (2011) had reported scant evidence for an inhibitory-control advantage, they did find support for advantages in executive processing. Now, however, Klein suggests that his inspection of later (i.e. post-2011) analyses have undercut this: in fact, 'support for BEPA [bilingual executive processing advantage] had surprisingly more or less evaporated' (Klein, 2015: 30). He cites publication bias (see below) as a possible reason for the pre-2011 results, and now recommends that 'the pendulum of scientific opinion on this question [i.e. of a "bilingual advantage"] be put into neutral' (Klein, 2015: 30). Although pendulums are not 'put into neutral', Klein's point is clear – and, again, reinforces what I wrote in 1995 (see above).

While commenting specifically on the language-and-aging relationship, Zahodne and Manly (2015: 45) make some observations which, *mutatis mutandis*, are relevant to finding the proper resting position of that research pendulum. First, they argue that 'there has not been a true experiment in which individuals are randomized to bilingualism or not' and that 'longitudinal studies, with direct standardized observation of cognitive performance and determination of dementia onset, should be the gold standard' – in this area, as in virtually all areas of social-scientific enquiry, such studies are regrettably rare. The difficulty, as the authors add, is that 'retrospective studies often rely in part or in whole on informant reports of functional decline' without taking on board – or, we might add, without being able to take on board – all sorts of other social and cultural information. It is almost superfluous for them to note that 'bilingual older adults may be antecedently different from monolingual older adults'.

Among the commentaries, we find Paap (2015) agreeing with Valian's arguments. In a series of earlier studies (Paap, 2014; Paap & Greenberg, 2013; Paap & Liu, 2014), he and his colleagues expand upon what they think is the 'artifactual' nature of positive bilingualism-intelligence correlations. Central here are two biases, neither of which is rare in social-scientific literature. There is, first, a 'confirmation bias', by which evidence supporting one's position is more actively sought, and more likely to be recalled, assessed and worked into emerging theory than is disconfirming information. There are also 'publication biases': on the one hand, editors are often more favourably disposed towards studies that provide significant, and significantly positive, results; on the other, researchers sometimes shelve disconfirming or ambiguous findings. De Bruin *et al.* (2015) assessed a large number

(169, in fact) of abstracts dealing with language and cognition, from conferences held between 1999 and 2012. About half the papers supported the 'bilingual advantage' position. Of these, 68% re-emerged as publications. Of those reporting mixed but broadly supportive positions, mixed but less supportive positions, and no advantage (or, in some few instance, advantages attached to *monolingualism*), the publication percentages were 50%, 39% and 29%, respectively. (See also the very recent overview by De Bruin & Della Sala, 2016.)

Such results do not in themselves negate the possibility of a bilingual or multilingual advantage, of course – but they may well lend at least some support to Valian's (2015a) summary statements. Relatedly, De Bruin and her colleagues cite comments by Kroll and Bialystok (2013) which, they think, make seemingly unfair criticisms of work that shows no such advantage: 'the considerable literature that reports group differences between monolingual and bilingual participants is greatly more informative than the attempted replications that fail to find significance' (Kroll & Bialystok, 2013: 502); and 'unless all conditions have been accounted for and all other explanations have been exhausted, it is misleading to call into question the reliability of the phenomena themselves' (Kroll & Bialystok, 2013: 503).

In a study similar to that of De Bruin *et al.* (2015), Kirk *et al.* (2014) replicated the methodology of one of the studies reported in Bialystok *et al.* (2004). They used a wider range of informants than is usually the case, including monolingual and mono-dialectal speakers of English, Scottish bi-dialectal speakers, and Gaelic-English and other types of bilinguals. Their findings revealed no important differences in 'cognitive control' tasks. Kempe (2014), under whose supervision the study was conducted, wrote in an Abertay University online newsletter that their initially surprising results turn out to join those of a 'number of studies that fail to find that bilingualism makes you smarter'. (This assessment is, of course, rather too blunt; a more temperate and more nuanced statement might have been nearer the mark.) She refers, too, to the 'publication bias' in a scholarly climate in which 'there is so much pressure to demonstrate novelty and real-life impact'. She sensibly concludes, however, by noting that – whether or not bilingualism entails cognitive benefits – the development of multilingual competence is intrinsically a good and useful thing: 'perhaps being able to see the world from another point of view is the most beneficial and mind-enhancing effect that comes with learning languages.'

A Concluding Note

This brief overview of individual multilingualism has tried to make one or two central points. There is, first of all, more multilingualism than monolingualism in the world, and the broad factors that bring it about are easily understood. The sometimes peculiar views of those lucky – or unfortunate – enough to be born into 'big' language communities, and whose lives require no linguistic excursions beyond the mother tongue, are just that. At the same time, common sense dictates that multiple fluencies are rarely equally developed within the individual; it would be uneconomical to 'over-develop' certain language skills. The essential and immediate perceptions of *necessity* are what differentially fuel and maintain these skills. If we were to draw on a literature not dealt with in this lecture, we would also find, however, that people are quite capable of enlarging hitherto restricted varieties should their circumstances change. There is a seemingly natural human flexibility here, even though (again) it often goes unrecognized by monolinguals. This multilingual elasticity can take a great many forms, which is why both assessments of language abilities and meaningful comparisons across individuals are so difficult. Variations in motivation, attitude and, of course, levels of fluency are the most important contributors to this complicated picture.

Multilingualism has often been ignored or treated with benign neglect, with language variations coming to official attention only when their speakers have been seen as potential barriers to desired political or collective policies. And it is of course the *speakers* who are important here, their languages being merely the team jerseys that highlight social and psychological differences. We come, then, to the language-and-identity nexus – which is generally the underlying factor of importance in many situations of contact. If languages were only communicative tools, we would still expect their speakers to resent the necessity of change and to resist shift; we could also fold into this picture concerns about intra-language mixing and switching, and about some of the subtler aspects of translation. When we add the symbolic and identity-bearing potential of language to this instrumental function, however, then we come more closely to the fullness of what language *means* to people. It is impossible to maintain a clear distinction between social and individual multilingualism here (as, indeed, in other parts of the discussion) because historical and contemporary realities, perceptions and prejudices have always led to strong judgments about the relative worth of different languages. Relevant here, too, are the names that people give themselves, and are given by others.

Perhaps the most important parts of this lecture are those dealing with intelligence and polyglossia. Some flavour of the arguments linking multilingual abilities with cognitive advantages has been provided under the first heading. A non-specialist in this area, I nevertheless weighed in with my own assessment a number of years ago: on the basis of information in the literature, of discussions with experts, of my own observations of bilingual and multilingual individuals – and of what common sense suggested – I argued that it was probably mistaken to think that expanding linguistic repertoires had a direct link to improved thought processes and mental agility. Of course, we are not seeing some return to the ignorance of the past, when bilingualism was sometimes seen as detrimental, nor is there the slightest rejection of the idea that adding languages is in itself a good thing. So, becoming multilingual *does* make you 'smarter' – if by 'smarter' we mean an expanded specific repertoire rather than an expanded general cognitive capability.

If multilinguals are – in this limited sense – 'smarter' than others, then are the most talented among them also stranger than others? The central point of the discussion here was to suggest, first of all, that polyglots and 'hyper-polyglots' are not magicians. Supporting this point is the fact that the awesome linguistic skills that some of them possess coexist with startling inadequacies in other areas of life. In turning to the relevant autism literature, no suggestion of any easy distinction that might link autism with polyglossia *tout court* was made – but it was suggested that, among exceptionally talented, creative and driven individuals, polyglossia may often be accompanied by a strengthening of certain traits and personality dimensions that are at once common to all of us, and exceptionally developed in cases of clinical autism. There are two main advantages in understanding these matters from the perspective of a continuum, an autistic spectrum. We see more clearly that there is no facile us-versus-them distinction possible, and that inaccurate black-and-white perceptions must give way to a virtual infinity of shading. At the same time, however, we can appreciate that some points on that continuum are more extreme than others. It may be objected that these are all observations that apply to a very small category of multilingual individuals. To the extent, however, to which we can better understand their motivations, limitations, and of course their capacities, we can demystify their achievements (without lessening them), and develop a fuller and perhaps more broadly applicable sense of individual multilingual possibilities.

> ## Questions for Students' Reflection
>
> 1. What are the implications of individual multilingualism for personal identity?
> 2. Discuss the methods – and the difficulties – involved in assessing multilingual competence.
> 3. Discuss the evidence bearing upon possible links between multilingualism and heightened cognitive flexibility.
> 4. What might the study of 'polyglots' tell us about more 'ordinary' multilingual capacities?

Suggestions for Further Reading

Aronin, L. and Singleton, D. (2012) *Multilingualism*. Amsterdam: John Benjamins.

Bhatia, T. and Ritchie, W. (eds) (2013) *The Handbook of Bilingualism and Multilingualism*. Oxford: Wiley-Blackwell.

Edwards, J. (2012) *Multilingualism: Understanding Linguistic Diversity*. London: Continuum/Bloomsbury.

Grosjean, F. (2010) *Bilingual: Life and Reality*. Cambridge, MA: Harvard University Press.

Stavans, A. and Hoffmann, C. (2015) *Multilingualism*. Cambridge: Cambridge University Press.

Notes

1. This lecture draws and expands upon previous work, particularly Edwards (2013a, 2013b).
2. This section draws largely from Edwards (in press).

References

Abutalebi, J. and Clahsen, H. (2015) Bilingualism, cognition, and aging. *Bilingualism: Language and Cognition* 18, 1–2.

Aronin, L. and Singleton, D. (2012) *Multilingualism*. Amsterdam: John Benjamins.

Baker, C. and Jones, S.P. (1998) *Encyclopedia of Bilingualism and Bilingual Education*. Clevedon: Multilingual Matters.

Bates, D. (2010) Learn another language to help protect yourself from Alzheimer's disease. *Daily Mail*, 13 October.

Bialystok, E. (2001) *Bilingualism in Development: Language, Literacy and Cognition*. Cambridge: Cambridge University Press.

Bialystok, E. (2009) Bilingualism: The good, the bad and the indifferent. *Bilingualism: Language and Cognition* 12, 3–11.

Bialystok, E. (2010) Global-local and trail-making tasks by monolingual and bilingual children. *Developmental Psychology* 46, 93–105.

Bialystok, E., Craik, R., Klein, R. and Viswanathan, M. (2004) Bilingualism, aging and cognitive control: Evidence from the Simon task. *Psychology and Aging* 19, 290–303.

Bialystok, E., Craik, F. and Freedman, M. (2007) Bilingualism as a protection against the onset of symptoms of dementia. *Neuropsychologia* 45, 459–464.

Bialystok, E., Craik, F., Binns, M., Ossher, L. and Freedman, M. (2014a) Effects of bilingualism on the age of onset and progression of MCI and AD: Evidence from executive function tests. *Neuropsychology* 28, 290–304.

Bialystok, E., Peets, K. and Moreno, S. (2014b) Producing bilinguals through immersion education: Development of metalinguistic awareness. *Applied Psycholinguistics* 35, 177–191.

Carlyle, T. (1859) *History of Friedrich II of Prussia, Called Frederick the Great*. London: Chapman & Hall. [this third edition is in four volumes: the passage cited is in Volume 1, Book 4, Chapter 3].

Chadwick, O. (1970) *The Victorian Church: Part II (1860–1901)*. London: A. & C. Black.

Craik, F., Bialystok, E. and Freedman, M. (2010) Delaying the onset of Alzheimer disease: Bilingualism as a form of cognitive reserve. *Neurology* 75, 1726–1729.

De Bruin, A. and Della Sala, S. (2016) How biases inflate scientific evidence. *The Psychologist* 29 (1), 36–39.

De Bruin, A., Treccani, B. and Della Sala, S. (2015) Cognitive advantage in bilingualism: An example of publication bias? *Psychological Science* 26, 99–107.

De Quehen, H. (1979) *Samuel Butler: Prose Observations*. Oxford: Clarendon.

Dewaele, J.-M. and Nakano, S. (2013) Multilinguals' perceptions of feeling different when switching languages. *Journal of Multilingual and Multicultural Development* 34, 107–120.

Edwards, J. (1995) *Multilingualism*. London: Penguin.

Edwards, J. (2012) *Multilingualism: Understanding Linguistic Diversity*. London: Continuum/Bloomsbury.

Edwards, J. (2013a) Bilingualism and multilingualism: Some central concepts. In T. Bhatia and W. Ritchie (eds) *The Handbook of Bilingualism and Multilingualism* (2nd edn) (pp. 5–25). Oxford: Wiley-Blackwell.

Edwards, J. (2013b) *Sociolinguistics: A Very Short Introduction*. Oxford and New York: Oxford University Press.

Edwards, J. (in press) Solomon Caesar Malan: Personality, polyglossia and the autistic spectrum. In L. Pfister (ed.) *The Life and Works of Solomon Caesar Malan*. Sankt Augustin: Monumenta Serica.

Erard, M. (2012) *Babel No More: The Search for the World's Most Extraordinary Language Learners*. New York: Free Press.

Firth, J. (1970) *The Tongues of Men and Speech*. London: Oxford University Press.

Foer, J. (2011) *Moonwalking with Einstein: The Art and Science of Remembering Everything*. London: Penguin.

Frith, U. (2014) Autism: Are we getting any closer to explaining the enigma? *The Psychologist* 27 (10), 744–745.

Gellner, E. (1983) *Nations and Nationalism*. Oxford: Blackwell.

Genesee, F. (2015) Myths about early childhood bilingualism. *Canadian Psychology* 56, 6–15.

Goodenough, F. (1926) Racial differences in the intelligence of school children. *Journal of Experimental Psychology* 9, 388–397.

Grosjean, F. (1982) *Life with Two Languages*. Cambridge, MA: Harvard University Press.

Grosjean, F. (2010) *Bilingual: Life and Reality*. Cambridge, MA: Harvard University Press.

Hamers, J. and Blanc, M. (2000) *Bilinguality and Bilingualism* (2nd edn). Cambridge: Cambridge University Press.

Hazlitt, W. (1920 [1821]) *Table Talk, or Original Essays*. London: Dent.

Hilchey, M. and Klein, R. (2011) Are there bilingual advantages on non-linguistic interference tasks? Implications for plasticity of executive control processes. *Psychonomic Bulletin & Review* 18, 625–658.

Howe, M. (1991) *Fragments of Genius: The Strange Feats of Idiots Savants*. London: Routledge.

Hudson, R. (2003) A 'gene' for hyper-polyglottism? *Linguist List* (26 October). See http://linguistlist.org/issues/14/14-2923.html

Jespersen, O. (1922) *Language*. London: Allen & Unwin.

Kellman, S. (2000) *The Translingual Imagination*. Lincoln, NE: University of Nebraska Press.

Kempe, V. (2014) Being bilingual does not make you smarter. See https://www.abertay.ac.uk/news/2013/being-bilingual-does-not-make-you-smarter/.

Kirk, N., Fiala, L., Scott-Brown, K. and Kempe, V. (2014) No evidence for reduced Simon cost in elderly bilinguals and bidialectals. *Journal of Cognitive Psychology* 26, 640–648.

Klein, R. (2015) Is there a benefit of bilingualism for executive functioning? *Bilingualism: Language and Cognition* 18, 29–31.

Kroll, J. and Bialystok, E. (2013) Understanding the consequences of bilingualism for language processing and cognition. *Journal of Cognitive Psychology* 25, 497–514.

Lewis, E.G. (1976) Bilingualism and bilingual education: The ancient world to the Renaissance. In J. Fishman (ed.) *Bilingual Education* (pp. 150–200). Rowley, MA: Newbury House.

Malan, A.N. (1897) *Solomon Cæsar Malan, D.D.: Memorials of his Life and Writings*. London: John Murray.

Malan, S.C. (1889–1893) *Original Notes on the Book of Proverbs, According to the Authorised Version* (3 vols). London: Williams & Norgate.

Mårtensson, J., Eriksson, J., Bodammer, N.C., Lindgren, M., Johansson, M., Nyberg, L. and Lövden, M. (2012) Growth of language-related brain areas after foreign language learning. *NeuroImage* 63, 240–244.

Milton, J. (1958 [1644]) *Prose Writings*. London: Dent.

Moreno, S., Bialystok, E., Wodniecka, A. and Alain, C. (2010) Conflict resolution in sentence processing by bilinguals. *Journal of Neurolinguistics* 23, 564–579.

Murray, K. (1977) *Caught in the Web of Words*. New Haven, CT: Yale University Press.

Paap, K. (2014) The role of componential analysis, categorical hypothesising, replicability and confirmation bias in testing for bilingual advantages in executive functioning. *Journal of Cognitive Psychology* 26, 242–255.

Paap, K. (2015) Do many hones dull the bilingual whetstone? *Bilingualism: Language and Cognition* 18, 41–42.

Paap, K. and Greenberg, Z. (2013) There is no coherent evidence for a bilingual advantage in executive processing. *Cognitive Psychology* 66, 232–258.

Paap, K. and Liu, Y. (2014) Conflict resolution in sentence processing is the same for bilinguals and monolinguals: The role of confirmation bias in testing for bilingual advantages. *Journal of Neurolinguistics* 27, 50–74.

Peal, E. and Lambert, W. (1962) The relation of bilingualism to intelligence. *Psychological Monographs* 76, 1–23.

Poplack, S. (1980) Sometimes I'll start a sentence in English *y terminó en español*. *Linguistics* 18, 581–618.

Ramírez-Esparza, N., Gosling, S., Benet-Martínez, V., Potter, J. and Pennebaker, J. (2006) Do bilinguals have two personalities? A special case of cultural frame switching. *Journal of Research in Personality* 40, 99–120.

Reiterer, S. and Festman, J. (eds) (2014) Multilingual brains: Individual differences in bi- and multilinguals. *International Journal of Bilingualism* 1 (special issue).

Russell, C. (1858) *The Life of Cardinal Mezzofanti, with an Introductory Memoir of Eminent Linguists, Ancient and Modern*. London: Longman, Brown.

Smith, N. (2005) *Language, Frogs and Savants*. Oxford: Blackwell.

Stavans, A. and Hoffmann, C. (2015) *Multilingualism*. Cambridge: Cambridge University Press.

Steiner, G. (1992) *After Babel: Aspects of Language and Translation* (2nd edn). Oxford: Oxford University Press.

Treffert, D. (1989) *Extraordinary People: Understanding 'Idiot Savants'*. New York: Harper & Row.

Tuckwell, W. (1900) *Reminiscences of Oxford*. London: Cassell.

Valian, V. (2015a) Bilingualism and cognition. *Bilingualism: Language and Cognition* 18, 3–24.

Valian, V. (2015b) Bilingualism and cognition: A focus on mechanisms. *Bilingualism: Language and Cognition* 18, 47–50.

Watts, T. (1852) On the extraordinary powers of Cardinal Mezzofanti as a linguist. *Proceedings of the Philological Society* 5 (115), 111–125.

Watts, T. (1859) On Dr. Russell's life of Cardinal Mezzofanti. *Transactions of the Philological Society* 6 (1), 227–256.

Weinreich, U. (1953) *Languages in Contact*. The Hague: Mouton.

Woumans, E., Santens, P., Sieben, A., Versijpt, J., Stevens, M. and Duyck, W. (2015) Bilingualism delays clinical manifestation of Alzheimer's disease. *Bilingualism: Language and Cognition* 18, 568–574.

Zahodne, L. and Manly, J. (2015) Does bilingualism improve cognitive aging? Commentary on Virginia Valian's target article, 'Bilingualism and cognition'. *Bilingualism: Language and Cognition* 18, 45–46.

Lecture 6

Cross-linguistic Influence and Multiple Language Acquisition and Use

Gessica De Angelis

Introduction

Research on cross-linguistic influence (CLI) aims to identify the mechanisms underlying the reliance on prior language knowledge in the acquisition, development or use of a target language. Prior language knowledge is widely understood to refer to the knowledge of any language an individual may be familiar with, so it includes the knowledge of the native language as well as of any other language previously acquired to varying degrees of proficiency.

The term *cross-linguistic influence* first appeared in the 1980s, when Sharwood-Smith and Kellerman (1986) introduced it to account for a range of phenomena arising from the interaction between languages, such as 'transfer, interference, avoidance, borrowing and L2 related-aspects of language loss' (Sharwood-Smith & Kellerman, 1986: 1). The term quickly established itself, becoming widely used in the field, along with the older term *language transfer*. In the present lecture, transfer and cross-linguistic influence are used as synonyms with no implied difference in meaning, unless otherwise specified.

This lecture provides an overview of studies on CLI that have influenced and shaped theoretical thinking from the 1940s to the present day and led scholars to conceive the notion of transfer in entirely new ways. As we shall see, transfer went from being a phenomenon almost exclusively associated with the first and second languages (L1, L2), to a phenomenon associated with several languages, often interacting with one another and at the same time. The lecture examines the role of a number of factors that are now known to trigger CLI phenomena in the acquisition and development of a target language.

Early Research on Cross-linguistic Influence: From a Focus on Language Teaching to a Focus on Language Learning

Research published in the 1940s already showed traces of an interest in language transfer and the awareness that the native language played a central role in language learning. Concerns at the time were mostly pedagogical in nature, and debates centred on how to write effective language teaching materials and on the need to compare the native language of the learner with the L2 being learnt in the classroom. Explanations based on behaviourism were used to describe how humans learned new languages, and such explanations reflected the common belief that in order to learn a language one needed to replace existing individual patterns of L1 use with those of the L2. Fries (1945), for instance, wrote an entire volume explaining how English language teaching materials were prepared at the University of Michigan throughout the 1940s, and presented articulated arguments in favour of a contrastive approach to language teaching. A few years later, Rosenbaum (1949) wrote an article which included an initial description of positive and negative transfer and provided support for the use of a contrastive approach in language teaching. The author also dedicated an entire section to the role of non-native languages in language teaching, acknowledging their potential role and explaining how useful they can be for the teacher's work in the classroom.

Many of Rosenbaum's arguments anticipate those of Lado (1957), who held the view that comparing the structure of languages was the best way to approach language teaching. He believed that differences between the elements of two languages implied difficulties for the learner, while similarities meant that learning would be easier to achieve. Lado's view, which became widely known as the contrastive analysis hypothesis (CAH), started a new phase in language learning research based on language comparisons and the identification of similarities and differences across language systems.

The association between languages is also at the heart of Weinreich's (1953) seminal work on bilingualism. Drawing on the well-known Saussurian distinction between signifier (sound of a word) and signified (concept of a word), he focused on the difference between form and meaning and proposed that the association between words in different languages is dependent on the association between the sound and the concept of a word. The resulting relationships can be of three main types: coordinate (form and meaning are kept separate and each word form is linked to a separate concept); compound (two sound forms are linked to the same concept); and subordinate (one language is subordinate and dominant in relation to the other). Weinreich also claimed that these associations may coexist in the mind and different words may establish a different type of relationship with one another, reflecting the level of proficiency or automaticity reached in the two languages.

As the wave of CAH research was taking place, in the late 1960s some scholars also started to question whether all errors in an L2 were the result of native language influence and consequently whether transfer could only come from the native language. Corder (1967) in particular presented a series of arguments to emphasize that not all errors are linked to the native language. While the L1 is the source of some errors, there are also other types of errors that can be born out of the L2 itself and are therefore meaningful in themselves. Corder's intuition proved to be accurate, and marked the beginning of research on L2 development and error analysis.

Also crucial to these theoretical developments was Selinker's (1972) interlanguage theory. He proposed that the language of an L2 learner is governed by rules which are different from those of the native language and from those of the target language. A learner does not simply rely on the L1, but creates a *novel* system which is governed by rules that are independent and systematic. Such a system is what he called interlanguage (Selinker, 1972). Similar notions were also proposed around the same time, such as the notions of *transitional idiosyncratic dialects* (Corder, 1971) and *approximative systems* (Nemser, 1971), but it is the term interlanguage that became widely known within the academic community.

Research during the 1970s continued to focus on patterns of non-native language development and typically aimed to identify sources of language transfer in addition to the L1. Some of these studies were highly descriptive in nature. Haggis (1973), for instance, gave a thorough descriptive account of phonetic influences in the language development of trilingual subjects coming from different villages in Ghana. His subjects spoke French, English and local dialects (Asante Twi, Akwapim Twi, Brong Twi). Chamot (1973) wrote on the phonetic influences in the English language development of a French-Spanish bilingual boy who had moved to the United States as a child with his family. She showed instances of transfer from both French and Spanish individually and simultaneously, and focused on the child's difficulties with phonetic features that were either absent or present in both French and Spanish. She claimed that whenever phonetic features were shared between the boy's two background languages, the acquisition of the same feature in the English L3 would be more difficult to achieve. Another study in which we find an early mention of the factors affecting the language acquisition process is Lococo (1976), who examined the written texts of German-Spanish bilinguals studying English in Mexico. The author was one of the first to show that factors such as age and proficiency level needed to be included in theoretical discussions on target language development. Another pioneer was Ringbom (1978), who showed the central role of cross-linguistic similarity in triggering instances of transfer, regardless of whether the source language was the L1 or the L2 for the speaker.

The cumulative effect of all these activities was that non-native languages began to be viewed as potential sources of influence in a more systematic manner, and the influence of more than one language started to be observed more closely (see Chamot, 1973; Chandresekhar, 1978; Singh & Carroll, 1979; Vildomec, 1963). During the following decades, research on multilingualism and CLI became more widespread and it gradually raised scholars' awareness of the broad role of non-native languages in multilingual language acquisition and language development.

Direction of Cross-linguistic Influence and Combined Influences

The presence of multiple languages in the mind entails an increase in the number of cross-linguistic interactions that are possible, and also an increase in the number of potential directions. For a long time, CLI was conceived as a unidirectional phenomenon, going from the L1 to the L2. We now know that the influence can also be bidirectional, that is from the L2 to the L1 (Jarvis & Pavlenko, 2008), as well as multidirectional, for instance from an L3 to an L2 or an L1 (for a review, see De Angelis, 2007). Additionally we know that CLI phenomena are not restricted to two languages and may occur from two or more languages at the same time. The latter is referred to as combined cross-linguistic influence, a term used in De Angelis (2007) to describe the simultaneous influence of two languages on the target language. In previous literature the same phenomenon was either described without the use of a specific term (Chandresekhar, 1978; Vildomec, 1963) or defined as 'double interference' (Chamot, 1973).

Several scholars have taken a special interest in combined CLI influence over the years, in particular from the 1960s onwards. Vildomec (1963), for example, reported a number of instances of this type of influence in his volume on multilingualism and openly acknowledged the existence of non-native language influence as well as combined CLI. Chamot (1973) called the phenomenon 'double interference' and put forward some arguments that challenged Lado's popular 'contrastive analysis'. She claimed that when two languages share a phonetic feature the influence on a third language tends to be negative rather than positive, as Lado would have predicted. Chandresekhar (1978) also commented on the production of a learner of German L3 whose native language was a form of Hindi-influenced English and was therefore a case of combined CLI.

Throughout the 1980s and 1990s we find brief mentions of combined CLI. In a discussion on the role of the proficiency factor and recency of use in language transfer, Möhle (1989) mentions instances of combined CLI involving Spanish, French, English or Latin. Clyne (1997) also identifies the effect of two languages interacting with one another, claiming that the similarity between two languages has a reinforcing effect and facilitates instances of language transfer in a third language.

The study of combined CLI has remained confined to a handful of studies to date, and this is mostly due to the difficulty of eliciting suitable empirical evidence in a quantity sufficient to carry out quantitative analysis. Nonetheless, the evidence we have is enough for us to understand that we cannot safely assume transfer to come from one source language whenever other languages are also in the mind. From a theoretical point of view, multiple language knowledge entails that, in addition to explaining why and how information from a source language is selected and transferred to a target language, we also need to explain why the additional language knowledge in the mind is excluded from selection. Combined CLI is of particular interest because of the reinforcing effect that similar information from different languages seems to exert on the target language.

Overt and Covert Transfer

Most of us have had the experience of hearing someone speak a language with an accent and understanding where the person is from. This is an example of *overt transfer*, a type of influence that can be easily noticed in oral or written production. Jarvis called it the 'you-know-it-when-you-see-it phenomenon' (Jarvis, 2000: 246), emphasizing how the source of the influence is often easy to detect for the reader or listener.

Transfer may also be less obvious and *covert*, and this type of influence is identified through the underuse, overuse or lack of use of a given element or structure in the target language. For example, an Italian L1 speaker learning English as an L2 may underuse the subject pronoun because Italian verb morphology allows the speaker to express gender and number without including an overt subject pronoun in production. A direct comparison between a French and an Italian native speaker at similar proficiency levels in English is then likely to show that the Italian native speaker is underusing the subject pronoun in production while the French native speaker is not, as overt subjects are compulsory in French as well as English. This phenomenon is commonly referred to as *avoidance*, which means that the learner will avoid an element or structure because he or she finds it difficult to produce it. The phenomenon was first highlighted in Schachter (1974). Focusing on the use of relative clauses in written production, Schachter compared the written compositions of native English speaking students with those of ESL learners. The ESL learners spoke different native languages: Chinese, Japanese, Persian and Arabic. The author then argued that Chinese and Japanese learners showed a lower rate of use of relative clauses because they found the structure more difficult to produce than speakers of Persian or Arabic.

Positive and Negative Transfer

The terms positive and negative transfer rank among the most popular in discussions about CLI because they convey a transparent message and are easy to understand. Scholars in the field, however, have not been very fond of these terms for several decades now, and for some good reasons.

CLI is a process that can be triggered or constrained by a range of external or internal factors. A process is neither negative nor positive per se; it is the outcome that can be subjectively classified as being positive or negative. For instance, if a French and a Japanese native speaker are learning Spanish as a second language, we are likely to find that the production of the French native speaker is much more elaborate (positive transfer) but also contains a higher number of mistakes (negative transfer) due to lexical guessing. Given similar exposure to the Spanish L2, the Japanese native speaker is not likely to resort to lexical guessing due to the distance between Spanish and Japanese, and the avoidance behaviour will lead the learner to write shorter texts that contain a lower number of mistakes. Is a short text with fewer mistakes an example of positive or negative transfer then? Whether transfer is judged as being positive or negative depends on a personal judgment, and the same outcome may in fact be classified as positive or negative by different individuals, depending on how they view it.

Internal Versus External Factors

A number of studies have focused on the triggering or constraining properties of external and internal factors for CLI. Of particular interest are the role of language distance, L2 status and recency of use, as well as the competition between some of these.

If on the one hand the history of CLI research shows a general interest in the role of different individual factors, we also see the opposite occurring, that is, a focus on the overall influence that one or more languages may exert upon another. Ringbom (2002) wrote about the existence of three levels of transfer: an overall level, an item level and a system level. The overall level is of concern here, as it describes the learners' overall perception of similarity between two or more linguistic systems, and the influence that may result from such a perception. The notion echoes Kellerman's (1978) claim of psychotypology being a trigger of CLI on a target language.

Thomas (1988) argued that receiving formal instruction in a non-native language leads the learner to develop a heightened awareness of language (metalinguistic awareness) which turns into an overall positive influence when learning an additional language. Swain *et al.* (1990) further claim that is not bilingualism per se that brings about benefits for the learner, but bilingual literacy. With respect to foreign language achievement, Griessler (2001) points to the positive influence that learning an L3 may have on the L2 learnt at school. More recently, Stavans (2015) has discussed the positive effect of exposure to foreign alphabets on the literacy development of multilingual children of preschool age. The children seemed to be positively affected by external input, even before they had learned to read and write any language.

There is a large body of evidence in support of an overall positive benefit from knowing one non-native language for the acquisition of subsequent ones, and such benefit seems to increase as the number of languages increases (Adesope *et al.*, 2010; Gold *et al.*, 2013; Lazaruk, 2007; Mårtensson *et al.*, 2012). The presence of multiple languages in the mind and their use on a frequent basis has further been linked to a protective effect against cognitive decline in old age (Bialystok *et al.*, 2007; Perquin *et al.*, 2013).

The following sections will review what we know about the most common triggers of CLI and multilingualism, placing special attention on three core triggers: language distance, L2 status and recency of use.

Language distance and the (psycho)typological factor

A substantial number of studies have examined multilingual speakers and the role of language distance in triggering CLI phenomena (Cenoz, 2001; Clyne, 1997; Clyne & Cassia, 1999; De Angelis, 2005a, 2005b; Odlin & Jarvis, 2004; Ringbom, 1987; Rivers, 1979; Rothman, 2011; Selinker & Baumgarten-Cohen, 1995; Singleton, 1987; Swarte *et al.*, 2015). Research findings have been consistent over the years and they seem to point to the same conclusion: the amount and degree of similarity between two languages are core triggers of CLI on a target language.

Language distance and language similarity, however, may mean different things to different authors. Some conceive similarity as being closely connected to typology and the actual relationship between languages. French, Spanish and German, for instance, are all Indo-European languages, but French and Spanish are Romance languages while German is a Germanic language. Language distance, in this case, identifies the typological difference between Germanic and Romance languages. The structures or elements of two languages may also be similar to one another even if the languages are typologically distant. For example, French (a Romance language) and English (a Germanic language) belong to different language families. They are typologically more distant than French and Spanish, yet for historical reasons the similarity between French and English vocabulary is extensive. Language similarity, in other words, does not necessarily imply typological closeness.

A third notion that is fundamental for any discussion on CLI and multilingualism relates to the learner's individual perception of language distance. This is referred to as *psychotypology* in the literature, and the proposal stems from the publication of a seminal study in the field known as the Breken study (Kellerman, 1978).

Kellerman gave 81 Dutch native speakers a list of idiomatic expressions that contained the verb *breken* ('to break' in English) and asked whether the expressions could be translated into English. Learners rated the translatability of each item, scoring for instance 100% for expressions such as 'he broke his leg' and 11% for opaque expressions such as 'some workers have broken the strike'.

Kellerman then argued that transfer is constrained by two interacting factors: psychotypology and prototypicality. The first refers to the individual's perception of closeness between the expressions of two languages, and the second to the prototypical meaning of a given form (Kellerman, 1987). Of concern here is the first factor, psychotypology, which remains one of the most cited notions in the literature on CLI and multilingualism. For the first time, Kellerman (1978) showed that what individuals perceive as being close or distant between two languages does not necessarily match what linguists define as being typologically close or distant. He further showed that judgments of transferability are closely connected to the prototypical meaning of idiomatic expressions and vary depending on what the learner is judging. Transfer, in other words, has a subjective connotation as well as an objective one.

Around the same time as Kellerman (1978), Chandrasekhar (1978) proposed another hypothesis based on language similarity: the base language hypothesis, which posits that learners are most influenced by the language that is most similar to the target language, and that it is this language that becomes the base language for the learner.

Some support for this position can be found in the literature. Focusing on Swedish and Finnish as native and non-native languages, Ringbom (1987) showed the dominant role of Swedish as an L2 in learners' written production of the English L3. The dominant role mostly concerned formal rather than semantic transfer, where the L1 continued to retain a strong role.

Finnish is a Finno-Ugric language and Swedish is a Germanic language like English. Odlin and Jarvis (2004) also compared the English L3 texts written by Finnish L1 and Swedish L1 speakers with Finnish and Swedish as second languages, reaching conclusions that are similar to Ringbom's. Learners in both groups were strongly influenced by Swedish, the language most similar to the English target language, regardless of whether Swedish was an L1 or an L2 for the learner, thus confirming the central role of language similarity and the ease with which it overrides second language status (see L2 status factor below).

While there is some support for the base language hypothesis, the literature on multilingualism seems to confirm it only in part. On the one hand, we have evidence that from time to time non-native languages may become the preferred source of information, regardless of language distance between the source and the target language. On the other hand, we also know that CLI influence is triggered or constrained by additional factors such as source and target language proficiency or how recently a language was last used.

With respect to transfer from languages that are more distant from the target language, we have evidence that it may occur in production as long as words in the source and the target language are phonetically similar to one another (Rivers, 1979). Phonetic similarity is identified as a prerequisite, while actual typological distance is not. Additional evidence and arguments of this kind can be found in the work of Selinker and Baumgartner-Cohen (1995), who also believe phonetic similarity to be a precondition for this type of transfer to occur. Their discussion further highlights that, in addition to being phonetically similar to the target, learners transfer items that tend to belong to the same word class and where the speaker seems to be somewhat familiar with the target form. Other types of transfer may also occur regardless of the distance between languages or the phonetic similarity between structures or items, such as semantic, pragmatic and conceptual transfer. In other words, phonetic similarity is often but not always a prerequisite for transfer to occur.

More recent discussions on the role of language distance and multilingualism focus on syntax and the initial state. Rothman (2011) in particular is the proponent of the typology primacy model (TPM). Using data on adjectival interpretation, he puts forward the claim that typological proximity – a notion here closely connected to Kellerman's psychotypology – takes precedence over L2 status (Bardel & Falk, 2007).

Second language status

Research on CLI traditionally examined instances of transfer from the L1 to the L2, showing L1 influence to be a strong and pervasive type of influence in L2 acquisition and development. When more languages started to be added to the learners' repertoire, however, it soon became apparent that the L1 was not the privileged source many had assumed it to be. Learners frequently relied on their non-native languages, even when it seemed illogical for them to do so, for instance when they were familiar with languages typologically closer to the target language. Learners' behaviour then started to be examined more closely, leading scholars to consider *L2 status* as a triggering factor in its own right.

The term L2 status is now broadly used to define learners' tendency to transfer information from non-native languages to a target language and, despite its name, it refers to any non-native language an individual may be familiar with, so it is not restricted to the L2. Research on L2 status typically highlights under what circumstances a non-native language becomes the preferred source of information for the learner, and under what circumstances it comes to override influence from the L1 or other languages in the mind.

Falk and Bardel (2010) attribute the first mention of a foreign language effect in language learning to Meisel (1983). We then find the notion discussed in several other studies, but from very different angles. Hammarberg and Hammarberg (1993), for instance, mention it to explain the seemingly odd behaviour of an English L1 learner of Swedish L3, who was deliberately trying not to sound English and sounded German (the L2) instead. An additional and more articulated discussion of the L2 status as a deliberate strategy can be read in Williams and Hammarberg (1998). Here the authors proposed that L2 status plays a central role in selecting the main supplier language for the learner, i.e. the language from which the learner tends to transfer the most information into the target language.

De Angelis (2005b) provides a different interpretation of the role of L2 status in triggering language transfer phenomena as she does not believe L2 status to be a deliberate strategy. She argues that transfer in multilinguals is constrained by two interacting factors: perception of correctness and association of foreignness. She explains that multilinguals will resist the use of L1 words because they instinctively know they do not belong to the target language (perception of correctness). Multilinguals also establish a cognitive association between foreign languages (association of foreignness) which will increase the likelihood that words from non-native languages will be selected instead of the native ones. Trude and Tokowicz (2011) also maintain that learners are better at inhibiting/suppressing the native language than the L2.

While several studies have found a close link between foreign languages (Aronin & Toubkin, 2002; Cohen, 1995; De Angelis & Selinker, 2001; Rivers, 1979; Schmidt & Frota, 1986; Selinker & Baumgarten, 1995), reliance on non-native language knowledge is more likely to occur during the early stages of acquisition when proficiency in the target language is still relatively low (Hammarberg & Hammarberg, 1993; Selinker & Baumgartner-Cohen, 1995; Williams & Hammarberg, 1998; Wrembel, 2009).

More recent discussions on L2 status focus on syntax and the initial state (Bardel & Falk, 2007; Cabrelli Amaro *et al.*, 2012; Falk & Bardel, 2011; Leung, 2005). Bardel and Falk in particular have argued in support of a strong role of L2 status in language transfer, which takes precedence over typological proximity (Bardel & Falk, 2007; Falk & Bardel, 2011). Their arguments are based on data obtained from German L3 learners with English L1 or L2 and French L1 or L2. Using grammaticality judgment/correction tasks, they focused on object pronouns in German main and subordinate clauses, showing the privileged role of the L2 as a preferred source of information.

A somewhat similar design but a different language combination and a focus on voice onset times is found in the work of Llama *et al.* (2010), who examined Spanish L3 learners with knowledge of English and French as either L1 or L2. The authors confirmed the strong role of L2 status, providing additional support for the proposal of Bardel and Falk (2007) and Falk and Bardel (2011).

In addition to the L2 status model (Bardel & Falk, 2007) and the TPM (Rothman, 2011), discussion of CLI and syntax typically includes a third model, namely the cumulative enhancement model (Flynn *et al.*, 2004), which claims that the L1 does not have a privileged status in language transfer, as other languages cumulatively enhance the learning process. Along similar lines, but with a slight difference in focus, is a fourth model: the linguistic proximity model (Westergaard *et al.*, 2017). This last model maintains that transfer may occur when a given property receives strong input from the background languages, regardless of distance or L2 status.

Recency of use

One other factor that has proved to be central in triggering CLI phenomena in multilinguals is *recency of use*. Most multilingual speakers know that the languages used recently tend to influence language production to a greater extent than those that go unused for a long time. Vildomec (1963) was perhaps the first to make a clear link between what he called the 'vividness' of languages and language use. Early confirmation of the central role of recency of use also comes from Albert and Obler (1978). The authors discuss the factor in relation to recovery patterns after brain injury and find that the speed and success of patients' language recovery was substantially affected by how recently they had used that language.

In the earlier literature on CLI, Schmidt and Frota (1986) comment on the role of this factor in relation to language proficiency. While the authors generally maintain that language proficiency is a stronger trigger of CLI, they also acknowledge that in some cases the recent use of a language may facilitate the introduction of non-target forms into production. The same claim can be found in Mohle (1989) and Williams and Hammarberg (1998). The latter, in particular, highlighted the importance of recency of use for CLI and turned the idea into a popular notion in the literature. Recency of use is also closely linked to the notion of frequency of use, and the frequency factor is a well-known trigger in psychology, whereby it is easier to retrieve a word used frequently than a word that is rarely used (Levelt & Mayer, 2000; Levelt *et al.*, 1999).

A Look Ahead

As we have seen in this lecture, over the past few decades much progress has been made in the field of CLI and multilingualism, and evidence of non-native language influence has been identified from low- to high-proficiency background languages and in all domains (for a review, see De Angelis & Dewaele, 2011).

While the field remains very young and our knowledge partial at best, an important benefit stemming from these research activities is that there is now an increased awareness among scholars that language transfer does not necessarily mean transfer from the L1. Given the pervasive nature of L1 influence and its central role in language acquisition and language development, this increased awareness brings with it the realization that general theories about language acquisition and language development will never be adequate if they continue to be based on evidence from the L2 alone. Ignoring the presence of non-native languages in the mind means providing models and theories that apply to a restricted number of learners rather than the general population. Multilingualism is a reality in our world, and the activities of the last few decades show that scholars are quickly learning to account for it. CLI is one of the fields of research that is providing meaningful contributions to our understanding of multilingualism, along with many other fields that have taken an interest in the multilingual mind and how it functions from a variety of perspectives.

Questions for Students' Reflection

1. How many languages have you studied in your life? Do you find that having learnt other non-native languages has helped you in learning additional ones? If so, what advantages have you noticed?

2. Have you ever found traces of your non-native languages in your writing or in your speech?

3. What do you consciously do in order to keep your languages apart?

4. Can you think of some personal examples where you have experienced transfer from your L1 and from one of your non-native languages?

Suggestions for Further Reading

Cabrelli Amaro, J., Flynn, S. and Rothman, J. (2012) *Third Language Acquisition in Adulthood*. Amsterdam: John Benjamins.

De Angelis, G. and Dewaele, J.M. (2011) (eds) *New Trends in Crosslinguistic Influence and Multilingualism Research*. Bristol: Multilingual Matters.

De Angelis, G., Jessner, U. and Kresić, M. (2015) *Crosslinguistic Influence and Crosslinguistic Interaction in Multilingual Language Learning*. London: Bloomsbury.

Jarvis, S. and Pavlenko, A. (2008) *Crosslinguistic Influence in Language and Cognition*. New York and London: Routledge.

References

Adesope, O.O., Lavin, T., Thompson, T. and Ungerleider, C. (2010) A systematic review and meta-analysis of the cognitive correlates of bilingualism. *Review of Educational Research* 80, 207–245.

Albert, M.L. and Obler, L.K. (1978) *The Bilingual Brain*. New York: Academic Press.

Aronin, L. and Toubkin, L. (2002) Language interference and language learning techniques transfer in L2 and L3 immersion programmes. *International Journal of Bilingual Education and Bilingualism* 5 (5), 267–278.

Bardel, C. and Falk, Y. (2007) The role of the second language in third language acquisition: The case of Germanic syntax. *Second Language Research* 23, 459–484.

Bialystok, E., Craik, F.I.M. and Freedman, M. (2007) Bilingualism as a protection against the onset of symptoms of dementia. *Neuropsychologia* 45 (2), 459–464.

Cabrelli Amaro, J., Flynn, S. and Rothman, J. (2012) *Third Language Acquisition in Adulthood*, Amsterdam: John Benjamins.

Cenoz, J. (2001) The effect of linguistic distance, L2 status and age on cross-linguistic influence in third language acquisition. In J. Cenoz, B. Hufeisen and U. Jessner (eds) *Cross-linguistic Influence in Third Language Acquisition: Psycholinguistic Perspectives* (pp. 8–20). Clevedon: Multilingual Matters.

Chamot, A.U. (1973) Phonological problems in learning English as a third language. *International Review of Applied Linguistics* XI (3), 243–250.

Chandrasekhar, A. (1978) Base language. *International Review of Applied Linguistics* XVI (1), 62–65.

Clyne, M. (1997) Some of the things trilinguals do. *International Journal of Bilingualism* 1 (2), 95–116.

Clyne, M. and Cassia, P. (1999) Trilingualism, immigration and relatedness of languages. *ITL: Review of Applied Linguistics* 123–124, 57–54.

Cohen, A.D. (1995) In which language do/should multilinguals think? *Language, Culture and Curriculum* 8 (2), 99–113.

Corder, S.P. (1967) The significance of learners' errors. *International Review of Applied Linguistics* 5, 160–170; doi:10.1515/iral.1967.5.1-4.161.

Corder, S. (1971) Idiosyncratic dialects and error analysis. *International Review of Applied Linguistics* IX, 149–159.

De Angelis, G. (2005a) Interlanguage transfer of function words. *Language Learning* 55 (3), 379–414.

De Angelis, G. (2005b) Multilingualism and non-native lexical transfer: An identification problem. *International Journal of Multilingualism* 2 (1), 1–25.

De Angelis, G. (2007) *Third or Additional Language Acquisition* (pp. i–vii, 1–152). Clevedon: Multilingual Matters.

De Angelis, G. and Dewaele, J.M. (2011) (eds) *New Trends in Crosslinguistic Influence and Multilingualism Research* (pp. i–xv, 1–128). Bristol: Multilingual Matters.

De Angelis, G. and Selinker, L. (2001) Interlanguage transfer and competing linguistic systems in the multilingual mind. In J. Cenoz, B. Hufeisen and U. Jessner (eds) *Cross-linguistic Influence in Third Language Acquisition: Psycholinguistic Perspectives* (pp. 42–58). Clevedon: Multilingual Matters.

De Angelis, G., Jessner, U. and Kresić, M. (2015) *Crosslinguistic Influence and Crosslinguistic Interaction in Multilingual Language Learning* (pp. i–x, 1–259). London: Bloomsbury.

Falk, Y. and Bardel, C. (2010) The study of the role of the background languages in third language acquisition. The state of the art. *International Review of Applied Linguistics in Language Teaching (IRAL)* 48 (2–3), 185–220.

Falk, Y. and Bardel, C. (2011) Object pronouns in German L3 syntax: Evidence for the L2 status factor. *Second Language Research* 27 (1), 59–82.

Flynn, S., Foley, C. and Vinnitskaya, I. (2004) The cumulative-enhancement model of language acquisition: Comparing adults' and children's patters of development in first, second and third language acquisition of relative clauses. *International Journal of Multilingualism* 1 (1), 3–16.

Fries, C.C. (1945) *Teaching and Learning English as a Foreign Language*. Ann Arbor, MI: University of Michigan Press.

Gold, B.T., Johnson, N.F. and Powell, D.K. (2013) Lifelong bilingualism contributes to cognitive reserve against white matter integrity declines in aging. *Neuropsychologia* 51 (13), 2841–2846.

Griessler, M. (2001) The effect of third language learning on second language proficiency: An Austrian example. *International Journal of Bilingual Education and Bilingualism* 4 (1), 50–60.

Haggis, B.M. (1973) Un cas de trilinguisme. *Linguistique* 9, 37–50.

Hammarberg, B. and Hammarberg, B. (1993) Articulatory re-setting in the acquisition of new languages. *Reports from the Department of Phonetics, University of Umeå, PHONUM* 2, 61–67.

Jarvis, S. (2000) Methodological rigour in the study of transfer: Identifying L1 influence in the interlanguage lexicon. *Language Learning* 50 (2), 245–309.

Jarvis, S. and Pavlenko, A. (2008) *Crosslinguistic Influence in Language and Cognition*. New York and London: Routledge.

Kellerman, E. (1978) Giving learners a break: Native language intuitions as a source of prediction about transferability. *Working Papers on Bilingualism* 15, 59–92.

Kellerman, E. (1987) Aspects of transferability in second language acquisition. PhD thesis, University of Nijmegen.

Lado, R. (1957) *Linguistics Across Cultures*. Ann Arbor, MI: University of Michigan Press.

Lazaruk, W. (2007) Linguistic, academic and cognitive benefits of French immersion. *Canadian Modern Language Review* 63 (5), 605–628.

Leung, Y. (2005) L2 vs. L3 initial state: A comparative study of the acquisition of French DPs by Vietnamese monolinguals and Cantonese-English bilinguals. *Bilingualism: Language and Cognition* 8 (1), 39–61.

Levelt, W.J.M. and Meyer, A.S. (2000) Word for word: Multiple lexical access in speech production. *European Journal of Cognitive Psychology* 12 (4), 433–452.

Levelt, W.J.M., Roelofs, A. and Meyer, A. (1999) A theory of lexical access in speech production. *Behavioural and Brain Sciences* 22, 1–75.

Llama, R., Waleir, C. and Collins, C. (2010) The influence of language distance and language status on the acquisition of L3 phonology. *International Journal of Multilingualism* 7 (1), 39–57.

Lococo, V. (1976) A cross-sectional study on L3 acquisition. *Working Papers on Bilingualism* 9, 44–75.

Mårtensson, J., Eriksson, J., Bodammer, N.C., Lindgren, M., Johansson, M., Nyberg, L. and Lövdén, M. (2012) Growth of language-related brain areas after foreign language learning. *NeuroImage* 63 (1), 240–244; doi:10.1016/j.neuroimage.2012.06.043.

Meisel, J. (1983) Transfer as a second language strategy. *Language and Communication* 3, 11–46.

Möhle, D. (1989) Multilingual interaction in foreign language production. In W.H. Dechert and M. Raupach (eds) *Interlingual Processes* (pp. 179–194). Tübingen: Gunter Narr.

Nemser, W. (1971) Approximative systems of foreign language learners. *International Review of Applied Linguistics* IX, 115–123.

Odlin, T. and Jarvis, S. (2004) Same source, different outcomes: A study of Swedish influence on the acquisition of English in Finland. *International Journal of Multilingualism* 1 (2), 123–140.

Perquin, M., Vaillant, M., Schuller, A.-M., Pastore, J., Dartigues, J.-F., Lair, M.-L. and Diederich, N. (2013) Lifelong exposure to multilingualism: New evidence to support cognitive reserve hypothesis. *PLoS ONE* 8 (4), 1–7.

Ringbom, H. (1978) The influence of the mother tongue on the translation of lexical items. *Interlanguage Studies Bulletin* 3, 80–101.

Ringbom, H. (1987) *The Role of the First Language in Foreign Language Learning*. Clevedon: Multilingual Matters.

Ringbom, H. (2002) Levels of transfer from L1 and L2 in L3-acquisition. In J. Ytsma and M. Hooghiemstra (eds) *Proceedings of the Second International Conference on Trilingualism*. Leeuwaarden: Fryske Akademie (CD).

Rivers, W.M. (1979) Learning a sixth language: An adult learner's daily diary. *Canadian Modern Language Review* 36 (1), 67–82.

Rosenbaum, E. (1949) The application of transfer between foreign languages. *The Modern Language Journal* 33 (4), 287–294.

Rothman, J. (2011) L3 syntactic transfer selectivity and typological determinacy: The typological primacy model. *Second Language Research* 27 (1), 107–127; doi:10.1177/0267658310386439.

Schachter, J. (1974) An error in error analysis. *Language Learning* 24 (2), 205–214.

Schmidt, R.W. and Frota, S.N. (1986) Developing basic conversation ability in a second language: A case study of an adult learner of Portuguese. In R. Day (ed.) *Talking to Learn: Conversation in Second Language Acquisition* (pp. 237–326). Rowley, MA: Newbury House.

Selinker, L. (1972) Interlanguage. *International Review of Applied Linguistics* 10 (3), 209–231.

Selinker, L. and Baumgartner-Cohen, B. (1995) Multiple language acquisition: 'Damn it, why can't I keep these two languages apart?' *Language, Culture and Curriculum* 8 (2), 115–121.

Sharwood Smith, M. and Kellerman, E. (1986) Crosslinguistic influence in second language acquisition: An introduction. In E. Kellerman and M. Sharwood Smith (eds) *Crosslinguistic Influence in Second Language Acquisition* (pp. 1–9). New York: Pergamon Press.

Singh, R. and Carroll, S. (1979) L1, L2 and L3. *Indian Journal of Applied Linguistics* 5, 51–63.

Singleton, D. (1987) Mother and other tongue influence on learner French: A case study. *Studies in Second Language Acquisition* 9, 327–346.

Stavans, A. (2015) 'If you know Amharic you can read this': Emergent literacy in multilingual pre-reading children. In G. De Angelis, U. Jessner and M. Kresić (eds) *Crosslinguistic Influence and Crosslinguistic Interaction in Multilingual Language Learning* (pp. 149–172). London: Bloomsbury.

Swain, M., Lapkin, S., Rowen, N. and Hart, D. (1990) The role of mother tongue literacy in third language learning. *Language, Culture and Curriculum* 3 (1), 65–81.

Swarte, F., Schüppert, A. and Gooskens, C. (2015) Does German help speakers of Dutch to understand written and spoken Danish words? The role of non-native language knowledge in decoding an unknown but related language. In G. De Angelis, U. Jessner and M. Kresić (eds) *Crosslinguistic Influence and Crosslinguistic Interaction in Multilingual Language Learning* (pp. 173–198). London: Bloomsbury.

Thomas, J. (1988) The role played by metalinguistic awareness in second and third language learning. *Journal of Multilingual and Multicultural Development* 9 (3), 235–246.

Trude, A. and Tokowicz, N. (2011) Negative transfer from Spanish and English to Portuguese pronunciation: The roles of inhibition and working memory. *Language Learning* 61, 259–280.

Vildomec, V. (1963) *Multilingualism*. Leyden: A.W. Sythoff.

Weinreich, U. (1953) *Languages in Contact*. New York: Linguistic Circle of New York.

Westergaard, M., Mitrofanova, N., Mykhaylyk, R. and Rodina, Y. (2017) Crosslinguistic influence in the acquisition of a third language: The linguistic proximity model. *International Journal of Bilingualism* 21 (6), 666–682; doi:10.1177/1367006916648859.

Williams, S. and Hammarberg, B. (1998) Language switches in L3 production: Implications for a polyglot speaking model. *Applied Linguistics* 19 (3), 295–333.

Wrembel, M. (2009) L2-accented speech in L3 production. *International Journal of Multilingualism* 7 (1), 75–90; doi:10.1080/14790710902972263.

Lecture 7

Motivation and Multilingualism

Ema Ushioda

> *I speak Spanish to God, Italian to women, French to men and German to my horse.*
> Attributed to Charles V, Holy Roman Emperor, 1500–1558

Why Motivation is Important in Multilingualism

In human psychology, motivation is broadly defined in terms of the choice of a particular action, the effort expended in it and the persistence with it (Dörnyei & Ushioda, 2011: 4). Thus questions about human motivation tend to revolve around why people choose to do something (reasons, goals, motives, values), how much they invest (effort, time, attention, energy) and how far they go (progress, achievement, challenges). When it comes to speaking multiple languages, learning multiple languages or functioning in a multilingual environment, issues of motivation will always come into play at some level, whether individual or societal. At an *individual* level, for example, motivation comes into play as we make choices and decisions about what languages to learn and why (or find that we have little freedom of choice), or as we invest and sustain effort (or not) in developing our language skills and enriching our linguistic repertoire. Motivation also shapes our behaviours and experiences when we use certain languages to express ourselves in particular contexts or communicate with particular people, or when we code-switch between languages for particular reasons. At the level of *societal* multilingualism, for example, there may be politico-cultural motivation shaping decision making in national and regional language policies, or inspiring language movements and linguistic revivals. More locally in relation to particular multilingual communities, motivation may be implicated in how languages are used to express membership or affiliation, or in how languages serve to include or exclude, to integrate or divide.

In short, issues of motivation are relevant and sometimes critically important to the analysis of both *individual* and *societal* multilingualism – that is, the analysis of how and why individuals and communities engage with multiple languages. This latter *societal* perspective clearly broadens our research interest in motivation beyond its traditional focus as a psychological construct and aspect of *individual* human behaviour. As we shall see later in this lecture, motivation has important social, cultural, political and sociological as well as psychological dimensions when it is applied to the analysis of multilingualism.

Overview of this Lecture

Nevertheless, in keeping with traditional perspectives in motivational psychology and language motivation research, I will begin with a focus on the individual level, and on the motivation of the *language learner* in particular. As I will explain, motivation has been a major topic within the field of second language acquisition (SLA) research since the 1960s. While this field of research has largely been concerned with the processes of acquiring a single additional language (L2) rather than more than one language (e.g. L3 or L4), its findings and implications have core relevance to our concerns in this lecture. I will therefore provide a historical account of key theories and concepts in motivation research in SLA, before bringing the reader up to date with contemporary thinking in the field.

Expanding the focus from language learning to *language use* and from individual to societal perspectives, I will then consider some critical issues in language motivation in today's multilingual societies and globalized world. This section will highlight how notions of identity are often implicated in the motivation to speak particular languages, and will discuss how these extend beyond static categorizations of linguistic or ethnic identity to encompass multiple, fluid and transformative identity processes. The section will also discuss motivational perspectives on language policy and practices in various multilingual contexts, thus broadening the analysis beyond psychological to sociological, cultural and political perspectives on motivation.

I will then review the relatively small body of recent research that has investigated motivational perspectives in the simultaneous learning of two or more languages or the learning of multiple languages. I will discuss what these studies tell us about the factors that motivate people to become multilingual, and what theoretical implications they offer for how we understand motivation in relation to individual multilingualism.

In the final part of the lecture, I will very briefly touch on methodological issues in researching motivation and multilingualism. I will consider the limitations of the traditional quantitative methodologies that have tended to prevail in language motivation research, and discuss the value of adopting qualitative and mixed methods approaches.

The Origins of Motivation Research in Second Language Acquisition and Multilingualism

Historically speaking, research interest in motivation in L2 learning grew out of a concern to understand why people learning a second or foreign language achieve rather variable degrees of success, despite exposure to similar learning conditions and language input. This was effectively the question posed by the two Canadian researchers, Robert Gardner and Wallace Lambert (1959, 1972), who pioneered work in this field of enquiry and established a major tradition of empirical research on motivation in SLA through the 1970s and 1980s.

Gardner and Lambert speculated that motivation was a significant factor in explaining individual variability in L2 learning success, and that the impact of this affective factor was independent of cognitive factors such as a person's aptitude for language learning. They further speculated that a person whose motivation to learn a language was shaped by a strong interest in the target language culture and community was likely to be more successful than a language learner motivated by purely pragmatic goals such as gaining a qualification. This was because motivation was likely to be more sustained when deeply rooted in a personal interest in the target language community and especially a desire 'to be like valued members' integrated into this community (Gardner & Lambert, 1959: 271). This latter kind of motivational orientation became labelled an *integrative orientation*, to contrast with the more *instrumental orientation* of pragmatic language learning goals.

Here I would like to make two important points about the origins of this research on L2 motivation which are particularly relevant to our concerns. First, it is worth noting that this field of enquiry was established in Canada, a country with two major language groups (English and French) where language-related policies have historically been high-profile concerns at national and regional level. Much of the early empirical work investigated L2-related motivation and attitudes among English or French Canadians, or in other bilingual or multilingual settings such as the US states of Louisiana and Maine (Gardner & Lambert, 1972), the Philippines (Gardner & Santos, 1970) or India (Lukmani, 1972). In other words, the research focus on language learning motivation and associated attitudes towards target language speakers originated in the context of societal bilingualism and multilingualism where opportunities for social contact and integration with members of the other language community exist and are theorized to interact with individual motivation to develop L2 skills. In short, while the empirical focus in this research tradition is on motivation for learning a single L2 rather than more than one, its theoretical and contextual concerns are very relevant to the analysis of motivation and multilingualism.

At the same time, the second point to be made is that this research tradition on L2 learning motivation is firmly situated in the field of SLA where the primary concern has been to explain how and why L2 learning differs from first language (L1) learning in terms of learning processes, behaviours and outcomes. Although there are of course many people who achieve remarkable levels of proficiency in an L2 that parallel or even surpass their L1 skills, the field of SLA research essentially derives its *raison d'être* from the fact that, on the whole, most people who learn an L2 do not reach such levels, as for example Towell and Hawkins (1994) have described in a typical statement about SLA:

> For most of us the acquisition of second languages is less spectacular. If we are past the age of around 7–10 years the acquisition of an L2, in marked contrast to the way we acquired our first language (L1), can turn out to be rather slow, laborious and, even in talented L2 learners, tends to stop short of native-like proficiency. (Towell & Hawkins, 1994: 2)

This focus on 'native-like proficiency' as the comparative benchmark for measuring L2 learning success has powerfully shaped the research agenda and research questions in SLA, as epitomized in the study of individual difference factors such as motivation, aptitude or personality characteristics to explain variability in L2 learning success (for a detailed overview of individual difference factors in SLA, see Dörnyei, 2005). The underlying theoretical rationale for much research in SLA is that L2 learning is rarely quite as successful an enterprise as L1 learning. Some L2 learners reach higher levels of proficiency than others, some persist in their learning while others give up, and many L2 speakers achieve a limited or functional level of competence beyond which they do not seem able to progress – a phenomenon characterized by Selinker (1972) as linguistic fossilization.

In short, interest in L2 motivation as a research topic was grounded in this kind of deficit view of SLA as a learning enterprise. Moreover, the concern with examining how motivation may explain variable levels of success and persistence in L2 learning continues to remain core to this field of enquiry in the 21st century, even if the theories and concepts have evolved significantly since Gardner and Lambert's original work, as we shall see in the sections to follow. This deficit view of SLA as a learning enterprise goes against the grain of much contemporary research within the field of multilingualism, where the concern is rather to characterize and understand the practices, experiences and motivations of people who engage with several languages in particular contexts and who develop 'linguistic multi-competence' – defined most recently by Cook (2016) as the overall system of a mind (or a community) that uses more than one language. As Murahata *et al.* (2016) put it:

> In a way, the multi-competence perspective takes the 'descriptive' approach central to all linguistics and tries to describe how L2 users are, rather than the 'prescriptive' approach, which prescribes how L2 users should be. (Murahata *et al.*, 2016: 38)

Despite its origins in bilingual and multilingual social contexts, L2 motivation research is more closely aligned with the 'prescriptive' concerns of SLA as it seeks to investigate associations between L2 learners' motivation and their progression (or lack thereof) towards target language proficiency. This is an important caveat to bear in mind as we continue with our overview of the L2 motivation field and examine its relevance to understanding multilingualism.

Types of Motivation Associated with Second Language Learning Success

From its origins to the present day, L2 motivation research has therefore been preoccupied with exploring relationships between the types of motivation that people bring to learning an L2 and how successful or not they are in this learning endeavour. Success might be measured in terms of ultimate L2 attainment or proficiency levels, or of behavioural outcomes such as persistence in or withdrawal from learning. In a broad sense, theoretical developments in this field have primarily been concerned with how we conceptualize *the kinds of motivation that shape (or impede) successful L2 learning*. In this section I will trace how these concepts of motivation have evolved from Gardner and Lambert's original work to the present day.

Social-psychological concepts of second language motivation

In developing their theory of L2 learning motivation, Gardner and Lambert (1972) pursued the idea that the motivation to learn a new language had important social and psychological dimensions which made it qualitatively different from motivation in other areas of learning such as history or science. This was because L2 learning entailed not simply acquiring new knowledge but also a willingness 'to identify with members of another ethnolinguistic group and to take on very subtle aspects of their behaviour, including their distinctive style of speech and their language' (Gardner & Lambert, 1972: 135). *Social* attitudes towards another community and their cultural and linguistic practices were thus theorized to be implicated in a person's *psychological* disposition to change their own cultural and linguistic practices by adopting those of the other community. In the *social-psychological* tradition of L2 motivation research which ensued through the 1970s and 1980s, much attention was focused on attitudinal-motivational variables reflecting how L2 learners regarded the target language community and the degree to which they felt oriented to engage with or integrate into this community (for a comprehensive theoretical and empirical account, see Gardner, 1985). In effect, a major goal of this programme of empirical research was to examine the robustness of the *integrative motivation* concept in characterizing L2 learners' motivation in different social contexts, and in explaining patterns of successful L2 learning alongside more *instrumental* types of motivation (for a meta-analysis of empirical studies in this social-psychological tradition, see Masgoret & Gardner, 2003).

The social-psychological perspective on L2 motivation thus laid particular emphasis on whether members of one ethnolinguistic community identified with another ethnolinguistic community sufficiently strongly to want to be able to engage with them and ultimately gain full membership through learning their language. As we shall see later, the implied one-to-one association between a specific language and a community or between a specific language and a culture (reflected in the label 'ethnolinguistic') does not adequately reflect the more complex and fluid multilingual realities of today's globalized world. Yet, as Dörnyei (2005: 67) observes, this socially grounded analysis of motivation in the language learning domain in the 1970s and 1980s was in some senses ahead of its time, since social and contextual perspectives did not really begin to feature in mainstream motivational psychology until the 1990s.

Among the motivation-related concepts and theories to emerge in the social-psychological research period, there are a few that have particular relevance to the discussion of multilingualism, as they focus on contact and relations between minority and majority language groups in bilingual or multilingual settings.

First, Schumann (1978, 1986) developed the concept of *social* and *psychological distance* to describe the perceived relationship between the language learner (such as a newly arrived immigrant from an ethnic minority group) and target language speakers (i.e. members of the host community who speak the majority language). The factors determining such distance may be social or structural, relating for example to degree of cultural congruence, attitudinal evaluations or patterns of dominance or assimilation between majority and minority groups. The factors may also be psychological, such as the individual's experience of culture shock or culture stress, and of course the strength of motivation to learn the target language. Developing a theory of *acculturation*, Schumann hypothesized that the greater the social and psychological distance between the individual and the target language community, the stronger the impediments would be to the process of acculturation, and the more likely that the person's developing L2 skills would fossilize at a basic functional level with a rudimentary grammar and vocabulary. Here Schumann drew a parallel with the restricted communicative functions and simplified linguistic systems characterizing pidgin languages, which typically develop in situations of language contact where there is considerable social distance between two language groups. He illustrated his theory of acculturation and linguistic fossilization through a case study of Alberto, a Spanish-speaking immigrant worker from Costa Rica living in the United States who showed little development in his simplified English language system through the 10 months under focus.

While Schumann's interests were primarily in the processes of (non-)acculturation and (unsuccessful) L2 learning when a person moves to a new cultural and linguistic environment, Giles and Byrne (1982) developed an *intergroup model* to characterize the relations between minority and majority ethnolinguistic groups in multicultural settings, and to specify 'the social psychological conditions which facilitate or inhibit members of a subordinate ethnic group achieving near native-like proficiency' (Giles & Byrne, 1982: 17) in the language of the majority group. (Note the characteristic SLA research preoccupation with native-speaker standards as the target benchmark.) Adopting a social-psychological approach to language and ethnicity, Giles and Byrne drew on *social identity theory* (Tajfel, 1974, 1982), where social identity refers to a person's sense of who they are based on perceived membership of particular social groups or categories, such as social class, ethnicity, religion or gender. Social identity is an important aspect of our self-concept, and achieving a positive self-concept may entail enhancing the perceived status of the social group to which we belong (*ingroup*) relative to the status of other social groups (*outgroups*) along particular valued dimensions such as wealth, language or cultural capital. This *ingroup–outgroup* or 'us and them' line of thinking may, of course, form the psychological basis for stereotyping, prejudice and discrimination if we accentuate the negative attributes of an outgroup to give our ingroup superior status (an issue to which we will return later in our discussion of critical perspectives on motivation and multilingualism). On the other hand, members may evaluate their own ingroup negatively along certain dimensions and strive to achieve a more positive social identity by aspiring towards membership of the outgroup – a phenomenon characterized as *individual mobility*. Individual mobility and the process of social identification with the outgroup can then shape how well the language of the outgroup is acquired.

In this respect, Giles and Byrne (1982) considered a group's *ethnolinguistic vitality* to be a key factor in determining the extent to which individual mobility takes place across groups and languages. The ethnolinguistic vitality of a group is determined by sociostructural factors relating to status, demography and institutional support. Status factors include social, political, economic and sociohistorical status as well as the status (local, national or international) of the language associated with the group. Demographic factors refer to the relative size and distribution of the ethnolinguistic group, while institutional support factors concern how extensively the ethnic group is represented in the mass media, education, government, industry, religion and culture. (For an original analysis of ethnolinguistic vitality, see Giles *et al.*, 1977; for more recent discussions, see Noels *et al.*, 2014; Yagmur, 2011.) Where ingroup ethnolinguistic vitality is strong, thus favouring a positive ingroup social identity, motivation for individual mobility and acquisition of the majority language of the outgroup may be correspondingly weak. Under these conditions, it is likely that individuals will retain more in the way of linguistic markers (such as accent, non-standard grammatical features) characterizing their own ethnolinguistic identity as they acquire and use the majority language. On the other hand, where ingroup ethnolinguistic vitality and social identification are weak and where group boundaries are open enough to facilitate mobility, there may be stronger motivation to aspire towards the outgroup and acquire more 'native-like' proficiency in the majority language.

Limitations of social-psychological concepts of second language motivation

As hinted earlier, the social-psychological perspective on motivation and SLA originated in an era when the associations between language and ethnicity or between language and cultural community seemed somehow simple and straightforward. In essence, this 'older' world view sees motivation for L2 learning as a process of 'moving' (physically, linguistically, culturally, psychologically) to some extent from one ethnolinguistic group to another or of situating oneself somewhere in between, depending on one's relative degree of social identification with the two groups. This binary line of thinking, together with the assumption that 'successful' L2 learning entails convergence towards 'native-speaker' target language norms, does not sit comfortably with the more complex sociolinguistic realities of our contemporary multicultural societies and globalized world. The idea that L2 learning motivation is underpinned by social identification with a particular culture or ethnolinguistic community will not go far in explaining, for example, what motivates a Cantonese speaker working in the casino tourism industry in Macau to develop communication skills in Mandarin Chinese, English and Japanese, or what motivates a Swedish teenager attending an English-medium international school in Kenya to learn French and Kiswahili.

Of course, there are still situations where a clearly perceived association between a language and a particular culture may shape individual motivation to learn that language and identify with that culture. This may happen, for example, in the case of motivation for learning heritage languages representing one's cultural roots and identity, such as the learning of Italian among people of Italian descent in New Zealand (e.g. Berardi-Wiltshire, 2013), or the learning of an endangered heritage language such as Scottish Gaelic (e.g. Armstrong, 2013; MacIntyre *et al.*, 2017). In fact, not surprisingly, motivation and attitudes often constitute an important focus in empirical research on heritage language learning. In a review of the first decade of the journal *Heritage Language Journal*, attitudinal-motivational perspectives accounted for 28% of the empirical studies published (Lynch, 2014).

However, in many contemporary contexts of language learning and use, the association between a target language and a specific culture or community of speakers is more difficult to define. This can be the case for languages that are widely spoken across several geographical areas (e.g. Spanish, Arabic), and languages that are used as a lingua franca between speakers of different regional languages (such as Russian across the territory of the former Soviet Union and in parts of Central and Eastern Europe – see Pavlenko, 2006). The notion of an 'ethnolinguistic community' identified with a particular language and culture becomes impossible to sustain when we consider the case of English as target language. This is partly because of its sheer geographical spread and the existence of so many Englishes as a legacy of colonialism (e.g. Indian English, Jamaican English, South African English). It is also because of the unassailable status that English has as both a global language and the language of globalization, and because of its widespread use as an international lingua franca in multicultural communication settings across the world. While estimates vary, on a global scale L2 speakers of English now substantially outnumber L1 speakers of English (see Crystal, 2003), making it conceptually difficult to define who would constitute a 'target language community' for a student of English in a particular country. Is the target language community associated with a particular geographical entity, such as the United States or Great Britain, or with a more amorphous 'Western' culture, or perhaps with a socially elite group of fluent English speakers in the local region (as, for example, in parts of India or Pakistan)?

Moreover, the social-psychological binary line of thinking that individuals may be motivated to 'move' from a minority to a majority language group or to relinquish one social identity in favour of another more positively valued one does not reflect the more complex social realities of today. This is a major criticism levelled at social-psychological approaches to L2 motivation by Pavlenko (2002), who argues that such approaches 'do not reflect the complexity of the modern global and multilingual world, where more than a half of the inhabitants are not only either bilingual or multilingual but also members of multiple ethnic, social and cultural communities' (Pavlenko, 2002: 279). Similarly, writing from the perspective of postcolonial settings, Coetzee-Van Rooy (2006) finds the concept of integrative motivation 'untenable' in such settings. As she argues, the context of immigrants or minority groups acquiring the language of the majority group or host community ('the prototype situation for the study of integrative motivation', Coetzee-Van Rooy, 2006: 447) is significantly different from postcolonial contexts of language learning and use such as South Africa. What she calls the 'simplex' view of social identity in social-psychological theories of L2 motivation 'does not take into account the complex, multidimensional identity construct prevalent in multilingual and multicultural societies' (Coetzee-Van Rooy, 2006: 447), such as among multilingual speakers of African languages and local Englishes. (See also Coleman, 2011, for a range of critical perspectives in relation to English and multilingualism in developing country contexts.)

On a much broader scale too, with the phenomenal growth in political, economic and student migration over the past few decades as well as advances in communication technologies, social contexts of language learning and use in the globalized world 'are becoming fluid, flexible, mobile, transitory, borderless' and 'not so easily definable in geographical, cultural, social or linguistic terms' (Ushioda, 2013: 5). For example, in cultural, social or linguistic terms, how might one characterize an international university setting geographically located in central China where the medium of instruction is English and where Chinese students attend alongside students from a range of Anglophone and non-Anglophone countries including India, Nepal, the United States, Vietnam, Korea, the Maldives, Denmark, Norway, Germany and Italy (Hu & Chen, 2011)? Or how might one characterize the sociolinguistic context of massive open online courses (MOOCs), where thousands of students situated in different parts of the world can enrol in online courses provided by various institutions in various countries (e.g. El-Hmoudova, 2014)?

Clearly, traditional social-psychological concepts such as integrative motivation, social distance, ethnolinguistic vitality or in-groups and outgroups are no longer adequate to address the complexities of language learning motivation in today's multilingual and multicultural societies. In what follows I will turn to consider more recent perspectives on L2 motivation research and identify the key theoretical approaches and concepts that are shaping current thinking in the field. Yet it is worth remembering that, despite these changing conceptions, the field of L2 motivation research nevertheless remains largely preoccupied with understanding what forms of motivation shape (or impede) *successful* SLA. In relation to the study of motivation and multilingualism, this is a limitation of the SLA field and I will return to discuss this issue later.

Towards current concepts of self and identity in second language motivation research

Since the 1990s and turn of the millennium to the present day, two closely related concepts in particular have come to feature extensively in the literature on L2 motivation – the notions of *self* and *identity*, where identity has a broader and more complex set of connotations than Tajfel's (1974, 1982) original concept of social identity or the social-psychological focus on ethnolinguistic identity. This growth of interest in notions of self and identity in relation to L2 motivation mirrors developments in the wider field of mainstream motivational psychology – a field whose influence on L2 motivation research remained relatively limited during its pioneering social-psychological phase (for further discussion, see Ushioda, 2012).

In motivational psychology in general, the notion of *self-concept* and associated *self-related* perceptions have come to occupy a central position in theorizing, as reflected in the abundance of motivational concepts such as self-efficacy, self-worth, self-esteem, self-determination, self-regulation (for an overview of self-related concepts of motivation, see Dweck, 2000; see also Csizér & Magid, 2014; Mercer & Williams, 2014 for comprehensive accounts of self-related theories in SLA). Since the turn of the century, moreover, theories of motivation in educational psychology have begun to move away from a traditionally strong focus on achievement-oriented frameworks towards more *identity-oriented* frameworks (see Kaplan & Flum, 2009). In other words, traditional achievement-related concepts of motivation such as a student's achievement goals, need for achievement or expectancy of success (e.g. Atkinson & Raynor, 1974) are becoming reframed in terms of identity development and construction, whereby a student pursues identity goals reflecting personal, social, academic or peer-related values and relationships as well as more long-term aspirations about what kind of person they want to be in the future (e.g. Brophy, 2009; Oyserman, 2013).

Given these significant developments in mainstream motivational and educational psychology, it is perhaps not surprising that self and identity concepts have also come to prominence in the L2 motivation field. Moreover, across the field of research in SLA and applied linguistics in general, identity-related issues have increasingly moved to centre stage in critical discussions around language learning, language use and language practices in education and society at large (see, for example, Block, 2007, 2014; Lin, 2007; Pavlenko & Blackledge, 2004a; Preece, 2016). The recent focus on identity issues and associated self-related concepts in L2 motivation research is thus very much in keeping with these broader thematic developments within and beyond the SLA field.

I will begin by discussing influential self-related concepts in L2 motivation research, and then consider perspectives on identity.

Self-related concepts of second language motivation

Two major theories under focus here are *self-determination theory* and *possible selves theory*. Both emanate from mainstream motivational psychology and have grown to have significant influence on current thinking in the L2 motivation field. At the core of each theory is the notion of a person's self-concept, which shapes our behaviours and our motivation to pursue or avoid particular courses of action, and which is affected by external social and cultural influences.

Self-determination theory (SDT) is a general theory of motivation, human growth and social development associated with the work of Edward Deci and Richard Ryan (Deci & Ryan, 1985; Ryan & Deci, 2000, 2002). A basic principle of SDT is that we have an inborn propensity for psychological growth, with a natural desire to explore and master new challenges, to develop our skills and competences, and to integrate these into an increasingly elaborated yet coherent sense of self – i.e. our self-concept. When we behave in ways and pursue courses of action that are true to our sense of self, our motivation is *self-determined*, expressing our personal autonomy and values. On the other hand, when our motivations and behaviours are largely controlled by external social forces (such as teachers, parents, employers), we act in ways that are less self-determined and less true to our self-concept, often resulting in more negative experiences and poorer quality engagement.

One form of clearly self-determined motivation is classified as *intrinsic motivation*, such as where we freely engage in a favourite activity simply for the pleasure and enjoyment it gives us (e.g. hobbies and leisure pursuits) or for the sense of challenge and skill development we derive (e.g. doing crossword puzzles or playing a musical instrument). An alternative form of motivation is *extrinsic motivation*, where we engage in an activity in order to achieve some separate goal or outcome, such as doing a part-time job in order to earn some money, or learning a foreign language in order to go travelling or to improve one's career prospects. While some extrinsic goals may be imposed on us (e.g. coursework requirements, sales targets), extrinsic goals may be more, or less, self-determined, depending on how far they align with our own self-concept and values, or indeed are fully integrated with our sense of self. Across the field of educational research, much attention has focused on how such alignment can be achieved between curriculum goals and values and students' interests and self-concepts, in order to foster more self-determined forms of motivation which typically lead to high-quality engagement in learning (see, for example, Anderman & Anderman, 2010).

Within the SLA field, it has largely been through the programme of research led by Kim Noels and her colleagues that SDT has become influential (e.g. Noels, 2001, 2009; Noels *et al.*, 2000, 2001). This body of work has usefully drawn attention to the importance of more self-determined forms of motivation in shaping successful L2 learning, particularly internalized goals and values rather than intrinsic motivation per se (Noels *et al.*, 2000). While intrinsic motivation factors such as enjoyment and sense of challenge may enhance the quality of student learning, it would seem that intrinsic motivation may not be sufficient in itself to sustain the long-term learning engagement that is needed to achieve a high level of proficiency in an L2. This may be especially so as the cognitive and learning demands increase after the early stages of learning a new language (for further discussion, see Ushioda, 2014).

SDT perspectives on L2 motivation have also been useful in focusing attention on social and environmental factors that may foster (or hinder) more self-determined forms of learning motivation. Particularly important in this regard are pedagogical strategies and communication styles that are perceived to support students' sense of autonomy rather than control their behaviour (see Noels *et al.*, 1999). Supporting students' sense of autonomy might be achieved, for example, by involving them in making meaningful choices and decisions about their learning, or in setting personal goals and targets (for detailed discussion, see Ushioda, 2003; for a very accessible account about supporting people's sense of autonomy in general, see Deci & Flaste, 1996). In SDT, the development of self-determined motivation is thus viewed in 'dialectical' terms (Ryan & Deci, 2002: 6), emerging through the interactions between the individual and the social environment, and being supported (or constrained) by these social interactions. This *dynamic interaction between self and environment* is a significant aspect of recent perspectives on motivation within and beyond the SLA field and, as we shall see later, has an important bearing on our understanding of motivation and language use in multilingual settings.

While SDT highlights how we are motivated to act in ways that are true to our current self-concept, *possible selves theory* focuses on the future-oriented dimension of the self-concept. The origins of this psychological theory are associated with Hazel Markus and Paula Nurius (1986), who define *possible selves* as representing the selves that people believe they might become, would like to become or are afraid of becoming. In other words, possible selves represent imagined aspects of the self-concept projected into the near or distant future. As such, they can serve to channel personal motivation to pursue certain courses of action in order to attain desired future self-states (e.g. visualizing oneself as a graduate student at an internationally prestigious university), or to avoid negative future self-states (e.g. visualizing oneself as a school leaver with no qualifications). Possible selves are thus positively or negatively valenced, and some possible selves may be more desirable than others. Since we cannot realistically pursue all our imagined future possible selves, it is theorized that our motivation is more likely to be channelled by those that represent our ideal future self-representations, because of our natural psychological desire to minimize the discrepancy between our current and ideal selves (Higgins, 1987). Possible selves are thus theorized to function as internal self-guides that can regulate motivation and behaviour. The role of possible selves in shaping motivation and behaviour has been extensively investigated in the context of school and academic learning (e.g. Oyserman *et al.*, 2006) as well as transitions to the world of work and career paths (e.g. Hardgrove *et al.*, 2015), and in relation to psychological wellbeing at other stages of life (e.g. Bolkan *et al.*, 2015). (For a comprehensive collection of research on possible selves, see Dunkel & Kerpelman, 2006.)

Within the SLA field, the influence of possible selves theory has largely come about through the work of Zoltán Dörnyei, who developed a theoretical framework called the *L2 motivational self system*, originally proposed in 2005 and more fully elaborated in 2009. The move towards a possible selves approach to theorizing L2 motivation was shaped by a growing sense that the integrative motivation concept was losing explanatory power for learning English in many sociolinguistic contexts, as discussed earlier. Instead of conceptualizing motivation for learning English in terms of social identification with an external reference group or community of speakers, it may be more meaningful to reframe it as a process of internal identification with a desired future self-representation – for example, a possible self as a fluent speaker of English, or perhaps as a global citizen. This was the line of thinking that led Dörnyei to develop his new framework of an L2 motivational self system, which is characterized by three key components (Dörnyei, 2005: 106):

- an *ideal L2 self*, representing the L2-related attributes and qualities we would ideally like to possess, such as being a fluent and proficient speaker of the language;
- an *ought-to L2 self*, representing the L2-related attributes and qualities we feel we should possess, in order to meet the expectations of others (e.g. parents, society at large) or to avoid negative consequences;
- *L2 learning experience*, referring to the situated process of motivation in a particular social learning environment and the ongoing interactions between learning experience and motivation.

An important difference between the ideal and ought-to L2 selves is in their relative degree of internalization within the person's self-concept, akin to the difference between more and less self-determined forms of motivation in SDT. Theoretically, it is assumed that those who have developed a plausible ideal L2 self are more likely to be strongly motivated and successful in their learning than those with a less internalized ought-to L2 self. (Note the continuing preoccupation with the association between motivation type and successful SLA.)

Although the L2 motivational self system evolved from a reconsideration of English learning motivation in particular, its self-related concepts are thought to be applicable to other target language contexts and, in this respect, to be compatible with the more traditional social-psychological concepts of integrative and instrumental motivation. As Dörnyei (2009: 29–31) explains, the ideal L2 self subsumes integrative motivation in cases where desired social relations with or membership of the target language community constitute part and parcel of one's ideal future self-representation as an L2 speaker. At the same time, the ideal L2 self may also subsume internalized forms of instrumental motivation (such as wanting to be able to speak the target language competently for professional purposes), while the ought-to L2 self may correspond to less internalized forms of instrumental motivation (such as studying hard to meet parental expectations or to avoid failure).

Since its first formulation in 2005, Dörnyei's L2 motivational self system has generated a growing body of empirical research, much of which has focused on examining the prevalence and explanatory power of the ideal L2 self concept in various educational settings (e.g. Csizér & Kormos, 2009; Lamb, 2013; Ryan, 2009; Taguchi et al., 2009; You & Dörnyei, 2014) or on investigating pedagogical strategies to help language learners develop ideal L2 selves (e.g. Mackay, 2014; Magid & Chan, 2012). However, it is worth noting that the bulk of this research to date has focused on students learning English rather than other target languages. Nevertheless, as we shall see later, there is a small body of research that has begun to apply possible selves approaches to analyzing motivation for learning multiple languages. The possible selves framework would thus seem to hold promise in illuminating issues of motivation in relation to multilingualism. I will return to these issues later after completing our review of motivation research in the SLA field with a look at identity-related concepts.

Identity-related concepts of second language motivation

While analyzing L2 motivation in terms of possible selves represents a significant conceptual departure from traditional social-psychological perspectives, we can trace a parallel and more continuous thread of development around the concept of identity. In the L2 motivation field, the notion of identity has evolved from its associations with ethnolinguistic identity and (ingroup or outgroup) social identity to a more varied and complex set of connotations in the contemporary literature. As noted earlier, these recent developments in the L2 motivation field reflect a wider critical concern with issues of identity in relation to language learning and use across the fields of SLA and applied linguistics, as well as a general shift towards identity-based theories of motivation in mainstream educational psychology.

At one level, concepts of identity in relation to L2 motivation have diversified in response to the social and cultural changes to the world order brought about through globalization, the widespread dominance of English and the growth of communication technologies. In a significant paper in this regard, for example, Lamb (2004) questioned the relevance of integrative motivation for junior high school students learning English in Indonesia. Although students in his study report strong motivation for learning English, his analysis suggests that, as English becomes less identified with specific Anglophone cultures, these students' motivation may be better explained in terms of an aspiration towards a 'bicultural' identity both as 'an Indonesian world citizen' who speaks English and as 'a Sumatran (or other ethnic group) Indonesian' (Lamb, 2004: 15). While these 'global' and 'local' identities are perceived as connected rather than at odds with one another, Lamb speculates that as students' sense of bicultural identity develops and their aspirations evolve, they may experience some tension or confusion between the 'global' and 'local' dimensions of their identity, which may in turn affect their motivation for studying English (Lamb, 2004: 16). As he notes, such changes in students' motivation may partly be associated with the processes of identity development and construction which are characteristic of adolescence, and which (as we saw earlier) feature prominently in current identity-oriented frameworks of motivation in educational psychology. In this respect, students' language learning histories and current experiences as well as their future-oriented aspirations may be significant in shaping their evolving identity-based motivations (see, for example, the collection of studies in Murray *et al.*, 2011).

In short, current concepts of identity in relation to L2 motivation have moved beyond the relatively static categorizations of ethnolinguistic identity or ingroup social identity to take account of the more complex, evolving and *multidimensional identities* of language learners and users in today's globalized yet multicultural societies (see earlier discussion on language users' identities in postcolonial contexts reported by Coetzee-Van Rooy, 2006). Moreover, these multidimensional and hybrid identities may relate not only to the various languages and cultures traversed (see, for example, Aronin & Singleton, 2012), but also to the complex range of social identities we inhabit (e.g. as mother, friend, colleague) in our personal, social and professional interactions in particular contexts (see Ushioda, 2009), or to the private versus public identities we may choose to express in our interactions with others (see, for example, Taylor, 2013).

However, at this more situated level of L2 learner/users' interactions and experiences, we find that a more *critically oriented perspective on identity* has emerged in the analysis of motivation, which has especial relevance for our focus on multilingual contexts. Earlier, when concluding the discussion on SDT, I drew attention to the 'dialectical' interactions between the individual and the social environment through which self-determined forms of motivation may develop or be impeded. The dynamic interaction between self and social environment in shaping (or constraining) motivation has become a significant aspect of how we now theorize motivation both within the SLA field (e.g. Dörnyei *et al.*, 2015) and in mainstream motivational psychology (e.g. Volet & Vauras, 2013). In other words, the theoretical focus is not only on the kinds of motivation that individuals may bring to a particular social setting but also on how their motivation may be affected (in positive, negative or more complex ways) by the motivational agendas and behaviours of others with whom they interact. The mediating and often unpredictable nature of these interactions between individual and social processes makes it more difficult to delineate relationships between 'motivation' and 'successful L2 learning' in the traditional sense pursued in the SLA field. Moreover, such interactions point to the importance of considering relevant criteria other than just L2 learning success when examining L2-related motivation in particular social settings (such as the classroom or the workplace), since individuals may bring a variety of motivations to such settings (e.g. motivation to learn, to work, to speak, to participate, to be heard).

In multilingual and multicultural settings, differences in linguistic and social power between speakers are particularly likely to affect how people's motivations and identities are played out. This has given rise to critically oriented analyses of motivation in interactional encounters in such settings. Since our focus of attention here clearly extends beyond contexts of *language learning* to contexts of *language use* in multilingual environments, I will now move on from the SLA field to consider critical perspectives on motivation, identities and language use in relation to individual and societal multilingualism.

Critical Perspectives on Motivation and Multilingualism

The idea that individual motivation to engage with an L2 may be affected by the social context of language use and by particular interactional experiences with target language speakers is of course not new. As far back as 1983 and working within the dominant social-psychological research tradition of the time, Genesee *et al.* highlighted the motivational importance ascribed by immigrant L2 users to the level of support they expected from host community members in their social interactions with them. Working in the same tradition, Clément (1980, 1986; Clément *et al.*, 1977) identified quality of contact with target language speakers as a significant factor in shaping linguistic self-confidence and motivation for engaging with the target language and culture. Integrating perspectives on identity, communication and adaptation from both social psychology and cross-cultural psychology, Clément and Noels (1992: 205) drew attention to situational factors that may affect people's sense of ethnolinguistic identity in bilingual or multilingual contexts, causing them to 'slip in and out of particular group memberships as required by immediate contextual demands'. In essence, as Clément et al. (2001) highlighted in a later study, situational factors and the mediating and moderating roles of communication have significant influences on people's language-related motivations, identities and intercultural engagement in multilingual environments.

However, the more critically oriented perspectives on these issues to emerge have originated from outside the traditions of social psychology and cross-cultural psychology, and are grounded instead in *poststructuralist* perspectives on identity that have come to influence thinking across the social sciences. Of relevance to our concerns here is the poststructuralist critique of traditional views of identity in terms of fixed social categories (e.g. ethnicity, gender, social class). As we noted earlier, this kind of social categorization approach to identity can lead to stereotyping or essentializing tendencies and discriminatory practices, such as ascribing generalized negative attributes to people simply because of the colour of their skin or their religion. From a poststructuralist perspective, identities are not fixed and predetermined but are viewed instead as multiple, complex, fluid, unstable, fragmented, in a constant state of flux, and as continually constructed, performed, negotiated and contested through our social relations and interactions with others (see, for example, Pavlenko & Blackledge, 2004b). In effect, language, discourse and interaction are fundamental to current theoretical perspectives on identity across the social sciences (see, for example, Benwell & Stokoe, 2006). As a consequence, it is perhaps not surprising that identity has become such a major theme of interest in applied linguistics in the 21st century, although the reasons why this has come about are complex and beyond the scope of our motivation-related concerns in this lecture (but see Block, 2014, for an excellent historical overview).

Norton's concepts of identity and investment

In a sense, however, we can say that motivation-related concerns are core to the origins of critically oriented identity research in the applied linguistics field. As Block (2014) acknowledges and others have emphasized (e.g. Kramsch, 2013), a significant foundation for current critical perspectives on identity and language is the work of Bonny Norton, who published a seminal paper in 1995 in which she questioned the construct of motivation in language learning (Norton Peirce, 1995). Norton subsequently developed her groundbreaking ideas into a major monograph on language learning, language use and identity in multilingual settings (Norton, 2000), which has now appeared in an extended revised edition (Norton, 2013).

Norton critically interrogated how L2 motivation is traditionally conceptualized with reference to an 'ahistorical' language learner or user who can be characterized as possessing certain types of motivation (e.g. integrative, instrumental, extrinsic) and a particular social identity. In her view, motivation and identity are processes that are socially constructed, changing over time and space, and often in inequitable relations of power in multilingual settings. Influenced by Weedon's (1987) ideas of 'subjectivity' in feminist poststructuralist thought, Norton argued for a view of *identity* as multiple, changing and a site of struggle, being locally constructed and negotiated through our discursive interactions with others. Instead of a traditional psychological view of motivation, she proposed a more sociological concept of *investment* to describe the 'socially and historically constructed relationship of learners to the target language, and their often ambivalent desire to learn and practice it' (Norton, 2000: 10). As she explains (Norton, 2000, 2013), drawing on Bourdieu's (1986, 1991) ideas on forms of human capital and on language as symbolic power, when people invest in an L2 they do so with the understanding that they will be able to acquire a wider range of symbolic and material resources. These resources will enhance their social and cultural capital, and their sense of identity and of possibilities (or imagined identities – see Kanno & Norton, 2003) for the future. Yet people's investment in an L2 may also be mediated by other investments that can conflict with the desire to speak or to participate in particular social interactions. This may happen, for example, if they fear being negatively positioned as an immigrant or feel that their professional status and background are not valued in these interactional spaces. As Darvin and Norton (2015) explain, the extent to which people are able to invest in a target language is contingent on the dynamic negotiation of power relations in a particular social setting. In this respect, investment is always 'complex, contradictory, and in a state of flux', and in this sense differs from motivation:

> For example, a student may be a highly *motivated* learner, but may not be *invested* in the language practices of a given classroom if the practices are racist, sexist, or homophobic. (Darvin & Norton, 2015: 37, italics in original)

Norton's (2000) original research focused on case studies of migrant women engaging with English and with life in Toronto, while her more recent work has extended her focus to investments in the English language and in digital literacy among students and teachers in poorly resourced African multilingual settings, especially in Uganda (e.g. Early & Norton, 2014; Norton *et al.*, 2011). In short, through its core concern with local and globalized power dynamics shaping individual investment in language and social practices, this critical perspective highlights the motivational issues faced in particular by L2 learner/users who experience disadvantage or marginalization in multilingual settings. At the same time, in bringing these issues into sharp focus, this critical perspective draws attention to such individuals' motivational aspirations and their agentive potential 'to negotiate the constraints and opportunities of their social location' (Darvin & Norton, 2015: 47). Indeed, this agentive potential of the individual to navigate, challenge or resist dominant language practices in multilingual or globalized environments is a key dimension of Darvin and Norton's (2015) latest comprehensive model of investment.

Over the years, many other researchers have drawn on Norton's concepts of investment and identity to investigate the experiences of L2 learner/users in various settings, particularly in North America and in Asia (see, for example, Pittaway, 2004, for a review; see also Arkoudis & Davison, 2008). Not surprisingly, much of this research focuses on social contexts where English is the target language under focus, which perhaps reflects how the dominant status of English in the globalized world has become so central to critically oriented analyses of L2 motivation and identity. Yet it is worth noting that these critically oriented perspectives on motivational investment and identity also extend to multilingual contexts where the focus is on other locally dominant languages, such as the case of Chinese language learning and use among South Asian immigrants in Hong Kong (see Shum *et al.*, 2011).

Motivation and language policy in multilingual societies

In relation to both individual and societal multilingualism, the critical perspectives on motivation and identity that have been strongly voiced by Norton (2000, 2013) as well as the likes of Pavlenko (2002) and Coetzee-Van Rooy (2006) constitute part of a much wider contemporary critical discourse on the sociolinguistics of postmodern societies, where issues of migration, inequality, language, identity and diversity are under scrutiny – whether in the workplace (e.g. Duchêne *et al.*, 2013), the internationalized university setting (e.g. Preisler *et al.*, 2011), the language classroom (e.g. Menard-Warwick, 2009; Toohey, 2000), the study abroad context (e.g. Benson *et al.*, 2013; Pellegrino, 2005), or across society at large (e.g. Pavlenko & Blackledge, 2004a; see also Preece, 2016). While the relevance of motivation across these wider critical discourses on migration, identity and multilingualism is often implicit rather than explicit, it is clear that societal or macro-contextual features of language policy and practice in multilingual contexts can have significant repercussions for motivation. For example, there is considerable critical debate around the policy of using language tests as gatekeeping measures for controlling immigration and conferring citizenship (e.g. McNamara *et al.*, 2015). The stark association between language tests and rights of entry, citizenship and identity throws into sharp relief how individual motivation can be severely constrained by policy and legislation, becoming a matter of conforming to particular linguistic behaviours and standards in order to gain social acceptance and a recognized identity. This casts a rather cynical light on our traditional academic preoccupation with associations between 'motivation' and 'L2 learning success' in the SLA field.

More generally, national or regional language policy and legislation will inevitably have an impact on the motivation of local education providers to offer a more, or less, diversified languages curriculum, or on their motivation to cater for the range of home languages spoken by children in multicultural schools, or indeed to build on these children's multilingual resources (see Lecture 4 in this volume, on educational policy and multilingualism). Macro-contextual features of language policy and changing social and educational structures may also filter through to impact on individual students' L2-related motivations and identity profiles in multilingual environments (see, for example, Ceuleers, 2008, on the case of Belgium), or on the motivations of parents to make significant language choices when deciding on their children's education (see, for example, Kuchah Kuchah, 2013, on Francophone parents' motivations for choosing English-medium schooling in Cameroon).

At a sociopolitical level, moreover, individual motivation to speak (or not speak) particular languages may interact closely with larger questions of language rights, linguistic nationalism and language planning, particularly in the wake of political conflict and reconfiguration (see Ushioda, 2006). For example, with the outbreak of ethnic conflicts in Eastern Europe following the collapse of Communism in 1989, language rights and identity became highly politicized issues in the region, as Kymlicka and Patten (2003) have commented. In such contexts, motivation in the sense of language choice may well constitute a personal political statement and expression of identity (for extensive discussion, see May, 2012). The transitional politics of language policy and language rights in post-conflict pluralist societies will inevitably have a significant impact on people's motivations, attitudes and identities in relation to linguistic and cultural diversity in their community (see, for example, McMonagle & McDermott, 2014, for a discussion of the case of Northern Ireland following the peace process).

In short, at both the macro-contextual level of language policy and sociopolitical structures and the micro-contextual level of localized practices and experiences, we can see that interactions between the individual and the social environment play a significant role in shaping motivation to engage (or not) with particular languages in multilingual societies. As we have also seen, in contrast with much of the 'success-oriented' research on motivation within SLA (i.e. focused on the forms of motivation associated with successful L2 learning), perspectives on language-related motivation in macro-contextual and micro-contextual interactions tend to be rather more 'critically oriented' and often socially or politically charged.

Motivation and Learning Multiple Languages

Having explored issues of motivation in relation to L2 learning and L2 use in multilingual contexts, we turn now to consider perspectives on motivation in relation to learning multiple languages, whether simultaneously or in succession. This section is necessarily fairly brief for two reasons. First, the psycholinguistic and psychological aspects of learning and engaging with multiple languages are given extensive treatment elsewhere in this volume (Lectures 3, 9 and 10), as are analyses of highly successful multilinguals (Lecture 5). Secondly, the amount of motivation research that specifically addresses multiple language learning is very small, effectively just a tiny fraction of the vast body of literature on L2 motivation. In what follows, I will examine this small subset of research and draw out some insights relevant to understanding how learning multiple languages may have different motivational characteristics from learning a single second language (for a more extensive discussion, see Dörnyei & Al-Hoorie, 2017).

Variations in motivation across languages of study

Among motivation research studies that have investigated people learning two or more foreign languages, a common and perhaps unsurprising finding seems to be that their attitudinal-motivational dispositions may vary across the different languages they are learning. In particular, motivation may vary in quality or strength depending on whether students have freely chosen to learn a particular language or not. For example, in the context of Hong Kong, Humphreys and Spratt (2008) investigated tertiary students' motivations for learning two compulsory languages, English and Putonghua (i.e. standard Mandarin Chinese as opposed to locally spoken Cantonese), and an elective foreign language (French, German or Japanese). Clear patterns emerged in the data showing that the two compulsory languages were perceived to have stronger instrumental value than the electives, but that both English and the chosen foreign language were regarded more positively in affective terms, suggesting a qualitatively different kind of motivational orientation to these languages in comparison to Putonghua. In a very different tertiary education setting in Mexico, Desirée Castillo Zaragoza (2011) observed a somewhat similar pattern among students who use university self-access centres to pursue the learning of several languages. Such students' motivations for learning different languages may vary according to whether languages are compulsory and have instrumental value (such as English) or are freely chosen and studied for pleasure or interest (i.e. intrinsic motivation).

Language-specific motivational differences may also be observed in contexts where choice does not exist and all languages are in effect compulsory. For example, Bernaus *et al.* (2004) conducted a study of language learning motivation in multicultural classrooms in a secondary school in Barcelona where Catalan is the main communication language and medium of instruction except in Spanish and English lessons. The student sample included many immigrant children from different language and cultural backgrounds, and the study investigated their motivation and attitudes towards learning Catalan, Spanish and English. Bernaus *et al.* report that children's motivation in relation to learning Spanish and English was generally more positive than for Catalan. As they comment (Bernaus *et al.*, 2004: 86–87), despite the role of Catalan as a medium of instruction, it was not perceived by the children as their language of communication outside the classroom, where Spanish and English are attributed higher status (see also Lasagabaster, 2017, for a comprehensive overview of language learning motivation and attitudes in multilingual regions of Spain).

Motivational 'interferences' across languages of study

In this respect, of course, it is likely that the perceived status of a particular target language may have a significant bearing on relative patterns of motivation for learning different languages. In particular in the current era, the dominant status of English as a global language clearly plays a critical role in shaping motivational priorities among education ministries and local education providers as well as individual motivational priorities among students themselves (for further discussion, see Ushioda, 2013). At the level of the individual multilingual learner, this raises the question as to whether 'attitudinal interferences' (Csizér & Dörnyei, 2005: 643) may come into play, where positive attitudes towards a high status language such as English may interfere with motivation for learning other less valued languages even if these have local or regional importance.

This was a speculation developed by Dörnyei and his colleagues (Csizér & Dörnyei, 2005; Dörnyei *et al.*, 2006), based on the cumulative findings of a large-scale repeated survey of Hungarian teenagers' (aged 13–14) motivation and attitudes towards learning five target languages (English, German, French, Russian, Italian). The survey spanned a period of significant sociopolitical transformation in Hungary from 1993 (a few years after the end of Communism) to 2004 (shortly before Hungary's accession to the European Union), and pointed to a steady decline in this age group's motivation for learning additional foreign languages other than English. While the survey showed that having a wide interest in foreign languages in general was motivationally beneficial in helping students develop an ideal language self (which, as we saw earlier, may facilitate successful language learning), it also indicated that highly positive attitudes towards learning English may interfere with motivation for learning other languages. In a separate study focusing on Hungarian students learning English and German simultaneously, Csizér and Lukács (2010) suggest that the nature of such interference may depend on whether English or German is learnt as the first or the second foreign language. For students who begin with English as the first foreign language (L2), their motivational dispositions towards English seem to remain wholly positive. However, in relation to German as L2 or L3 and English as L3, there appear to be negative interferences between students' motivational dispositions towards the two languages.

Developing the idea of motivational interference between languages further, Henry (2010) reports on research among Swedish school students to support his hypothesis that those engaged in learning more than one foreign language may have separate L2 and L3 self-concepts as speakers of English (first foreign language) and as speakers of French, German or Spanish (additional foreign language). Moreover, as his findings suggest, students' L2 English self-concept may serve a referential function against which their L3 self-concepts are internally evaluated. A high degree of negative self-concept referencing may then be associated with low L3 motivation, particularly among boys. In a follow-up case study, Henry (2011) provides evidence to suggest that, while some L3 learners may be able to use positive thinking strategies to counteract such negative self-concept referencing, for others the impact of an L2 English self is such that it may be psychologically difficult to sustain a possible L3 self.

Positive motivational interactions across languages of study

While the notion of motivational interference between languages of study casts the motivational dimension of multiple language learning in a somewhat negative light, there is clearly an abundance of research literature that highlights the cognitive and affective benefits of individual multilingualism (see, for example, Aronin & Singleton, 2012; De Angelis, 2007), as well as plenty of evidence to show that many individuals achieve a high level of proficiency in several languages (see Lecture 5, this volume). For multilingual learners, it seems likely that the motivation-related interactions among the different languages of study may be positive as well as negative, particularly when motivation is shaped by an intrinsic interest in languages, or by a strong sense of purpose (see, for example, Lepp-Kaethler & Dörnyei, 2013, on the power of religious vocation in motivating the learning of multiple languages even in very challenging circumstances).

In this respect, multilingual learners' perception of positive interactions (cognitive, affective or linguistic) in their experiences of learning two or more languages in the past may have a significant influence on their motivation for learning subsequent languages. This idea has been put forward by Thompson (2013), embodied in her concept of 'perceived positive language interaction' (PPLI). Research evidence suggests that, in terms of motivational profiles, there are significant differences between multilingual learners who report PPLI and those who report either no such language interactions or only negative interactions in their previous language learning experiences (Thompson & Erdil-Moody, 2014). In essence, those who perceive a positive interaction between the foreign languages studied are more likely to report a strong ideal language self, which can help to facilitate further language learning.

In short, it would seem that multilingual learners' perceptions of cross-linguistic influences (see Lecture 6, this volume) may have important implications for motivation. Moreover, their perceptions of their language selves as separate or as integrated may also have important implications for motivation. As Henry (2017) discusses, those engaged in learning multiple languages may develop ideal future self-representations associated with particular languages as well as an ideal future self-representation as a multilingual speaker – i.e. *an ideal multilingual self*. Having an ideal multilingual self may in turn strengthen the motivational value of acquiring skills in each particular language. From a theoretical perspective, the notion of an ideal multilingual self helps to broaden the analysis of motivation beyond traditional SLA frameworks, where the focus is on the learning of a single L2, usually with L1 competence or 'native-speaker' competence as reference points for evaluating degrees of L2 learning success. By conceptualizing language learning motivation as the development of an integrated multilingual self (rather than only language-specific selves), we move from an SLA towards a linguistic multicompetence framework (Cook, 2016), and enable a more holistic focus on a person's composite linguistic repertoire as a multilingual speaker (see Ushioda, 2017, for more extensive discussion).

Ultimately, of course, a person's motivation to develop multicompetence in several languages will be shaped by a unique and complex mixture of internal and social-environmental factors, socialization experiences, individual circumstances, need, opportunity and evolving life trajectories. From a research perspective, this suggests that our attempts to make generalized claims and statements about motivation for learning multiple languages based on quantitative statistical evidence will always be limited. On the other hand, by focusing in depth on particular multilingual individuals' stories and perspectives, we may gain important qualitative insights into the processes whereby language learning motivation shapes and is shaped by interactions with lived experience. This brings me to the last section in this lecture where I will very briefly consider some methodological issues in researching motivation and multilingualism.

Researching Motivation and Multilingualism

In this short concluding section I do not aim to provide a detailed overview of research designs, methodologies and instruments for investigating language learning motivation. Comprehensive accounts of approaches to researching L2 motivation can be found in

Dörnyei and Ushioda (2011), including summaries of sample quantitative, qualitative and mixed methods studies and copies of motivation measurement instruments, as well as in Ushioda and Dörnyei (2012). My purpose here is rather to highlight some methodological issues that are relevant in particular to researching motivation in the context of multilingualism, where *context* is in fact a key word to consider.

As I have discussed elsewhere (Ushioda, 2009), traditional approaches to researching motivation in SLA have tended to conceptualize context as an independent background variable defined in broad general terms such as geographical, cultural or institutional setting (e.g. a public secondary school in a provincial capital city in southeast China). Such definitions of context in terms of background variable may then facilitate comparisons across contexts, such as comparing the L2 motivational self system profiles among learners of English in China, Iran and Japan (Taguchi *et al.*, 2009), or reviewing evidence of integrative motivation across a wide range of previous research in different settings (e.g. Masgoret & Gardner, 2003).

However, as we have seen in relation to language learning and language use in multilingual environments and also in relation to learning multiple languages, people's motivations to learn and speak particular languages are inescapably bound up with the macro-level and micro-level sociohistorical, cultural and interactional contexts in which they live and with which they engage. From the perspective of investigating motivation and multilingualism, this means that the notion of 'context' in our research designs is necessarily rather more complex than just a matter of location or setting. Our research designs need to take into account not only the contexts in which people are located but also their ongoing interactions with and lived experiences in these contexts through which their motivations evolve. Moreover, we must remember that people are also an integral part of the contexts with which they engage and which they *shape and change* through their interactions, behaviours and actions (see Ushioda, 2009, on 'person-in-context' perspectives on motivation). After all, in any multilingual 'context' or setting, it is the people who are part of that context who contribute to defining and shaping its multilingualism.

This suggests that research on motivation and multilingualism would particularly benefit from qualitative approaches that privilege participants' own contextually situated perspectives and experiences and that allow for richly detailed analyses of these situated perspectives and experiences to emerge. Such approaches might include the use of, for example, qualitative interviews (e.g. Kvale & Brinkmann, 2009; Wengraf, 2001), ethnographic fieldwork methods (e.g. Hammersley & Atkinson, 2007), case studies (e.g. Duff, 2008; Yin, 2009), or forms of narrative enquiry and narrative research (e.g. Barkhuizen, 2014; Chase, 2005; Clandinin & Connolly, 2000). These kinds of contextually grounded research approaches are certainly characteristic of the more critically oriented studies of investment and identity among L2 learner/users in multilingual environments (see, for example, Block, 2014; Darvin & Norton, 2015; Norton, 2000, 2013).

This does not mean, of course, that there is no place for more quantitative research approaches to investigating motivation and multilingualism. In terms of the language choices that people make and the types of motivation that they bring to language learning, there are clearly some patterns and commonalities shared across individuals and contexts for which the more generalizable insights yielded through quantitative statistical evidence are useful. Historically, such quantitative methodologies have typified research on motivation in SLA, which has traditionally followed a psychometric approach to measuring psychological traits using questionnaire-type instruments to yield quantifiable data for statistical analysis. Indeed, much of the research literature on motivation in the SLA field has been devoted to developing, piloting, analyzing, validating or adapting measurement scales and instruments in relation to new motivation constructs or in relation to different language and cultural contexts (e.g. Gardner, 1985; MacIntyre *et al.*, 2009; Ryan, 2009). At the broad level of characterizing certain types of motivation and how these may relate to the choices and progress people make in their language learning in a given setting, these kinds of statistical approaches will continue to serve a useful purpose.

Nevertheless, such approaches have limited value in helping us to understand the complexities of social-environmental interactions and individual experiences through which people's motivations and identities are played out in multilingual contexts of language learning and use. In this respect, an optimum strategy may be to integrate quantitative and qualitative approaches through a mixed-methods research design (for discussion of mixed-methods research, see Creswell & Plano Clark, 2007). A mixed-methods design can be particularly useful if we wish to engage in multilevel analysis, such as examining motivation and multilingualism at a societal level (e.g. a broad survey of the range of languages people choose to learn or speak in a particular community and why), and also at an individual level (e.g. undertaking case studies of how certain members of this community are motivated to engage with particular languages in their day-to-day lives).

Ultimately, of course, as any good research methods manual will tell us, the decisions we make about research design and methodology should always be shaped by the particular research questions we want to address. In this respect, the questions for reflection that follow may offer a starting point for thinking about what lines of enquiry might be pursued.

Questions for Students' Reflection

1. For each of the languages you have learnt in the past or are learning now, how would you describe your motivation for studying this language? Which of the following terms would you use to characterize your motivation to learn each language: *integrative; instrumental; intrinsic; extrinsic; self-determined; externally regulated; ideal L2 self; ought-to L2 self; investment; identity goals*? Or does none of these terms apply? Are your motivations very different or similar across the languages you have learnt?

2. In relation to your reflections on Question 1, do you notice any associations between the types of motivation you have and how successful you have been in learning those languages? And what defines 'success' for you?

3. For any of the languages that you have been learning or using, has your motivation towards this language changed over time? If so, in what ways has it changed and why?

4. Would you agree that motivation for learning and speaking languages is somehow different from motivation for pursuing other areas of study or activity in life? In what ways do you find it is similar or different?

5. For 'native English' speakers, particularly those living in Anglophone countries, the perceived need to learn foreign languages or other languages spoken in their local community can be low. What do you see as the motivational value of developing other language skills for English speakers?

6. In what ways do you think the experience of learning and speaking different languages engages, expands or changes your sense of identity? Do you feel that you are a different person when expressing yourself in another language, and if so, how does this affect your motivation to engage with that language or with people who speak that language?

7. In the country or region where you live, how do language-related policies or practices affect the motivations of different members of the community to engage with multilingualism or indeed with life in that society? Are you aware of any critical issues in this regard?

Suggestions for Further Reading

Block, D. (2014) *Second Language Identities*. London: Bloomsbury Academic.

Although this book makes little explicit reference to 'motivation' per se, issues of motivation are very relevant to its critical discussion of research on identity in language learning and use across three contexts: adult migration, foreign language classrooms and study abroad programmes.

Coleman, H. (ed.) (2011) *Dreams and Realities: Developing Countries and the English Language*. London: British Council.

This edited collection offers a range of perspectives on the role of English (and other national and local languages) in 15 countries across Africa and Asia. Its critical analysis of language policy and practice has important implications for motivation and multilingualism in developing country contexts.

Darvin, R. and Norton, B. (2015) Identity and a model of investment in applied linguistics. *Annual Review of Applied Linguistics* 35, 36–56.

This substantial article presents an updated comprehensive model of investment and identity in language learning and use in multilingual settings, reviewing and building on Norton's foundational critically oriented work in this area.

Dörnyei, Z. and Ushioda, E. (eds) (2009) *Motivation, Language Identity and the L2 Self*. Bristol: Multilingual Matters.

This volume represents the first collection of conceptual and empirical papers marking the 21st century theoretical reframing of L2 motivation in relation to concepts of self and identity. It also includes the fullest account of Dörnyei's influential L2 motivational self system.

Dörnyei, Z. and Ushioda, E. (2011) *Teaching and Researching Motivation* (2nd edn). Harlow: Pearson.

This provides a useful overview of theories of motivation in mainstream psychology, followed by a comprehensive survey of theory, research and practice in the field of language learning motivation. It includes a detailed illustrated discussion of approaches to researching L2 motivation and sample motivation measurement instruments.

References

Anderman, E.M. and Anderman, L.H. (2010) *Classroom Motivation*. Upper Saddle River, NJ: Pearson.

Arkoudis, S. and Davison, C. (2008) Chinese students: Perspectives on their social, cognitive, and linguistic investment in English medium interaction. *Journal of Asian Pacific Communication* 18 (1), 3–8.

Armstrong, T.C. (2013) 'Why won't you speak to me in Gaelic?': Authenticity, integration and the Heritage Language Learning Project. *Journal of Language, Identity and Education* 12 (5), 340–356.

Aronin, L. and Singleton, D. (2012) *Multilingualism*. Amsterdam: John Benjamins.

Atkinson, J.W. and Raynor, J.O. (eds) (1974) *Motivation and Achievement*. Washington, DC: Winston & Sons.

Barkhuizen, G. (2014) Narrative research in language teaching and learning. *Language Teaching* 47 (4), 450–466.

Benson, P., Barkhuizen, G., Bodycott, P. and Brown, J. (2013) *Second Language Identity in Narratives of Study Abroad*. Basingstoke: Palgrave Macmillan.

Benwell, B. and Stokoe, E. (2006) *Discourse and Identity*. Edinburgh: Edinburgh University Press.

Berardi-Wiltshire, A. (2013) Motivational implications of heritage language identity for heritage language learning. *Beyond Words* 1 (1), 68–87.

Bernaus, M., Masgoret, A.-M., Gardner, R.C. and Reyes, E. (2004) Motivation and attitudes toward learning languages in multicultural classrooms. *International Journal of Multilingualism* 1 (2), 75–89.

Block, D. (2007) The rise of identity in SLA research, post Firth and Wagner (1997). *The Modern Language Journal* 91 (5), 863–876.

Block, D. (2014) *Second Language Identities*. London: Bloomsbury Academic.

Bolkan, C., Hooker, K. and Coelho, D. (2015) Possible selves and depressive symptoms in later life. *Research on Aging* 37 (1), 41–62.

Bourdieu, P. (1986) The forms of capital. In J.F. Richardson (ed.) *Handbook of Theory and Research for the Sociology of Education* (pp. 241–258). New York: Greenwood Press.

Bourdieu, P. (1991) *Language and Symbolic Power*. Cambridge, MA: Harvard University Press.

Brophy, J. (2009) Connecting with the big picture. *Educational Psychologist* 44 (2), 147–157.

Ceuleers, E. (2008) Variable identities in Brussels. The relationship between language learning, motivation and identity in a multilingual context. *Journal of Multilingual and Multicultural Development* 29 (4), 291–309.

Chase, S.E. (2005) Narrative inquiry: Multiple lenses, approaches, voices. In N.K. Denzin and Y.S. Lincoln (eds) *The Sage Handbook of Qualitative Research* (3rd edn) (pp. 651–679). Thousand Oaks, CA: Sage.

Clandinin, D.J. and Connelly, F.M. (2000) *Narrative Inquiry: Experience and Story in Qualitative Research*. San Francisco, CA: Jossey Bass.

Clément, R. (1980) Ethnicity, contact and communicative competence in a second language. In H. Giles, W.P. Robinson and P.M. Smith (eds) *Language: Social Psychological Perspectives* (pp. 147–154). Oxford: Pergamon.

Clément, R. (1986) Second language proficiency and acculturation: An investigation of the effects of language status and individual characteristics. *Journal of Language and Social Psychology* 5, 271–290.

Clément, R. and Noels, K.A. (1992) Towards a situated approach to ethnolinguistic identity: The effects of status on individuals and groups. *Journal of Language and Social Psychology* 11 (4), 203–232.

Clément, R.. Gardner, R.C. and Smythe, P.C. (1977) Motivational variables in second language acquisition: A study of francophones learning English. *Canadian Journal of Behavioural Science* 9, 123–133.

Clément, R., Noels, K.A. and Denault, B. (2001) Interethnic contact, identity, and psychological adjustment: The mediating and moderating roles of communication. *Journal of Social Issues* 57 (3), 559–577.

Coetzee-Van Rooy, S. (2006) Integrativeness: Untenable for world Englishes learners? *World Englishes* 25 (3/4), 437–450.

Coleman, H. (ed.) (2011) *Dreams and Realities: Developing Countries and the English Language*. London: British Council.

Cook, V. (2016) Premises of multi-competence. In V. Cook and Li Wei (eds) *The Cambridge Handbook of Linguistic Multicompetence* (pp. 1–25). Cambridge: Cambridge University Press.

Creswell, J.D. and Plano Clark, V.L. (2007) *Designing and Conducting Mixed Methods Research*. Thousand Oaks, CA: Sage.

Crystal, D. (2003) *English as a Global Language* (2nd edn). Cambridge: Cambridge University Press.

Csizér. K. and Dörnyei, Z. (2005) Language learners' motivational profiles and their motivated learning behavior. *Language Learning* 55 (1), 613–659.

Csizér, K. and Kormos, J. (2009) Learning experiences, selves and motivated learning behaviour: A comparative analysis of structural models for Hungarian secondary and university learners of English. In Z. Dörnyei and E. Ushioda (eds) *Motivation, Language Identity and the L2 Self* (pp. 98–119). Bristol: Multilingual Matters.

Csizér, K. and Lukács, G. (2010) The comparative analysis of motivation, attitudes and selves: The case of English and German in Hungary. *System* 38, 1–13.

Csizér, K. and Magid, M. (eds) (2014) *The Impact of Self-Concept on Language Learning*. Bristol: Multilingual Matters.

Darvin, R. and Norton, B. (2015) Identity and a model of investment in applied linguistics. *Annual Review of Applied Linguistics* 35, 36–56.

De Angelis, G. (2007) *Third or Additional Language Acquisition*. Clevedon: Multilingual Matters.

Deci, E.L. and Flaste, R. (1996) *Why We Do What We Do: Understanding Self-Motivation*. New York: Penguin.

Deci, E.L. and Ryan, R.M. (1985) *Intrinsic Motivation and Self-Determination in Human Behavior*. New York: Plenum Press.

Désiree Castillo Zaragoza, E. (2011) Identity, motivation and plurilingualism in self-access centers. In G. Murray, X. Gao and T. Lamb (eds) *Identity, Motivation and Autonomy in Language Learning* (pp. 91–106). Bristol: Multilingual Matters.

Dörnyei, Z. (2005) *The Psychology of the Language Learner: Individual Differences in Second Language Acquisition*. Mahwah, NJ: Lawrence Erlbaum.

Dörnyei, Z. (2009) The L2 motivational self system. In Z. Dörnyei and E. Ushioda (eds) *Motivation, Language Identity and the L2 Self* (pp. 9–42). Bristol: Multilingual Matters.

Dörnyei, Z. and Al-Hoorie, A.H. (2017) The motivational foundation of learning languages other than global English: Theoretical issues and research directions. *The Modern Language Journal* 101 (3), 455–468.

Dörnyei, Z. and Ushioda, E. (2011) *Teaching and Researching Motivation* (2nd edn). Harlow: Pearson.

Dörnyei, Z., Csizér, K. and Németh, N. (2006) *Motivation, Language Attitudes and Globalisation: A Hungarian Perspective*. Clevedon: Multilingual Matters.

Dörnyei, Z., MacIntyre, P.D. and Henry, A. (eds) (2015) *Motivational Dynamics in Language Learning*. Bristol: Multilingual Matters.

Duchêne, A., Moyer, M. and Roberts, C. (eds) (2013) *Language, Migration and Social Inequalities: A Critical Sociolinguistic Perspective on Institutions and Work*. Bristol: Multilingual Matters.

Duff, P.A. (2008) *Case Study Research in Applied Linguistics*. New York: Lawrence Erlbaum.

Dunkel, C. and Kerpelman, J. (eds) (2006) *Possible Selves: Theory, Research and Applications*. Hauppauge, NY: Nova Science.

Dweck, C.S. (2000) *Self-Theories: Their Role in Motivation, Personality and Development*. Philadelphia, PA: Taylor & Francis/Psychology Press.

Early, M. and Norton, B. (2014) Revisiting English as medium of instruction in rural African classrooms. *Journal of Multilingual and Multicultural Development* 35 (7), 1–18.

El-Hmoudova, D. (2014) MOOCs motivation and communication in the cyber learning environment. *Procedia – Social and Behavioral Sciences* 131, 29–34.

Gardner, R.C. (1985) *Social Psychology and Second Language Learning*. London: Edward Arnold.

Gardner, R.C. and Lambert, W.E. (1959) Motivational variables in second language acquisition. *Canadian Journal of Psychology* 13, 266–272.

Gardner, R.C. and Lambert, W.E. (1972) *Attitudes and Motivation in Second Language Learning.* Rowley, MA: Newbury House.

Gardner, R.C. and Santos, E.H. (1970) Motivational variables in second language acquisition: A Philippine investigation. *Research Bulletin* 149. London, Ont.: University of Western Ontario, Department of Psychology.

Genesee, F., Rogers, P. and Holobow, N. (1983) The social psychology of second language learning. Another point of view. *Language Learning* 33, 209–224.

Giles, H. and Byrne, J.L. (1982) An intergroup approach to second language acquisition. *Journal of Multilingual and Multicultural Development* 3, 17–40.

Giles, H., Bourhis, R.Y. and Taylor, D.M. (1977) Towards a theory of language in ethnic group relations. In H. Giles (ed.) *Language, Ethnicity and Intergroup Relations* (pp. 307–348). London: Academic Press.

Hammersley, M. and Atkinson, P. (2007) *Ethnography* (3rd edn). London: Routledge.

Hardgrove, A., Rootham, E. and McDowell, L. (2015) Possible selves in a precarious labour market: Youth, imagined futures, and transitions to work in the UK. *Geoforum* 60, 163–171.

Henry, A. (2010) Contexts of possibility in simultaneous language learning: Using the L2 motivational self-system to assess the impact of global English. *Journal of Multilingual and Multicultural Development* 31 (2), 149–162.

Henry, A. (2011) Examining the impact of L2 English on L3 selves: A case study. *International Journal of Multilingualism* 8 (3), 235–255.

Henry, A. (2017) L2 motivation and multilingual identities. *The Modern Language Journal* 101 (3), 547–565.

Higgins, E.T. (1987) Self-discrepancy: A theory relating self and affect. *Psychological Review* 94, 319–340.

Hu, X. and Chen, Y. (2011) International students at China Three Gorges University: A survey. In B. Preisler, I. Klitgård and A.H. Fabricius (eds) *Language and Learning in the International University: From English Uniformity to Diversity and Hybridity* (pp. 193–211). Bristol: Multilingual Matters.

Humphreys, G. and Spratt, M. (2008) Many languages, many motivations. A study of Hong Kong students' motivation to learn different target languages. *System* 36 (2), 313–335.

Kanno, Y. and Norton, B. (2003) Imagined communities and educational possibilities: Introduction. *Journal of Language, Identity and Education* 2 (4), 241–249.

Kaplan, A. and Flum, H. (2009) Motivation and identity: The relations of action and development in educational contexts. An introduction to the special issue. *Educational Psychologist* 44 (2), 73–77.

Kramsch, C.J. (2013) Afterword. In B. Norton (ed.) *Identity and Language Learning: Extending the Conversation* (2nd edn) (pp. 192–201). Bristol: Multilingual Matters.

Kuchah Kuchah, H. (2013) From bilingual Francophones to bilingual Anglophones: The role of teachers in the rising 'equities' of English-medium education in Cameroon. In E. Ushioda (ed.)

International Perspectives on Motivation: Language Learning and Professional Challenges (pp. 60–81). Basingstoke: Palgrave Macmillan.

Kvale, S. and Brinkmann, S. (2009) *InterViews: Learning the Craft of Qualitative Research Interviewing* (2nd edn). Thousand Oaks, CA: Sage.

Kymlicka, W. and Patten, A. (2003) Language rights and political theory. *Annual Review of Applied Linguistics* 23, 3–21.

Lamb, M. (2004) Integrative motivation in a globalizing world. *System* 32, 3–19.

Lamb, M. (2013) 'Your mum and dad can't teach you!': Constraints on agency among rural learners of English in the developing world. *Journal of Multilingual and Multicultural Development* 34 (1), 14–29.

Lasagabaster, D. (2017) Language learning motivation and language attitudes in multilingual Spain from an international perspective. *The Modern Language Journal* 101 (3), 583–596.

Lepp-Kaethler, E. and Dörnyei, Z. (2013) The role of sacred texts in enhancing motivation and living the vision in second language acquisition. In M.S. Wong, C. Kristjánsson and Z. Dörnyei (eds) *Christian Faith and English Language Teaching and Learning: Research on the Interrelationship of Religion and ELT* (pp. 171–188). New York: Routledge/Taylor & Francis.

Lin, A. (ed.) (2007) *Problematizing Identity: Everyday Struggles in Language, Culture and Education*. Mahwah, NJ: Lawrence Erlbaum.

Lukmani, Y.M. (1972) Motivation to learn and learning proficiency. *Language Learning* 22, 261–273.

Lynch, A. (2014) The first decade of the *Heritage Language Journal*: A retrospective review of research on heritage languages. *Heritage Language Journal* 11 (3), 224–242.

MacIntyre, P.D., Mackinnon, S. and Clément, R. (2009) Toward the development of a scale to assess possible selves as a source of language learning motivation. In Z. Dörnyei and E. Ushioda (eds) *Motivation, Language Identity and the L2 Self* (pp. 193–214). Bristol: Multilingual Matters.

MacIntyre, P.D., Baker, S. and Sparling, H. (2017) Heritage passions, heritage convictions and the rooted L2 self: Music and Gaelic language learning in Cape Breton, Nova Scotia. *The Modern Language Journal* 101 (3), 501–516.

Mackay, J. (2014) Applications and implications of the L2 motivational self system in a Catalan EFL context. In K. Csizér and M. Magid (eds) *The Impact of Self-Concept on Language Learning* (pp. 377–400). Bristol: Multilingual Matters.

Magid, M. and Chan, L. (2012) Motivating English learners by helping them visualise their Ideal L2 Self: Lessons from two motivational programmes. *Innovation in Language Learning and Teaching* 6 (2), 113–125.

Markus, H. and Nurius, P. (1986) Possible selves. *American Psychologist* 41, 954–969.

Masgoret, A.-M. and Gardner, R.C. (2003) Attitudes, motivation, and second language learning: A meta-analysis of studies conducted by Gardner and his associates. *Language Learning* 53 (Suppl. 1), 167–210.

May, S. (2012) *Language and Minority Rights: Ethnicity, Nationalism and the Politics of Language* (2nd edn). New York: Routledge/Taylor & Francis.

McMonagle, S. and McDermott, P. (2014) Transitional politics and language rights in a multi-ethnic Northern Ireland: Towards a true linguistic pluralism? *Ethnopolitics* 13 (3), 245–266.

McNamara, T., Khan, K. and Frost, K. (2015) Language tests for residency and citizenship and the conferring of individuality. In B. Spolsky, O. Inbar-Lourie and M. Tannenbaum (eds) *Challenges for Language Education and Policy: Making Space for People* (pp. 11–22). New York: Routledge/Taylor & Francis.

Menard-Warwick, J. (2009) *Gendered Identities and Immigrant Language Learning*. Bristol: Multilingual Matters.

Mercer, S. and Williams, M. (eds) (2014) *Multiple Perspectives on the Self in SLA*. Bristol: Multilingual Matters.

Murahata, G., Murahata Y. and Cook, V. (2016) Research questions and methodology of multi-competence. In V. Cook and L. Wei (eds) *The Cambridge Handbook of Linguistic Multicompetence* (pp. 26–49). Cambridge: Cambridge University Press.

Murray, G., Gao, X. and Lamb, T. (eds) (2011) *Identity, Motivation and Autonomy in Language Learning*. Bristol: Multilingual Matters.

Noels, K.A. (2001) New orientations in language learning motivation: Towards a contextual model of intrinsic, extrinsic, and integrative orientations and motivation. In Z. Dörnyei and R. Schmidt (eds) *Motivation and Second Language Acquisition* (pp. 43–68). Honolulu, HI: University of Hawaii Press.

Noels, K.A. (2009) The internalisation of language learning into the self and social identity. In Z. Dörnyei and E. Ushioda (eds) *Motivation, Language Identity and the L2 Self* (pp. 295–313). Bristol: Multilingual Matters.

Noels, K.A., Clément, R. and Pelleter, L.G. (1999) Perceptions of teachers' communicative style and students' intrinsic and extrinsic motivation. *The Modern Language Journal* 83 (1), 23–34.

Noels, K.A., Pelleter, L.G., Clément, R. and Vallerand, R.J. (2000) Why are you learning a second language? Motivational orientations and self-determination theory. *Language Learning* 50, 57–85.

Noels, K.A., Clément, R. and Pelletier, L.G. (2001) Intrinsic, extrinsic and integrative orientations of French Canadian learners of English. *Canadian Modern Language Review* 57, 424–444.

Noels, K.A., Kil, H. and Fang, Y. (2014) Ethnolinguistic orientation and language variation: Measuring and archiving ethnolinguistic vitality, attitudes and identity. *Language and Linguistics Compass* 8 (11), 618–628.

Norton, B. (2000) *Identity and Language Learning: Gender, Ethnicity and Educational Change*. Harlow: Pearson.

Norton, B. (2013) *Identity and Language Learning: Extending the Conversation* (2nd edn). Bristol: Multilingual Matters.

Norton, B., Jones, S. and Ahimbisibwe, D. (2011) Learning about HIV/AIDS in Uganda: Digital resources and language learner identities. *Canadian Modern Language Review* 67 (4), 568–589.

Norton Peirce, B. (1995) Social identity, investment, and language learning. *TESOL Quarterly* 29 (1), 9–31.

Oyserman, D. (2013) Not just any path: Implications of identity-based motivation for disparities in school outcomes. *Economics of Education Review* 33, 179–190.

Oyserman, D., Bybee, D. and Terry, K. (2006) Possible selves and academic outcomes: How and when possible selves impel action. *Journal of Personality and Social Psychology* 91, 188–204.

Pavlenko, A. (2002) Poststructuralist approaches to the study of social factors in second language learning and use. In V. Cook (ed.) *Portraits of the L2 User* (pp. 277–302). Clevedon: Multilingual Matters.

Pavlenko, A. (2006) Russian as a lingua franca. *Annual Review of Applied Linguistics* 26, 78–99.

Pavlenko, A. and Blackledge, A. (eds) (2004a) *Negotiation of Identities in Multilingual Contexts*. Clevedon: Multilingual Matters.

Pavlenko, A. and Blackledge, A. (2004b) Introduction: New theoretical approaches to the study of negotiation of identities in multilingual contexts. In A. Pavlenko and A. Blackledge (eds) *Negotiation of Identities in Multilingual Contexts* (pp. 1–33). Clevedon: Multilingual Matters.

Pellegrino, V. (2005) *Study Abroad and Second Language Use: Constructing the Self*. Cambridge: Cambridge University Press.

Pittaway, D.S. (2004) Investment and second language acquisition. *Critical Inquiry in Language Studies* 1 (4), 203–218.

Preece, S. (ed.) (2016) *Routledge Handbook of Language and Identity*. London: Routledge.

Preisler, B., Klitgård, I. and Fabricius, A.H. (eds) (2011) *Language and Learning in the International University: From English Uniformity to Diversity and Hybridity*. Bristol: Multilingual Matters.

Ryan, R.M. and Deci, E.L. (2000) Self-determination theory and the facilitation of intrinsic motivation, social development and well-being. *American Psychologist* 55, 68–78.

Ryan, R.M. and Deci, E.L. (2002) Overview of self-determination theory: An organismic dialectical perspective. In E.L. Deci and R.M. Ryan (eds) *Handbook of Self-Determination Research* (pp. 3–33). Rochester, NY: University of Rochester Press.

Ryan, S. (2009) Self and identity in L2 motivation in Japan: The ideal L2 self and Japanese learners of English. In Z. Dörnyei and E. Ushioda (eds) *Motivation, Language Identity and the L2 Self* (pp. 120–143). Bristol: Multilingual Matters.

Schumann, J.H. (1978) *The Pidginization Process: A Model for Second Language Acquisition*. Rowley, MA: Newbury House.

Schumann, J.H. (1986) Research on the acculturation model for second language acquisition. *Journal of Multilingual and Multicultural Development* 7, 379–392.

Selinker, L. (1972) Interlanguage. *International Review of Applied Linguistics* 10 (3), 209–231.

Shum, M.S.K., Gao, F., Tsung, L. and Ki, W.-W. (2011) South Asian students' Chinese language learning in Hong Kong: Motivations and strategies. *Journal of Multilingual and Multicultural Developments* 32 (3), 285–297.

Taguchi, T., Magid, M. and Papi, M. (2009) The L2 motivational self system among Japanese, Chinese and Iranian learners of English: A comparative study. In Z. Dörnyei and E. Ushioda (eds) *Motivation, Language Identity and the L2 Self* (pp. 66–97). Bristol: Multilingual Matters.

Tajfel, H. (1974) Social identity and intergroup behaviour. *Social Science Information* 13, 65–93.

Tajfel, H. (1982) *Social Identity and Intergroup Relations*. Cambridge: Cambridge University Press.

Taylor, F. (2013) *Self and Identity in Adolescent Foreign Language Learning*. Bristol: Multilingual Matters.

Thompson, A.S. (2013) The interface of language aptitude and multilingualism: Reconsidering the bilingual/multilingual dichotomy. *The Modern Language Journal* 97 (3), 685–701.

Thompson, A.S. and Erdil-Moody, Z. (2014) Operationalizing multilingualism: Language learning motivation in Turkey. *International Journal of Bilingual Education and Bilingualism* 19 (3), 314–331.

Toohey, K. (2000) *Learning English at School: Identity, Social Relations and Classroom Practice*. Clevedon: Multilingual Matters.

Towell, R. and Hawkins, R. (1994) *Approaches to Second Language Acquisition*. Clevedon: Multilingual Matters.

Ushioda, E. (2003) Motivation as a socially mediated process. In D. Little, J. Ridley and E. Ushioda (eds) *Learner Autonomy in the Foreign Language Classroom: Teacher, Learner, Curriculum and Assessment* (pp. 90–102). Dublin: Authentik.

Ushioda, E. (2006) Language motivation in a reconfigured Europe: Access, identity and autonomy. *Journal of Multilingual and Multicultural Development* 27 (2), 148–161.

Ushioda, E. (2009) A person-in-context relational view of emergent motivation, self and identity. In Z. Dörnyei and E. Ushioda (eds) *Motivation, Language Identity and the L2 Self* (pp. 215–228). Bristol: Multilingual Matters.

Ushioda, E. (2012) Motivation: L2 learning as a special case? In S. Mercer, S. Ryan and M. Williams (eds) *Psychology for Language Learning: Insights from Research, Theory and Practice* (pp. 58–73). Basingstoke: Palgrave Macmillan.

Ushioda, E. (2013) Motivation and ELT: Global issues and local concerns. In E. Ushioda (ed.) *International Perspectives on Motivation: Language Learning and Professional Challenges* (pp. 1–17). Basingstoke: Palgrave Macmillan.

Ushioda, E. (2014) Motivation, autonomy and metacognition: Exploring their interactions. In D. Lasagabaster, A. Doiz and J.M. Sierra (eds) *Motivation and Foreign Language Learning: From Theory to Practice* (pp. 31–49). Amsterdam: John Benjamins.

Ushioda, E. (2017) The impact of global English on motivation to learn other languages: Toward an ideal multilingual self. *The Modern Language Journal* 101 (3), 469–482.

Ushioda, E. and Dörnyei, Z. (2012) Motivation. In S. Gass and A. Mackey (eds) *The Routledge Handbook of Second Language Acquisition* (pp. 396–409). London and New York: Routledge/Taylor & Francis.

Volet, S. and Vauras, M. (eds) (2013) *Interpersonal Regulation of Learning and Motivation: Methodological Advances*. London and New York: Routledge/Taylor & Francis.

Weedon, C. (1987) *Feminist Practice and Poststructuralist Theory*. Oxford: Blackwell.

Wengraf, T. (2001) *Qualitative Research Interviewing*. London: Sage.

Yagmur, K. (2011) Does ethnolinguistic vitality theory account for the actual vitality of ethnic groups? A critical evaluation. *Journal of Multilingual and Multicultural Development* 32 (2), 111–120.

Yin, R.K. (2009) *Case Study Research: Design and Methods* (4th edn). Thousand Oaks, CA: Sage.

You, C.J. and Dörnyei, Z. (2014) Language learning motivation in China: Results of a large-scale stratified survey. *Applied Linguistics* 37 (4), 495–519.

Lecture 8

Age and Multilingualism

Carmen Muñoz and David Singleton

Introduction

Ever more people are engaged in language learning, learning more languages and learning them at younger and older ages, from preschool to 'third age' programmes. There are personal, educational and economic benefits to knowing more than one language (Callahan & Gándara, 2014). And there is evidence that learning more than one language may yield cognitive advantages, particularly for individuals with advanced levels of proficiency and who use their languages actively on a regular basis (Bialystok *et al.*, 2014; but cf. De Bot, 2017; Paap *et al.*, 2015). There is also evidence that, in the most favourable circumstances, multilingualism may bring benefits for all ages, including the mitigation of cognitive decline in older individuals (Kavé *et al.*, 2008).

The relationship between age and additional language acquisition is complex and it can be examined through diverse theoretical and methodological approaches. A first distinction needs to be made between *starting age*, that is, the age at which the acquisition of an additional language begins, and *biological* or *chronological age*, that is, the individual's age at the moment of the study. This distinction is essential in order to be able to understand and interpret any suggested age effects on language learning. For example, younger learners' advantage is seen by some as related to maturational constraints, insofar as language learning may be more successful before a certain age (e.g. puberty in Lenneberg's (1967) original proposal for first language acquisition). This is the focus of the critical period hypothesis (CPH) or the maturational constraints approach, which contends that also in second language acquisition an early *starting age* leads to higher ultimate attainment, which may be native-like or near native-like (e.g. Abrahamsson & Hyltenstam, 2008). In contrast, starting to learn a language after the end of the critical period is claimed to result in less successful or non-native like attainment. Also relevant is learners' *biological age* in that older adults' language learning may be affected by aging processes that persist across the lifespan, such as declines in working memory capacity and decreases in processing speed (e.g. Birdsong & Paik, 2008; Craik & Bialystok, 2005; Salthouse, 2004). Research on L2 learning in adulthood is still very scarce but it suggests that cognitive skills play an important role. For example, the study by Mackey and Sachs (2012) showed that different aspects of working memory had strong effects on immediate and sustained L2 development, while factors such as age, years of residence and years of formal education affected the latter more than the former.

A crucial concept in CPH studies is that of *native-likeness*, used to refer to those learners of additional languages whose ultimate attainment in those languages is indistinguishable from that of native speakers. The difficulty of reaching native-likeness is reflected in the concept of *near native-likeness*, which is used to denote a close approximation to native-likeness (Birdsong & Gertken, 2013).

In this chapter we first consider the topic of multilingualism and different learning ages or stages of maturity. Then we address maturational constraints and ultimate attainment issues, and the ways in which the degrees of proficiency attained by multilingual school learners are influenced by the age at which they begin to learn their additional language. We end with a consideration of some crucial issues in school multilingualism/multilingual schools. Note that the term *multilingualism* is used here as the generic term to refer to two or more languages, and thus subsumes the term *bilingualism* (Aronin & Singleton, 2008).

Multi-language Acquisition at Different Ages

Two issues arise from any consideration of the topic of multilingualism and different stages of maturity. The first has to do with the relationship between age and the characterization of multilingualism; the second concerns the yardstick to be used in the evaluation of the attainment of later beginning learners of additional languages.

Fused or differentiated?

There is a variety of multilingualism labelled *simultaneous*, where the languages in question are acquired from infancy, and another labelled *successive* or *sequential*, where additional languages are added when the first is already to some extent established. The dividing line between simultaneity and sequentiality in this context has often been set at a particular age, that of three years. One notes that Baker (2006: 97), on the other hand, takes the line that '[t]here are no exact boundaries' in this regard.

The proposal of age three as the watershed between simultaneous and sequential multilingualism has been linked to the terms of the 'unitary language system hypothesis', which posits (see, for example, Volterra & Taeschner, 1978) differently characterized phases of simultaneous multilingualism according to stage of development. The hypothesis suggests that simultaneous multilinguals begin with a single, fused language system, and that 'it is only by age 3;0 that they begin to differentiate their ... languages' (Petitto *et al.*, 2001: 455). The claim has been made, for instance, that the child at an early stage is not in possession of translation-equivalents across languages, that he/she has a single lexical store, with one word from one or other of his/her languages for any given meaning.

This perspective has been shown to be questionable. Paradis (2007: 22) talks about more recent research which, she claims, 'has shown that bilingual children can differentiate their two languages according to their interlocutor, at least from the age of 2;0 and possibly earlier for some (Deuchar & Quay, 2000; Genesee *et al.*, 1995; Lanza, 1997; Nicoladis & Genesee, 1996)'. Paradis also points to evidence of pragmatic differentiation in multilingual children in relation to their ability 'to accommodate the language preference of familiar versus unfamiliar interlocutors (Genesee *et al.*, 1996; Maneva, 2004; Suyal, 2002), and to accommodate shifts in the amount of language mixing initiated by the interlocutor across different play sessions (Comeau *et al.*, 2003: 22–23)'. One further comment made by Paradis refers to indications that children much younger than three make 'overt metalinguistic statements' about the different languages at their disposal and engage in 'behaviour such as translating for parents' (Paradis, 2007: 23). In sum, there is sufficient research evidence to reject the 'unitary language system hypothesis', which reflects an early belief that infants' brains are essentially monolingual (Genesee, 2015).

An interesting sidelight is cast on this issue by Werker's (2012) discussion of infant speech perception. Werker points out that the infant facing the process of language development has to deploy:

> his/her perceptual knowledge of the rhythmical properties of the ... language, of the speech sound categories that distinguish one possible word from another, and of the sequences of sounds that are allowable within a word and/or the statistical learning of other cues to segmentation. (Werker, 2012: 50)

Only on this basis, she says, can the child isolate different words and structures and map them on to meaning. The child growing up in the environment of more than one language, she goes on to affirm, has to master the rhythmical properties, the phonetic categories, the phonotactic regularities, the word order patterns, the lexis–concept configuration and the conceptualization of the world of each of the languages involved. What is more, the infant bilingual must do this, she states, without interlingual confusion (see also Bosch & Sebastian-Galles, 2001, 2003; Werker & Byers-Heinlein, 2008).

Age and the monolingual native-speaker yardstick for successful multilingualism

Success in additional language learning tended traditionally to be interpreted as a level of achievement comparable to monolingual native-speaker proficiency. Cook (2002: 6) has long argued in this context, however, that, while on every side the user of additional languages is judged against the 'monolingual standard' of the unilingual native speaker, there is in fact no intrinsic reason why the level of proficiency of a user of additional languages *should* ever be the same as that of a monolingual native speaker (cf. Grosjean, 1992).

The interaction between language competencies inevitably has subtle and not so subtle effects on language performance (see, for example, Jarvis & Pavlenko, 2008). Birdsong (2006: 22) argues in relation to bilingual pronunciation that 'minor quantitative departures from monolingual values are artifacts of the nature of bilingualism, wherein each language affects the other and neither is identical to that of a monolingual'. The same argument applies at all levels of language. We return to this issue in the next section.

It seems to follow that a more appropriate comparison in the exploration of later multilingual acquisition than that between the performance of later multilinguals and that of monoglot native users of the language(s) in question would be a comparison between those who begin acquiring other languages later in life and those who begin to acquire them in early childhood (Ortega, 2010). Murahata *et al.* (2016) argue along these lines:

> Much of the research into effects of age of start in second language acquisition research is ... presented in terms of the extent to which L2 users are defective compared with adult native speakers. ... This research might in fact be reinterpreted as establishing whether the unique competence of the L2 user is affected by age, leaving the native speaker out of the equation. (Murahata *et al.*, 2016: 26–27)

To be noted, however, is that early and late multilinguals differ in terms of the degree to which languages are entrenched before others are acquired. It is widely recognized that 'adult L2 learners are at a potential disadvantage because of L1 entrenchment and interference' (Roehren-Brackin, 2015: 182; see also Hernandez *et al.*, 2005). Accordingly, the entrenchment variable will continue to confound comparisons.

Maturational Constraints and Ultimate Attainment Issues

One perspective on the idea that maturation puts constraints on what can be attained by language acquirers is the above-mentioned approach taken by advocates of the CPH (in its various versions! – cf. Singleton, 2005). Some researchers replace the term *critical period* with that of *sensitive period*, defined as 'the period during which a child can acquire language easily, rapidly, perfectly, and without instruction' (Richards & Schmidt, 2002: 145).

The idea of a critical/sensitive period

This critical/sensitive period hypothesis has been applied both to first language acquisition and to the acquisition of additional languages, and it has dominated discussion of differences of attainment between language acquirers for more than half a century. Some researchers have, however, always entertained doubts about it. In any case, for some time now researchers have increasingly regarded age as a very complex factor, a 'macrovariable' (Flege et al., 1999), and most have been calling for dimensions other than maturation to be taken into consideration in this context.

The term *critical/sensitive period* is applied to a limited phase in the development of an organism during which a particular capacity or behaviour must be acquired if it is to be acquired at all. One example is the case of imprinting in ducklings which, for a short time after hatching, become irreversibly attached to the first moving object they see – usually the mother duck – after which they develop a fear of and aversion to strange moving objects. If language acquisition in human beings is affected by the limits of such a critical/sensitive period, the implication would seem to be that, unless language acquisition begins before the period ends, it will not happen.

First language evidence

Some of the first language findings cited in favour of a critical/sensitive period refer to cases of children who because of parental neglect are deprived of the experience of language in childhood. Such children (see, for example, Jones, 1995) who are rescued in adolescence typically exhibit progress in language development – but of a limited or unusual kind. Eric Lenneberg, often called the 'father of Critical Period Hypothesis', was not convinced, however, of the value of such evidence in relation to his hypothesis, seeing such evidence as interpretable in terms simply of the general damage done to an individual by isolation and deprivation of interaction (Lenneberg, 1967: 142; cf. Chugani et al., 2001; Singleton & Muñoz, 2011: 407).

Other first language evidence comes from deaf subjects who were deprived of language input in their early years and who then acquired a sign language as their first language at a later age (e.g. Johnson & Newport, 1989; Lieberman et al., 2015; Mayberry & Lock, 2003; Newport & Supalla, 1987). Such studies have not found an abrupt cut-off point to successful language acquisition or that language completely fails to develop, but they have revealed some deficits in the language of the later signers. Being cut off from language-mediated social intercourse during the phase when cognitive development is at its most intense is likely to have general psychological/cognitive effects (see above); it may well be these general effects that are reflected in later language development.

Evidence from additional language acquisition

The evidence quoted in favour of the critical period notion in relation to additional languages is generally derived from immigrant studies. From the middle of the last century, there has been a wealth of research (e.g. Asher & García, 1969; Hyltenstam, 1992; Patkowski, 1980; Piske et al., 2002; Seliger et al., 1975) showing that younger arrivals in a country where the dominant language is different from the immigrants' home languages are more likely than older arrivals to end up passing for native speakers of the new language. It is worth saying that in these immigrant studies the 'younger = better' tendency is just that – a tendency. Not *all* immigrants who arrive in their new country in childhood end up with a perfect command of the language of the host country; nor do those who arrive later in life systematically fail apparently to attain the levels reached by younger arrivals. Some recent research (e.g. Granena & Long, 2013; Huang, 2014; Werker & Tees, 2005) has looked at the way in which age has differential effects at different stages depending on the linguistic domain in question (phonology, lexis, syntax, etc.). This is a kind of revival of the longstanding 'multiple critical periods hypothesis' (cf. Singleton, 2005), although recent research shies away from absolutism and tends to prefer the terms *optimal periods* or *sensitive periods*.

One might cite in connection with the success of some older immigrants Kinsella and Singleton's (2014) study. This involved 20 native English speakers whose average age of significant exposure to French (arrival in France) was 28;6 years. All were resident in France, and all reported at least occasionally passing for native speakers of French. These participants (and a control group of native French speakers) were asked to identify some regional French accents and to complete a test incorporating lexical and grammatical elements. Three of the 20 participants scored within native-speaker ranges on all tasks (outperforming many of the native speakers on the accent recognition task). Such cases as those of Kinsella and Singleton's most native-like subjects do not suffice, however, to falsify the critical/sensitive period hypothesis for its staunchest advocates (e.g. Abrahamsson & Hyltenstam, 2009; Long, 2013). For such researchers the criterion for falsification is 'scrutinized native-likeness' with regard to all linguistic features in the later learner (Abrahamsson & Hyltenstam, 2009). This brings us back to the matter of comparison with the monolingual native speaker. Birdsong (2014: 47) comments that, because of the mutual influence of a multilingual's knowledge of his/her languages, 'nonnativelikeness will eventually be found'. His conclusion is that if 'across-the-board nativelikeness is what is required to disconfirm the CPH, the CPH is invulnerable to falsification'.

Broader perspectives

The growing consensus is that multilinguals' relationship with their languages cannot be explained simply in terms of maturation. In immigrants, proficiency attainment in the host country language can also be related, for example, to the development of linguistico-cultural identity. As children grow, so they begin to identify with particular languages or cultural identities (cf. Skrzypek & Singleton, 2016). Thus, in multilingual nurseries children seem not to pay attention to the fact that their peers come from different linguistic backgrounds. They gradually become aware of this as they mature, and the friendships they form may become more restricted over time by language and cultural group.

To elaborate on the socio-affective dimension of age, we can refer to three studies which show that maturation is not necessarily determinative when it comes to learning other languages, and that a strong socio-affective factor often underlies success in this connection. In the first (Muñoz & Singleton, 2007), the participants were 12 female late learners of English resident in Ireland. Generally, the participants were rated as having a foreign accent, but two of the non-natives scored within the native-speaker range. It emerged that these exceptional learners had very close contact with English speakers they liked – an English-speaking husband and an English-speaking boyfriend, respectively. The other participants all operated in Spanish-speaking home contexts. The second study (Walsh & Singleton, 2013) focused on the lexical acquisition of nine Polish children of immigrants to Ireland, which was compared with that of nine Irish children. Particularly intriguing were individual differences found among the Polish children. These were explored by examining the profiles of the two highest scoring Polish children. Both used Polish at home with their families but also regularly enjoyed activities with friends in which English was used. Both children's parents had learned English, and so the possibility of parental support for their English was also similar. Again, we see elements which seem partly to account for differences in their performance from that of the others in the group which seem to relate to the enjoyable nature of the experience of English and the degree to which it was supported. To return to the Kinsella and Singleton (2014) research, most participants in this study performed below native-speaker level on one or more of the tasks they were given. As noted earlier, however, three of the 20 participants scored within native-speaker ranges on **all** of the tasks. It transpired (via interview data) that all three: (i) conducted their social life primarily through French; (ii) identified themselves closely with the Francophone community; and (iii) had French partners. In other words, the personal data reveal a factorial dimension involving the quality of the emotional experience of encountering a new language.

Moyer (2013, 2014) has offered the view, echoing an increasingly often expressed line of thinking, that ultimate attainment in additional languages is a function of the quantity and quality of language experience rather than simply a matter of maturation. She thus talks about the above-discussed identity question as well as the importance of consistency of contact with native speakers, the use of additional languages across multiple domains, motivation, and positive attitudes towards the target-language culture. She comments that 'insights from the empirical research highlight these relationships between age, affect and linguistic experience, signaling a welcome shift in the critical period paradigm' (Moyer, 2013: 19).

Age and Foreign Language Learning

The term *multilingualism* is often used simply to denote possession of knowledge of more than one language, whatever the age at which such knowledge was acquired and whatever the degree of proficiency in the languages in question. It is, though, frequently claimed that multilinguals are limited in terms of the proficiency they can aspire to in given languages when they begin to be exposed to such languages beyond the childhood years. This seems to be an over-simplistic generalization, as seen above, for immigrants or acquirers in an immersion situation. It is also an over-generalization for instructed learners (see the discussion in Muñoz & Singleton, 2011). In fact, the native-speaker model has also been challenged by the findings of research on additional language learning conducted in typical foreign language classrooms, showing that the model is inadequate in input-limited contexts where native-likeness is not achievable (Muñoz, 2008a).

The implementation of early foreign language teaching in the schools of many countries has allowed comparisons between school pupils who have started at different grades. The findings have partially differed from those obtained in immigration or naturalistic settings in a critical way. In the latter type of situation, older starters are observed to proceed faster in the beginning stages of language acquisition but to be outperformed by younger starters in the long term (Krashen et al., 1979). The next two sections address these two different types of findings: learning rate and long-term attainment in a foreign language setting.

Learning rate and efficiency in foreign language learning settings

Like in a naturalistic setting, older starters in an instructed setting are observed to be faster in the short term. Older starters' rate advantage has been widely supported by evidence showing that older pupils achieve higher proficiency levels in the additional language than younger ones after the same amount of instruction. An illustration of this line of research is the BAF (Barcelona Age Factor) project, which was conducted in schools in Catalonia (where students are Catalan-Spanish bilingual) when the introduction of English was changed from Grade 6 (11 years) to Grade 3 (eight years) (Muñoz, 2006a). Four groups of learners with different starting ages (8, 11, 14, 18+) were compared at three different points after the same amount of instruction in English (L3) (200, 416 and 726 hours, respectively). That is, learner groups were compared among themselves and not with native speakers, and the effects of starting age could be separated from those of amount of exposure by controlling for the latter factor. An extensive test battery was used in view of the fact that there may be different age effects for different language components (Snow & Hoefnagel-Höhle, 1978) (the observation in naturalistic contexts supporting the existence of sensitive periods from a maturational constraints perspective; see above). Cross-sectional and longitudinal analyses showed that the older starting learners outperformed the younger starting learners at all times: young adults' scores were higher than adolescents'; those of adolescents higher than older children's; and older children's better than younger children's. This confirmed the higher efficiency of older learners since they could achieve higher levels after the same amount of time/instruction. Interestingly, the results showed that the gap was wider in the short term than in the long term and wider too for cognitively demanding tasks (i.e. involving morphosyntax) than for non-cognitively demanding tasks (i.e. listening comprehension). This was interpreted as reflecting a diminution of the cognitive maturity gap existing between the age groups as the younger learners grew older and more mature (Muñoz, 2006b).

The same older starters' advantage has been found in other studies, including multilingual settings such as the Basque Country in Spain (see García-Mayo & García-Lecumberri, 2003) and Switzerland (Kalberer, 2007; Pfenninger, 2013, 2014a; Pfenninger & Singleton, 2017), and through behavioural and also neuroimaging data (Ojima et al., 2011). Older learners have also shown higher learning efficiency in studies in which younger and older starters are compared at the same age but after different amounts of instruction, which controls for the possible effects of age at testing (see Muñoz, 2008b). Findings from these studies have not found early starters, with many more hours of instruction, outperforming older starters. For example, in the above-mentioned research carried out in the Basque Country, when early and late starters were compared at the same age (15 years) the latter obtained higher scores on several tests in spite of having had 300 hours less of instruction

(Cenoz, 2003). Another study that shows late starters closing the gap was conducted in Germany with a very large sample of English learners distributed in two cohorts: age 8–9, late starters; and age 6–7, early starters (Jaekel *et al.*, 2017). The results showed that in Year 5 the early starters outperformed the late starters in reading and listening comprehension but that in Year 7 the late starters outperformed the early starters in spite of the longer period of instruction of the latter (5;5 years versus 4 years). The authors suggest that the late starters could apply their metacognitive knowledge and benefit from explicit language learning earlier and have a faster progression through learning. In a study carried out in Switzerland (Pfenninger, 2014b) where English was the L3/L4, the late starters (age of onset 13), who began English instruction five years after the early starters (age of onset eight), caught up with the written performance of the early starters within six months. This study also showed a strong correlation between writing skills in the students' main language of literacy (L2 Standard German) and L3 writing skills. Pfenninger suggests that the late starters were better equipped to transfer their conceptual vocabulary and grammatical knowledge to the L3, while the early starters' knowledge of the L2 may have been insufficient to have a positive influence on their learning of English (L3). These findings highlight the superiority of older learners particularly on literacy-related tasks. Literacy skills in the L1, or previous languages, are possibly being transferred to the additional language, enhancing older learners' literacy development in that language. Or, as Cummins (1984) explains in relation to immersion contexts, bilingual learners' use of common underlying (cognitive) abilities facilitates their cognitive academic language proficiency (CALP) (for school studies confirming the importance of L1 literacy in immersion contexts see, among others, Genesee, 2004, 2007; Harley & Hart, 1997; Swain, 1981; Swain *et al.*, 1990; Thomas & Collier, 2002).

Long-term attainment in foreign language learning settings

As seen above, in naturalistic or immigrant settings younger starters outperform older starters (and may even attain native-like levels of proficiency) in the long term (a minimum of ten years has been suggested as the period necessary to reveal ultimate attainment rather than rate results; DeKeyser, 2000). In foreign language learning settings, research evidence indicates that, given similar periods of instruction and learning conditions, younger starters do not outperform older starters in the long term (see the recent synthesis by Huang, 2016). This discrepancy may be explained in terms of differences in the amount and quality of contact with the target language that learners have in the two contexts (Muñoz, 2008a). First of all, the young learners' slow pace of learning may be related to the scarcity of input in typical foreign language learning settings. DeKeyser (2000) argued that young children are good at implicit learning, but that implicit learning mechanisms need massive amounts of input. Therefore, if the learning setting does not provide them with the amount of input required, implicit learning will not be facilitated and no long-term superiority is to be expected. In contrast, older children and adolescents will be better at explicit learning because of their more developed analytic skills, and explicit learning does not require so much input (cf. the relevant discussion in Singleton, 2014); furthermore, as noted above, the literacy skills they have already acquired in one language can facilitate literacy development in the new language through transfer or the use of common underlying cognitive abilities linked to reading and writing (Pfenninger, 2014b; Riches & Genesee, 2006).

However, in the long run this superiority may disappear because the younger starters will have reached similar levels of cognitive maturity and literacy. Indeed, recent studies that have conducted comparisons of long-term results (Al-Thubaiti, 2010; Harada, 2014; Huang & Chang, 2015; but see Larson-Hall, 2008) have found that starting age does not have as strong an influence as amount and type of input. For instance, investigating foreign language learners with more than ten years of exposure to English, Muñoz (2011) found that language proficiency was significantly associated with different measures of input rather than with starting age. Confirming results were found in a second study where the long-term oral performance of foreign language learners was not found to be associated with starting age and where different input measures significantly predicted different performance dimensions (fluency, lexical diversity, syntactic complexity and accuracy) (Muñoz, 2014). In both studies, more significant than measures of cumulative input were measures highlighting the value of intensive input as well as the quality of individuals' language experience, which reflect their orientations and predispositions to seek opportunities to learn the language and to use it in meaningful interactions.

Becoming Multilingual at School in a Foreign Language Setting

Multilingual schools are increasingly common these days, also in foreign language contexts. Most schools have become multilingual through using more than one language as the language of instruction and/or teaching one or more languages as school subjects. Furthermore, in many schools more and more pupils bring a home language that is different from the school languages (for studies in a variety of multilingual school contexts, see Cenoz & Gorter, 2015). As an illustration of multilingual policies concerned with pupils' starting age, consider the European Union's recommendation that children are introduced to two additional languages from an early age.

Learner, school and sociolinguistic factors are relevant to the choice of starting age for a first and a second foreign language and to the particular sequence in which languages are taught. With respect to the learner, as seen above, essential factors are quality, quantity and intensity of input, and the number of languages and literacies acquired prior to the school target language experience (cf. Pfenniger & Singleton, forthcoming), as well as the efficiency of learning mechanisms at each age; the linguistic distance between the languages will also affect learning difficulty. With respect to the school system, a crucial factor is the provision of teachers with adequate language competence and pedagogic training. The latter needs to be specific to the target age group and suitable for multilingual settings, including an awareness of the phenomena associated to multilingualism, such as the main psycholinguistic processes involved and of cross-linguistic influence and interaction. Decisive sociolinguistic factors are the different language configurations and needs (e.g. preservation of a minority language), the out-of-school exposure to the additional languages, and the status of the languages to be learned and attitudes towards them.

Learners' age is also a crucial concern for new developments in language teaching and learning, such as content and language integrated learning (CLIL) (i.e. the issue of when it is more efficient to integrate content and language; cf. Muñoz, 2015); and exchange or study abroad programmes (i.e. the optimum conditions for each age group to benefit from a language (and culture) immersion experience; cf. Llanes & Muñoz, 2013; Muñoz & Llanes, 2014).

Conclusions

In sum, research on multilingual acquisition has shown that the effects of age differ according to the learning environment. In relation to the younger = better belief, one can agree that an early start may lead to success but only provided that it is associated with enough significant exposure. In input-limited settings typical of foreign language learning situations, research findings indicate that older starters are more efficient learners: comparisons after the same amount of instructional time show that they progress further than younger learners, while comparisons at the same age show that they catch up with younger starters in most skills despite having had fewer hours of instruction. Research has also shown that learners' attitudes towards the target language and their motivation impact language learning in ways that pertain to each individual learner and that are not necessarily connected with the age at which they started learning that language. Finally, the crucial role of the learning context, including the quality of multilingual school programmes, needs to be highlighted, since in the appropriate conditions (including lifelong learning opportunities) learners at all ages may become successful multilingual individuals.

Questions for Students' Reflection

1. Have you ever met a non-native user of your language whom you initially took for a native speaker? At what age did they start learning the language? Under what conditions? Did they want to sound 'native'? Why or why not?

2. In what respects has the (monolingual) native speaker model associated with the maturational approach to age effects been challenged?

3. How would you define and characterize a 'successful learner' of an additional language? Would you use 'native-like' as a criterion? Why or why not?

4. What do you think is the most appropriate age to begin foreign language instruction?

5. If you were a school principal with students of all ages learning a foreign language, would you assign the more proficient and fluent foreign language teachers to the younger-age classes or to the older-age ones?

Suggestions for Further Reading

DeKeyser, R. (2013) Age effects in second language learning: Stepping stones toward better understanding. *Language Learning* 63 (Suppl. 1), 52–67.

Kinsella, C. and Singleton, D. (2014) Much more than age. *Applied Linguistics* 35 (4), 441–462.

Muñoz, C. (2008) Symmetries and asymmetries of age effects in naturalistic and instructed L2 learning. *Applied Linguistics* 29, 578–596.

Muñoz, C. and Singleton, D. (2011) A critical review of age-related research on L2 ultimate attainment. *Language Teaching* 44 (1), 1–35.

Murphy, V.A. (2014) *Second Language Learning in the Early School Years: Trends and Contexts*. Oxford: Oxford University Press.

Singleton, D. (2005) The critical period hypothesis: A coat of many colours. *International Review of Applied Linguistics in Language Teaching* 43 (4), 269–285.

References

Abrahamsson, N. and Hyltenstam, K. (2008) The robustness of aptitude effects in near-native second language acquisition. *Studies in Second Language Acquisition* 30 (4), 481–509.

Abrahamsson, N. and Hyltenstam, K. (2009) Age of onset and nativelikeness in a second language: Listener perception versus linguistic scrutiny. *Language Learning* 59 (2), 249–306.

Al-Thubaiti, K.A. (2010) Age effects in a minimal input setting on the acquisition of English morpho-syntactic and semantic properties by L1 speakers of Arabic. Unpublished PhD thesis, University of Essex.

Aronin, L. and Singleton, D. (2008) Multilingualism as a new linguistic dispensation. *International Journal of Multilingualism* 5, 1–16.

Asher, J. and García, R. (1969) The optimal age to learn a foreign language. *The Modern Language Journal* 53, 334–341.

Baker, C. (2006) *Foundations of Bilingual Education and Bilingualism* (4th edn). Clevedon: Multilingual Matters.

Bialystok, E., Peets, K.F. and Moreno, S. (2014) Producing bilinguals through immersion education: Development of metalinguistic awareness. *Applied Psycholinguistics* 35, 177–191.

Birdsong, D. (2006) Age and second language acquisition and processing: A selective overview. *Language Learning* 56 (1), 9–49.

Birdsong, D. (2014) The critical period hypothesis for second language acquisition: Tailoring the coat of many colors. In M. Pawlak and L. Aronin (eds) *Essential Topics in Applied Linguistics and Multilingualism* (pp. 43–50). Heidelberg: Springer.

Birdsong, D. and Gertken, L. (2013) In faint praise of folly: A critical review of native/non-native comparisons, with examples from native and bilingual processing of French complex syntax. *Language, Interaction and Acquisition* 4, 107–133.

Birdsong, D. and Paik, J. (2008) Second language acquisition and ultimate attainment. In B. Spolsky and F. Hult (eds) *Handbook of Educational Linguistics* (pp. 424–436). Oxford: Blackwell.

Bosch, L. and Sebastian-Galles, N. (2001) Evidence of early language discrimination abilities in infants from bilingual environments. *Infancy* 2 (1), 29–49.

Bosch, L. and Sebastián-Gallés, N. (2003) Simultaneous bilingualism and the perception of a language-specific vowel contrast in the first year of life. *Language and Speech* 46 (2–3), 217–243.

Callahan, R.M. and Gándara, P.C. (eds) (2014) *The Bilingual Advantage: Language, Literacy and the US Labor Market*. Bristol: Multilingual Matters.

Chugani, H.T., Behen, M.E., Muzik, O., Juhasz, C., Nagy, F. and Chugani, D.C. (2001) Local brain functional activity following early deprivation: A study of post-institutionalized Romanian orphans. *NeuroImage* 14 (6), 1290–1301.

Cenoz, J. (2003) Facteurs determinant l'acquisition d'une L3: Age, développement cognitif et milieu. *Acquisition et Interaction en langue étrangère* 18, 37–51.

Cenoz, J. and Gorter, D. (eds) (2015) *Multilingual Education. Between Language Learning and Translanguaging*. Cambridge: Cambridge University Press.

Comeau, L., Genesee, F. and Lapaquette, L. (2003) The modelling hypothesis and child bilingual code-mixing. *International Journal of Bilingualism* 7 (2), 113–126.

Cook, V. (2002) Background to the L2 user. In V. Cook (ed.) *Portraits of the L2 User* (pp. 1–28). Clevedon: Multilingual Matters.

Craik, F. and Bialystok, E. (2005) Intelligence and executive control: Evidence from aging and bilingualism. *Cortex* 41, 222–224.

Cummins, J. (1984) *Bilingualism and Special Education: Issues in Assessment and Pedagogy*. Clevedon: Multilingual Matters.

De Bot, K. (2017) The future of the bilingual advantage. In S.E. Pfenninger and J. Navracsics (eds) *Future Research Directions for Applied Linguistics* (pp. 15–32). Bristol: Multilingual Matters.

DeKeyser, R. (2000) The robustness of critical period effects in second language acquisition. *Studies in Second Language Acquisition* 22 (4), 499–533.

Deuchar, M. and Quay, S. (2000) *Bilingual Acquisition: Theoretical Implications of a Case Study*. Oxford: Oxford University Press.

Flege J.E. (2009) Give input a chance! In T. Piske and M. Young-Scholten (eds) *Input Matters* (pp. 175–190). Bristol: Multilingual Matters.

Flege, J.E., Yeni-Komshian, G.H. and Liu, S. (1999) Age constraints on second language acquisition. *Journal of Memory and Language* 41 (1), 78–104.

García-Mayo, M.P. and García-Lecumberri, M.L. (eds) (2003) *Age and the Acquisition of English as a Foreign Language: Theoretical Issues and Field Work*. Clevedon: Multilingual Matters.

Genesee, F. (2004) What do we know about bilingual education for majority language students? In T.K. Bhatia and W. Ritchie (eds) *Handbook of Bilingualism and Multiculturalism* (pp. 547–576). Malden, MA: Blackwell.

Genesee, F. (2007) Literacy outcomes in French immersion. *Encyclopedia of Language and Literacy Development*. London, ON: Canadian Language and Literacy Research Network.

Genesee, F. (2015) Myths about early childhood bilingualism. *Canadian Psychology/Psychologie Canadienne* 56 (1), 6–15.

Genesee, F., Nicoladis, E. and Paradis, J. (1995) Language differentiation in early bilingual development. *Journal of Child Language* 22 (3), 611–631.

Genesee, F., Boivin, I. and Nicoladis, E. (1996) Bilingual children talking with monolingual adults: A study of bilingual communicative competence. *Applied Psycholinguistics* 17 (4), 427–442.

Granena, G. and Long, M.H. (2013) Age of onset, length of residence, language aptitude, and ultimate L2 attainment in three linguistic domains. *Second Language Research* 29 (3), 311–343.

Grosjean, F. (1992) Another view of bilingualism. In R. Harris (ed.) *Cognitive Processing in Bilinguals* (pp. 51–62). Amsterdam: North-Holland.

Harada, T. (2014) Not age but length of learning matters in second language speech learning in a minimal input situation. Poster presented at the *2014 Conference of the American Association for Applied Linguistics (AAAL), 22–25 March, Portland, OR*.

Harley, B. and Hart, D. (1997) Language aptitude and second language proficiency in classroom learners of different starting ages. *Studies in Second Language Acquisition* 19 (3), 379–400.

Hernandez, A., Li, P. and MacWhinney, B. (2005) The emergence of competing modules in bilingualism. *Trends in Cognitive Sciences* 9 (5), 220–225.

Huang, B.H. (2014) The effects of age on second language grammar and speech production. *Journal of Psycholinguistic Research* 43 (4), 397–420.

Huang, B.H. (2016) A synthesis of empirical research on the linguistic outcomes of early foreign language instruction. *International Journal of Multilingualism* 13 (3), 257–273; doi:10.1080/14790718.2015.1066792.

Huang, B.H. and Chang, S. (2015) Not all early birds get the worm: The effect of early instruction on long-term foreign language outcomes. Paper presented at the *2015 Conference of the American Association for Applied Linguistics (AAAL), 21–24 March, Toronto*.

Hyltenstam, K. (1992) Non-native features of near-native speakers: On the ultimate attainment of childhood L2 learners. *Advances in Psychology* 83, 351–368.

Jaekel, N., Schurig, M., Florian, M. and Ritterb, M. (2017) From early starters to late finishers? A longitudinal study of early foreign language learning in school. *Language Learning* 67 (3), 631–664; doi:10.1111/lang.12242.

Jarvis, S. and Pavlenko, A. (2008) *Crosslinguistic Influence in Language and Cognition*. London: Routledge.

Johnson, J.S. and Newport, E.L. (1989) Critical period effects in second language learning: The influence of maturational state on the acquisition of English as a second language. *Cognitive Psychology* 21 (1), 60–99.

Jones, P.E. (1995) Contradictions and unanswered questions in the Genie case: A fresh look at the linguistic evidence. *Language and Communication* 15 (3), 261–280.

Kalberer, U. (2007) Rate of L2 acquisition and the influence of instruction time on 100 achievement. MEd thesis, University of Manchester.

Kavé, G., Eyal, N., Shorek, A. and Cohen-Mansfield, J. (2008) Multilingualism and cognitive state in the oldest old. *Psychology and Aging* 23 (1), 70–78.

Kinsella, C. and Singleton, D. (2014) Much more than age. *Applied Linguistics* 35 (4), 441–462.

Krashen, S., Long, M. and Scarcella, R. (1979) Age, rate and eventual attainment in second language acquisition. *TESOL Quarterly* 9, 573–582.

Lanza, E. (1997) *Language Mixing in Infant Bilingualism: A Sociolinguistic Perspective*. Oxford: Clarendon Press.

Larson-Hall, J. (2008) Weighing the benefits of studying a foreign language at a younger starting age in a minimal input situation. *Second Language Research* 24 (1), 35–63.

Lenneberg, E.H. (1967) *Biological Foundations of Language*. New York: Wiley.

Lieberman, A.M., Borovsky, A., Hatrak, M. and Mayberry, R.I. (2015) Real-time processing of ASL signs: Delayed first language acquisition affects organization of the mental lexicon. *Journal of Experimental Psychology: Learning, Memory, and Cognition* 41 (4), 1130–1139.

Llanes, À. and Muñoz, C. (2013) Age effects in a study abroad context: Children and adults studying abroad and at home. *Language Learning* 63, 63–90.

Long, M. (2013) Maturational constraints on child and adult SLA. In G. Granena and M. Long (eds) *Sensitive Periods, Language Aptitude and Ultimate Attainment* (pp. 3–41). Amsterdam: John Benjamins.

Mackey, A. and Sachs, R. (2012) Older learners in SLA research: A first look at working memory, feedback, and L2 development. *Language Learning* 62 (3), 704–740; doi:10.1111/j.1467-9922.2011.00649.x.

Maneva, B. (2004) 'Maman, je suis polyglotte' [Mommy, I'm a polyglot]: A case study of multilingual language acquisition from 0 to 5 years. *International Journal of Multilingualism* 1 (2), 109–122.

Mayberry, R.I. and Lock, E. (2003) Age constraints on first versus second language acquisition: Evidence for linguistic plasticity and epigenesis. *Brain and Language* 87 (3), 369–384.

Moyer, A. (2013) *Foreign Accent: The Phenomenon of Non-native Speech*. Cambridge: Cambridge University Press.

Moyer, A. (2014) Exceptional outcomes in L2 phonology: The critical factors of learner engagement and self-regulation. *Applied Linguistics* 35 (4), 418–440.

Muñoz, C. (2006a) (ed.) *Age and the Rate of Foreign Language Learning*. Clevedon: Multilingual Matters.

Muñoz, C. (2006b) The effects of age on foreign language learning: The BAF Project. In C. Muñoz (ed.) *Age and the Rate of Foreign Language Learning* (pp. 1–40). Clevedon: Multilingual Matters.

Muñoz, C. (2008a) Symmetries and asymmetries of age effects in naturalistic and instructed L2 learning. *Applied Linguistics* 29, 578–596.

Muñoz, C. (2008b) Age-related differences in foreign language learning: Revisiting the empirical evidence. *International Review of Applied Linguistics* 46, 197–220.

Muñoz, C. (2011) Is input more significant than starting age in foreign language acquisition? *International Review of Applied Linguistics* 49, 113–133.

Muñoz, C. (2014) Contrasting effects of starting age and input on the oral performance of foreign language learners. *Applied Linguistics* 35 (4), 463–482.

Muñoz, C. (2015) Time and timing in CLIL: A comparative approach to language gains. In M. Juan-Garau and J. Salazar-Noguera (eds) *Content-based Language Learning in Multilingual Educational Environments* (pp. 87–102). Berlin: Springer.

Muñoz, C. and Llanes, À. (2014) Study abroad and changes in degree of foreign accent in children and adults. *The Modern Language Journal* 98 (1), 432–449.

Muñoz, C. and Singleton, D. (2007) Foreign accent in advanced learners. Two successful profiles. *EuroSLA Yearbook* 7, 171–190.

Muñoz, C. and Singleton, D. (2011) A critical review of age-related research on L2 ultimate attainment. *Language Teaching* 44 (1), 1–35.

Murahata, G., Murahata, Y. and Cook, V. (2016) Research questions and methodology of multi-competence. In V. Cook and Li Wei (eds) *The Cambridge Handbook of Linguistic Multicompetence* (pp. 26–49). Cambridge: Cambridge University Press.

Newport, E.L. and Supalla, T. (1987) A critical period effect in the acquisition of a primary language. Unpublished manuscript, University of Illinois.

Nicoladis, E. and Genesee, F. (1996) A longitudinal study of pragmatic differentiation in young bilingual children. *Language Learning* 46 (3), 439–464.

Ojima, S., Matsuba-Kurita, H., Nakamura, N., Hoshino, T. and Hagiwara, H. (2011) Age and amount of exposure to a foreign language during childhood: Behavioral and ERP data on the semantic comprehension of spoken English by Japanese children. *Neuroscience Research* 70, 197–205.

Ortega, L. (2010) The bilingual turn in SLA. Plenary presentation given at the *Annual Conference of the American Association for Applied Linguistics (AAAL)*, March, Atlanta, GA.

Paap, K.R., Johnson, H.A. and Sawi, O. (2015) Bilingual advantages in executive functioning either do not exist of are restricted to very specific and undetermined circumstances. *Cortex* 69, 265–278.

Paradis, J. (2007) Early bilingual and multilingual acquisition. In P. Auer and Li Wei (eds) *Handbook of Multilingualism and Multilingual Communication* (pp. 15–44). Berlin: Mouton de Gruyter.

Patkowski, M.S. (1980) The sensitive period for the acquisition of syntax in a second language. *Language Learning* 30 (2), 449–468.

Petitto, L.A., Katerelos, M., Bronna, G., Levy, K.G., Tétreault, K. and Ferraro, V. (2001) Bilingual signed and spoken language acquisition from birth: Implications for the mechanisms underlying early bilingual language acquisition. *Journal of Child Language* 28 (2), 453–496.

Pfenninger, S.E. (2013) Quadrilingual advantages: Do-support in bilingual vs. multilingual learners. *International Journal of Multilingualism* 11 (2), 143–163.

Pfenninger, S. (2014a) The misunderstood variable: Age effects as a function of types of instruction. *Studies of Second Language Learning and Teaching* 4 (3), 529–556.

Pfenninger, S. (2014b) The literacy factor in the optimal age discussion: A five-year longitudinal study. *International Journal of Bilingual Education and Bilingualism* 17.

Pfenninger, S. and Singleton, D. (2017) *Beyond Age Effects in Instructional L2 Learning: Revisiting the Age Factor*. Bristol: Multilingual Matters.

Pfenninger, S. and Singleton, D. (forthcoming) Starting age overshadowed: The primacy of differential environmental and input effects on L2 attainment in an instructional context. *Language Learning.*

Piske, T., Flege, J.E., Mackay, I.R. and Meador, D. (2002) The production of English vowels by fluent early and late Italian-English bilinguals. *Phonetica* 59 (1), 49–71.

Richards, J.C. and Schmidt, R. (2002) *Longman Dictionary of Language Teaching and Applied Linguistics.* Harlow: Pearson Education.

Riches, C. and Genesee, F. (2006) Cross-linguistic and cross-modal aspects of literacy development. In F. Genesee, K. Lindholm-Leary, W.M. Saunders and D. Christian (eds) *Educating English Language Learners: A Synthesis of Research Evidence* (pp. 64–108). New York: Cambridge University Press.

Roehren-Brackin, K. (2015) Long-term development in an instructed adult L2 learner: Usage-based and complexity theory applied. In T. Cadierno and S.W. Eskildsen (eds) *Usage-based Perspectives on Second Language Learning* (pp. 181–206). Berlin: Mouton de Gruyter.

Salthouse, T.A. (2004) What and when of cognitive aging. *Current Directions in Psychological Science* 13, 140–144.

Seliger, H., Krashen, S. and Ladefoged, P. (1975) Maturational constraints in the acquisition of a native-like accent in second language learning. *Language Science*s 36, 20–22.

Singleton, D. (2005) The critical period hypothesis: A coat of many colours. *International Review of Applied Linguistics* 43 (4), 269–285.

Singleton, D. (2014) Apt to change: The problematic of language awareness and language aptitude in age-related research. *Studies in Second Language Learning and Teaching* 4 (3), 557–571.

Singleton, D. and Muñoz, C. (2011) Around and beyond the critical period hypothesis. In E. Hinkel (ed.) *Handbook of Research in Second Language Teaching and Learning, Vol. 2* (pp. 407–425). London: Routledge.

Skrzypek, A. and Singleton, D. (2016) Age and identity. In V. Regan, C. Diskin and J. Martyn (eds) *New Approaches to Multilingualism and Identity in Transnational Contexts* (pp. 83–97). Oxford: Peter Lang.

Snow, C. and Hoefnagel-Höhle, M. (1978) The critical period for language acquisition: Evidence from second language learning. *Child Development* 49, 1114–1128.

Suyal, C. (2002) Bilingual first language acquisition: Code-mixing in children who speak a minority language. Unpublished MA thesis, Department of Linguistics, University of Alberta.

Swain, M. (1981) Time and timing in bilingual education. *Language Learning* 31, 1–15.

Swain, M., Lapkin, S., Rowen, N. and Hart, D. (1990) The role of mother tongue literacy in third language learning. *Language, Culture and Curriculum* 3, 65–81; doi:10.1080/07908319009525073.

Thomas, W.P. and Collier, V.P. (2002) *A National Study of School Effectiveness for Language Minority Students' Long-term Academic Achievement.* Santa Cruz, CA and Washington, DC: Center for Research on Education, Diversity & Excellence. See http://www.thomasandcollier.com/assets/2002_thomas-and-collier_2002-final-report.pdf.

Volterra, V. and Taeschner, T. (1978) The acquisition and development of language by bilingual children. *Journal of Child Language* 5 (2), 311–326.

Walsh, P. and Singleton, D. (2013) Variation in English lexical acquisition among Polish migrant children in Ireland. In D. Singleton, V. Regan and E. Debaene (eds) *Linguistic and Cultural Acquisition in a Migrant Community* (pp. 156–182). Bristol: Multilingual Matters.

Werker, J.F. (2012) Perceptual foundations of bilingual acquisition in infancy. *Annals of the New York Academy of Sciences* 1251, 50–61.

Werker, J.F. and Byers-Heinlein, K. (2008) Bilingualism in infancy: First steps in perception and comprehension. *Trends in Cognitive Sciences* 12 (4), 144–151.

Werker, J.F. and Tees, R.C. (2005) Speech perception as a window for understanding plasticity and commitment in language systems of the brain. *Developmental Psychobiology* 46 (3), 233–251.

Part 3

The Psycholinguistics and Neurolinguistics of Multilingualism

Lecture 9

The Psycholinguistics of Multilingualism

Julia Festman

What is Psycholinguistics?

Linguistics is the science of *language*, and psychology the science of *behaviour*. As a field of science, linguistics describes the structures that underlie language whereas psychology explains behaviour in terms of mental processes (De Groot, 2011). Psycholinguistics is in fact an interdisciplinary discipline to explore human language behaviour in depth. In my view, we can probably grasp only half of the story if we investigate language behaviour from the viewpoint only of psychology or of linguistics. In psycholinguistics both disciplines conveniently converge to provide a comprehensive and detailed picture. Psycholinguistics is the science of linguistic behaviour; it is about how language is internally represented, how language is used and processed and how humans learn a language (Rickheit *et al.*, 2002).

Crucial questions

Psycholinguistics as a discipline centres on three crucial questions about language and behaviour: (1) How is language knowledge organized? (2) How do we process language? and (3) How do we acquire language? We will consider these three questions in this lecture.

1. *How is language knowledge organized?*
   One key goal of psycholinguistics is to describe the content and organization of language knowledge in our mind, i.e. we assume that our language knowledge is stored in a '*mental lexicon*' and we have assumptions about how grammar is represented in the mind. Researchers in this discipline are interested in the organization of word

knowledge (lexical knowledge) and how words can be combined (grammatical knowledge) in order for conveyed information to be comprehensible to the reader/listener.

2. *How do we process language?*
A second key goal of psycholinguistics is to explore the mechanisms of language processing (Dietrich, 2007). Psycholinguists are searching for generally valid patterns of language production and language perception in order to find answers to the key questions of how we produce language output (i.e. *language production*) and how we understand language input (i.e. *language perception*). Four linguistic skills are hereby distinguished along the lines of modality: listening and speaking belong to the oral modality, whereas reading and writing are written forms of language. The four *language skills* can also be considered as areas of language production (speaking, writing) and of language perception (listening/comprehension, reading).

3. *How do we acquire language?*
The third key goal of psycholinguistics is to reveal valid patterns of language acquisition (regarding first and home languages) and patterns of language learning (regarding foreign languages) and the cognitive processing of language(s) necessary in the acquisition and learning processes.

Experimental paradigms and methods

Psycholinguistics is an empirical discipline in which a diversity of methods and experimental paradigms are commonly employed, as shown in Table 9.1. Most of these paradigms used in psycholinguistic research and listed in the table reveal two main behavioural output measures: (a) *reaction times* (that is, the time until a response/reaction can be recorded to a certain stimulus, sometimes called *response latency*); and (b) the quality of the response (usually measured in terms of *accuracy*).

Here is one example: in a *picture naming paradigm*, the participant sees a visually presented object – usually on a computer screen – and is asked to name it (see Figure 9.1). For example, the picture of a dog appears on the computer screen and the participant correctly says 'dog' (see Figure 9.1). A number of cognitive stages have to be mastered in order to be able to produce the correct name: the object (that is the picture of the dog) has to be perceived visually, recognized and the adequate name that matches the picture has to be accessed in the mental lexicon; then the auditory representation has to be activated and verbally produced. Of interest is quantitatively how fast the participant can produce the correct object name, which implies information about how fast s/he can pass through these stages. Therefore, the time elapsing between presentation of the visual object and the onset of the verbal response is measured in milliseconds (this is known as reaction time). Qualitatively, it can be investigated how correct the response is. When the picture of a dog is shown, the participant might just say 'animal' or 'poodle' or 'mammal' at 'it has four legs'. These are likely within-language substitutions (i.e. alternatives at different levels of specificity) that both mono- and multilingual participants might produce instead of the expected word (i.e. the *target word*). A multilingual might produce a response such as 'Katze' (see Figure 9.1). This is German for 'cat'. Such a response would indicate on the one

Table 9.1 *Some examples of experimental paradigms and psycholinguistic studies which use these paradigms with mono-/bilingual and trilingual participants*

Experimental paradigms	Selected studies on mono-/bilinguals	Selected studies on trilinguals
Priming	Bosch and Clahsen (2016); Duñabeitia et al. (2010)	Francis and Gallard (2005); Tytus (2017)
Grammaticality judgment	Gangopadhyay et al. (2016); Sato and Felser (2010); Prior et al. (2017)	Charkova (2003)
Lexical decision	De Groot et al. (2002); Frost (1998); Mosca and de Bot (2017)	Alonso et al. (2016); Ibrahim and Eviatar (2012)
Picture naming	Bobb and Wodniecka (2013); Costa and Santesteban (2004); Festman (2012); Gollan et al. (2005); Kleinman and Gollan (2018); Mosca and De Bot (2017)	Costa et al. (2006); Festman (2008); Guo et al. (2013); Poarch and Van Hell (2012)
Picture-word interference	Hermans et al. (1998); Marian et al. (2008); Schriefers et al. (1990)	Abunuwara (1992); Shao et al. (2015)
Word recognition	Dijkstra et al. (1999)	Lemhöfer et al. (2004)
Verbal fluency	Festman (2012); Sandoval et al. (2010)	Schwieter and Sunderman (2011)
Self-paced reading	Bultena et al. (2015); Jacob and Felser (2016)	
Translation task	Poarch et al. (2015)	Cenoz (2001)
Language switching	Hut and Leminen (2017); Meuter and Allport (1999); Philipp and Koch (2009); Prior and Gollan (2011)	Festman and Mosca (2016); Hut et al. (2017); Linck et al. (2012); Marian et al. (2013); Mosca (2018)

hand that it is the wrong language (if a red frame indicates that the response should be given in English rather than in German, i.e. *cross-language interference*), and on the other hand that it is the name of another animal (cat rather than dog, i.e. *semantic interference*). From among all given trials in an experiment the number of correct trials is determined and usually calculated as percentage of correct responses. The responses differ in specificity and reveal information about the organization and size of the mental lexicon and the participant's ability to access this kind of information. We then know how long it took a participant to retrieve and produce the name of the presented picture, and whether or not it was correct in terms of semantics and language, or how close the given response was to the target word.

There are also non-invasive neurophysiological methods which will be listed below to provide an initial overview, but they will not be the focus of this lecture. Since language

Figure 9.1 Example of a *picture naming paradigm*: the picture of an object (e.g. a dog) appears on the computer screen and the participant is asked to name it as accurately and as fast as possible. In multilingual set-ups the language in which the picture should be named is indicated, e.g. by a coloured frame on the screen, and before the start of the experiment the participant learns to associate one frame colour with one of her languages (e.g. red = English; yellow = German; green= French)

processing has a physiological brain basis, common methods to observe language processing in even more depth are:

- measures of eye movements (eye-tracking during reading or in visual word paradigms);
- changes of the pupil as an indication of processing (pupillometry);
- measures of electrophysiological changes relative to specific information (visual, auditory), which represent an event (event-related potentials, ERP);
- measures of electromagnetic changes of the brain (MEG);
- and measures of local distribution of brain activity (in particular, functional magnetic resonance imaging, fMRI).

Language processing is constituted by the orchestration of functionally distinct subsystems and functionally distinct levels of processing. In particular, individual, situated and medial factors influence language knowledge, language processing and language acquisition.

What is Multilingualism?

Defining bilingualism, trilingualism and multilingualism

Let us start with bilingualism. In this lecture *bilingualism* is defined as the knowledge and use of two languages, *trilingualism* as the knowledge and use of three languages and *multilingualism* as the knowledge and use of more than two languages. Consequently and

Table 9.2 List of most relevant criteria for classifying bilinguals

Criteria	Type	Explanation
Role of language	First language	Learned from birth
	Second/additional/foreign	Learned later
Current level of fluency in L2	Proficient bilinguals	(Near-)native level of proficiency
	Non-proficient bilinguals	Far from native level of proficiency
Language competence L1–L2	Balanced bilinguals	Possess similar levels of proficiency in both languages, but not necessarily high levels of language proficiency in both
	Dominant/unbalanced bilinguals	Possess a higher level of proficiency in one language than in the other
Age at acquisition of L2	Early bilinguals	Start to acquire L2 in childhood (between ages 0 and 3)
	Late bilinguals	Start to acquire L2 after age 6
	Simultaneous bilinguals	Exposed to both languages simultaneously
	Sequential/consecutive bilinguals	Learn first L1, then L2
Influence of L2 on L1 (cf. Lambert, 1975)	Additive bilinguals	The L2 is an addition to the L1, as it serves as an enrichment (e.g. in the context of immersion)
	Subtractive bilinguals	The L1 is not frequently used any longer and is usually replaced by the stronger, more dominant language (e.g. in the context of migration)
Context/manner of acquisition	Formal	at school
	Informal	At home, from parents

strictly speaking, trilingualism is thus part of multilingualism, but bilingualism is not (see Cenoz, 2013, for more information on defining multilingualism).

There are a number of *classifications for bilingualism*, some of which are presented in Table 9.2. They are crucial when relating findings of studies to certain types of bilinguals. For example, De Groot (2011) warns: '(…) the bilingual community are a colorful lot. One should therefore think twice before generalizing a conclusion based on the results of a study testing bilinguals of a specific type to another type, and it behooves the author of any bilingual study to provide details about the type of bilinguals tested.' A seminal paper by Francois Grosjean (1998) provides an even longer list of 'methodological and conceptual issues' when studying bilinguals. It has not lost at all its relevance and should be read by everyone planning studies with bilingual or multilingual participants. The list in Table 9.2 is by no means exhaustive, but it provides the most relevant criteria when thinking about bilinguals as a heterogeneous group.

What is special about trilingualism?

Hoffmann (2008) claimed that trilingualism is quite distinct from bilingualism. She argued that we cannot automatically assume that trilingualism involves exactly the same processes and interplay factors as bilingualism. The main difference is a quantitative one, but a closer comparison between the two reveals a high degree of complexity involved in the latter. In addition, certain social, cultural and above all psychological and personality-related factors may assume disproportionately high significance in influencing trilingual acquisition and use. (Hoffmann, 2008: 13)

Aronin and Jessner (2015: 270) stated that 'studies conducted by neurolinguists, psycholinguists, sociolinguistic scholars as well as ordinary daily observations and experiences, indicate systemic and significant differences between bilingualism and multilingualism'. While the definition of bilingualism has not been clear-cut, including the knowledge and use of two or more languages, the definition of multilingualism is just as unclear. Multilinguals speak three or more languages, they are quite experienced language learners and they know what it means to learn a second or foreign language. It is likely that this also applies to children who grow up trilingually, since the acquisition of multiple languages presumably triggers thinking about languages. Such metalinguistic awareness is characterized by two components: the analysis of linguistic knowledge into structured categories, and the control of attention when selecting and processing specific linguistic information (Bialystok, 1986).

Although the criteria to classify multilinguals (Table 9.3) are, of course, heavily based on those used for bilinguals, some additional criteria (in italics in Table 9.3) seem to attract more attention and might be even more relevant to multilingualism in future research (see also De Bot & Jaensch, 2015).

What is the Psycholinguistics of Multilingualism?

The psycholinguistics of multilingualism is the science focusing on managing more than two languages in the mind, from acquisition to representation and processing. More specifically, it aims at furthering our understanding of an individual's knowledge of several languages (lexicon, grammar), how a multilingual is able to produce and perceive a number of languages, and how a multilingual acquires several languages.

Psycholinguistic processes in individual multilingualism

Think about the difference between doing two or three things at the same time. Maybe you immediately think about multitasking mothers: for example, [task1 – cooking] while [task 2 – watching a child] and [task 3 – talking on the phone]. The more tasks this person has to fulfil and concentrate on, the harder or more exhausting it is. Therefore, thinking about multilingual representation and processing, it is most likely more complex than

Table 9.3 *List of most relevant criteria for classifying multilinguals; italics show those that have lately received more attention and will most likely play a more crucial role in future research*

Criteria	*Type*	*Explanation*
Role of language	First language/*source language?*	Learned from birth
	Second/additional/foreign/ *reference language?*	Learned later
Current level of fluency in L2, L3, … (proficiency)	Proficient multilinguals	(Near-)native level of language proficiency
	Non-proficient multilinguals	Far from native level of proficiency
Language competence/ dominance	Balanced multilinguals	Possess similar levels of proficiency in all languages, but not necessarily high levels of language proficiency in each of them
	Dominant/unbalanced multilinguals	Possess higher levels of language proficiency in one language than in the others
Age at acquisition (AoA) of L2, L3, …	Early multilinguals	Start to acquire L2/L3… in childhood (between ages 0 and 3/6)
	Late multilinguals	Start to acquire L2/L3… after age 6/ beyond childhood
	Simultaneous multilinguals	Exposed to all languages simultaneously
	Sequential/consecutive multilinguals	Learn first L1, then L2/L3…
Influence of L2 on L1	Additive multilinguals	The L3 is an addition to the first two languages, as it serves as an enrichment
	Subtractive multilinguals	The first language is not frequently used any longer and is usually replaced by the stronger, more dominant languages
Context/manner of acquisition	Formal	Formal, at school
	Informal	At home, from parents
Status of languages	*High-prestige-language multilinguals*	*All languages are socially valued*
	Lower-prestige-language multilinguals	*One language is devalued*
Typology of languages	Close/similar/same language family	e.g. Spanish-French-Italian (all Romance languages with much lexical and grammatical overlap)
	Far/different	e.g. German, Farsi, Japanese (each language from a different language family, no overlap)

(continued)

Table 9.3 *(Continued)*

Criteria	Type	Explanation
Frequency/recency of using each language	Equal	Frequency and recency of using each language is equally distributed across a day/week, ...
	Unequal	One language is more often used than the other(s); use of language(s) is some time ago
Purpose of use	Work, academia, etc.	The use of each language is at certain points in time linked to certain domains, e.g. the language(s) used while working
	Private, conversations, internet, reading books	Or the language(s) used in the private domain
Control ability Festman, J. et al. (2010)	Switchers	Have trouble with using only the intended language
	Non-switchers	Have no trouble with using only the intended language; no unintentional switching
Switching habits Rodriguez-Fornells, A. et al. (2012)	Frequent switching	Frequent switching between two or three languages
	No switching	Use of only one language in a specific situation (e.g. a conversation, writing a letter, etc.)
Socio-economic status (SES)	Low	Low income, low level of education
	High	High income, high level of education

bilingualism. Just to give one example, a trilingual speaker has knowledge in three languages. In some circumstances, e.g. at school, during an exam or job interview, in a business meeting, etc., it is crucial that only one of them is used (the so-called *target language*, i.e. the appropriate language in the communicative situation or experimental setting). Therefore, a trilingual has to focus on this one target language while the other two languages (the so-called *non-target languages*) need to be kept out of the 'production line'. It is now known that both non-target languages can facilitate (*'positive transfer'*) or disturb (*'negative transfer'*) processing in the target language. The assumption that in order to use a certain language for production, the target language is activated (i.e. made more available) and the other has to be *inhibited* (i.e. made less available) is very central to bilingualism theories and follows Green's very influential inhibitory control model (1986, 1998). If only one language is the target language, then in trilingual processing more languages have to be inhibited than are used for current production (the ratio for a trilingual would be 2:1, meaning inhibit two and use one). Thus trilingual processing is more effortful than bilingual processing (with a ratio of 1:1) or monolingual processing (no ratio since the one available language is used and no other needs to be inhibited). This is due to the condition unique to trilingualism that two non-target languages could *interfere with* (i.e. disturb) processing and production in the target language. Therefore, efficient organization is in high demand for trilingual processing and production in order to manage the impact the other languages known to the speaker might exert on target language processing.

Research on trilingualism plays a major role when we talk about the psycholinguistics of multilingualism. Not only are most of the studies involving multilingual participants focused on the processing of three languages, but also, and perhaps even more importantly, trilingualism is at the heart of current investigations. Recent studies have clearly attempted to verify the applicability for trilingualism of assumptions or theoretical suggestions generated from or for bilingualism research. The key issues are:

- how the current non-target languages are involved in the processing of one target language;
- the impact of language dominance/proficiency/typology/AoA and other crucial factors (see Table 9.3) on language representation and processing; and
- the how exactly inhibition mechanisms work during lexical selection (i.e. how a word is chosen from the lexicon to be produced). Selection processes are particularly important when only one language should be used, e.g. due to the communication partner's language knowledge or requirements of work, school, etc. So the main question here is whether many words are initially activated and then later inhibited (local inhibition), or if one or more languages are disregarded during the selection process (global inhibition), and how the time course of inhibition proceeds, before the selection takes place or during the process (proactive or reactive inhibition).

This leads to a more general (and currently hotly debated) question regarding the impact of frequent switching and inhibition (the *cognitive advantage* for bilinguals) on multilingual processing, and it is unclear

- whether multilinguals profit even more from juggling with languages in terms of frequent switching and inhibition which might reveal an even larger cognitive advantage than for bilinguals.

Areas of psycholinguistic research on individual multilingualism

In the following section, the psycholinguistic issues targeted so far in research on individual multilingualism will be outlined and key articles as well as recent studies will be reviewed.

Knowledge about language as knowledge about structures and functions of languages

Language is assumed to be stored in terms of *representations* in *long-term memory*, fragmentized as words, phonemes, perhaps grammatical rules. And the mechanism of *activation* as a very general concept for processing (see below) also guides our thinking about the use of one, two or three languages, as will be described in the next section.

Part 3: The Psycholinguistics and Neurolinguistics of Multilingualism

In the case of trilingualism, trilingual language competence contains the linguistic component (i.e. knowledge of three language systems) and the pragmatic component (i.e. sociolinguistic discourse and strategic competences pertaining to the three languages involved) and it includes the ability to function in monolingual, bilingual and trilingual contexts. This means that a trilingual can use either one, two or three languages in a certain situation.

Language modes

In order to encapsulate the language situation in which multilinguals produce language behaviour, Grosjean (e.g. 1998) put forward a systematic description, which is based on the observation that apparently bilinguals willingly choose the number of languages they use (i.e. *language choice*). Grosjean (2001) extended his concept, which originally accounted for bilingual language behaviour, to include multilinguals. In general, language choice is made according to a communication partner's language knowledge: one would speak in one language to monolinguals but one would employ both languages when talking to bilinguals. Grosjean established the concept of *language modes*. Language mode is used to reflect the speaker's use of her languages in a conversation. Language mode is defined as the 'state of activation' of the speaker's languages and processing mechanisms (Grosjean, 1998: 136). The state of activation of each language is relative to how much this language is currently needed for the conversation. This is said to be determined by the speaker's language choice, which is influenced by factors such as the interlocutor's language knowledge, the situation and the topic of the conversation. In Figure 9.2, the three language modes for the trilingual speaker are represented: monolingual, bilingual and trilingual modes.

In a *monolingual mode* (in Figure 9.2, first diagram) a trilingual uses one of her languages when speaking to a monolingual. For example, Trina, a German-English-French trilingual, speaks only in English to Mona (an English monolingual). The language in use is active (in Figure 9.2, Language A as a black square), whereas the trilingual's 'unused' languages are inactive (Languages B and C are represented as white squares). In our example, Trina's language A is English, while French and German (Languages B and C) are the unused languages when speaking to Mona.

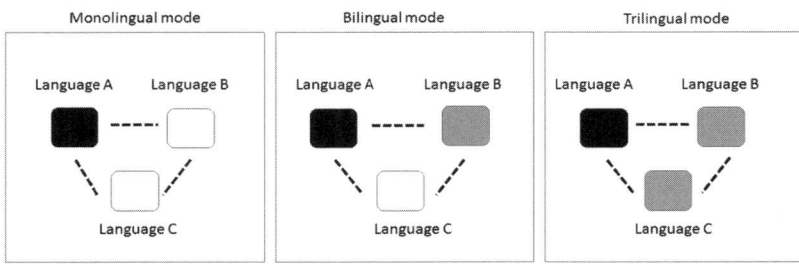

Figure 9.2 Three language modes, adapted from Grosjean's (2001) visual representation of a trilingual in a monolingual, bilingual, and trilingual mode. The level of activation of a language is indicated by the degree of darkness of the squares (black = most active; grey = active; white = inactive)

In a *bilingual mode* (Figure 9.2, second diagram), two languages are used (Languages A and B). With the speakers in our example, Trina would speak English and French to Bill (an English-French bilingual). The two languages usually differ in their degree of activation: Language A (in black) is more active than B (in grey); the third language (Language C, in white) is inactive. The most active language is called the *base language*, i.e. the main language of processing and communication (Grosjean, 2001). For example, Trina uses English, Bill's first language, as the base language, and sometimes switches to French, Bill's second language, but does not make use of German, a language which is unknown to Bill.

The *trilingual mode* (Figure 9.2, third diagram) is characterized by having three languages in use at different levels of activation, one of which functions as base language (in Figure 9.2 it is Language A). The other two languages (B and C) are less active than A, and are both represented in grey (Grosjean, 2001: 19). For example, when talking to Trevor, an English-French-German trilingual, Trina employs English as a base language, but also uses some words from French and German, since her friend Trevor, a native speaker of English, knows these two languages too. The bi- and trilingual modes indicate that the productive and creative use of multilinguals' language repertoire when using more than one language in a conversation is 'allowed'.

Grosjean (2001) stated that the base language and activation level of any of the languages could be changed independently of one another at any given point in time. Such changes rely on the language-choice decision in the speaker's mind, i.e. which language(s) should be used in the following part of the conversation. A bilingual example will illustrate these changes. Our bilingual Bill (English-French) is talking to Brigitte (French-English) with English as base language and occasional use of French. During the conversation Bill changes the base language to Language B (French) instead of Language A (English), e.g. because he notices that Brigitte feels more comfortable using her native language to tell him a very touching story. Language A is still active and used for code-switches and borrowings. This means that Bill only changed the base language (from English to French), but remained in the same language mode (bilingual). A third interlocutor, Monique, joins the conversation. She is monolingual in French (Language B). The language mode of Bill's conversation with Brigitte moves now towards the monolingual mode (French). Both initial interlocutors, Bill and Brigitte, change/reduce the activation level of Language A (i.e. *deactivate* English) in order not to use this language while talking to Monique.

As regards language production, Grosjean attempted to relate frequently occurring *interlingual phenomena* (e.g. interference, code-switching and borrowing) to different language modes. He observed that, in a monolingual mode, multilingual speakers experience *interference*, i.e. 'speaker-specific deviations' from the language being spoken (Grosjean, 1998: 136). Since a monolingual interlocutor is not able to understand instances from other languages, the trilingual speaker is assumed to try to avoid using those languages. For example, Trina would not use English and German when talking to Monique, her French-monolingual friend. In bi- and trilingual language modes, instances of code-switching and borrowing are found. *Code-switch* is a complete shift to the other language – this is done for either a word, a phrase or a sentence. *Borrowing* is using a word or short expression from a less activated language and morphosyntactically (and sometimes phonologically) adapting it into the base language (Grosjean, 1998). The simultaneous high activation of two or three languages is suggested to enable the speaker to produce code-switches and borrowing. (For an interesting view on Grosjean's language mode theory, see De Groot, 2011: 288–294; Dewaele, 2001).

Following Grosjean, trilinguals probably acquire and use their languages for different purposes, in different domains of life, with different people. Since the needs and uses of the languages are usually quite different, trilinguals rarely develop equal fluency in their languages. Grosjean claims that the level of fluency attained in a language (more precisely, in a language skill) will depend on how much one needs that language and will be domain specific. Trilinguals are therefore likely to have a more specific distribution of functions and uses of their languages than bilinguals (Hoffmann, 2008: 19).

Metalinguistic awareness

Metalinguistic awareness is the ability to focus on systematic elements of language and the ability to think about language in an abstract way. Multilinguals have a strategic advantage over monolinguals for further language learning, since metalinguistic awareness is thought of as a key component of multilingual competence (e.g. Jessner, 2008). Dating back to Vygotsky (1986), understanding of a first language is said to be enhanced by learning a foreign language. In experimental studies, mainly the awareness of words or grammar is assessed (Bialystok, 2001). According to Bialystok (2001), bilingual children often show a better understanding of relations between words and their meaning and show a more refined understanding of ambiguities of names than monolingual children. They are better able to focus on structural similarities and differences. When children had to make up nonsense sentences by replacing the word 'we' with 'spaghetti', bilingual children accepted these sentences more easily than monolingual controls. This indicates that the former are less tied to the strict meaning of words; they are more liberal in the use of word meaning.

Herdina and Jessner (2000) suggested that multilingual learners can rely on a particularly heightened monitoring mechanism which fulfils the usual control functions in speech production (anticipating problems, correcting misunderstandings, using compensatory strategies to keep the communicative flow, etc.). Moreover, this enables learners to draw on common resources in their linguistic repertoire and to keep their language systems apart by checking for possible transfer phenomena (Bono, 2011). In general, bilingual learners have been found to outperform monolingual learners when acquiring the same language as their second or third languages (L3, L2), respectively (Sanz, 2000). Multilinguals *coactivate* and thus exploit their prior language knowledge regarding grammar (e.g. Goldrick *et al.*, 2016, for parallel activation of grammatical structures in bilinguals) and lexical knowledge (e.g. Bates *et al.*, 1982). That those multilinguals who already know a number of languages learn more easily even more languages is explained by a general cognitive principle called the 'Matthew effect'. Gibson and Hufeisen (2003) presented a very interesting application of this effect for multilinguals' language learning abilities. The more languages participants in their translation study knew, the higher their accuracy score in the task, since they had more sources to be exploited (languages, general knowledge, metalinguistic knowledge).

Language membership

One unsolved riddle is how exactly several language systems are organized in a multilingual's mind in terms of *language membership*. There are several proposals. Paradis (1981, 2004) suggested a *subset hypothesis* in which every language is organized in a separate subset. All elements within each subset are strongly interconnected, and these connections, for example between words, get stronger if they co-occur in speech, linguistic expression, etc. If a linguistic unit is represented in a certain language subset, it thereby belongs to it. In the second proposal, the *bilingual interactive activation model* (BIA; Dijkstra & Van Heuven, 1998, 2002), all linguistic units in each language are connected to a *language node*; there is one node per language, and language membership of each linguistic unit is defined by a connection to a node. This model incorporates approaches known from connectionist models. Evidence supporting it comes mainly from language perception (in particular reading, lexical decision, homographs, etc.). In the third proposal, the *inhibitory control model* (IC-model; Green, 1998), language membership of every single linguistic unit is implemented in terms of a so-called *language tag*. This is a piece of information that is attached, for example, to each lemma and which specifies to which language this lemma belongs. A lemma is composed of the meaning, syntactic properties and grammatical functions of a lexical entry (Kempen & Huijbers, 1983). For instance, the meaning of *give* is the transfer of something to someone; the syntactic category of *give* is that it is a verb. Its grammatical functions denote that it requires a subject, an indirect object and a direct object (someone gives something to someone).

The IC-model has been related mainly to studies on language production. It seems very difficult to prove which of the three models is most likely to best represent the overall organization of multiple languages. Hence one can take these proposals as assumptions, but empirical evidence for one or the other is lacking. It is of particular interest to reveal how multiple languages interact during processing, which is in the focus of the next section.

Grammar

Another issue still under debate is how grammar is represented in the mind. While it is commonly assumed that the mental lexicon contains all lexical information, grammar is different. It probably works in terms of abstract linguistic rules which have to be applied to lexical units. One of the key topics in psycholinguistic research is the English past tense formation for regular and irregular verbs. One possibility is that, according to the *dual-route model*, a rule is used for regular verbs whereas the past tense forms of irregular verbs are stored in the lexicon. Thus, the past tenses for regular verbs are formed by the action of abstract linguistic rules (regular verb, singular past tense, add *-ed* to the stem) (Pinker & Prince, 1988). An alternative view is put forward by proponents of *distributed processing models*, who suggest patterns learned by neural networks after repeated exposures to words rather than abstract rules (Rumelhart & McClelland, 1986). All forms of a verb are stored separately in the lexicon and can be retrieved without applying rules to word stems.

Language processing including production and perception

The still dominant view on language production is essentially a monolingual one, in which language production is described for only one language (for a critique, see Festman, 2013). A recent prominent example is the theoretical model put forward by Pickering and Garrod (2013), which integrates language production and comprehension framed within embodied cognition. To date, existing psycholinguistic proposals for the processing of two or three languages have been extensions of earlier suggested monolingual processing models, based on two principal assumptions (e.g. De Bot, 1992; Green, 1986, 1998; Grosjean, 1997; Paradis, 1984, 1997): that we always speak the currently most *activated* language, and that language systems are represented as subsystems which are kept apart by each having a different level of activation. This view replaced earlier proposals of switch models, which assumed allowing a speaker to switch a particular language on or off (e.g. Macnamara, 1967), but could not account for occurrences of code-switch and interference. Some studies investigated the organization of the trilingual lexicon (e.g. Abunuwara, 1992; De Groot & Hoeks, 1995; Schönpflug, 2000; Wei, 2002a, 2000b). More recently published experimental studies on the language production of trilingual adults (e.g. Clyne, 1997; Dewaele, 1998, 2001; Ecke, 2001; Ecke & Hall, 2000; Singleton, 2002; Williams & Hammarberg, 1998), although more plentiful, relate their findings to bilingual production models.

Mono, bi- and multilingual language production

Psycholinguistic models of monolingual language production (e.g. Levelt, 1989) suggest a number of discrete stages that occur during the preparation of speech production, until a word or sound is uttered. Roughly speaking, first of all, an idea, message or speaker intention is planned. This has to pass through the stages of conceptualization (segmentation, structure of abstract information), formulation (world knowledge, lexical selection in terms of the lemma containing the meaning, grammatical encoding in terms of lexemes containing grammatical information, and phonological encoding, temporal order of message, cultural appropriateness) and finally production (articulation) until a verbal utterance is expressed. The processes are monitored for incoherence with the original idea or message, and adaptations are made throughout the process. The question that remains is how words in a multilingual's mind are selected in the intended language.

For perception, one of the most influential models is the bilingual interactive activation model (BIA+, see above; Dijkstra & Van Hell, 2003), which can easily be extended to trilingualism to include three language systems. The same mechanisms work for bi- and trilingual perception (namely activation and inhibition). In this model, language membership of a language unit (word, sound, etc.) is represented via language nodes or 'tags' attached to each unit at the lexical and sublexical level. Words from the L3 are assumed to be represented via a link from the L3 language node to the orthographic representation of that word.

For bilingual production, one attempt to adapt Levelt's model for bilingualism was undertaken by De Bot (2004). He suggested that two languages are coordinated via a language node in the conceptualizer. Here, the decision about language choice or language switching is made. For every stage of Levelt's model, language-specific subunits are assumed. And De Bot suggested that at every stage of the process, a checking procedure assesses language membership of every selected unit, most crucially at the lemma level. Although this model focuses exclusively on bilingual language production it can easily be extended and adapted to trilingualism, assuming a third language node and a more complex mental lexicon containing L3 information with processing based on the bilingual model.

The role of a language node seems to be changeable. Under certain conditions, the L3 is more strongly related to the L2 language node, so that the L2, the other 'foreign' language, is the reference language for interference, borrowing, code-switching, etc. Under other conditions, the L3 more often relates back to the first language (L1) language node. In his study on bilingual adults who became trilingual following migration to Australia, Clyne (1997) outlined that the trilinguals show a relative influence of the languages on one another depending on a number of factors, such as the amount of use, language typology (more or less distance between them) and the role each language plays in the individual's triculturalism. Other important studies for this topic are published by Williams and Hammarberg (1998), Hufeisen (2000) and Cenoz (2001). The conditions are modulated by factors such as language proficiency, language typology, etc. In Cenoz's (2001) study, bilingual Spanish-Basque and Basque-Spanish learners of L3 English used Spanish (even if it was L1) more for lexical transfer whereas Basque was often used for transfer of function words. Hoffmann (2008: 20) states: 'I have come across very little linguistic evidence of subjects using three languages within the same utterance.' There seems to be bidirectionality (use of only two languages within the same utterance even when more languages are theoretically available to the speaker).

Parallel activation

It is generally assumed that whenever one of the languages is used (when thinking about a trilingual speaker) the other languages are involved to some degree. The knowledge of additional languages seems to have an impact on processing for all languages in the multilingual's mind. Empirical support comes from experimental studies on bilingual language processing. There is a growing body of evidence that bilinguals continually access both of their languages even if the task does not involve the other language at all. This is called *parallel activation* or 'language co-activation' and it has been found at every level of processing (see, for example, Kroll & Tokowicz, 2005; Kroll *et al.*, 2006; Starreveld *et al.*, 2014; Kroll *et al.*, 2013, for a review).

The question that arises is how the bi- and multilingual deals with this co-activation, which on the one hand seems to facilitate code-switching, but on the other hand might increase the likelihood of errors of interference. In the course of the production process, lexical access is necessary in order to access the relevant representation for retrieval and production. Thus, the more specific question is whether *lexical access* is *language-specific* (lemmas are limited to one language only) or *unspecific* (lemmas from all languages are included). This is also an open question for perception. Language-specific access is likely and possible if stimuli are presented in only one language to a bilingual, if the target language is the stronger language and if no other language was invoked prior to the experiment proper. As soon as words from non-target language(s) are presented, they boost activation of this/these non-target language(s) and perception will be more likely to be language-nonspecific.

States of activation

One fundamental idea as to how to think about a number of language systems in the mind and their parallel activation is that put forward by Green (1986). In an attempt to provide a theoretical account for both the condition (1) that two language systems can be used separately and (2) that two language systems can be mixed (e.g. for code-switching), Green (1986) suggested that every language has a certain level of activation. He proposed three possible states of activation to describe the actual activation level of a language during speech production (Green, 1986, 1993, 1998). These states of activation, visualized in Figure 9.3, differ in their degree of activation as a function of their use at any given moment.

1. The *selected* language is the most activated, currently spoken and used language.
2. The *active* language is currently unselected, but nevertheless active.
3. The *dormant* language is the least activated language, and generally not in use.

Green's distinction is based on two factors, *selection* and *activation*. The currently produced language is (+selected +activated), the 'active' language is (−selected +activated), and the 'dormant' language is (−selected −activated). Green's (1986) original proposal was made with a bilingual speaker in mind. It is important to notice that only one language can be the 'selected' language at any one time (Green, 1986: 215). The two languages of a bilingual

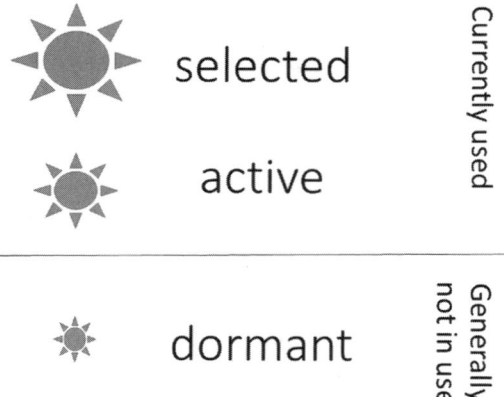

Figure 9.3 Graphic representation of the three states of activation (according to Green, 1986). The size of the star icon symbolizes the degree of activation. The horizontal line separates the three activation states into two subdivisions: the upper layer contains the activation states for currently used languages ('selected' and 'active'), while the activation state of the language which is generally not in use ('dormant') is located in the lower layer

The Psycholinguistics of Multilingualism

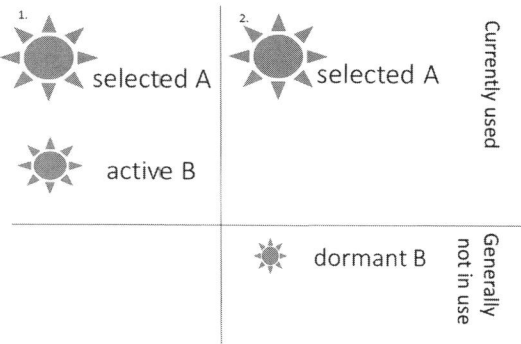

Figure 9.4 Graphic representation of a bilingual's states of activation (according to Green, 1986). The two possible combinations for Languages A and B are illustrated: 1. Selected A – Active B; and 2. Selected A – Dormant B

could be envisioned as in either of the two combinations of activation states: one language (e.g. Language A) is the selected language; the other (e.g. Language B) is either in an active (Figure 9.4, Section 1) or a dormant state (Figure 9.4, Section 2). Figure 9.4 represents these combinations graphically.

Figure 9.4 shows one language in the selected state (Language A), and two different activation states for the L2 (Language B) – active or dormant. A language remains active when it is in regular use but declines to a dormant state when not used for long periods of time. This difference is crucial for the impact on the processing of the selected language: the dormant language does not have any influence on current processing, whereas the activation level of an active language is high enough to cause interference or to be available for code-switching and borrowing. In this way the model accounts for involuntary production and intentional use of the other language. But this questions the language choice concept. If a speaker chooses to speak Language A and interference occurs from Language B, although not intended, then how efficient is language choice? It could be the case that a multilingual might attempt to use but never be capable of using one of the available languages exclusively. Green (1986: 215) maintained that a language can be activated in multiple ways, not only intentionally by language choice, but also by actively making use of the language in daily life, by speaking, reading, writing or hearing it. This view includes the possibility of activation of languages beyond the speaker's intention.

To date, we still lack a clear-cut and validated model for trilingual processing. In the next section, we will consider an elaboration of Green's original bilingual model to account for trilingual processing (Festman, 2008). It is suggested that the three languages of a trilingual could be envisioned in one of the three combinations of activation states, represented in Figure 9.5. The first section shows one language (e.g. Language A) as the selected language, a second language (e.g. Language B) as active and a third language as dormant. In the second section, one language is selected (e.g. Language A), and the other two languages are active (e.g. Languages B and C). The third combination has one language as the selected language (e.g. Language A), while the other two languages are dormant (e.g. Languages B and C).

Part 3: The Psycholinguistics and Neurolinguistics of Multilingualism

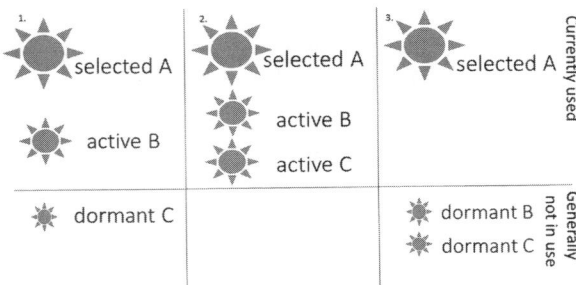

Figure 9.5 Graphic representation of a trilingual's states of activation (according to Green, 1986). Three combinations for Languages A, B and C are shown: 1. Selected A – Active B – Dormant C; 2. Selected A – Active B and C; and 3. Selected A – Dormant B and C

The second section of Figure 9.5 is unique to trilingualism. The relative activation level of two 'unselected' but active languages can directly influence current language processing in the selected language. This might result in trilingual code-switching and/or interference from two unselected languages. An unexplored question to date is whether these two active languages have the same level of activation or whether one of them is more activated than the other.

It is not clear (1) whether the first section of Figure 9.4 is similar to the first section of Figure 9.5, because in both conditions only the active language influences the selected language and the dormant language in the trilingual setting is said not to have any impact on the selected language, and (2) whether the second section of Figure 9.4 resembles the third section of Figure 9.5 in that the selected language is uninfluenced by the dormant language(s).

Three advantages emerge when comparing Green's bilingual model with Grosjean's (2001) extension of language modes to trilingualism. For capturing the language situation in which multilinguals produce language behaviour, Grosjean (1985, 1997, 1998, 2001) put forward a systematic description based on language modes (see above), which is based on the observation that bilinguals choose the number of languages they use (i.e. 'language choice') according to their communication partner's language knowledge: with monolinguals they speak with one language, but they employ both languages when talking to bilinguals (e.g. Grosjean, 1982). The notion of language mode is used to reflect the speaker's use of her languages in a conversation and is defined as the 'state of activation' of the speaker's languages and processing mechanisms (Grosjean, 1998: 136).

First, the account presented by Green is very detailed regarding the possible impact of a certain activation state on other languages, whereas Grosjean is generally concerned with the language situation and suggests that the language choices, which a speaker makes depending to their interlocutor, their situation or the topic of the conversation, are realized in terms of language modes.

As regards language production, Green explicitly includes occurrences of interference, whereas Grosjean is more focused on code-switching and borrowing, arguing that a proficient bilingual does not have any 'permanent interference' (Grosjean, 1982: 300).

Green's model can be applied to three subgroups of trilingual speakers, i.e. learners, users and attriters (speakers that do not use a certain language any more), while Grosjean's model only accounts explicitly for the user subgroup, the '"true" bilingual, that is, the person equally fluent in two languages' (Grosjean, 1982: 300). Commonly, learners and users have three languages in general use (as selected or active languages); however, their level of proficiency differs across their languages and distinguishes both groups. Attriters have two languages in general use and one language in a dormant state.

The detection of the mechanisms by means of which a multilingual speaker changes the activation states of her languages is the key to an explanation of how language choice is realized and may further our understanding of why involuntary language production occurs. For this purpose the next section presents the notions of inhibition and control, as incorporated in the inhibitory-control model by Green (1998).

Inhibition

Green (1998) assumed that language processing could not function without inhibition (see also Tzelgov *et al.*, 1990). Inhibition is understood as the opposite process to activation. While activation usually raises the activation level, e.g. of a language, the role of inhibition is to reduce that activation level. As a consequence of this action, immediate reactivation is prohibited.

Inhibition occurs in multiple ways in language processing. This counter-action is said to be necessary for the execution of two general processes: first to prevent repetition of an already produced word, and secondly to reduce the probability of interference and avoid its production (Green, 1998). Two further functions are attributed to inhibition in multilingual processing: in Green's opinion, activation and inhibition are necessary to realize language choice (i.e. to enable a bilingual speaker at any point in time to use one language but not the other), and to switch between languages (for studies on trilingual switching, see Festman & Mosca, 2016; Philipp *et al.*, 2007). The necessity for an inhibitory mechanism has been questioned (e.g. Costa & Santesteban, 2004) and the debate is ongoing.

It is commonly assumed that at any point in time we produce the word with the highest activation level. After its production its activation level remains high. Without inhibition the same word would be produced over and over again. Inhibition, however, quickly reduces the activation level of the word and allows the production of the next word. It is generally said that mental representations of information that have undergone inhibition tend to be less accessible (Neumann *et al.*, 1993). For language processing, this means that words that have been inhibited after their production could not be reproduced immediately.

Generally, inhibitory processes are used to suppress irrelevant, distracting information which could interfere with current processing, e.g. which could prevent the accomplishment of processes that are currently being carried out (Neumann *et al.*, 1999: 1052; Querné *et al.*, 2000: 172–173). The mechanism of inhibition is employed to reduce or avoid such interference (Bjork, 1989: 324–325). For example, Trina, a trilingual speaker (German-English-French), sees a seagull and wants to say to her monolingual friend Mona (E) 'look at this beautiful seagull'. But Trina has problems with finding the exact English name of the bird that is flying above her. These difficulties might be due to remembering words such as 'animal' and 'airplane', none of which would describe precisely what she sees. If the activation level of any of these 'inexact' or 'incorrect' words is very high, it might be produced. Since these words seem so wrong to Trina, she does not want to use them to refer to the seagull. Not only does the production of these words have to be inhibited by her language system, but the level of activation also has to be decreased in order to allow for further search for the appropriate word.

The two functions of inhibition that are particularly involved in multilingual processing will be presented in the next section.

Language choice

The IC-model by Green (1986: 215; 1998) proposed that inhibition is the mechanism to realize language choice. In order to speak in one language a bilingual has to inhibit the other to allow for processing of the selected language and to avoid interference from the unselected language.

Language modes (monolingual: just one; bilingual: monolingual A, monolingual B, bilingual AB) for trilinguals present more options (up to seven). What mechanisms enable multilinguals to switch languages, with regard to perception and production? To what degree are two or more of the trilingual's languages deactivated when the speaker is in a monolingual or bilingual mode? To what extent and in what relation to each other do both or all three languages become activated when s/he is in a bilingual or trilingual mode?

For example, if Bill (an English-French bilingual) talks to Monique (a French monolingual) on the phone, he has to speak in French to her. To be able to use French he has to inhibit English. Continuous inhibition of the currently unselected language (in our example, English) is said to prevent interference from that language and to ensure production in the selected language (in this example, French). For trilinguals, this would mean that when using only one of their languages, both of the other languages have to be inhibited. For example, when Trina (our speaker of German, English and French) wants to speak to Monique in French, she has to inhibit her other languages, German and English.

Language switch

According to the IC-Model by Green (1998), activation and inhibition cooperate when switching languages. In order to perform a language switch from one language to the other, the previously spoken language must be inhibited and the previously inhibited language must be activated. For example, immediately after having ended his conversation in French with Monique, Bill (English-French) wants to make another phone call and talk to Mona (English monolingual). With her he has to speak in English. He has to perform two processes that constitute the switch to using his English: he has to inhibit the language (i.e. French) he spoke before (with Monique), and has to activate his other language which was inhibited during this conversation (i.e. English).

In order to perform a language switch, it was assumed that the previously spoken language must be inhibited and the previously inhibited language must be activated. An example will help to illustrate this theoretical issue. Our bilingual Bill (English-French) is talking to Brigitte (French-English). Bill is more proficient in English and Brigitte in French. They started off speaking in English and used French very occasionally. But during the conversation Bill switched to French, because he noticed that Brigitte felt more comfortable using her native language to tell him that very touching story.

Green claimed that mere activation of the other language would not be sufficient to perform a switch, because the currently selected language is always the one with the highest activation. It is likely that the reason why inhibition is necessary as a complementary mechanism is that strongly activating the other language would lead, in the long run, to a continuous increase of activation, because each language would have to be more highly activated than the former selected language. Inhibition, however, is a mechanism that prevents such endless activation increase and keeps activation levels in balance. The high activation of the previously selected language is reduced by means of inhibition, and the new increase in activation of another language is made possible.

Green (1998) concluded from the relationship between proficiency and general activation that the amount of inhibition necessary for a language to be suppressed is relative to the speaker's proficiency in that language. This means that an unbalanced bilingual has to attribute more inhibition to suppress the dominant over the weaker language, because the dominant language has a higher general activation level than the weaker language. This asymmetry is important when describing in detail how multilingual speakers execute a new language choice, i.e. how they switch between their languages.

In order to switch back from using the weaker language to using the dominant language, two similar processes have to be executed: the previously inhibited language has to be reactivated, and the currently selected language re-inhibited. With Bill and Brigitte, we could imagine that after they switched to French, Bill wanted to tell Brigitte what happened to him that day at work. He carries out his work in English and never speaks French when working. Since he feels more at ease talking about his job in English, he switches back to the language they had used before. The previously inhibited language that has to be reactivated is English, and the currently selected language, French, has to be re-inhibited.

The amount of inhibition that was allotted while the weaker language was selected strongly influences the ease of reactivation. Had the language been strongly inhibited, then a high amount of activation would be necessary to overcome the previous inhibition and bring it into a functional selected state; the inhibition of a weaker language would be easier to overcome, because it is less strong. For Bill and Brigitte, this means that since Bill is more proficient in English and Brigitte in French, it is difficult for Bill to reactivate his strongly inhibited English, while for Brigitte it is comparably easier to reactivate her weaker language, English.

It follows from these assumptions that the cost of switching is asymmetric when the speaker's proficiency in the languages is unbalanced. For unbalanced bilinguals it takes longer to switch into the dominant language, which was more strongly suppressed, than to switch from the dominant to the weaker language (for example, it took Brigitte longer to switch from English to French, her native language, than from French to English). Evidence for this asymmetric inhibition pattern across languages is provided, for example, in Meuter and Allport's (1999) study of digit naming on unbalanced bilinguals. They examined switch costs in a numeral-naming task in which the required language of response was signalled by a colour background and each trial comprised the presentation of one single-digit number. Switch reaction times from the weaker L2 to the stronger L1 were consistently slower than switches from L1 to L2. They concluded that the size of the language-switch cost depended only on the direction of the switch (L1 → L2 versus L2 → L1), since it remained constant over successive switches within a list.

For balanced bilinguals, however, the switch cost should be equal, and not related to the switch direction. The amount of activation and inhibition that are applied to two languages of an equal general level of activation should be identical, so that switching to either direction is equally time consuming. Evidence for this prediction is provided in a categorization-naming task on balanced bilinguals. Meuter (1994) found switch costs to either language were identical.

So far, we have considered the language switching of bilinguals (for a recent review, see Festman & Schwieter, 2015) for two reasons: first, Green's original theory focused on the bilingual speaker; and secondly, it can be assumed that for trilinguals, the same principles apply. More inhibition is necessary for inhibiting a stronger language, less for a weaker language, if the proficiencies in the languages are unbalanced. Overcoming the inhibition of a stronger language is more difficult (i.e. time consuming and effortful) than reactivating a weaker language. Compared to bilingual switching, trilingual switching would be a lot more effortful, because with three languages in mind two are unselected and need to be inhibited (for a recent review, see Festman & Mosca, 2016).

The major difficulty a multilingual is faced with when attempting to switch between languages is the general level of activation. Unbalanced proficiency in a multilingual's languages is found to result in asymmetric inhibition patterns, i.e. the stronger language has to be more strongly inhibited than the weaker language, and to overcome the stronger inhibition of the dominant language is more time consuming than to reactivate an inhibited weaker language. The two mechanisms, activation and inhibition, have to be executed effectively and in time, otherwise the new language choice would not be implemented in the language systems. In order to monitor processing, the idea of control has been introduced and will be elaborated on in the next section.

Control in multilingual language production

The control of cognitive processes is generally defined as the ability to sustain information-processing activity over time in the face of distraction. It includes the ability to consider and if necessary avoid concurrent activities, to interrupt the execution of one goal-directed activity and to resume it later, and to coordinate the course of all such activities (Parasuraman, 1998: 7). Control can be seen as playing the role of a 'manager' or 'director' in cognitive processing that takes care of focused, efficient and correct processing. The IC-model (Green, 1998) provides a detailed account of the control mechanisms and control processes involved in language production. Green suggested three basic loci for the execution of control during language production: (1) an executive locus known as the supervisory attentional system (SAS); (2) a locus at the level of language task schemas; and

(3) a locus at the lemma level, within the lexical system itself. These three locations of control will now be described in turn.

Task selection

The main function of the SAS is the management of processing. According to Green (1998), the SAS selects the appropriate task schema for a goal by means of increasing the activation level of this task schema. A task 'consists of producing an appropriate action in response to a stimulus' (Monsell, 2003: 134), and its schema 'implements a declarative representation of the instructions in order to achieve the control of action' (Green, 1998). For example, Monique (French) wants to speak to Bill (English-French) on the phone. Monique selects the task schema 'talking on the phone'. As a monolingual, Monique executes this task in French. In Green's IC-model schemas concern language actions (e.g. naming a picture in one language, L1 rather than in another, L2).

Language task schemas

For multilinguals the language in which a certain task should be executed has to be specified. Task schemas that are related to a certain language are termed 'language task schemas' and contain information about both the task and the language. According to Green (1998), a multilingual has a language task schema for each task in each language. For example, Bill has two language task schemas for 'talking on the phone': 'talking on the phone in French' and 'talking on the phone in English'. For Bill, the language task schema 'talking on the phone in French' is, when talking to Monique, more highly activated than 'talking on the phone in English'. In order to perform a task switch from a previous task schema to a newly selected task schema, the activation level of the previous task schema has to be inhibited. Earlier in our example, Bill spoke to Mona in English before he called Monique for a chat. The previously activated task schema was 'talking to Mona on the phone in English'. This task schema had to be inhibited to enable the execution of the new task schema, 'talking to Monique on the phone in French'.

The function of language task schemas is to execute control over processing in the appropriate language. The selected language task schema (e.g. 'talking to Mona on the phone in English') controls the input and output from the lexical system, which was chosen for the realization of this task (i.e. English), while the language task schema for the same task ('talking on the phone') is inhibited for all other languages (e.g. French). Language tags (i.e. language labels) are said to be attached to each lemma specifying its language. Only lemmas with the language tag of the language task schema are 'allowed' to leave the lexical system.

Lemma level

Within the lexical system control is executed in two ways. On the one hand, the activation states of the languages are changed according to the language choice, which influences the activation state of lemmas in the lexicons; lemmas from the selected language are more highly activated than lemmas from the unselected languages, which makes them more easily available for lexical processing. On the other hand, control could be implemented in lexical processing by means of check-procedures. In general, three different check-procedures can be distinguished: they are used to ascertain the appropriateness and correctness of the selected lemma with regard to its content, task and language.

The first procedure checks whether the selected lemma matches the content of the intention ('Am I going to say what I wanted to say?'), and is assumed to function between the concept and the lemma. The second check-procedure tests whether the selected lemma matches the intended task ('Am I going say it the way I wanted to say it?'). This refers to the pragmatic, contextual and social appropriateness of the word with regard to the intention (Levelt, 1983). The third check-procedure assesses whether the lemma was selected from the intended language ('Am I going to say it in the correct language?') by determining the language tag of the lemma (Albert & Obler, 1978; Green, 1986, 1993; Paradis, 1985).

The third check-procedure plays a key role in multilingual processing. Representations are thought to be activated in the mental lexicon at some *baseline level*, almost 'ready to use'. However, in order to use a certain word, a critical threshold of its *activation level* has to be surpassed, so that its representation is sufficiently activated and clearly 'ready to use'. The word can then be recognized, produced, etc. Boosting activation in the mental lexicon is, however, not limited to a single representation. Activation is *spreading*, which means that in the course of activating a certain representation, those representations which are similar in certain features (spelling, sound or meaning, e.g. homographs, homophones, synonyms) are activated as well. Not only are lemmas from the selected language activated, but also from the active language(s). This leads to *competition* between the target unit and those which are similar. Research since the 1970s (e.g. Fromkin, 1973) has focused on monolingual error production such as speech errors providing a sort of window into the speaker's mind.

De Bot (1996) put forward a detailed outline of the process of the first check-procedure (i.e. concept-lemma appropriateness). He suggested that before a selected lemma reaches articulation an internal feedback loop translates it back into its conceptual terms. Secondly, the control process is executed by comparing the intended content in the preverbal message and the selected lemma (De Bot, 1996: 542–543, 551). When a mismatch between intended content and selected word (i.e. concept and lemma) is detected, the production system stops the planned output. Nooteboom (1980: 95) suggested that in this situation two possibilities are available: either the wrong lemma is substituted with the correct one and the original phrase is restarted, or a completely new phrase is prepared. Both ways result in internally corrected production.

Processing load and its influence on control

Processing load, a concept from cognitive psychology, is said to influence our ability and efficiency in executing control over processing. Laver (1973: 140) stated that despite constant monitoring it is possible for errors to get past the check-procedures undetected, and he suggested the notion of attention to be responsible for such malfunctioning. He proposed different factors that influence attention and thus the efficiency of check-procedures: besides fatigue and stress, reduced efficiency of control can also be due to distraction or division of attention. Attention is less focused when divided among different demands, tasks or levels of speech control (Laver, 1973).

Two kinds of load need to be distinguished: the first concerns language production in general, and the second the processing of several languages. During production, the language system is under pressure in terms of available time and cost to produce the intended messages, because the objective of the system is to work as efficiently as possible, to avoid errors and to achieve fluency (Green, 1993). Control aims at all levels for fluent and error-free production of the intended message. For example, when Trina wanted to draw her interlocutor's attention to the seagull, we said that she had problems in finding the exact English word. The alternative words she remembered ('animal' and 'airplane') seemed so wrong to her that she refrained from using them to refer to the seagull. The mechanism of control is suggested to be responsible for the avoidance of this possible error (i.e. saying 'animal' instead of seagull).

Considering the use of three languages, Green (1986) infers from his bilingual model that the more languages that are active, the greater the processing load. Processing in a trilingual system needs to be highly controlled, as it is more complex due to the number of language subsystems involved (Mägiste, 1979: 85; 1986: 115). For example, in trilingual processing three languages could be active, with one of them being the selected language (see Figure 9.5, Section 2). For example, Trevor (English-French-German trilingual) is talking to Trina (German-English-French). They employ English as the selected language and use some words from French and German. All three languages were active and used in this trilingual conversation.

Trilingual processing has been described in particular as more demanding than bilingual or monolingual processing because more languages have to be inhibited in order to allow for processing in the selected language, for instance when Trina speaks in English to Mona (English monolingual), she has to inhibit both German and French. Moreover, switching has been said to involve more complex patterns of activation and inhibition. For example, our trilingual friends Trina (German-English-French) and Trevor (English-French-German) were on their way to visit Monique, the French monolingual. Trina and Trevor preferred to speak one another's native language, German and English. As soon as they met Monique they both had to switch to Monique's native language, which is assumed to be realized by means of inhibition of the other two languages, German and English.

From among the four factors brought up by Laver (i.e. fatigue, stress, distraction and division of attention), the last one seems to be most fitting to capture the complexity of trilingual processing. Attention is divided between the regulation of the current state of activation of **three** languages (selected, active, dormant), which involves the inhibition of two unselected languages, and monitoring that processing is executed in the intended language and that check-procedures for correctness of content, task and language are efficient and accurate.

When resources (i.e. 'energy' or 'fuel' for processing) for the control of processing and production are insufficient, the additional cognitive load of multilingualism is said to reduce the effectiveness of control, which results in error production (Green, 1986). In general, the effects of load for the entire language system are evident in two respects: the performance is less accurate (with regard to content, task and language) or less fluent (i.e. the speed of processing is slowed down) (Mägiste, 1984, 1986).

Language acquisition of the native language, foreign language and literacy

Krashen (1985) distinguished between language acquisition as being informal and language learning as being formal. While in the former, acquisition is subconscious – it is like 'picking up' the language from interaction in the family, workplace, media, communities – learning in the latter is usually associated with formal instruction in foreign language classrooms. The big issue is how the acquisition of new words is actually realized and whether learners access the meaning of an L2 or L3 word independently from the translation in their native language. One theory holds that languages are interconnected conceptually (e.g. Potter *et al.*, 1984; Snodgrass, 1984). According to this bilingual model, the establishment and strengthening of the conceptual connection between the L1 and L2 makes the acquisition of new words possible. The concept mediation model (Potter *et al.*, 1984) holds that L2 words always rely on concept mediation from the L1. Meaning in the L2 is not accessed directly, but rather via concept mediation in the L1.

Another model, the revised hierarchical model (Kroll & Stewart, 1994), suggests that at first the L2 is mediated through direct access to meaning in the L1, and only later through the conceptual link. With increasing proficiency in the L2 there is a shift from relying on form to relying on meaning. Evidence supporting this model comes from translation studies (e.g. Kroll *et al.*, 2002; see Van Hell & Kroll, 2013, for a review). For example, Talamas and colleagues (1999) compared beginning and more advanced adult L2 learners on a translation recognition task. In this task the participant has to decide whether from among two presented words the second word is the first word's translation or not. Another task is the forward and backward translation task. In a trilingual translation study by Francis and Gallard (2005), proficient participants with English-Spanish-French had to translate in all six language combinations. They found no qualitative differences between translating from weaker to stronger languages or from the native language to the weaker L2 or L3. In sum, all translation is likely to be mediated via a common conceptual store. A recent bilingual study by Poarch *et al.* (2015) revealed that whether children at early stages of L2 acquisition rely on conceptual or lexical mediation is mainly task dependent. The translation recognition task showed that in a task when no verbal response is required, even beginning L2 learners activate concepts. In the translation production task, however, beginning L2 learners relied more on the lexical link and less on the conceptual link. This was even more apparent during backward translation when, after reading the L2 word, the L1 lexicon is accessed and the lexical items retrieved in order to allow for verbal production. Whether child beginning L2 learners use conceptual and lexical links seems to depend on task demands.

High proficiency in an additional language can only be achieved if the L2 vocabulary becomes independent from the L1. This is a complex process which involves the strengthening of connections between L2 words, the automatization of L2 access and retrieval, and adding L2 meaning nuances; moreover, this process takes years of learning and much exposure and input in an L2 naturalistic environment. But, as has been outlined before, lexical access is rather nonselective, languages are activated in parallel and the degree of this cross-language activation seems to be modulated by the proficiency levels (even for highly proficient speakers and readers, e.g. Libben & Titone, 2009), language typology (the more overlap the higher the co-activation, e.g. Van Hell & Dijkstra, 2002), and task demands and stimuli (cognates, homographs, homophones, words in isolation or with syntactic context, etc.).

Skilled language performance requires a great deal of cognitive control. Moreover, lexical competition and selection is thought to be regulated in a network of brain structures which are associated with executive functions (for a review on control over bilingual speech production, see Abutalebi & Green, 2007). One task through which to explore language control is language switching (for a review, see Festman & Schwieter, 2015).

Currently Open Research Areas

In this lecture, a number of concepts used in psycholinguistic research and current assumptions have been described and empirical evidence has been summarized. The picture one gets from this might still be rather vague. One might wonder:

- What do we know about language processing in individual mono-, bi- and multilingualism?
- What are the specific differences between bi- and trilingualism on a processing level?
- In which aspects is the representation of the first language and later learned languages similar or different?
- In which psycholinguistic aspects are the processes involved in the acquisition of the first language and later learned languages similar or different?

All of these huge questions are a matter of ongoing debate. And in a way it shows that this field of research is: (a) rigorous in testing theoretical models; (b) challenging in accepting the necessity for incorporating more background variables in order to obtain a clear picture of whether the participant is bi- or multilingual; and (c) careful before applying single research findings to a larger population or more general questions. Many studies on bilingualism have been conducted with L3 speakers but only the L2 was of interest; as long as it is not clear in which aspects bilinguals differ from multilinguals, there is most likely no clear-cut evidence for bilingualism either.

There is a tendency towards larger groups (i.e. more participants per group) and the acknowledged need for more careful matching on a number of variables (see Table 9.3), such as language learning history information (previous exposure and current use). Language typology needs to be taken into account, since it seems not to be irrelevant which languages had been learned before. The impact of earlier learned languages can be found in the knowledge of grammatical structures and of vocabulary as it appears that more similar languages are more difficult to keep apart. There seems to be a shift in the selection of participant groups: no longer are differences between mono- and bilingual processing in focus, but rather between subgroups of bilinguals (e.g. Festman, 2012) or of multilinguals, or between bi- and multilinguals. As regards language proficiency, self-ratings are informative but not sufficient; more objective outcome measures include indicators for vocabulary knowledge (verbal fluency, picture naming), the ability to maintain a conversation, or grammar knowledge. And finally it might be advisable to conduct more studies involving triangulation or mixed-methods which provide a broader view and an in-depth picture of the multilingual psycholinguistic phenomena under investigation. For one such example of multilingual language acquisition in linguistically diverse settings, see Festman (2018).

Questions for Students' Reflection

1. Which three key questions are at the heart of psycholinguistics?
2. Which experimental paradigms and methods are used in psycholinguistic research and which behavioural output measures are useful? What can they tell us about multilingual processing and acquisition?
3. What is special about and unique for trilingualism when comparing it with bilingualism?
4. Which criteria are the most relevant for classifying multilinguals? Why is the list of criteria more extended than for bilinguals?
5. What is a language mode, and why is it a very useful concept when thinking about multilinguals' conditions when communicating?
6. Which theoretical accounts are available for the organization of multiple languages? Which are supported by empirical evidence?
7. Which are the main stages in language production, and how does multilingualism influences the processing?

Suggestions for Further Reading

Aitchison, J. (1987) *Words in the Mind: An Introduction to the Mental Lexicon*. Oxford: Blackwell.

De Groot, A. (2011) *Language and Cognition in Bilinguals and Multilinguals*. Philadelphia, PA: Psychology Press.

Kroll, J.F. and De Groot, A.M. (2005) (eds) *Handbook of Bilingualism: Psycholinguistic Approaches*. Oxford: Oxford University Press.

Schwieter, J.W. (2015) (ed.) *The Cambridge Handbook of Bilingual Language Processing*. Cambridge: Cambridge University Press.

Singleton, D. (2003) Perspectives on the multilingual lexicon: A critical synthesis. In J. Cenoz, B. Hufeisen and U. Jessner (eds) *The Multilingual Lexicon* (pp. 167–176). Dordrecht: Springer.

Yu, Z. and Schwieter, J. W. (2018) Recognizing the effects of language mode on the cognitive advantages of bilingualism. *Frontiers in Psychology*, 9, 366.

References

Abunuwara, E. (1992) The structure of the trilingual lexicon. *European Journal of Cognitive Psychology* 4 (4), 311–322.

Abutalebi, J. and Green, D. (2007) Bilingual language production: The neurocognition of language representation and control. *Journal of Neurolinguistics* 20 (3), 242–275.

Albert, M.L. and Obler, L.K. (1978) *The Bilingual Brain: Neuropsychological and Neurolinguistic Aspects of Bilingualism*. New York: Academic Press.

Alonso, J.G., Villegas, J. and Mayo, M.D.P.G. (2016) English compound and non-compound processing in bilingual and multilingual speakers: Effects of dominance and sequential multilingualism. *Second Language Research* 32 (4), 503–535; doi:0267658316642819.

Aronin, L. and Jessner, U. (2015) Understanding current multilingualism: What can the butterfly tell us? In U. Jessner and C. Kramsch (eds) *The Multilingual Challenge: Cross-disciplinary Perspectives* (pp. 269–287). Berlin: Walter de Gruyter.

Bates, E., McNew, S., MacWhinney, B., Devescovi, A. and Smith, S. (1982) Functional constraints on sentence processing: A cross-linguistic study. *Cognition* 11 (3), 245–299.

Bialystok, E. (1986) Factors in the growth of linguistic awareness. *Child Development* 57 (2), 498–510.

Bialystok, E. (2001) *Bilingualism in Development: Language, Literacy, and Cognition*. New York: Cambridge University Press.

Bjork, R.A. (1989) Retrieval inhibition as an adaptive mechanism in human memory. In H.L. Roediger and F.I.M. Craik (eds) *Varieties of Memory and Consciousness: Essays in Honour of Endel Tulving* (pp. 309–330). Hillsdale, NJ: Lawrence Erlbaum.

Bobb, S.C. and Wodniecka, Z. (2013) Language switching in picture naming: What asymmetric switch costs (do not) tell us about inhibition in bilingual speech planning. *Journal of Cognitive Psychology* 25 (5), 568–585.

Bono, M. (2011) Crosslinguistic interaction and metalinguistic awareness in third language acquisition. In G. De Angelis and J.-M. Dewaele (eds) *New Trends in Crosslinguistic Influence and Multilingualism Research* (pp. 25–52). Bristol: Multilingual Matters.

Bosch, S. and Clahsen, H. (2016) Accessing morphosyntax in L1 and L2 word recognition: A priming study of inflected German adjectives. *The Mental Lexicon* 11 (1), 26–54.

Bultena, S., Dijkstra, T. and Van Hell, J. G. (2015) Language switch costs in sentence comprehension depend on language dominance: Evidence from self-paced reading. *Bilingualism: Language and Cognition* 18 (3), 453–469.

Cenoz, J. (2001) The effect of linguistic distance, L2 status and age on cross-linguistic influence in third language acquisition. In J. Cenoz, B. Hufeisen and U. Jessner (eds) *Cross-linguistic Influence in Third Language Acquisition: Psycholinguistic Perspectives* (pp. 8–20). Clevedon: Multilingual Matters.

Cenoz, J. (2013) Defining multilingualism. *Annual Review of Applied Linguistics* 33, 3–18.

Charkova, K.D. (2003) Early foreign language education and metalinguistic development: A study of monolingual, bilingual and trilingual children on noun definition tasks. *Annual Review of Language Acquisition* 3 (1), 51–88.

Clyne, M. (1997) Some of the things trilinguals do. *International Journal of Bilingualism* 1 (2), 95–116.

Costa, A. and Santesteban, M. (2004) Lexical access in bilingual speech production: Evidence from language switching in highly proficient bilinguals and L2 learners. *Journal of Memory and Language* 50, 491–511.

Costa, A., Santesteban, M. and Ivanova, I. (2006) How do highly proficient bilinguals control their lexicalization process? Inhibitory and language-specific selection mechanisms are both functional. *Journal of Experimental Psychology: Learning, Memory, and Cognition* 32 (5), 1057–1074.

De Bot, K. (1992) A bilingual production model: Levelt's 'speaking' model adapted. *Applied Linguistics* 13, 1–24.

De Bot, K. (1996) The psycholinguistics of the output hypothesis (Review article). *Language Learning* 46 (3), 529–555.

De Bot, K. (2004) The multilingual lexicon: Modelling selection and control. *International Journal of Multilingualism* 1 (1), 17–32.

De Bot, K. and Jaensch, C. (2015) What is special about L3 processing? *Bilingualism: Language and Cognition* 18, 130–144.

De Groot, A.M.B. (2011) *Language and Cognition in Bilinguals and Multilinguals*. Philadelphia, PA: Psychology Press.

De Groot, A.M.B. and Hoeks, J.C.J. (1995) The development of bilingual memory: Evidence from word translation by trilinguals. *Language Learning* 45 (4), 683–724.

De Groot, A.M., Borgwaldt, S., Bos, M. and Van den Eijnden, E. (2002) Lexical decision and word naming in bilinguals: Language effects and task effects. *Journal of Memory and Language* 47 (1), 91–124.

Dewaele, J.-M. (1998) Lexical inventions: French interlanguage as L2 versus L3. *Applied Linguistics* 19(4), 471–490.

Dewaele, J.-M. (2001) Activation of inhibition? The interaction of L1, L2, and L3 on the language mode continuum. In J. Cenoz, B. Hufeisen and U. Jessner (eds) *Cross-linguistic Influence in Third Language Acquisition: Psycholinguistic Perspectives* (pp. 69–89). Clevedon: Multilingual Matters.

Dietrich, R. (2007) *Psycholinguistik* (2nd edn). Stuttgart and Weimar: J.B. Metzler.

Dijkstra, A., Grainger, J. and Van Heuven, W. (1999) Recognition of cognates and interlingual homographs: The neglected role of phonology. *Journal of Memory and Language* 41, 496–518.

Dijkstra, T. and Van Hell, J.G. (2003) Testing the language mode hypothesis using trilinguals. *International Journal of Bilingual Education and Bilingualism* 6 (1), 2–16.

Dijkstra, T. and Van Heuven, W.J. (1998) The BIA model and bilingual word recognition. In J. Grainger and A.M. Jacobs (eds) *Localist Connectionist Approaches to Human Cognition* (pp. 189–225). New York: Psychology Press.

Dijkstra, T. and Van Heuven, W.J. (2002) The architecture of the bilingual word recognition system: From identification to decision. *Bilingualism: Language and Cognition* 5 (3), 175–197.

Duñabeitia, J.A., Dimitropoulou, M., Uribe-Etxebarria, O., Laka, I. and Carreiras, M. (2010) Electrophysiological correlates of the masked translation priming effect with highly proficient simultaneous bilinguals. *Brain Research* 1359, 142–154.

Ecke, P. (2001) Lexical retrieval in a third language: Evidence from errors and tip-of-the-tongue states. In J. Cenoz, B. Hufeisen and U. Jessner (eds) *Cross-linguistic Influence in Third Language Acquisition: Psycholinguistic Perspectives* (pp. 90–114). Clevedon: Multilingual Matters.

Ecke, P. and Hall, C.J. (2000) Lexikalische Fehler in Deutsch als Drittsprache: Translexikalischer Einfluß auf 3 Ebenen der mentalen Repräsentation. *Deutsch als Fremdsprache* 1, 31–37.

Festman, J. (2008) Cross-language interference during trilingual picture naming in single and mixed language conditions. In M. Gibson, B. Hufeisen and C. Personne (eds) *Mehrsprachigkeit: lernen und lehren, Multilingualism: Learning and Instruction, Le Plurilinguisme: apprendre et enseigner, O Pluilinguismo: aprender e ensinar* (pp. 109–119). Selected papers from the L3-Conference in Fribourg, Switzerland, 2005.

Festman, J. (2012) Language control abilities of late bilinguals. *Bilingualism: Language and Cognition* 15 (3), 580–593.

Festman, J. (2013) The complexity-cost factor. Commentary on Pickering & Garrod's theory of language perception and production. *Behavioral and Brain Sciences* 36 (4), 27–28; doi:10.1017/S0140525X12001495.

Festman, J. (2018) Vocabulary gains of mono-and multilingual learners in a linguistically-diverse setting: results from a German-English intervention with inclusion of home languages. *Frontiers in Communication* 3, 26.

Festman, J. and Mosca, M. (2016) Influence of preparation time on language control: A trilingual digit-naming study. In J.W. Schwieter (ed.) *The Cognitive Control of Multiple Languages: Experimental Studies and New Directions* (pp. 145–170). Amsterdam: John Benjamins.

Festman, J. and Schwieter, J.W. (2015) Behavioural measures of language control: Production and comprehension. In J.W. Schwieter (ed.) *The Cambridge Handbook of Bilingual Language Processing* (pp. 527–547). Cambridge: Cambridge University Press.

Festman, J., Rodriguez-Fornells, A. and Münte, T.F. (2010) Individual differences in control of language interference in late bilinguals are mainly related to general executive abilities. *Behavioral and Brain Functions* 6 (1), 5.

Francis, W.S. and Gallard, S.L. (2005) Concept mediation in trilingual translation: Evidence from response time and repetition priming patterns. *Psychonomic Bulletin & Review* 12 (6), 1082–1088.

Fromkin, V.A. (1973) Introduction. In V.A. Fromkin (ed.) *Speech Errors as Linguistic Evidence* (pp. 1–45). The Hague: Mouton.

Frost, R. (1998) Toward a strong phonological theory of visual word recognition: True issues and false trails. *Psychological Bulletin* 123 (1), 71.

Gangopadhyay, I., Davidson, M.M., Weismer, S.E. and Kaushanskaya, M. (2016) The role of nonverbal working memory in morphosyntactic processing by school-aged monolingual and bilingual children. *Journal of Experimental Child Psychology* 142, 171–194.

Gibson, M. and Hufeisen, B. (2003) Investigating the role of prior foreign language knowledge: Translating from an unknown into a known foreign language. In J. Cenoz, B. Hufeisen and U. Jessner (eds) *The Multilingual Lexicon* (pp. 87–102). Dordrecht: Springer.

Goldrick, M., Putnam, M. and Schwarz, L. (2016) Coactivation in bilingual grammars: A computational account of code mixing. *Bilingualism: Language and Cognition* 19, 857–876.

Gollan, T.H., Montoya, R.I., Fennema-Notestine, C. and Morris, S.K. (2005) Bilingualism affects picture naming but not picture classification. *Memory & Cognition* 33 (7), 1220–1234.

Green, D.W. (1986) Control, activation, and resource: A framework and a model for the control of speech in bilinguals. *Brain and Language* 27, 210–223.

Green, D.W. (1993) Towards a model of L2 comprehension and production. In R. Schreuder and B. Weltens (eds) *The Bilingual Lexicon* (pp. 249–277). Amsterdam: John Benjamins.

Green, D.W. (1998) Mental control of the bilingual lexico-semantic system. *Bilingualism: Language and Cognition* 1 (2), 67–81.

Grosjean, F. (1982) *Life with Two Languages: An Introduction to Bilingualism*. Cambridge, MA: Harvard University Press.

Grosjean, F. (1985) The bilingual as a competent but specific speaker-hearer. *Journal of Multilingual and Multicultural Development* 4 (6), 467–477.

Grosjean, F. (1997) Processing mixed language: Issues, findings, and models. In A.M.B. De Groot and J.F. Kroll (eds) *Tutorials in Bilingualism: Psycholinguistic Perspectives* (pp. 225–253). Mahwah, NJ: Lawrence Erlbaum.

Grosjean, F. (1998) Studying bilinguals: Methodological and conceptual issues. *Bilingualism: Language and Cognition* 1, 131–149.

Grosjean, F. (2001) The bilingual's language modes. In J. Nicol (ed.) *One Mind, Two Languages: Bilingual Language Processing* (pp. 1–22). Oxford: Blackwell.

Guo, T., Ma, F. and Liu, F. (2013) An ERP study of inhibition of non-target languages in trilingual word production. *Brain and Language* 127 (1), 12–20.

Herdina, P. and Jessner, U. (2000) The dynamics of third language acquisition. In J. Cenoz and U. Jessner (eds) *English in Europe: The Acquisition of a Third Language* (pp. 84–98). Clevedon: Multilingual Matters.

Hermans, D., Bongaerts, T., De Bot, K. and Schreuder, R. (1998) Producing words in a foreign language: Can speakers prevent interference from their first language? *Bilingualism: Language and Cognition* 1, 213–229.

Hoffmann, C. (2008) The status of trilingualism in bilingualism studies. In J. Cenoz, B. Hufeisen and U. Jessner (eds) *Looking Beyond Second Language Acquisition: Studies in Tri- and Multilingualism* (2nd edn) (pp. 13–25). Tübingen: Stauffenberg.

Hufeisen, B. (2000) How do foreign language learners evaluate various aspects of their multilingualism? *Tertiär- und Drittsprachen. Projekte und empirische Untersuchungen* (pp. 23–56). Tübingen: Stauffenberg.

Hut, S.C., Helenius, P., Leminen, A., Mäkelä, J.P. and Lehtonen, M. (2017) Language control mechanisms differ for native languages: Neuromagnetic evidence from trilingual language switching. *Neuropsychologia* 107, 108–120.

Hut, S.C., and Leminen, A. (2017) Shaving bridges and tuning kitaraa: The effect of language switching on semantic processing. *Frontiers in Psychology* 8, 1438.

Ibrahim, R. and Eviatar, Z. (2012) The contribution of the two hemispheres to lexical decision in different languages. *Behavioral and Brain Functions* 8 (1), 1.

Jacob, G. and Felser, C. (2016) Reanalysis and semantic persistence in native and non-native garden-path recovery. *Quarterly Journal of Experimental Psychology* 69 (5), 907–925.

Jessner, U. (2008) A DST model of multilingualism and the role of metalinguistic awareness. *The Modern Language Journal* 92 (2), 270–283.

Kempen, G. and Huijbers, P. (1983) The lexicalization process in sentence production and naming: Indirect election of words. *Cognition* 14 (2), 185–209.

Kleinman, D. and Gollan, T.H. (2018) Inhibition accumulates over time at multiple processing levels in bilingual language control. *Cognition* 173, 115–132.

Krashen, S. (1985) *The Input Hypothesis: Issues and Implications*. London: Longman.

Kroll, J.F. and De Groot, A.M. (eds) (2005) *Handbook of Bilingualism: Psycholinguistic Approaches*. Oxford: Oxford University Press.

Kroll, J.F. and Stewart, E. (1994) Category interference in translation and picture naming: Evidence for asymmetric connections between bilingual memory representation. *Journal of Memory and Language* 33, 149–174.

Kroll, J.F. and Tokowicz, N. (2005) Models of bilingual representation and processing. In J.F. Kroll and A.M. De Groot (eds) *Handbook of Bilingualism: Psycholinguistic Approaches* (pp. 531–553). Oxford: Oxford University Press.

Kroll, J.F., Michael, E., Tokowicz, N. and Dufour, R. (2002) The development of lexical fluency in a second language. *Second Language Research* 18 (2), 137–171.

Kroll, J.F., Bobb, S.C. and Wodniecka, Z. (2006) Language selectivity is the exception, not the rule: Arguments against a fixed locus of language selection in bilingual speech. *Bilingualism: Language and Cognition* 9, 119–135.

Kroll, J.F., Gullifer, J.W. and Rossi, E. (2013) The multilingual lexicon: The cognitive and neural basis of lexical comprehension and production in two or more languages. *Annual Review of Applied Linguistics* 33, 102–127.

Lambert, W.E. (1975) Culture and language as factors in learning and education. In A. Wolfgang (ed.) *Education of Immigrant Students* (pp. 55–83). Toronto: Ontario Institute for Studies in Education.

Lemhöfer, K., Dijkstra, T. and Michel, M. (2004) Three languages, one ECHO: Cognate effects in trilingual word recognition. *Language and Cognitive Processes* 19 (5), 585–611.

Levelt, W.J.M. (1983) Monitoring and self-repair in speech. *Cognition* 14, 41–104.

Levelt, W. (1989) *Speaking: From Intention to Articulation*. Cambridge, MA: Bradford.

Laver, J.D. (1973) The detection and correction of slips of the tongue. *Speech Errors as Linguistic Evidence*, 132–143.

Libben, M.R. and Titone, D.A. (2009) Bilingual lexical access in context: Evidence from eye movements during reading. *Journal of Experimental Psychology: Learning, Memory, and Cognition* 35 (2), 381.

Linck, J., Schwieter, J. and Sunderman, G. (2012) Inhibitory control predicts language switching performance in trilingual speech production. *Bilingualism: Language and Cognition* 15 (3), 651–662.

Macnamara, J. (1967) The bilingual's linguistic performance – a psychological overview. *Journal of Social Issues* XXIII (2), 58–77.

Mägiste, E. (1979) The competing language systems of the multilingual: A developmental study of decoding and encoding processes. *Journal of Verbal Learning and Verbal Behavior* 18, 79–89.

Mägiste, E. (1984) Learning a third language. *Journal of Multilingual and Multicultural Development* 5 (5), 415–421.

Mägiste, E. (1986) Selected issues in second and third language learning. In J. Vaid (ed.) *Language Processing in Bilinguals: Psycholinguistic and Neuropsychological Perspectives* (pp. 97–122). Hillsdale, NJ: Lawrence Erlbaum.

Marian, V., Blumenfeld, H.K. and Boukrina, O.V. (2008) Sensitivity to phonological similarity within and across languages. *Journal of Psycholinguistic Research* 37 (3), 141–170.

Marian, V., Blumenfeld, H.K., Mizrahi, E., Kania, U. and Cordes, A.K. (2013) Multilingual Stroop performance: Effects of trilingualism and proficiency on inhibitory control. *International Journal of Multilingualism* 10 (1), 82–104.

Meuter, R.F.I. (1994) Language switching in naming tasks. Unpublished PhD thesis, University of Oxford.

Meuter, R.F.I. and Allport, A. (1999) Bilingual language switching in naming: Asymmetrical costs of language selection. *Journal of Memory and Language* 40, 25–40.

Monsell, S. (2003) Task switching. *Trends in Cognitive Sciences* 7, 134–140.

Mosca, M. and De Bot, K. (2017) Bilingual language switching: Production vs. recognition. *Frontiers in Psychology* 8, 934.

Mosca, M. (2018) Trilinguals' language switching: A strategic and flexible account. *Quarterly Journal of Experimental Psychology*, 1747021818763537.

Neumann, E., Cherau, J.F., Hood, K.L. and Steinnagel, S.L. (1993) Does inhibition spread in a manner analogous to spreading activation? *Memory* 1, 81–105.

Neumann, E., McCloskey, M.S. and Felio, A.C. (1999) Cross-language positive priming disappears, negative priming does not: Evidence for two sources of selective inhibition. *Memory & Cognition* 27 (6), 1051–1063.

Nooteboom, S.G. (1980) Speaking and unspeaking: Detection and correction of phonological and lexical errors in spontaneous speech. In V.A. Fromkin (ed.) *Errors in Linguistic Performance: Slips of the Tongue, Ear, Pen, and Hand* (pp. 87–95). New York: Academic Press.

Paradis, M. (1981) Neurolinguistic organization of a bilingual's two languages. In J.E. Copeland and P.W. Davis (eds) *The Seventh LACUS Forum 1980* (pp. 486–494). Columbia, SC: Hornbeam.

Paradis, M. (1984) Aphasie et traduction. *META Translators' Journal* 29, 57–67.

Paradis, M. (1985) On the representation of two languages in one brain. *Language Sciences* 61, 1–39.

Paradis, M. (1997) The cognitive neuropsychology of bilingualism. In A.M.B. De Groot and J.F. Kroll (eds) *Tutorials in Bilingualism: Psycholinguistic Perspectives* (pp. 331–354). Mahwah, NJ: Lawrence Erlbaum.

Paradis, M. (2004) *A Neurolinguistic Theory of Bilingualism*. Amsterdam: John Benjamins.

Parasuraman, R. (1998) The attentive brain: Issues and prospects. In R. Parasuraman (ed.) *The Attentive Brain* (pp. 3–15). Cambridge, MA and London: MIT Press.

Philipp, A. and Koch, I. (2009) Inhibition in language switching: What is inhibited when switching between languages in naming tasks? *Journal of Experimental Psychology: Learning, Memory, and Cognition* 35, 1187–1195.

Philipp, A.M., Gade, M. and Koch, I. (2007) Inhibitory processes in language switching: Evidence from switching language-defined response sets. *European Journal of Cognitive Psychology* 19, 395–416.

Pickering, M.J. and Garrod, S. (2013) An integrated theory of language production and comprehension. *Behavioral and Brain Sciences* 36, 329–392.

Pinker, S. and Prince, A. (1988) On language and connectionism: Analysis of a parallel distributed processing model of language acquisition. *Cognition* 28 (1), 73–193.

Poarch, G.J. and Van Hell, J.G. (2012) Cross-language activation in children's speech production: Evidence from second language learners, bilinguals, and trilinguals. *Journal of Experimental Child Psychology* 111 (3), 419–438.

Poarch, G.J., Van Hell, J.G. and Kroll, J.F. (2015) Accessing word meaning in beginning second language learners: Lexical or conceptual mediation? *Bilingualism: Language and Cognition* 18 (3), 357–371.

Potter, M.C., So, K.-F., Von Eckardt, B. and Feldman, L.B. (1984) Lexical and conceptual representation in beginning and proficient bilinguals. *Journal of Verbal Learning and Verbal Behavior* 23, 23–38.

Prior, A. and Gollan, T. (2011) Good language-switchers are good task-switchers: Evidence from Spanish–English and Mandarin–English bilinguals. *Journal of the International Neuropsychological Society* 17, 682–691.

Prior, A., Degani, T., Awawdy, S., Yassin, R. and Korem, N. (2017) Is susceptibility to cross-language interference domain specific?. *Cognition* 165, 10–25.

Querné, L., Eustache, F. and Faure, S. (2000) Interhemispheric inhibition, intrahemispheric activation, and lexical capacities of the right hemisphere: A tachistoscopic, divided visual-field study in normal subjects. *Brain and Language* 74, 171–190.

Rickheit, G., Sichelschmidt, L. and Strohner, H. (2002) *Gedanken ausdrücken und Sprache verstehen: Psycholinguistik. Arbeitsbuch Linguistik* (pp. 382–405). Paderborn: Schöningh.

Rodriguez-Fornells, A., Kramer, U., Lorenzo-Seva, U., Festman, J. and Münte, T.F. (2012) Self-assessment of individual differences in language switching. *Frontiers in Psychology* 2, 388.

Rumelhart, D.E. and McClelland, J.L. (1986) *Parallel Distributed Processing: Explorations in the Microstructure of Cognition, Vol. 1. Foundations*. Cambridge, MA: MIT Press.

Sandoval, T.C., Gollan, T.H., Ferreira, V.S. and Salmon, D.P. (2010) What causes the bilingual disadvantage in verbal fluency? The dual-task analogy. *Bilingualism: Language and Cognition* 13 (2), 231–252.

Sanz, C. (2000) Bilingual education enhances third language acquisition: Evidence from Catalonia. *Applied Psycholinguistics* 21, 23–44.

Sato, M. and Felser, C. (2010) Sensitivity to morphosyntactic violations in English as a second language. *Second Language* 9, 101–118.

Schönpflug, U. (2000) Word-fragment completions in the second and third language: A contribution to the organization of the trilingual Speaker's lexicon. In J. Cenoz and U. Jessner (eds) *English in Europe: The Acquisition of a Third Language* (pp. 121–142). Clevedon: Multilingual Matters.

Schriefers, H., Meyer, A.S. and Levelt, W.J. (1990) Exploring the time course of lexical access in language production: Picture-word interference studies. *Journal of Memory and Language* 29 (1), 86–102.

Schwieter, J.W. (ed.) (2015) *The Cambridge Handbook of Bilingual Language Processing*. Cambridge: Cambridge University Press.

Schwieter, J.W. and Sunderman, G. (2011) Inhibitory control processes and lexical access in trilingual speech production. *Linguistic Approaches to Bilingualism* 1 (4), 391–412.

Shao, Z., Roelofs, A., Martin, R.C. and Meyer, A.S. (2015) Selective inhibition and naming performance in semantic blocking, picture-word interference, and color–word Stroop tasks. *Journal of Experimental Psychology: Learning, Memory, and Cognition* 41 (6), 1806.

Singleton, D. (2002) Crosslinguistic interactions in the multilingual mental lexicon. In M. Hooghiemstra (ed.) *Selected Papers from the Second International Conference on Third Language Acquisition*. Leeuwaarden: Fryske Akademie (CD).

Singleton, D. (2003) Perspectives on the multilingual lexicon: A critical synthesis. In J. Cenoz, B. Hufeisen and U. Jessner (eds) *The Multilingual Lexicon* (pp. 167–176). Dordrecht: Springer.

Snodgrass, J.G. (1984) Concepts and their surface representations. *Journal of Memory and Language* 23 (1), 3.

Starreveld, P.A., De Groot, A.M., Rossmark, B.M. and Van Hell, J.G. (2014) Parallel language activation during word processing in bilinguals: Evidence from word production in sentence context. *Bilingualism: Language and Cognition* 17 (2), 258–276.

Talamas, A., Kroll, J.F. and Dufour, R. (1999) From form to meaning: Stages in the acquisition of second-language vocabulary. *Bilingualism: Language and Cognition* 2 (1), 45–58.

Tytus, A.E. (2017) Asymmetrical priming effects: An exploration of trilingual German–English–French lexico-semantic memory. *Journal of Psycholinguistic Research* 46 (6), 1625–1644.

Tzelgov, J., Henik, A. and Leiser, D. (1990) Controlling Stroop interference: Evidence from a bilingual task. *Journal of Experimental Psychology: Learning, Memory, and Cognition* 16, 760–771.

Van Hell, J.G. and Dijkstra, T. (2002) Foreign language knowledge can influence native language performance in exclusively native contexts. *Psychonomic Bulletin & Review* 9 (4), 780–789.

Van Hell, J.G. and Kroll, J.F. (2013) Using electrophysiological measures to track the mapping of words to concepts in the bilingual brain: A focus on translation. In J. Altaribba and L. Isurin (eds) *Memory, Language, and Bilingualism: Theoretical and Applied Approaches* (pp. 126–160). Cambridge: Cambridge University Press.

Vygotsky, L.S. (1986) *Thought and Language* (revised edn). Cambridge, MA: MIT Press.

Wei, L. (2002a) The bilingual mental lexicon and speech production process. *Brain and Language* 81 (1–3), 691–707.

Wei, L. (2002b) The multilingual mental lexicon: Language separation/activation in trilinguals. In M. Hooghiemstra (ed.) *Selected Papers from the Second International Conference on Third Language Acquisition*. Leeuwaarden: Fryske Akademie (CD).

Williams, S. and Hammarberg, B. (1998) Language switches in L3 production: Implications for a polyglot speaking model. *Applied Linguistics* 19 (3), 295–333.

Lecture 10

The Neurolinguistics of Multilingualism

McLoddy Kadyamusuma, Eve Higby and Loraine Obler

Most present-day societies consist of various ethnic groups, cultures and languages. This mingling of diverse sets of people frequently results in multiple languages being used on a daily basis by members of these different linguistic communities in their social and professional interactions and all other spheres of life. The fact that most societies are linguistically diverse has resulted in multilingualism being the norm and not the exception for most individuals when communicating. In fact, more than 50% of the world's population can be characterized as bilingual (Ansaldo *et al.*, 2008; De Bot, 1992). The terms *bilingual* and *multilingual* as used in this lecture refer to individuals who regularly speak or utilize two or more different languages or dialects in their daily communication (Fabbro, 2001; Grosjean, 1994, 1998). In this lecture we use the terms interchangeably. The terms L1 and L2 are used to describe a multilingual's first- and second-learned languages, respectively, and the term Ln is used to refer to any language learned after the native language.

In the past, multilingualism has often been defined as the mastery of verbal language skills or high fluency in all the languages the speaker knows. This strong version of multilingualism will not be used in this lecture since we know that the language skills of multilingual individuals can vary depending on the individual's circumstances at a given point in time, as well as on the modality (e.g. oral versus written skills), context and method of acquisition (Muñoz & Qualls, 2005). Individuals who speak two or more languages usually use their languages with different people in different spheres of life. Different facets of their lives may require different languages. We therefore do not restrict ourselves to the notion that bilingualism or multilingualism requires near-native skill in all languages and do not expect that multilingual speakers behave as if they were two (or more) monolinguals.

The way the brain organizes the languages of multilingual speakers is influenced by factors such as brain hemispheric lateralization, the semantic organization of the lexicons, the proficiency level of each of their languages, and the age and manner of acquisition. In the first part of this lecture we will focus on how these factors affect the performance of multilingual brain-damaged patients. In the final section we will consider what the consequences of multilingualism are for cognition and the brain, and how these consequences interact with aging and dementia.

Representation of Multiple Languages

The way the brain is organized among those who speak two or more languages has captivated researchers, motivating them to explore whether multilinguals have special neural mechanisms for processing language. Much of the research has focused on whether there is one brain mechanism for all languages or whether they are processed independently.

Brain hemispheric lateralization

Our knowledge of how the brain is organized has benefited from brain imaging techniques such as computer tomography (CT), magnetic resonance imaging (MRI), positron emission tomography (PET), magnetoencephalography (MEG) and electroencephalography (EEG), among others. These techniques permit us to visualize the brain's anatomy and the brain regions that are involved when performing different tasks. Our knowledge of brain organization has also been informed by linking brain-damaged areas and associated cognitive and linguistic behaviours. From these different techniques, we know that the brain is divided into two hemispheres, left and right. Both hemispheres play important roles and complement each other for most brain functions (Hull & Vaid, 2007). However, there is also some degree of specialization within each of the two hemispheres. This hemispheric specialization for different functions is referred to as *lateralization*.

In most people, the left hemisphere is primarily responsible for processing language. Right-handed people nearly always show left-hemisphere lateralization for language (Brookshire, 2014: 188). Since each hemisphere is primarily responsible for controlling the opposite side of the body, that means that the left hemisphere controls handedness in right-handed people, which is the same hemisphere that is usually used for language processing. Figure 10.1 shows some of the brain areas in the left hemisphere involved in language processes. About 85% of left-handed monolingual speakers also use the left hemisphere for most language processes, while the remaining 15% use the right hemisphere as their language-dominant hemisphere.

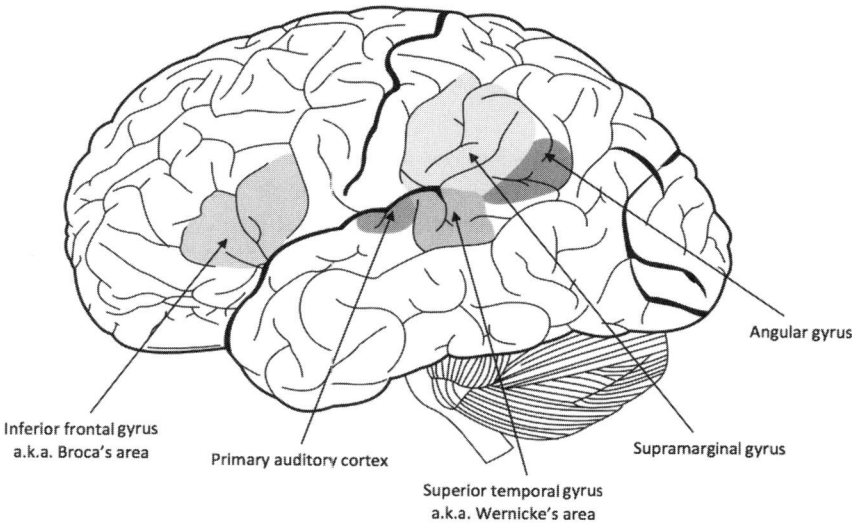

Figure 10.1 The central language-processing regions of the left hemisphere

One of the foundational questions in the neurobiology of multilingualism is whether language is organized in similar ways for multilinguals and monolinguals. For example, is the left inferior cortex involved in language production in similar ways for people who speak one language and those who speak two? The literature demonstrates that, as in monolinguals, most multilinguals are also left-hemisphere dominant for all their languages (Kovelman *et al.*, 2008). However, the strength of the dominance can vary across individuals. In other words, for some people the left hemisphere is predominant for language processing tasks, while for others the right hemisphere may contribute a bit more, which is referred to as stronger or weaker degrees of language lateralization. Compared to monolinguals, multilinguals sometimes show weaker lateralization, in other words, more involvement from both hemispheres (Moreno *et al.*, 2010; Park *et al.*, 2012). This may be because the right hemisphere often supports the processing of the second language due to different acquisition contexts and proficiency levels (Albert & Obler, 1978; Marshall *et al.*, 2015; Proverbio *et al.*, 2004; Sussman *et al.*, 1982).

Organization of the lexicon

Words are stored in a mental dictionary called the lexicon. According to Weinreich (1953), multilingual speakers can be classified based on the relationship of how words and their meanings are stored in the lexicon. Weinreich's classifications include compound, coordinate and subordinate multilinguals. *Compound* multilinguals learn all their languages in the same environment, and they have two or more lexicons but one semantic system. *Coordinate* multilinguals are thought to have separate semantic systems for each language as well as distinct lexicons for each one, since they learn their languages in different contexts (e.g. home, school or work). *Subordinate* multilinguals have one dominant language and semantic system, and they learn their second languages by reference to their dominant L1. Research has since shown that the compound state is the most common for multilinguals, although L2 learners with low proficiency may show more of a subordinate relationship.

Some researchers have argued that the lexicons are not as distinct as was once assumed. The *shared* hypothesis states that all words are integrated in a single memory system (*shared storage*, Kolers, 1963; *bilingual interactive activation + model*, Dijkstra & Van Heuven, 2002). The *separate* hypothesis argues that words from each language are represented separately (*the independence hypothesis*, e.g. Obler & Gjerlow, 1999). A third possibility for how the lexicon of a multilingual is organized is neither fully integrated nor fully independent but rather some aspects are shared while others are not. This hypothesis claims, like the shared storage one, that all the languages of the speaker are connected to the same conceptual information store, but it focuses on the extent to which the speaker's languages are interconnected at the lexical and conceptual levels and not just whether there is a single multilingual system or not (*the subset hypothesis*, Paradis, 2004; Szubko-Sitarek, 2015: 130).

Two variables that affect the degree to which the word forms in the lexicon are connected to concepts are proficiency level and the age of acquisition of the L2. These will be discussed next.

Proficiency

Language proficiency is the level of mastery attained by individuals in their different languages. The level of mastery can vary across language domains such as reading, writing, speaking and listening. A few multilinguals attain expert proficiency in all modalities and languages, but most reach different levels of proficiency across the different modalities and languages. The scenarios and communication contexts to which multilingual speakers are exposed and in which they use each of their languages affect the level of mastery attained in each language. Languages acquired in early childhood that continue to be used are likely to be maintained at a high level of proficiency, whereas those learned later on, such as in adulthood, often do not reach the same level of mastery. Consistent exposure to the languages, the variety of context, the speakers with whom the languages are used and high motivation also contribute to higher levels of proficiency as well as their maintenance. High motivation to become proficient in a new language is usually evident in those individuals who want to become fully functional and integrated in a new society.

The level of proficiency influences the degree to which similar areas of the brain are recruited when processing language. In multilinguals with high proficiency in both languages, the brain regions that are involved when processing all their languages generally overlap (e.g. Bai *et al.*, 2011; Higby *et al.*, 2013; Kotz *et al.*, 2008; Sebastian *et al.*, 2011). That is, all languages spoken at high proficiency are processed within the same central left-hemisphere regions of the brain, using substantially overlapping networks. For less proficient languages, additional regions in the brain – for example, some areas in the right hemisphere (Marshall *et al.*, 2015) and additional areas in the left hemisphere – are recruited as well (Liu *et al.*, 2010). This may be due to the fact that processing languages with lower proficiency levels requires more effort (e.g. Indefrey, 2006). In general, a lower level of proficiency in the Ln results in different brain activation patterns for the proficient and less proficient language(s); as proficiency increases, the differences become less obvious.

Age of acquisition

Different ages of language acquisition can sometimes result in different linguistic profiles in multilingual speakers. Simultaneous multilinguals learn more than one language during infancy, whereas successive multilinguals learn their languages at different points in time (Ansaldo *et al.*, 2008). Age of acquisition and proficiency are generally correlated; the earlier the age at which a language is acquired, the higher the proficiency will usually be later on. However, the two can dissociate depending on how the languages of the multilingual were acquired and how they are used.

According to Wattendorf *et al.* (2014), the age of acquisition affects how the languages are processed in the brain. If simultaneous multilinguals continue to be exposed to their languages, there are few or no differences in the general brain activation patterns when performing language tasks in all of their languages, whereas there is a greater amount of variability across languages for successive multilinguals (Bloch *et al.*, 2009). This demonstrates that being exposed to one or to more than one language in early childhood indeed affects how the languages are processed in the brain. However, Perani *et al.* (1998) tested one group of early bilinguals (age of L2 acquisition before four years of age) and another of late bilinguals (age of acquisition after 10 years of age), and they found that oral comprehension was processed in the same brain areas as long as the level of proficiency was very high in the L2 whether or not the L2 was acquired in early childhood or later in life.

Summary

The factors summarized here are just a small part of a complex set of interactions between age of acquisition, proficiency and patterns of language use. The patterns of language processing seen for multilinguals are a result of when and how they acquired their languages and their continued use. All these factors in turn affect how the languages are organized and processed in the brains of these individuals. For those languages that are acquired early in infancy and remain highly used, speakers by and large attain a high level of proficiency. These languages will be processed in the same central peri-Sylvian brain regions, in the language-dominant hemisphere in simultaneous multilinguals as in monolinguals. More regions may be recruited for processing languages in late, successive multilinguals as a sign of the difficulty of processing the later acquired languages, especially those that are not used frequently.

How the Multilingual Brain Deals with Damage or Decline

The first part of this lecture explored what multilingualism is and the different factors that affect how multilingualism manifests in the brains of healthy speakers. We will now turn our attention to how brain damage, as seen in *aphasia*, and how brain decline, as seen in *dementia*, affect the different languages of the multilingual, relative to what happens in these cases for monolingual individuals, and what these patterns tell us about the organization of languages in the human brain.

Bilingual aphasia

Before the advent of sophisticated technological inventions for studying the human brain, most of what we knew about the organization of the brain for language came from deductions linking brain-damaged regions and language behaviours in individuals with aphasia. Some of the first ground-breaking discoveries and documentation on how the brain is wired for language took place during the classical aphasia period between 1860 and 1890 through the work of Paul Broca and Carl Wernicke. Aphasia is a language impairment resulting from brain trauma that affects the ability to understand and produce language (Davis, 2000; Kohnert, 2004, 2013). Lesions in various cortical regions around the left Sylvian fissure may result in language impairments in articulation, the internal structure of words, the grammatical elements of the sentence and/or the availability of individual words.

Since the majority of people around the world use more than one language, aphasia in bilingual individuals offers important insights in the neurobiology of languages. Researchers use the information we know about the organization of language in the brain of healthy multilinguals to understand how each language recovers in multilinguals with aphasia and to make inferences about the neurological representations of their languages (Muñoz & Qualls, 2005; Paradis, 1977). While the most common pattern is comparable impairment in a speaker's two or more languages, not infrequently one language is more impaired than the other, even when we take into consideration the patient's relative proficiency in the languages before the aphasia (e.g. Albert & Obler, 1978; Weekes, 2010).

Recovery patterns

Adults' brains are less malleable than children's. Most healthy adults find it extremely difficult to fully master a second or third language. Similarly, recovering from aphasia, which usually occurs in mid- to late adulthood, is quite difficult (Paradis, 2008). Bilingual individuals with aphasia normally exhibit similar recovery patterns in the languages they spoke before brain damage. Paradis (1977) identified six language recovery patterns in bilingual speakers, with parallel and differential recovery as the two major patterns observed. Of these recovery patterns, parallel recovery occurs about 61% of the time, differential recovery occurs about 18%, selective recovery (including antagonistic recovery) 7%, blended recovery 9% and successive recovery 5% (Paradis, 2001).

Parallel recovery is the most frequent pattern in multilinguals with aphasia. In parallel recovery all languages improve at similar rates. In an assessment of 20 Friulian-Italian bilinguals with aphasia, 65% of the patients displayed parallel recovery (Fabbro, 2001). Recall that a similar percentage of 61% was observed in a study done by Paradis (2001). One can infer that a bilingual speaker with aphasia has a greater than 50% chance of exhibiting parallel recovery of the two languages after brain damage. This is in line with what we know about the organization of language in healthy multilinguals – that balanced, simultaneous bilinguals process both of their languages in virtually overlapping brain regions.

The second most frequent form of recovery is differential recovery (Muñoz & Marquardt, 2003; Paradis, 2008). In differential recovery patterns, one of the languages shows recovery but the others show less recovery or none at all. *Differential recovery* may be more likely to occur in successive or unbalanced multilinguals, but it may also occur in simultaneous multilinguals. This may be because the languages of successive or unbalanced bilinguals may be processed using not only the classical language areas, but also additional brain regions. This means that brain damage may affect the languages or components of the languages differentially, which may also lead to differential patterns of recovery.

Successive recovery occurs when the recovery of one language comes before the recovery of the other. This implies that both languages are recoverable, although not simultaneously. Weeks or months after one language has stopped recovering, the other language spontaneously shows improvements (Paradis, 2008). In *antagonistic recovery*, one language shows signs of recovery first, but then it regresses as the other language improves. Paradis *et al.* (1982) describe a patient with an antagonistic recovery pattern. Their patient spoke Arabic one day and French the next day. The language most available to the patient would change every few days. *Selective recovery* occurs when only one language recovers. In some cases, only one language is affected by the brain trauma with no apparent deficits in the other language – a very rare phenomenon if it occurs at all (Lorenzen & Murray, 2008). More commonly for this type of recovery, both languages show impairment but recovery is seen in only one language (Gil & Goral, 2004). *Blended recovery* occurs when speakers lose control of their ability to keep their languages apart and unintentional mixing of elements from their languages ensues. The patients might mix sounds, words and/or phrases – even syntactic structures – from both languages in their speech even when they are expected to use only one language at a time.

One explanation that has been given for the differential recovery patterns is that the languages of the multilingual may still be fully represented in the brain, but the individual may lose the ability to access the information necessary to use the languages appropriately (Gil & Goral, 2004). For this to occur, the focal brain damage will have spared the peri-Sylvian language centres, but the language networks in these areas may still be inaccessible to the speaker (Fabbro, 2001; Pitres, 1895). One may infer that the pathways in the brain that are used to access necessary components of the language may be damaged.

An attempt to explain differential recovery led to what is known as Ribot's rule. The rule states that the language that was acquired first will be the first to be recovered. An alternative proposal for differential recovery argued that the language that was most frequently used prior to the brain damage would recover first (Hyltenstam, 1995: 309; Pitres, 1895). However, neither of these explanations can account for all the recovery patterns we see in multilingual individuals with aphasia.

What is clear from these studies is that the level of proficiency, exposure and age of acquisition influence how each language recovers after trauma to brain areas involved in language. Even in the two studies that observed parallel recovery in most lexical subtests (McCann et al., 2012; Venkatesh et al., 2012), some differences between the languages were observed in other tasks such as repetition and syntactic comprehension (McCann et al., 2012; Venkatesh et al., 2012). These different patterns are testament to the diversity that exists across multilingual individuals and how a number of different interacting factors influence the final outcome of what recovery patterns are exhibited in the individuals.

Earlier we demonstrated how different factors, such as proficiency, age of acquisition and language use, affect the brain organization for the language of healthy multilingual speakers. Below we will examine how these factors can predict language recovery in speakers with bilingual aphasia. We will demonstrate how recovery may depend on the age and manner of acquisition, the language most familiar at the time of brain damage, the most socially useful language, the language of the environment, and the context in which the languages were acquired.

Age and manner of acquisition

Age of acquisition is highly linked to how the languages were acquired, with early multilinguals learning their languages without instruction, and late multilinguals, as a rule, learning Ln in a formal or academic context. If the age and manner of acquisition affect how the brain is wired for language, the impact of lesion location on a bilingual speaker with aphasia might be predicted by the age and manner of acquisition (Paradis, 2004). Paradis (2004) hypothesized that different neural connections form depending on the age and manner of acquisition. Languages that are acquired implicitly, i.e. informally in a naturalistic environment, will develop different neural connections from those learned in an explicit teaching situation.

A number of studies have been conducted to investigate the effect of age of L2 acquisition on the recovery patterns in speakers with multilingual aphasia (Amberber & Cohen, 2012; Diéguez-Vide et al., 2012; McCann et al., 2012; Venkatesh et al., 2012). The results from McCann et al. (2012) demonstrate a parallel recovery pattern in their multilingual speaker of Mandarin, English, Guan Xi and Cantonese after a stroke in the left hemisphere. The speaker performed at the same level in most subtests of the Bilingual Aphasia Test for both English and Mandarin despite having learned them at different ages. Similarly, Venkatesh et al. (2012) examined two proficient multilingual speakers with transcortical aphasia who spoke Gujarati as their native language and also had a good command of Swahili, English and Hindi before brain damage. Their aphasia symptoms primarily affected their native tongue, with both Hindi and English showing mostly intact lexical performance. The later age of acquisition of Hindi and English may have led to some differences in how the languages were stored in the brain, resulting in the different levels of impairment between the native and later learned languages. Diéguez-Vide et al. (2012) report a differential recovery pattern for a multilingual speaker whose native language was Mandarin who had learned Catalan and Spanish after childhood. The patient had aphasia after a haemorrhage to the left frontoparietal region. There was superior recovery in the native language followed by the L2 (Spanish), which was better than the L3 (Catalan).

If patients who learned the Ln via formal instruction suffer brain damage in regions subserving the networks involved in explicit memory, this should predominantly affect those languages rather than the naturally acquired L1 (Ansaldo et al., 2008). However, if the individuals had obtained a full command of their languages in an informal environment, damage to explicit memory networks should leave the languages largely intact. Brain damage to the neural connections subserving explicitly learned materials may result in differential or successive recovery in late bilinguals since they typically acquired their languages in different environments (Ansaldo et al., 2008; Diéguez-Vide et al., 2012). The same level of impairment in all languages could occur in those individuals who acquired their languages early in childhood in a natural environment when the neural connections for implicitly learned materials are damaged (Ansaldo et al., 2008).

Proficiency

The level of proficiency before brain damage in different modalities and across languages also plays an important role in recovery patterns. Patients show better recovery for languages that they use more often and also in the domains in which they used their languages (Green, 1998; Paradis, 2004). If speakers had high levels of proficiency across their languages before the aphasia-producing incident, they are likely to exhibit parallel recovery. Conversely, patients with different proficiency levels may show differential recovery rates in each language (Centeno, 2005). Hence, it is important to acquire information about the patient's level of proficiency in each language before the brain damage. This is very important so that differences in performance across languages are not attributed to brain damage when they may simply reflect differences in premorbid proficiency.

Lexical-semantic organization

The way the lexicon is organized in the memory is also likely to impact on language recovery patterns. If the languages are more highly integrated, then therapy in one language should facilitate improvement in the others (Paradis, 2004). If the lexicons are distinct, then generalization should be difficult. To test the latter prediction, Kohnert (2004) used cognitive-based treatment to test general improvement in a Spanish-English multilingual individual with aphasia. The patient was trained using cognate words, which have the same form and meaning across languages, such as *biography/biografía* in English and Spanish. Kohnert found generalization gains for the cognates only from Spanish to English. This demonstrates that treatment gains are transferrable when the lexicons are more integrated, at least for cognates, although it is unclear why the benefit was only seen in one language. This is consistent with the finding that, in healthy adults with high proficiency in their languages, words in both languages may be processed in the same brain regions (Dijkstra et al., 1999; Kadyamusuma, 2016; Kohnert, 2004).

Code-switching and code-mixing in bilingual aphasia

Code-switching is a term used to describe the perfectly normal use of more than one language in the same conversation with another multilingual who shares the same languages as the speaker. Switching involves alternating phrases between two or more languages within the same sentence or conversation, whereas mixing involves inserting a word from one language into the other, or applying the grammatical rules or structure of one language to the vocabulary of another language. Code-switching that results from brain damage, however, is termed 'pathological' by some researchers. However, that term is considered by others to be too derogatory in English. Non-brain damaged individuals do both mixing and switching, but only when they are talking to other multilinguals who share the same languages. Obviously, problems in communication arise if such switching and mixing is done in the presence of a monolingual, as can happen after brain damage.

Among healthy multilingual individuals, code-switching is not a haphazard, unpredictable phenomenon but rather a rule-governed interaction. Many factors, such as the setting, the conversation participants, the proficiency in each language, the topic of conversation, the availability of words, and so forth guide this alternate use of two or more languages within the same discourse (e.g. Grosjean, 1982). The multilingual speaker has the choice of which language to use and also when and how often to code-switch. Healthy multilinguals monitor the language status of their conversation partners in order to determine whether they should stay in a 'monolingual mode' during the conversation or whether they are allowed to switch between languages. If everyone involved in the conversation knows the same languages, then switching and mixing generally does not impair comprehension. Multilingual individuals with brain damage may switch languages when speaking with monolinguals (Stilwell *et al.*, 2016). The nature of this involuntary code-switching provides valuable insights into the neurolinguistic mechanisms involved in inhibiting or selecting the desired language to speak.

Language mixing often occurs as a result of word-finding difficulties or because of the inability to suppress the other languages. The brain areas thought to control mixing are the left anterior cingulate, and to control switching, areas in the frontal and parietal lobes (Abutalebi & Green, 2007, 2016; Fabbro *et al.*, 2000). Abutalebi *et al.* (2000) posit that damage to the basal ganglia may disturb the inhibition/disinhibition process (i.e. the inability to select) necessary to appropriately switch back and forth between languages. Patients are sometimes aware that their switching is inappropriate, but may still not be able to stay in one language, switching unintentionally in the presence of monolingual speakers (e.g. Abutalebi *et al.*, 2000).

In summary, one effect of brain injury among multilinguals is the failure to speak the expected language in a particular situation. This has normally been attributed to the temporary or permanent inability to reach the required language but not a permanent loss of the language (Paradis, 1989: 134). During this brain damage-related switching and mixing, the multilingual speakers are usually not aware of speaking a language that is not appropriate. Even in those instances when they are aware of it, they do not normally manage to switch back to the appropriate language.

Multilingual Dementia

Language impairments can also occur as a result of progressive decline affecting the brain (Stilwell *et al.*, 2016). Dementia results from a set of progressive diseases that cause gradual damage to the brain cells and their connections, resulting in various symptoms of cognitive decline, which manifest themselves in progressive impairments of communication, personality and intelligence (Bayles & Kaszniak, 1987: 1). Whereas aphasia is caused by focal brain injuries, the neurological deterioration that takes place in dementia is somewhat more global in nature. These changes may involve progressive deterioration of memory first and then language deficits later, or vice versa (Faber-Langendoen *et al.*, 1988; Manchon *et al.*, 2015; Stilwell *et al.*, 2016).

Language decline in Alzheimer's disease

Patients with Alzheimer's dementia typically produce a lot of words, but these words lack the typical richness in their semantic content and therefore do not add a lot to the general meaning of the discourse. Their discourse usually includes a small number of nouns (Bencini *et al.*, 2011; Gomez & White, 2006). It may not be the knowledge of the words that is affected, but rather an inability to find the words they want to say. How frequently words are used in the language may affect how strong their mental representations are and hence how resistant they are to decline. Words that are less frequently used are likely to decline earliest both in the dominant and non-dominant languages, while frequently used words are likely to decline last (Ivanova *et al.*, 2014).

During the early stages of the disease, the neurodegeneration is primarily in the frontal lobe and the superior temporal cortex (Manchon *et al.*, 2015; Mattsson *et al.*, 2014). The neurodegeneration then typically extends to the subcortical nuclei. Obler and Albert (1984) posited a six-stage model of linguistic regression for both monolingual and multilingual patients with Alzheimer's disease. The model illustrates that the characteristics of monolingual and multilingual Alzheimer's dementia patients start out very mild in the *early phases* (Stages I–II). Some of the early symptoms of language decline are impairments of complex comprehension and verbal fluency, whereas linguistic automatisms such as counting are preserved (Manchon *et al.*, 2015). As the progression continues in the *middle phases* (Stages III–IV), there is a general drop in the quantity and quality of their general conversational capabilities (Heller *et al.*, 1992). Written comprehension and production slowly deteriorate as the disease advances. New problems are added in *later phases* (Stages V–VI), the predominant characteristics of which include echolalia (repetition) and logorrhoea (muteness).

Although there are similarities in the linguistic characteristics of monolingual and multilingual speakers, there are also differences due to the fact that multilingual speakers have approximately twice as many linguistic options as monolinguals. As a result, there are linguistic phenomena that are likely to appear only in multilingual speakers and not in monolingual speakers.

Code-switching and code-mixing in multilingual dementia patients

Multilingual speakers have few problems with language choice or with keeping the languages apart when needed, two highly developed multilingual skills. Multilinguals suffering from Alzheimer's dementia, by contrast, often display involuntary code-switching and code-mixing during conversations. Alzheimer's patients often lack the ability to choose the appropriate language according to the setting or conversational partner, which can lead to serious communication breakdown (Friedland & Miller, 1999) and worsens as the disease progresses (De Santi *et al.*, 1990).

The inability of multilinguals with Alzheimer's dementia to select the appropriate language has been attributed to limited cognitive control capacity, which is a by-product of deteriorating cognitive functions (Hyltenstam, 1995: 319). Languages acquired in adulthood are likely to be affected by cognitive control declines earlier than the native language. This sometimes results in individuals with Alzheimer's dementia using their native language as a default language even when communicating with a monolingual speaker who does not speak or understand that language. De Santi *et al.* (1990) noted that their patient had greater difficulties in suppressing the dominant language (L1) when speaking the less dominant one (L2). During L1 interactions there were a number of L2 intrusions. This same pattern was exhibited by a patient in another study, GM, who was initially able to respond in the correct language (L2) but then would mix the languages and continue in the L1 (Hyltenstam & Stroud, 1989).

In the early stages, patients with Alzheimer's dementia are sometimes aware of their inappropriate language mixing and attempt to repair the mistake. However, this ability to repair deteriorates with the progression of the disease. As disorientation and lapses in attention worsen, it becomes more difficult to repair the inappropriate mixing. Friedland and Miller (1999) reported that at least three of their four patients managed to correct their own errors within a very short span of time in those cases in which their code-switching resulted in communication breakdown. This demonstrates that the individuals were aware of what was causing the language breakdown. However, sometimes patients with Alzheimer dementia are clearly unaware of the fact that they are not using the same language as their conversation partner (Hyltenstam, 1995: 322).

Language-specific deficits in multilinguals with Alzheimer's dementia

The way in which neurodegenerative disease affects each language can also tell us something about the organization of language in multilingual speakers. Evidence from some earlier studies suggested that this neurodegenerative disease impacts the L2 more than the L1 (De Santi *et al.*, 1990: 233). Dronkers *et al.* (1986) examined Dutch-English bilinguals with Alzheimer's disease and discovered that they primarily produced Dutch even when speaking to an English-speaking monolingual. Dronkers and colleagues initially attributed this language choice to memory impairments. However, on further testing they discovered that their subjects' linguistic abilities were actually equally affected in both languages.

More recent evidence suggests that, for multilinguals who acquire their languages in early childhood and also for later bilinguals, Alzheimer's dementia results in parallel progressive deterioration in the L1 and L2 (Gómez-Ruiz et al., 2012; Manchon et al., 2015). According to Manchon et al. (2015), Alzheimer's disease impairs all the languages at the same rate when patients are processing words at the semantic and the syntactic level. This is in line with findings that the two languages share neural representations at the lexico-semantic level (Costa et al., 2012). Manchon and colleagues argue that this supports the idea that even individuals who acquire their languages late in adulthood have shared neural networks for both their L1 and L2. Their argument is that Alzheimer's disease impairs the regions of the brain that are responsible for processing both the L1 and L2, resulting in their languages manifesting the same deficits.

The results of Manchon and colleagues are in line with what is proposed by the convergence hypothesis, that the lexical-semantic neural networks are shared between the languages of bilinguals (Abutalebi & Green, 2007). Processing the later acquired languages may require recruitment of additional brain regions if the level of proficiency is not comparable to the L1; however, as the level of proficiency before the onset of dementia increases, there will be a convergence of brain regions responsible for processing both languages (Abutalebi, 2008; Wartenburger et al., 2003).

What the neuroimaging studies and patient studies show us is that the different languages of multilingual speakers with dementia decline similarly over the course of the disease. Some language problems, such as inappropriate code-switching and code-mixing, are specific to multilinguals by virtue of their speaking at least two different languages. The parallel decline of all languages in multilinguals with Alzheimer's dementia is in line with the common finding of similar degrees of impairments and recovery patterns observed after stroke (e.g. Tschirren et al., 2011). These support the neuroimaging findings showing that the extent to which the languages involve the same brain regions or networks depends on the age at which the languages were acquired (Ivanova et al., 2014) and the level of proficiency (Abutalebi, 2008; Gómez-Ruiz et al., 2012).

Consequences of Multilingualism

Cognitive consequences of multilingualism

A fascinating yet controversial proposal is that bilingualism leads to improved executive control. One aspect of executive control is inhibitory control, or resistance to interference. A number of studies have demonstrated better performance by bilinguals on tasks measuring inhibitory control compared to monolinguals (e.g. Bialystok et al., 2004). However, some aspects of inhibition, such as inhibiting making a response, do not appear to be better performed by multilinguals (Colzato et al., 2008). Likewise, bilinguals have demonstrated superior performance in tasks involving flexible mental shifting (e.g. Prior & MacWhinney, 2009) and conflict resolution (e.g. Bialystok, 2010); these findings, too, have sometimes not been replicated (e.g. Hilchey & Klein, 2011; Paap & Greenberg, 2013). Some researchers have attributed the inconsistent findings to the diverse characteristics of the bilinguals being tested (Luk, 2015) and the lack of a consensus with regard to what different tasks measure (Marton, 2015).

Neuroimaging evidence has helped to clarify this issue in two ways. First, when behavioural differences between groups are not found, that does not necessarily mean that differences do not exist. It may be the case that the groups do differ but that the tasks used were not sensitive enough to detect that difference. Or perhaps the groups are not sufficiently distinct; if the 'monolingual' group has in fact had some foreign language experience such as time spent abroad, that may reduce the degree to which they differ from the bilinguals. Thus, null findings are inconclusive with regard to whether there is a group effect or not. In some cases where behavioural differences are not observed we can detect distinct patterns of brain activation between the groups. In this way, neuroimaging data contribute information that may coincide with behavioural findings or may not but is nonetheless revealing about the nature of the bilingual advantage in executive control.

The second important contribution that neuroimaging studies provide is clarity regarding what control mechanisms are involved in the tasks being used and how language groups may use those control mechanisms differently. The activation patterns seen during tasks of executive control can be compared with those of other studies to deduce the kinds of control needed to perform the task. For example, the anterior cingulate cortex is frequently activated when conflict monitoring is needed (Botvinick *et al.*, 2004), while the putamen is involved in motor movements, including articulatory control (Abutalebi *et al.*, 2013). When these structures are recruited differently by multilinguals and monolinguals, this information allows us to draw conclusions about how the brains of these groups function that behavioural data may not be able to reveal.

Controlling two languages engages much of the same neural network as other types of non-linguistic control. Two structures that are involved in bilingual control include the anterior cingulate cortex and the caudate nucleus (Crinion *et al.*, 2006; Hervais-Adelman *et al.*, 2014). These structures show greater activation during word retrieval in a bilingual context (in which either language may be needed) compared to a monolingual context (when only one language is needed) and are more activated when using the second (less proficient) language than the first (Abutalebi *et al.*, 2007). As we learn more about the different brain structures involved in language control, we see that there may be multiple levels of language control. One level may involve a *supervisory attentional system*, which engages the anterior cingulate cortex and pre-supplementary motor area (Branzi *et al.*, 2016). This system is recruited when monitoring demands are increased. Another level involves a *response selection system*, which includes inferior parietal cortex, prefrontal areas and caudate nucleus, and is recruited with increased demands on both local control (previously encountered items) and global control (over the whole language).

An influential model that incorporates cognitive control and language control in multilinguals was presented by Abutalebi and Green (2007). Their model comprises four brain areas and their connections: the prefrontal cortex, the anterior cingulate cortex, the basal ganglia (including the caudate and putamen) and the inferior parietal lobule. Language selection and planning is proposed to take place in basal ganglia structures while the maintenance of those representations in working memory engages the inferior parietal lobule. The other two structures, the prefrontal and anterior cingulate cortices, are widely involved in non-linguistic control but also play an important role in language control through response selection and inhibition, conflict monitoring and error detection.

Perhaps due to their greater use of control mechanisms during language processing compared to monolinguals, multilinguals are more efficient users of these control systems. In non-language tasks involving dealing with conflict, which typically involves the anterior cingulate, bilinguals show less activity in the anterior cingulate compared to monolinguals but better task performance (Abutalebi *et al.*, 2012). Multilinguals also show a more extensive network of control regions when suppressing interference as well as less susceptibility to interference (Coderre & Van Heuven, 2014; Luk *et al.*, 2010; Wu & Thierry, 2013). These findings from neuroimaging support the behavioural studies summarized earlier showing enhanced performance by multilinguals.

Neuroimaging evidence supports the proposal that multilinguals employ greater use of executive control during language tasks than monolinguals do, and that their use of executive control during non-linguistic tasks is more efficient than it is for monolinguals. This literature has provided important contributions to our understanding of how executive control is modified as a result of multilingualism and has led to more specific proposals of how control networks are implemented by multilinguals.

Structural changes as a consequence of multilingualism

The notion of neuroplasticity is that our brains adapt to our life experiences. Language acquisition and use are some of those experiences, so we would expect there to be differences in the way in which the brains of multilinguals and monolinguals are structured. Moreover, we might expect there to be differences among multilinguals with different types of language experience, such as differing ages of acquisition or proficiency.

Bilinguals have nearly twice the vocabulary size of monolinguals when words from both languages are counted. What is the neural consequence of this vocabulary expansion? The density of grey matter in a region in the right hemisphere (the posterior supramarginal gyrus) increases with vocabulary size in monolinguals and bilinguals (Mechelli *et al.*, 2004), and density in this region is greater for bilinguals than monolinguals and for multilinguals who speak three or more languages compared to bilinguals who speak only two (Grogan *et al.*, 2012; Mechelli *et al.*, 2004). Among multilinguals, individual differences in lexical use may lead to different patterns of neural adaptation. For example, lexical efficiency in the non-native language (the speed and accuracy of word recognition and the number of words produced during a timed word retrieval task) varies among bilinguals, and those with greater lexical efficiency show higher grey matter density in the left hemisphere in a portion of the frontal lobe called the pars opercularis (Grogan *et al.*, 2012). This region is involved in speech sound processing and word retrieval (Parker Jones *et al.*, 2012), which may be more demanding for bilinguals than for monolinguals, leading to the changes in neural density observed for bilinguals.

Bilinguals also need to produce a wider variety of speech sounds and master a larger number of grammatical structures compared to monolinguals. The articulatory demands of mastering the sound systems of multiple languages requires the adaptation of subcortical structures such as the putamen, which has higher grey matter density in multilinguals than monolinguals (Abutalebi *et al.*, 2013). Furthermore, bilinguals have higher grey matter volume in the cerebellum, a structure at the base of the brain which is used when applying grammatical rules (Pliatsikas *et al.*, 2014). In fact, the volume in the cerebellum is directly related to how well bilinguals process the grammar of their L2 (Pliatsikas *et al.*, 2014).

Besides the local brain areas involved in different language tasks, we also find differences between bilinguals and monolinguals in the white matter tracts connecting various brain regions. For example, bilinguals show greater connectivity along white matter tracts connecting frontal lobe regions to parietal/temporal and occipital lobe regions (García-Pentón *et al.*, 2014; Mohades *et al.*, 2012; Pliatsikas *et al.*, 2015). These pathways are important for language processing and may indicate that language information is processed more rapidly by bilinguals. A different tract was found to have greater connectivity for monolinguals; this tract connects the front part of the corpus callosum (the bundle of tracts connecting the right and left hemispheres) to the orbital lobe, the bottom, most-front portion of the frontal lobe (Mohades *et al.*, 2012). Precisely what role these tracts play in bilingualism and language processing more generally is yet to be seen.

Not only are there structural differences in regions underlying language functions, but also in regions involved in executive control. As described in the previous section, the anterior cingulate cortex and the left caudate nucleus are frequently called upon to deal with conflict and control, and bilinguals recruit these regions when applying language control whereas monolinguals do not. This enhanced use appears to lead to structural changes as well. Bilingual older adults have higher grey matter volume in these structures than monolinguals (Abutalebi *et al.*, 2015; Zou *et al.*, 2012). Furthermore, the amount of activity in the anterior cingulate correlates with grey matter volume in bilinguals (Abutalebi *et al.*, 2012), and better behavioural performance on a switching task is associated with higher grey matter volume (Zou *et al.*, 2012).

As with the neuroimaging data, age of acquisition also influences structural changes in multilingualism. Earlier age of L2 acquisition is associated with greater volume in the right parietal cortex and left pars opercularis (in the frontal lobe) (Grogan *et al.*, 2012; Wei *et al.*, 2015). However, in some cases, later age of acquisition appears to lead to greater structural changes, possibly because of the greater demands placed on later ages of acquisition. In one study, the later the age of L2 acquisition, the thicker the cortex was in the left inferior frontal gyrus, but the thinner the cortex was in the same region in the right hemisphere (Klein *et al.*, 2014). In another study successive L2 learners had greater grey matter volume in multiple areas of the frontal, temporal and parietal lobes compared to simultaneous bilinguals (Kaiser *et al.*, 2015). What these studies suggest is that language learning experience interacts with developmental patterns in the brain at different stages, resulting in specific patterns of localized changes.

Interestingly, it does not take a lifetime of bilingualism to result in brain changes; some structural changes have been observed in just a few months. Three months of intensive language study was found to increase the volume of the hippocampus and the cortical thickness of several areas in the frontal and temporal lobes (Mårtensson et al., 2012). The structural changes observed in immersion language environments are related to the degree of proficiency attained; the greater the proficiency increase, the greater the structural brain change (Mechelli et al., 2004; Stein et al., 2012).

The evidence summarized here clearly points to multilingualism as a source of neuroplasticity. There is even evidence that learning a third language changes brain organization over and above the changes brought about by learning a second one (Watterndorf et al., 2014). The neural adaptations involve language-related structures as well as areas engaged in executive control. Although age of acquisition appears to influence the degree of neuroplasticity, the effects of immersion in a foreign language environment can be quite rapid, even when they are observed in adults. Therefore, brain changes appear to occur in both childhood and adulthood in response to challenging linguistic environments.

Multilingualism effects during aging and onset of dementia

As we age, our brains tend to shrink. This is less noticeable in middle adulthood but becomes more noticeable in older age. Bilingualism may offset some of this decline, however, by contributing to 'brain reserve capacity'. Brain reserve refers to the ability of the brain to continue to support functioning despite the accumulation of various kinds of lesions or insults (Valenzuela, 2008). What this means practically is that individuals with higher brain reserve can continue to live their lives normally even in the presence of declining neural structure such as the atrophy associated with aging. Bilingual older adults have increased grey matter volume in the parietal lobe compared to bilingual younger adults (Abutalebi et al., 2015). They also have more robust white matter tracts in the frontal lobe and corpus callosum, as well as tracts connecting anterior and posterior areas (Luk et al., 2011; Olsen et al., 2015). Furthermore, with increasing age, monolinguals show decreases in the cortical thickness of the temporal pole and the prefrontal cortex while no change with age is found in this region for bilinguals (Abutalebi et al., 2014, 2015; Olsen et al., 2015).

The protective effects of bilingualism also extend to disease conditions like dementia. Bilinguals tend to be older than monolinguals when diagnosed with dementia or displaying symptoms, by about four to five years (Alladi et al., 2013; Bialystok et al., 2007; Chertkow et al., 2010; Craik et al., 2010; Freedman et al., 2014; Gollan et al., 2011). There is some debate, however, about whether the benefit is due to using more than one language or to other typically co-occurring situations like immigration. One study reported that dementia occurred later only among bilinguals who were immigrants (Chertkow et al., 2010), while another study showed that one had to speak at least four languages to show the delay in onset of dementia if not an immigrant but only two languages if an immigrant (Freedman et al.,

2014). Furthermore, the effect of bilingualism may be more pronounced in older adults with lower levels of education than in those with higher levels of education (Gollan *et al.*, 2011).

While the concept of brain reserve is based on the idea that brain functions can be maintained even while brain volume or connectivity declines, the concept of 'cognitive reserve' is based on the idea that cognitive functions persevere despite brain atrophy. The bilingualism findings discussed above are consistent with the cognitive reserve hypothesis of neural decline in aging. Cognitive reserve refers to the brain's ability to maintain cognitive functions in the face of atrophy that would be expected to produce deficits (Stern, 2002). Several types of life experience are thought to contribute to a person's cognitive reserve: higher education, engagement in intellectually stimulating leisure activities and a dense social network (Scarmeas & Stern, 2003). Furthermore, the effects of these activities are cumulative; the risk of developing dementia is reduced by about 12% for each additional leisure activity beyond the first (Scarmeas *et al.*, 2001). Bilingualism may also be one of those lifestyle factors that improves cognitive reserve (Valian, 2014).

One clever way that cognitive reserve has been tested is by comparing the degree of brain atrophy among individuals with similar levels of cognitive performance. Those with greater cognitive reserve exhibit worse atrophy. This test has been done for bilinguals and monolinguals. When the brains of patients with Alzheimer's disease were examined for degree of atrophy, the brains of bilinguals showed a greater amount of atrophy even though they could perform as well as the monolinguals on tests of cognitive function (Gold *et al.*, 2013; Schweizer *et al.*, 2012). These results support the idea that bilingual individuals have higher levels of cognitive reserve than monolinguals, although it is unclear whether this is due to using two languages or to other factors that differ between the two groups such as immigration. The evidence suggests that immigration may exert a greater effect on cognitive reserve than bilingualism does (Freedman *et al.*, 2014). Moreover, we do not yet know whether different types of bilingual characteristics provide greater benefit than others, such as daily use of both languages, age of acquisition, proficiency, contexts of language use, and other factors that differentiate individuals' bilingual experiences.

Conclusions

Clearly the cortical regions underlying bilingualism in the brain form a complex system, but it is safe to say that there are not altogether different regions subserving each language. Rather, the left hemisphere language region is most crucial for both languages of the bilingual and for all the languages of a multilingual. Other regions of the brain – perhaps particularly the right hemisphere – may contribute during the early stages of learning a language, or for processing low-proficient languages, which will tend to be those learned after childhood and those that are less used. Nevertheless, the evidence reviewed from rare instances of differential aphasia – when two languages are impaired, or recover disproportionately to how they were known before the aphasia – suggests that the two or more languages' networks are not altogether overlaid one on the other in all individuals.

As well, there is substantial literature suggesting regions regulating switching in bilinguals and the inhibition of switching when appropriate. These include particular cortical and subcortical regions that form an executive control network, that is, the brain systems that control other brain systems' processing for activities like making decisions, monitoring what is going on in the brain and in the environment, and planning.

Most interesting is the bilingualism research suggesting brain plasticity, in that learning an L2 at different ages appears to result in slightly different forms of cortical organization for the languages' representation and processing. Intriguing as well is the possibility that the years of practice in inhibiting one language in order to speak another appear to provide a buffer against the behavioural changes associated with dementing diseases that affect some individuals in advanced age.

Questions for Students' Reflection

1. Why would it make sense that a language learned after childhood is rarely mastered to native-like proficiency?

2. Have you spent time with a bilingual who had dementia? What did you notice about their choice of language when talking with you or with caregivers who did not know all the same languages?

3. How is bilingualism (or multilingualism) an advantage? A disadvantage?

4. What else do you think might contribute to the different types of language recovery patterns in multilingual speakers with aphasia?

5. What other types of expertise might, like being bilingual, lead to cognitive reserve in older adults?

Suggestions for Further Reading

Fabbro. F. (1999) *The Neurolinguistics of Bilingualism: An Introduction*. New York: Psychology Press.

Grosjean, F. (2010) *Bilingual: Life and Reality*. Cambridge, MA: Harvard University Press.

Obler, L.K. and Gjerlow, K. (1999) *Language and the Brain*. Cambridge: Cambridge University Press.

Paradis, J. (2007) Early bilingual and multilingual acquisition. In P. Auer and Li Wei (eds) *Handbook of Multilingualism and Multilingual Communication* (pp. 15–44). Berlin: Mouton de Gruyter.

Paradis, M. (2004) *A Neurolinguistic Theory of Bilingualism*. Studies in Bilingualism series. Amsterdam: John Benjamins.

De Groot, A.M.B. (2011) *Language and Cognition in Bilinguals and Multilinguals: An Introduction*. New York: Psychology Press.

References

Abutalebi, J. (2008) Neural aspects of second language representation and language control. *Acta Psychologica* 128, 466–478.

Abutalebi, J. and Green, D.W. (2007) Bilingual language production: The neurocognition of language representation and control. *Journal of Neurolinguistics* 20, 242–275.

Abutalebi, J. and Green, D.W. (2016) Neuroimaging of language control in bilinguals: Neural adaptation and reserve. *Bilingualism: Language and Cognition* 19 (4), 689–698.

Abutalebi, J., Miozzo, A. and Cappa, S.F. (2000) Do subcortical structures control 'language selection' in polyglots? Evidence from pathological mixing. *Neurocase* 6, 51–56.

Abutalebi, J., Annoni, J.-M., Zimine, I., et al. (2007) Language control and lexical competition in bilinguals: An event-related fMRI study. *Cerebral Cortex* 18 (7), 1496–1505.

Abutalebi, J., Della Rosa, P.A., Green, D.W., et al. (2012) Bilingualism tunes the anterior cingulate cortex for conflict monitoring. *Cerebral Cortex* 22 (9), 2076–2086.

Abutalebi, J., Della Rosa, P.A., Gonzaga, A.K.C., Keim, R., Costa, A. and Perani, D. (2013) The role of the left putamen in multilingual language production. *Brain and Language* 125, 307–315.

Abutalebi, J., Canini, M., Della Rosa, P.A., Sheung, L.P., Green, D.W. and Weekes, B.S. (2014) Bilingualism protects anterior temporal lobe integrity in aging. *Neurobiology of Aging* 35 (9), 2126–2133.

Abutalebi, J., Canini, M., Della Rosa, P.A., Green, D.W. and Weekes, B.S. (2015) The neuroprotective effects of bilingualism upon the inferior parietal lobule: A structural neuroimaging study in aging Chinese bilinguals. *Journal of Neurolinguistics* 33, 3–13.

Albert, M.L. and Obler, L. (1978) *The Bilingual Brain: Neuropsychological and Neurolinguistics Aspects of Bilingualism*. New York: Academic Press.

Alladi, S., Bak, T.H., Duggirala, V., et al. (2013) Bilingualism delays age at onset of dementia, independent of education and immigration status. *Neurology* 81 (22), 1938–1944.

Amberber, A.M. and Cohen, H. (2012) Assessment and treatment of bilingual aphasia and dementia using the Bilingual Aphasia Test. *Journal of Neurolinguistics* 25, 515–519.

Ansaldo, A.I., Marcotte, K., Scherer, L. and Raboyeau, G. (2008) Language therapy and bilingual aphasia: Clinical implications of psycholinguistic and neuroimaging research. *Journal of Neurolinguistics* 21, 539–557.

Bai, J., Shi, J., Jiang, Y., He, S. and Weng, X. (2011) Chinese and Korean characters engage the same visual word form area in proficient early Chinese-Korean bilinguals. *PLoS ONE* 6, e22765.

Bayles, K.A. and Kaszniak, A.W. (1987) *Communication and Cognition in Normal Aging and Dementia*. New York: Taylor & Francis.

Bencini, G., Pozzan, L., Biundo, R., McGeown, W., Valian, V., Venneri, A. and Semenza, C. (2011) Language-specific effects in Alzheimer's disease: Subject omission in Italian and English. *Journal of Neurolinguistics* 24 (1), 25–40.

Bialystok, E. (2010) Global-local and trail-making tasks by monolingual and bilingual children: Beyond inhibition. *Developmental Psychology* 46 (1), 93–105.

Bialystok, E., Craik, F.I.M., Klein, R. and Viswanathan, M. (2004) Bilingualism, aging, and cognitive control: Evidence from the Simon task. *Psychology and Aging* 19 (2), 290–303.

Bialystok, E., Craik, F.I.M. and Freedman, M. (2007) Bilingualism as a protection against the onset of symptoms of dementia. *Neuropsychologia* 45 (2), 459–464.

Bloch, C., Kaiser, A., Kuenzli, E., *et al.* (2009) The age of second language acquisition determines the variability in activation elicited by narration in three languages in Broca's and Wernicke's area. *Neuropsychologia* 47, 625–633.

Botvinick, M.M., Cohen, J.D. and Carter, C.S. (2004) Conflict monitoring and anterior cingulate cortex: An update. *Trends in Cognitive Sciences* 8 (12), 539–546.

Branzi, F.M., Della Rosa, P.A., Canini, M., Costa, A. and Abutalebi, J. (2016) Language control in bilinguals: Monitoring and response selection. *Cerebral Cortex* 26 (6), 2367–2380.

Brookshire, R.H. (2014) *Introduction to Neurogenic Communication Disorders* (8th edn). St. Louis, MO: Mosby.

Centeno, J. (2005) Working with bilingual individuals with aphasia: The case of a Spanish-English bilingual client. *Perspectives on Communication Disorders and Sciences in Culturally and Linguistically Diverse Populations* 12, 2–7.

Chertkow, H., Whitehead, V., Phillips, N., Wolfson, C., Atherton, J. and Bergman, H. (2010) Multilingualism (but not always bilingualism) delays the onset of Alzheimer disease: Evidence from a bilingual community. *Alzheimer Disease & Associated Disorders* 24 (2), 118–125.

Coderre, E.L. and Van Heuven, W.J.B. (2014) Electrophysiological explorations of the bilingual advantage: Evidence from a Stroop task. *PLoS ONE* 9 (7), e103424.

Colzato, L.S., Bajo, M.T., Van den Wildenberg, W., Paolieri, D., Nieuwenhuis, S., La Heij, W. and Hommel, B. (2008) How does bilingualism improve executive control? A comparison of active and reactive inhibition mechanisms. *Journal of Experimental Psychology: Learning, Memory, and Cognition* 34, 302–312.

Costa, A., Calabria, M., Marne, P., *et al.* (2012) On the parallel deterioration of lexico-semantic processes in the bilinguals' two languages: Evidence from Alzheimer's disease. *Neuropsychologia* 50, 740–753.

Craik, F.I.M., Bialystok, E. and Freedman, M. (2010) Delaying the onset of Alzheimer disease: Bilingualism as a form of cognitive reserve. *Neurology* 75 (19), 1726–1729.

Crinion, J., Turner, R., Grogan, A., *et al.* (2006) Language control in the bilingual brain. *Science* 312 (5779), 1537–1540.

Davis, G.A. (2000) *Aphasiology: Disorders and Clinical Practice*. Boston, MA: Allyn & Bacon.

De Bot, K. (1992) A bilingual production model: Levelt's 'speaking' model adapted. *Applied Linguistics* 13 (1), 1–24.

De Santi, S., Obler, L.K., Sabo-Abrahamson, H. and Goldberger J. (1990) Discourse abilities and deficits in multilingual dementia. In Y. Joanette and H.H. Brownell (eds) *Discourse Ability and Brain Damage: Theoretical and Empirical Perspectives* (pp. 224–235). New York: Springer.

Diéguez-Vide, F., Gich-Fullà, J., Puig-Alcántara, J., Sánchez-Benavides, G. and Peña-Casanova, J. (2012) Chinese-Spanish-Catalan trilingual aphasia: A case study. *Journal of Neurolinguistics* 25 (6), 630–641.

Dijkstra, T. and Van Heuven, W.J.B. (2002) Modeling bilingual word recognition: Past, present and future. *Bilingualism: Language and Cognition* 5 (3), 175–197.

Dijkstra, A., Grainger, J. and Van Heuven., W.J.B. (1999) Recognition of cognates and interlingual homographs: The neglected role of phonology. *Journal of Memory and Language* 41 (4), 496–518.

Dronkers, N.F., Koss, E., Friedland, R.P. and Wertz, R.T. (1986) 'Differential' language impairment and language mixing in a polyglot with probable Alzheimer's disease. *Journal of Clinical and Experimental Neuropsychology* 8, 139.

Fabbro, F. (2001) The bilingual brain: Bilingual aphasia. *Brain and Language* 79, 201–210.

Fabbro, F., Skrap, M. and Aglioti, S. (2000) Pathological switching between languages after frontal lesions in a bilingual patient. *Journal of Neurology, Neurosurgery, and Psychiatry* 68, 650–652.

Faber-Langendoen, K., Morris, J.C., Knesevich, J.W., LaBarge, E., Miller, J.P. and Berg, L. (1988) Aphasia in senile dementia of the Alzheimer type. *Annals of Neurology* 23, 365–370.

Freedman, M., Alladi, S., Chertkow, H., et al. (2014) Delaying onset of dementia: Are two languages enough? *Behavioural Neurology* 22, 1–8.

Friedland, D. and Miller, N. (1999) Language mixing in bilingual speakers with Alzheimer's dementia: A conversation analysis approach. *Aphasiology* 13 (4), 427–444.

García-Pentón, L., Fernández, A.P., Iturria-Medina, Y., Gillon-Dowens, M. and Carreiras, M. (2014) Anatomical connectivity changes in the bilingual brain. *Neuroimage* 84, 495–504.

Gil, M. and Goral, M. (2004) Nonparallel recovery in bilingual aphasia: Effects of language choice, language proficiency, and treatment. *International Journal of Bilingualism* 8 (2), 191–219.

Gold, B.T., Johnson, N.F. and Powell, D.K. (2013) Lifelong bilingualism contributes to cognitive reserve against white matter integrity declines in aging. *Neuropsychologia* 51 (13), 2841–2846.

Gollan, T.H., Salmon, D.P., Montoya, R.I. and Galasko, D.R. (2011) Degree of bilingualism predicts age of diagnosis of Alzheimer's disease in low-education but not in highly educated Hispanics. *Neuropsychologia* 49 (14), 3826–3830.

Gomez, R.G. and White, D.A. (2006) Using verbal fluency to detect very mild dementia of the Alzheimer type. *Archives of Clinical Neuropsychology* 21, 771–775.

Gómez-Ruiz, I., Aguilar-Alonso, A. and Espasa, M.A. (2012) Language impairment in Catalan-Spanish bilinguals with Alzheimer's disease. *Journal of Neurolinguistics* 25, 552–566.

Green, D.W. (1998) Mental control of the bilingual lexico-semantic system. *Bilingualism: Language and Cognition* 1, 67–81.

Grogan, A., Parker Jones, O., Ali, N., et al. (2012) Structural correlates for lexical efficiency and number of languages in nonnative speakers of English. *Neuropsychologia* 50, 1347–1352.

Grosjean, F. (1982) *Life with Two Languages. An Introduction to Bilingualism*. Cambridge, MA: Harvard University Press.

Grosjean, F. (1994) Individual bilingualism. In R.E. Asher (ed.) *The Encyclopedia of Language and Linguistics* (pp. 1656–1660). Oxford: Pergamon Press.

Grosjean, F. (1998) Studying bilinguals: Methodological and conceptual issues. *Bilingualism: Language and Cognition* 1, 131–149.

Heller, R.B., Dobbs, A.R. and Rule, B.G. (1992) Communicative function in patients with questionable Alzheimer's disease. *Psychology and Aging* 7, 395–400.

Hervais-Adelman, A., Moser-Mercer, B., Michel, C.M. and Golestani, N. (2014) fMRI of simultaneous interpretation reveals the neural basis of extreme language control. *Cerebral Cortex* 25 (12), 4727–4739.

Higby, E., Kim, J. and Obler, L.K. (2013) Multilingualism and the brain. *Annual Review of Applied Linguistics* 33, 68–101.

Hilchey, M.D. and Klein, R.M. (2011) Are there bilingual advantages on nonlinguistic interference tasks? Implications for the plasticity of executive control processes. *Psychonomic Bulletin & Review* 18 (4), 625–658.

Hull, R. and Vaid, J. (2007) Bilingual language lateralization: A meta-analytic tale of two hemispheres. *Neuropsychologia* 45, 1987–2008.

Hyltenstam, K. (1995) The code switching behavior of adults with language disorders – with special reference to aphasia and dementia. In L. Milroy and P. Muysken (eds) *One Speaker, Two Languages: Cross-disciplinary Perspectives on Code Switching* (pp. 302–343). Cambridge: Cambridge University Press.

Hyltenstam, K.K. and Stroud, C. (1989) Bilingualism in Alzheimer's dementia: Two case studies. In K. Hyltenstam and L.K. Obler (eds) *Bilingualism and Regression in Language: Sociocultural, Neuropsychological and Linguistic Perspectives* (pp. 202–226). Cambridge: Cambridge University Press.

Indefrey, P. (2006) A meta-analysis of hemodynamic studies on first and second language processing: Which suggested differences can we trust and what do they mean? *Language Learning* 56, 279–304.

Ivanova, I., Salmon, D. and Gollan, T. (2014) Which language declines more? Longitudinal versus cross-sectional decline of picture naming in bilinguals with Alzheimer's disease. *Journal of the International Neuropsychological Society* 20, 1–13.

Kadyamusuma, M.R. (2016) Transfer of treatment in multilingual individuals after brain damage. *The Communicator* 46 (1), 17–20.

Kaiser, A., Eppenberger, S., Smieskova, R., *et al.* (2015) Age of second language acquisition in multilinguals has an impact on grey matter volume in language-associated brain areas. *Frontiers in Psychology* 6, 638.

Klein, D., Mok, K., Chen, J.K. and Watkins, K.E. (2014) Age of language learning shapes brain structure: A cortical thickness study of bilingual and monolingual individuals. *Brain and Language* 131, 20–24.

Kohnert, K. (2004) Cognitive and cognate-based treatments for aphasia: A case study. *Brain and Language* 91, 294–302.

Kohnert, K. (2013) *Language Disorders in Bilingual Children and Adults* (2nd edn). San Diego, CA: Plural.

Kolers, P.A. (1963) Interlingual word associations. *Journal of Verbal Learning and Verbal Behavior* 2, 291–300.

Kotz, S.A., Holcomb, P.J. and Osterhout, L. (2008) ERPs reveal comparable syntactic sentence processing in native and non-native readers of English. *Acta Psychologica* 128, 514–527.

Kovelman, I., Baker., S. and Petitto, L.A. (2008) Bilingual and monolingual brains compared: A functional magnetic resonance imaging investigation of syntactic processing and a possible 'neural signature' of bilingualism. *Journal of Cognitive Neuroscience* 20, 153–169.

Liu, H., Hu, Z., Guo, T. and Peng, D. (2010) Speaking words in two languages with one brain: Neural overlap and dissociation. *Brain Research* 1316, 75–82.

Lorenzen, B. and Murray, L.L. (2008) Bilingual aphasia: A theoretical and clinical review. *American Journal of Speech-Language Pathology* 17, 299–317.

Luk, G. (2015) Who are the bilinguals (and monolinguals)? *Bilingualism: Language and Cognition* 18 (1), 35–36.

Luk, G., Anderson, J.A.E., Craik, F.I.M., Grady, C.L. and Bialystok, E. (2010) Distinct neural correlates for two types of inhibition in bilinguals: Response inhibition versus interference suppression. *Brain and Cognition* 74 (3), 347–357.

Luk, G., Bialystok, E., Craik, F.I.M. and Grady, C.L. (2011) Lifelong bilingualism maintains white matter integrity in older adults. *Journal of Neuroscience* 31 (46), 16808–16813.

Manchon, M., Buetler, K., Colombo, F., Spierer, L., Assal, F. and Annoni, J.-M. (2015) Impairment of both languages in late bilinguals with dementia of the Alzheimer type. *Bilingualism: Language and Cognition* 18 (1), 90–100.

Marshall, N., Borodkin, K., Maliniak, O. and Faust, M. (2015) Hemispheric involvement in native and non-native comprehension of conventional metaphors. *Journal of Neurolinguistics* 35, 96–108.

Mårtensson, J., Eriksson, J., Bodammer, N.C., Lindgren, M., Johansson, M., Nyberg, L. and Lövdén, M. (2012) Growth of language-related brain areas after foreign language learning. *Neuroimage* 63 (1), 240–244.

Marton, K. (2015) Theoretically driven experiments may clarify questions about the bilingual advantage. *Bilingualism: Language and Cognition* 18 (1), 37–38.

Mattsson, N., Insel, P.S., Nosheny, R., *et al.* (2014) Emerging β-amyloid pathology and accelerated cortical atrophy. *JAMA Neurology* 71 (6), 725–734.

McCann, C., Lee, T., Purdy, S.C. and Paulin, A.K. (2012) The use of the Bilingual Aphasia Test with a bilingual Mandarin-New Zealand English speaker with aphasia. *Journal of Neurolinguistics* 25 (6), 579–587.

Mechelli, A., Crinion, J.T., Noppeney, U., O'Doherty, J., Ashburner, J., Frackowiak, R.S. and Price, C.J. (2004) Neurolinguistics: Structural plasticity in the bilingual brain. *Nature* 431, 757.

Mohades, S.G., Struys, E., Van Schuerbeek, P., Mondt, K., Van de Craen, P. and Luypaert, R. (2012) DTI reveals structural differences in white matter tracts between bilingual and monolingual children. *Brain Research* 1435, 72–80.

Moreno, S., Bialystok, E., Wodniecka, Z. and Alain, C. (2010) Conflict resolution in sentence processing by bilinguals. *Journal of Neurolinguistics* 23, 564–579.

Muñoz, M.L. and Marquardt, T. (2003) Picture naming and identification in bilingual speakers of Spanish and English with and without aphasia. *Aphasiology* 17, 115–132.

Muñoz, M.L. and Qualls, C.D. (2005) Application of a monolingual-bilingual continuum to research and clinical practice in neurogenic communication disorders. *E-Journal for Black and Other Ethnic Group Research and Practices in Communication Sciences and Disorders* 1, 22–56.

Obler, L.K. and Albert, M.L. (1984) Language in aging. In M.L. Albert (ed.) *Clinical Neurology of Aging*. New York: Oxford University Press.

Obler, L.K. and Gjerlow, K. (1999) *Language and the Brain*. Cambridge: Cambridge University Press.

Olsen, R.K., Pangelinan, M.M., Bogulski, C., Chakravarty, M.M., Luk, G., Grady, C.L. and Bialystok, E. (2015) The effect of lifelong bilingualism on regional grey and white matter volume. *Brain Research* 1612, 128–139.

Paap, K.R. and Greenberg, Z.I. (2013) There is no coherent evidence for a bilingual advantage in executive processing. *Cognitive Psychology* 66 (2), 232–258.

Paradis, M. (1977) Bilingualism and aphasia. In H. Whitaker and H.A. Whitaker (eds) *Studies in Neurolinguistics, Vol. 3* (pp. 65–121). New York: Academic Press.

Paradis, M. (1989) Bilingual and polyglot aphasia. In F. Boller and J. Grafman (eds) *Handbook of Neuropsychology II* (pp. 117–140). Amsterdam: Elsevier Science.

Paradis, M. (2001) Bilingual and polyglot aphasia. In R.S. Berndt (ed.) *Handbook of Neuropsychology* (2nd edn) (pp. 69–91). Oxford: Elsevier Science.

Paradis, M. (2004) *A Neurolinguistic Theory of Bilingualism*. Amsterdam: John Benjamins.

Paradis, M. (2008) Language and communication disorders in multilinguals. In B. Stemer and H. Whitaker (eds) *Handbook of the Neuroscience of Language* (pp. 341–349). Amsterdam: Elsevier Science.

Paradis, M., Goldblum, M.C. and Abidi, R. (1982) Alternate antagonism with paradoxical translation behavior in two bilingual aphasic patients. *Brain and Language* 15, 55–69.

Park, H.R.P., Badzakova-Trajkov, G. and Waldie, K.E. (2012) Language lateralization in late proficient bilinguals: A lexical decision fMRI study. *Neuropsychologia* 50, 688–695.

Parker Jones, O., Green, D.W., Grogan, A., *et al.* (2012) Where, when and why brain activation differs for bilinguals and monolinguals during picture naming and reading aloud. *Cerebral Cortex* 22 (4), 892–902.

Perani, D., Paulesu, E., Galles, N.S., *et al.* (1998) The bilingual brain: Proficiency and age of acquisition of the second language. *Brain* 121, 1841–1852.

Pitres, A. (1895) Aphasia in polyglots. In M. Paradis (ed.) *Readings on Aphasia in Bilinguals and Polyglots* (pp. 26–49). Montreal: Didier.

Pliatsikas, C., Johnstone, T. and Marinis, T. (2014) Grey matter volume in the cerebellum is related to the processing of grammatical rules in a second language: A structural voxel-based morphometry study. *Cerebellum* 13 (1), 55–63.

Pliatsikas, C., Moschopoulou, E. and Saddy, J.D. (2015) The effects of bilingualism on the white matter structure of the brain. *Proceedings of the National Academy of Sciences* 112 (5), 1334–1337.

Prior, A. and MacWhinney, B. (2009) A bilingual advantage in task switching. *Bilingualism: Language and Cognition* 13 (2), 253–262.

Proverbio, A.M., Leoni., G. and Zani, A. (2004) Language switching mechanisms in simultaneous interpreters: An ERP study. *Neuropsychologia* 42, 1636–1656.

Scarmeas, N. and Stern, Y. (2003) Cognitive reserve and lifestyle. *Journal of Clinical and Experimental Neuropsychology* 25 (5), 625–633.

Scarmeas, N., Levy, G., Tang, M.X., Manly, J. and Stern, Y. (2001) Influence of leisure activity on the incidence of Alzheimer's disease. *Neurology* 57 (12), 2236–2242.

Schweizer, T.A., Ware, J., Fischer, C.E., Craik, F.I.M. and Bialystok, E. (2012) Bilingualism as a contributor to cognitive reserve: Evidence from brain atrophy in Alzheimer's disease. *Cortex* 48 (8), 991–996.

Sebastian, R., Laird, A.R. and Kiran, S. (2011) Meta-analysis of the neural representation of first and second language. *Applied Psycholinguistics* 32, 799–819.

Stein, M., Federspiel, A., Koenig, T., *et al.* (2012) Structural plasticity in the language system related to increased second language proficiency. *Cortex* 48, 458–465.

Stern, Y. (2002) What is cognitive reserve? Theory and research application of the reserve concept. *Journal of the International Neuropsychological Society* 8 (3), 448–460.

Stilwell, B.L., Dow, R.M., Lamers, C. and Woods, R.T. (2016) Language changes in bilingual individuals with Alzheimer's disease. *International Journal of Language and Communication Disorders* 51 (2), 113–127.

Sussman, H.M., Franklin, P. and Simon, T. (1982) Bilingual speech: Bilateral control? *Brain and Language* 15, 125–142.

Szubko-Sitarek, W. (2015) *Multilingual Lexical Recognition in the Mental Lexicon of Third Language Users*. New York: Springer.

Tschirren, M., Laganaro, M., Michel, P., Martory, M.D., Di Pietro, M., Abutalebi, J. and Annoni, J.-M. (2011) Language and syntactic impairment following stroke in late bilingual aphasics. *Brain and Language* 119, 238–242.

Valenzuela, M.J. (2008) Brain reserve and the prevention of dementia. *Current Opinion in Psychiatry* 21 (3), 296–302.

Valian, V. (2014) Bilingualism and cognition. *Bilingualism: Language and Cognition* 18 (1), 3–24.

Venkatesh, M., Edwards, S. and Saddy, D. (2012) Production and comprehension of English and Hindi in multilingual transcortical aphasia. *Journal of Neurolinguistics* 25 (6), 615–629.

Wartenburger, I., Heekeren, H.R., Abutalebi, J., Cappa, S.F. and Villringer, A. (2003) Early setting of grammatical processing in the bilingual brain. *Neuron* 37, 159–170.

Wattendorf, E., Festman, J., Westermann, B., *et al.* (2014) Early bilingualism influences early and subsequently later acquired languages in cortical regions representing control functions. *International Journal of Bilingualism* 18 (1), 48–66.

Weekes, B.S. (2010) Issues in bilingual aphasia: An introduction. *Aphasiology* 24 (2), 123–125.

Wei, M., Joshi, A.A., Zhang, M., *et al.* (2015) How age of acquisition influences brain architecture in bilinguals. *Journal of Neurolinguistics* 36, 35–55.

Weinreich, U. (1953) *Language in Contact: Findings and Problems*. New York: Linguistic Circle of New York.

Wu, Y.J. and Thierry, G. (2013) Fast modulation of executive function by language context in bilinguals. *Journal of Neuroscience* 33 (33), 13533–13537.

Zou, L., Ding, G., Abutalebi, J., Shu, H. and Peng, D. (2012) Structural plasticity of the left caudate in bimodal bilinguals. *Cortex* 48 (9), 1197–1206.

Part 4

Forms of Multilingualism in the Past and Present

Part 2

Lecture 11

Historical Multilingualism*

Kurt Braunmüller

Introduction

Preliminaries

What is the difference between contemporary and historical multilingualism? Is there any fundamental difference at all? Strictly speaking, multilingualism in any period of the past is not different from multilingualism today, due to the so-called *uniformitarian principle*. According to this principle, 'the linguistic processes taking place around us are the same as those that have operated to produce the historical record' (Labov, 1972: 101). One might add that it is therefore unreasonable to assume that other forces may have operated in the past, disregarding of course such modern phenomena as the influence of mass media.

Investigating historical multilingualism is therefore simply looking back in human history, based on those insights we have gained from similar investigations of the present. This means that all the information about other aspects of multilingualism in the preceding chapters and in the next chapter can be applied to the issues of historical multilingualism as well. The major (obvious) difference is, however, that the data come from earlier periods. The problems that may arise when investigating earlier forms of multilingualism concern the dearth of (sound) data: we may have only fragmentary or incomplete sources (such as inscriptions on stones, documents written on vellum, broadsheets, etc.) for some of our questions or we may have no (direct) testimonies at all. Thanks to the uniformitarian principle we may, however, have good reasons to believe that, in any given situation, the same state of affairs that holds for the well-described contemporary or recent setting will, in principle, also hold for the past. These conclusions can of course not claim the status of natural laws, but they are by far the best guesses in order to come to grips with (similar or comparable) situations in the past to which we otherwise have no direct access. Other more specific differences between historical and contemporary multilingualism cannot be treated in this survey but are discussed, for example, in Aronin and Singleton (2012: 33–50).

To give an example, most of the inhabitants in the constantly expanding Roman Empire had to learn Latin as a second language (L2), especially as a lingua franca (similar in its functions to English as a lingua franca for most people in the world today), in order to be able to communicate with the authorities, as a trade language and, not to forget, as the language of the army. These new 'Romans' were bi- or multilingual speakers who once acquired Latin as a second (or third) language, mastering it at different levels of proficiency, either as early sequential bilingual children or much later as adults. Their linguistic situation can thus be compared to similar groups of L2 learners today who have learnt a foreign language, e.g. at school, as migrants to another country or as a lingua franca. But when the influence of the proficient speakers of Latin began to vanish in Late Antiquity because the bulk of the Romanized speakers were on the retreat, the former lingua franca Latin was subject to more and more fundamental changes. These changes were essentially comparable to the changes typically made by foreign language learners (such as simplifications, overgeneralizations and the replication of widely disseminated mistakes), which later became fossilized. Thus different new regional vernaculars emerged, which were often labelled 'Vulgar Latin' (cf. also Kiesler, 2006: 7–14). This term refers to diverging manifestations of colloquial non-standard Latin showing traces of speakers' first languages (for further reading on other forms of bilingualism based on Latin, see the broad survey presented in Adams, 2003).

Some basic concepts

It makes general sense to distinguish between *individual* and *societal* multilingualism. They are interrelated but differ in scope (one individual versus a group of individuals). Moreover, we have to distinguish between (a) learning languages *step by step*, beginning with the first language, informally also called 'mother tongue' (L1), then augmented by other languages (L2, L3, L4, etc.) acquired later from peers, at school, at work or at university, in marriage or when working abroad. Other individuals may be privileged (b) to grow up with more than one language *from birth* (2L1; in Africa and Asia in many instances also 3L1/4L1 and additionally other languages and dialects). But what are the consequences of these two ways of becoming and being a multilingual person? Are bi-/multilingual individuals from birth in a better position? Are they more proficient, resembling the typically 'perfect' native speakers of the languages in question? Putting the frequently raised question aside of whether there are perfect speakers of any language at all (including its varieties, i.e. dialects, sociolects, stylistic registers, languages for specific purposes, not to mention ancient types of texts such as anthems or Bible texts), there are of course obvious differences between these two types of being bi- or multilingual. If you have grown up with only one language (and all its varieties, also called a linguistic *diasystem*; cf. Weinreich, 1954), you still have the chance to learn more languages up to a high degree of proficiency – if you try hard enough and get sufficient practice and assistance and, of course, as much native input as possible. On the other hand, bi-/multilingual speakers from birth (2[/3]L1) are clearly in a better position because languages are acquired and used differently at various ages, whereby the rule of thumb holds: 'the earlier, the better (i.e. the easier, the more effective)'. But in many cases the dominant (or the individual's 'best') language is the language that receives more input and stimuli from the environment than the other language which is, for example, only practised at home and/ or spoken by only one parent, or which is only used in its formal register as an educational language at school. The other languages may then often turn out to be the weaker ones (cf. also Montrul, 2008: 102–107), with obvious consequences for the individual's performance in that language: the other weaker languages might have been acquired imperfectly or otherwise in an incomplete way (e.g. only orally, and in their colloquial registers); acquisition might have come to a premature end, for example due to migration, where linguistic competence will fossilize at some stage during the process of acquisition (what has nowadays been labelled as 'heritage speakers', cf. Benmamoun *et al.*, 2013); or when the linguistic output shows many features of incomplete (e.g. simplifying) acquisition, as does the output of speakers who have learnt the language as a 'second' language later in life.

All these aspects have to be accounted for in historical multilingualism as well, since they are in a way universal and thus applicable to any form of language acquisition. Therefore we also have to reckon with interferences between languages in contact, mistakes due to insufficient practice or incomplete literacy, and overgeneralizations and simplifications in historical sources, including all the occasional divergences from the presupposed unified norm that tend to be not accounted for in historical surveys or grammatical overviews of the former stages of a language. On the contrary, if one expects or takes for granted that older testimonies reflect the grammatical rules of those languages, one will soon come across instances which are not accounted for in historical grammars or which are deviant in one way or another. Therefore, one has to bear in mind that historical grammars and surveys are based on a *selection of sources*, very often the most important ones by virtue of their contents, or documents which are most characteristic for the further development of the language in question, neglecting most of the many other sources that can be found in peripheral types of text, e.g. in lists of articles, minutes of meetings, cookery books, drafts or notes on margins, etc.

Interaction between the languages acquired

When individuals master more than one language (which is the default assumption of this book and in modern postnationalist linguistics as well), an *interaction* between these languages is *inevitable*: there is mutual contact and influence. The crucial issue is, however, to what extent and under what circumstances this process will take place. This also means that a bilingual person cannot be considered a conjunction of two monolinguals in one and the same person but represents something different and unique (Grosjean, 2010).

One of the main issues in (multilingual) language history is the role and *impact of language contact*, seen from both the individual's and the societal perspective. It is therefore important to keep in mind that any contact between languages ultimately happens in the brain of the multilingual individuals and does not, for example, fall over a border region, a whole country or members of a population like rain from a cloud. Any language has to be learnt individually – only the ways and the circumstances in which this process takes place may (and will) diverge.

Of course, individuals, even young children, are able to keep their languages apart. But it has been observed when discussing the mutual effects of bi- and multilingualism that the lower the degree of separation between the languages, the lower the cognitive cost will be (Matras, 2009: 151, 235). One of the negative aspects of this lack of separation has formerly been called *interference*, i.e. the negative (undesired) import of features from one language onto another. For example, mastering two genetically very closely related languages such as Dutch and German or Danish and Norwegian certainly has a low cost profile because the linguistic structures and the lexicons of these languages are quite similar, in part even identical. But the challenge when learning or practising closely related languages is still demanding, since any form of *code-mixing*, which is not desirable (at least) from the native speakers' point of view because it may offend established societal norms, is sooner or later inevitable (see Braunmüller, 2009: 66–67, where a code-mixing hierarchy is presented).

However, not all parts of the (core) grammar of a language seem to be open for non-deliberate code-mixing, such as, for example, the pronominal or the conjunctional systems, because they represent a highly frequent as well as manageable part of the vocabulary without much variation. But a comparative study conducted from a multilingual perspective (Braunmüller, 2015) has produced arguments as to why, for example, the Scandinavian demonstrative pronouns could have entered the system of Old English personal pronouns as far as the third person plural is concerned. The reason for this kind of unexpected code-mixing in one of the core parts of the linguistic system is evident when we take incomplete acquisition by foreign language learners into account: the mostly illiterate Scandinavian invaders learnt local English dialects only to a rudimentary extent, encouraged by the fact that the languages in contact were more or less mutually intelligible, at least in face-to-face communication where speakers could point to things whenever they did not know the appropriate term. So they used their Scandinavian demonstrative pronouns (in modern terms *they/them*, originally meaning 'these', and not the Old English personal pronouns *hīe/hira/him*) when pointing to things or more generally when talking about things they wanted to refer to. This was the simplest way of referring to things that were not related to the person of the speaker or the addressee. Why should they learn more grammar than necessary? They just wanted to be understood, which was enough in many cases. Quite a few languages have, therefore, no personal pronouns in the third person – Korean, for example. From a theoretical and multilingual perspective, this means that *L2 learners*, as representatives of *unbalanced bilinguals*, are the best indicators for detecting grammatical redundancy: they tend to prefer the most general (i.e. non-specific) ways of verbalization, neglecting anything they consider 'superfluous', such as [here] third person pronouns in the plural or articles. But this strategy may also be extended onto different forms of the past tense (imperfect, preterit, present/past perfect, aorist, etc.) and separate forms for expressing the future tense, passives, prepositions etc., not to forget variation in word order.

Covert code-mixing, i.e. the disguised transfer between related structures in terms of using another language's wording (presented in more detail in the section on 'Traces of covert multilingualism', p. 318), may only be an option if almost all speakers of a certain community master both languages and will thus understand transferred structures and wordings due to their bilingual competence. This is, for example, the case on the Faroe Islands, where all speakers of Faroese (L1) also speak Danish (L2; originally the colonial language) at a very high level of proficiency. Due to the rather close genetic relationship between Faroese, a western Scandinavian language in the North Atlantic, and Danish, a Mainland Scandinavian language, transferred constructions and calques occur as *shortcuts*, inadvertently and largely unnoticed. But it may happen that some utterances produced by (bilingual) speakers of Faroese will not be fully accepted as native Danish or sometimes actually not be completely understood by monolingual speakers in Denmark, as the grammatical system of the non-activated language, Faroese, is not available (for details and examples, see Petersen, 2010). Such a scenario also holds for other bilingual speakers of minor, especially minority, languages, when they interact with speakers of the majority language who have no access to those speakers' coexistent other grammatical resources.

Bilinguals strive to minimize the *cognitive costs*, i.e. the expense of acquiring more than one grammatical system, by making use of structures and wordings closest to each other (sometimes at the expense of the societal norms of that language). Thus gradual *converging changes* may occur when languages come into contact with one another (in the brain). As research on bilinguals has shown (see Muysken, 2000: chapter 5), they tend to prefer and produce parallel structures between their languages, known as *congruent lexicalizations*. If possible, they give preference to those structures that are closest to each other but that do not violate the principles of the linguistic systems themselves. Since language change is mainly based on choices between different, more or less equivalent varieties, bilingual speakers will prefer those structures which best bridge the gap between 'their' languages and even ignore (or avoid) completely some structures of the other language which they consider 'redundant'. Thus, the changes made by bilinguals primarily affect the linguistic *norm*, viz. the preferred selections of equivalent terms and structures, as used by the dominant or the (by and large) non-multilingual population, and not the linguistic system itself. Research into historical multilingualism will exploit this situation in order to: (a) find the reasons for these deviations from the dominant local societal norm – are they due to foreign language learning, incomplete acquisition, migration (with a yet rudimentary linguistic knowledge of the local vernacular) or due to the impact of the dominant erudite language, e.g. Latin, Classical Greek or French?; and (b) reveal the dominant language of the writers/speakers in question based on interferences or non-received shortcuts between their languages. In other words, *covert multilingualism* (in descriptive historical linguistics also known as *substrata*), as this shining-through phenomenon of the formerly dominant language should be called in a multilingual framework, may open the door to the structures of other languages, which we otherwise might have no access to.

To give an example, definite articles are rare in the oldest Old High German texts, which is actually not very surprising because the original texts are written in Latin, a language without articles, and because the earliest translations started out as word-for-word translations or glosses. But things are more complicated when we look at the oldest testimonies of Germanic, the Runic inscriptions in the so-called older Futhark (ca. AD 150–750), where articles are completely absent. Is this due to the model language the Runic writers used (presumably the ubiquitous lingua franca Latin; cf. Braunmüller, 2005b for a short summary in English) or has the emergence of articles a completely other status in the evolution of languages, since many modern languages such as Finnish, Turkish, the Slavic languages and very many other languages have not developed this grammatical category at all? This observation is meant here to serve as a caveat insofar as one has to look for other supporting observations whenever using arguments based on multilingualism and its acquisition. 'Multilingualism' is by no means the ultimate answer to all unsolved problems in language evolution and history! Nevertheless it is a fundamental aspect of any study of the history of human behaviour one has to account for.

Why is it meaningful to study multilingualism from a historical point of view?

There are two reasons why a historical approach may be useful when dealing with issues of multilingualism: (a) by *looking back* from the present or a well-documented earlier period of the past, we can observe how and under which conditions contact-induced linguistic changes have taken place; and (b) by *looking forward*, we can hypothesize the likelihood that certain developments will occur in a particular multilingual scenario, based on insights we have gained from analyzing changes under equivalent circumstances in the past. Are certain languages endangered due to a very intense contact with a much bigger, dominating language? Are languages subject to restructurings due to intense immigration? Are new contact-induced varieties likely to emerge? Let me give four examples:

i. In the late Middle Ages and in Early Modern Times, *mixed dialogues* with German and Latin, elsewhere probably considered an incomprehensible lingo, were quite common among highly educated people (see the analysis of Luther's table talks by Stolt, 1964 [only available in German]; but cf. Braunmüller, 2010, for a summarizing description in English; Braunmüller, 2000, for a broader North European perspective). The interesting observation to be gained from these mixed dialogues in Luther's table talks is that they basically follow German in their sentence formation and word order, which means that there is an underlying blueprint based on the interlocutors' native language of German, and no clutter as one might suspect when hearing an apparently uncontrolled mixture of two languages.

ii. In late Medieval London English, so-called *macaronic* business documents from the Thames occurred, which show many forms of mixing and intertwining, not least in well-established abbreviations and suspensions ('*p*' could, for example, stand for 'par, per, pre' or 'pur'; for further details see the documentation in Wright, 1996; cf. also Schendl, 2000). From both instances we can learn that modern forms of code-mixing which can be observed from expert talks or youngsters in in-group communication are by no means new or unique. At first glance, they might be regarded as products of linguistic thoughtlessness or serve as paradigms for the decline of linguistic awareness, but actually they function, comparable to Luther's table talks, as very colloquial shortcuts among highly proficient multilingual/multilectal speakers in informal in-group conversations which serve as rapid effective communication interchange.

iii. In the 18th and 19th centuries many loan words from French entered the German language and sometimes they prevailed in certain types of text. In former times, French was not only a prestigious *à la mode* language in the German speaking territories, it was also the common language of the European aristocracy, of diplomacy and within the international postal system. Today the bulk of these French words have disappeared without leaving many visible traces. Only the word formation element, (Ger.) *-ieren*, originally occurring in foreign verbs such as *ras<u>ieren</u>* 'to shave', *praktiz<u>ieren</u>* 'to practise' or *renov<u>ieren</u>* 'to renovate', is still productive.

iv. To give a more recent example, after WWII numerous new words borrowed from (American) English entered the German language, in the first five decades predominantly in the western regions of Germany, due to various reasons and motivations (the so-called 're-education', imitating the American way of life, English as an international language, etc.). It may very well be that speakers of German, even those with a satisfying command of colloquial English, are unable to conceive the contents of certain types of [German] texts, e.g. in national economy, business administration or informational technology areas, due to their heavy English superstratal impact. Based on experience with lexical loans from French and Latin in history, we may assume that in the long run many of these words will disappear again, at least in non-technical colloquial German. The average native speaker of German will, however, never become a real bilingual person through being exposed to English professional terminology or other forms of confrontation with the American culture via mass media.

We might classify such a situation as *pseudo-bilingualism*. Although the prestigious contact language (American English today, French and Latin in former times) occurs everywhere and in many contexts, if used in this way it will never become part of the active linguistic competence of the domestic speakers. Of course, some words/terms will be understood and used more or less properly, but this partial lexical competence will never lead to a fully bilingual competence, as the grammatical rules and the rules for proper application of the terminology are missing.

Convergence, Stability and Divergence in Language Contact Scenarios

Convergence: The only and inevitable outcome of language contact and change?

As noted above, there is a strong tendency for the two languages used by bilinguals, especially L2 language learners, to converge at least in some respects, e.g. in parts of their syntax and word order and in the use of modal verbs or prepositions. Two simple examples may illustrate this observation:

i. An obvious 1:1 transfer of an English phrasal construction with the preposition *to* can be seen from the German phrase *willkommen <u>zu</u> ...*, influenced by its English cognate *welcome <u>to</u> ...*, whereas the more traditional, more idiomatic use would have been *bei, auf* or *in*, depending on the context: *willkommen <u>bei</u> unserem Fest/<u>auf</u> unserer Party; <u>in</u> unserer Stadt '... to our party; our town'*.

ii. Some word-for-word translations from English into German become more and more acceptable for whatever reason and tend to supersede their idiomatic equivalents, as can be seen from the phrase *not really* which is generally rendered into German as *nicht wirklich*, whereas its idiomatic equivalent *eigentlich nicht* loses more and more ground, especially in short replications such as *Are you tired? – Not really. > [...] – Nicht wirklich.* The ultimate reason for these converging developments is that a considerable amount of effort is needed to keep all one's languages completely separated from each other. In careless colloquial dialogues among L2 bilinguals many more transfers and deviations from the societal norm may and do actually occur, which might be acceptable for a change but will certainly not become the default mode of communication. Otherwise a diffuse *interlanguage* such as foreigner talk or a tourist pidgin may be the result. Both are undesired forms of uncontrolled merging, which will not be accepted as the default in most societies and will therefore be stigmatized as forms of incomplete language acquisition. At best, they could become a new restricted non-standard or in-group language (such as foreigner talk among younger immigrants).

Convergence is predominantly ruled by individual cognitive factors, viz. by creating shortcuts in the brain of a bilingual individual. As mentioned above, this makes life with two (or more) languages in many cases easier to manage. Reverse developments may, however, also occur. (More details on this issue can be seen in Chapter 10.)

However, as we have just seen, not all forms of language contact are subject to converging/assimilating processes. It may also be the case that the two languages in contact do not converge but remain stable or increase the distance between their grammatical systems, e.g. as a result of language cultivation or language policy. Such diverging developments have largely been overlooked by most of the researchers in the past (a more elaborate discussion is given in Kühl & Braunmüller, 2014).

On other outcomes of language contact

It therefore makes sense to find out which cases besides the allegedly default form of language evolution in a multilingual setting, namely (a) linguistic *convergence*, may also occur. We should also envisage (b) contact-induced *stability*, (c) stability despite contact, (d) contact-induced *divergence* and (e) divergence despite contact. To give some examples:

I. Isolated minority languages or in-group languages which are spoken mainly in some indigenous families and in cultural clubs, as is for example the case for the North Frisian varieties/languages along the western littoral regions of Schleswig-Holstein in northern Germany, are good candidates for Case (b); otherwise these small languages/dialects would be absorbed by the majority language, in this case colloquial northern Standard

German (or in earlier times Low German), and fade away. In this case, language cultivation and social as well as political motivations play a crucial role in keeping the status of this vernacular stable and largely unchanged. Even standardizations between these closely related varieties, on the one hand on the islands Föhr, Amrum and Sylt, and on the other hand on the mainland including the islands located in the mudflats, seem to be prohibited by various language cultivation movements and not because this undertaking would be an impossible task. The intention is that each of these minority languages should be preserved as they are now for cultural or traditional reasons, although a unification process would increase the survival chances for these small West Germanic languages. As such a unification will apparently not happen in the years to come, language death will sooner or later be the inevitable result.

II. Stability despite contact, Case (c), can be observed in the instance of the sociolinguistic situation in Norway, from the beginning of the 19th century until today. Two very closely related (written) languages, Dano-Norwegian (*bokmål*) and New Norwegian (*nynorsk*), were elaborated after Norway had become independent from Denmark and they have been competing heavily for supremacy since the end of the 19th century. It is exclusively due to historical and cultural reasons that these two varieties of (written) Norwegian did not merge, although this would have been quite an easy task because most of their structures and a very great portion of the vocabulary are shared by both varieties. All the other differences are rather marginal and would, under other circumstances, go along with any normal linguistic variation within one and the same diasystem. Establishing fusion varieties (explicitly Pan-Norwegian (*samnorsk*), but also that version of Dano-Norwegian which strives to integrate forms of New Norwegian language use) failed because of a fundamental social and cultural antagonism between the proponents of these two varieties of Norwegian (cf. also Jahr, 2014, for a sociohistorical account).

III. Contact-induced divergence, Case (d), can be exemplified by what has occurred during recent decades in the Balkans and beyond: Serbian and Croatian have diverged more and more, caused by well-known political reasons. The same holds for the current linguistic situation between Czech and Slovakian.

IV. Divergence despite contact, Case (e), can be illustrated by the divergent developments between Swedish in Sweden and Swedish in Finland, Portuguese as spoken in Portugal and in Brazil, or between the colloquial varieties of German spoken in Germany, Switzerland and Austria. In the latter instance we find minor differences in vocabulary which are, however, kept alive, although language-internal Swiss and Austrian accommodations between the local (rural) dialects and the roofing standard vernaculars also occur (such as *Erdäpfel* > *Kartoffeln* 'potatoes'). But converging with Standard German as used in Germany is not an option since this would endanger the independence of the Swiss and Austrian German vernaculars, respectively.

Cases where the distances between language-internal varieties are intentionally enlarged and often exaggerated are known as *hyperdialectisms* (i.e. forms that highlight and exaggerate typical dialectal features), in both sociolinguistics and dialectology (cf. Trudgill, 1988: 550ff.). What we may learn from those developments is that convergence, as we have argued above, while clearly favourable for the individual's bilingual competence, can be prevented by social and/or political tendencies. The mental energy multilingual speakers spend in upholding these small idiosyncratic divergences including the creation of additional new ones between very closely related varieties might be motivated by the satisfaction they feel when being considered 'different' or 'special' by fellow speakers of essentially the same linguistic community.

Types of Language Change in Multilingual Settings

The most basic types of changes in the linguistic systems are (a) the augmentative and (b) the reductive change. But also (c) typological chain reactions, (d) unnoticed word order and other changes and (e) language change due to second language acquisition (SLA), code-mixing and covert multilingualism are likely to occur in bi- as well as in multilingual environments.

Augmentative change

Augmentative change means that the linguistic *complexity* of a language will increase, induced by intense language contact, as new linguistic patterns and structures borrowed from a model language have become integrated into (one of) the speaker's languages. This process is closely associated with certain grammatical changes that have been called 'grammatical replication' (Heine & Kuteva, 2005: chapter 2), 'code-copying' (Johanson, 2008) or 'additive borrowing' (Trudgill, 2011: 27ff.). This means that speakers of the recipient language incorporate several grammatical structures of a model language that lead, as a direct consequence, to more complexity in their own language. A precondition for such a development is bilingualism, either of an influential group of speakers or of the society as a whole. One of the results may be the emergence of new regional varieties/languages. Contact on equal terms will of course facilitate such processes.

A well-known example of such a linguistic change, actually an upheaval, is the intense contact between English and Anglo-Norman, a northern French dialect, after AD 1066. The French-speaking upper class not only invaded Britain, but their French dialect also penetrated the local variety spoken by the Germanic speaking population in that area. This was the starting point for a dramatic increase of complexity in the vocabulary of the English language, a typical superstratal effect. But it was also the origin of the Romanization of English and its typological change due to SLA developments such as generalizations and simplifications, restricted word order, etc.

At first glance, augmentative changes seem unfavourable for those speakers who have to learn divergent patterns and rules to which they are not accustomed. From a bilingual's perspective things may turn out to be slightly different: admittedly, the original linguistic system, i.e. the one before the intense contact took place, becomes more complex and is thus more difficult to master. On the other hand, these bilingual speakers are thus given easier access to the new language, which facilitates frequent code-switching and the fixing of the new language in their brains, since these recently acquired structures now function as *ties*, bridging the gap between the divergent languages bilinguals have to cope with in everyday life.

Reductive change

Reductive change, the opposite development, means a *decrease* in linguistic complexity, e.g. the loss of grammatical categories and distinctions in comparison with the original languages. Such a development is often due to SLA by adults or children beyond puberty. Trudgill (2011: 21ff.) mentions, among other things, the regularization of irregularities, the increase in lexical and morphological transparency and the loss of redundancy. In other words, reductive changes cause the languages in contact to lose some of their original (idiomatic) structures and grammatical categories and become in a way 'simpler'. Only very intense and asymmetric contacts are able to trigger those far-reaching modifications within the speakers' linguistic competence, including the loss of grammatical categories. A precondition for successfully turning a reduced linguistic variety into a new vernacular is, again, the social and/or political dominance of the (invaded/immigrated) learner group in that society. As these new speakers had to learn this language as adults, they will in most cases not be able to acquire the complete linguistic system of that (target) language. The reasons for this failure are manifold: among others, the unfavourable late age of these learners, their indifference towards grammatical correctness and/or discrimination against the local natives' variety as something not very important and therefore not worthy of being acquired in all details. The ultimate results will be structural simplifications and alignments between grammatical idiosyncrasies and underspecification with respect of certain grammatical categories (see McWhorter, 2007, for a more general discussion). The most important question occurring when analyzing this kind of contact is, however, how much simplification and which kind of reduction is possible and still tolerable. One conclusion we may come to might be: the structurally simpler a language is developing in a contact situation, the more context-dependent it will become (at least towards the end of such a development).

This leads us to the issue as to whether there are simple languages and degrees of simplicity between languages at all. Of course there are simple languages, e.g. the earliest stages of child language (with two- or three-word utterances), all kinds of learner varieties (also called interlanguages) and compromise (trade) languages such as pidgins, to name some of the most obvious candidates (cf. also Gil, 2009, and for more a more theoretical discussion of linguistic complexity, Braunmüller, 2016).

Standardization belongs to this kind of change, since as a consequence of the process of language cultivation local varieties will be downgraded or completely given up, and many fine-grained distinctions (especially in the lexicon) will be dropped. On the other hand, speakers exposed to language standardization become new bilinguals in respect of their native linguistic knowledge, which will find its place as a more peripheral variety within this new diasystem. However, these individuals have to learn new rules, and they have to use more generalized (viz. underspecified) words and constructions for this new standardized language, while they will still adhere to their local dialect and its idiosyncrasies in face-to-face communication. The price to pay is the partial *reorganization* of their linguistic competence, but they will also win a broader range of communication skills.

Augmentative versus reductive changes

Strictly speaking, these two types of language change are two faces of the same coin. It seems to be a question of a benefit-cost analysis, i.e. which kind of development is the most favourable in certain situations and for the society to which those bilingual speakers belong: what one may win on the one hand has to be paid for on the other, in other words, a zero-sum game. But this also means that being a bi- or multilingual person is never a static state of affairs. The language you use most frequently in everyday life will occupy a much larger amount of your mental storage than the other language(s) you once learnt but now use infrequently or not at all. The crucial point of this scenario is that this development cannot be (fully) reversed at any time, i.e. the language used hardly at all for years or decades may vanish. It will become your weaker language and may in the long run show features that otherwise can be observed by (non-native) L2 learners. In other words, one (or more) of your native (or very early acquired) languages will be *unlearnt*. You will become a *heritage speaker* (cf. section on 'Some basic concepts', p. 298), with a fairly good receptive competence but with obvious deficits in the active use of this language, because calques from the dominant language will permanently enter your other language(s), for example as ad hoc replications (calques) and translinguistic wordings (also called 'negative transfer' or 'interferences').

Typological chain reactions

Typological chain reactions are *successive replications* from a proto-model language to a language that has borrowed some grammatical structures and later forms from another contact language, which in turn has integrated some grammatical replications earlier. We are here talking about language contact in terms of a third and/or fourth cycle. These replications in terms of chain reactions have not been described before but may represent a natural outcome of any secondary contact with contact (i.e. previously restructured) languages.

Such a process, which turns out to be rather complicated, can best be visualized by presenting a concrete example. Before discussing any details, one has to know that simple verbs in Ancient Germanic could only be modified by postposed particles (often identical with adverbs or prepositions, mirrored by the Modern English type: *to come/get/stand up*, *to look/search/wait for* etc.). Preverbal constructions (cf. the Modern English type *to forgive, to invent,* etc.) were unknown. Moreover, one has to recall that Latin was the dominant and model language for the elaboration of most non-Latin based vernaculars in western and central Europe since Late Antiquity. Some of these languages were not influenced directly by the model language Latin but later via intermediating contact languages. When translating texts of the Bible many new terms were needed, including more differentiated verb forms for rendering abstract (theological or philosophical) concepts. (An example of a productive Latin pattern of prefix verbs is the paradigm of *venire* 'to come': *convenire* 'to gather', *invenire* 'to invent', *obvenire* 'to gather; to provide', *pervenire* 'to arrive', *revenire* 'to come home', etc.) The Old High German translators code-copied (or replicated) many prefix verbs from Latin. Later Middle Low German authors did the same, but mostly based on southern German translations. In the Middle Ages and beyond, Danish, Swedish and Norwegian texts were inspired by the lingua franca of the Baltic, Low German, which soon gained ground in the Scandinavian countries based on intense trade activities during the era of the Hanseatic League. In the end, Low German became an important model language itself for the speakers of the Scandinavian vernaculars. On top of that, Luther's High German Bible translations influenced the remodelled Scandinavian languages and the norms in their texts to a high extent. This means that many West Germanic typological features (represented by the superstratal languages Low and High German) were code-copied into the North Germanic/Scandinavian vernaculars (especially into the bordering language, Danish). As mentioned above (see section on 'Covert code-mixing', p. 300), Faroese was heavily influenced by the colonial language Danish, which represented the dominant written language on the Faroe Islands up to the middle of the 20th century. At the end of this chain development, prefix verbs also entered the Faroese language via the contact language Danish. (Most of the prefix verbs that were earlier found in the sister language of Faroese, Icelandic, which also existed under the roof of the colonial language Danish, were later sorted out and banned due to strong puristic regulations.)

To cut a long story short and to conclude, prefix verbs became part of the Faroese language system via Danish, based on balanced local bilingualism, with Danish itself being influenced by Middle Low German, and Low German more or less influenced by High German, which was itself the first Germanic vernacular in central Europe that code-copied prefix verbs from Latin, motivated by the need to find equivalent verb constructions when translating texts of the Latin Bible, the Vulgate. This was a very challenging task and required sometimes radically new solutions (for details, see Braunmüller & Höder, 2012).

Invisible changes

Invisible changes are very strong candidates when it comes to explaining why grammatical systems undergo sustainable restructurings. The obvious question for which we have to find an answer is how this can happen. As is well known, all natural languages are encoded with a considerable amount of redundancy which is needed whenever, for example, disorders or interruptions in information interchange occur. But redundancy makes language learning more demanding and in principle more complicated than is absolutely necessary, although it also has advantages and we may rank some of the redundancies as alternative expressions, i.e. as (stylistic) *variation*. This means that any (elaborate) language displays several alternative possibilities in order to denote more or less the same content.

To give a simple example, one can say in English (a) *Peter cuts Mary a piece of cake* or (b) *Peter cuts a piece of cake for Mary*. The content of these utterances is by and large the same, although the phrase *for Mary* indicates some emphasis or contrast. If we assume that one has overlooked the (b) version when learning English, nothing dramatic will happen: only one alternative pattern has not become part of the learner's linguistic competence which, strictly speaking, does not really matter. In a similar way, Low German L2 learners of Medieval Scandinavian languages will probably have overlooked the possibility of using the V1 word order in declarative sentences, simply because this pattern was infrequent (or outdated) in colloquial Middle Low German. V1 declarative sentences have no obvious counterpart in these learners' L1 system, Low German, and would thus demand some effort to learn them. The default (unmarked) word order in declarative sentences is, however, SVO/V2, both in Low German and in Mainland Scandinavian languages. A very basic structure of one's L1 can therefore also be applied unchanged to the second (or target) language. By neglecting, or rather by overlooking, V1 declarative sentences nothing actually happened which might be called crucial when, for example, a German merchant, located in the Hanseatic trading place in Bergen (Norway), tried to learn Norwegian. But when in the end all Low German speakers fail to acquire this 'superfluous' V1 word order, its frequency in use will decrease, first among this particular group of L2 learners but later potentially also among the local population, if the German traders and craftsmen form a prestigious part of the population (as was actually the case) and influence the locally spoken norm. 'Invisible changes' such as ignoring equivalent structures may happen in any language learning process. Heine and Kuteva (2005: 158) have called such instances 'word-order change without word-order change'. This is not a contradictory statement as it seems to be at first glance; rather, it describes the unnoticed changes within the societal norm, often triggered by a group of L2 learners who did not acquire all equivalent alternative constructions of the target language. The ultimate result of such developments may be that the variation within a linguistic system to be learnt decreases, leaving behind what one may call the 'essence' of a grammatical system and ignoring much redundancy and variation. *Variation*, a well-known fact from sociolinguistic studies, can therefore be considered one of the primary sources of language change – a well-known fact that can be learned from studies in sociolinguistics. All other changes will suddenly become obvious and be considered mistakes as they cause violations of the linguistic system.

Language change due to incomplete second language acquisition

This kind of change can undoubtedly be considered the major cause of far-reaching restructurings of linguistic systems – in contrast to those theories that maintain that language change primarily occurs during its transmission from the parents' to the children's generation. But why should small children deviate from the medium that guaranties successful contact with their parents and other caretakers on whom they are ultimately depending? Of course, many errors and mistakes occur during this learning process, but they will be corrected (or in certain cases ignored) and will thus disappear as a consequence of absent reinforcement. Small children want to learn this vital code, along with many other things, in order to manage their lives successfully and become more and more independent. This does, however, not exclude *innovations*, e.g. caused by peer groups or when these young people become independent and enter other social groups and networks.

The decisive impact of changes due to SLA is the social power behind them – if practised by an influential group. Otherwise they will stigmatize their speakers' variety as 'foreigner talk'. But if those *deviations* from the societal norm that also may be called 'innovations' occur more frequently and are shared by other speakers of that speech community, then these deviations have a fair chance, at least in the long run, of becoming the default way of verbalization. In other words, the two steps accompanying SLA are (a) the modification of the societal norm and, in the long run, (b) some structural (or even typological) changes. Systemic changes without any preceding modification of the norm are most typical of the emergence of new contact languages such as jargons or pidgin languages, where far-reaching simplifications occur and where the grammars of the source languages are largely abandoned. To give two examples of changes caused by SLA:

i. The substitution of the Old English third person pronouns by Scandinavian pronouns (see p. 300) seems to be a counter example, because a direct change in the system of the core grammar of the target language itself occurred, but this is not really an adequate description of what happened. The Vikings, who learnt the local English varieties only incompletely and predominantly in face-to-face communication, simply used deictic pronouns and ignored the third person pronouns because they seemed to be 'superfluous', as other means of reference could do that job in the same way.

ii. During and after the very intense Low German-Scandinavian contact, not only the V1 declaratives (cf. section on 'Invisible changes', p. 309) vanished, but also the internal variation in the default SVO/V2 word order fossilized. As summarized [in English] in Braunmüller (2006), the variation in the constituents to the left of the finite verb, _VO, decreased. Whereas in all varieties of German, any constituent often emphasized/left-dislocated objects may be transferred into this position, subjects and (shorter) adverbs will primarily occur in this position in post-contact Scandinavian texts (in our sample, around 84%, both in older Danish and Swedish). Pronominal object forms are at least rare. The effect of this fossilization can still be noticed today, as prose texts in all Mainland Scandinavian languages have lost a considerable amount of their internal variation. Their texts reveal some remarkable uniformity. As far as the default sentence initial constituents are concerned, they are in most cases subjects and adverbs. Nominal objects have to be marked, e.g. by cleft sentences. These constructions are not very popular because they make texts clumsy. If someone intended to propose that this development is a direct consequence of the loss of case markings, one has to observe that only the reverse chronology really makes sense: unless the default word order has become fixed – subjects to the left and objects to the right of the finite verb V – inflectional endings could not be neglected or dropped, because this would have been harmful to the interpretation of the most basic syntactic relations. This can be demonstrated by a German sentence with OVS word order, e.g. *den Mann*$_{accusative}$ *beißt der Hund* [meaning: 'the dog bites the man']. This sentence pattern can, however, not be directly transferred into English because speakers of English (and of the Mainland Scandinavian languages) rely on the default SVO order such that the constituent immediately preceding the finite verb is the position of the subject (often the agent) of the sentence: **the man*$_{accusative}$ *bites the dog* – and not of an object constituent (unless it is a personal pronoun, where these languages have retained a distinction between subject and object pronouns, cf. Danish *ham*$_{object}$ *har jeg ikke set i lang tid* '[litt.] him I have not seen for a long time').

Societal, Lexical and Structural Traces of Change Based on Multilingualism

Inter-linguistic correspondences and transfer

As is well known, changes may leave behind some residual outdated structures which are still part of most native speakers' (receptive/'passive') linguistic competence. This is also the case with multilingual speakers: traces as well as remnants of outdated structures and items can be found in each of the diasystems, e.g. in some dialects or sociolects, in older texts or as stylistically highly marked words or constructions.

When becoming an L2 or L3 speaker of genetically related languages, outdated words in either language may help to strengthen the mental ties between the languages to be acquired. To give some examples, Scand. *smör/smør* 'butter' has historical equivalents in Ger. *Schmer* 'fat' and *Schmiere* 'grease', and Scand. *öl/øl* has a counterpart in Eng. *ale* (cf. also Dan. s<u>k</u>jorte [sǵj-]/Swed. s<u>k</u>jorta [ʃ-] 'shirt' versus English both <u>shirt</u> and <u>skirt</u>). Such etymological correspondences might be useful for (academic) L2 learners but will not automatically be noticed by 2L1-bilinguals because their acquisition process from birth is directly linked to the current language use of each of their parents.

Some translingual correspondences might, however, cause some misunderstandings; this is a well-known phenomenon, for example in unmediated inter-Scandinavian communication by means of the respective mother tongues (for more details, see Chapter 12 in this volume) but will disappear with more practice in this asymmetric form of communication. Very few of these divergences are harmful for sufficient mutual understanding, such as the differences between Swed. *by* 'village' and Dan. *by* 'town'. But there are also many diverging expressions for the same concept. These will, however, be learnt step by step with increased practice in this kind of communication. Consider here, for example, the divergent words for 'window': in Danish *vindue* (< Old Norse *vind-auga* 'wind-eye'; ≈ Eng. *wind|ow*) but in Swedish *fönster* (< Ger. *Fenster* < Lat. *fenestra*), or for 'flower': in Danish *blomst* versus Swedish *blomma*, whereas the corresponding verbs for 'to blossom' are the same: *blomstre/a*. Other pseudo-parallels, in language learning research ambiguously known as 'false friends', will obviously not be recognized at once. See for example Danish *rar* 'nice' and Norwegian *rar* 'strange': if you know that these words are misleading matches, you will try to avoid using them in the wrong way because you have obtained some comparative insights into the two linguistic systems you must cope with. In other words, you have already acquired an all-encompassing *metalinguistic competence* between these genetically related varieties, which gives you the opportunity to recognize coincidences and divergences between the two linguistic systems in question.

Even young children bilingual from birth (2L1) have such metalinguistic insights at their disposal. To give an example, my bilingual son (German-Danish) wondered as a boy of about four years why there is no direct 1:1 counterpart of German *Eisen|bahner* 'railwayman' in Danish – *isen|baner* – although both parts of this compound do occur in other Danish compounds: (a) *jern|bane* 'railway' (≈ Ger. *Eisen* 'iron' + *Bahn* 'railway') and (b) *isen|kræmmer* 'hardware dealer' (≈ Ger. [litt.] *Eisen|krämer* = sc. *Eisen-waren-händler*). This *metalinguistic awareness* has to be considered a vital part of the bilingual speakers' competence of genetically related languages because it makes the burden of mastering two closely related varieties easier to bear: these bilingual speakers are able to recognize cases where they can rely on cross-linguistic correspondences (here, in word formation), and they are also aware of all those cases where they need to learn words and structures separately. (L2 learners have no such insights at their immediate disposal.)

So far, so good, but when in the course of language history the almost symbiotic relations between Danish and German as the once preferred language for many purposes in Denmark (German was, for example, the language of command in the Danish army) were cut off due to political reasons (the Struensee Affair of 1772), it has become difficult for the Danish population living outside the Danish kingdom proper to follow up with the internal developments. Bilingual speakers have been used ever since for very many German-Danish *loan translations* and calques, which are now considered obsolete, having been replaced by other terms (cf. Older Dan. *afhang* [< Ger. *Abhang*] > Mod. Dan. *skråning* 'slope'; *bekomme* [< *bekommen*] > *opnå, få* 'to get'; or *opsats* [< *Aufsatz*] > *artikel, stil* 'essay'). (A similar development took place in the local dialects when the northern part of the Duchy of Schleswig became an integrated part of Denmark in 1920.) Translingual productive word formation patterns and word-for-word loan translations could no longer be used uncritically without offending the ruling language norms. Border-crossing communication was in earlier times no problem because many Danes were used to German as they are used to English today. But these Danish minority speakers south of today's border with Germany can no longer rely on the existence of the (non-activated) German language in Denmark. Moreover, they may risk not being understood without difficulty or that their way of using the Danish language seems to display features of SLA, which is obviously face threatening for a minority that has very strong sentiments towards Denmark and its culture. Also their potential role as mediators between Germans and Danes tends to become problematic because their way of speaking and writing Danish may show traces of *negative transfer* from the majority language, which they otherwise have to master perfectly. As a member of a bilingual minority outside the 'mother country' one must always cope with the difficulty that the majority language is the dominant language in almost every context, which actually turns out to became a danger in that your main or, rather, your preferred language might become the weaker language in the long run (cf. also Kühl, 2015, for the varieties of Danish as used on the Faroe Islands). This effect is, at least to a certain extent, inevitable because the whole social life and most of the relationships with other people take place in the majority language and its culture. Unimpeded transfers will facilitate their lives but are also a risk, not only for the integrity of the minority language but also for linguistic awareness. Genetically related varieties are especially vulnerable for unintended transfers and deviations from the societal norm.

The easiest and most frequent solution to be observed in such cases is to create *shortcuts* between these languages in order to make code-switching and everyday life easier.

(We have earlier mentioned this solution when describing the linguistic situation in the Faroe Islands; cf. section on 'Covert code-mixing', p. 300). Ad hoc solutions may occur as well as regionally conventionalized wordings, which help to bridge the gaps between the majority and minority languages. Communication will, however, not be endangered because these shortcuts are calques based on the majority language as a virtually underlying structure. Let me give two further examples, one from Swedish and the other from Low German language history.

Until 1809 Finland had been part of the Swedish kingdom for about 600 years. (From 1809 to 1917 Finland was part of Russia and then became independent.) After the political separation from Sweden as a consequence of the defeat of the Swedish army near Poltava in 1809, the local Swedish vernacular and their speakers came increasingly under the influence of the majority language, Finnish, which in the long run replaced the former colonial language, Swedish. The final result was that the genuine Swedish speaking population shrunk, both in terms of the native population and in their territories. As has been shown by Tandefelt (1988), it does not take more than three generations and mixed marriages to make Swedish disappear in a family: the starting point (1) is that two bilinguals with Swedish and Finnish as the dominant language, respectively, marry and have children; the next step (2) is asymmetric bilingualism, as the majority language Finnish now also represents the dominant language within this family; the last step (3) to be observed is that only remnants of the native Swedish language are passed on to the third generation, such as some songs, rhymes or poems. Strictly speaking, the death of Swedish as a native language already happens in this generation, if not yet completely then definitely in the following generation. (Similar developments were reported from immigrants and the loss of their inherited language.)

Today, the former politically and socially dominating Swedish population, now only about 5% of the total population, lives marginalized in some coastal areas in the northwest, the southwest and around the capital, Helsinki. Almost all of them are bilingual with a sufficient or even excellent command of Finnish. In spite of the rather close vicinity to the 'homeland' Sweden, their way of speaking Swedish is clearly different, both in pronunciation (with perceivable indirect influences from Finnish, such as non-aspirated *p*, *t*, *k*, no [ʉ] vowel and no retroflex consonants, etc.), in the lexicon and in some parts of their grammar. Generally speaking, the local Swedish variety spoken in Finland is in some instances more conservative compared to the standard language in Sweden (cf. for example, *sagde* 'said': Fi.-Swed. [`sɑːdə] versus Sw.-Swed. ['sɑː]). The main differences occur in the vocabularies: on the one hand, we find forms that are considered outdated in Sweden today, such as *aktionär* (Sw.-Swed. *aktieägare* 'share holder') or *lektor* (Sw.-Swed. *adjunkt* 'teacher at a grammar school'), which has a direct equivalent in Finnish *lehtori* and is a former loan translation from Swedish(!). On the other hand, there are direct translations from Finnish: *fylld kaka* < Fi. *täyte|kakku* versus Sw.-Swed. *tårta* (< Ger. *Torte*) 'fancy cake'. The Fi.-Swed. word can be regarded as semi-transparent for other speakers of Swedish because it contains the well-known noun *kaka*, which in other contexts just means 'cake', here: [litt.] 'filled cake'. But some words, such as *kavera* (Sw.-Swed. *prata*) 'to converse/to gossip' are totally incomprehensible without knowledge of the corresponding local Finnish terms.

The conclusion to be drawn is that *dislocated varieties* will in the long run definitely diverge from the norms of the (former) 'mother tongue'. They might develop into varieties in their own right, and become received vernaculars or even new national languages, as happened with American English < British English, Brazilian Portuguese < (European) Portuguese, or Afrikaans < Dutch, to name only a few examples. In all these instances some other local languages in contact are involved in these historical developments. This can best be observed when studying the so-called 'World Englishes', which is also the name of a journal dealing with the variation in the use of English in the world, often as a lingua franca, e.g. in Singapore or Hong Kong.

Upgrading a regional language must also be viewed from a bilingual speaker's perspective. It may happen that, for example due to nation building, the locally spoken variety becomes upgraded and is supposed to function now as the new standard language which should finally be able to cover all domains of everyday life.

As regional languages are ultimately linked to their speakers' *local identity*, it might be an option to revitalize, elaborate and expand this vernacular again, originally the first language in this region. It is therefore necessary to find many new L2 speakers who are willing to support this indigenous culture and identity by learning and practising this language, although it is on the decline and definitely not needed for managing everyday life in this region. Why should people learn a new language which has no longer any domains of its own? Just for fun or for demonstrating their local identity?

In the past decades, the process of attempting to revitalize a dying language has taken place in many regions of northern Germany, where local associations tried to promote the daily use of Low German among the local residents (cf. the slogan: *We snakt Platt* 'We speak [sc. are able to talk] Low German'). Meanwhile, Low German has become a teaching subject at schools, e.g. in Hamburg and Schleswig-Holstein, in conformity with the European Charter of Lesser Used Languages.

This is not the right place to discuss whether such efforts make sense and/or will be successful in the long run. The interesting aspect here is to look at the consequences for bilingualism. Is it possible to teach speakers of a northern German (colloquial) standard variety a genetically very closely related language, which was in former times a vital vernacular, spoken by farmers, craftsmen and many other people, but which has no distinct domain of its own any longer? What will happen when (half-proficient) L2 speakers try to speak this kind of school Low German to some older bilingual native speakers? Will they be generally accepted, will they be looked upon as some sort of *semi-speakers* (cf. also Dorian, 1981) or will the addressees rather feel treated as uneducated rural speakers who are not able to master the standard language?

When teaching this vernacular as an L2 in the classroom, one can build upon certain rules that distinguish Low from High German, e.g. the second (or Old High German) sound shift: *Appel ~ Abbel – Apfel* 'apple', *Schipp – Schiff* 'ship', *Water ~ Wodder – Wasser* 'water', *maken – machen* 'to make'; which facilitates the construction of many equivalents terms: *Apfel|kuchen > Abbel|koken* 'apple pie', *Mutter|sprache > Mod(d)er|spraak* 'mother tongue', etc. But these rules will also generate many pseudo or secondary terms, such as

Fuß|boden > **foot|bod(d)en* 'floor' instead of the genuine word *Deel* (cf. the by far less frequent Standard German equivalent *Diele*) or *Mohr|rübe* > **Moor|rööf* 'carrot' [Germanic *b̵* > *b/f*] instead of *Wuddel* (cf. Stand. Ger. *Wurzel* /-ts-/ 'root', in northern German varieties also meaning 'carrot', originally transferred from Low German). Further details about such bilingual speakers and their strategies can be retrieved from Hansen-Jaax (1995). Moreover, Höder (2014) has presented a diasystematic model based on the principles of construction grammar which is capable of mapping these closely related morphophonological varieties onto a unified model.

The main issue is whether it makes sense to re-establish or recreate new L2 bilinguals for cultural or folkloristic reasons. It might make some sense having lessons in vanishing vernaculars at elementary schools as far as very small minority languages, such as the (five?) North Frisian dialects, are concerned, where at least some of the oldest members of a family are able to speak this language proficiently. This fact may motivate children to learn, for example, grandma's language, especially when later practised together with her. But when teaching Low German by using L2 or semi-speakers as teachers (!), things will become problematic because they can never guarantee that their pupils will learn more than a superficially adopted version of Low German, based on Standard German syntax and, for example, ignoring the typical *doon* 'to do'-paraphrase in subordinated clauses. To come straight to the point: does it make sense to reverse language history and to re-establish a formerly existing *diglossia*, i.e. a functional distribution between a High and a Low variety, even though such a distribution no longer exists and has been replaced by different registers of (colloquial) Standard/High German?

Substrata and covert multilingualism in language history
Substratal influence and bilingualism

As is well known, languages change over time, which also has consequences for bi-/multilingual approaches. One of the outcomes may be that the internal dominance between two (or more) languages changes, for instance when one's dialect can no longer be used for trans-regional communication or when one language, e.g. Latin or French, recedes in importance as a lingua franca. More in-depth results can be observed when a vernacular is suppressed by a new language, due to occupation (cf. the heavy impact of Anglo-Norman French on English by the end of the 11th century and later on), or when a population of a certain region prefers the national language (for example, Standard French) and does not place special value on the local (e.g. Alemannic) dialect, as can be observed in Alsace and elsewhere (cf. also the case of Low German in the northern lowlands of Germany discussed above).

One of the results of such a development is that some *traces* of the (former) vernacular remain noticeable in the new preferred or dominating language, leaving structures behind that are caused by the L1 which violate some structures and norms of the recently acquired language. This kind of remnant has traditionally been called *substrata* in language history and presupposes *unbalanced bilingualism*.

A good example of traces of (Insular) Celtic dialects in English is the very special use of possessive pronouns when speaking about unalienable possessions (and articles of clothing), such as *he broke his leg*. This use of the possessive pronoun, more precisely of an internal possessive construction, has no equivalent in any other modern Germanic variety, as can be seen, for example, in the corresponding German translation: *er brach sich*$_{dative}$ *das Bein*$_{accusative}$ '[litt.] he broke himself the leg', which shows an external possessive construction and an 'affected' possessor. In these languages and in Old and Middle English texts as well, the reference to the subject is indicated by a reflexive pronoun (*sich*), followed by a definite noun phrase, whereas the modern English phrase marks reflexivity by using [± reflexive] possessive pronouns, following the rules of Old and Middle Celtic syntax. (The presupposed reading is 'his own leg', of course.) Translations into a Mainland Scandinavian language will result in phrases like Danish *han brak __ benet* 'he broke __ leg-the', where no reflexive pronoun will occur but no possessive pronoun either. In Insular Scandinavian, phrases like Faroese *fótin hjá mér* 'my foot' (litt. 'the foot at/with me') is the unmarked way to express an unalienable possession, again with an external possessor but again unlike modern English. More details of this special kind of impact from Insular Celtic varieties due to cross-linguistic transfer (and on other much earlier substratal influences due to contacts with a non-European language) can be retrieved in Vennemann (2002) and, from a more general perspective, in Vennemann (2011). The examples above illustrate how substratal structures may be used to reveal ancient bilingualism as those remnants reflect traces of incomplete SLA.

Deviant ways of using a language are normally considered mistakes and will be corrected at once by proficient speakers. But when all or a majority of L2 learners make the same mistakes, these deviations from the norm may in the end become accepted by most of the native speakers as well. (The opposite development, *superstratal* influence, has been dealt with in the section on 'Convergence: The only and inevitable outcome of language contact and change?', p. 303: Ger. *willkommen* zu ... and *nicht wirklich*, replicated from the dominant lingua franca English by native speakers of German.) Are interferential influences and mistakes made by (foreign) L2 learners and others rather a question of quantity and the degree of impact caused by a socially and/or economically dominant part of the society? The typological changes in the Mainland Scandinavian languages (cf. the transfer of Low German word formation and derivation patterns) due to a group of socially dominant speakers of Low German seem to support this hypothesis (cf. the survey in Braunmüller, 2005a).

Another case of substratal influence is the way of writing and producing texts in the oldest Germanic runic inscriptions. There is considerable evidence that Latin was the model language as far as the earliest Germanic writing practice is concerned. (The issue of the ultimate origin of the letters of the Germanic runic alphabet touches on a completely different matter of dispute, which cannot be discussed here; for the hitherto most convincing explanation, see Vennemann, 2015). Curse tablets, in Latin 'defixiones', and their performative functions have obviously been one of the most inspiring types of texts. Historical or documentary inscriptions and poems are unknown as far as the earliest period, the runic inscriptions written in the Older Futhark, is concerned.

To give a few examples: among others, we find (i) wordings without lexical meaning, so-called 'voces mysticae', e.g. Runic *gagaga ginu-ga* (spear shaft of Kragehul, early

6th century) as we also do in Roman texts, such as Latin *huat, hauat, huat, ista pista sista* or *dannabo dannaustra* (Önnerfors, 1991: 7); moreover, we find (ii) '(self-)speaking' or prosopopeial inscriptions, such as Runic *mk mrla wrta* 'I was made by Merila' (Etelhem, AD 450–500, starting with a marked object pronoun *mk* (= *mik*) 'me', almost consistently written without vowels); as well as (iii) inscriptions with hyperbata (i.e. a stylistically motivated separation of syntactically closely related terms), such as Runic *hariuha haitika farauisa | gibu̱ auja* 'Hariūha [i.e. the first among warriors] I am called, the travel-wise | I̱ give good luck' (on a bracteate from Sjælland/Køge, Denmark, about AD 500; cf. Antonsen, 1975: 65f.). In the normal unmarked word order, in Latin called 'ordo naturalis', this phrase should have been rendered as Run. *hariuha, farauisa, haitika* 'H., the travel-wise [apposition], I am called'.

However, there are many more indications that this Germanic speaking elite became acquainted with the Latin language, with classical rhetoric and generally with Latin culture and practices. Moreover, these writers were able to transfer their knowledge acquired by learning Latin as an L2 (cf. section on 'Preliminaries', p. 297), onto their native language. They also used (iv) the general Latin orthographical practice, as can best be seen from the use of the letter *c* for the phoneme /k/ in Germanic: *c* was the default letter for all allophones of /k/ in Latin whereas *k* only occurs in one single loan word from the (prestigious language) Greek, *kalendae* 'the first day of a month', and in the place name *Kartago*. Its form has nothing to do, as widely assumed in runology, with an intentional modification of the Roman capital letter *K*, where the writers have left out the 'I' and maintained only the '‹'.

(v) There is also some evidence that these Germanic writers (in the inscriptions called *erilar* [nom.sing.masc.]) code-copied parts of the passive inflection from Latin, because Ancient Germanic was a typical *contact language* that was heavily influenced by non-Indo-European L2 learners and had therefore lost many of its basic grammatical categories, such as: the passive mode (with very few remains in Gothic), almost all forms of the past tenses (among them the aorist), the future tense(s), the subjunctive (which was replaced by the optative mode), the locative and the ablative case (for my argumentation related to the replication of the Latin passive mode into early North-West Germanic, see Braunmüller, 2017).

Traces of covert multilingualism

As pointed out above, the relationship between two (or more) varieties spoken by an individual may change over the course of time. Such a situation may occur when the local population has to learn a new language because of changes in sovereignty. This happened in Norwegian history when this country came under the rule of Denmark in 1380 and became an integrated part of it. With the increase of literacy and scribality in the early 19th century, many Norwegians, especially those living in towns, had to acquire Danish as an L2, in both its written and oral forms, in order to manage their daily lives. They became (late) *sequential bilinguals* in a *diglossic* setting, with a local dialect as L1 and the low variety on the one hand and Danish as L2 and the high variety on the other. But their pronunciation still exhibited many features of their mostly rural dialects: they spoke varieties with overt traces of their home dialects and signs of SLA and imperfect language learning. 'Imperfect' means, in this case, that there was no need to completely achieve the norm of the target language Danish, as (a) Danish and the local Norwegian varieties were genetically closely related and thus to a certain degree mutually intelligible, and (b) this variety was exclusively used in Norway and in its modified way easier to understand for the local population than the non-customized Danish pronunciation, as spoken by the governmental representatives from the capital Copenhagen.

Similar observations can be made when the inhabitants of the Faroe Islands and Iceland speak the originally colonial language Danish. One can still hear that their pronunciation has been modified towards their own dialects, with the result that their version of Danish is easier to understand for many other Scandinavians than the fully idiomatic pronunciation of Danish. The ultimate reason for this observation is that Danish pronunciation has undergone several far-reaching weakening processing since the High Middle Ages, which have not come to an end yet. To give some examples:

i. the devoicing of the voiced obstruents in the interlude and coda (Dan. *b, d, g* > Norw. *p, t, k*: Dan. *kage* > Norw. *kake* 'cake'; 'Norw.' is understood here as Dano-Norwegian/*bokmål*); or

ii. the reinterpretation of the Danish orthography of the 19th century in terms of the locally used palatalizations: *kjær*-: Dan. [kʰæːʔR] versus Norw. [ç/(ʃ)æːr/(R)] or *gjort*: [gj-] > [j-] 'done' etc.

iii. Frequently used forms changed their lexical codifications because they were considered counterintuitive and confusing, such as: (α) the use of dissimilating *d*'s in orthography (Dan. *mand* [manʔ] > Norw. *mann* [manː] 'man', *falde* > *falle* 'to fall' – but with many exceptions, e.g. Norw. *kveld*; cf. Swed. *kväll*); (β) simplifications that are supposed to facilitate both pronunciation and spelling: Dan. *anden* > Norw. *annen* [aːnː] 'other; second', Dan. *tvivl* > Norw. *tvil* 'doubt', Dan. *give* [giː] > Norw. *gi* 'to give', or *blive* [bliː] > Norw. *bli* 'to become, remain'; (γ) reductions of the allomorphy in the Danish plural system (giving up the complementary distribution between *e*- and *er*- plurals: Dan. = Norw. *by|er* 'towns' versus Dan. *hest|e* turned into Norw. *hest|er* 'horses'); (δ) the simplification of inflectional morphology, which is characteristic of any form of SLA, such as adjectives in neuter singular and adverbs ending on -*ig* no longer inflect: -*ig* (Dan.: -*ig* versus -*igt*), preteritum and past perfect participles were merged: Dan. *vaskede*, *vasket* versus Norw. *vasket* (or *vaska*) 'washed'; (ε) simplifying the distributional use of prepositions, e.g. Dan. *kvart i tolv* versus Norw. *kvart på tolv* 'quarter to twelve' (*på* is the most general or least specified preposition in Scandinavian).

The result of all these and many other diverging developments is that the local Norwegian implementation of Danish shows several 'inconsistencies', especially in terms of pronunciation and orthography. Some former Danish pronunciations still occur and seem to remain for ever, e.g. the pronunciations of *regn* 'rain' /-ai-/ and *løgn* 'lie' /-oi-/ with (covert) diphthongs as in Danish. (However, exceptions of this kind do not occur in the other Norwegian variety New Norwegian/*nynorsk* as it has its roots in the local dialects. There, *regn* and *løgn/(lygn)* are pronounced as suggested by their spelling.) Other peculiarities occur in the contextually dependent and thus rather intricate pronunciation of the consonant cluster -*rd*-: *nord|lig* 'northern' [ˋnuːr.lɪ]

(< Dan. *nord* [noːʔ(R)/ɐ]) but *Norden* 'Scandinavia' [ˈnʊr.dən], occasionally with locally diverging realizations, e.g. in northern Norway (and parallel to Swedish) [ˈnuːɖən] with a retroflex *d*. (For more details on the nature of this kind of contact language, called 'creoloid' [in contrast to 'creole'], see Braunmüller, 2018.)

All these examples are supposed to give a more detailed impression of what might happen when speakers of closely related dialects had to practise another related language, but stuck to their habits in pronunciation on the one hand and tried to simplify some of the other features because this was possible without disturbing communication with speakers of (homeland) Danish and, furthermore, because it was socially accepted. A welcome side effect was the fact that the new local variety of Danish as spoken especially by the educated middle and upper class (called *dannet dagligtale*: 'educated colloquial speech') became more and more distinct from the original Danish language and could thus develop into a new variety in its own right. But the traces of multilingualism can still be observed.

This phenomenon may be called *covert multilingualism*, since some of the underlying dialectal structures can still be seen. Contrary to the idea of distinguishing between the activated and the invisible (but still present) non-activated language (cf. p. 299 on the interaction between languages), covert multilingualism can be seen in the activated language as either modifications of the common societal norm or as structural changes in the new language.

Different Forms of Multilingualism in Language History: A Short Survey

The main distinction to be made is between *individual* and *societal* multilingualism. In both cases the languages involved *interact* with each other but the outcomes are different.

There is a strong tendency for the individual bilingual speakers to minimize the cost of managing two (more or less diverging) languages side by side. Therefore it seems only natural to establish *shortcuts* between these languages, e.g. by congruent lexicalizations or, more generally speaking, by *converging* these languages to a certain extent. But convergences may come into conflict with societal norms. The least conflict laden way is to select and/or prefer only those grammatical structures that are closest to one's dominant (or first) language. Neglecting some structures will not conflict with societal norms, but will be at the expense of the stylistic variation of the other (weaker?) language. So one might feel inhibited when speaking the other language and will use it only when necessary. Proficient speakers of this variety might thus get the impression that your variety is more similar to a reasonably competent L2 learner than to a native speaker.

Other reasons may also be an obstacle to any converging attempts, such as the wish to indicate that your variety is different from similar dialects of the same language. So you might enlarge the differences to your fellow speakers by using hyperdialectisms (see p. 305, Point IV). All other causes for non-convergence are due to societal causes as well.

It may therefore happen that two varieties/languages remain stable although spoken in adjacent areas and in spite of the fact that they are genetically related. They may even diverge in order to emphasize more recent historical or political differences. Seen from a societal perspective, language contact will not always lead to converging structures but contact may also trigger *stability* and *divergence* between adjacent languages or dialects. The price for learning and memorizing all those (smaller) differences and idiosyncrasies might be high, but other arguments might be more important, which obviously justifies extra efforts and expenses. To give an example, in interactions with Germans, speakers of Swiss German will keep at least some of their special Swiss characteristics in phonetics and especially in vocabulary in order to indicate that they do not want to be considered Germans, but speakers of German in their own right. However, they have to know the corresponding expressions in the neighbours' variety (e.g. Swiss Ger. *allfällig* ≈ *etwaig* 'possible', *ūsschaffe* ≈ *ausweisen/*hin-ausschaffen* 'to expel', *büssen* ≈ *eine Strafe verhängen/*büßen* 'to inflict a punishment' or *öppis* ≈ *etwas* 'something'). Moreover, there are hundreds of Swiss German nouns which are totally incomprehensible for most speakers of German. Many Standard German expressions occur, however, in written texts, which in most cases follow a common German writing norm. Swiss speakers actually profit from the *media diglossia* in their country, but the other speakers of German, especially those in northern Germany will feel that this language is rather remote from their own German variety like, for example, Dutch, which is actually an offspring of Low German acknowledged after the Thirty Years' War in 1648.

Keeping the differences between genetically very closely related varieties alive is extremely difficult and demanding. That is why many inadvertently converging forms and structures will occur. In the end (partial) *convergences* will be an inevitable outcome. This development can best be studied in inter-Scandinavian communication. Danish, Norwegian and Swedish have formerly (and until Early Modern Times) been dialects of one and the same linguistic (dia)system, which split up into more or less distinct national varieties. These three languages are, however, still mutually intelligible. Ad hoc accommodations are therefore very common but not desirable, since they may come into conflict with the local lexical and phraseological usage. They are generally avoided in writing but acknowledged and sometimes even gratefully welcomed in face-to-face communication (see Braunmüller, 2002).

Cross-Scandinavian mixtures in text production will, however, not be accepted since convergences of that kind would threaten the national linguistic norms. Therefore one will find translations from Danish into Dano-Norwegian/*bokmål* and vice versa, although this is strictly speaking entirely unnecessary. But translations of foreign poems and novels into the national standard language are part of the national identity and therefore indispensable. (Even inter-Norwegian 'translations'/adaptations occur, such as theatre productions of Henrik Ibsen's dramas into from Dano- into New Norwegian – due to purely ideological reasons.) However, specialist literature as well as articles in journals will never be translated.

Receptive multilingualism has its primary domains in oral communication (permitting spontaneous queries in problematic cases), trade contacts or in scientific interchange. One of the main obstacles for this kind of communication is the laziness of the interlocutors/readers, since this kind of asymmetric communication involves learning divergent words and phrases and the activation of (potentially all) varieties of your own diasystem, especially some regional, stylistically highly marked as well as outdated forms (cf. Ház, 2005, for forms of *intercomprehension* between Dutch and Standard as well as Low German). A recent investigation has shown that English as the universal lingua franca threatens inter-Scandinavian communication for the youngest generation (cf. Delsing & Lundin Åkesson, 2005). This clearly shows that expanding the knowledge of one's own L1 diasystem and learning many correspondence rules as well as new or divergently used words is not a free good. Until recently, language history has shown that most Scandinavians were willing to make these extra efforts as they felt that this form of direct/unmediated communication would not only support the ancient historical ties but also the solidarity between the inhabitants of the Scandinavian countries. However, these insights and efforts seem to have now come to an end: the youngest generation have obviously considered the pros and cons of receptive multilingualism and the efforts needed for mastering English as an international languages with a high level of proficiency, and an increasing number of members of the younger generation have come to the conclusion that one has to learn English anyway, and that it does not make much sense to spend time and effort in distinguishing and learning local Scandinavian varieties. This attitude is gaining ground in all Scandinavian countries and it is the reason why this famous example of receptive (or asymmetric) multilingualism, often misleadingly called 'semi-communication' (a term coined by Haugen, 1966), is on the decline. On top of this, its model function can no longer be invoked when arguing for more direct ways of communication interchange within language families (for more details on the Scandinavian and the Slavic language family, see Besters-Dilger & Braunmüller, 2013).

This survey of some of the most important aspects of multilingualism in (European) language history has shown that in multilingualism we find *conflicting priorities* regarding the benefits for: (a) the individual when processing more than one standard language, often including some or most of their varieties; and (b) the individual as an integrated part of a social environment which values other arguments than brain economy and mental (here: cross-linguistic) shortcuts. Both aspects occur in language history, as demonstrated above, but in diverging and constantly changing parts.

Questions for Students' Reflection

1. What are the main differences between forms of current multilingualism and historical multilingualism?
2. How is multilingualism related to language contact? Give examples.
3. Languages in contact may converge, remain stable or may diverge. Give and interpret examples that you have come across and explain why these developments happened in that way.
4. What are model languages? Which effects may be triggered by them – and why?

Note

* This lecture is primarily based on the author's own research in this field and the examples mentioned are taken from Germanic languages. Unlike literature reviews and summarizing research surveys, this lecture gives priority to a coherent, readily accessible presentation of the subject and the currently discussed controversies. Preference is given to literature published in English. I would like to thank my colleague Juliane House for her help with proofreading and correcting this manuscript.

Suggestions for Further Reading

The following *reference books* should be available in most academic libraries and are thus easy to access. The articles or chapters suggested for further reading focus on important aspects of historical change and multilingualism. They are concise and deliver more details about topics that could not be examined here in more detail.

Bhatia, T.K. and Ritchie, W.C. (eds) (2014) *The Handbook of* **Bilingualism** (2nd edn). Malden, MA and Oxford: Blackwell; Articles No. 2 and 6.

Hickey, R. (ed.) (2010) *The Handbook of* **Language Contact**. Malden, MA and Oxford: Wiley-Blackwell; Articles No. 1, 7, 13 and 20.

Joseph, B.D. and Janda, R.D. (eds) *The Handbook of* **Historical Linguistics**. Malden, MA and Oxford: Blackwell; Articles No. 5, 18 and 23.

Matras, Y. (2009) **Language Contact**. Cambridge: Cambridge University Press; esp. Chapters 3, 6, 9 and 10.

Winford, D. (2003) *An Introduction to* **Contact Linguistics**. Malden, MA and Oxford: Blackwell.

Collections of case studies in European historical multilingualism may also be useful for obtaining deepening insights into the various mechanisms of linguistic change caused by individual and societal multilingualism:

Braunmüller, K. and Ferraresi, G. (eds) (2003) *Aspects of Multilingualism in European Language History*. Amsterdam and Philadelphia, PA: John Benjamins.

Filppula, M., Klemola, J. and Pitkänen, H. (eds) (2002) *The Celtic Roots of English*. Joensuu: University of Joensuu.

Stenroos, M., Mäkinen, M. and Særheim, I. (eds) (2012) *Language Contact and Development around the North Sea*. Amsterdam and Philadelphia, PA: John Benjamins.

Trotter, D.A. (ed.) (2000) *Multilingualism in Later Medieval Britain*. Woodbridge and Rochester, NY: Brewer.

References

Adams, J.N. (2003) *Bilingualism and the Latin Language*. Cambridge: Cambridge University Press.

Antonsen, E.H. (1975) *A Concise Grammar of the Older Runic Inscriptions*. Tübingen: Niemeyer.

Aronin, L. and Singleton, D. (2012) *Multilingualism*. Amsterdam and Philadelphia, PA: John Benjamins.

Benmamoun, E., Montrul, S. and Polinsky, M. (2013) Heritage languages and their speakers: Opportunities and challenges for linguistics. *Theoretical Linguistics* 39, 129–181.

Besters-Dilger, J. and Braunmüller, K. (2013) Sociolinguistic and areal factors promoting or inhibiting convergence within language families. In J. Besters-Dilger, C. Dermarkar, S. Pfänder and A. Rabus (eds) *Congruence in Contact-induced Language Change: Language Families, Typological Resemblance, and Perceived Similarity* (pp. 390–410). Berlin and Boston, MA: De Gruyter.

Braunmüller, K. (2000) On types of multilingualism in Northern Europe in the late Middle Ages: Language mixing and semicommunication. In G. Thórhallsdóttir (ed.) *The Nordic Languages and Modern Linguistics* (pp. 61–70). Reykjavik: Institute of Linguistics.

Braunmüller, K. (2002) Semicommunication and accommodation: observations from the linguistic situation in Scandinavia. *International Journal of Applied Linguistics* 12, 1–23.

Braunmüller, K. (2005a) Language contacts in the Late Middle Ages and in Early Modern Times. In O. Bandle, K. Braunmüller, E.H. Jahr, A. Karker, H.-P. Naumann and U. Teleman (eds) *The Nordic Languages: An International Handbook of the History of the North Germanic Languages, Vol. 2* (pp. 1222–1233). Berlin and New York: De Gruyter.

Braunmüller, K. (2005b) Variation in word order in the oldest Germanic runic inscriptions: A case for bilingualism? *Papers on Scandinavian and Germanic Language and Culture*. NOWELE, Vol. 46/47 (pp. 15–30). Odense: University Press of Southern Denmark. [Many more details on that issue can be retrieved from Braunmüller, K. (2004) Zum Einfluss des Lateinischen auf die ältesten Runeninschriften. In O. Bandle, J. Glauser and S. Würth (eds) *Verschränkung der Kulturen. Der Sprach- und Literaturaustausch zwischen Skandinavien und den deutschsprachigen Ländern* (pp.23–50). Tübingen and Basel: Francke.]

Braunmüller, K. (2006) Left periphery of C – a vulnerable domain in language contact situations? Studies in older Danish and Swedish syntax and discourse structure. In W. Kürschner and R. Rapp (eds) *Linguistik International. Festschrift für Heinrich Weber* (pp. 41–49). Lengerich: Pabst. [A more detailed analysis is to be found in: Braunmüller, K. (2006) Wortstellung und Sprachkontakt: Untersuchungen zum Vorfeld und Nebensatz im älteren Dänischen und Schwedischen. *Amsterdamer Beiträge zur älteren Germanistik* 62, 207–241.]

Braunmüller, K. (2009) Converging genetically related languages: *Endstation code mixing*? In K. Braunmüller and J. House (eds) *Convergence and Divergence in Language Contact Situations* (pp. 53–69). Amsterdam and Philadelphia, PA: John Benjamins.

Braunmüller, K. (2010) On the role of finite verbs in overtly mixed and in converged languages. In M. Petzell, K. Jóhannesson, I. Larsson, S.-G. Malmgren, L. Rogström and E. Sköldberg (eds) *Bo65. Festskrift till Bo Ralph* (pp. 242–251). Göteborg: Göteborgs Universitet (*Meijerbergs arkiv för svensk ordforskning* 39).

Braunmüller, K. (2015) Competing tendencies in Germanic pronominal and deictic systems: The most general principle will prevail. In M. Hilpert, J.-O. Östman, C. Mertzlufft, M. Rießler and J. Duke (eds) *New Trends in Nordic and General Linguistics* (pp. 11–27). Berlin, Munich and Boston, MA: De Gruyter.

Braunmüller, K. (2016) On the origins of complexity: Evidence from Germanic. In G. Seiler and R. Baechler (eds) *Complexity and Isolation* (pp. 47–69). Berlin, Munich and Boston, MA: De Gruyter.

Braunmüller, K. (2017) Zum Passiv im Nordgermanischen: Drei unterschiedliche Ansätze zur Wiedereinführung einer verloren gegangenen grammatischen Kategorie. *Årsbok 2015* of the *Kungl. Humanistiska Vetenskaps-Samfundet i Uppsala* (pp. 5–27). Uppsala: Swedish Science Press.

Braunmüller, K. (2018) Creating a creoloid as a national language: The case of Dano-Norwegian. In E. Håkon Jahr (ed.) *Perspectives on Two Centuries of Norwegian Language Planning and Policy: Theoretical Implications and Practical Lessons.* Uppsala: Gustav Adolf's Academy.

Braunmüller, K. and Höder, S. (2012) The history of complex verbs in Scandinavian languages revisited: Only influence due to contact with Low German? In E. Håkon Jahr and L. Elmevik (eds) *Contact between Low German and Scandinavian in the Late Middle Ages: 25 Years of Research* (pp. 151–169). Uppsala: Gustav Adolf's Academy.

Delsing, L.-O. and Lundin Åkesson, K. (eds) (2005) *Håller språket ihop Norden?* [*Does the Language Hold the Nordic Countries Together?*]. Copenhagen: Nordic Council of Ministers.

Dorian, N. (1981) *Language Death: The Life Cycle of a Scottish Gaelic Dialect.* Philadelphia, PA: University of Pennsylvania Press.

Gil, D. (2009) How much grammar does it take to sail a boat? In G. Sampson, D. Gil and P. Trudgill (eds) *Language Complexity as an Evolving Variable* (pp. 19–33). Oxford: Oxford University Press.

Grosjean, F. (2010) *Bilingual: Life and Reality.* Cambridge, MA and London: Harvard University Press.

Hansen-Jaax, D. (1995) *Transfer bei Diglossie. Synchrone Sprachkontaktphänomene im Niederdeutschen.* Hamburg: Kovač.

Haugen, E. (1966) Semicommunication: The language gap in Scandinavia. *Sociological Inquiry* 36, 280–297.

Ház, É. (2005) *Deutsche und Niederländer. Untersuchungen zur Möglichkeit einer unmittelbaren Verständigung.* Hamburg: Kovač.

Heine, B. and Kuteva, T. (2005) *Language Contact and Grammatical Change.* Cambridge: Cambridge University Press.

Höder, S. (2014) Phonological elements and diasystematic construction grammar. *Constructions and Frames* 6 (2), 202–231.

Jahr, E.H. (2014) *Language Planning as a Sociolinguistic Experiment: The Case of Modern Norwegian.* Edinburgh: Edinburgh University Press.

Johanson, L. (2008) Remodeling grammar: Copying, conventionalization, grammaticalization. In P. Siemund and N. Kintana (eds) *Language Contact and Contact Languages* (pp. 61–79). Amsterdam and Philadelphia, PA: John Benjamins.

Kiesler, R. (2006) *Einführung in die Problematik des Vulgärlateins.* Tübingen: Niemeyer.

Kühl, K. (2015) Faroe Danish: An unknown variety. In E. Torgersen, S. Hårstad, B. Mæhlum and U. Røyneland (eds) *Language Variation – European Perspectives V* (pp. 157–168). Amsterdam and Philadelphia, PA: John Benjamins.

Kühl, K. and Braunmüller, K. (2014) Linguistic stability and divergence: An extended perspective on language contact. In K. Braunmüller, S. Höder and K. Kühl (eds) *Stability and Divergence in Language Contact: Factors and Mechanisms* (pp. 13–38). Amsterdam and Philadelphia, PA: John Benjamins.

Labov, W. (1972) Some principles of linguistic methodology. *Language in Society* 1, 97–120.

Matras, Y. (2009) *Language Contact.* Cambridge: Cambridge University Press.

McWhorter, J. (2007) *Language Interrupted: Signs of Non-native Acquisition in Standard Language Grammars.* Oxford: Oxford University Press.

Montrul, S.A. (2008) *Incomplete Acquisition in Bilingualism: Re-examining the Age Factor.* Amsterdam and Philadelphia, PA: John Benjamins.

Muysken, P. (2000) *Bilingual Speech: A Typology of Code-mixing.* Cambridge: Cambridge University Press.

Önnerfors, A. (1991) *Antike Zaubersprüche: Griechisch/Lateinisch/Deutsch.* Stuttgart: Reclam.

Petersen, H.P. (2010) *The Dynamics of Faroese-Danish Language Contact.* Heidelberg: Winter.

Schendl, H. (2000) Linguistic aspects of code-switching in medieval English texts. In D.A. Trotter (ed.) *Multilingualism in Later Medieval Britain* (pp. 77–92). Woodbridge and Rochester, NY: Brewer.

Stolt, B. (1964) *Die Sprachmischung in Luthers Tischreden: Studien zum Problem der Zweisprachigkeit.* Stockholm: Almqvist and Wiksell.

Tandefelt, M. (1988) *Mellan två språk: en fallstudie om språkbevarande och språkbyte i Finland.* [*Between Two Languages: A Case Study on Language Retention and Language Shift in Finland*]. Uppsala: University.

Trudgill, P. (1988) Dialect contact and interdialect in linguistic change. In J. Fisiak (ed.) *Historical Dialectology: Regional and Social* (pp. 555–564). Berlin and New York: Mouton de Gruyter.

Trudgill, P. (2011) *Sociolinguistic Typology: Social Determinants of Linguistic Complexity.* Oxford: Oxford University Press.

Vennemann, T. (2002) On the rise of 'Celtic' syntax in Middle English. In P.J. Lucas and A.M. Lucas (eds) *Middle English from Tongue to Text: Selected Papers from the Third International Conference on Middle English: Language and Text, held at Dublin, Ireland, 14 July 1999* (pp. 203–234). Frankfurt am Main: Peter Lang.

Vennemann, T. (2011) English as a contact language: Typology and comparison. *Anglia* 129, 217–257.

Vennemann, T. (2015) Origins of runic writing: A comparison of theories. In R. Mailhammer, T. Vennemann, gen. Nierfeld and B.A. Olsen (eds) *The Linguistic Roots of Europe* (pp. 295–341). Copenhagen: Museum Tusculanum.

Weinreich, U. (1954) Is a structural dialectology possible? *Word* 10, 388–400.

Wright, L. (1996) *Sources of London English: Medieval Thames Vocabulary.* Oxford: Clarendon Press.

Lecture 12

Receptive Multilingualism

Jan D. ten Thije[1]

Introduction

Receptive multilingualism (RM) refers to the communicative mode by which interlocutors use different languages and still understand each other on the basis of the passive language competencies of each interlocutor. This communicative mode has been used ever since the Middle Ages, as languages were not yet standardized at that time and various multilingual modes were applied by travellers in interlingual contacts. Recently, attention to RM has increased considerably as this mode facilitates mutual understanding in times of structural mobility and worldwide transnational and international cooperation. Researchers from the social sciences and humanities contribute to this field of research by analyzing its core issues such as mutual intelligibility, occurrence in different communicative practices, language planning, acquisition and educational impact. In actual fact, studies of RM profit from multi- and interdisciplinary approaches that sometimes use different names to denote this communicative mode. Therefore, this lecture begins by next discussing terminology: the notions you may find in the literature are considered in their different theoretical and social backgrounds. In the subsequent sections an overview is given regarding the linguistic and social features that characterize this phenomenon. These sections concern intelligibility, occurrence, choice, interaction and planning. In the conclusion it is stated that many everyday language users apply RM without being aware of doing so. If their awareness were raised, they might be able to handle the potential and the restrictions of RM more adequately.

Terminology

Although scientific awareness nowadays suggests that RM is a recent phenomenon in Europe related to labour mobility and globalization, it has to be said that actually the concept of monolingualism has a shorter history than is generally assumed, since it results from the emergence of nation-states predominantly in the 18th century. The process of the homogenization of one language variant into the national standard in many – not all – European countries brought an end to the multilingualism that in fact was the default for a very long time. No factual documentation is available, but written documents reveal that communication between foreigners was not infrequently realized on the basis of the simultaneous use of a multitude of dialects and languages (Braunmüller, 1995, 2007; Vogl, 2012). In fact, the concept of one national language was not yet developed at that time. Consequently, communicative practices of RM in which interlocutors understand each other on the basis of some receptive knowledge of the other's linguistic repertoire, each making productive use of his/her own verbal and non-verbal repertoire, could have been the default in many contacts.

The multilingual constellation in the Middle Ages may resemble situations nowadays where people travel to foreign countries where they do not know the local languages and a lingua franca (English, French, Spanish, Arabic, Mandarin) is not always an option. What people often do under such conditions is just start talking and gesturing according to all the communicative conventions they have at their disposal and see if they can reach a minimum of understanding. Often they do reach the communicative purposes they were aiming for. The underlying theoretical point here is that *native competence* or *native speaker* are not the concepts we need in order to clarify success in these communicative events (Coulmas, 1981). It makes more sense to consider and elaborate concepts such as *multilingual repertoire* and *multilingual speaker* in order to understand how these communicative efforts can be successful at all (Grosjean, 1982). We will come back to these theoretical concepts later from different disciplinary perspectives. In any case, we have created a starting point to introducing the notions that have been proposed to denote the phenomenon of RM.

Table 12.1 contains 10 concepts that have been proposed over the years to cover the phenomenon of RM. The origin of all these concepts is somehow related to the formation and growth of sociolinguistics and pragmalinguistics, starting in the 1960s. These new disciplines studied language variation, language contact and speech actions on the one hand and language acquisition and language teaching in formal and non-formal learning situations on the other. In fact, the development of these concepts reflects the paradigmatic switch within linguistics from a formal paradigm (Chomsky, 1957) to a functional paradigm (Hymes, 1972).

The concepts of *receptive bilingualism* (Hockett, 1958), *mutual intelligibility of closely related languages* (Wolff, 1959) and *semi-communication* (Haugen, 1987) orient themselves more to the formal paradigm since they investigate *intelligibility* among related languages or dialects due to *close genetic relationship* (e.g. syntactic, lexical, phonological and phonetic characteristics). Semi-communication presumes that similarity can occur in the linguistic

Table 12.1 *Receptive multilingualism and its related concepts*

Semi-communication (Haugen, 1953, 1966, 1987)
Receptive bilingualism (Hockett, 1958)
Mutual intelligibility of closely related languages (Gooskens & Van Bezooijen, 2013; Wolff, 1959)
Polyglot dialogue (Posner, 1991)
Plurilingualism (CoE, 2001)
Pluri-lingual discourse (Clyne, 2003)
Intercompréhension (Meissner, 2008)
Plurilingual repertoire (Lüdi, 2007)
Receptive multilingualism (Braunmüller, 2007)
Lingua receptiva (Rehbein *et al.*, 2012)

forms of different languages, and that reaching understanding requires little education and/or practice in a non-native language with such similarities to one's own language. This concept assumes an incomplete mode of communication in which only a kind of 'half-understanding' takes place: 'semi-communication, the trickle of messages through a rather high level of "code-noise"' (Haugen, 1966: 153). In contrast, the concept of *receptive bilingualism* (Hockett, 1958) emphasizes the benefits rather than the shortcomings of making use of the similarities of your first language to another language in order to understand speakers of the latter. Hockett (1958) states:

> Among educated Danes and Norwegians, however, communication is quite unimpeded: each speaks his own personal variety of his own language, but has learned by experience to understand the speech patterns of the others. The result may be called semi-bilingualism: receptive bilingualism accompanying productive monolingualism. (Hockett, 1958: 327)

In actual fact, the concept of semi communication is rather confusing since it remains unclear what is meant by *semi*, exactly.

In sum, the focus of interest of these three concepts remains on the formal linguistic characteristics and, therefore, these concepts align more with the formal paradigm.

Concepts in the category covering the range from *polyglot dialogue* (Posner, 1991) to *lingua receptiva* (Rehbein *et al.*, 2012) take *language use* as the central focus of investigation and, therefore, seem to be oriented more to the functional paradigm in linguistics. The differences associated with the latter concepts can be understood from the societal domains and fields of interest in which they have been developed. *Plurilingualism* (CoE, 2001) and *Intercompréhension* (Meissner, 2008) originate primarily from studies into language teaching, whereas *Pluri-lingual discourse* (Clyne, 2003), *plurilingual repertoire* (Lüdi, 2007) and *lingua receptiva* (Rehbein *et al.*, 2012) were developed in discourse analyses concerned with authentic multilingual communication (e.g. workplace, family interaction or professional communication). Since all the latter concepts integrate more and more pragmatic and discursive characteristics of multilingual communication, they align more to the functional paradigm within linguistics.

An important distinction between all the concepts represented in Table 12.1 concerns the typological distances between the languages that are covered by the concepts. The key notion in this perspective is *language family* (e.g. the Germanic, Romance, Slavic and Finno-Ugric families of languages). The concepts of *mutual intelligibility, receptive bilingualism, semi-communication* and *receptive multilingualism* (Braunmüller, 2007) refer to the potential understanding between native speakers of typologically related languages. This relates to the understanding between speakers of different languages within the same language family – for instance, when a Danish speaker communicates with a Swedish speaker. These other concepts also cover cases of understanding between speakers across language family borders – for instance, when a speaker of German understands a speaker of French. Whereas the former concepts primarily rely on the formal linguistic characteristics in order to explain mutual comprehension, the latter also incorporate functional characteristics (such as proficiency, exposure, interaction and attitude) to construe potential mutual understanding.

Verschik (2012) proposes the distinction between *inherent* and *acquired* receptive multilingualism in order to clarify the explanatory power of the various concepts in Table 12.1. She states that the distinction between inherent and acquired RM can be compared to a dichotomy between languages that are mutually intelligible and those that are not. The acquisition of receptive competencies in a second language (L2) facilitates interaction with first language (L1) speakers of that language. The important issue for studies of RM concerns the question of what is the degree of acquisition or threshold competence that is needed for minimal understanding. The hypothesis would be that: the more the languages are typologically distanced, the more acquisition is prerequisite for achieving mutual understanding.

The question of the degree of minimal understanding also has historical cultural and ideological dimensions. For instance, in case of Scandinavian languages the mutual understanding has been influenced by the pan-Scandinavian movement and identity that positively determined the attitude and intention towards mutual understanding (Doetjes, 2007). In contrast, especially after WWII, German-Dutch RM was for a long time determined by negative attitudes (Beerkens, 2010). When people do not want to understand each other, typological closeness seems to be of little or no importance.

With respect to the incorporation of languages involved in RM, the concept of *lingua receptiva* has the broadest coverage. In actual fact, this concept also covers multilingual constellations that are not included in the other concepts. According to Rehbein *et al.* (2012), *lingua receptiva* also refers to multilingual interaction in which speakers do not use their L1 but another language – an L2 or a lingua franca – in order to attain understanding. For instance, an L1 speaker of Estonian may use English for interaction with a speaker of Dutch when the Estonian speaker understands Dutch but the Dutch speaker does not understand Estonian and receptively understands English.

Another dimension that should be discussed when elaborating the various RM notions concerns the distinctions between oral versus written communication. The processes of understanding differ in oral and written communication. Reading a text in an unknown language is often easier then hearing someone speaking an unknown language. One can reread the text and make use of orthographic and other similarities with other known languages in order to reconstruct its meaning, whereas speech is evanescent, which implies the impossibility of rehearing the utterance without an interactive move to invite the interlocutor to do so in face-to-face communication. Moreover, sound correspondences between languages are often not immediately recognizable. On the other hand, RM in oral communication is facilitated by other communication means, such as gesturing, face expression and intonation which are not or are less available in written communication. Some notions have been developed and studied especially in face-to-face interaction, such as polyglot dialogue, plurilingual discourse and plurilingual repertoire, whereas other concepts have been primarily investigated in written communication (e.g. reading), such as intercomprehension. The other concepts have been used for the analysis of RM in oral and written as well as mediated communication.

In conclusion, the phenomenon of RM has been defined over the last four decades by more than 10 different concepts. The quintessence of all these concepts is that they address the multilingual mode in which interlocutors use different language variants and still understand each other on the basis of receptive knowledge of the language in which they do not have productive proficiency. In short, one asks a question in a language one knows and gets an answer in a language one does know at least receptively. The concepts differ primarily in terms of the coverage of the language combinations that can be explained (e.g. *closely related* versus *not related languages*) and, secondly, in terms of the formal and/or functional paradigms within linguistics and the corresponding interactive, social and cognitive processes of RM on which they focus. The next section discusses mutual intelligibility in more detail.

Intelligibility

Mutual intelligibility studies concentrate on the question of how linguistic and non-linguistic factors may account for potential understanding between closely related languages. This research has a long tradition starting especially with studies of the Scandinavian languages. In fact RM between Norwegian, Swedish and Danish has been one of cornerstones of the pan-Scandinavian movement and identity (Doetjes, 2007), as was mentioned earlier. Haugen (1953) was the investigator who started to research the mutual intelligibility between Nordic languages by developing the use of questionnaires asking people whether they understood other related dialects.

Nowadays, the linguistic scope has expanded and the relevant research instruments have grown tremendously in sophistication. Scandinavian languages are still being studied, however, in the more general framework of the Germanic languages. Other closely related languages are also being investigated within the framework of the Romance languages and Slavic language family, respectively (see Table 12.2 for details).

Gooskens (2013) provides an overview of methods for measuring mutual intelligibility between closely related languages. Work on the instrumentation for investigating mutual

Table 12.2 *Research into the mutual intelligibility of closely related languages in Europe*

Germanic languages (Beerkens, 2010; Braunmüller, 2002; Gooskens & Van Bezooijen, 2013; Haugen, 1967, 1987; Ház, 2005; Marx, 2012; Schüppert, 2011; Swarte, 2016; Zeevaert, 2004)
Romance languages (Conti & Grin, 2008; Jensen, 1989)
Slavic languages (Golubović, 2016; Kompasová, 1999/2000; Nekvapil, 2013)

intelligibility and language attitude has drawn on sociolinguistic and psycholinguistic expertise. Gooskens and Van Heuven (2017) developed the following test battery: a word recognition test, cloze tests, a picture test and a word translation test. These tests are applied in experimental settings between closely related languages within the language families mentioned above. They address the following research questions. In the first place, researchers aim to document mutual intelligibility with special attention to the symmetry regarding the intelligibility of related languages. For instance, does a native Danish speaker understand Swedish more easily than, vice versa, a Swedish speaker can understand Danish, which apparently is an issue (Schüppert, 2011). Secondly, researchers aim to explain their results by correlating their findings to linguistic factors (lexical, phonetic, orthographic, morphological and syntactic distances) and (what they call) non-linguistic factors such as language contact, exposure and attitude towards the other language and culture. Finally, they are interested in the explanation of their findings with respect to genealogical relations within the language families which have been reconstructed by historical and typological linguists (Gooskens *et al.*, 2017).

In sum, this research programme combines sociolinguistic, psycholinguistic and language typological expertise and can be oriented within the formal paradigm. This research tradition does not aim to explain processes of *real* understanding of speakers and hearers in multilingual interaction both using their different native tongues, but rather seeks to account for *potential* understanding between native speakers and hearers and writers and readers of related languages on the basis of primarily structural linguistic (e.g. syntactic, morphological, lexical, phonetic or phonological) characteristics.

Until recently, the intelligibility studies consisted primarily of studies focusing on one language family (see Table 12.2); however, a recent large-scale research project on 'Mutual Intelligibility between Closely Related Languages' (MICReLA) has changed this scene (Gooskens & Van Heuven, 2017; Gooskens *et al.*, 2017). This project compares mutual intelligibility between 16 closely related European languages within three language families (see Table 12.3). This is an extraordinary example of research in this field; we discuss the relevant results since they survey the state of affairs in this tradition.

The project developed an online test battery consisting of six tests (e.g. word recognition, cloze text, text understanding in both an oral and written format). Data from about 13,000 (out of a broader dataset of 40,000) respondents were analyzed. The respondents included highly educated men and women in the age range 18–34 years, who were born and raised in one of the 16 relevant countries. The 16 languages included in the study are the standard languages of the respective nation-states. If a language is an official language in more than one country, they only included the variety from the country with the largest number of speakers. For example, Dutch is an official national language in both Belgium and the

Table 12.3 *Languages studied in the MICReLA project*

Germanic		Romance		Slavic	
Danish	Da	French	Fr	Bulgarian	Bu
Dutch	Du	Italian	It	Croatian	Cr
English	En	Portuguese	Pt	Czech	Cz
German	Ge	Romanian	Ro	Polish	Pl
Swedish	Sw	Spanish	Sp	Slovak	Sk
				Slovene	Sn

Source: Gooskens and Van Heuven (2017, in preparation); Gooskens *et al.* (2017).

Netherlands, but since the larger number of speakers lives in the Netherlands, Netherlandic Dutch was included as test language and Flemish Dutch was not. A questionnaire collected non-linguistic data of respondents (e.g. attitude, exposure and education).

The results of the intelligibility measure on the basis of spoken cloze tests are presented in Figure 12.1: Germanic languages, Romance languages and Slavic languages (Gooskens *et al.*, 2017). The study reveals that 'mutual intelligibility between related languages within the three major language families within Europe, differs per language family' (Gooskens *et al.*, 2017). The figures also reveal that intelligibility within one language family differs enormously. A huge difference in understanding is found within combinations with English. English is well understood by Dutch, Danish, Swedish and German listeners ranging from 94% down to 86%, but the other way around the understanding is around 8–28%. In the Romance family the top scores can be found in Romanian participants listening to, in descending order, Italian (58%), Spanish (54%), French (47%) and Portuguese (23%). Romanian, on the other hand, is barely understood by listeners of other languages. The highest degree of mutual intelligibility within the Slavic family is found for Slovak for Czech listeners (93%) and Czech for Slovak listeners (95%), followed by Slovene for Croatian listeners (44%) and Croatian for Slovene listeners (79%). Mutual intelligibility within the Slavic family in general emerges as lower than in the other two language families.

With regard to the explanation of intelligibility, the study reveals that non-linguistic factors are more important than linguistic factors. Especially *exposure* has a high predictive value for mutual intelligibility. The authors state that positive or negative attitudes towards the stimulus language do not make a significant contribution to the prediction of mutual intelligibility (Gooskens & Van Heuven, in preparation).

The MICReLA study is an important contribution to the field of RM, because for the first time a survey is available that compares mutual intelligibility within and between the three greatest language families in Europe. The ranking of language pairs within the three families clearly reveals the asymmetry in understanding and enables comparison between the families. The finding that exposure has the most explanatory power to account for all these relationships is an important outcome which has impact on language education and language planning, as we will discuss in more detail in the penultimate section on Planning.

Part 4: Forms of Multilingualism in the Past and Present

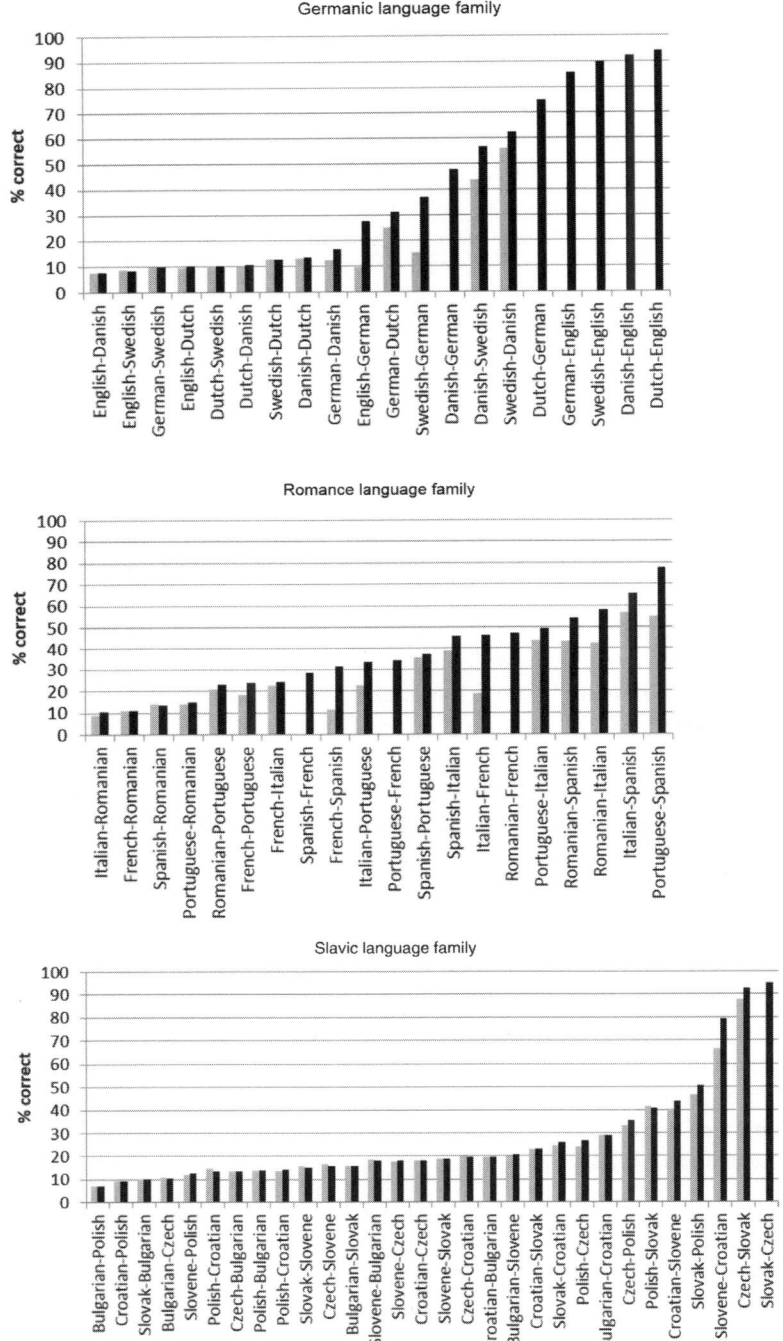

Figure 12.1 Mutual intelligibility in Germanic, Romance and Slavic language families
Source: Gooskens et al. (2017).

Some critical questions can be formulated regarding the MICReLA results. First, because of the large scale of the project, the researchers chose to consider only nation-states with a single standard national language as units of analysis. Nation-states with multilingual traditions (e.g. Switzerland and Belgium) were excluded. This may have reduced the coverage of the outcomes regarding mutual intelligibility, since the inhabitants of these multilingual countries might have been more experienced in and exposed to RM (for Switzerland, see Lüdi, 2007). Secondly, the outcome that *language attitude* does not influence mutual intelligibility was only based on one question in the questionnaire ('Do you like language X?', Gooskens & Van Heuven, in preparation). Language attitude also regularly refers to attitudes towards speakers of that language and the country and cultures in which the language is spoken. If these aspects had been included the outcomes could have been different. For instance, Rehbein and Romaniuk (2014) developed a Pragmatic Index of Language Distance (PILaD) usable to measure mutual understanding in RM. This model also includes discourse characteristics such as attitude of the speaker–hearer interaction, which will be discussed below.

In the next section we first focus on the occurrence of RM; this communicative mode appears to be a phenomenon in cross-border communication, in particular regions and in specific transnational and international institutions.

Occurrence

Sociolinguistic research poses the question as to which linguistic and social factors determine the occurrence and success of RM in various multilingual and organizational settings. Table 12.4 contains reference to research that documents RM in transnational situations, multilingual regions and cross-border contacts.

The first empirical studies regarding RM were carried out in Scandinavia. As we stated earlier, it was Haugen who distributed questionnaires in 1954 to hundreds of respondents in Norway, Sweden and Denmark in order to investigate the occurrence of what he called 'semi-communication' (Haugen, 1966). The crucial question in the questionnaire was 'Do you understand X speech without difficulty?'. His results not only documented the occurrence of RM in Scandinavia, but also started a debate with regard to the *(a)symmetry of understanding* between speakers of Norwegian, Swedish and Danish (see the previous section on Intelligibility). Although research has revealed many varieties and degrees characterizing these asymmetries, a consensus seems to be that Danish is the most difficult to understand by the other speakers of the related languages (Swarte, 2016).

The occurrence of RM is historically interesting in Nordic countries because it was used by the ideological movement of 'Scandinavism', as we indicated above. This cultural and political group tried to reinforce the common cultural and historical roots of Nordic countries in the 19th century (Braunmüller & Zeevaert, 2001). In actual fact, Braunmüller (2007) shows how already in the Middle Ages RM was the default communicative mode for international travellers in the Nordic countries. Nowadays, RM still exists in international

Table 12.4 *Occurrence of receptive multilingualism in transnational areas and multilingual regions*

Transnational areas and multilingual regions
Nordic countries (Braunmüller & Zeevaert, 2001; Delsing & Åkesson, 2005; Zeevaert, 2004)
Cantons in Switzerland (Lüdi, 2007; Werlen, 2007)
Romance languages (Blanche-Benveniste, 2008; Conti & Grin, 2008)
Catalonia and Galicia (Strubell i Trueta, 2007, cited in EC, 2012)
Netherlands, Province of Friesland (Riemersma, n.d., cited in EC, 2012)
Polish, Ukrainian and Russian (Rehbein & Romaniuk, 2014)
Turkish and Kazakh (Massakowa, 2014)
Cross-border communication
Northern Italy – Austria: Tirol (Risse, 2015)
Italy and France: Valle d'Aosta (Almaskati, 2002, cited in EC, 2012)
Spanish and Portuguese (Jensen, 1989)
Dutch – German (Beerkens, 2010; Ház, 2005; Snijkers, 2014)
Flemish – Wallonia (Belgium) (Niesen, 2016)
Azerbaijani – Turkish (Sağın-Şimşek & König, 2012)

contacts, although young people increasingly choose to use English as a lingua franca on these occasions (Delsing & Åkesson, 2005).

Within the transnational area of the Romance languages, Blanche-Benveniste (2008) also points to early occurrences of RM which she designates as *intercomprehension*. Travellers in the Middle Ages, when traversing different European countries, made themselves understood by making use of the correspondences between the Romance languages. At the time of the formation of nation-states in Europe in the 17th and 18th centuries, the establishment and ideology of national languages suppressed the use of RM. In recent times RM has attracted new attention as a result of the support of regional minority languages in Europe (e.g. in Catalonia and Galicia; Strubell i Trueta, cited in EC, 2012: 16).

Rindler-Schjerve and Vetter (2007) document the occurrence of RM (also denoted as *polyglot dialogue*) in the Habsburg Empire, including references to German, Italian and various Slavic languages. Since there was no overall state language in the Habsburg Empire, linguistic diversity facilitated various kinds of multilingualism including the use of different languages next to each other. After the collapse of the empire, standards for national languages were set up and RM disappeared from the scene. In Eastern Europe – especially during the Soviet Union – the Russian language had an overall dominant relevance. Sloboda *et al.* (2016) and Nekvapil (2013) document the state of affairs of the former Eastern Bloc countries after two decades of the regime change, but do not devote much attention to RM.

The *Swiss model* and *plurilingual repertoire* are the notions Lüdi (2007, 2013) and colleagues propose to designate RM in Switzerland. The Swiss multilingual situation involves four languages: French, German, Italian and Romansh. Most Cantons in Switzerland choose only one of these languages. Three cantons accept two official languages but these language areas are strictly separated. In fact, only in the district of Biel/Bienne and in the environment of Fribourg/Freiburg is RM an everyday practice (Werlen, 2007).

This short and incomplete survey exemplifies that RM has a longstanding history which can be traced back to the Middle Ages. The historical development thereafter varies as the result of conflicts between the ruling powers that created European borders, which changed frequently and often did not correspond to language borders. However, the constitution and consolidation of nation-states in Europe in the 18th century supported the language ideology of 'one nation, one culture and one language', with the result that multilingualism was suppressed and national monolingualism was officially promoted throughout Europe. RM returned to the scene only recently, mostly in cross-border contacts and institutional constellations.

Although this lecture is primarily focused on RM in Europe, it has also been studied in other parts of the world. For instance, Greer (2013) investigated encounters between a Japanese hairdresser and his Bolivian client, who tacitly negotiate a receptive bilingual Japanese–lingua franca English interaction mode.

The complexity of current international and transnational communication has been studied in various institutional organizations with the result that occurrences of RM could be detected. No Europe-wide overview is available, but Table 12.5 lists some relevant studies of institutional constellations.

The economic, political and cultural integration of Europe in recent decades has resulted in the opening of national borders and the increase of transnational cooperation in all kinds of social domains. This has changed institutional relations between governmental bodies in all European countries. Although monolingualism still characterizes communication between European nation-states, it has become clear that various institutions have also developed modes of communication to cope with the multilingualism that characterizes Europe as a

Table 12.5 *Occurrence of receptive multilingualism in institutions (including in companies and the media)*

Institutions
International Criminal Tribunal for the Former Yugoslavia (EC, 2012)
Governmental organizations (Ribbert & ten Thije, 2007)
Army (Berthele & Wittlin, 2013)
EU institutions (De Vries, 2013; Van Klaveren, 2013)
Education (Sağın-Şimşek, 2014; Vetter, 2012; Zeevaert, 2004)
Families (Afshar, 1998; Fiorentino, 2017; Herkenrath, 2012; Korevaar, 2009)
Media, digital communication
Talk shows (Nábělková, 2008)
Chat rooms (Melo-Pfeigfer, 2014)
Websites (Sloboda & Nábělková, 2013)
Business discourse
Sales talks (Dresemann, 2007; Verschik, 2012)
Workplace (Lüdi, 2007; Werlen, 2007)

whole. Even RM has become one of the communicative modes that contribute to attaining societal purposes in, for instance, international courts, governmental organizations and EU institutions. It should be stressed, however, that RM is not the only communicative mode that is applied. It is quite clear that *English as a lingua franca* is the most important mode next to regional linguae francae (RELF; e.g. German in Eastern Europe) and translation and interpretation services (Backus *et al.*, 2013). With the announcement of Brexit, French has regained some of its historical importance for trans- and international communication. Studies (listed in Table 12.5) reveal that RM can also contribute to the communicative purposes of education, families and media discourse. Finally, international commercial communication has integrated the option of RM next to the other multilingual modes in the organization of workplace communication and sales talk. Discourse characteristics of the institutional application of RM will be discussed below.

Choice

One topic that is often investigated in the framework of sociolinguistic studies into language contact and multilingualism concerns the question of *language choice*. This appears to be a key question with regard to the occurrence of RM, namely which factors determine the choice of RM as the multilingual mode in a specific exchange. As Spolsky (2004) argues, in every exchange people decide anew which language they will use. In other words, in multilingual constellations people have to choose between RM and another communicative mode for their interaction.

In fact, little is known about the process of choosing communicative modes (e.g. Werlen, 2007). Snijkers (2014) has reconstructed the process of language choice in German–Dutch RM communication in detail. She aims to find out which factors influence the choice between the RM mode and other multilingual modes (e.g. English as lingua franca (ELF), code-switching (CS) or accommodating to one of the languages of the interlocutors). On the basis of ethnographic research, she compares governmental and commercial discourse in cross-border communication. Her field of research concerns Limburg in the south of the Netherlands. Specifically, Snijkers (2014) investigates, on the one hand, cross-border governmental meetings and, on the other, sales interaction in shops and entertainment events in the same border region. Her study exemplifies the determining factors for (not) choosing RM. Besides the national standard varieties of Dutch and German, in Limburg local inhabitants also have local dialects at their disposal to communicate with people across the German-Dutch border. As is often the case, dialect borders do not correspond to national borders. In Figures 12.2 and 12.3 the process of making language choices in the case of a Dutch and a German interlocutor is graphically systematized. The findings are of multiple interest: first, how does the hearer react upon hearing the choice of the first speaker? Secondly, how does the first speaker react upon hearing the choice of the second speaker? This threefold sequence is crucial, because it contains the quintessence of RM (Rehbein *et al.*, 2012): the third contribution reveals whether RM is used.

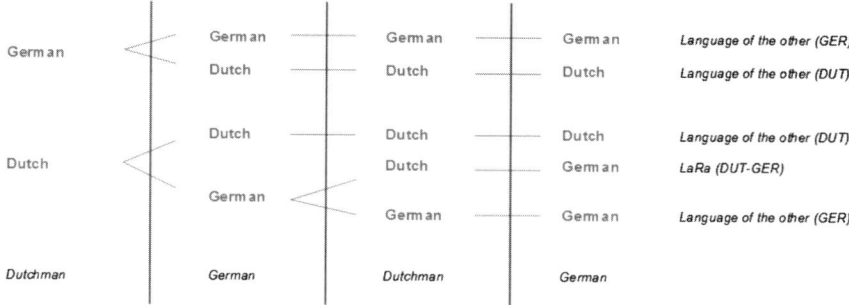

Figure 12.2 Language choice in governmental German-Dutch receptive multilingualism
Source: Snijkers (2014: 71).

The flow chart in Figure 12.2 reveals the options for language choice between Dutch and German from a Dutch perspective. Dutch may accommodate to German and vice versa. Only in the case where the Dutch person continues to speak in Dutch and the German answers in German does it result in the RM mode. Interestingly, another RM option is to be found in the commercial domain (see Figure 12.3) which is not found in the governmental domain. The Dutch interlocutor may use dialect and continue speaking dialect even in the case where the German answers in German.

Snijkers (2014) concludes, with regard to the distribution of the possibilities of language choice at governmental meetings, that in fact RM is often chosen. She explains that local and regional officials have determined a language policy for cross-border communication that favours RM. However, in cases where the receptive proficiency of one of the interlocutors appears not to be sufficient, a change to the language of the other is allowed.

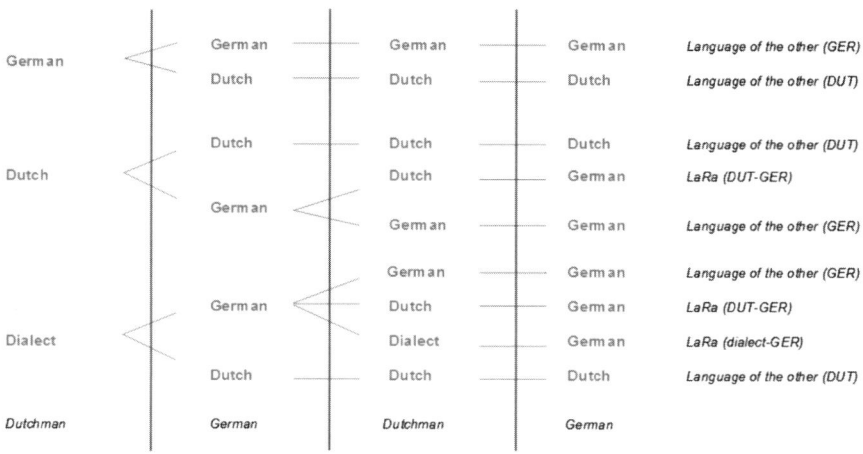

Figure 12.3 Language choice in commercial German-Dutch receptive multilingualism
Source: Snijkers (2014: 73).

At meetings where no language policy has been determined, the degree of receptive proficiency in the language of the other is also decisive. Moreover, the number of speakers present of each of the languages as well as the location (whether in the Netherlands or in Germany) is likely to determine the choice of mode. Interestingly, ELF does not occur in oral communication at these governmental meetings at all. Only in written communication is English used. The factors involved in choosing the communicative mode in the commercial domain appear different (see Figure 12.3).

Snijkers (2014) observes that RM occurs in shops on both sides of the border and is especially applied by younger people. Their productive proficiency in the other language is not enough to prompt them to switch completely to the other language. Nevertheless, their receptive proficiencies in each other's languages enable them to apply RM. Nowadays many German pupils in the border region learn some Dutch at school, just as Dutch pupils have been learning some German at school for a long time now. Moreover, on both sides they have already experienced exposure to RM. Choice in favour of dialect by young speakers does not occur. Dialect was found to be used by young people in a receptive multilingual mode only where the interlocutors were more or less familiar with one another. Thus, for instance, a Dutch salesperson may speak in dialect and the German client may speak in German. In a case where the German client does not possess enough receptive dialect proficiency, the Dutch salesperson will immediately switch to German. On the other hand, elderly people on both sides of the border speak only German to each other. Dutch elderly people have learned German, whereas German elderly people have not learned Dutch. English as a lingua franca is not found in interaction in the commercial domain in the border region at all.

Snijkers (2014) exemplifies in her analysis the factors that determine the application of RM (see Table 12.6). These factors are also known from sociolinguistic research into language choice in other language contact situations (Eastman, 1983; Fasold, 1984; ten Thije, 2013). The hierarchy and relevance of the factors depend on the specific constellation and should be the subject of further research.

In the next section more interaction structures will be discussed – those that occur when interlocutors have chosen to apply RM.

Table 12.6 *Factors for choosing receptive multilingualism*

Location (distance to border)
Language policy
Institutional constellation
Exposure
Attitude
Proficiency
Status
Age
Common communicative history

Interaction

The previous section discussed the factors that determine the choice of the RM mode. In this section we address the factors that determine RM success in cases where interlocutors have indeed chosen to apply this mode. Pragmatic research and discourse analytical studies focus on interaction strategies that facilitate mutual understanding between speaker and hearer while using RM. A central issue in these studies is what the specific interactive characteristics are of attaining comprehension in RM. As was mentioned earlier, RM is characterized by a 'production-to-comprehension switch'. This so called *turn-over* occurs 'between speaking in one language (the speaker's role) and understanding in the other (the hearer's role)' (Rehbein *et al.*, 2012: 251). To stress the special relevance of hearer competencies for RM, Rehbein *et al.* (2012) introduce the concept of *lingua receptiva*. They state:

> By definition, lingua receptiva is the ensemble of those linguistic, mental, interactional as well as intercultural competencies which are creatively activated when interlocutors listen to linguistic actions in their 'passive' language or variety. The essential point is that speakers apply additional competencies in order to monitor the way in which hearers activate their 'passive knowledge' and thus attempt to control the ongoing process of understanding. (Rehbein *et al.*, 2012: 249)

In order to distinguish the notion of RM from lingua receptiva, Blees and ten Thije (2016) indicate:

> Receptive multilingualism is a mode of interaction in which speakers with different linguistic backgrounds use their respective preferred languages while understanding the language of their interlocutor. The mechanisms and competences contributing to mutual understanding in this constellation are described by the concept of lingua receptiva (LaRa). (Blees & ten Thije, 2016: 335)

In this section we discuss investigations in the field of lingua receptiva that analyze *interaction strategies*. The research in Scandinavia that Braunmüller (2006) and Zeevaert (2004) mention was primarily focused on giving advice to future users of RM. This advice concerns issues such as how to cope with and prevent problems of misunderstanding using RM. In order to support these recommendations they analyzed authentic data. Zeevaert (2004) analyzed workgroup sessions of the Nordic Association of University Administrators. These sessions included presentations and panel discussions between Danish, Norwegian and Swedish professionals making use of RM. On the basis of this analysis the authors were able to distinguish between the interactive characteristics of the *monolingual speaker*, the *bilingual speaker* and the *hearer*. The difference between the monolingual and bilingual speaker concerns the level of proficiency of the speaker in the language of the hearer. Monolingual speakers do not have any or have only very little relevant receptive proficiency, whereas bilingual speakers have moderate or good proficiency. It is hypothesized that the strategies that speakers and hearers have at their disposal depend on their passive proficiency in the language of the

Table 12.7 *Discourse strategies in receptive multilingualism (RM) for the monolingual and bilingual speaker and the hearer (based on Braunmüller, 2006: 18–20; Zeevaert, 2004, 2007)*

Discourse strategies within RM		
Monolingual speaker	**Bilingual speaker**	**Hearer**
1. Repetition	1. Nonce-borrowing	1. 'Let-it-pass' principle
2. Reformulation	2. Flagged-term strategy	2. Await using RM
3. Cognitive prophylactic reformulation	3. 'Accommodation at every price'	3. Counter-question
4. Echo	4. Code-switching as an accommodation strategy	4. Preparation for the topic
	5. Await using RM	5. Back-channelling
	6. Slow and enunciated speech	
	7. Avoidance of colloquial expressions	

Source: Beerkens (2010: 33).

other. Beerkens (2010) provides us with a concise summary of the work of Braunmüller and Zeevaert in Table 12.7.

A short explanation will clarify the strategies in Table 12.7 that are not self-evident. The monolingual strategies of *repetition*, *reformulation* and *echo* concern simple activities in order to signal non-understanding to the hearer and to request explanation of the wording used. In the case of *cognitive prophylactic reformulation*, the speaker anticipates non-understanding of lexical features on the part of the hearer and avoids these words. The bilingual strategies are based on restricted proficiency in the language of the hearer. *Nonce-borrowing* concerns specific use of words from the other language to show understanding. *Flagged-term strategy* refers to the use of frequent and distinctive words from the other language to show willingness to accommodate to the other's language. *Accommodation at any price* refers to the discourse strategy that speakers with little knowledge of the other's language try to accommodate on the basis of overgeneralization of correspondence rules to show eagerness to be comprehensible to the hearer. Much the same account covers the strategy of *code-switching as accommodation*. In his authentic material, Zeevaert (2004) found the strategy whereby the interlocutor first assesses and checks the receptive proficiency of the hearer before using their own language, which he designates as *await using RM*. The strategies *slow and enunciated speech* and *avoidance of colloquial words* both aim at improving mutual understanding. The hearer strategy *let-it-pass* refers to postponing an interpretation of the other in order to receive more information. *Preparing for a topic* refers to the strategy that Braunmüller (2002) observed in cases where interlocutors anticipate potential problematic wordings and formulate understandable solutions in advance of an RM meeting. This collection of strategies has inspired other researchers to elaborate on and systematize the interactive structure of the *turn-over* between hearer and speaker while using RM.

Beerkens (2010) investigates RM in Dutch-German cross-border communication. She analyzed meetings in the governmental domain and in so-called civil society organizations such as playground, kindergarten and ecclesial meetings. Whereas in the former a top-down language policy determines the use of RM, such a policy is not in force in the latter and, therefore, RM is more a result of bottom-up determination. In order to systematize the speaker–hearer interaction in relation to aiming for understanding, Beerkens concentrates on the repair pattern within RM. According to Rehbein (1984), the repair pattern consists of four phases: (1) *utterance element*, (2) *intervention*, (3) *repair* and (4) *confirmation*.

The first important finding of Beerkens (2010) is that in her corpus of ten RM encounters, with a total duration of 14 hours, only 9.5% of the utterances were non-native. That means that 90.5% were from German speakers speaking German and Dutch speakers speaking Dutch. In other words, RM was indeed the main communicative mode being applied in these encounters (see previous section on Occurrence). The second interesting finding was that only 63 occurrences of repairs were found. The utterances realizing together the four steps of the repair pattern account for less than 1% of the complete corpus of 14 hours. Beerkens concludes that the level of mutual understanding in the analyzed team meetings using RM is rather good.

Analysing the distribution of the four steps over German and Dutch interlocutors, the patterns in Table 12.8 resemble the most frequently occurring sequence. An utterance of a Dutch person speaking Dutch triggers an intervention by a German hearer speaking German. The repair is realized by the Dutch hearer speaking Dutch and accepted by the German hearer speaking German. Table 12.9 contains an example of such an interaction. It is interesting to note that Beerkens does not take the *linguistic form* of RM as a starting point for her analysis but the *function* of an utterance in the repair pattern.

This discourse fragment contains a problem of reception which illustrates the general distribution between Dutch and German interactants. The Dutch speaker (S6mDut [vDUT]) reports on the production of a new website (Step 1). The German interactant (S2mGer) does not understand the utterance element and formulates the intervention 'What?' (Step 2). The Dutch speaker rephrases the main utterance (Step 3) which subsequently is accepted by the German speaker, 'Oh, OK yes' (Step 4). Beerkens (2010) explains this distribution of the four steps by using the results of a self-evaluation survey regarding the active and passive proficiencies of the German and Dutch interactants under investigation. On the whole, the active and passive proficiencies of Dutch speakers appear slightly higher than those of the Germans, so that the latter signal more reception problems.

Subsequently, Beerkens analyses the linguistic realization of the four steps. With regard to the utterance elements that trigger a reception problem (Step 1), her study confirms the findings from research into mutual intelligibility (see above): *acoustic, syntactic* and

Table 12.8 *Most frequently occurring sequence of the repair pattern in the corpus*

(a) Utterance element	(b) Intervention	(c) Repair	(d) Confirmation
D-D	G-G	D-D	G-G

Source: Beerkens (2010: 274).

Table 12.9 Transcription fragment

[1]

	190	191				
S4mDut [vDUT]	Nee dat is uh...					
S4mDut [ENGtr]	No that's uh...					
S6mDut [vDUT]	Ja, dat is heel belangrijk, want er komt dus uh een/ • • die website is op dit					
S6mDut [ENGtr]	Yes, that is very important, because a uh/ • • that website is currently under construction,					

[2]

	192	193	194
	..		
S4mDut [vDUT]	Ja˙		
S4mDut [ENGtr]	Yes˙		
S1mDut [vDUT]			
S6mDut [vDUT]	moment in bewerking, • die wordt gemaakt, • • en die is vijf juni klaar.		
S6mDut [ENGtr]	• it is being worked on, • • it is ready on fifth of June.		

[3]

	195	196	197	198	199	200
	..					
S2mGer [vGER]		Was?		Ach so, ja.		
S2mGer [ENGtr]		What?		Oh ok, yes.		
S1mDut [vDUT]	hm¨˙					
S6mDut [vDUT]			Vijf juni is die klaar, die website.			
S6mDut [ENGtr]			Fifth of June it is finished, the website.			

[4]

	..	
S6mDut [vDUT]	bij TVA in Doetinchem, ik weet niet of jullie dat bedrijf kennen,	((3s)) En uh ((2,5s)) dat doen ze
S6mDut [ENGtr]	TVA in Doetinchem, I don't know whether you known that company,	((3s)) And uh ((2,5s)) this is done at

Source: Beerkens (2010: 241f.).

especially *lexical elements* trigger reception problems. However, 50% of problematic utterance elements concern *knowledge differences* either verbalized in the discourse itself or represented in written documents. It is striking that authentic data reveal results in this respect which differ from the experimental studies that were presented earlier in the section on Intelligibility. In actual fact, the hearers do not understand the information that the speakers try to transmit. It will not be a surprise that most analyzed interventions that signal non-understanding (Step 2) concern *questions about the content* or *meta-communication*. The repair itself (Step 3) reveals interesting characteristics for RM. Besides *elucidations*, *repetitions* and *summaries*, this step is realized by means of a *reformulation*. Therefore, speakers make use of their native language as well as of their non-native language. In the latter case they utter a code-switch in the language of the hearer. In other words, they neglect the turn-over between speaker role and hearer role that typically characterizes lingua receptiva. Production and comprehension are realized in the same language. Most *confirmations* in Step 4 concern hearer signals and interjections such as 'ja' (yes), 'hm', 'ach' and 'aha'.

Interestingly, most strategies mentioned by Braunmüller and Zeevaert (see Table 12.7) are incorporated by Beerkens (2010); however, the form–function relation is made more transparent within the repair pattern. Beerkens (2010) also accounts for interaction strategies that are not directly part of the repair pattern such as *await using RM* and *preparation of the topic*. She elaborates on the planning of the speaker and hearer before the use of RM. Both interlocutors assess the language skills of the other in their own languages. This deployment of assessment is an important part of the competency that lingua receptiva includes.

Bahtina-Jantsikene (2013) elaborates on Beerkens' (2010) findings with regard to form and function relations in connection to interaction strategies in RM. Bahtina-Jantsikene takes a different approach in order to focus on issues that are shown by Beerkens (2010) to remain difficult to isolate and control. Bahtina-Jantsikene (2013) investigates lingua receptiva between Estonian and Russian. Whereas Dutch and German belong to the same Germanic language family, Estonian and Russian belong, respectively, to the Finno-Ugric language family and the Eastern-Slavic language family. Thereby the author is able to investigate *acquired lingua receptiva* (e.g. lingua franca beyond boundaries of language families). Also, her investigation is set up as a task-oriented dialogue through the use of Skype. This set-up enables scrutiny of controlling factors such as the *success rate* in achieving the purposes of the interaction in relation to the *levels of proficiency* of speaker and hearer. In other words, it allows answers to questions about the extent to which interactive success depends on the use of specific interaction strategies and about the extent to which the use of such strategies depends on the relationship between the proficiency levels of speaker and hearer. In actual fact, the receptive proficiencies of the respondents were tested and, subsequently, the experiment was executed using pairs of participants that were organized as follows: (1) high–high, (2) low–low, (3) high–low, (4) low–high. High and low refer to receptive proficiency. Moreover, Estonian native pairs (five) and Russian native pairs (six) were included in the experiment. Since Estonian and Russian are not mutual intelligible, this set-up made it possible to analyze the factor of receptive proficiency in successful lingua receptiva interaction.

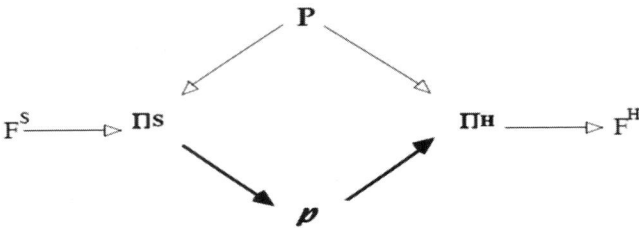

Figure 12.4 Knowledge model of functional pragmatics: the relationship between reality (**P**), language (*p*) and knowledge (π)
Source: Ehlich and Rehbein (1986).

The study by Bahtina-Jantsikene (2013) focuses on *meta-communication*, which appeared to be an important interaction strategy in the investigations discussed previously (e.g. Beerkens, 2010; Braunmüller, 2006; Zeevaert, 2004, 2007). The author's analyses lead to the distinction of four *meta-communicative devices* (see Figure 12.4). Again the functionality of linguistic forms is taken as a starting point of the analysis. The distinction is based on the knowledge model of functional pragmatics (Ehlich & Rehbein, 1986). This model differentiates between reality (P), the knowledge of the speaker (π^S) and hearer (π^H), and the propositional content of the utterance (*p*). The flow chart (see Figure 12.4) starts with the speech action (F^S) the speaker realizes in interaction and ends with the follow-up action of the hearer (F^H). The gist of the FP model is that: (1) knowledge of the speaker and hearer mediate between the propositional content of speech and reality; and (2) understanding can only be realized on the basis of the knowledge of the speaker and hearer being congruent. In this sense the FP knowledge model is clearly differentiated from the simple transmission model in which the message is represented as being transferred from sender to receiver (Shannon & Weaver, 1949).

Taking this knowledge model as a starting point, Bahtina-Jantsikene (2013) was able to discern four meta-communicative devices (MCDs; see Table 12.10). The first MCD concerns meta-communication with regard to the *action constellation* (e.g. the purpose of the interaction). The second MCD concerns the *conceptual orientation system*. The third refers to *lexical meaning* and the fourth concerns the *overall checking* of the hearer.

Table 12.10 *Meta-communicative devices for achieving understanding in lingua receptiva*

MCD1 ensures the common understanding of the action constellation and a presumed set of actions that are to be taken in order to reach communicative purposes.
MCD2 aims at securing a common conceptual orientation system in the time and space given.
MCD3 assures understanding of linguistic realizations within ongoing discourse. Determined by: (1) interactants' plurilingual background and experiences; (2) speaker's anticipation as to what the hearer would understand; and (3) hearer's anticipation as to what would the speaker would aim at.
MCD4 concerns overall checking.

Source: Bahtina-Jantsikene (2013).

Bahtina-Jantsikene (2013) concludes that L2 proficiency is not the decisive factor that predicts successful application of RM. In fact it emerged that low L2 proficiency can be compensated for by *exposure* to the multilingual constellation in everyday life together with a positive *attitude* towards the other language. The results contradict the findings within the mutual intelligibility framework we discussed earlier in the section on Intelligibility. With regard to the application of the four MCDs, a clear difference was able to be established between the native pairs and the various mixed pairs. Generally speaking, MCD2 (aimed at mutual orientation) was used more by pairs that had higher L2 proficiency, whereas MCD3 (aimed at linguistic alignment) was applied by pairs with low and mixed L2 proficiency. Furthermore, it emerged that HH couples were not always the most successful in lingua receptiva mode. The author explains that they apparently were more used to speaking in either their L1 or their L2. Consequently, they may have been prevented from accommodating to the language of the other. In fact the mixed HL pairs were the most efficient couples because they were purpose oriented. In sum, the author states: '[g]enerally, the speakers were able to monitor and adapt their speech as well as model their knowledge for the benefit of the dialogue: by making the best use of their interactive and plurilingual resources' (Bahtina-Jantsikene, 2013: 105). In the end, the author proposes developing a RM training programme in order to test the outcome of the application of lingua receptiva in real-life situations. We will discuss educational measurements, including an example of training in RM, in the next section.

Finally, Massakowa (2014) should be mentioned. She investigates Turkish and Kazakh RM in Germany, Turkey and Kazakhstan. The two languages belong to the same Turkic language family and, therefore, RM involving Turkish and Kazakh speakers can be designated as *inherent lingua receptiva*. However, the students who were recorded in multilingual discussion meetings did not have any or had only little receptive proficiency in the other language. Therefore, their communication was far from efficient and successful. Nevertheless, in the course of their discussions they developed elementary knowledge of the other language. They started to understand each other by making use of formal linguistic correspondences between the languages (i.e. mutual intelligibility, see section on Intelligibility) as well as by making use of common institutional and cultural knowledge. Moreover, knowledge of a third contact language (i.e. Persian) functioned as a mediator, as a bridge to facilitate understanding. Her study also takes the functional pragmatic approach towards lingua receptiva. Within this approach she is able to develop an overview of various *types of discourse-related understanding* such as *intuitive, successive, partial, delayed* and *rejected* understanding. These types of understanding can also be considered as stages in a learning process in relation to another language. It is hypothesized that the increase of receptive proficiency promotes productive proficiency.

In conclusion, the interaction strategies that Braunmüller (2006) and Zeevaert (2004) have observed in authentic RM interaction have inspired researchers to develop theories that systematize these strategies either in the occurrences of the *repair pattern* (Beerkens, 2010), as *meta-communicative devices* (Bahtina-Jantsikene, 2013) or as *types of discourse-related understanding* (Massakowa, 2014). These proposals are elaborations of *mechanisms and competences contributing to mutual understanding* that are denoted by the notion of lingua receptiva. Bahtina-Jantsikene (2013) has elaborated these mechanisms in detail. Furthermore, she shows convincingly that and how RM is possible between languages that are not from the same language family. Further research is desirable into the other language combinations that are presented in Table 12.4.

Planning

Studies in the field of language planning concerning RM address the question as to how RM can be organized and implemented in various social and institutional settings. In that connection, Backus *et al.* (2013) summarize the advantages of RM as follows:

> The main advantages of this communicative mode are its inherent fairness, as no interlocutor is at a disadvantage because of limited speaking skills (Beerkens, 2010), and the fact that it naturally induces cooperative behaviour: a seemingly universal by-product, reported by most studies, is that speakers engaged in this mode are very attuned to misunderstandings and to any problems the listener might have understanding the content of what is being said (Conti & Grin, 2008). The main restrictions of this mode concern the settings in which it used. Studies confirm that it is especially effective in informal settings (Beerkens, 2010). (Backus *et al.*, 2013: 199)

In addition, Braunmüller summarizes the five main hindrances for implementing RM. He states:

> (1) the general lacking awareness of this possibility, though RM has been proved to be successful in acquiring a reading competence in genetically related languages (...), (2) the missing flexibility of the interlocutors in oral communication due to the dominance of standardised languages in almost all domains, (3) the decline of dialects and multilectality in many (European) countries in favour of the default use of standard languages, (4) the laziness in accommodating to other varieties due to the dominance of written standards, (5) the dominance of the world-wide lingua franca English, which prevents people from expanding their implicit receptive knowledge L1 towards other related varieties. (Braunmüller, 2013: 221)

Although RM is a multilingual communication mode and not a language in its own right, it may be helpful to discuss the above-mentioned advantages and hindrances of RM within the framework of language planning. The relevant literature discerns three dimensions with regard to language planning. These are *status and prestige planning*, including attention to the vitality of languages/language varieties, *corpus planning* in respect of the standardization and modernization of languages and, finally, *acquisition planning* regarding educational issues related to national standard languages and the question of how to handle multilingualism (Coulmas, 1991; Eastman, 1983; Fasold, 1984; Haugen, 1966). These three dimensions of language policy will be discussed in what follows.

First, *status and prestige planning* will be discussed. In this connection, we refer back to occurrences of RM in Tables 12.5 and 12.6. It can be observed from this survey that RM is particularly a *local* phenomenon in border regions on the one hand and a *transnational* phenomenon in supranational institutions on the other. No European studies are available that document RM language policies at a national level. It can be inferred that actually RM has a non-official status and low prestige at national level – at least within Europe. In the section on Occurrence this was illustrated with the Swiss model: although Switzerland has four official languages, only three cantons accept two languages and are in fact multilingual, whereas in only one canton does RM occur in everyday communication (Werlen, 2007). Therefore, it can be stated that RM only has an official status at a local level. Elsewhere, in European institutes like Euregio, RM is also accepted as a regular communicative mode at a regional level. German and Dutch governmental officials apply RM during their official cross-border meetings (Beerkens, 2010). The prestige and status of RM at a transnational level become clear when we consider the European Union's policy on multilingualism.

From its start the EU Commission has developed a language policy on multilingualism (Nic Craith, 2006; EC, 2008). We cannot discuss this European multilingual policy in any detail, but the most important features are the following. National standard languages are treated equally. Every European citizen may address EU institutions in their national standard language. In order to execute this democratic principle, extensive interpretation and translation services are available. Minority and regional languages are supported. Member states are recommended to organize language education according to the principle 'mother tongue plus two'; this means that the national standard should be taught as well as an international language (e.g. English) and a neighbouring language. As a result of enlargement, the EU nowadays includes 24 languages, which has increased the relevance of and urgency for a European policy on multilingualism. For instance, there is an ongoing debate about which language is to function as the EU's working language: French, English or German.

It is interesting to point out that in official EU documents RM has gradually received more prestige and status. For instance, the High Level Group on Multilingualism in 2007 stresses the importance of RM as one of seven topics for the management of multilingualism in Europe in a variety of contexts. The report states as its seventh key issue:

Receptive multilingualism

Key issue: communication strategies used by speakers of Scandinavian, Romance and Slavonic languages and their relevance to improved intra-European communication. High level report. (EC, 2007: 21)

It is striking that the EU Commission refers to *intra-European* communication. Because of enlargement and the increase of languages, the coherence of the nation-states and cultures have to be strengthened. Apparently, RM could be one of the relevant resources. Accordingly, the EU Commission has supported comprehensive research projects into multilingualism over the last 15 years (see Table 12.11).

Table 12.11 *European research projects on multilingualism*

DYLAN (http://www.dylan-project.org): Language Dynamics and Management of Diversity
LINEE (http://www.linee.info/): Languages in a Network for European Excellence
LUCIDE (http://www.urbanlanguages.eu/): Languages in Urban Communities – Integration and Diversity for Europe
MIME (http://www.mime-project.org/): Mobility and Inclusion in Multilingual Europe
AThEME (http://www.atheme.eu/): Advancing the European Multilingual Experience

In these projects RM has received some attention. In the final brochure on the DYLAN project, authors for instance represent a scheme for the systematization of multilingual interaction strategies, in which lingua receptiva is allocated its place:

> One axis compares 'monolingual' strategies ('one language only' or OLON and 'one language at a time' or OLAT) with 'multilingual' ones – known as ALAST ('all the languages at the same time') or ALAAT ('all language at all times') – and the other axis compares the 'exolingual' pole (greatly asymmetrical repertoires) with the 'endolingual' one (participants share the same repertoire) ... Another solution is the lingua receptiva mode, in which everybody speaks his/her own language and is expected to understand the ones used by the other speakers. (Berthoud *et al.*, 2012: 13)

Furthermore, the MIME project includes a study regarding intercomprehension for the integration of adopted children (Fiorentino, 2017), which corresponds to the project aims connecting mobility with inclusion.

In sum, at national level RM has no status, since the monolingual ideology of European nation-states appears still to be hegemonic (Vogl, 2012). However, at local and supranational levels RM is one of the multilingual modes promoted by the EU and local officials in order to cope with multilingualism in Europe. According to professionals, multilingualism should not be considered as a problem but rather as an asset for societal cohesion or for organizations as well as for companies to increase their international activities and earnings. However, the final decisions on language planning are being made at the level of national member states.

Secondly, we consider *corpus planning*. In the pertinent literature this concept refers to the modernization and standardization of one language. For instance, the written or oral standards have to be adapted to new social developments in order to gain social functionalities that were connected to existing standards. However, the concepts of modernization and standardization are considered here in relation to a discussion of the implications of changes in the form and functions of RM for language policy. What could a modernization of language policy look like? What should the new standards be?

From the perspective of multilingual Europe as we have suggested, it is important to prepare European citizens to cope more *effectively* and *adequately* with the multilingual constellation. They should be made aware of the possibility of making use of all the language proficiencies that they have at their disposal even if these are not native-like. The norm for successful multilingual communication does not necessarily depend on native standards but could be replaced by norms for *effective understanding*. This means that the standard of the native speaker that underpins monolingual language policies could become less important. Over the years various concepts have been proposed to meet these needs, such as *translingual practice* (Canagarajah, 2009, 2013), *polylingualism* (Jørgensen *et al.*, 2011), *metrolingualism* (Otsuji & Pennycook, 2010), *translanguaging* (García, 2009), *the ecology of multilingual settings* (Kramsch, 2008) or *semiotic resources* (Blommaert, 2010: 47). The concept that explicitly integrates RM is called *inclusive multilingualism* (Backus *et al.*, 2013).

The concept of inclusive multilingualism integrates RM with English as Lingua Franca (ELF), Regional Lingua Franca (RELF), Code Switching (CS), and translation and interpretation. These multilingual communicative modes together provide language users with the communicative tools with which to cope with multilingual constellations. Backus *et al.* (2013) state:

> Inclusive Multilingualism involves a theoretical framework in which the communicative modes used to overcome limitations in linguistic competence are considered the core means for achieving multilingual understanding, rather than as undesired deviations of monolingual communication. (Backus *et al.*, 2013: 189)

The five communicative modes have common characteristics. RM can be considered as a type of CS. Interaction strategies achieving and securing mutual understanding correspond to those active for ELF, RELF and CS. Inclusive multilingualism brings these modes under one overarching concept. Within this framework it can be made clear that RM never will be the solution for multilingualism on its own. When modernization of language planning is the matter in hand RM will be part of the collection of communicative modes having the same purpose. The authors formulate the following vision for modernization and standardization:

> The goal of Inclusive Multilingualism is reached once people become aware of, have access to, and make wise use of the linguistic resources that can get the communicative job done most efficiently and, importantly, once this flexible multilingual behaviour becomes widely accepted as common sense and is taken for granted. (Backus *et al.*, 2013: 209)

In conclusion, it is important to emphasize that RM is not in competition with ELF, but can be considered as complementary (cf. Hülmbauer, 2014; Zeevaert & ten Thije, 2007). Modernization and standardization in achieving inclusive multilingualism will be the challenge for professionals, including applied linguists. In fact, the analyses of interaction strategies that have been proposed by discourse analytical experts (see previous section on Interaction) describe new communicative standards that have been implemented in acquisition planning in respect of RM, which we will discuss below.

The European Commission also presents a very concrete example of how the modernization of multilingual policy involves RM. This instance concerns the attempts of the Directorate General for Translation (DGT) of the EU to optimize their translation services regarding 24 languages. DGT investigates the possibility of incorporating *intercomprehension* into their translation workflow (EC, 2012). The translation procedures changed after the extension of the member states. Nowadays, almost all official documents are written in English before they are translated into the other languages of all member states. DGT has organized a pilot in which *intercomprehension* is applied. This means that documents are translated from English to Spanish and subsequently from Spanish to Portuguese, or vice versa, from English to Portuguese and then from Portuguese to Spanish. It is hypothesized that making use of the language correspondences within the Romance languages may shorten and ease the translation procedure and, consequently, will lead to cost reductions. This pilot exemplifies clearly how RM contributes to the modernization of EU multilingual policy.

Thirdly, *acquisition planning* will be considered. This dimension of language planning concerns the question of how *language status* and *literacy* with regard to RM can be changed through educational measurement. On the basis of literature study, one may state that RM has attracted a lot of attention from educational institutes at various levels.

The *Common European Framework of Reference for Languages* (CEFR) is well known because of its role as an auxiliary instrument for (self-)assessment of oral and written proficiencies, often in relation to recruitment procedures (e.g. the European Language Portfolio). Less well known is the fact that the introduction to this framework contains clear references to RM. In fact, the concept of *plurilingualism* incorporates that of RM. The authors state:

> The plurilingual approach emphasises the fact that as an individual a person's experience of language in its cultural contexts expands, from the language of the home to that of society at large and then to the languages of other peoples (whether learned at school or college, or by direct experience), he or she does not keep these languages and cultures in strictly separated mental compartments, but rather builds up a communicative competence to which all knowledge and experience of language contributes and in which languages interrelate and interact. In different situations, a person can call flexibly upon different parts of this competence to achieve effective communication with a particular interlocutor. (CoE, 2001: 4f)

The emphasis on the flexibility of communicative competence which enables receptive and productive competences in more than one language to collaborate in order to achieve effective communication is in complete alignment with the concept of inclusive multilingualism and with RM in particular. It is a pity that the concept of plurilingualism is no longer used for description of the proficiency levels and has been replaced by the rather traditional division into the five components: writing, reading, speaking, listening and interaction. Moreover, the levels of description are all restricted to the assessment of a single language. Multilingual communication is not addressed in the CEFR.

The European Centre for Modern Languages of the Council of Europe has initiated the development of another framework in order to meet these objections. This framework is called the *Framework of Plurilingual and Intercultural Education* (FREPA; Candelier *et al.*, 2013). If one has a close look at the elaborated descriptions, there is one skill in FREPA that includes RM explicitly. The framework states:

> Can make interlingual transfers (e.g. transfers of recognition (i.e. which establish a link between an identified feature of a known language and a feature one seeks to identify in

an unfamiliar language) or transfers of production (i.e. an activity of language production in an unfamiliar language)) from a known language to an unfamiliar one. (Candelier *et al.*, 2013: 95)

In the account of the framework, the authors explain that the framework comprises four approaches: language awareness, the intercultural approach, the integrated didactic approach and the intercomprehension approach. They state that in the 1990s this latter approach was supported by the European Commission and has resulted in materials for schools, but few developments have recently been observed in schools concerning intercomprehension. (CoE, 2011).

Within the framework of the Lifelong Learning Programme of the EU Commission a third framework has been developed (Räsänen *et al.*, 2013). Whereas FREPA aims at secondary education, the MAGICC project is meant to address higher education. This MAGICC project also is an instrument for (self-)assessment. The abbreviation stands for *Modularising Multilingual and Multicultural Academic and Professional Communication Competence* for BA and MA level. The framework aims at integrating intercultural competencies into professional competencies (Neuner-Anfindsen & Meima, 2016). RM is included in one of the skills to increase effective listening, thus:

Apply effectively translanguaging and/or other inferring and decoding strategies to optimise understanding of speech and retrieve information and meaning (intercomprehension strategies, inferring from content text type and structure, anticipation). (MAGICC, n.d.)

The MAGICC framework has been launched recently and is not yet able to report on its implementation in tertiary education.

The next project is one that actually precedes the previously discussed frameworks, namely the *EuroCom* project (Klein & Stegeman, 2000; McCann *et al.*, 2002). Whereas FREPA and MAGICC include all proficiencies, EuroCom is restricted to reading and focuses on Romance, Germanic and Slavic languages (see Table 12.12).

Table 12.12 *Teaching and learning receptive multilingualism*

EuroCom-ROM: Listening and Reading Competence of the Romance Languages (Klein & Stegeman, 2000)
EuroCom-GER: Germanische Interkomprehension (Hufeisen & Marx, 2007)
EuroCom-SLA: (Zybatow, 2003)

EuroCom is not a framework for self-assessment but a reading course which helps to make an intelligent guess when reading a text in a language that is not one's mother tongue but that belongs to the same family. On the basis of linguistic analyses, the authors have developed seven grids that make language correspondences within a language family transparent. Table 12.13 summarizes these grids for the Romance language family, which are represented as constituting an *optimal deduction model*. By using these grids, readers can infer the meaning of a text in another language, the formal correspondences between languages being made transparent.

Table 12.13 *Seven grids of intercomprehension in reference to the Romance languages*

International vocabulary
Pan-Romance vocabulary
Sound correspondences
Spelling and pronunciation
Pan-Romance syntactic structures
Morphosyntactic elements
Lists of prefixes and suffixes

The EuroCom reading courses are very elaborated in their linguistic descriptions (Hufeisen & Marx, 2007). Little is known about their implementation. It would be an excellent idea for its use to be surveyed by various readers with different competencies in the respective languages. Marx (2012) exemplifies this research interest.

The last example in which RM could be considered to be part of an acquisition planning programme concerns a crash course in oral communication which aims to enable Czech students to understand Croatian by using RM. Golubović (2016) set up a didactic teaching experiment in which Czech university students received four hours of training in understanding Croatian. The course included instruction in recognizing, among others, cognates, and in making use of common phoneme correspondences and syntactic similarities. The statistical comparison of the results of a pre-test versus a post-test that was administered to the group that underwent the above training as well as to the relevant control group showed a significant difference. The trained group was far better at executing the task after training. The author concludes that it makes sense to study linguistic correspondences in order to improve one's capacities in understanding a closely related language (e.g. RM).

In sum, the above five instances of acquisition planning reveal that RM has gained more attention in relation to acquisition planning compared to the status/prestige issue and to corpus planning. However, increasing the prestige and status of RM would have increased the visibility of many RM practices, and it can be assumed that the implementation of RM in all kinds of educational settings would have been more successful. As has become clear from the language policy literature, the three dimensions should be in balance in order to be effective.

Conclusions

This 12th lecture on multilingualism has presented six perspectives on the state of affairs of RM in Europe, specifically by elaborating on (1) terminology, (2) intelligibility, (3) occurrence, (4) choice, (5) interaction and (6) planning. These six perspectives come together in the notion of *awareness*. In general, language awareness concerns 'explicit knowledge about language, and conscious perception and sensitivity in language learning, language teaching and language use' (Association of Language Awareness, 2007, cited by Svalberg, 2007: 288). The awareness of RM has an individual component, an institutional component and a societal component which have all been discussed extensively in this lecture.

The crucial characteristic of all concepts relating to RM discussed in this lecture is that it focuses on the reception that is realized with respect to another language rather than the production. The relationship between the language of production and the language of reception accounts for the differences between the concepts. In the case of *mutual intelligibility* and *intercomprehension*, the languages in question belong to the same language family. In the case of *receptive multilingualism* and *lingua receptiva* language, combinations beyond family borders are included; understanding depends here on the degree of acquisition of the other language. *Lingua receptiva* focuses on the mechanisms and competences contributing to mutual understanding in RM.

Studies in the occurrence of RM have revealed a tendency for RM to be a local cross-border phenomenon as well as a supranational phenomenon, but for it rarely to be overtly addressed at a national level. Studies concerning *language choice* as well as *interaction strategies* in RM have revealed factors for successful RM, including: location, language policy, institutional constellation, exposure, attitude, proficiency, status, age, and commonality of communicative history of speaker and hearer. Further research is needed to determine the hierarchy between these factors in various language combinations.

The language planning literature makes clear that the *prestige and status* of RM are low at national level, even though it is the subject of various *acquisition* projects. Finally, it is argued that RM can be successful at the social and national level when it is part of the overarching concept of *inclusive multilingualism*, which also integrates other modes of multilingual communication such ELF, RELF, CS, and interpretation and translation.

The quintessence of lingua receptiva is to be aware of its restrictions in order to know its potential.

Questions for Students' Reflection

1. Have you ever experienced receptive multilingualism yourself? Describe this experience with the help of the categories in this lecture (oral or written RM, language combinations, setting and purpose of the contact, level of proficiencies in the others' language, exposure and attitude towards the others' language, negotiations regarding the RM choice, specific interaction strategies, etc.). How did you evaluate RM at that time and how do you reflect upon this experience after reading this lecture? Consider the advantages and the disadvantages for yourself and the other participants.

2. Do you know of any organizations or companies in which employees make use of RM? Is any formal or informal language planning available within the organization regarding RM? Try to formulate explicit planning to introduce and elaborate RM in this organization. Address the three domains of language planning (status and prestige, corpus, and acquisition) in your proposal.

3. In this lecture ten notions are discussed that have been introduced to denote RM (see Table 12.1). Choose three of these notions and compare how they cope with the distinction acquired and inherent RM.

4. This lecture discusses factors for successful RM, including: location, language policy, institutional constellation, exposure, attitude, proficiency, status, age, and commonality of communicative history of speaker and hearer. Can you imagine any other factors that could determine RM's success or failure?

5. On the internet you can find RM reading courses (e.g. EuroCom). Read a text in an unknown language that belongs to the same language family as your first language and, subsequently, look for examples of the seven sieves that EuroCom has detected between the two languages. How do these sieves help your reading comprehension in the unknown language?

6. The lecture concludes with the statement: 'The quintessence of lingua receptiva is to be aware of its restrictions in order to know its potential.' How could you explain this statement? Do you agree?

Note

(1) I would like to thank Gerda Blees, Kurt Braunmüller, Charlotte Gooskens, Karen Schoutsen and the editors of this book for their valuable comments on earlier drafts of this lecture.

Suggestions for Further Reading

Backus, A., Gorter, D., Knapp, K., Schjerve-Rindler, R., Swanenberg, J., ten Thije, J.D. and Vetter, E. (2013) Inclusive multilingualism: Concept, modes and implications. *European Journal of Applied Linguistics* 1 (2), 179–215.

Braunmüller, K. and Zeevaert, L. (2001) *Semikommunikation, rezeptive Mehrsprachigkeit und verwandte Phänomene. Eine bibliographische Bestandsaufnahme.* Arbeiten zur Mehrsprachigkeit, B/19. Hamburg: SFB.

Conti, V. and Grin, F. (eds) (2008) *S'Entendre entre Langues Voisines: Vers l'Intercompréhension* (pp. 33–51). Chêne-Bourg: Georg.

ten Thije, J.D. and Zeevaert, L. (eds) (2007) *Receptive Multilingualism: Linguistic Analyses, Language Policies and Didactic Concepts.* Amsterdam: John Benjamins.

References

Afshar, K. (1998) *Zweisprachigkeit oder Zweitsprachigkeit? Zur Entwicklung einer schwachen Sprache in der deutsch-persischen Familienkommunikation.* Münster: Waxmann.

Backus, A., Gorter, D., Knapp, K., Schjerve-Rindler, R., Swanenberg, J., ten Thije, J.D. and Vetter, E. (2013) Inclusive multilingualism: Concept, modes and implications. *European Journal of Applied Linguistics* 1 (2), 179–215.

Bahtina-Jantsikene, D. (2013) *Mind your Languages: Lingua Receptiva in Estonian-Russian Communication*. Utrecht: Landelijke Onderzoekschool Taalwetenschap.

Beerkens, R. (2010) *Receptive Multilingualism as a Language Mode in the Dutch-German Border Area*. Münster: Waxmann.

Berthele, R. and Wittlin, G. (2013) Receptive multilingualism in the Swiss Army. *International Journal of Multilingualism* 10 (2), 181–195.

Berthoud, A.C., Grin, F. and Lüdi, G. (2012) *The DYLAN Project Booklet. Dylan Project, Main Findings*. See http://www.dylan-project.org/Dylan_en/home/home.php (accessed 13 January 2017).

Blanche-Benveniste, C. (2008) Comment retrouver l'expérience des anciens voyageurs en terres de langues romanes? In V. Conti and F. Grin (eds) *S'entendre entre Langues Voisines: Vers l'Intercompréhension* (pp. 33–51). Chêne-Bourg: Georg.

Blees, G. and ten Thije, J.D. (2016) Receptive multilingualism and awareness. In J. Cenoz, D. Gorter and S. May (eds) *Language Awareness and Multilingualism, Encyclopedia of Language and Education* (pp. 333–345). Dordrecht: Springer; doi:10.1007/978-3-319-02325-0_25-2.

Blommaert, J. (2010) *The Sociolinguistics of Globalization*. Cambridge: Cambridge University Press.

Braunmüller, K. (1995) Semikommunikation und semiotische Strategien. Bausteine zu einem Modell für die Verständigung im Norden zur Zeit der Hanse. In K. Braunmüller (ed.) *Niederdeutsch und die skandinavischen Sprachen II* (pp. 35–70). Heidelberg: Winter.

Braunmüller, K. (2002) Semicommunication and accommodation: Observations from the linguistic situation in Scandinavia. *International Journal of Applied Linguistics* 12 (1), 1–23.

Braunmüller, K. (2006) Vorbild Skandinavien? Zur Relevanz der rezeptiven Mehrsprachigkeit in Europa. In K. Ehlich and A. Hornung (eds) *Praxen der Mehrsprachigkeit* (pp. 11–31). Münster: Waxmann.

Braunmüller, K. (2007) Receptive multilingualism in Northern Europe in the Middle Ages: A description of a scenario. In J.D. ten Thije and L. Zeevaert (eds) *Receptive Multilingualism: Linguistic Analyses, Language Policies and Didactic Concepts* (pp. 25–49). Amsterdam: John Benjamins.

Braunmüller, K. (2013) Communication based on receptive multilingualism: Advantages and disadvantages. *International Journal of Multilingualism* 10 (2), 214–223.

Braunmüller, K. and Zeevaert, L. (2001) *Semikommunikation, rezeptive Mehrsprachigkeit und verwandte Phänomene. Eine bibliographische Bestandsaufnahme*. Arbeiten zur Mehrsprachigkeit, B/19. Hamburg: SFB.

Canagarajah, S. (2009) The plurilingual tradition and the English language in South Asia. *AILA Review* 22 (1), 5–22.

Canagarajah, S. (2013) *Translingual Practice: Global Englishes and Cosmopolitan Relations*. London: Routledge.

Candelier, M., Camilleri Grima, A., Castellotti, V., *et al.* (2013) *FREPA – A Framework of Reference for Pluralistic Approaches to Languages and Cultures: Competences and Resources*. Graz: ECML.

Chomsky, N. (1957) *Syntactic Structures*. The Hague and Paris: Mouton.

Clyne, M. (2003) *Dynamics of Language Contact: English and Immigrant Languages*. Cambridge: Cambridge University Press.

CoE (Council of Europe) (2001) *Common European Framework of Reference for Languages: Learning, Teaching, Assessment.* Cambridge: Cambridge University Press.

CoE (Council of Europe) (2011) *Pluralistic Approaches to Languages and Cultures.* Graz: European Centre for Modern Languages of the Council of Europe. See http://carap.ecml.at/Keyconcepts/tabid/2681/language/en-GB/Default.aspx (accessed 7 January 2017).

Conti, V. and Grin, F. (eds) (2008) *S'entendre entre Langues Voisines: Vers l'Intercompréhension.* Chêne-Bourg: Georg.

Coulmas, F. (1981) *Conversational Routine: Explorations in Standardized Communication Situations and Prepatterned Speech.* Berlin: Walter de Gruyter.

Coulmas, F. (1991) *A Language Policy for the European Community: Prospects and Quandaries.* Berlin: Walter de Gruyter.

Delsing, L.-O. and Åkesson, K.L. (eds) (2005) *Håller språket ihop Norden? En forskningsrapport om ungdomars förståelse av danska, svenska och norska.* TemaNord Report 2005: 573. Copenhagen: Nordic Council of Ministers.

De Vries, J. (2013) Lingua receptiva in de schriftelijke communicatie van de Europese Commissie. Een onderzoek naar de praktijk en potentie van lingua receptiva voor een efficiënter vertaalproces binnen het directoraat-generaal Vertaling voor de Europese Commissie. Master's Thesis, Utrecht University.

Doetjes, G. (2007) Understanding differences in inter-Scandinavian language understanding. In J.D. ten Thije and L. Zeevaert (eds) (2007) *Receptive Multilingualism: Linguistic Analyses, Language Policies and Didactic Concepts* (pp. 217–230). Amsterdam: John Benjamins.

Dresemann, B. (2007) Receptive multilingualism in business discourses. In J.D. ten Thije and L. Zeevaert (eds) (2007) *Receptive Multilingualism: Linguistic Analyses, Language Policies and Didactic Concepts* (pp. 179–195). Amsterdam: John Benjamins.

Eastman, C.M. (1983) *Language Planning: An Introduction.* San Francisco, CA: Chandler & Sharp.

EC (European Commission) (2007) *High Level Group on Multilingualism. Final Report.* Luxembourg: Office for Official Publications of the European Communities. See https://www.scribd.com/document/251229225/High-Level-Group-on-Multilingualism.

EC (European Commission) (2008) *A Rewarding Challenge – How Language Diversity Could Strengthen Europe. Proposals from the Group of Intellectuals for Intercultural Dialogue Set up at the Initiative of the European Commission.* Brussels: European Commission, Education and Culture DG.

EC (European Commission) (2012) *Studies on Multilingualism and Translation: Intercomprehension.* Luxembourg: Publications Office of the European Union. See http://ec.europa.eu/dgs/translation/publications/studies/.

Ehlich, K. and Rehbein, J. (1986) *Muster und Institution. Untersuchungen zur schulischen Kommunikation.* Tübingen: Narr.

Fasold, R.W. (1984) *The Sociolinguistics of Language.* Oxford: Blackwell.

Fiorentino, A. (2017) Strategies for language maintenance in transnational adoption: Which role for the parents? *Journal of Home Language Research (JHLR)* 2, 5–22.

García, O. (2009) *Bilingual Education in the 21st Century: A Global Perspective.* New York: Wiley-Blackwell.

Golubović, J. (2016) *Mutual Intelligibility in the Slavic Language Area*. Groningen Dissertations in Linguistics No. 152. Groningen: University of Groningen.

Gooskens, C. (2013) Experimental methods for measuring intelligibility of closely related language varieties. In R. Bayley, R. Cameron and C. Lucas (eds) *The Oxford Handbook of Sociolinguistics* (pp. 195–213). Oxford: Oxford University Press.

Gooskens, C. and Van Bezooijen, R. (2013) Explaining Danish-Swedish asymmetric word intelligibility – an error analysis. In C. Gooskens and R. Van Bezooijen (eds) *Phonetics in Europe: Perception and Production* (pp. 59–82). Frankfurt am Main: Peter Lang.

Gooskens, C. and Van Heuven, V.J. (2017) Measuring cross-linguistic intelligibility in the Germanic, Romance and Slavic language groups. *Speech Communication* 89, 25–36.

Gooskens, C. and Van Heuven V.J. (in preparation) How well can intelligibility of closely related languages in Europe be predicted by linguistic and non-linguistic variables? *Linguistic Approaches to Bilingualism*.

Gooskens, C., Van Heuven, V.J., Golubović, J., Schüppert, A., Swarte, F. and Voigt, S. (2017) Mutual intelligibility between closely related languages in Europe. *International Journal of Multilingualism* 15 (2), 169–193; doi:10.1080/14790718.2017.1350185.

Greer, T. (2013) Establishing a pattern of dual-receptive language alternation. *Australian Journal of Communication* 40, 47–62.

Grosjean, F. (1982) *Life with Two Languages: An Introduction to Bilingualism*. Cambridge, MA: Harvard University Press.

Haugen, E. (1953) *The Norwegian Language in America: A Study in Bilingual Behavior*. Philadelphia, PA: University of Pennsylvania Press.

Haugen, E. (1966) Semicommunication: The language gap in Scandinavia. *Sociological Inquiry* 36 (2), 280–297.

Haugen, E. (1967) Semicommunication: The language gap in Scandinavian. In S. Lieberson (ed.) *Explorations in Sociolinguistics* (pp. 152–169). Bloomington, IN: Indiana University Press.

Haugen, E. (1987) Semicommunication. In E. Haugen (ed.) *Blessings of Babel: Bilingualism and Language Planning* (pp. 71–76). Berlin: Mouton de Gruyter.

Ház, E. (2005) *Deutsche und Niederländer. Untersuchungen zur Möglichkeit einer unmittelbaren Verständigung*. Hamburg: Kovač.

Herkenrath, A. (2012) Receptive multilingualism in an immigrant constellation: Examples from Turkish–German children's language. *International Journal of Bilingualism* 16 (3), 287–314.

Hockett, C.F. (1958) *Language Learning*. Wiley Online Library.

Hufeisen, B. and Marx, N. (eds) (2007) *EuroComGerm – Die sieben Siebe: Germanische Sprachen lesen lernen*. Aachen: Shaker.

Hülmbauer, C. (2014) A matter of reception: ELF and LaRa compared. *Applied Linguistics Review* 5 (1), 273–295.

Hymes, D. (1972) *Sociolinguistics*. Harmondsworth: Penguin.

Jensen, J.B. (1989) On the mutual intelligibility of Spanish and Portuguese. *Hispania* 72 (4), 848–852.

Jørgensen, J.N., Karrebæk, M.S., Madsen, L.M. and Møller, J.S. (2011) Polylanguaging in superdiversity. *Language and Superdiversities* 13 (2). See http://unesdoc.unesco.org/images/0021/002147/214772e.pdf#214780 (accessed 8 January 2017).

Klein, H.G. and Stegmann, T.D. (2000) *EuroComRom – Die sieben Siebe: Romanische Sprachen sofort lesen können*. Aachen: Shaker.

Kompasová, S. (1999/2000) Čeština ve vysílání slovenské televizní stanice Markíza [Czech in the broadcasts of the Slovak television channel Markíza]. Češtinář 10, 156–163.

Korevaar, M. (2009) Met mes en vork! Een functioneel-pragmatisch onderzoek naar het gebruik van de receptief meertalige gespreksmodus in Nederlands-Duitse gezinnen met kinderen in de leeftijd tot twaalf jaar. Master's thesis, Utrecht University.

Kramsch, C. (2008) Ecological perspectives on foreign language education. *Language Teaching* 41 (3), 389–408.

Lüdi, G. (2007) The Swiss model of plurilingual communication. In K. Bührig and J.D. ten Thije (eds) *Beyond Misunderstanding. Linguistic Analyses of Intercultural Communication* (pp. 159–178). Amsterdam and Philadelphia, PA: John Benjamins.

Lüdi, G. (2013) Receptive multilingualism as a strategy for sharing mutual linguistic resources in the workplace in a Swiss context. *International Journal of Multilingualism* 10 (2), 140–158.

MAGICC (n.d.) *Modularising Multilingual and Multicultural Academic and Professional Communication Competence for BA and MA Level*. See http://sepia.unil.ch/magicc/ (accessed 7 January 2017).

Marx, N. (2012) Reading across the Germanic languages: Is equal access just wishful thinking? *International Journal of Bilingualism* 16 (4), 467–483.

Massakowa, G. (2014) *Rezeptive Mehrsprachigkeit in der intertürkischen Kommunikation*. Münster: Waxmann.

McCann, W.J., Klein, H.G. and Stegmann, T.D. (2002) *EuroComRom – the Seven Sieves: How to Read All the Romance Languages Right Away*. Aachen: EuroCom.

Meissner, F. (2008) La didactique de l'intercompréhension à la lumière des sciences de l'apprentissage. In V. Conti and F. Grin (eds) *S'entendre entre Langues Voisines: Vers l'Intercompréhension* (pp. 229–250). Chêne-Bourg: Georg.

Melo-Pfeifer, S. (2014) Intercomprehension between Romance languages and the role of English: A study of multilingual chat rooms. *International Journal of Multilingualism* 11 (1), 120–137.

Nábělková, M. (2008) *Slovenčina a čeština v kontakte: Pokračovanie príbehu* [Slovak and Czech in Contact: Continuation of the Story]. Bratislava: Veda, Filozofická fakulta Univerzity Karlovy v Praze.

Nekvapil, J. (2013) The main challenges facing Czech as medium-sized language: The state of affairs at the beginning of the 21st century. In F. Xavier Vila (ed.) *Survival and Developments of Language Communities: Prospects and Challenges* (pp. 18–37). Bristol: Multilingual Matters.

Neuner-Anfindsen, S. and Meima, E.J. (2016) MAGICC: A project of the EU Lifelong Learning programme: Modularising multilingual and multicultural academic communication competence. *European Journal of Applied Linguistics* 4 (2), 341–347.

Nic Craith, M. (2006) *Europe and the Politics of Language: Citizens, Migrants and Outsiders*. Basingstoke: Palgrave Macmillan.

Niessen, M. (2016) De rol van Lingua Receptiva in het West-Vlaamse grensgebied. Een etnografisch onderzoek naar de keuze tussen dialect, tussentaal, algemeen Nederlands en Frans in Lendelede, West Vlaanderen. Master's thesis, Utrecht University.

Otsuji, E. and Pennycook, A. (2010) Metrolingualism: Fixity, fluidity and language in flux. *International Journal of Multilingualism* 7 (3), 240–254.

Posner, R. (1991) Der Polyglot Dialog. *Sprachreport* 3, 6–10.

Räsänen, A., Natri, T., Forster Vosicki, B., et al. (2013) *MAGICC: Conceptual Framework Modularising Multilingual and Multicultural Academic Communication Competence for BA and MA level*. See http://www.unil.ch/magicc/home.html (accessed 8 January 2017).

Rehbein, J. (1984) *Reparative Handlungsmuster und ihre Verwendung im Fremdsprachenunterricht*. Rolig Papir No. 30. Roskilde: Universitetscenter.

Rehbein, J. and Romaniuk, O. (2014) How to check understanding across languages: An introduction into the Pragmatic Index of Language Distance (PILaD) usable to measure mutual understanding in receptive multilingualism, illustrated by conversations in Russian, Ukrainian and Polish. *Applied Linguistics Review* 5 (1), 131–171.

Rehbein, J., ten Thije, J.D. and Verschik, A. (2012) Lingua receptiva (LaRa) – remarks on the quintessence of receptive multilingualism. *International Journal of Bilingualism* 16 (3), 248–264.

Ribbert, A. and ten Thije, J.D. (2007) Receptive multilingualism in Dutch-German intercultural team cooperation. In J.D. ten Thije and L. Zeevaert (eds) *Receptive Multilingualism: Linguistic Analyses, Language Policies and Didactic Concepts* (pp. 73–101). Amsterdam: John Benjamins.

Rindler-Schjerve, R. and Vetter, E. (2007) Linguistic diversity in Habsburg Austria as a model for modern European language policy. In J.D. ten Thije and L. Zeevaert (eds) *Receptive Multilingualism: Linguistic Analyses, Language Policies and Didactic Concepts* (pp. 49–70). Amsterdam: John Benjamins.

Risse, S. (2015) *Deutsch als Zweitsprache für Jugendliche mit Migrationshintergrund an der Landesberufsschule für Industrie und Handwerk Bozen*. Bolzano: Freie Universität Bozen.

Sağın-Şimşek, Ç. (2014) Receptive multilingualism in Turkish-Turkmen academic counseling sessions. *Applied Linguistics Review* 5 (1), 195–210.

Sağın-Şimşek, Ç. and König, W.K. (2012) Receptive multilingualism and language understanding: Intelligibility of Azerbaijani to Turkish speakers. *International Journal of Bilingualism* 16 (3), 1–17.

Schüppert, A. (2011) Origin of asymmetry: Mutual intelligibility of spoken Danish and Swedish. Doctoral dissertation, University of Groningen.

Shannon, C.E. and Weaver, W. (1949) *A Mathematical Model of Communication*. Urbana, IL: University of Illinois Press.

Sloboda, M. and Nábělková, M. (2013) Receptive multilingualism in 'monolingual' media: Managing the presence of Slovak on Czech websites. *International Journal of Multilingualism* 10 (2), 196–213.

Sloboda, M., Laihonen, P. and Zabrodskaja, A. (2016) *Sociolinguistic Transition in Former Eastern Bloc Countries: Two Decades after the Regime Change*. Frankfurt am Main: Peter Lang.

Snijkers, L. (2014) Grensoverschrijdende communicatie in Zuid-Limburg. Een etnografisch onderzoek naar de keuze van Lingua Receptiva en dialecten in grensoverschrijdende communicatie in Zuid-Limburg. Master's thesis, Utrecht University. See http://dspace.library.uu.nl/handle/1874/292766 (accessed 7 January 2017).

Spolsky, B. (2004) *Language Policy*. Cambridge: Cambridge University Press.

Svalberg, A.M. (2007) Language awareness and language learning. *Language Teaching* 40 (4), 287–308.

Swarte, F. (2016) Predicting the mutual intelligibility of Germanic languages from linguistic and extralinguistic factors. Doctoral dissertation, University of Groningen.

ten Thije, J.D. (2013) Lingua Receptiva (LaRa). In: J.D. ten Thije and J. Rehbein (eds) *Receptive Multilingualism*. Special Issue of *International Journal of Multilingualism* 10 (2), 137–139.

ten Thije, J.D. and Zeevaert, L. (eds) (2007) *Receptive Multilingualism: Linguistic Analyses, Language Policies and Didactic Concepts*. Amsterdam: John Benjamins.

Van Klaveren, S. (2013) Lingua receptiva in mondelinge communicatie. Een onderzoek naar de praktijk van lingua receptiva voor een efficiëntere communicatie binnen het Directoraat-Generaal Vertaling van de Europese Commissie. Master's thesis, Utrecht University. See http://dspace.library.uu.nl/handle/1874/273887 (accessed 7 January 2017).

Verschik, A. (2012) Practising receptive multilingualism: Estonian–Finnish communication in Tallinn. *International Journal of Bilingualism* 16 (3), 265–286.

Vetter, E. (2012) Exploiting receptive multilingualism in institutional language learning: The case of Italian in the Austrian secondary school system. *International Journal of Bilingualism* 16 (3), 348–365.

Vogl, U. (2012) Multilingualism in a standard language culture. In M. Hüning, U. Vogl and O. Moliner (eds) *Standard Languages and Multilingualism in European History* (pp. 1–42). Amsterdam: John Benjamins.

Werlen, I. (2007) Receptive multilingualism in Switzerland and the case of Biel/Bienne. In K. Bührig and J.D. ten Thije (eds) *Beyond Misunderstanding. Linguistic Analyses of Intercultural Communication* (pp. 137–157). Amsterdam and Philadelphia, PA: John Benjamins.

Wolff, H. (1959) Intelligibility and inter-ethnic attitudes. *Anthropological Linguistics* 1 (3), 34–41.

Zeevaert, L. and ten Thije, J.D. (2007) Introduction. In J.D. ten Thije and L. Zeevaert (eds) *Receptive Multilingualism: Linguistic Analyses, Language Policies and Didactic Concepts* (pp. 1–21). Amsterdam: John Benjamins.

Zeevaert, L. (2004) *Interskandinavishe Kommunikation. Strategien zur Etablierung von Verständigung zwischen Skandinaviern im Diskurs*. Philologia No. 64. Hamburg: Kovač.

Zeevaert, L. (2007) Receptive multilingualism and inter-Scandinavian semicommunication. In J.D. ten Thije and L. Zeevaert (eds) (2007) *Receptive Multilingualism: Linguistic Analyses, Language Policies and Didactic Concepts* (pp. 103–135). Amsterdam: John Benjamins.

Zybatow, L. (2003) EuroComSlav – a road to Slavic languages. *Wiener Slawistischer Almanach* 52, 281–295.

Subject Index

acquisition, 4, 11, 15, 38, 43, 69, 137, 258, 285, 306, 356
age of acquisition, 275, 278, 288
age of onset, 221
aging, 287–288
à la mode languages, 305
Alzheimer's disease, 153, 281–282, 288
antagonistic recovery, 276–277
aphasia, 276–277, 279
approximative systems, 165
augmentative vs. reductive changes, 310
autism, 149–150
attainment, 213–214, 220
awareness, xiii– xvii, 47, 66, 121, 222, 329

bilingual *(noun)*, 12, 18, 70, 72, 91, 116, 144
   balanced, 254
   unbalanced, 253–254, 277, 302
   successive, 277, 279
Bilingual
   aphasia, 276
   stage of development, xiv–xv
   education, 86, 112, 114–116, 125
Bilingualism, xviii–xix, 3, 11, 14, 37, 67, 73, 91, 114, 124, 138, 153, 216, 259, 287
Biotic Model of Multilingualism (Aronin and Ó Laoire), 13
Brain, xxii, 39, 151, 259, 272, 274, 281, 286, 289, 306
brain damage, 278
   brain decline, 276
   brain hemisphere, 39
   brain organization, 272
   brain structure, 284

changes
   augmentative vs. reductive, xxii–xxiii, 310
code mixing/code-mixing, xxi, 280, 282–283, 302, 304, 308
code switching/code-switching, 17, 39, 42, 57, 124, 309, 315–316, 344
cognitive advantage, 74, 151, 241
cognitive costs, 303
cognitive consequences of multilingualism, xxii, 283–285
competence
   metalinguistic, 38, 74, 314
CLI (cross-linguistic influence/crosslinguistic influence), 44, 57, 163, 169, 172

CLIL (content and language integrated learning), 112–114, 223
complexity, 13, 27, 43, 187, 257, 308, 339
communication, 6, 52, 66, 102, 108, 119, 149, 192, 198, 241, 314, 333
conceptualization, 14–15, 215, 246
context, 4, 8–10, 20, 51, 71, 118, 181–182, 201, 274, 278, 284
control, 86, 123, 153, 218, 240, 254, 257, 277, 280, 284
continua of multilingual education, xx, 115–119
convergence vs. divergence in language contact, 305–308
costs
   cognitive, 303
   switching, xix, 12
creoloid (Dano-Norwegian), 322
Critical/Sensitive Period Hypothesis, 216–217
cross-linguistic similarity, 165
CT (computer tomography), 272

dementia, xxii, 276, 281, 283, 287
development
   trilingual, 37
   early, 12
   language, viii, 56, 77, 165, 217
   multilingual, 37, 41, 68, 72, 77, 84, 90
dialect, 69, 146, 340, 342
differential recovery, 276–279
differences between multilingualism and bilingualism, 3, 12, 37,
diversity, 8, 9, 15–17, 234
dislocated varieties, 317
distinctive features of multilingualism, 10–17
Dominant Language Constellation (DLC), 20–25
Dynamic Model of Multilingualism (DMM) (Herdina and Jessner), x, 41, 77–79

education
   trilingual, 12
   multilingual, viii, x, 102, 114
      bilingual, 114
      of multilinguals, 115–119
      of bilinguals, 114–115
educational policy/educational policies, 101–126
electroencephalography (EEG), 272
ethnolinguistic vitality, 71, 185

factor model (Hufeisen), 79–81
Focus on multilingualism (approach), 120–122
fossilization, 182, 184, 313
foreign language effect, 73, 171
foreignness, xxi, 171
forms of multilingualism, 4–7
fundamentals of multilingualism, 4
functional MRI, 236

globalization, 6, 8–10, 101, 114, 186, 330
grammar, 11–12, 47, 75, 82, 89, 141, 245, 316

hemisphere (brain), 39
hemispheric specialization, 272
heritage language, 18, 92, 103, 115, 124, 186
heritage speaker, 301, 310
home languages, 15–16, 101, 116, 196
hyperdialectisms, 307, 322–323
hypothesis, 39, 78, 170, 199, 215, 274, 319

identity
  ethnolinguistic, 185, 188, 192, 194
  local, 317
  multilingual, xxi, 13, 19, 40,
independence hypothesis 274
inhibition, 241, 251–252, 254,289
immersion, 110–112, 221, 287
intelligibility, 329, 333–337
Interaction
  of linguistic systems, 39
    cross-linguistic, xiii, 10, 78, 121
intercomprehension, 76, 324, 331, 333, 353–354, 356
interference, 13, 37, 126, 144, 199, 216, 250, 283–284, 302
interlanguage, 80, 82, 165, 306, 309
inter-linguistic correspondences, 314–318
introspection, 54, 57

L1, 11, 37–39, 51
L2, 11, 37–39, 51
L3, 37, 38–39, 51
language (a language; **the** language; langua**ges**), xv, 3, 5, 15, 20, 22, 25, 51, 65, 82, 89, 103, 105, 117–118, 124, 171, 184–185, 215, 247, 251, 277, 333, 349, 355
language*(noun)*
  additional, xvi, xix, 11, 67, 76, 87, 91, 110, 167, 213, 217–218, 222
  à la mode, 305
  colonial, 311, 316, 321
  heritage, 18, 71, 87, 92, 103, 115, 186
  lesser-used, 5, 317
  majority, 103, 105, 109–114
  minority, 18, 65–66, 71, 103–109
  national, 18, 87, 185, 317, 330, 334–335, 338
  native, xiv, 12, 43, 163–164, 171
  non-native, xvi, xviii, 12, 43, 164, 166, 171
  official, 5, 18, 27, 71, 103, 142, 351
  regional, 16, 180, 196,351
  received, 19
  subsequent, 12, 136–137, 141, 199–200
language acquisition, 12–13, 20, 42, 72, 139–140, 217, 220, 234
language choice, 66, 74, 196, 201–202, 242, 250, 341
language community, 181, 184
language competence, xiv, 141, 153, 242
language conflict, 285–286, 322
language contact, 13, 184, 301–302, 305–308
language distance, 169–171
language impairment, 276, 281
language knowledge, 167, 233, 241
language learner, 18, 180–181, 184
language learning, 44–45, 57, 66, 68, 104, 180, 186, 193, 200, 202, 214, 234
language learning strategies, 11, 69, 75, 80, 85, 89
language loss, 72, 103–104, 163
language modes, 242, 250
language nominations, 18–19, 20, 27
language perception, 234, 245
language planning, 329, 350, 353, 357
language policy, 102, 141, 180, 196–197, 306
language practices, 7, 17, 27, 122, 188, 195
language production, 245–246, 254, 273
language processing, 56, 234, 236, 286
language proficiency, 51, 65, 77, 172, 183, 260
language repertoire, 17, 20, 22, 42, 84–85
language specific deficits, 282–283
language transfer, 36, 42, 44, 48, 57, 75, 166, 172
language teaching, 35, 92, 164, 223, 330
language typology, 37, 43–44, 75, 247, 259
language use, 15–16, 25, 47, 109, 144, 190, 201, 278
language varieties, 4, 12, 15, 146
lateralization, 272
lexical transfer, xviii, 44, 46, 53, 247
lexicon mental
  multilingual, 36, 38, 50–51
lingua franca, 12, 102, 186, 300, 317, 338, 350
lingua receptive, 330
linguistic practices, 9, 183
linguistic typology, 75
literacy, 168, 221–222, 320
localization (in brain), 10, 39

magnetic resonance imaging (MRI), 272
mastery, 17, 271, 274
material culture of multilingualism, vii, 15, 91
maturational constraints, 213, 214, 216–219
memory
   long-term, 54, 241
     mental lexicon, 47–51, 233, 245
mental processes, 233
metacommunication, 347
metalinguistic competence, 314
metalinguistic awareness, 10, 38, 75, 125, 168, 238, 244–245, 315
metalinguistic knowledge, 245
metaphors, 14, 91
method, 35, 53, 54, 76, 84, 234
methodology of multilingualism, 13–15
migration, 8–9, 10, 72, 301, 303
minority language speakers, 15, 57, 102, 103–114
minority language, 15, 18–19, 102, 103–114, 307, 318
modality, 54, 234, 271
models of multilingualism, xviii–xix, 13, 36–38
   of bilingualism, xviii–xix, 36–38
mother tongue, xvi, 10, 19, 52, 141, 142, 300, 317
motivation, 179–202
multi-competence/multicompetence, xvii, 14, 36, 38–43, 91, 120, 182, 200
Multilingual(noun)
   additive, 239
   compound, 273
   coordinate, 273
   non-proficient, 239
   proficient, 239
   simultaneous, 239
   subordinate, 273
   subtractive, 239
multilingual classroom, 119–126
multilingual communicative modes, 353
multilingual dementia, 281–283
multilingual education, xx, 86, 92, 102, 103–119
multilingual pedagogical practices, 84, 124–126
Multilingual Processing Model (Franz-Joseph Meißner), 13, 82–83
multilingual speaker, xvi, 77, 120–124, 144, 172, 200, 243, 272, 273, 280, 282, 330
M(ultilingualism)-factor, 78, 91
Multilingualism
   African, 16
   current, 6–25
   individual, xxi, 4–6, 238–259
   integrative, 6
   inclusive, 353–354, 357

   in school contexts, 101–102
   historical, 6–7
   proximate, 5
   receptive, 323, 324, 329–356
   societal, 4–6, 15–17
multiple language learning, xx, 65–92, 197, 199
multiple language teaching, xiii, xx, 65–92
mutual Intelligibility, 329, 330, 332–337, 357

native language, 19, 163, 164, 165, 258–259, 282
native speaker, xv, 120, 168, 186, 200, 330, 353
nativelikeness and near-nativelikeness, 214, 218
neurolinguistics, xvi, 11, 271–288
neural mechanisms, xxii, 272
neuroimaging, 220, 283, 284, 285, 286
New Linguistic Dispensation, xx, 23, 25–27,
non-native lexical transfer, 11

pattern, 9, 21, 37, 72, 165
perception, 19, 121, 168, 171, 246
personality, 139, 150–151
philosophy of multilingualism, 15
polyglossia, 141, 147, 149–151, 156
positron emission tomography (PET), 272
processing
   processing of the first language, 247
   processing of the second language, 247
   processing of the third language, 247
proficiency, xvi, 66, 86, 274–275, 279, 301
pseudo-bilingualism, 305
psycholinguistics, xxii, 65–92, 233, 234, 238–260
psychotypology, xxi, 43, 73, 168, 169

recency, xxi, 73, 166, 172
representation (of languages in brain), xix, 11
role-function model (Williams and Hammarberg), 13

'savants', xxi, 149–150, 151
second language acquisition (SLA), xxi, 36, 38, 36, 180, 181–183, 308, 312–313
semantic organization, 272, 279
small-scale multilingualism, 16
southern multilingualisms, 17
speaker, 103–114
   monolingual, 68, 77, 303, 343, 344
   bilingual, 124, 153, 251, 303, 309, 315, 343, 344
   multilingual, 77, 120, 121, 122, 137, 144, 172, 200, 273, 283, 330
   of minority languages, 15, 57, 102, 103–114
spontaneous hypothesis grammar, 82, 85

Stages of the Graded Intergenerational
    Disruption Scale, 130
subset hypothesis, 245, 274
substrata, 303, 318–320
substratal influence, 318–320
successive recovery, 277, 279
super-diversity/superdiversity, xvi, 9, 10
switchers and non-switchers, 240
switching cost, xix, 12

target language, 43, 73, 76, 82, 83, 85, 163, 167, 170, 171, 181, 186, 191, 193, 195, 198, 240, 312
teachers' proficiency, 108
teaching through the minority language, 105
the two trends, 26
third language, x, xvi, 10, 11, 19, 78, 81, 166, 287
threshold, xv, xviii, 11, 75, 91, 332
transfer
    positive, xxi, 85, 164, 167–168, 240
    negative, xxi, 44, 164, 167–168, 240, 310, 315

cross-linguistic, 319
    overt, 167
    covert, 167
translanguaging, xvi, 17, 46, 57, 122–125
translation, xxii, 52, 142, 143, 235, 258, 353–354
trilingual *(noun)*, xxii, 10, 12, 37, 75, 165, 240, 241, 242, 243, 249, 257
trilingual language competence, 242
trilingual lexicon, 246
trilingual processing, xxii, 240, 249, 257
trilingual's states of activation, 250
typology, 45, 115, 116, 239

ultimate attainment, 213, 214, 216–219
unitary language system hypothesis, 214, 215

verbal repertoire, 20

whole school language curriculum, xx, 88–89
world Englishes, 12, 317